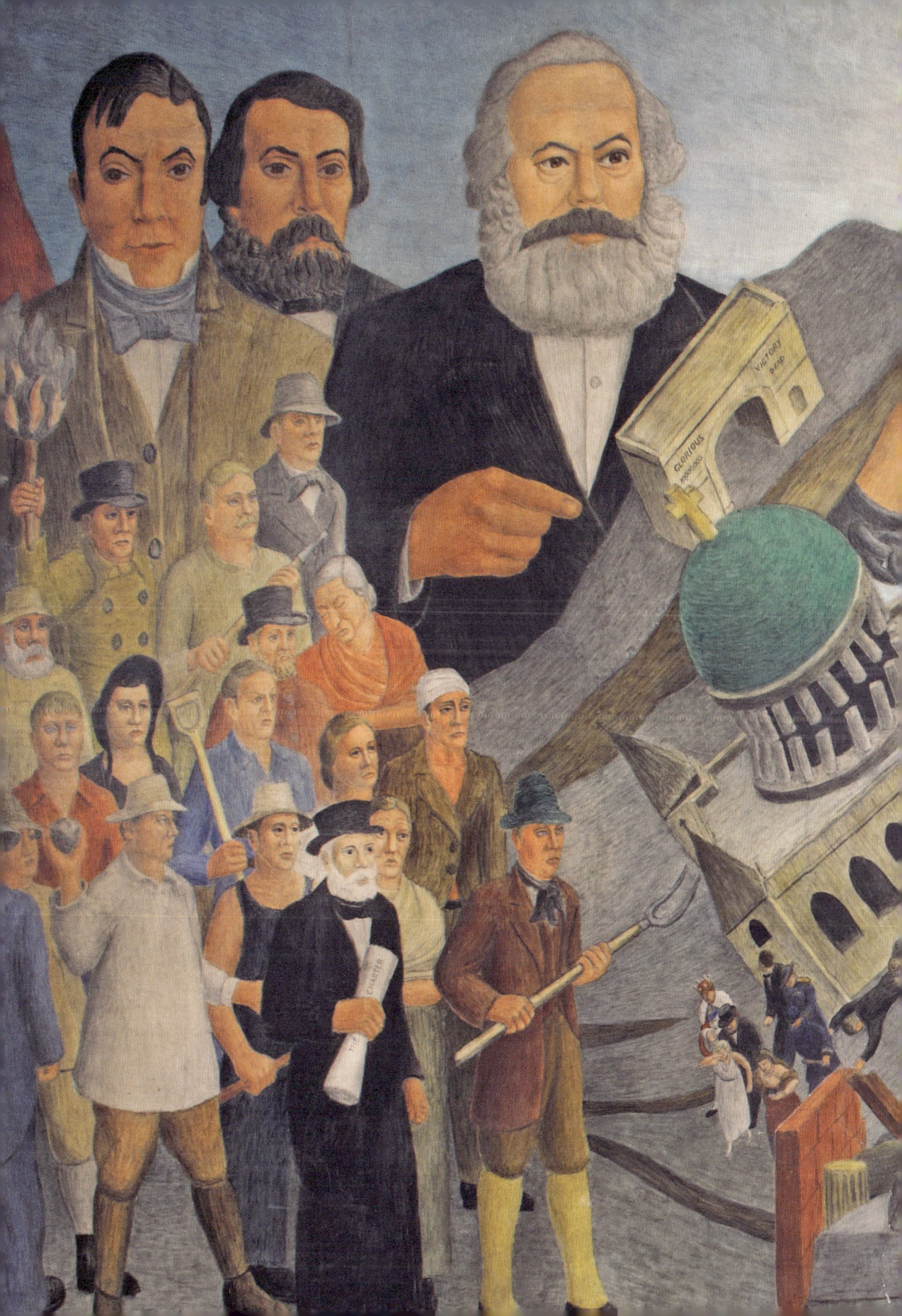

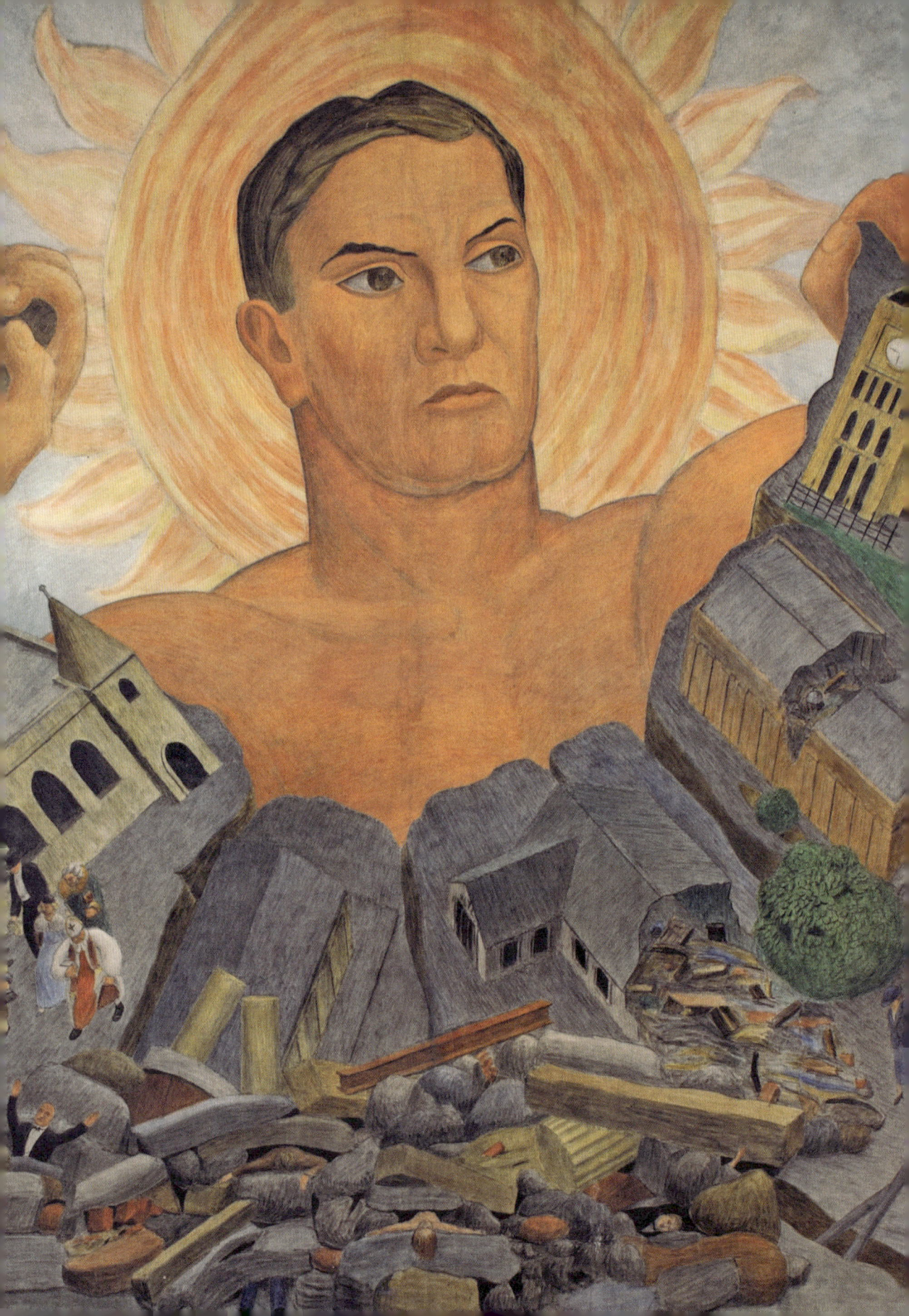

ANDY FRIEND

COMRADES IN ART

ARTISTS AGAINST FASCISM
1933–1943

FOREWORD BY
FRANCES SPALDING

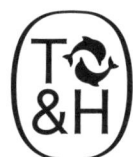

IN HONOUR OF THOSE WHO ORGANIZED
IN MEMORY OF THOSE WHO WERE NOT SAVED

ON PAGES 1, 2 AND 6
Jack Hastings,
The Worker of the Future Clearing Away the Chaos of Capitalism,
fresco, 1935

First published in the United Kingdom
in 2025 by Thames & Hudson Ltd,
6–24 Britannia Street, London WC1X 9JD

First published in the United States of America
in 2025 by Thames & Hudson Inc., 500 Fifth
Avenue, New York, New York 10110

Comrades in Art:
Artists Against Facism 1933–1943
© 2025 Thames & Hudson Ltd, London

Foreword © 2025 Frances Spalding
Text © 2025 Andy Friend

Jacket designed by Steve O Connell
Interior layout designed by Lisa Ifsits

All Rights Reserved. No part of this publication may be reproduced or transmitted in any form or by any means, electronic or mechanical, including photocopy, recording or any other information storage and retrieval system, without prior permission in writing from the publisher.

EU Authorized Representative: Interart S.A.R.L.
19 rue Charles Auray, 93500 Pantin, Paris, France
productsafety@thameshudson.co.uk
interart.fr

A CIP catalogue record for this book is available from the British Library

Library of Congress Control Number 2025934592

ISBN 978-0-500-02741-7
01

Printed and bound in China by
C&C Offset Printing Co. Ltd

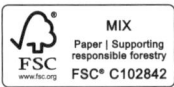

Be the first to know about our new releases, exclusive content and author events by visiting
thamesandhudson.com
thamesandhudsonusa.com
thamesandhudson.com.au

CONTENTS

FOREWORD
6

CHAPTER 1
SEVEN DIALS
10

CHAPTER 2
CHARLOTTE STREET
52

CHAPTER 3
SOHO SQUARE
88

CHAPTER 4
CHARING CROSS ROAD
124

CHAPTER 5
GROSVENOR SQUARE
164

CHAPTER 6
WHITECHAPEL HIGH STREET
210

CHAPTER 7
CAMDEN STREET AND SENATE HOUSE
246

CHAPTER 8
HOLLES STREET
278

AFTERWORD
310

ABBREVIATIONS 313 NOTES 314
BIOGRAPHIES 336 BIBLIOGRAPHY 345
ACKNOWLEDGMENTS 349 PICTURE CREDITS 350
INDEX 353

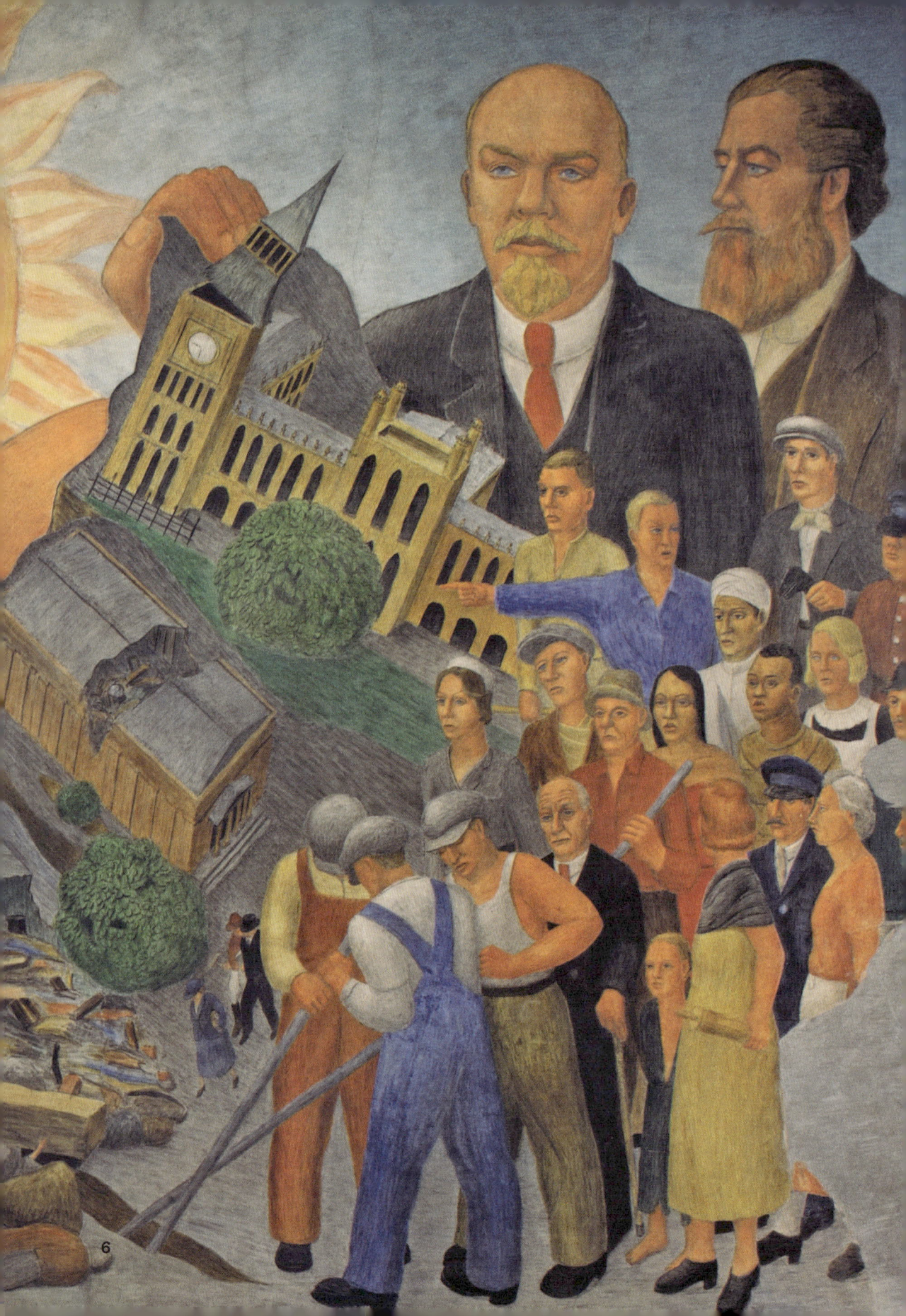

FRANCES SPALDING

FOREWORD

This book gifts the reader with a record of one of the boldest and most imaginative artistic developments in England during the twentieth century, namely the formation of the Artists International Association in 1933 and its existence during its first ten years. It grew large but began small – also informally, for only a dozen or so men and women, mostly impoverished jobbing commercial artists in their twenties, attended its first meeting. It was held in a London studio belonging to the twenty-two-year-old Misha Black, a versatile designer and organizer with a gift for leadership. The room was candle-lit, not for any romantic or nostalgic reason, but simply because Black was moving from Little Earl Street into Charlotte Street the following day, and the electricity had already been cut off.

This room served, however, to create a dramatic and memorable setting for what was perhaps the keynote item – an enthusiastic report delivered by the twenty-nine-year-old Pearl Binder of her recent visit to Russia. Coming from a working-class background, she had of necessity done factory work after leaving school. Yet, concurrently, she learned about art by taking evening classes at Manchester School of Art and gained a diploma. This young woman moved to London in 1925 at the age of twenty-one, spent time in Paris, and by 1933 had gained a reputation as a distinctive lithographic book illustrator. In this role she had recently contributed to Thomas Burke's *The Real East End* (1932). Before leaving for Russia, she had been asked to bring with her albums of her work, for possible exhibition, and was not disappointed: a temporary show of her art was mounted in Moscow by the Museum of New Western Art, gifting her with a singular honour. In Russia she also enjoyed conversations with professors and other persons high up in the art and museum worlds, and learned much about how artists were treated. She reported to the candle-lit group that thousands of artists were supported, organized and satisfactorily employed, given contracts or travelling scholarships, or were sponsored by trade unions or the Red Army. She could not but contrast this in her mind with the precarious, directionless work of her artist friends in England, struggling, in the wake of the Wall Street crash and the subsequent Depression, to please dilettante London collectors and gallery owners.

Also present in the room that night was Clifford Rowe. He too was an artist, and had been to Russia on what he intended to be a short visit as he wanted to experience communism. On arriving in Moscow, he learned that, owing to severe shortages, he would not be allowed to stay unless he found a job and a room within seven days. He found a job with a co-operative publishing society, and stayed not two weeks but eighteen months. Like Pearl Binder, he too had been impressed by the role of the artist in Soviet society, but he was critical of the recent decision to move Soviet propaganda art towards Socialist Realism, which he thought mere story-telling. While in Russia he himself had contributed to a celebration of the Red Army's fifteenth anniversary, which welcomed evidence of revolutionary activities in other countries. Rowe painted *The Struggle between the Unemployed and the Police Forces*, drawing on reports and photographs in arriving copies of the *Daily Worker*, which he amalgamated into one large canvas. What he wanted was a sense of social responsibility in art and a willingness to relate artistic practice to radical political ideas. A seemingly chance meeting between Rowe and Binder, before she returned to England, gave him a chance to inform her of what he had in mind. According to Andy Friend, she voiced enthusiastic support. Rowe's experience of Russia must have been a major ingredient during the candle-lit meeting, and he was to become and remain one of the Association's most central figures.

At its second meeting, attendance doubled in size. The intention was clear – to initiate something akin to a revolutionary union for artists. Those present agreed on its title: 'Artists International'. Radical in intent and clear-sighted as to what needed doing, it seemed in these early days a very English phenomenon. Yet the word 'international' was very definitely intended to imply unity with similarly inclined artists in other countries, a unity that could transcend the bitter nationalist barriers that had begun to take shape. In 1935, after two years had passed, it added the word 'Association' to its title, becoming the Artists International Association, and was from then on familiarly known as the AIA. This softened its identity, adding a suggestion of ideological tolerance and a broadening of purpose, which made it attractive to a broader range of artists. This was in step with what was happening elsewhere, namely a move towards a popular front. At the same time, with the advancing threat of fascism in Europe, it became necessary for the AIA to clarify its mission statement. It did so, announcing: 'The AIA stands for Unity of Artists against Fascism and War and the Suppression of Culture.'

It needs mentioning here that the story of the AIA was initially told in 1983 by the Museum of Modern Art, Oxford, by means of the exhibition *AIA: The Story of the Artists International Association 1933–1953*, curated by Lynda Morris and Robert Radford. A summary history of the AIA followed four years later when Radford published *Art for a Purpose*, which included a chapter on the main ideas feeding into the 1930s art and politics debate. But Andy Friend is nevertheless right to say in this book that the story of the AIA has been a neglected topic in the annals of mid-twentieth-century British art history. Although largely run by a nucleus of committed activists, under Misha Black's chairmanship it was brilliant at networking and showed great ingenuity in pursuit of collective endeavour, drawing a very respectable list of well-known or leading artists into its orbit. Very few instances of this have been mentioned in biographies and monographs of these more famous associates. As the biographer of Vanessa Bell, I am shamefully aware that, until I read this book, I did not know Bell was a founder member of the AIA Advisory Council in early 1939 and served on it throughout the Second World War.

Andy Friend brings to this study of the AIA the narrative skills already encountered in his two previous books, the biographies *Ravilious & Co* and his life of John Nash. He has a flair for achieving both breadth and depth in his handling of information, while maintaining a lively pace. As a historian, he recognizes the need to identify the nucleus of intelligent, committed activists at the core of AIA's identity, while also reaching far into the multiple activities with which it engaged. Particularly successful were its exhibitions. These included *Artists Against Fascism and War*, mounted in November 1935, with which it was readily identified, but also small touring shows sent out to factory canteens or provincial libraries. Its success is registered by its growing membership numbers, which soon reached just over a thousand. But it is the richness of its story that makes this book such a pleasure to read. Each new proposition or shift of ideas within this artists' group is neatly tied into the historical moment, with expert understanding of the tensions behind the world's crises that led up to another world war. The result is a massive contribution to our knowledge of British art in the mid-twentieth century, at a time when the dialogue between art and politics could and did play such an urgent and influential role.

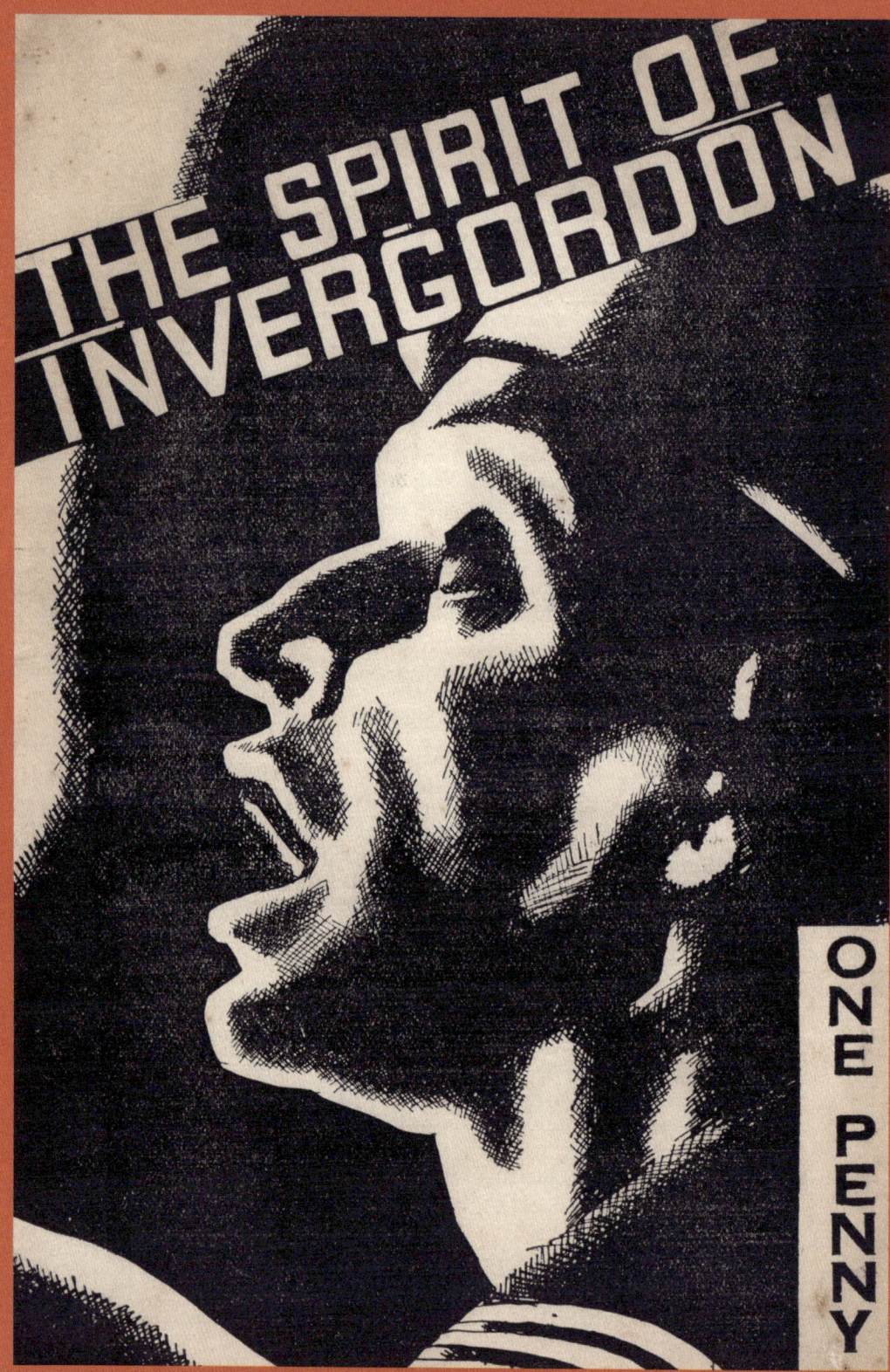

CHAPTER ONE

SEVEN DIALS

One early autumn day in 1933 a letter addressed to twenty-two-year-old Misha Black arrived at the premises of Studio Z in London's Covent Garden, two third-floor rooms above a lock-up shop on Little Earl Street, Seven Dials.[1]

For three years, Black – he would not become Sir Misha until 1972 – had been sleeping in the back room, working in the front one. After struggling through slump conditions, at first with a female business partner, then by himself, his effort to keep his fledgling design business afloat during the Depression was nearing its end.[2]

The letter, probably written in haste as the artist Cliff Rowe was preparing to leave Moscow, brought news that its author would shortly arrive back in London after eighteen months in the Soviet Union. We are unlikely ever to see its detail but can be reasonably certain that the letter was intercepted at the depot serving the Covent Garden area, the neighbourhood where Rowe had lived in Endell Street before leaving for Russia with a married lover.[3]

After transcription Rowe's text would have been circulated within the Security Service, as an earlier letter of his to the same address had been the previous December:

> I was talking to an English comrade who gives us political classes now and again and he mentioned with bated breath our joint 'works' for the Invergordon leaflet and the ILD,[4] without knowing we did them. He was very pleased with the idea of us forming an artist revolutionary union in London and he knows Pollitt[5] and the other leaders very well so I think we could get them to send us on the spot during demonstrations to help with banners, street newspapers, caricatures, posters, etc. etc.[6]

1.1 Cliff Rowe, cover design for *The Spirit of Invergordon*, pen and ink, 1932. 18.2 × 12.5 cm (7¼ × 5 in.)

On reading this, Security Service officer S.9 asked: 'Have you any idea which Invergordon leaflet is referred to? ... If the underlined remarks in this intercept indicate that the writer is concerned in the production of subversive leaflets for circulation among Naval Ratings, the writer becomes of great interest. Can you tell me anything of him?' S.6 replied: 'The part played by the writer and by Misha Black will probably have to do with illustrations or the design on the cover, as both these people are artists.'

'I did not realise BLACK was an artist', noted S.9. 'It seems not unlikely that the English comrade, referred to at 41a., page 2, might be WINCOTT, as the latter is believed to be in Russia at the present time. It seems equally possible that the leaflet referred to is the "Spirit of Invergordon", which was partly written by WINCOTT and has a picture of a gaunt, Bolshevik blue jacket on the cover.'

The full text of Rowe's letter remained in Black's file, while this exchange was copied to communist activist Len Wincott's file, since released to the National Archives. Black had come under surveillance in October 1932 as a result of contact with the London office of Russian Oil Products Ltd while designing a poster.[7] Cliff Rowe had been under observation since late 1931 and, given the rise of artists' organization against fascism and war that followed their reunion in London, the personal files on both men must have burgeoned in the decade ahead. Since then, they have either been destroyed or are still being withheld by the British government.

* * * * *

Fifty years later Misha recalled his teenage disappointments trying to make it as a fine artist in the late 1920s after 'anxious evenings at the Central School drawing the big toe of Greek casts', and noted that Cliff, coming from 'a completely working-class family had failed to make any impression as an artist, though a magnificent draughtsman'.[8]

They had probably first met as jobbing commercial artists at Olympia or Wembley around 1928, when a youthful Misha was designing and assembling trade-show stands.[9] By then Rowe, the elder by six years, was attracting more notice as a painter than Black subsequently remembered, but not enough to live off. And while Misha would be knighted as a pre-eminent industrial designer, Cliff continued to develop as a painter of consequence and integrity over the six decades to come.

Rowe's father had been one of London's black-coated workforce, a clerk commuting from Wandsworth to the City; after his mother died when he was eight, an aunt who kept a corner shop looked out for Cliff and his siblings. As a teenager he developed a streak of determined independence and a conscience about potentially wasting slight family resources. Five years at Wimbledon School of Art were punctuated by work at an advertising agency and a growing friendship with Ronald Ossory Dunlop, a conscientious objector in the Great War, who was also working in advertising while giving himself ten years to succeed as an artist. In autumn 1923 Rowe won a place at the Royal College of Art (RCA), but left after

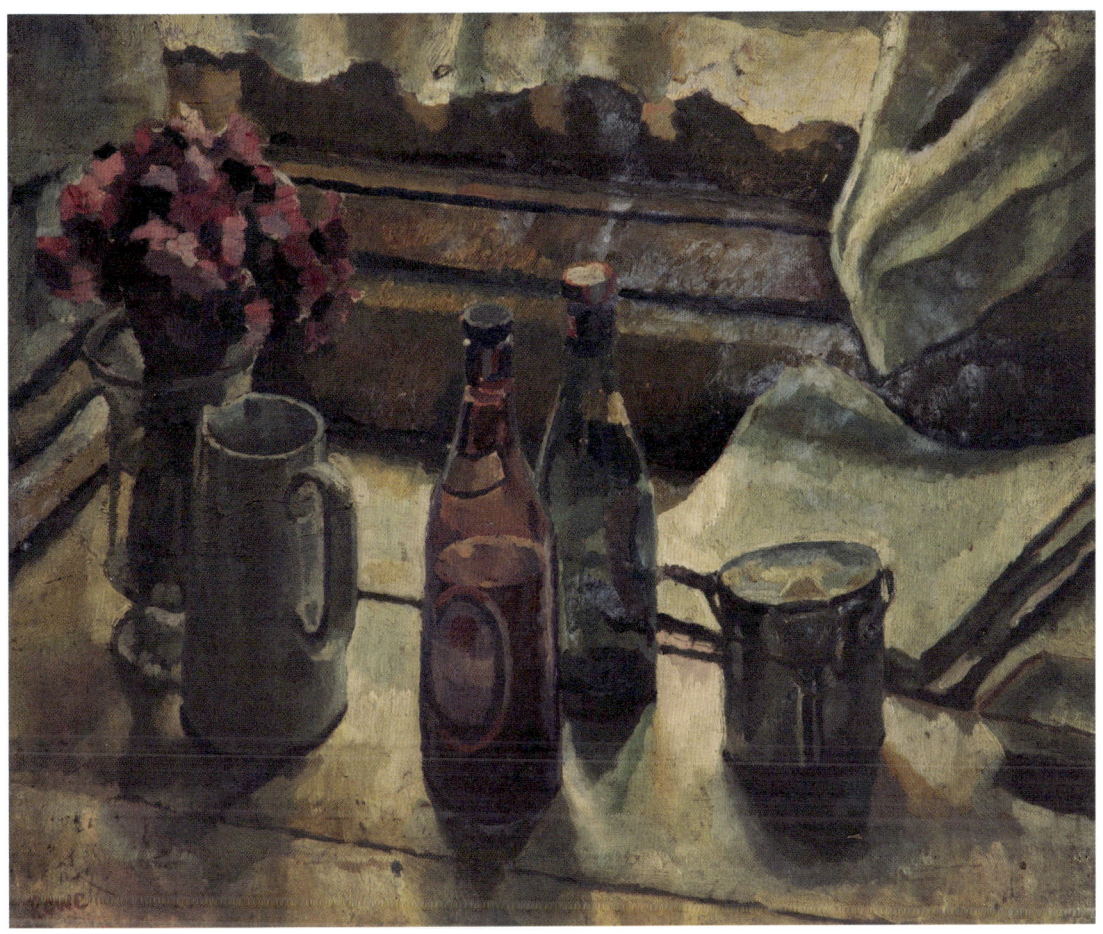

1.2 Cliff Rowe, *Still Life*, oil on canvas, c. 1931. 44 × 54 cm (17⅜ × 21⅛ in.)

two terms, his presence too questioning, his style too experimental for the Painting School and its principal, William Rothenstein.[10]

Dunlop, meanwhile, had formed the Emotionist Group, whose signature tenet was a Clive Bell-esque assertion that artists must emotionally engage with their subject in order to invoke an aesthetic response in the viewer.[11] Whether or not Rowe fully subscribed to this sub-Bloomsbury variant of 'art for art's sake', the brief flowering of the group's salon at Chelsea's Hurricane Lamp Gallery gave him a temporary entrée to a very different intellectual milieu and, more importantly, the opportunity to exhibit.[12] In 1928 *The Times* praised Clifford Hooper Rowe for his responsive execution and feeling for design in a largely critical review of the group's heavy impasto ('you have to dodge the paint to see the picture'), but thereafter, although Dunlop's career as a portraitist thrived, the group dissolved.[13]

Cliff, however, had attracted the attention of Cicely Marchant, proprietor of the Regent Street Goupil Gallery, who included several London

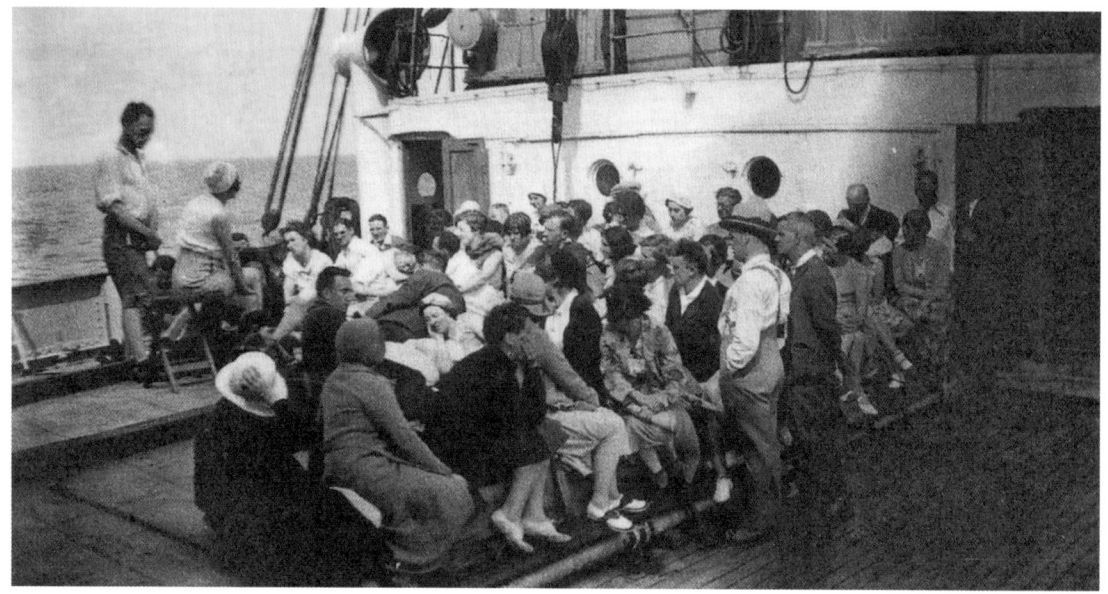

1.3 Unknown photographer, Shipboard lecture en route to Leningrad, 1932

night scenes in a mixed show in December 1930.¹⁴ When these sold she required more, but an artistically restless Rowe produced still lifes instead of the requested urban nocturnes. This soured the relationship at a time when collectors on both sides of the Atlantic were suffering from the Wall Street crash, most galleries were avoiding all but the safely established, and commercial work of every type was becoming scarcer, the rate for the task ever meaner. If you were a young artist 'there would be at least ten people in front of you for every job', Rowe recalled; 'we were all living in poverty, there was no doubt about that.'¹⁵

At this juncture he produced a poster for the Workers' Bookshop near his lodgings, attracting the attention of communist organizer Pat Dooley, who asked him to design pamphlet covers. Initially unconvinced by their content, Rowe nevertheless responded – which explains why on 7 November 1931 the Special Branch recorded Jack Cohen, the Communist Party's publications manager, leaving a dwelling occupied by 'an artist named Hooper Rowe', a minor occurrence in a season of international turmoil.¹⁶

Six weeks before, steep pay cuts had provoked mutiny among the Atlantic Fleet anchored at Invergordon – the most serious British naval rebellion since Spithead and the Nore during the French Revolutionary Wars – and such a substantial assault on the credibility of the National Government that within five days sterling had left the gold standard.¹⁷ Less than forty-eight hours after the mutiny subsided, Japanese agents destroyed railway lines at Mukden, a false-flag pretext for Emperor Hirohito's Kwantung Army to annexe the Chinese region of Manchuria, an action which would in due course shred the credibility of the League of Nations. In Germany the failure of a big four bank, Danatbank, had precipitated financial contagion and, amid spreading middle-class anxiety, a ratcheting up of National Socialist anti-Semitism was now in train. Fearing the United States would soon follow Britain and Germany into an economic abyss, investors stampeded to sell dollar assets for gold; by the end of the year more than two thousand banks worldwide had failed, global trade was stalling, and tariffs were being raised on all sides.

As 1932 opened the capitalist system appeared to be rocking violently on its axis, and for a growing number only the reported success of the USSR's first five-year plan held out hope of escape from depression. Rowe, however, had preserved his scepticism until Dooley lent him, and he read, *The Communist Manifesto*: 'It solved so many intellectual problems about advertising and my work as a commercial artist that I felt the scales fall from my eyes. It was at this point that I decided to go to Russia ... I thought propaganda was one thing, but reality was the acid test.'[18]

At this time, going to the Soviet Union usually meant joining a tour organized either by Intourist or by VOKS, the Moscow-based All-Union Society for Cultural Relations with Foreign Countries, arranged through the Society for Cultural Relations between the Peoples of the British Commonwealth and the Union of Soviet Socialist Republics (SCR). The London-based SCR had been formed in 1924 after a mendacious press campaign about Bolshevik plots which helped destroy the first Labour government; its objective was promotion of exchange about arts and the sciences, and its vice-presidents included Virginia Woolf, E. M. Forster, John Maynard Keynes, Aldous Huxley, H. G. Wells and William Rothenstein.[19] In spring 1932 many were attracted to the idea of Soviet Russia but far fewer actually went; for Rowe a factor urging departure was probably his citation as co-respondent in a divorce petition lodged by the husband of Dr May Tilney Miles;[20] a passport application soon followed, as did a fire sale of paintings to fund a seven-day tour. The month of May was probably drawing to a close when the lovers boarded a Soviet steamer at Hay's Wharf, Southwark, bound for Leningrad.

*****

When Misha Black received Rowe's letter from Moscow the following December, its writer was at work on another painting of London by night, but one with a very different resonance from those previously displayed at the Goupil. A major undertaking, it was the best supported commission he had ever had – and as he painted a conviction that unity among artists could transcend bitter nationalist barriers was taking shape.

When he first arrived, Cliff had observed 'Russia was in a hell of a state. There were shortages of just about everything.' He had seven days to find both a job and a room – without the latter he would not get permission to remain in Moscow and without the former he would have no means to do so: 'On the sixth day I decided to just wander around, until I saw an English sign. This led me to the Foreign Workers' Publishing House and, believe it or not, on the walls were covers I had done for the Communist Party in London.'[21]

Once hired, he worked at the Co-operative Publishing Society of Foreign Workers in the USSR for nearly eighteen months, volunteering on weekends producing a wall newspaper at a factory on the outskirts of the city. His output was considerable and his style varied, employing bold

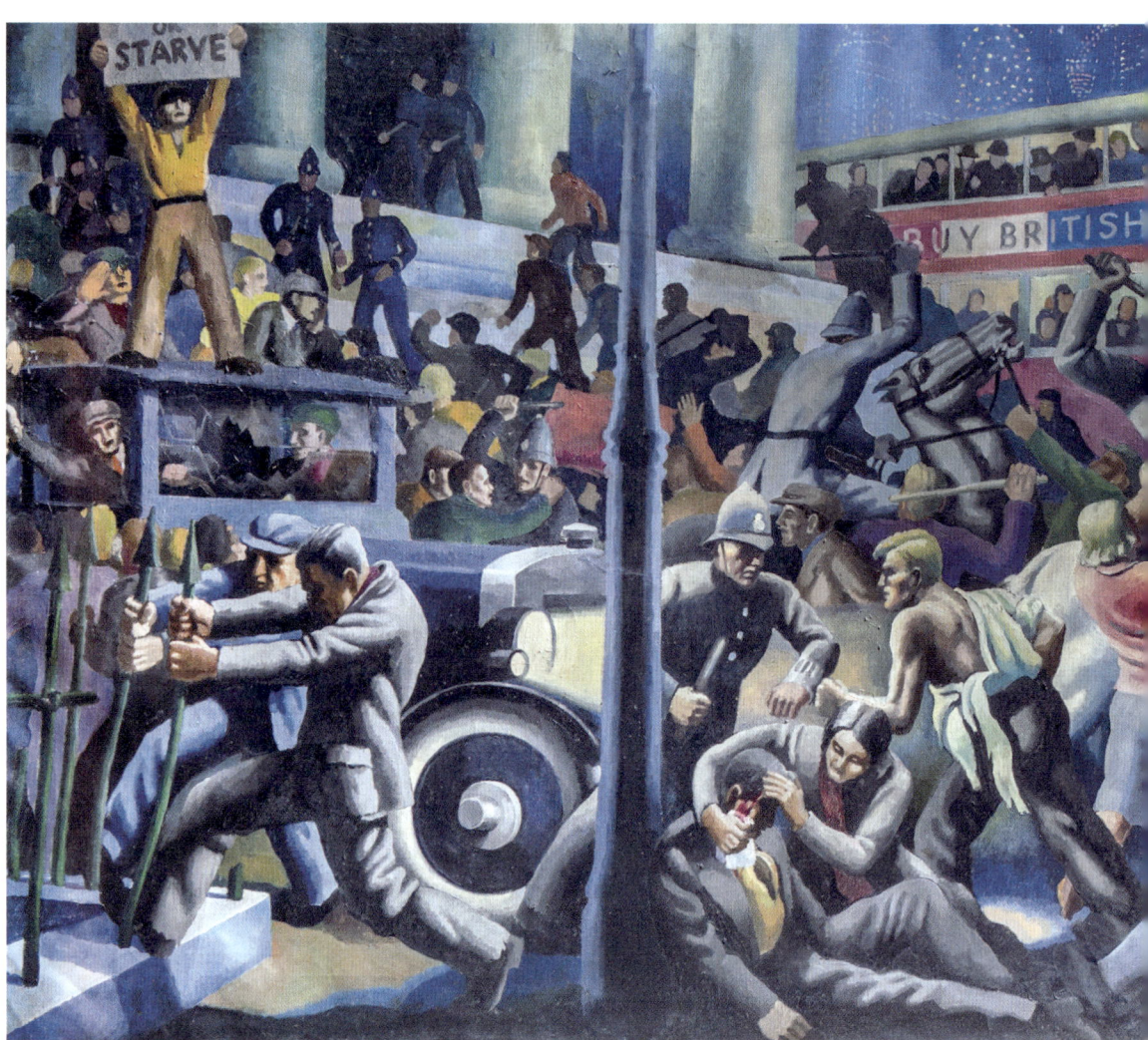

1.4 Cliff Rowe, *The Struggle between the Unemployed and the Police Forces*, oil on canvas, 1932–33. 137 × 329.5 cm (54 × 129¼ in.)

typography matched to photography for the cover of the graphic-rich publication *9th Congress of Trade Unions*, or lithography and a stripped-down constructivism to render eye-catching such volumes as *The Development of Socialist Methods and Forms of Labour*. At first he was living with May, who it is thought was working as a medic, but their attempt at making a new life plainly failed; after a few months she returned to England and the divorce petition her husband had lodged was never finalized.

Around this time Rowe was called to a meeting organized by the Red Army. Preparations were in train to celebrate its fifteenth anniversary with an extensive exhibition including foreign artists' work to evidence 'international solidarity of the revolutionary detachments of the world proletariat'.²² 'I was very impressed with what went on at this meeting',

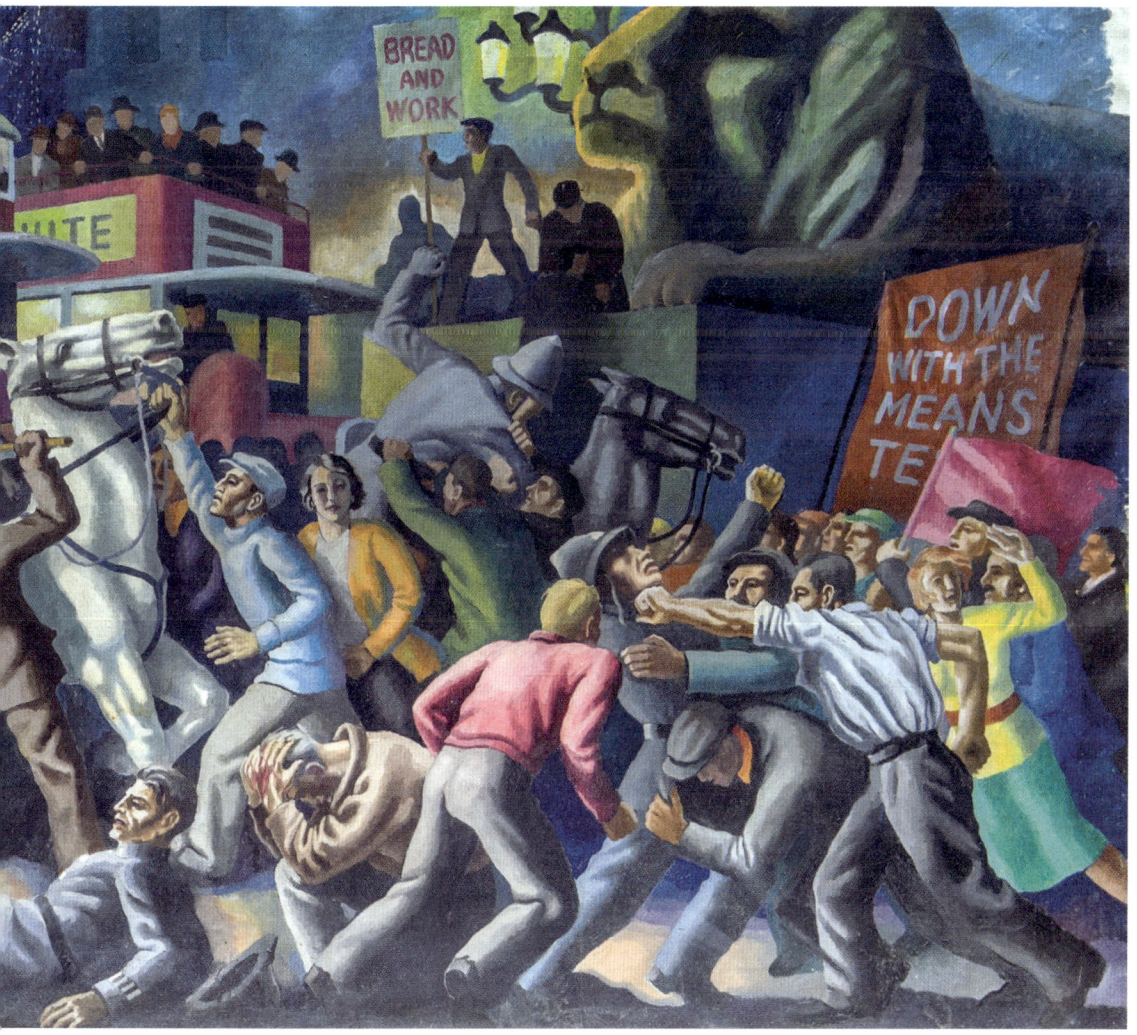

he recalled. 'At the time Japan was invading Manchuria but the Chinese and Japanese artists were discussing together what paintings they would do. No one was at loggerheads; the artists were together for peace and anti-fascism.'[23]

The woman organizing the exhibition favoured 'almost photographic realism', disliked abstraction and wanted a work on 'class struggle, the English class struggle'. Although Rowe 'could not take' the then dominant strain of Soviet propaganda art – 'most of it was literature, story-telling in academic terms, and therefore illustration' – he clearly saw that she who was going to pay the painter could call the tune. But after deciding to produce 'a very realistic night scene of Hunger Marchers Entering Trafalgar Square', unfaultable on grounds of abstraction or choice of subject, he nevertheless went on to create a work of extraordinary dynamism, vivid design and vibrant colouring that was anything but mere illustration; as a work on canvas at 3.5 metres wide by 1.3 metres high (11½ × 4¼ ft), it was evidently intended to be both monumental and transportable to other Soviet republics.[24]

Faced with the task of projecting the class struggle in oils, he drew on events in central London described in arriving issues of the *Daily Worker*, developing a design which amalgamated specific incidents from the eleven-day lead-in to a mass lobby of Parliament on Tuesday 1 November 1932. A fortnight before this, more than two thousand hunger marchers in seventeen regional contingents had converged on the capital; warmly welcomed in many places on their journey, they had faced police violence and been harassed into workhouses in many others. Knowing this, the organizers arranged a delegation to the London County Council (LCC) to demand provision of accommodation for those arriving; but as groups from south London gathered in Southwark at St George's Circus on the evening of Tuesday 20 October, mounted police waded into them. The next day's *Daily Worker* carried a front-page report of this assault, illustrated with a photo of a policeman on a rearing white horse; caught at the moment his truncheon strikes down at a woman, this became a central motif for Rowe's painting.

Six days later, an aggressively policed mass rally assembled in Hyde Park to welcome the marchers; as running battles broke out demonstrators tore up railings to defend themselves, an episode transposed to Trafalgar Square in Rowe's depiction of events. As an estimated 150,000 assembled there the following Sunday, police tried but failed to prevent the entry of banners and placards attacking the Means Test – and Rowe portrayed this to good effect in dramatizing the marchers' demands. A million-signature petition against benefit cuts had been brought to London and the mass lobby of Parliament on Tuesday night was an attempt to deliver

1.5 Cliff Rowe, *The Struggle between the Unemployed and the Police Forces*, detail of central scene

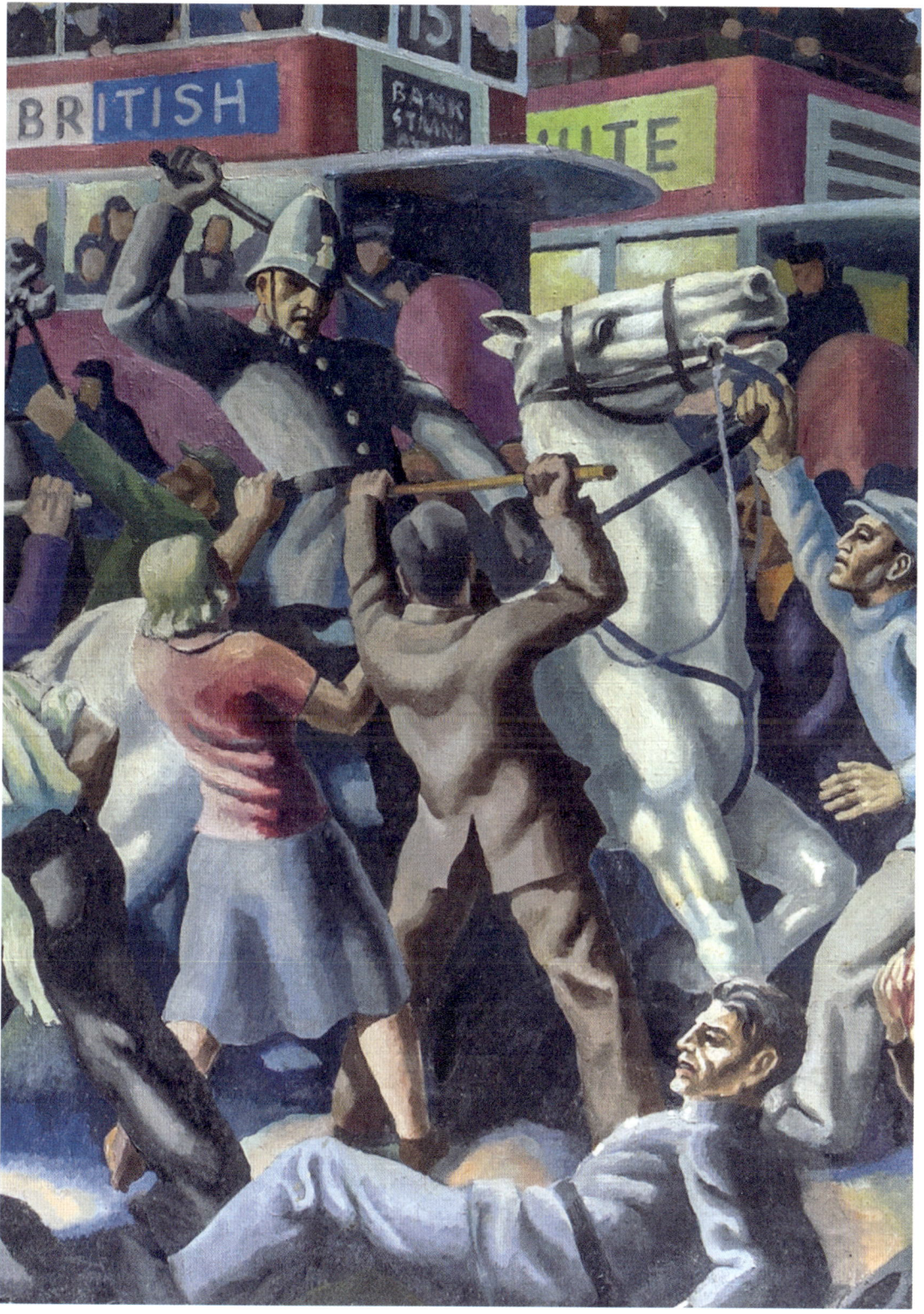

SEVEN DIALS

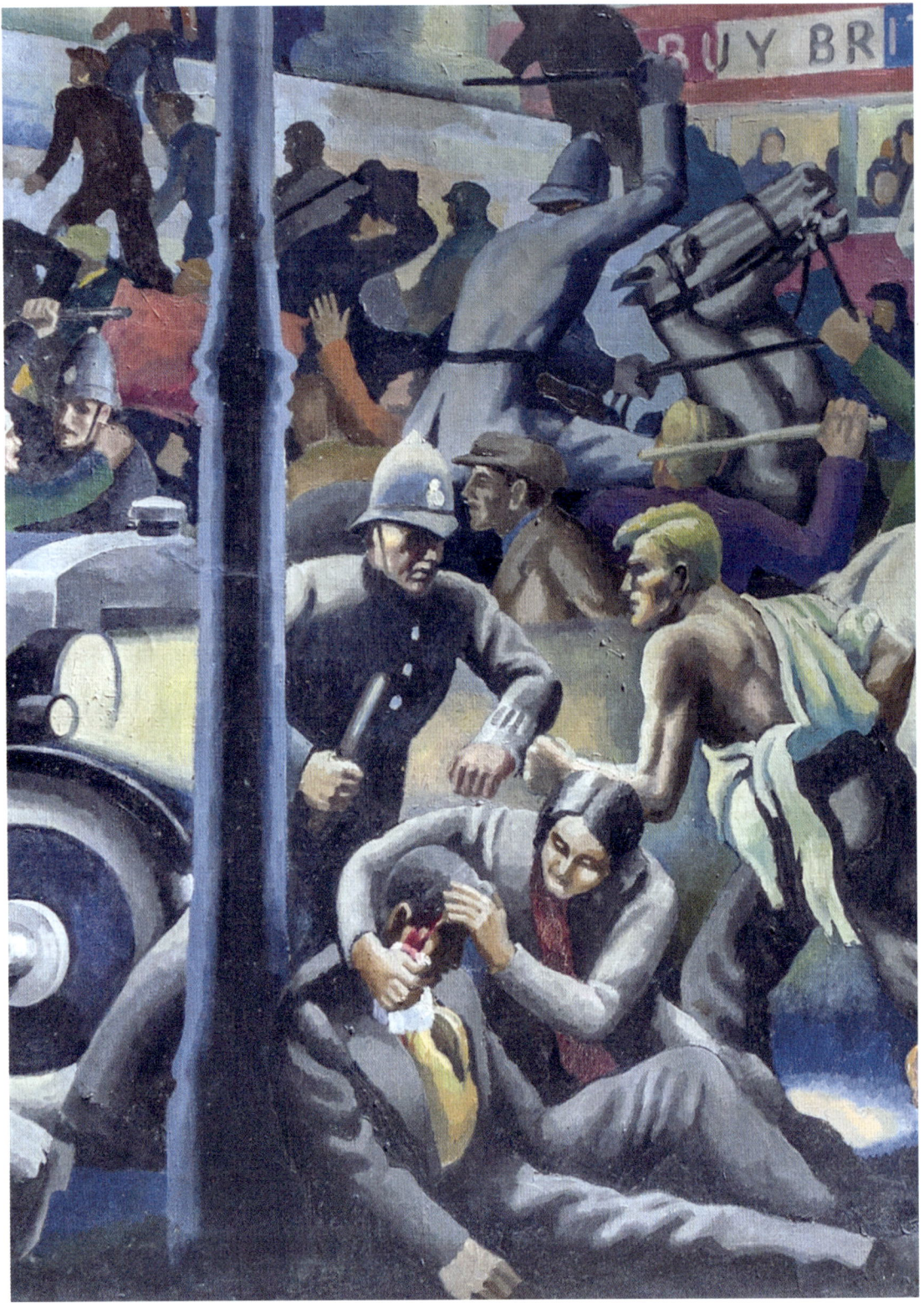

it; as clashes broke out from Farringdon to Victoria, on the south bank of the Thames demonstrators mounted vehicles attempting to get through the police lines and reach Westminster. At just after nine o'clock the most vicious confrontations of all took place in Trafalgar Square at the foot of the National Gallery steps, during which protesters were clubbed to the ground and trampled by horses.[25] Rowe made this tumult central to the work exhibited two months later, and in doing so made plain his own allegiance by including, front and left of centre, a portrait of himself as a shirtless combatant.

It may have been a wry joke for, as he painted, the Writers International, a Comintern organization 'under the careful but firm guidance' of Stalin's party, was issuing revised marching orders to Soviet writers and artists; two years before in Kharkov a 'mirthless' congress had determined that in the fight to defend the Soviet Union 'every proletarian artist must be a dialectic materialist', eschewing bourgeois experimentalism and 'using art as a weapon'.[26] As the results since had frequently been dire, a new definition of Socialist Realism was now being promoted: 'Reproduction of *truth* is demanded of the artist. Not in the sense of a photographic copy of reality which cannot see the wood for the trees ... but in the sense of an artistically true reproduction which shows up the leading, decisive tendencies [and] expresses the unambiguous inner participation of the socialist artist in the represented incidents, his justified emotion in face of the real mass heroism of the struggle.'[27] Rowe had more than fulfilled this new brief.

At some point during his stay in Russia, Rowe visited Kharkov in eastern Ukraine and, whether or not he knew the full extent of devastating famine unfolding in the countryside, a drawing he did there suggests a growing ambivalence towards the results of Soviet policy. In *Lenin and the Peasants*, a towering statue of Vladimir Ilyich on a plinth looks to a distant horizon, while below, oblivious, a forlorn peasant, his wife and their child sit at an empty kitchen table. Back in Moscow, Rowe had now met and was living with Anna Meblin, a woman his own age from the USA who was teaching part-time at the Anglo-American school; against the grain of his libertine twenties, he was now ready to marry and this they did, shortly before circumstances combined to precipitate another sudden journey.

The catalogue entry at the Red Army exhibition had talked up Rowe's proletarian credentials ('In the first period of his artistic career, focused mostly on sketches of London's working-class neighbourhoods and docks ... Later, he began to collaborate as an artist with Communist periodical editions'),[28] but early 1933 was a time of paranoia about subversion and heightened scrutiny of foreigners in Moscow, and it appears probable that the Co-operative Publishing Society came under pressure to justify

1.6 Cliff Rowe, *The Struggle between the Unemployed and the Police Forces*, detail of self-portrait as combatant

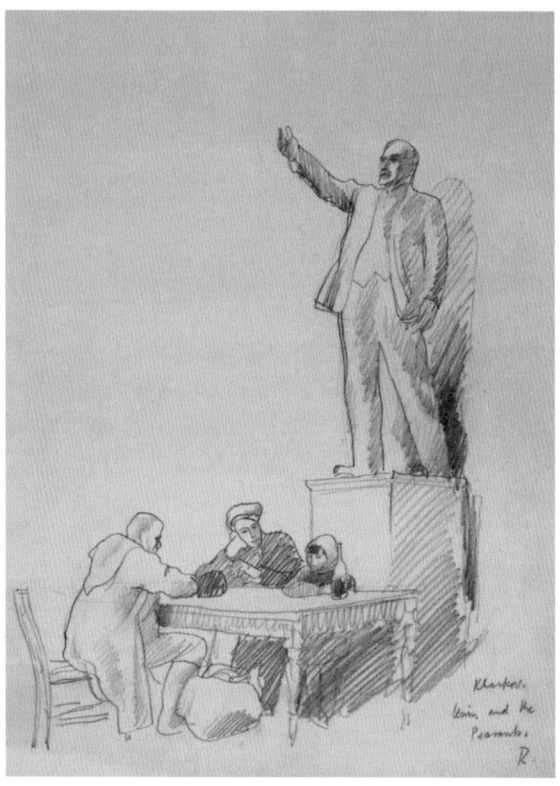

1.7 Cliff Rowe, *Lenin and the Peasants*, pencil on paper, 1932. 29 × 21 cm (11½ × 8⅜ in.)

employment of someone with petit-bourgeois shopkeeping links. At some point, too, satirical content in a factory newspaper failed to amuse both management and local party bosses, a potentially very dangerous transgression.

Much later Rowe would recall: 'I left only because I realised they did not really need me. The class struggle was really going on back in England, so I decided to come back.' This was part of the story, but whatever the precipitating events (which were sufficiently compelling to persuade a reluctant Anna to leave with him), he departed with his belief in internationalism and the potential of unity among artists intact. Before the voyage back he and Anna met Pearl Binder, another accomplished and determined artist visiting Moscow for the first time.[29] Rowe explained what he had in mind, and she voiced her enthusiastic support.[30]

* * * * *

Pearl – Polly to family and friends – had disembarked at Leningrad in July 1933 a couple of weeks after her twenty-ninth birthday; as she recalled later, she had read Dostoevsky and as a theatre lover she had seen the Diaghilev ballets in London after moving south from Manchester, but at that time 'Russia was to me a completely unknown continent'.[31]

Arriving as part of a two-week Intourist tour believing 'the best remedy for wishful thinking was to go and see for oneself', she walked towards customs carrying a rucksack, a mackintosh, very little money and a portfolio of drawings and lithographs.[32]

Art and a quick intelligence had already carried Pearl far from the Salford streets where, when she was seven, the family name had changed from Binderofski to Binder. Having won a scholarship to the technical school, she started to attend classes at Manchester School of Art while clerking in a textile mill. When *The Studio* covered the college's 1925 graduation show, it was Pearl's caricatures that stood out ('she has imagination, a Puckish sense of humour and a power of quickly sizing up a personality'); if she could restrain an 'undue admixture' of savage indignation, the reviewer concluded, 'Miss Binder should make her mark'.[33]

Moving to London, she had done just that as an illustrator with line drawings that satirized well-heeled bohemians in Bloomsbury; a spell working in Paris and a short-lived marriage back in London followed before – separated but not divorced – she moved east to Whitechapel.[34] Based in Spread Eagle Yard, she had explored the East End, getting to know its people and communities, its markets and watersides, so similar to and yet so different from the neighbourhoods poor Jews had made home in Manchester. This terrain had provided the motifs for sixteen lithographs illustrating Thomas Burke's *The Real East End*, published in 1932 – and, in the two years following her first visit to Moscow, she would complete ten superb full-page lithographs for *Odd Jobs*, her own book of London lives.[35]

Autolithography, the complex process of drawing with waxed crayon on polished stones to produce unique but directly reproducible images, had entered her repertoire four years before when she began attending classes at the LCC's Central School of Arts and Crafts. The Central on Southampton Row boasted good equipment and a practical ethos which had long attracted fine art students seeking more marketable skills. For fifteen years its thrice-weekly lithography evening classes had been led by the distinguished artist-lithographer A. S. Hartrick; and after retiring in 1929 he ensured that an outstanding pupil, James Fitton, became his successor but one four years later.[36]

Fitton was another working-class Mancunian. His path to becoming an artist had involved leaving school at fourteen ('won't be good at anything – except drawing' was the headmaster's farewell), short-lived insecure employment at a calico printer and a newspaper office, and becoming, like Polly, a non-fee-paying evening class student at Manchester School of Art. Although Fitton was eleven years younger, fellow pupil

L. S. Lowry became his closest friend, sharing many sketching outings and theatre visits over six years, before another redundancy saw James move to London before 1924.

Unlike Polly, Fitton was following his family because his father, a courageous blacklisted activist in the north-west labour movement, had been appointed national organizer of the Amalgamated Engineering Union, headquartered in Peckham Rye.[37] Once there, James found varied employment as a letterer, an assistant at a printers, and a copy artist turning black-and-white stills into oil paintings for film posters before securing a mural commission for the British Gas Association stand at Olympia. Like Rowe, he had ambitions as a painter, and in 1930 alone had work accepted by the London Group, the New English Art Club and the Royal Academy Summer Exhibition.[38]

Barnett Freedman was another East End attendee at the Central, on his way to becoming a lithographer of extraordinary inventiveness. He would eventually undertake many celebrated commercial commissions, but his present goal was to succeed as an easel painter; 'Jim, I'd rather cut my "frote" than do commercial work', he joked. Fitton himself could not afford such qualms and Russian Oil Products' acceptance of a poster design which had 'a fleeting glance at Léger and Kandinsky' led to him, like Black, visiting the company's Moorgate offices. Special Branch surveillance followed, his movements reported to Downing Street during the second Labour government, which had come to office in June 1929.[39]

A friendship between Fitton's father and the Labour politician John Clynes, Ramsay MacDonald's Leader of the Commons in 1924, who always had a soft spot for his friend's young son, gave James temporary entrée to very different circles after his arrival in London. One consequence was his subsequent lifelong 'dread of social and political pretence' and a lively cynicism about establishment double standards, which in due course would combine with his admiration for the art of Honoré Daumier to produce searing satirical imagery.

Even in 1928 Hartrick must have known where his protégé's sympathies lay when Fitton produced a lithograph on two stones titled *May Day*, depicting demonstrators marching behind a banner through poorly lit streets, columns of smoke and distant fire visible on the other side of a railway embankment. The feel is Central European, the subject a departure from safely conventional subject matter – Fitton may have had the previous year's abortive uprising of Viennese workers in mind[40] – but whatever its antecedents it heralded a style, striking in its dramatic use of black masses and lithographic chiaroscuro, which anticipated and probably encouraged the emerging work of fellow classmates Pearl Binder and James Boswell.

1.8 James Fitton, *Russian Oil Products*, poster design, *c.* 1930. 75.7 × 50.2 cm (29⅞ × 19⅞ in.)

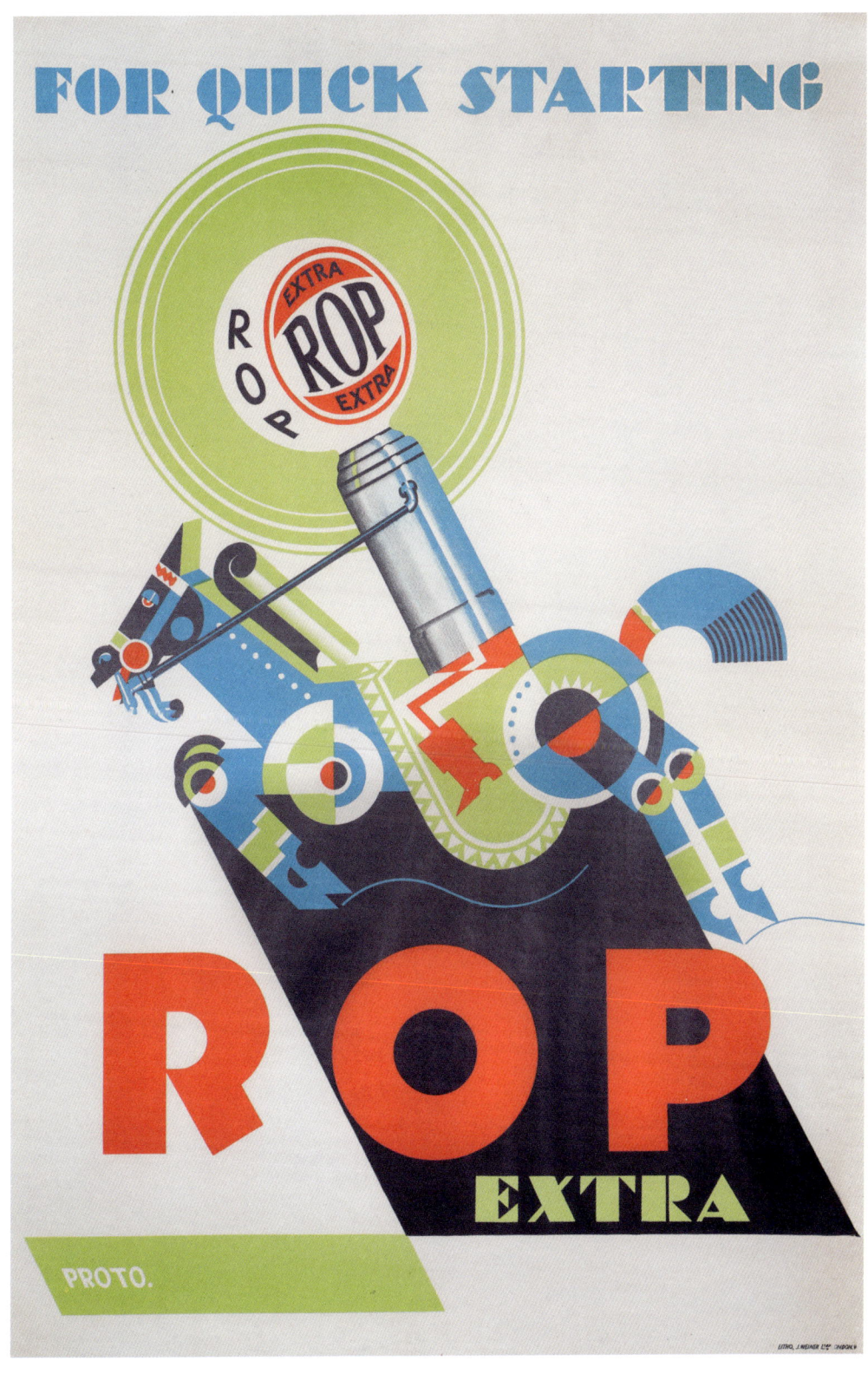

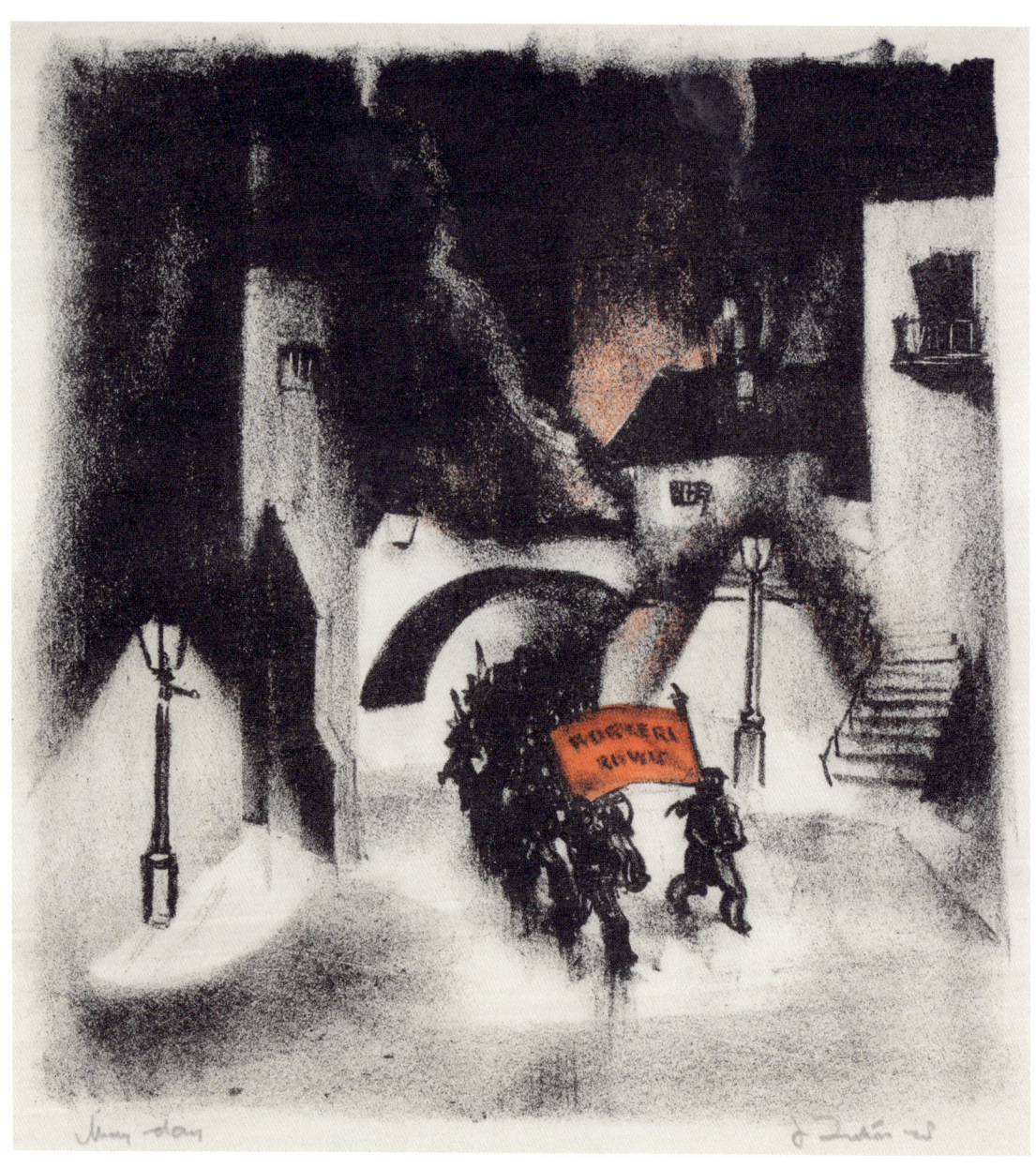

1.9 James Fitton,
May Day,
lithograph, 1928.
31.4 × 28 cm
(12⅜ × 11⅛ in.)

Formally taking over at the beginning of the new autumn term, while Binder was still in Moscow, Fitton decided to build on group camaraderie in egalitarian fashion, modestly recalling: 'I limited the class to about a dozen students. They all knew as much about lithography as I did and they were all as good artists as I was, even better.'[41] A new arrival that term was Hans Feibusch, a thirty-five-year-old Jewish refugee and prize-winning member of the Frankfurt Künstlerbund, whose paintings had been burnt in the streets by Nazi thugs earlier that year. Another was sixteen-year-old Edith Simon, whose Berliner father – a previously prosperous decorated war veteran – fearing for family survival had already chosen the poverty of exile. As Edith noted, as she struggled to survive as sweated labour, doing her own artwork 'betweenwhiles', Fitton's class 'was a great stand-by besides serving us as a crypto discussion club: for 10/6d a term you got the use of materials and equipment thrown in'.[42]

* * * * *

As Pearl approached the Leningrad customs shed, a uniformed officer indicated she should open her portfolio, but as she did 'his face broke into smiles of delight. Eagerly he beckoned the other customs officials and they all pored over my sketches with the deepest interest.' Behind her the luggage-laden queue grew restless, but a lively appraisal of her images of the East End and backstage theatre life continued until 'they tied up my portfolio and returned it to me with smiles and bows, which I found extraordinarily gratifying'. For Binder it was a first taste of a very un-English popular enthusiasm for art she witnessed across 'all kinds' of people: 'Red soldiers and sailors, busy housewives, street-sweepers, chauffeurs, shopkeepers, teachers and children, farmers.'[43]

She had come to Russia with the hope of exhibiting her own art and perhaps picking up work as a cartoonist – as she had done in Paris – or possibly as an illustrator of children's books. The previous autumn her friend Peggy Angus, another attendee at Central lithography classes, had brought back a dozen examples, strikingly fresh and beautifully realized. After visiting as part of an art teachers' delegation, Angus reported back on the literacy campaigns they supported, the barely believable hundred-thousand publishing runs and the demand for artists to work on them.[44]

Two days after her arrival Polly found her way to the VOKS office, as recorded in its daybook for Sunday 16 July 1933: 'Binder – artist (graphist), member of Cultural Contacts Society, came to Moscow with a group ... to become familiar with Soviet art. Had a conversation with Tchernyavsky and Amdur – showed them the albums of her works, which were, after Tchernyavsky, interesting. She wants to gift them to a Soviet art

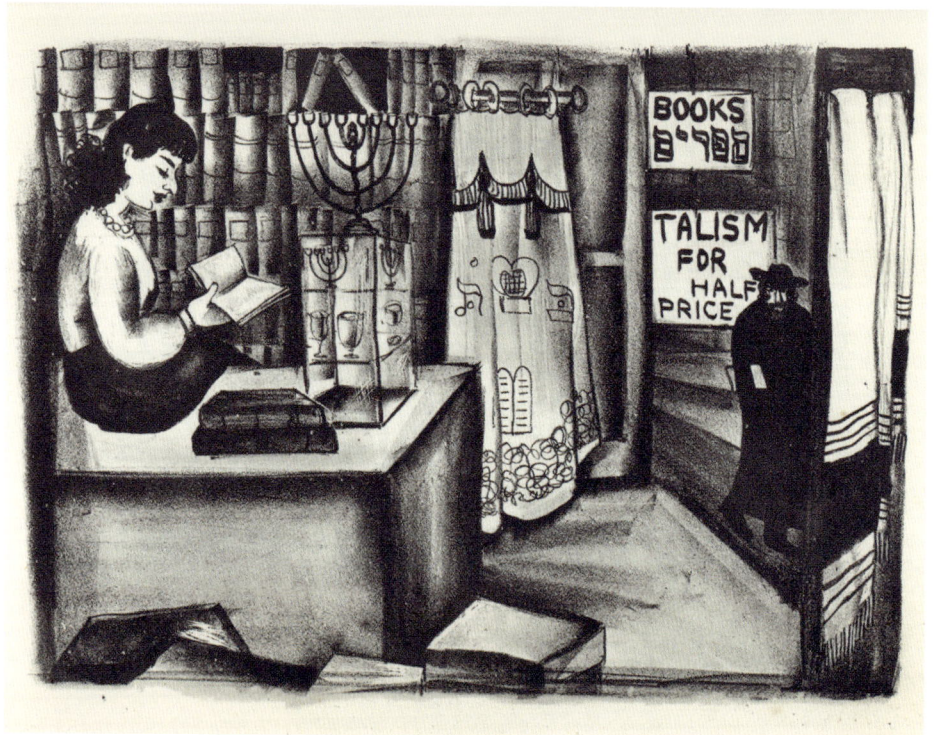
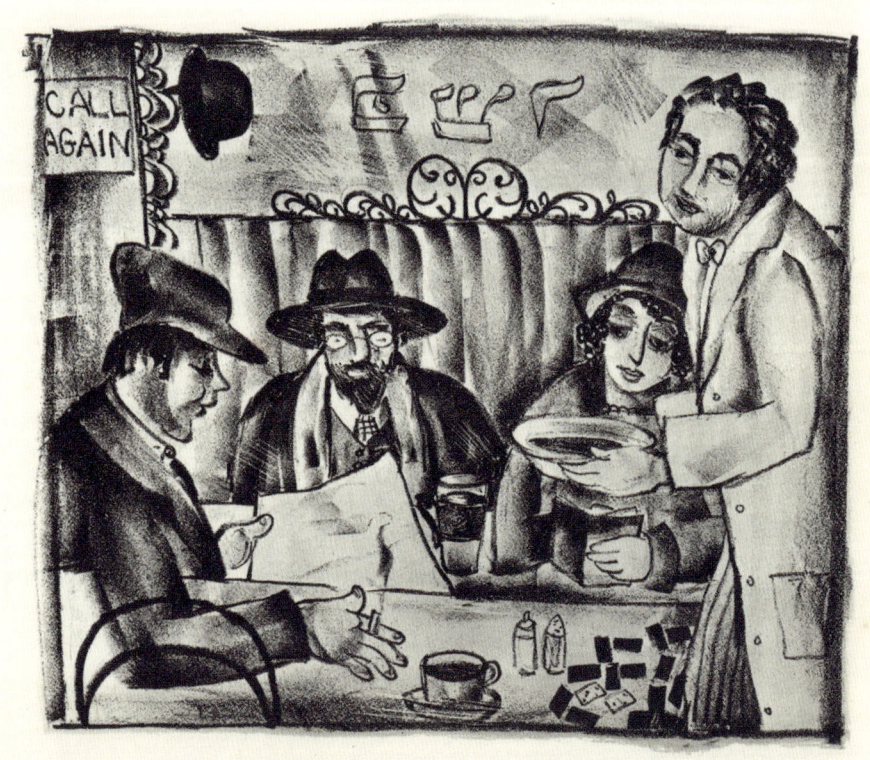

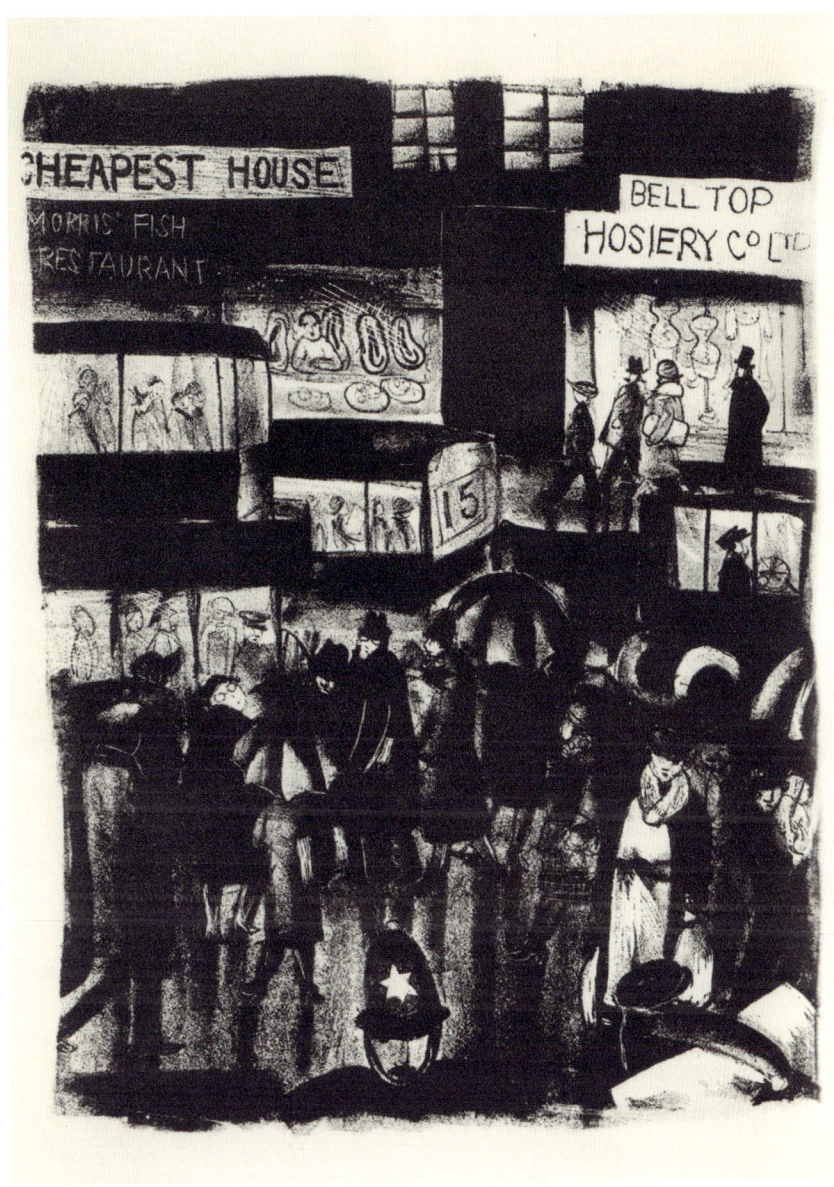

1.10 Pearl Binder, *Jewish Bookshop, Wentworth Street*, lithograph, *c.* 1932. 12.5 × 18 cm (5 × 7⅛ in.)

1.11 Pearl Binder, *Jewish Restaurant, Brick Lane*, lithograph, *c.* 1932. 12.5 × 18 cm (5 × 7⅛ in.)

1.12 Pearl Binder, *Evening in Aldgate*, lithograph, *c.* 1932, one of sixteen full-page lithographs illustrating Thomas Burke's *The Real East End*, 1932. 22 × 15.5 cm (8¾ × 6⅛ in.)

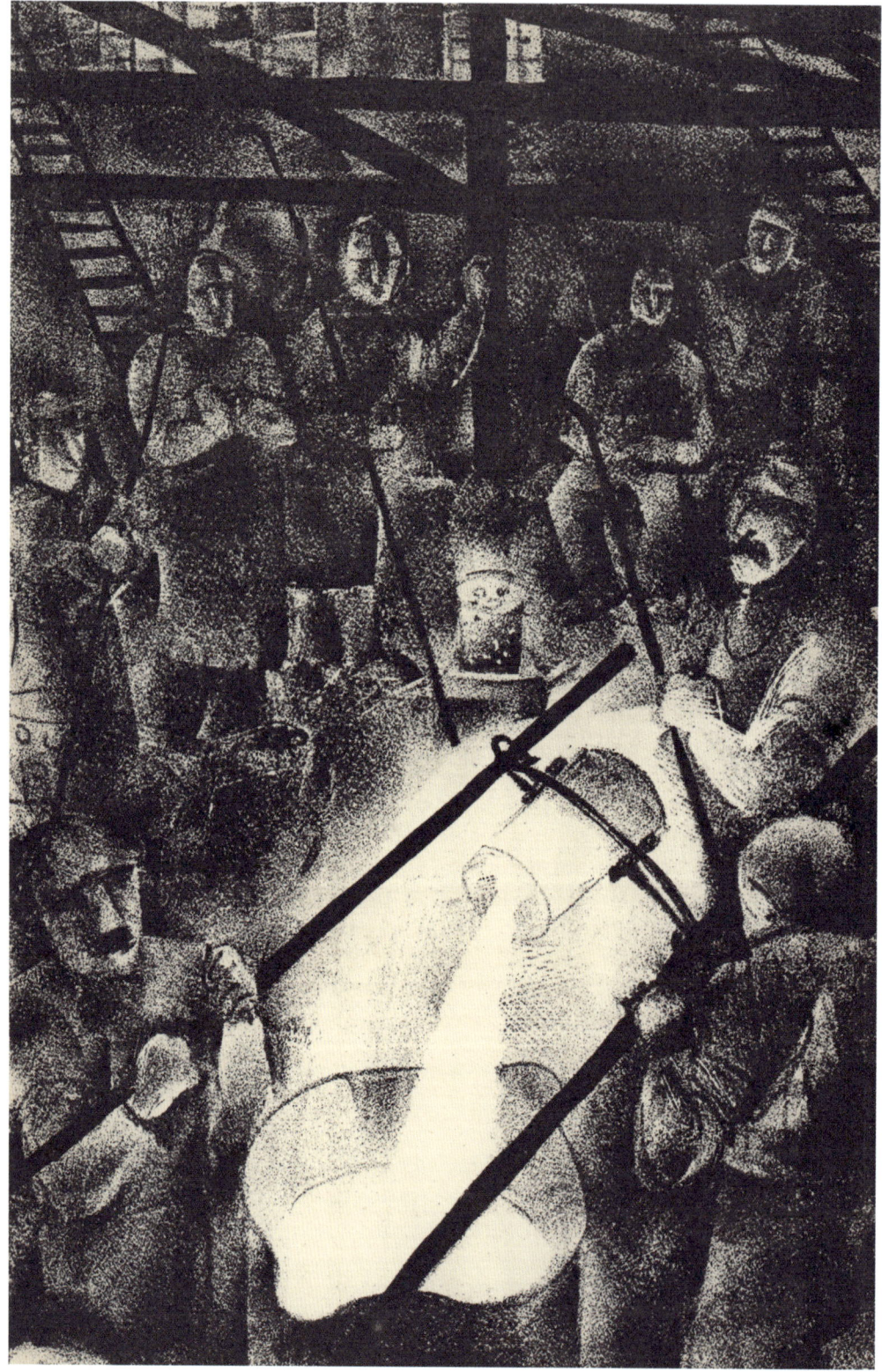

organization. Wanted to illustrate Soviet books for Children. Promised to link her with prof. Ternovets (Museum of New Western Art) and prof. Sidorov (Fine Arts Museum).'[45]

Pearl Binder would later talk with affection, understandably so, about the 'venerable, humorous Ternovets', a sculptor, and his 'lively staff of quite young people'. The response to her work was as enthusiastic at the Museum of New Western Art as it had been at the customs post, and in short order an exhibition of her work was hung in the room set aside for temporary shows. Given an official opening, it attracted large inquisitive crowds in the weeks that followed. Having seen it himself, the editor of the satirical magazine *Krokodil* sent for Binder to offer her work, an opportunity she would take up again on her next visit a year later.

By the time she met Rowe and Anna Meblin on the way home, Polly had had time to marvel at the very different way thousands of artists were supported, organized and employed, sometimes in co-operative studios, sometimes sponsored by trade unions or the Red Army, often on contracts and travelling scholarships.[46] It seemed a world away from the precarious, directionless work of her friends and the dilettante London collectors, gallery owners, agents and editors they had to court, and indeed from a metropolitan avant-garde where 'revolutionary innovation' meant obscure experimentation ever more remote from the life of people as a whole. By contrast, while she was in Moscow the new turn towards Socialist Realism was being launched, and for her what was most striking, as she overheard getting her hair cut one afternoon, was how it 'dominated every other topic, and the most unlikely people discussed every aspect of it passionately'.

Pamphlets published while Cliff Rowe was at the Co-operative Publishing Society testified to a world order of all against all: the World Disarmament Conference at Geneva was on course to fail and the London Economic Conference – where sixty-six nations ostensibly convened to chart a means of escape from global slump – had just collapsed. In Germany the proletariat had not triumphed as the Comintern had forecast; over the previous eight months Adolf Hitler had destroyed both the Socialist and Communist parties.[47] Yet despite this darkening horizon of international events, Pearl Binder evidently brought back to London enthusiasm and a strong sense of possibility; Cliff Rowe, whose lengthier experience of pre-Terror Moscow was more nuanced, carried with him an urgent sense that now was the time for their generation of artists to organize.

*****

'It was in the early days of the Autumn term ... people came into work there and to talk and meet friends on Mondays, Wednesdays and to some

1.13 Pearl Binder, *The Bell Foundry*, lithograph, *c.* 1934, one of eight full-page lithographs illustrating Binder's 1935 book *Odd Jobs*. 22 × 14 cm (8¾ × 5⅝ in.)

extent Fridays ... Pearl turned up one evening and said we must all go and hear Cliff Rowe ... so off some of us went to Misha's place in Seven Dials', recalled James Boswell in the early 1980s, outlining the genesis of two meetings that shaped the embryonic 'Artists International British Section'. The 'some of us' who left the lithography class that night to hear Rowe on his return included James Fitton and James Holland, who – along with Boswell – would make up the 'three Jameses', the graphic heart of so much that lay ahead.[48]

Now twenty-seven, Boswell remembered Cliff Rowe from the Emotionists, whose brief flowering had occurred when he too had been at the RCA. It was an opportunity Boswell had travelled across the globe for, only to find the work its Painting School promoted 'dreary, academic and rubbishy'. Born on the remote west coast of New Zealand's South Island, where his father, Edward, was an art-loving, specimen-collecting deputy headmaster, Boswell's teenage years had been spent in Auckland, where the family moved after his father retired. There the family kept an open house in which, his son recalled, 'being a painter seemed to me the most natural and easy thing in the world'. As his talent as a watercolourist emerged, teachers persuaded his parents that he should train in Europe, whereupon his mother, Ida, twenty years younger than Edward, packed their bags and brought James and his sister to live in London.[49]

Arriving at Tilbury in September 1925, Boswell started at the Royal College ten days later, where James Holland, embarking on his second year, remembered the appearance of 'a stockily built and raw-boned New Zealander who made it apparent that he had not arrived in any mood of colonial humility'.[50] The new arrival had a slow genial smile and an impressive breadth of education, being widely read in both English and French; a powerful swimmer, he was not averse – despite the gentle lilt of his accent – to being seen as 'a Wild Colonial Boy'.[51] But his pilgrimage to the imperial heart of the home country had not begun well: London struck him as 'provincial and awful'. With an outsider's eye he soon discerned that English society was perversely class-obsessed and that the RCA Painting School was a backwater: 'I was fascinated by modern painting but couldn't find anyone to talk to about it.'[52] Disliking the young antipodean's work, William Rothenstein – for whom abstraction was 'a cardinal sin', 'Modernism' an aberration – suspended Boswell with an injunction not to return 'until you can do better than *that*'.[53]

Rothenstein's cursory dismissal was, however, more than compensated for by the generosity of Freddie Porter, a fellow Aucklander who had arrived in London a decade earlier via Melbourne and Paris and gained recognition as a painter of landscapes, townscapes and still lifes. Porter, a radical socialist, took Boswell into his studio at 8 Fitzroy Street, where

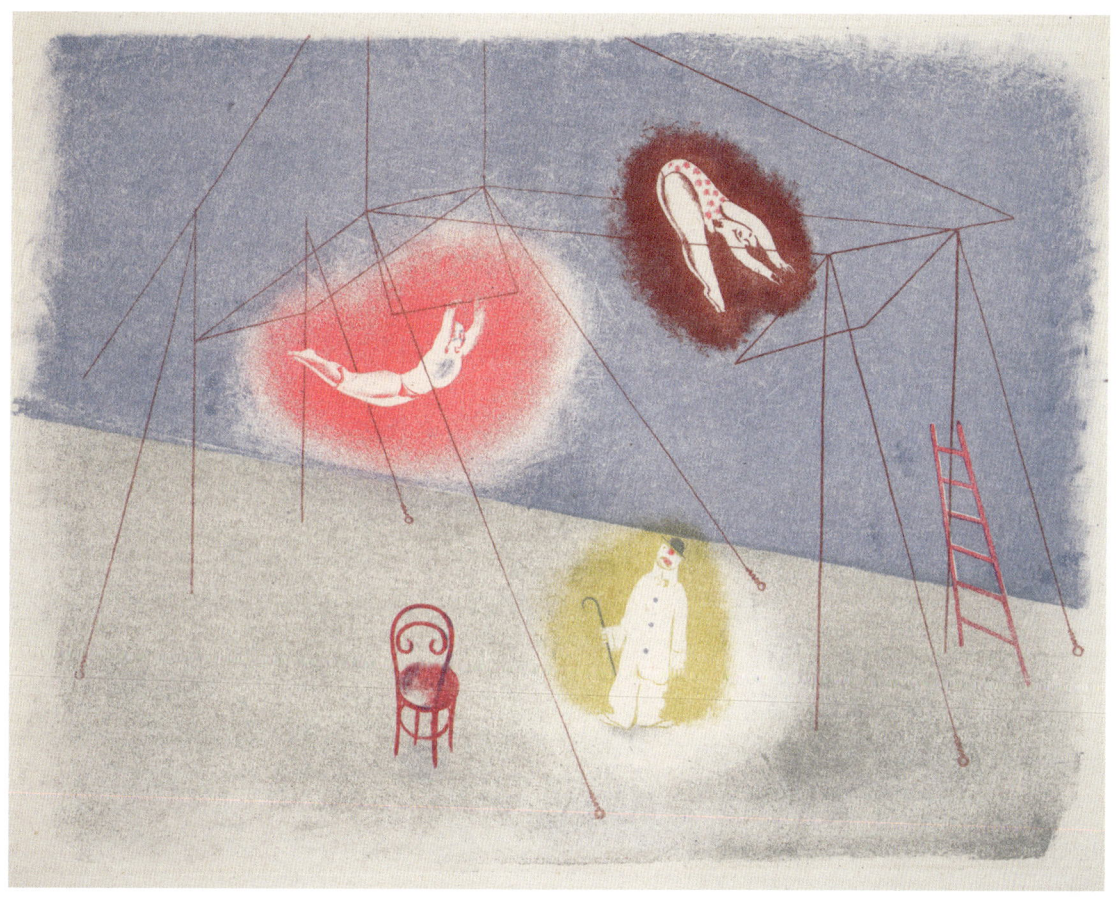

1.14 James Fitton, *Trapeze II*, lithograph, 1935, based on the artist's *Trapeze I*, oil on board, 1934. 40 × 54 cm (15¾ × 21⅜ in.)

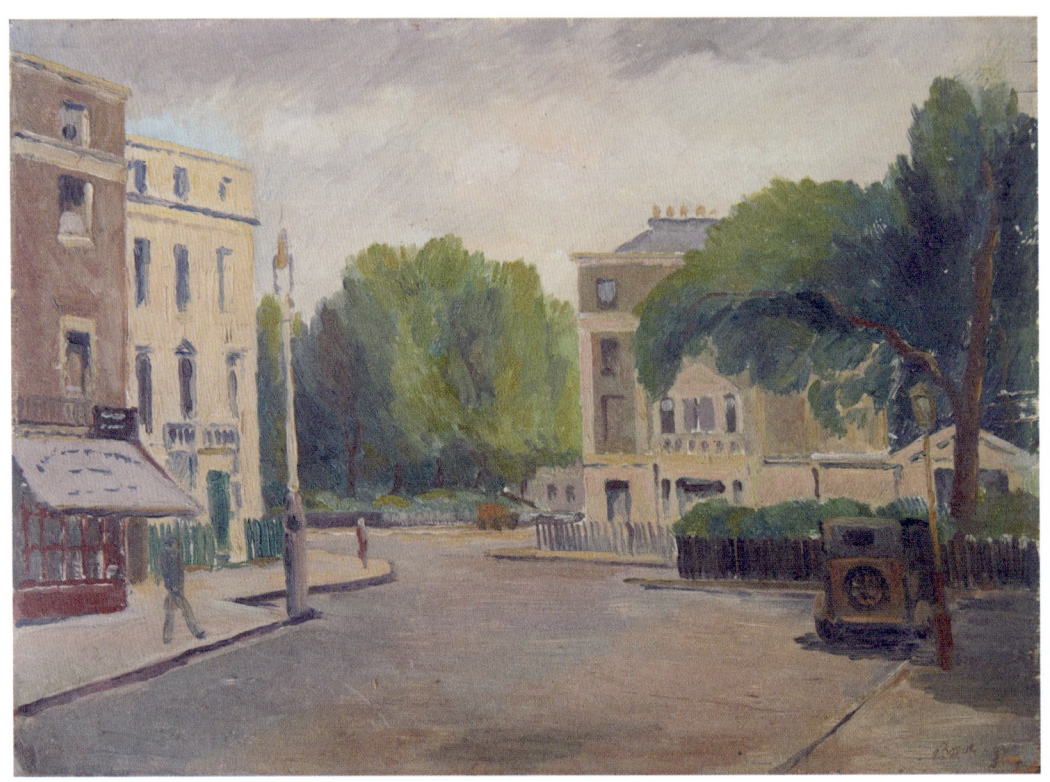

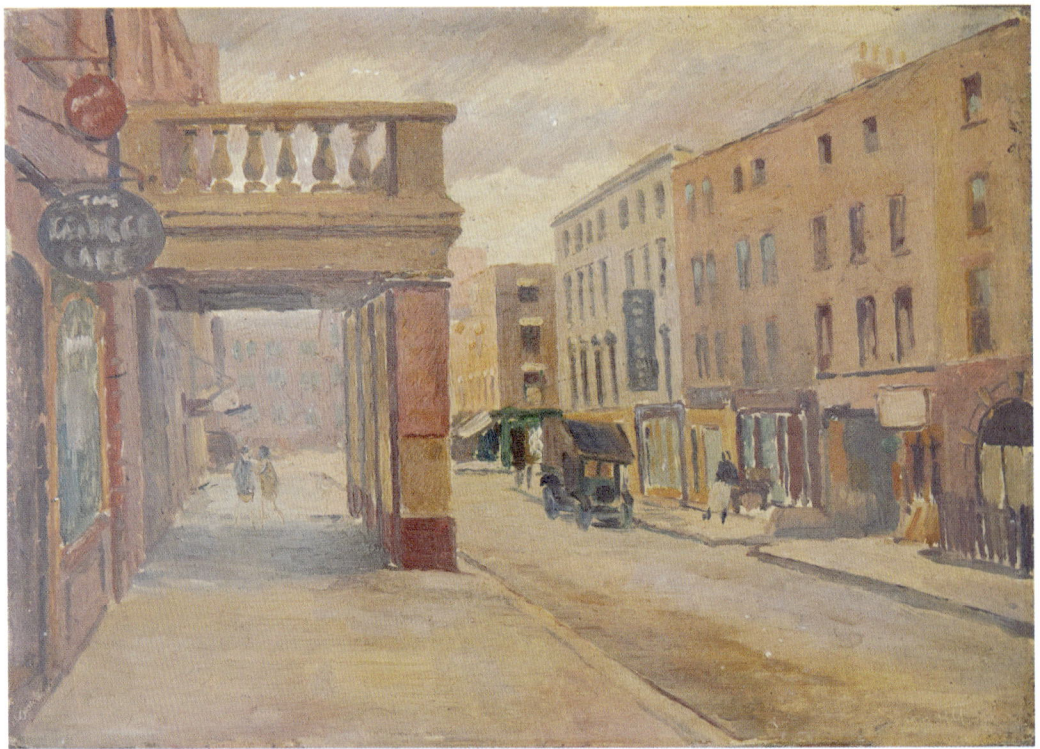

his own first solo exhibition had been held in 1916 and where he now lived in the rambling house in which the Camden Town Group had first met in Walter Sickert's rooms; the London studios of Vanessa Bell and Duncan Grant were in a rear annexe reached by a complicated walkway. Inheriting an attic room with a skylight, Boswell had accidentally arrived at the ramshackle crossroads of the London Group's artistic network.

Porter had become London Group vice-president in 1925, and his status was further reinforced in 1926 when John Maynard Keynes endowed the London Artists' Association; this was the latest in the economist's long line of generous moves to support his former lover Grant and Bell, the mother of Grant's child, Angelica. Porter became one of seven artists guaranteed an annual income by the Association.[54] A decade later this web of connection would bring benefits for more political initiatives, but the principal consequence for Boswell and Holland in the late 1920s was a welcome opportunity to submit non-member work to both exhibiting bodies, so gaining a little traction in their struggle to survive as fine artists.[55]

Boswell's confidence and range grew under Porter's influence, and by 1927 an Auckland paper was reporting the young émigré's success in showing seven oil sketches, eight watercolours, a backcloth design for a ballet, three pen-and-ink drawings and three woodcuts which were 'progressive, a little daring and extremely original'.[56] A return to the RCA, however, was short-lived: 'I took my diploma and won a scholarship to go on painting. But I was too restive to work in the place and spent most of my time in my studio so they fired me again.'[57]

Boswell and Holland had been wary on first meeting, but 'in a matter of weeks [that] changed to considerable enjoyment of each other's company, perhaps chiefly because our backgrounds and experiences had been so different'.[58] James Holland's journey to South Kensington had been much shorter in terms of distance, but more stretching in terms of family expectation. His father was a naval blacksmith working in the Chatham Dockyard, as had both his grandfathers, one dying before he was born, leaving his maternal grandmother penniless with a large family of small children, forced to sew for long hours in the flag loft. With the ending of the war, retrenchment cut into the industrial workforce of the Medway Towns 'and men employed at levels of responsibility suddenly found themselves demoted, back at the workbench and lucky to be there'.[59] Every year boys of fourteen sat the Dockyard Exam, those successful gaining admission to the Dockyard School, the route to a trade. Holland, however, had gained entry to the Mathematical School, where his visual talent was spotted by the visiting principal of Rochester Art College, which in turn became a stepping stone to the Royal College. But the ships, the slums, the disabled ex-servicemen and the funeral processions, the returning sailors and

1.15 James Boswell, *The Entrance to Gordon Square*, oil on board, *c.* 1931. 27.5 × 39.5 cm (10⅞ × 15⅝ in.)

1.16 James Boswell, *The Scala Stage Door, Tottenham Street*, oil on board, *c.* 1931. 40.6 × 50.8 cm (16 × 20 in.)

SEVEN DIALS

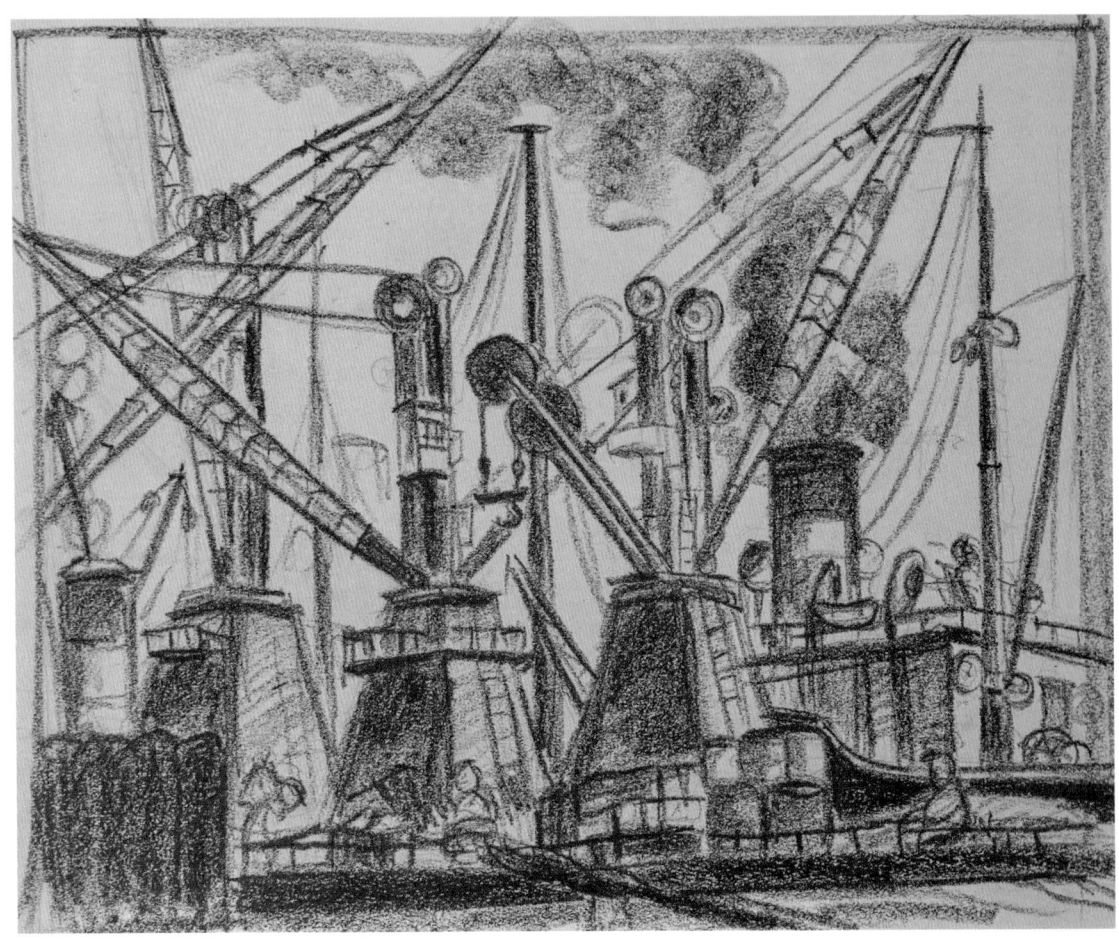

1.17 James Holland, *Docks*, crayon on paper, early 1930s. 33 × 42.5 cm (13 × 16¾ in.)

skilled men laid off – these were the remnants of lean years in the Medway Towns he carried with him.

When Duncan Grant went to France in 1929 and let his studio, Holland moved in, and shortly after a visiting New Zealander found the two friends leading a 'rather dowdy vie de Bohème' there, reporting how one night 'having an embarrassing number of paintings on their hands, they went round Fitzroy Square distributing a neglected masterpiece in each doorway'.[60] Scant picture sales were supplemented by very erratic freelance earnings, which improved marginally for Boswell as he won book cover work for the progressive publisher Boriswood,[61] and for Holland when Shell-Mex's new publicity officer Jack Beddington commissioned a series of press adverts.[62]

But the shock waves of financial crash followed. By 1932 Boswell had decided to abandon oil painting in favour of graphic art and moved from the Fitzroy Street studio to Chalk Farm; equally decisively, appalled by the

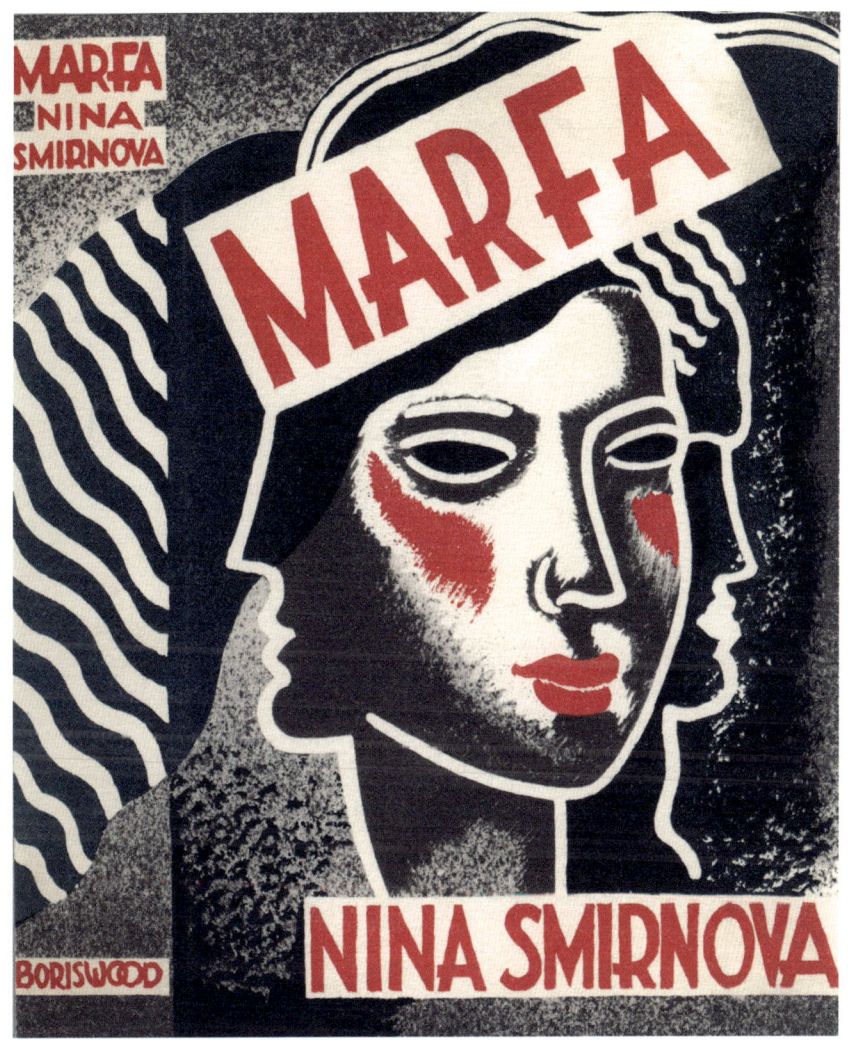

1.18 James Boswell, cover design for *Marfa* by Nina Smirnova, 1934; one of fifteen cover designs Boswell created for Boriswood between 1932 and 1936. 19 × 16.2 cm (7½ × 6½ in.)

way Britain's rulers were treating the poor and unemployed, he became 'an active though not uncritical' member of the Communist Party.[63] His major artwork the following year, carried out at the Central, was *The Fall of London*, a series of eight small, highly accomplished, darkly evocative lithographs which, as his daughter Sal Shuel has written, 'depicted the city destroyed by violence and anarchy; buildings in ruins, bodies littering the ground. They are his apocalyptic version of Goya's *Disasters of War*.'[64]

Three years later Holland wrote to an exiled German art critic living in Moscow describing the times they had lived through: 'Economic crisis killed the active but undiscriminating patronage that the younger English artists had enjoyed since the war ... these artists were faced with a choice of a cut-throat competition for what crumbs of patronage remained, continuing to paint until overtaken by starvation, giving up art, or using their abilities to discredit a system that makes art and culture dependent on the caprices of the money markets. The last has always seemed to me the only realistic course.'[65] It was in this frame of mind on a September evening that he and Boswell walked the half mile to Misha Black's rooms to hear what Cliff Rowe had to say.

* * * * *

Memoirs are distinct: one witness recalls particular details omitted by another; those present remember meeting a different person for the first time, but perhaps not the presence of another comrade in the coming endeavour. But all accounts are consistent in two meetings having taken place in quick succession, that in the interval some seeking of views and spreading of news occurred, and that this led to an embryonic organization forming, with chair, secretary and an initial committee, and a name being selected. By early October 1933 a core group was reaching out to others and a trajectory of activity had been set, which would be pursued with slight resources but astounding determination in the months – and then the years – ahead.

On that first candle-lit evening in Little Earl Street there were about a dozen people present, nearly all in their twenties, almost equally split between men and women.[66] The electricity had been disconnected because Misha Black was in the process of closing down Studio Z, moving his living quarters to a rented room in Charlotte Street and, by the following spring, his working endeavours to Bassett-Gray, a consultancy in Bedford Square.[67] Styled as 'the distributing organisation of a body of artists who design for industrial and commercial purposes' by 'working individually or collaboratively', Bassett-Gray would in due course become the Industrial Design Partnership (IDP) and Black's base for servicing a wide variety of

1.19 James Boswell, *The Colosseum*, from the series *The Fall of London*, 1933. Each lithograph measures 13.5 × 9.5 cm (5⅜ × 3¾ in.)

1.20 James Boswell, *Through the City*, *The Fall of London*, 1933

1.21 James Boswell, *Waterloo*, *The Fall of London*, 1933

1.22 James Boswell, *The British Museum*, *The Fall of London*, 1933

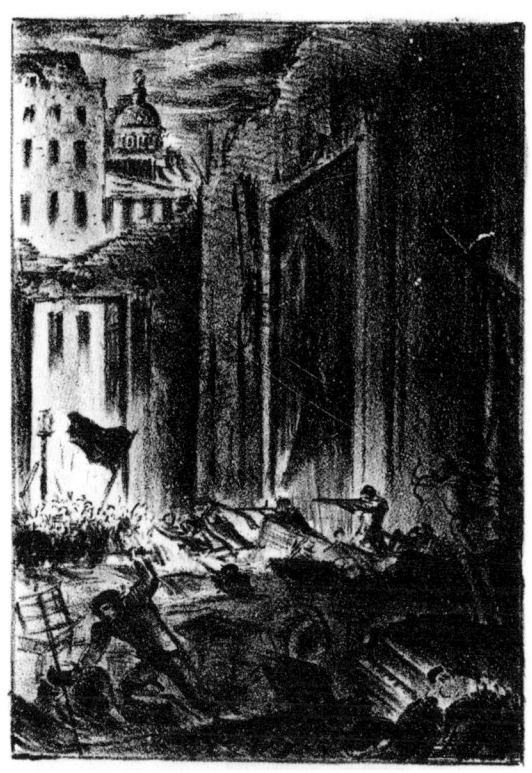
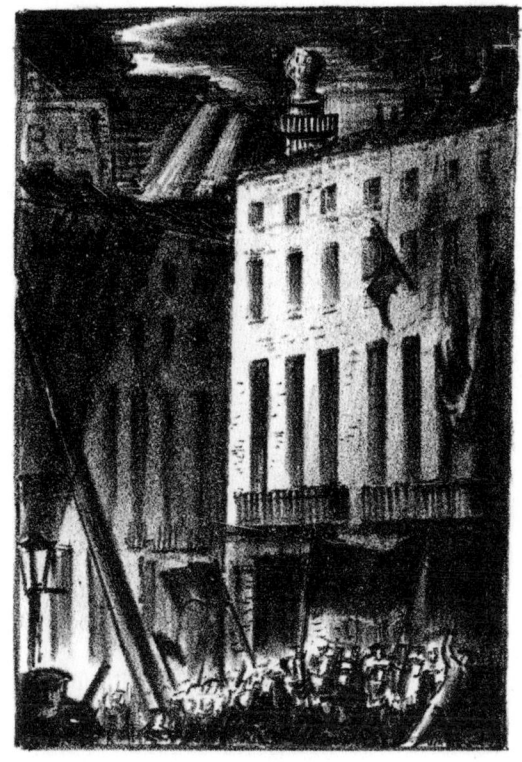
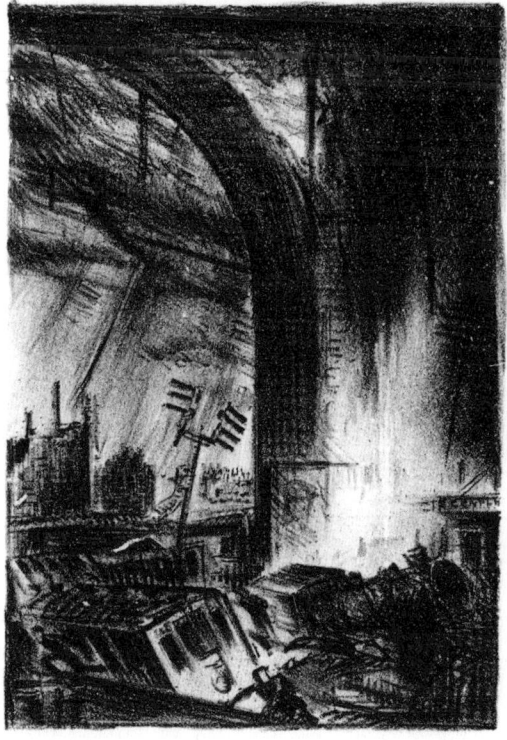
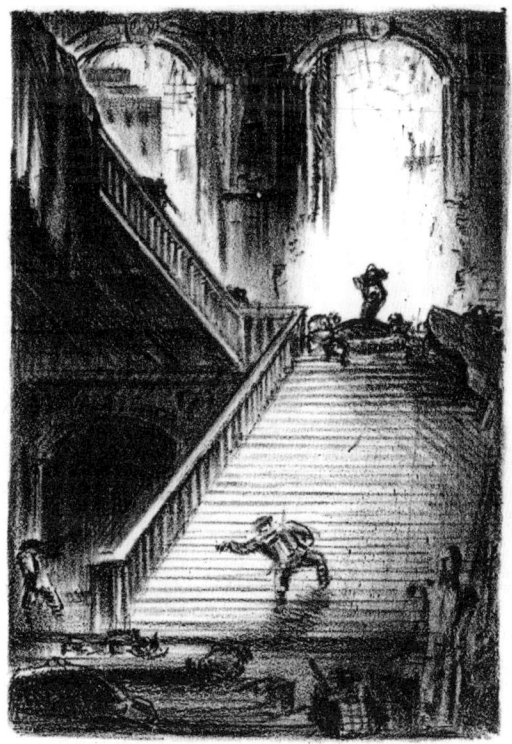

SEVEN DIALS

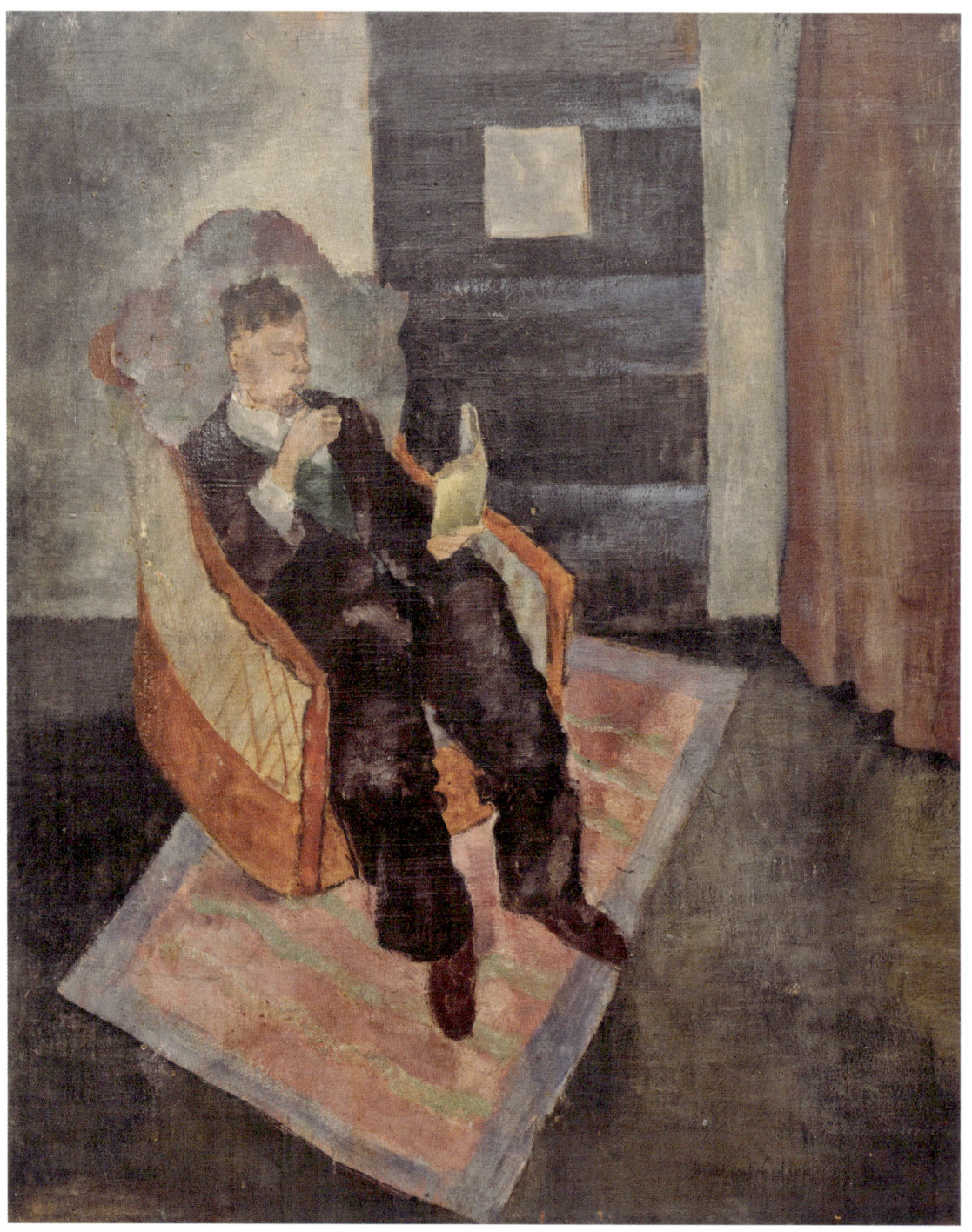

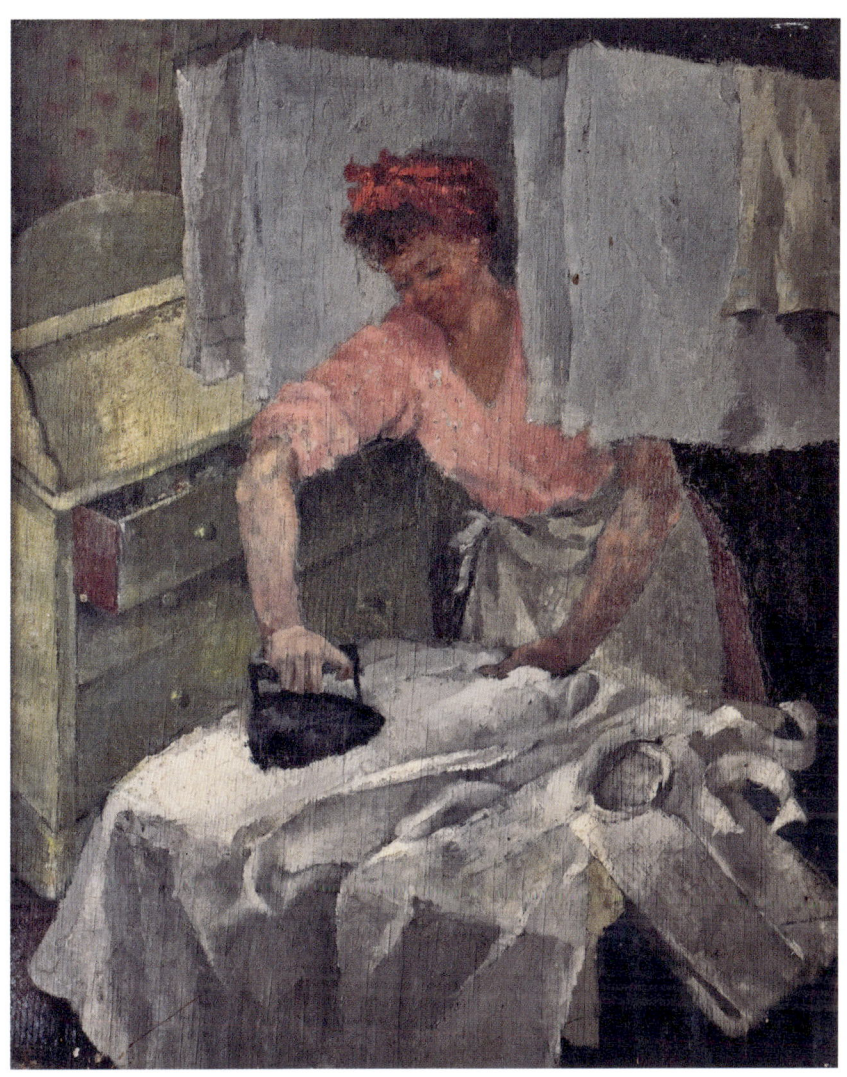

1.23 Margaret Fitton, *Man in a Wicker Chair*, oil on canvas, *c.* 1934. 61 × 49 cm (24⅛ × 19⅜ in.). The subject is her husband, James Fitton, at 10 Pond Cottages, Dulwich, where the couple moved after their marriage. This painting was exhibited as cat. 53 at *Artists Against Fascism and War*, 1935

1.24 Margaret Fitton, *Ironing and Airing*, oil on canvas, mid-1930s. 62 × 50 cm (24½ × 19¾ in.). Fitton was a founder member of the AIA, exhibiting at all its major exhibitions during its first decade

clients, but he long remembered how at this time 'we were all very poor … £3 a week was really doing rather well'.⁶⁸

What was evident that night, however, was a quality of leadership in twenty-three-year-old Misha, whose knack of identifying common ground urged his selection as 'chairman' to a group whose average age was five years older. Mild in manner, amusing and ironic, more of 'a diplomat than a philosopher intent on expounding personal views', he would have to stretch himself in the years ahead to give meaning and unity 'to what might be seen as conflicting ideas and events'.⁶⁹ But his visitors' choice would be endorsed and re-ratified for the next eleven years, even as the number of members approached a thousand and many of the artistic great and good were brought into the fold.

Those present felt the political situation was becoming intolerable, oppressive at home, ever more dangerous internationally, their situation as artists increasingly fragile. No one in the room had been to Oxbridge; no one was in revolt – however temporary – against their adolescence at Eton or Harrow; none were members of avant-garde groups such as Paul Nash's Unit One; and few had even the slenderest of savings to ride out the slump or any expectations of even modest inheritances to come.⁷⁰ And

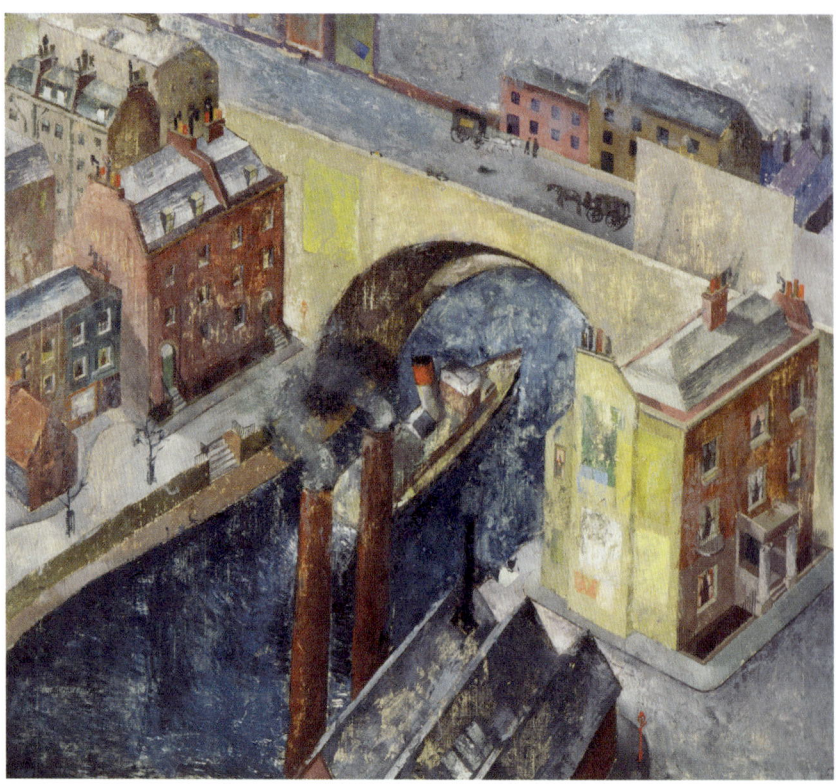

1.25 James Fitton, *The Canal Bridge*, oil on board, 1933. 69.1 × 76.8 cm (27¼ × 30¼ in.)

1.26 Edith Simon, *Self-portrait*, oil on board, 1935. 35.6 × 25.4 cm (14 × 10 in.)

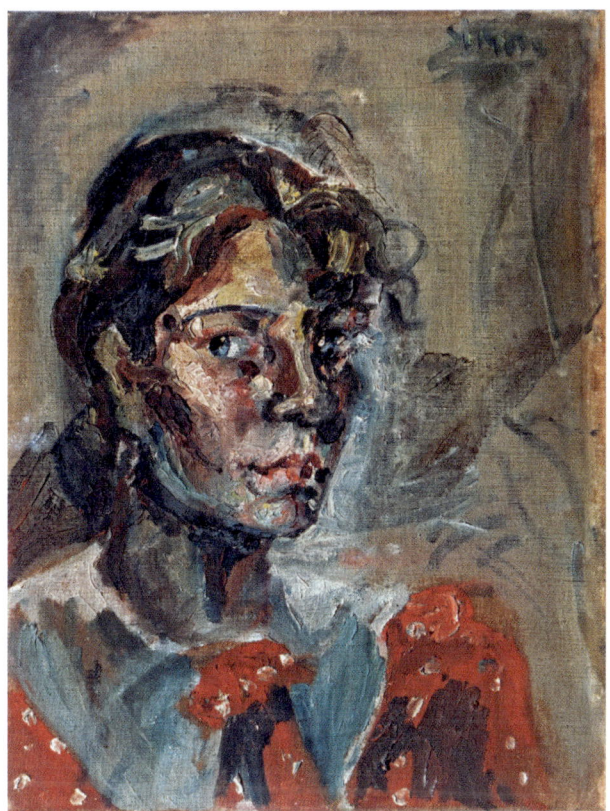

while there were theoretical debates not far ahead, with the British Union of Fascists (BUF) already on the streets and reports of German artists being incarcerated in Dachau, the urge to collective action was born of integrity and pragmatism. As Black said later, it 'had no intellectual basis ... it was purely socially and politically motivated [and] sprang from a real feeling of social responsibility'.[71]

Into this milieu, the three USSR returnees brought news of alternative possibilities, as sixteen-year-old Edith Simon, the youngest person present, observed. Alongside colouring cartoon films for the under-age wage of 10/6d a week, one of Simon's odd jobs had been copy-typing 'at the rate of threepence per 1000 words, top and 2 carbons'. Invited along to Charlotte Street for her keyboard skills, she witnessed both the new organization's naming and the sense of optimism that accompanied it: 'Can you imagine the upsurge of energy and will from the news that art could actually help to revolutionise society? that art and the values it embodies are a fundamental part of society? that thorough integration of art into everyday life must enhance the quality of both? ... Clearly artists formed the natural vanguard in the fight for peace, freedom and full employment.'[72]

SEVEN DIALS

As note-taker that night it fell to her to record the first name suggested: 'The International Association of Artists for Revolutionary Proletarian Art'; and later, after listening to much discussion, to type out its marginally punchier replacement, 'Artists International – British Section', more generally called the 'AI'.

*****

Ahead of its publication that October, Faber and Faber had been sending out review copies of Herbert Read's *Art Now: An Introduction to the Theory of Modern Painting and Sculpture.* It was the book that secured Read's reputation as modernism's most enthusiastic London advocate, and its preface referenced the unfolding Nazi assault on freedom of artistic expression, coupled with a plea for art to be separated from politics. The public, he argued, mired in the drabness of modern life, desired entry to the inner world of the imagination, the key to which was held by artists who 'the more modern they are in spirit as artists, the more disinterested and detached they become. In short the good artist is very rarely interested in anything but his art.'[73] Read's theorizing bridged both abstraction and automatism – of which Surrealism was the principal strand – and this viewpoint, plus his Hampstead social connections, made him the natural choice for his next editorial task: pulling together a book of essays for Unit One, the newly minted grouping fostered by Paul Nash which sought to unite an artistic elite straddling both tendencies.

Nash had announced Unit One's formation in a letter to *The Times* the previous June, expanding on it in *The Listener* as 'an adventure in art' to be pursued by eleven painters, sculptors and architects who stood 'for the expression of a truly contemporary spirit'.[74] Unashamedly exclusive, by invitation only, it was to bring together 'artists of established reputations who are not very concerned as to how other English artists paint or make sculpture or build', its name signalling that 'though as persons, each artist is a unit, in the social structure they must, to the extent of their common interests, be *one*'.

This unity among leading contemporary artists was intended to realize a strategic purpose for English art, which had long been hampered by 'lack of structural purposefulness', insularity and the 'crippling weakness' of proceeding too exclusively 'by the light of nature'. In the face of this, Nash asserted, 'the international character of modern art, by destroying false values of nationalism' was opening the way for imaginative research and exhibition activity that could revolutionize the 'imprisoned spirit' of English tradition in a specifically English way.

When the second founding meeting of the AI occurred, many of Unit One's participants had work on display at the Mayor Gallery in Cork Street, Mayfair. This exhibition was timed to coincide with the publication of *Art Now*, which carried plates of works by Henry Moore, Barbara Hepworth, Ben Nicholson, Paul Nash, Edward Burra, John Bigge, Edward Wadsworth and Tristram Hillier. Nash had announced that the Mayor would be Unit One's headquarters and it was there that it held its sole member exhibition six months later, after which it immediately began to break up, riven by personalized aesthetic disputes.[75] When unanimous approval was made the test of continued membership, only Henry Moore and Paul Nash survived the vote. Tellingly, however, all its members would come to participate in the AI in the coming years.

For the AI's young founding core neither exhibition nor sales activity was the central purpose, still less the forging of an epochal contribution to English art or any self-conscious aesthetic agenda. The goal was not to improve art or artistic life by separating it from politics, but the total reverse, to serve shared political goals through their art and to develop an artists' organization that would act as an auxiliary to progressive causes; from the first there was an aspiration that internationalism was to be a terrain for action, not a cultural reservoir to be drawn on for local furthering of 'contemporary spirit'.

The AI's first *Bulletin*, cyclostyled from stencils typed by Simon, defined its aim as 'The International unity of artists against Imperialist War, War on the Soviet Union, Fascism and Colonial Oppression', and explained:

> It is intended to further these aims by the following practical measures:
> 1. The uniting of all artists, in Great Britain, sympathetic with these aims, into working units ready to execute posters, illustrations, cartoons, book-jackets, banners, tableaux, stage decorations, etc
> 2. The spreading of propaganda by means of exhibitions, the press, lectures and meetings
> 3. The maintaining of contacts with similar groups in 16 other countries

Cliff Rowe and Pearl Binder were two of the *Bulletin*'s five signatories and it was probably one of them who sent a copy and covering letter to *International Literature* in Moscow, which explained in its first issue for 1934 that the group now had thirty-two members[76] and outlined its activities and aims:

> We have instituted fortnightly discussions on Communism and Art from all angles. We are working closely with the Marx Library and the Workers' School.

We have taken part in strikes and elections producing mimeographed newspapers on the spot, backed up by cartoons and posters. This will give us the experience we need of direct contact with the masses.

We have made contact with Revolutionary art groups abroad and plan International Exhibits.

Among our activities have been posters done for the Marxist Club of London University, preliminary work for an animated film cartoon for the Workers Film Movement; drawings and illustrations for the first number of the New Challenge, our new workers' sports paper; a puppet show to be shown on the streets for the ILD, etc.

We are also decorating halls for revolutionary meetings among other activities.

*****

Boswell recalled how he and James Lucas were the only card-carrying members of the Communist Party present at the first Little Earl Street discussion – others there joining subsequently – and that they consulted more experienced members before the next meeting. One who offered both advice and practical support in building a new organization was Percy Horton, who both Rowe and Boswell had previously crossed paths with at the Royal College of Art.

Now thirty-six, Horton was the epitome of someone who was radical and always humane in politics but conservative in art. Imprisoned as an absolutist conscientious objector in 1916, he had been subjected to brutal punishment in Edinburgh's Calton jail and faced both ill health and discrimination after the war before being accepted into Hartrick's painting classes at the Central; from there he had won a scholarship to the RCA where, favoured by Rothenstein, he had become a fine portraitist. In 1927, keenly alive to Percy's personal qualities and lack of money (but only dimly aware of the depth of his politics), Rothenstein had recommended Horton to reorganize the evening art classes at the Working Men's College in Crowndale Road, Camden, which had now thrived under his guidance for the last six years.[77] While working there and living in Mecklenburgh Square, not far from the Mount Pleasant sorting depot, he had painted *The Postman* in the year after the general strike, one of a series of works in which he both used and subverted the conventions of society portraiture to imbue working people with dignity and agency. It was almost certainly through their common membership of the Communist Party St Pancras branch that he first met Francis Klingender, a student activist who was involved with producing *Red Letter*, the factory newspaper for post workers.[78] Klingender required posters to advertise London University

1.27 Percy Horton, *The Postman*, oil on canvas, 1927. 50 × 40.5 cm (19¾ × 16 in.)

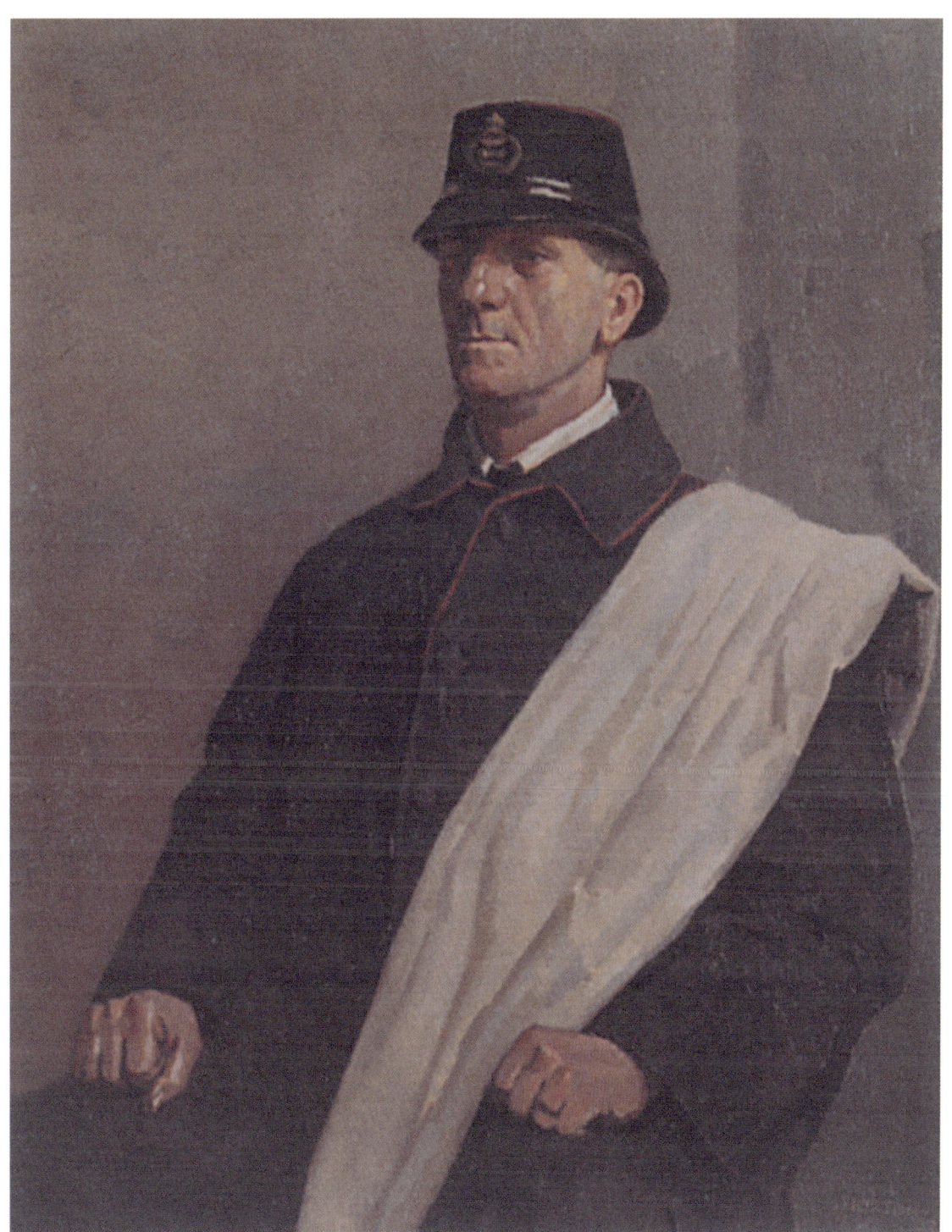

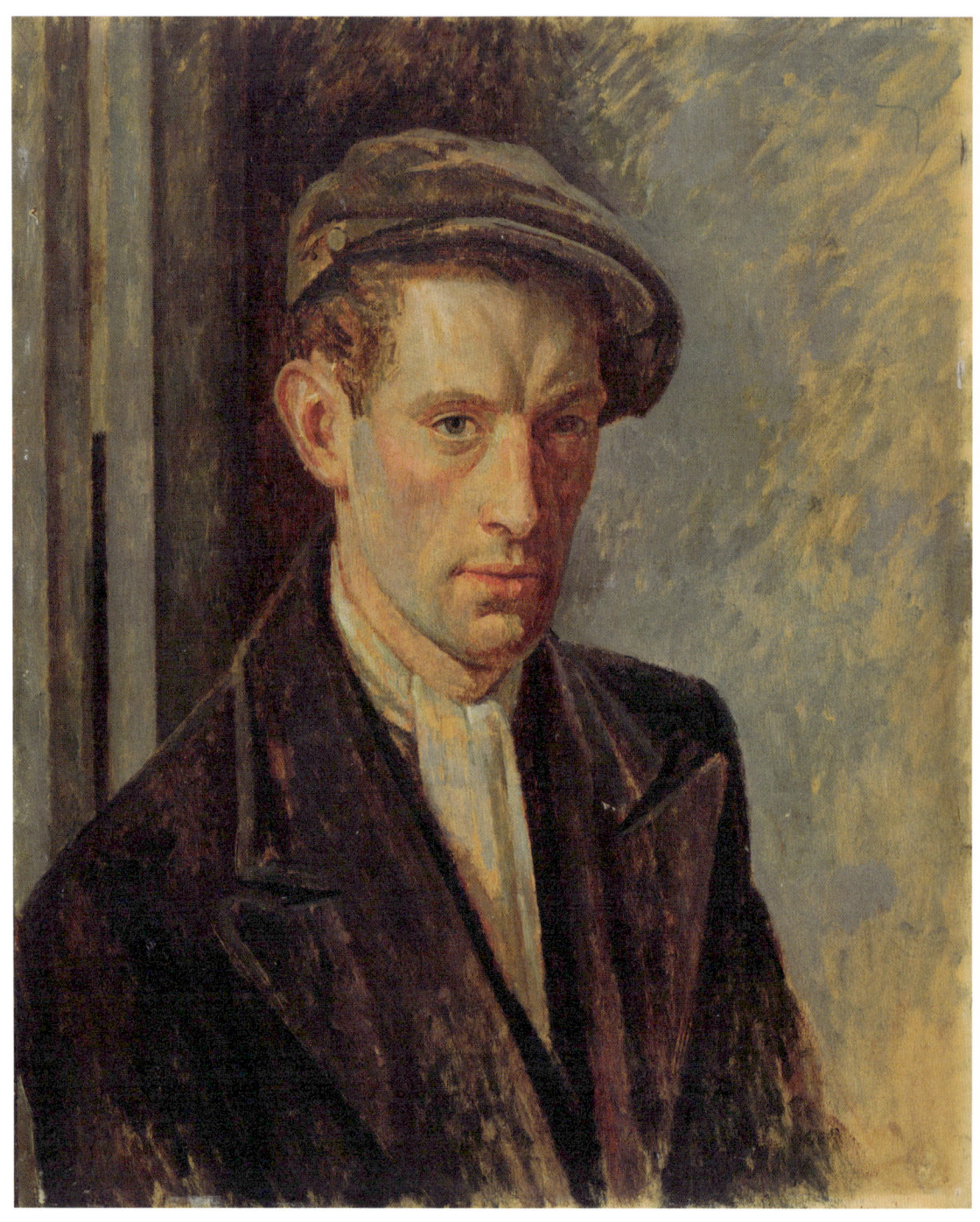

1.28 Percy Horton,
Unemployed Man,
oil on panel, *c.* 1929.
44.5 × 36.2 cm
(17⅝ × 14⅜ in.)

Marxist Club events and soon became a leading participant in the early AI's fortnightly discussions, to which he brought both self-confident intellectual heft and a strong awareness of colonial oppression.

Klingender, who spoke fluent English with a lifelong German intonation, had arrived in London soon after 1926, having already witnessed the beginnings of the slow, angry dissolution of the Weimar Republic. Now twenty-six and in his last year as a PhD student at the London School of Economics (LSE), he had been born in Goslar in the Harz mountains of north-east Germany, where his father Louis – a migrant from Liverpool three decades before – had a successful career as a painter of hunting scenes, woodcarver and museum curator. Interned as a suspected spy during the war, Klingender senior suffered social ostracism in the 1920s and his art fell from fashion even as Francis, his teenage son, already interested in socialism and writing on art and culture in the local press, faced hostility from right-wing teachers and nationalist students.

His father's former artistic prowess may well have helped Francis get his first employment in London as an editorial assistant in an advertising agency owned by a Berlin collector, but for the next twenty years it was the frequently impoverished son who supported the bewildered exiled father. Further radicalized while studying at the LSE and as a result of returning briefly to Germany in 1931, after which he had joined the party, Klingender was now completing his thesis on 'The Black-Coated Worker in London', which would be published as a book two years later, wrapped in a cover designed by Misha Black. The LSE had a sizeable number of students from the Indian subcontinent who supported the Comintern-sponsored League Against Imperialism; Klingender's Security Service file, opened in June 1931, recorded his association with the League as well as his role in editing the nationally circulated *Student Vanguard*. He co-edited this with John Cornford, the radical young scion of the Darwin family intellectual dynasty, who after studying at the LSE for six months had just returned to Cambridge as an undergraduate. These connections with an emerging student militancy, far removed from Oxford Union mimicry of Westminster politics, were already in place as the fledgling AI prepared to help welcome the next National Hunger March to London eighteen months after the Trafalgar Square battle Rowe had memorialized in Moscow.

* * * * *

Arriving back in London, Cliff Rowe and Anna Meblin had camped in an outhouse behind a friend's place in Old Gloucester Street, Bloomsbury, other friends chipping in with pots and pans, clothes and groceries.[79]

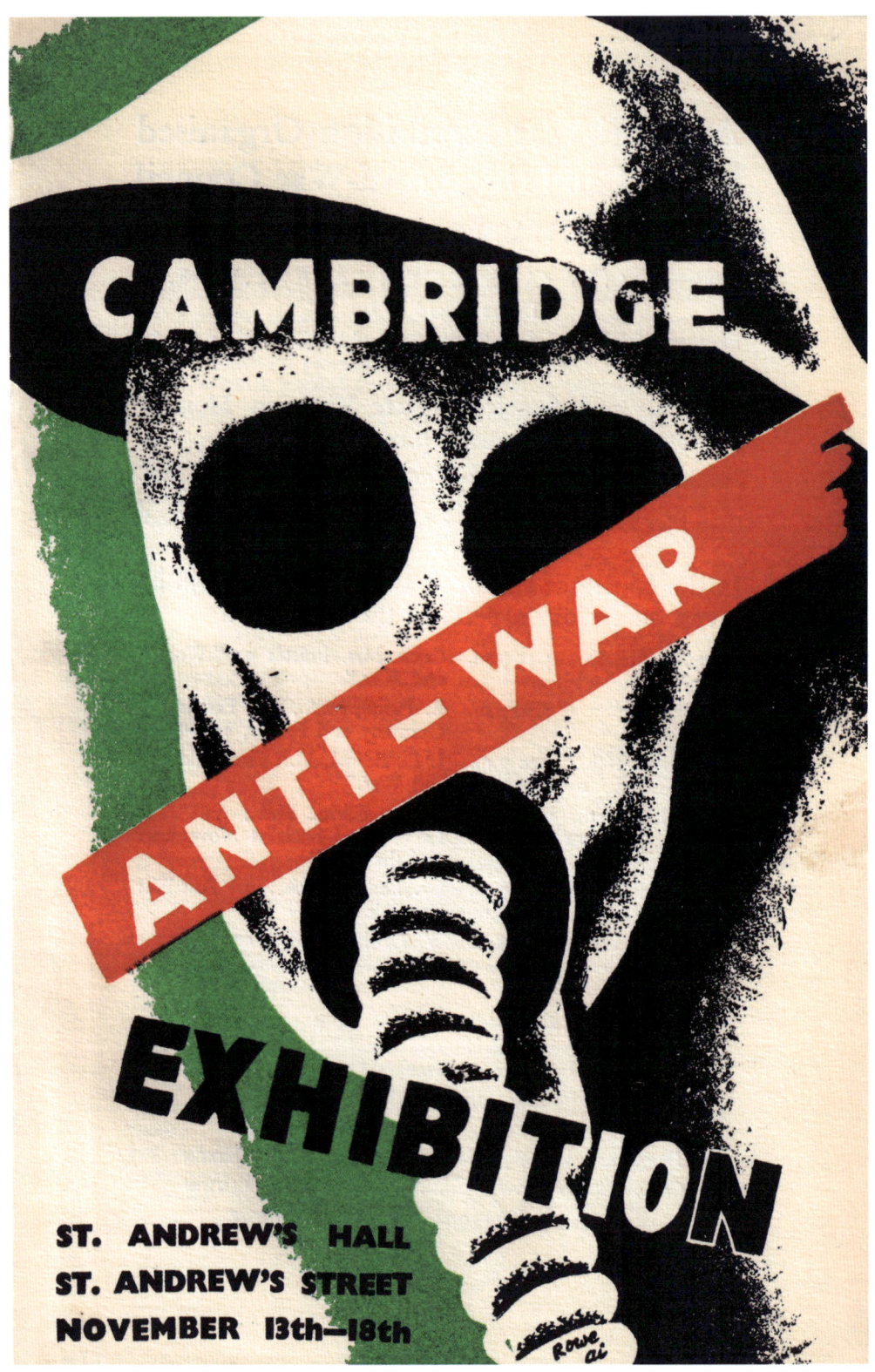

1.29 Cliff Rowe, *Cambridge Anti-War Exhibition*, design for lithographed cover and poster, 1933. 22 × 13.5 cm (8¾ × 5⅜ in.)

Shortly after, Anna became the first in a long line of women (and one man) who would act as AI or AIA honorary secretary during the next four decades;[80] not long after that she must have been aware she was pregnant, a development that made better accommodation essential. By the time her son was born early the following June, it had been found not far away, above a laundry at 65 Marchmont Street, Tel: Terminus 3969, an address and telephone number which now invited surveillance as the AI's advertised base.[81]

Prior to this, Misha Black's new rooms in Charlotte Street functioned as a banner-making workshop ahead of the hunger march's arrival in London in February 1934 and the subsequent May Day parade. Portraits of Lenin and Georgi Dimitrov, the communist leader put on trial by the Nazis after Hitler's seizure of power, figured prominently on cheap sign-painter's cloth held aloft on the latter occasion; this gives us a rough dating for the time Helen, Misha's future wife, moved out of their chaotic rooms. Three nights of banner-painting on porous cloth had reduced the place to a shambles and she could no longer endure the sight of 'Lenin's blood' running down the walls.[82]

At the Hyde Park rally, 100,000 welcomed the marchers and the iconography of the banners and posters was more domestic. The main targets were two measures in the National Government's newly announced Unemployment Bill which threatened savage benefit cuts and incarceration of the long-term workless in labour camps. In a foretaste of publications to come, *Why We Are Marching!*, a book of eighteen cartoons hurriedly produced by the AI for sale in the park, turned an angry satirical eye on both.

18 cartoons

WHY
WE ARE MARCHING

CHAPTER TWO

CHARLOTTE STREET

In October 1932 the National Unemployed Workers' Movement (NUWM) published *Why Are We Marching?*, explaining the hunger marchers' case and mapping the routes they would take to London. The journey was to culminate in a Parliamentary lobby to present a mass petition calling for an end to the Means Test and the hardship it imposed.

The cartoon book produced by the fledgling Artists International British Section in support of the next march in January 1934 dropped the question mark. *Why We Are Marching!* was an affirmation of militancy in the face of past provocation; this time the focal point would be a National Congress of Action, arranged to coincide with the marchers' arrival in London as a determined step in a long campaign.

Fifteen months earlier, the lobby of Parliament had been due to take place two days after the Trafalgar Square events depicted in Cliff Rowe's painting. The evening before, an agent provocateur delivered a letter to national organizer Wal Hannington, implicating the NUWM in the preparation of terrorist acts. Hannington immediately burnt the letter and a police raid on the NUWM offices the following morning found no trace of it, despite the removal of 5 hundredweight of documents; Hannington was nevertheless arrested and refused bail.[1] Early in the evening of 1 November 1932, the delegation to Parliament was surrounded at Charing Cross Station and the petition seized, never to be seen again. That night running battles broke out as five thousand police and special constables blocked the routes to Parliament from Camden, the East End and south London.

As the hunger marchers once again took to the roads in 1934, the Metropolitan Police commissioner Lord Trenchard, a veteran imperialist not averse to using colonial methods of repression at home, was making careful preparations.[2] Criticized for the reckless ferocity of mounted police operations in 1932, he now demanded that newsreels 'abstain from taking or publishing cinematograph pictures of the hunger marchers', stepped up surveillance of the NUWM offices – where volunteers were guarding against the possibility of a British Union of Fascists Blackshirt attack – and made use of three inside informers.[3] Through them Scotland Yard received reports of efforts to find accommodation for the marchers, activity James

2.1 Cliff Rowe, cover design for *Why We Are Marching!*, 1934. 29 × 23.3 cm (11½ × 9¼ in.)

Boswell – now living in Camden – was part of, even as he was drawing three cartoons for *Why We Are Marching!*, a series of images very much in the political moment.

Introducing new unemployment legislation the previous November, when evidence of malnutrition among children of the unemployed was accumulating, National Government ministers had expressed satisfaction that £54 million had been saved in two years through benefit cuts and the Means Test; but the Cabinet was aware that the savings would have been higher were it not for the local campaigns mounted by the NUWM mobilizing the unemployed and bringing pressure to bear on the local authority Public Assistance Committees.[4] In London, Trenchard had imposed a ban on meetings outside Labour Exchanges as soon as he was appointed,[5] but now the new Unemployment Bill proposed to undermine campaigning nationwide through central imposition of 'a complete national system of relief of unemployment', introduction of compulsory labour for unemployed youths 'to avoid the temptation of even a small dole', and the setting up of work camps to house the persistently unemployed.

Beyond Parliament, these were measures that appealed to many Conservative admirers of Benito Mussolini's fascist corporatism and the arrival of Reich Chancellor Hitler as a 'bulwark against Bolshevism'.[6] But to those on the left, and certainly for attendees at Fitton's lithography class, the proposed measures echoed both Britain's use of concentration camps in the Boer War and Ireland and – even more alarmingly – news of Dachau, Oranienburg and Hohenstein, 'retraining' camps for political opponents and trade unionists known to have been recently set up in Germany. Peter László Peri, Francis Klingender, Edith Simon and Hans Feibusch were early AI participants with personal connection to those at risk.

Government expenditure figures, a recent Hammersmith medical officer's report on malnutrition, the cruelty of the Means Test, the attempts to divide employed and unemployed, the similarity of actions in Germany and Britain – these were the disparate but highly topical materials out of which seven or eight founders of the Artists International fashioned their book of eighteen cartoons to distribute at the congress and its accompanying rally in Hyde Park. It was a cheap affair, produced by incising drawings into waxed sheets before placing them on the revolving inked drum of a cyclostyle machine, probably a Gestetner.[7] This was not a medium most had used before and, despite contributions from artists who would soon revolutionize English satirical drawing, the overall effect achieved belied how good most of the book's creators already were as graphic artists.[8]

The book's penultimate cartoon by 'RL' – believed to be Roy Laurier – is something of an exception, executed with a sureness of touch which suggests prior experience, possibly in a business or advertising setting. It is

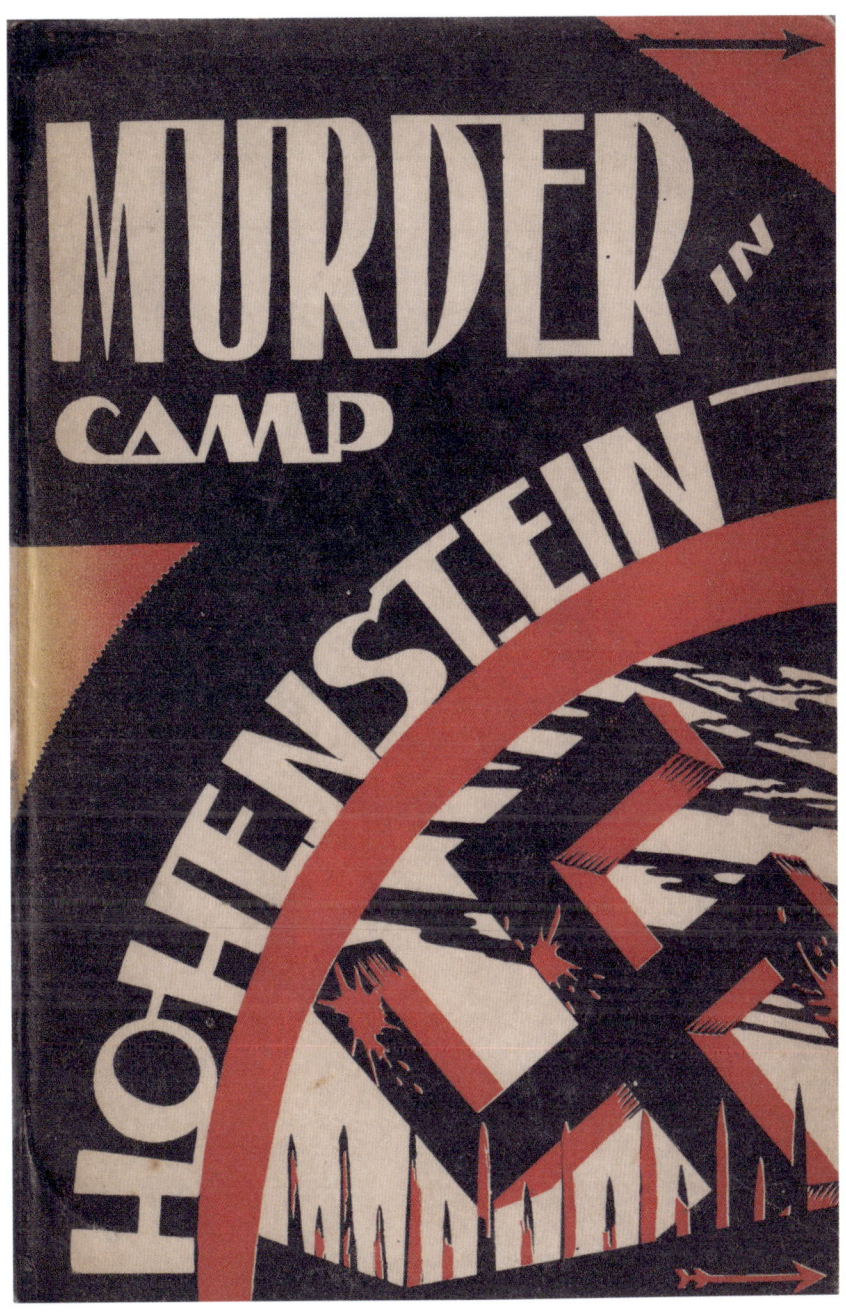

2.2 Unidentified artist, *Murder in Camp Hohenstein*, cover design for Martin Lawrence, 1933. 18.4 × 12.5 cm (7¼ × 5 in.)

also the image that expresses the cartoonists' collective political perspective most holistically: enthroned as overseers of the proposed 'fascist scheme' are Ramsay MacDonald, the incumbent National Government and former Labour prime minister, and Stanley Baldwin, his Conservative and Unionist successor-in-waiting, his hand already on the lever of power. Baldwin manipulates a Whitehall mandarin, who is standing atop the new national administrative body, pulling a New Unemployment Bill cord to manipulate a Local Authorities marionette, which mechanically lops off benefit expenditure to feed the armaments bin below. On the wall behind, portraits of Hitler and Mussolini flank one of Oswald Mosley awaiting enlargement, a tartly creative allusion to the fact that the proprietor of the Conservative-supporting *Daily Mail*, Viscount Rothermere, had just authored an opinion piece praising Mosley's British Union of Fascists as 'a well organised party of the Right ready to take over responsibility for national affairs with the same directness of purpose and energy of method as Hitler and Mussolini have displayed'.[9]

As the marchers reached London's outskirts, the Home Secretary, Sir John Gilmour, issued an inflammatory warning that shops should be shuttered and children kept indoors 'because of possible bloodshed', stoking press calls for those protesting to be 'laid by their heels' and the NUWM leadership

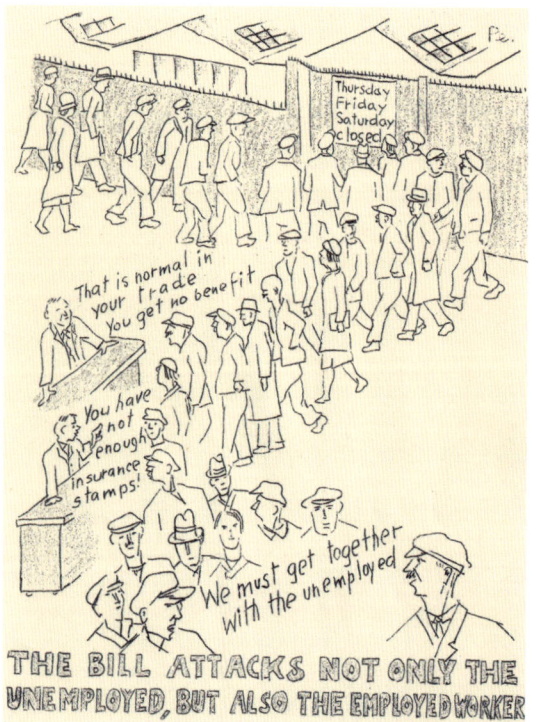

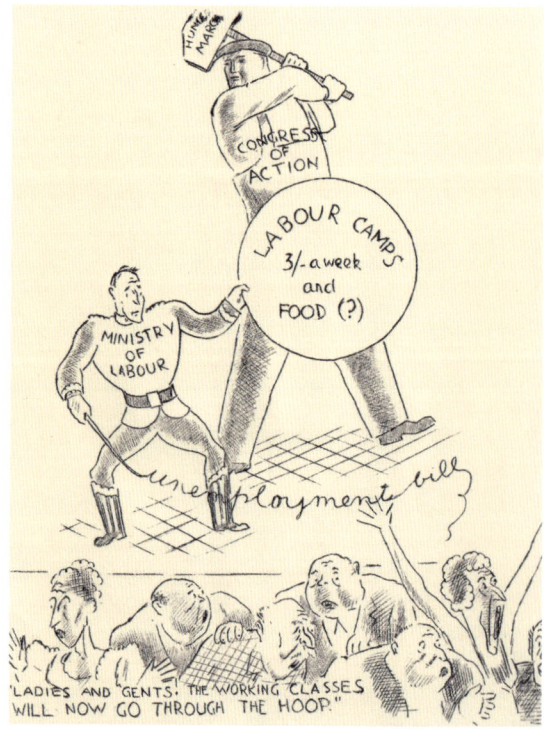

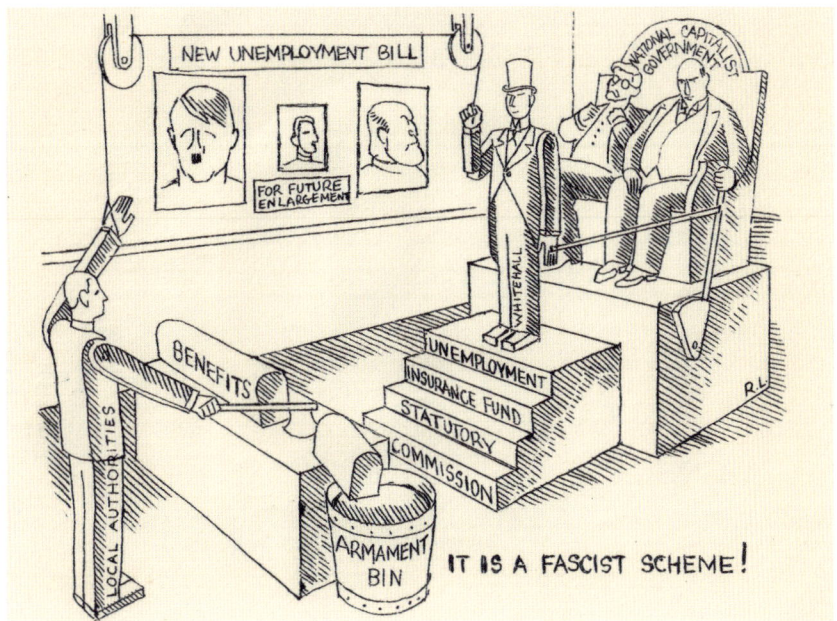

detained, a demand both the Labour Party and the official trade unions failed to condemn. It would take until 1936 and the Jarrow March before the Labour leadership endorsed a hunger march, and in 1934 they opposed the NUWM as part of the 'Communist Solar System' of front organizations, proscribing local branches from affiliating with, as they saw it, a sectarian network that had habitually denounced moderates as 'social fascists'.

In a pamphlet the previous September, the Labour Party had forecast that other 'sympathising organisations for special purposes' would arise in the Comintern universe, and by allying so closely with the NUWM the young founders of the AI risked being dismissed as a mere Communist Party front by nearly all other artists. As it turned out, a combination of their own energetic networking and a rip tide of threatening events would see them beginning to achieve precisely the opposite result.

The National Congress of Action – a gathering of 1,494 delegates made up of Communist and Independent Labour Party members, NUWM and trade union activists and a handful of left-wing Labour MPs – was held over a day and a quarter at Bermondsey Town Hall, adjourning mid-morning on Sunday 25 February 1934 to march as one through drizzle to join the 100,000-strong crowd welcoming the hunger march in Hyde Park. The Scottish contingent, which had set out from Glasgow five weeks before, was the first to enter the park led by fifes, drums and bagpipes as waves of cheers and intermittent downpours punctuated the appearance of each group of marchers; Boswell would publish an AIA lithograph five years

2.3 Unidentified artist, *The Bill Attacks Not Only the Unemployed ...*, from *Why We Are Marching!*, 1934. 29 × 23.3 cm (11½ × 9¼ in.)

2.4 Edward Ardizzone, *Through the Hoop*, from *Why We Are Marching!*, 1934. 29 × 23.3 cm (11½ × 9¼ in.)

2.5 Roy Laurier, *It is a Fascist Scheme!*, from *Why We Are Marching!*, 1934. 23.3 × 29 cm (9¼ × 11½ in.)

later showing a footsore marcher at the margins of such a rally, which possibly relates to this occasion. Unlike the running battles of 1932, it was a largely peaceful afternoon and set the tone for more sympathetic mainstream press coverage. Ramsay MacDonald, however, refused to receive a delegation, complaining privately that he was not obligated to meet everyone who chose to walk to London, and via his private secretary: 'The deputation can do no service to the unemployed. The communist purpose of these marches is common knowledge. The Government is responsible for a Bill which, when in operation, will facilitate the most satisfactory treatment of the whole question of unemployment.'[10]

Another observer in Hyde Park that afternoon was forty-two-year-old Ronald Kidd, who fifteen months earlier had witnessed Metropolitan Police use of agents provocateurs to incite violence on the night of the aborted Parliamentary lobby.[11] For over a year Kidd and his companion Sylvia Crowther-Smith, an actress he met while employed as a provincial stage manager, had been working to raise awareness of threats to peaceful protest. The previous Thursday they had convened a meeting in the vestry of St Martin-in-the-Fields in Trafalgar Square, and that Saturday morning a letter had appeared in the *Manchester Guardian* announcing the formation of a Council for Civil Liberties; its fourteen signatories included H. G. Wells, Vera Brittain, Dr Edith Summerskill and Clement Attlee.[12] What none of them knew at that point, however, was that within six weeks the National Government would publish an Incitement to Disaffection Bill, creating a substantial threat to free expression and an urgent focus for both the Artists International and the nascent Council for Civil Liberties.

*****

In early 1934 the dark horizon of events in Europe weighed on the spirits of some young artists more than others, even as violence in both Paris and Vienna underscored how their generation faced a time of democratic failure and fascist advance. Since the Versailles Treaty of 1919, authoritarian regimes had already come to power in Hungary, Italy, Turkey, Poland, Portugal and Germany, and while the marchers were on the road that February it appeared the French Third Republic would fall.

Two years earlier, Socialist gains had altered the balance in the French National Assembly, triggering press vilification of the succession of scandal-ridden radical party coalitions that followed. Amid exaggerated fears of a 'red threat', a campaign of xenophobia and shrill nationalism unfolded, creating a climate which led writers and artist-designers to found the Association des Écrivains et Artistes Révolutionnaires (AEAR).[13] As paralysis in the Assembly hampered efforts to address economic crisis, the semi-fascist Croix-de-Feu and Action Française gained in strength, and on 6 February 1934 thirty thousand of their supporters besieged the Palais Bourbon calling for parliament to be suspended and the reactionary Paris police prefect Jean Chiappe to take power. Fifteen died that night and 1,400 were injured, and the next day Édouard Daladier's government resigned; three days later the police killed six at a communist counter-demonstration in the Place de la République. On 12 February more than a million answered the socialist Confédération Générale du Travail's call for a regional general strike in defence of democracy, a call the smaller communist trade unions supported; five days later, in an unprecedented move that sowed seeds of future unity, socialists took part in a funeral procession for the communist demonstrators who had been killed.[14] A new, more right-wing coalition had taken power in the Assembly, but the French Republic had just about survived an attempted coup. In Austria, however, those same February days saw a different outcome.

On 16 February Peggy Angus wrote to the artist Eric Ravilious from Furlongs, her cottage on a flank of the South Downs, thanking him for the weekend she had just enjoyed at Great Bardfield in Essex. It was the first time she had spent with Ravilious and Edward Bawden since they were all students at the RCA Design School in 1925, and so relaxing that she had felt liberated from the weight of political events: 'But my hat! Didn't I come back to it with a vengeance. Don't you feel pains in the stomach over the unholy terror in Vienna? You see I know the places they've been blowing up. I was there about 3 years ago and made drawings of these very blocks of workers' flats they've been destroying. I don't see how we are to escape the same massacre. I met several artists in Vienna and they were all sympathetic towards Socialism … They are probably dead by now or soon will be … How lucky you are to feel so remote and aloof from it all. I get so tied up – I can't see to paint.'[15]

One person who had joined Angus in the AI that spring could certainly not feel detachment as she read how the Austrian army and fascist auxiliaries had shelled and assaulted the Karl-Marx-Hof in the Viennese neighbourhood of Heiligenstadt four nights earlier. Born Edith Suschitzky in Vienna in 1908, Edith Tudor-Hart had photographed the public housing complex in the 19th district the year before, and her socialist-humanist father still ran a progressive bookshop and publisher on Favoritenstrasse in the 10th district.[16] Edith had originally come to London in April 1925 to train as a Montessori nursery teacher, meeting Beatrix Tudor-Hart, a progressive educationalist, and her brother Alex, who was training to become a surgeon; friendship, further trips to London and reciprocal visits to Vienna followed. Artistically talented and socially engaged, Edith studied at the Bauhaus in Dessau in 1928; already a member of the small

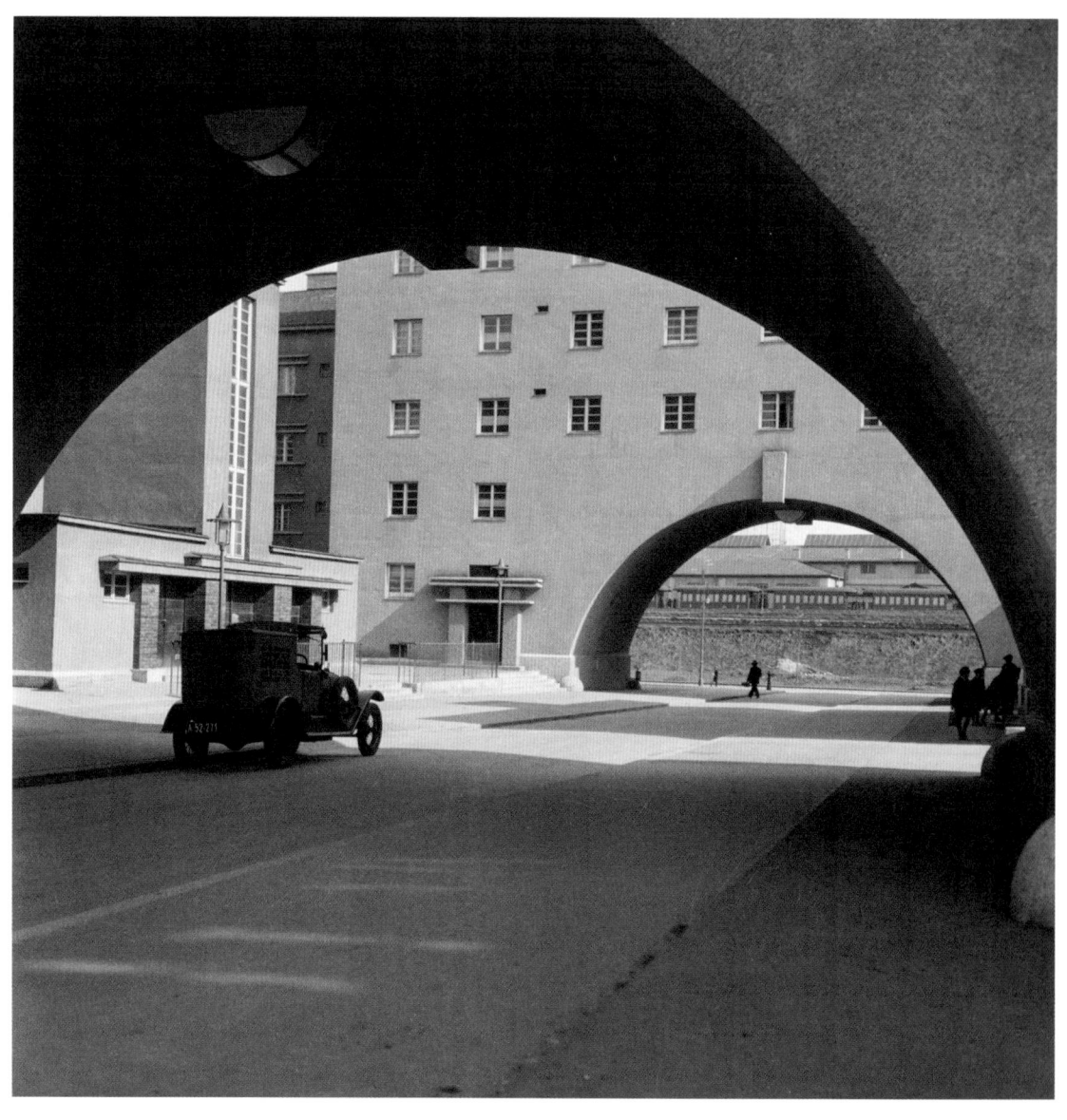

2.6 Edith Tudor-Hart
(Edith Suschitzky),
Karl-Marx-Hof, Vienna,
silver gelatin print, 1933

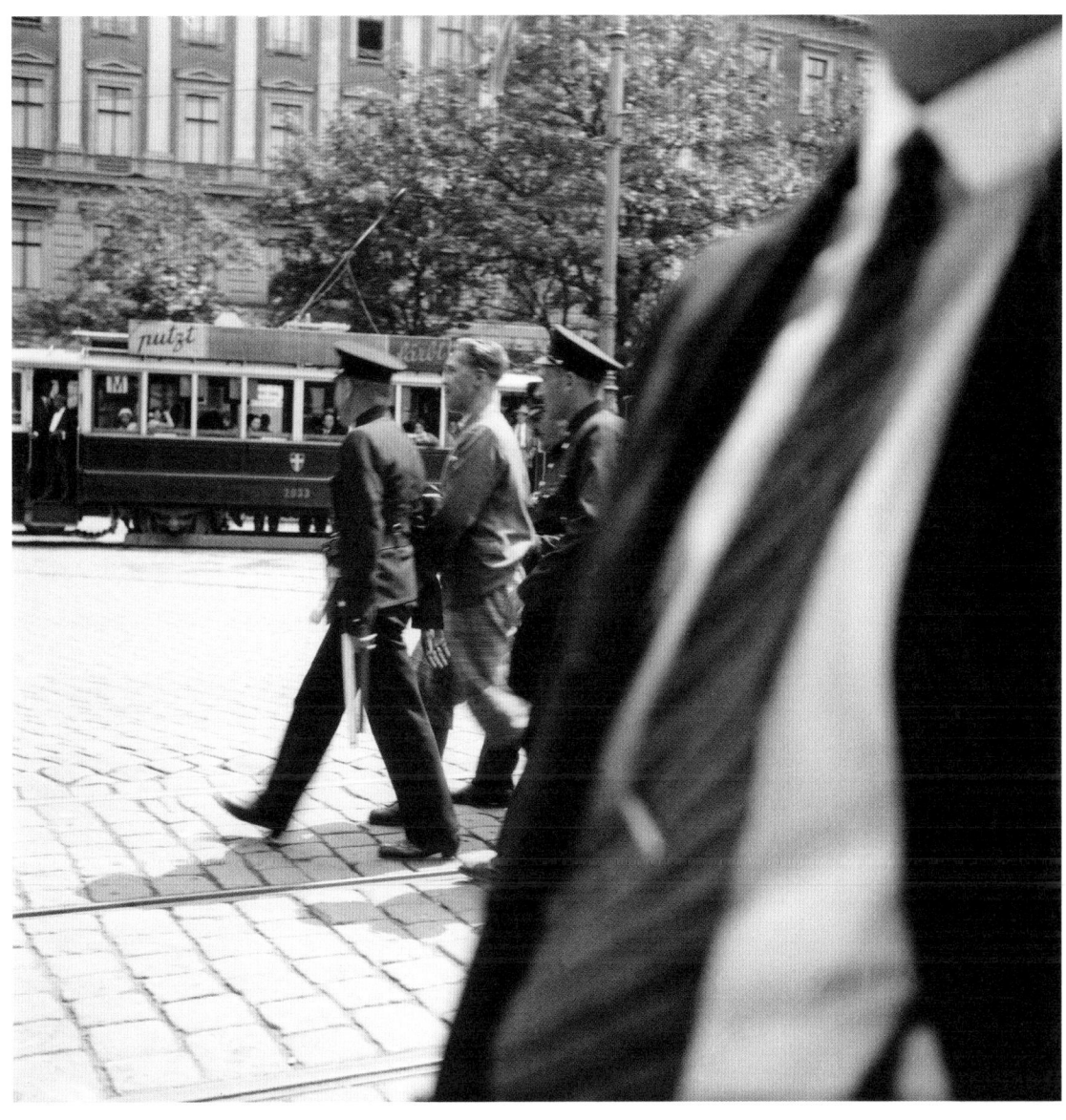

2.7 Edith Tudor-Hart
(Edith Suschitzky),
An Arrest, Vienna,
silver gelatin print, 1933

Austrian Communist Party, she had also taken up photography with the intent of documenting social injustices.

Living back in London with Alex in October 1930, she attracted Special Branch attention talking to Communist Party leaders at a Trafalgar Square rally, and soon after was served with a notice to leave the country. After failed appeals she complied in January 1931, but not before she had completed a body of photojournalism on working-class life in Whitechapel, where Pearl Binder was already living and at work and where the two probably first met.[17] On returning to Vienna, Edith was able to publish photo-essays in *Der Kuckuck*, a Social Democratic illustrated magazine, and *Die Bühne*, a liberal monthly, before getting work as a photojournalist for the Soviet news agency TASS. She also began to use photomontage, designing a cover for an edition of John Reed's eyewitness account of the Russian Revolution, *Ten Days That Shook the World*.

In March 1933 the Austrian Chancellor Engelbert Dollfuss, threatened by local Nazis and events across the German border, suspended parliamentary government and moved to rule by decree, openly allying with the reactionary Heimwehr militia while repressing the socialist paramilitary

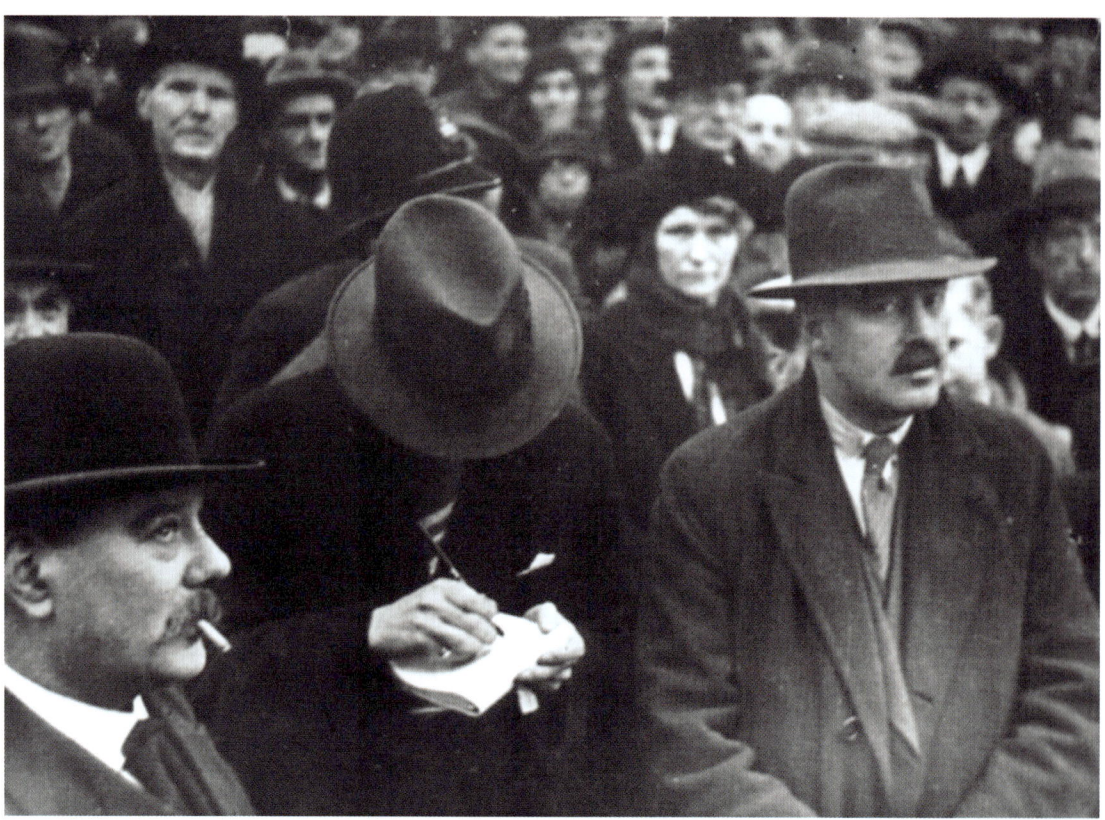

2.8 Edith Tudor-Hart (Edith Suschitzky), *Sedition*, photograph reproduced in *Left Review*, March 1935

organization Schutzbund. During this rolling crisis Edith made clandestine use of her medium-format Rolleiflex camera, held at waist height to capture dramatic images of arrests and police barricades. May Day was followed by the summary imprisonment of more than eight hundred communists and socialists, and shortly after Edith was picked up carrying a leaflet calling for a united front to support political prisoners; a search of her home led to seizure of further material and, although released, it was now too dangerous for her to stay. After marrying Alex in Vienna that August she was able to leave for London as Mrs Tudor-Hart, her new status overriding the previous exclusion order. There, while the Special Branch became frustrated at losing track of her on arrival, she was able to begin re-establishing her photographic career, not least when R. S. Lambert started to publish her work in *The Listener*.[18]

One of Tudor-Hart's photographs attests to her presence in Hyde Park on May Day 1934. But it was probably back in Trafalgar Square that she took an image of three Special Branch officers undertaking surveillance, capturing the sidelong hostility of one as he suddenly becomes aware of a woman with a camera.[19] *Sedition* would be exhibited five months later when the Artists International held its first exhibition in a vacant motorcycle showroom at 64 Charlotte Street, where, although hung in a basement passage, Edith's photographs were for Herbert Read the best 'works of art' on display, 'admirable in lighting and composition and, *incidentally*, efficient propaganda'.[20] Before this, in a less explicitly political vein, *The Listener*'s cover in mid-May had carried her haunting bird's-eye view of Vienna seen through the girders of the Great Wheel on the Prater, using it to highlight a BBC foreign correspondent's studiedly neutral reporting of 'Austria in Transition'.[21]

By then Edith knew that her father, Wilhelm, overwhelmed by the destruction of the democratic workers' movement he had championed, had taken his own life. After four nights of watching the same fighting from her window, Oskar Kokoschka's mother suffered a fatal stroke and, once her funeral had taken place, the expressionist painter left Vienna – the city of his birth – for Prague, never to live in his homeland again.[22]

* * * * *

The same spring weeks saw Peggy Angus painting in company with Eric Ravilious, who started making regular trips to Furlongs following their weekend at Great Bardfield. Less than half a mile away over downland lay the Alpha Cement Works, enveloping Asheham House, Vanessa Bell and Virginia Woolf's former shared base in Sussex. Now the scene was a moonscape of chalk workings, industrial buildings, rails, gantries, dusted vegetation and workers labouring under clouded skies by day and arc-lights by night. It was a controversial intrusion into a pastoral landscape that provoked the first demands for a South Downs national park, and its overseer Mr Brown was 'surprised but pleased to meet two artists who could see beauty in his works'.[23] The two friends made successive expeditions there, working side by side on occasion, and a few months later Peggy responded to the AI call for 'work executed with a definite social purpose' by sending two paintings of the complex up to its Charlotte Street show.[24]

Titled *The Social Scene* and organized on a shoestring, the exhibition was in effect a public launch for the Artists International British Section, coming at the end of a year in which, as James Boswell recalled, it was evolving as 'a mixture of agit-prop body, Marxist discussion group, exhibitions and anti-war, anti-fascist outfit', and the pre-publicity reflected some of the dilemmas involved in such multitasking.[25] On the one hand, if art was indeed to be 'a weapon in the struggle' as suggested in discussion group debates, the organizers wanted to both proclaim their mission and also attract works suitable 'to be sent to the USSR to represent Great Britain in an International Exhibition, which will travel to the capital cities of the republics'.[26] On the other, as Misha Black reflected, there was a strong feeling that to gain momentum it had to be 'a very pragmatic organisation … a broadly based united front' capable of attracting sympathizers regardless of generation, artistic métier, stylistic persuasion and whether or not individuals were signed-up true believers in the Soviet five-year plan. To this end it was announced 'paintings, drawings, sculpture, photographs and architecture have been invited from artists throughout the country under the general heading of "The Social Conditions and Struggles of Today" and over 120 works have already been promised. Among others, Edmund Burra [*sic*], Eric Gill and Henry Moore have agreed to exhibit.'[27]

No copy of the exhibition catalogue is known to have survived but three detailed reviews have, as well as a printed recruiting leaflet outlining AI aims and a cordial invitation for 'all professional architects and photographers to join the Artists' International'.[28] In sum we know the names of some twenty of the artists who exhibited and a good deal of information about the catalogue's introductory manifesto and different elements of the exhibition, which included a display of political posters, an analysis of the housing crisis, and sections on sculpture and the Workers Film and Photo League, accompanied by lectures on civil liberties under threat, 'Revolutionary Proletarian Art' and 'Marxist Art History'.[29] From these sources it is unclear what items were exhibited by the misnamed Edward Burra, Henry Moore and Paul Nash but it is clear all three did contribute, as well as artists such as Clare Leighton and Robert Medley.[30] Eric Gill

2.9 Peggy Angus, *Cement Works*, oil on board, 1934. 86 × 65 cm (33⅞ × 25⅝ in.)

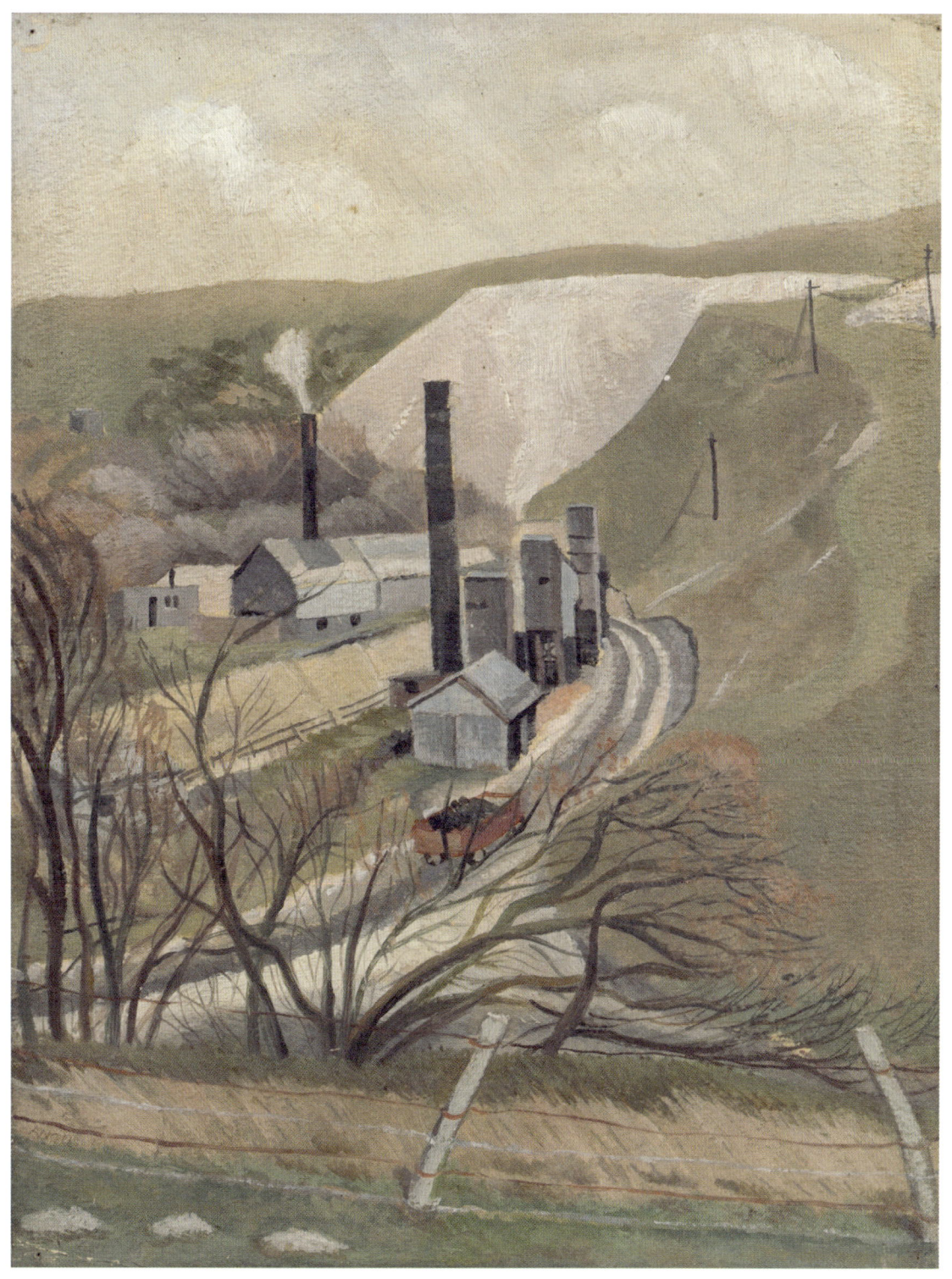

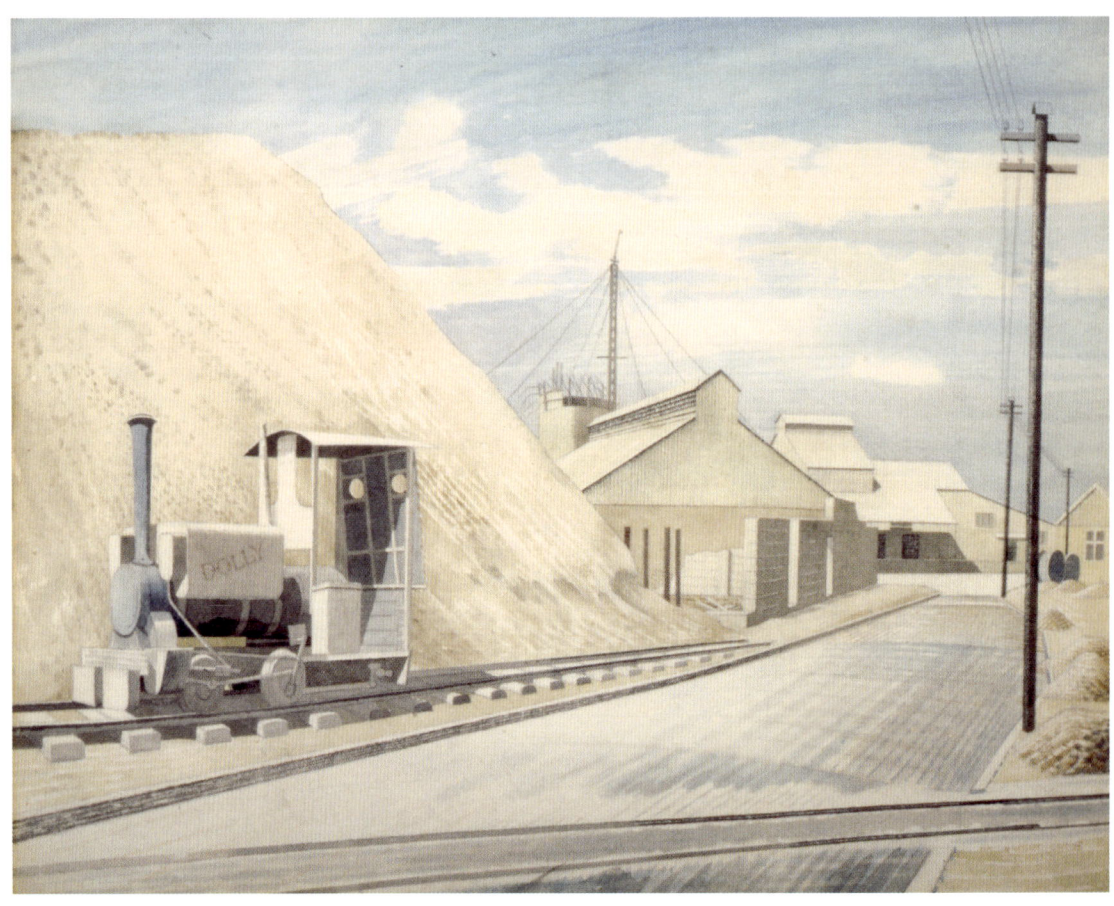

2.10 Eric Ravilious, *Cement Works*, watercolour on paper, 1934. 46 × 58 cm (18⅛ × 22⅞ in.)

not only sent in work and visited, but would also, after it closed, mount a sustained defence of *The Social Scene* and his own participation in it.

All three of the major reviews highlighted a gap between aspiration and achievement. In *The Studio*, the apolitical Douglas Goldring confessed to having approached the exhibition with optimism because 'Communism, for its adherents, is a political religion and sincere religious convictions are often productive of great art', but averred, 'Judged on its merits as an exhibition, rather than in the light of the intentions expressed in the manifesto, it is on the whole disappointing and much of the work shown seemed to be crude and bad'. Nevertheless he cited a range of work he liked: an excellent portrait of Lenin by Norman Walkington, two good pictures of cement works by Margaret Angus, *Lunch Hour Politics*, an attractive painting by Jean Garside, and several forceful groups in coloured concrete by 'Perry', the work of Peter László Peri.[31] He also noted satirically effective propaganda drawings and James Lucas's *Haunting Europe* as 'the most powerful and ominous of the purely political exhibits', before concluding:

66 CHAPTER TWO

'Everything must have a beginning and perhaps I have not been quite fair to the "Artists' International". Something surprising may come from this group in the near future.'

Tom Wintringham opened his analysis in *Left Review* by stating 'this first effort by a young organisation was remarkably successful', but observed that exhibitors who were AI members 'have come fairly recently to realise that politics are of dominating importance to them in their work, fairly recently have decided to put their ability at the service of the working class movement; their work – naturally – shows more real acquaintance with, more real feeling for, the working class movement than for the working class itself'.[32] He too picked out exceptions: Lucas's painting of a street meeting at night, two drawings by Boswell and 'one outstanding painting of men at work: a bakery by A. E. Webster. It gives the feeling of the cellar, of the warm choking steam and the smell of new bread; details are put in with simple certainty – tap, oven, bench, loaves belong where they are. The painter has worked in a bakery; it makes a difference.' By contrast he found C. H. Rowe's large canvas of a pit rescue gang carrying a stretcher, surrounded by women watching for the rescued and the dead, 'monumental in its solidity' but lacking in tension because 'the artist has not perhaps felt entirely the continual unquiet, the undertone of anxiety and waiting, that dominates a pit village every day'; in a similar vein, he noted that two pictures of cement works by Margaret Angus 'are pictures from the outside of the works'. For Wintringham, the show was 'a big start' and a 'great and cheering contrast to the work of bourgeois cliques and individuals', but also one that demonstrated 'a clear need for these artists to get closer to the working class, more inside the class struggle, if they are to do the work they can do'.

Wintringham's concluding qualification, penned from the perspective of a political activist, was nevertheless silent about how such a rapprochement might be effected. In the *London Mercury* Herbert Read, writing as a cultural commentator, took on the show's professed theoretical underpinnings, quoting from both the catalogue introduction and an early, now lost, *AI Bulletin*, and in so doing he gave a foretaste of numerous debates about style, subject and meaning to come, some of which he would soon participate in under AI auspices. He began by noting that the exhibition had promised 'to be of exceptional interest, but even the most sympathetic of critics would have to confess it was disappointing in quality', save for Gill's woodcut, two paintings by Robert Medley and Tudor-Hart's photographs. Professing that he counted himself 'on the side of the working class and against the capitalist class', did not support 'art for art's sake', and that he could even accept, with qualifications, that 'all art is the outcome of the mode of material production of its period', he nevertheless stressed 'we are not excused the process of aesthetic valuation. There are good and bad artists in every period, and the better an artist is the more he transcends the limitations of his period.'

The aspect Read took greatest exception to was an article in the *AI Bulletin* which claimed that 'art in its most representative "modern" form [is] an art of obscurantism, a petty-bourgeois sectarian, clique art completely out of touch with the life of the people ... which finds its final absurdity when the individual yields all conscious part in his work as has been advocated recently when a group of artists put forward the claim that they placed arbitrary marks on a canvas and allowed the picture to evolve of itself.' Read identified this as an attack on the French 'Surréalistes' but noted that Picasso had described his work in similar terms, before concluding: 'When the writer of the article in the *AI Bulletin* has realised that in denying Picasso and his type he is denying the only artists who are breaking down the conventions of petty bourgeois art and thus preparing the way for the art of the socialist state, he will perhaps be able to organise something more inspiring than this first exhibition.'[33]

* * * * *

At this time, aside from the International Bureau of Revolutionary Artists (IBRA) in Moscow, the John Reed Clubs (JRC) in the USA were the clear first among equals of the overseas artists' organizations that the London AI was in touch with. From these channels, those putting together *The Social Scene* would have been aware that the New York John Reed Club had staged *The Social Viewpoint in Art* in January 1933, an exhibition held in the interregnum between Franklin Delano Roosevelt winning the presidential election and his arrival in the White House the following March.[34] Like the London event, its title had sought to encompass the idea that art might be a 'weapon in the struggle', but also to avoid any stridency that might repel artists who did not yet, or would never, see themselves as signed-up members of a politicized 'cultural front'.

Announced at a moment when the private gallery market was at a nadir and exhibiting possibilities slight, the exhibition attracted attention. By the time it opened in the Manhattan loft that served as the John Reed clubrooms, over a hundred artists, a minority of whom were invitees, had sent in work – and when it closed in mid-February after a two-week extension, over three thousand people had visited, many in parties organized by union and community groups. By then, some art scene limelight had been cast on the John Reed Club and, more significantly, the 'first large and important enterprise of the club in promoting an active revolutionary art' had attracted individuals who would drive the launch of the American

2.11 James Boswell, *His Majesty's Servants*, line-drawn cartoon in *Left Review*, March 1935. 24.6 × 15.7 cm (9¾ × 6¼ in.). The inspiration for this image, Tudor-Hart's photograph *Sedition*, was reproduced in the same issue

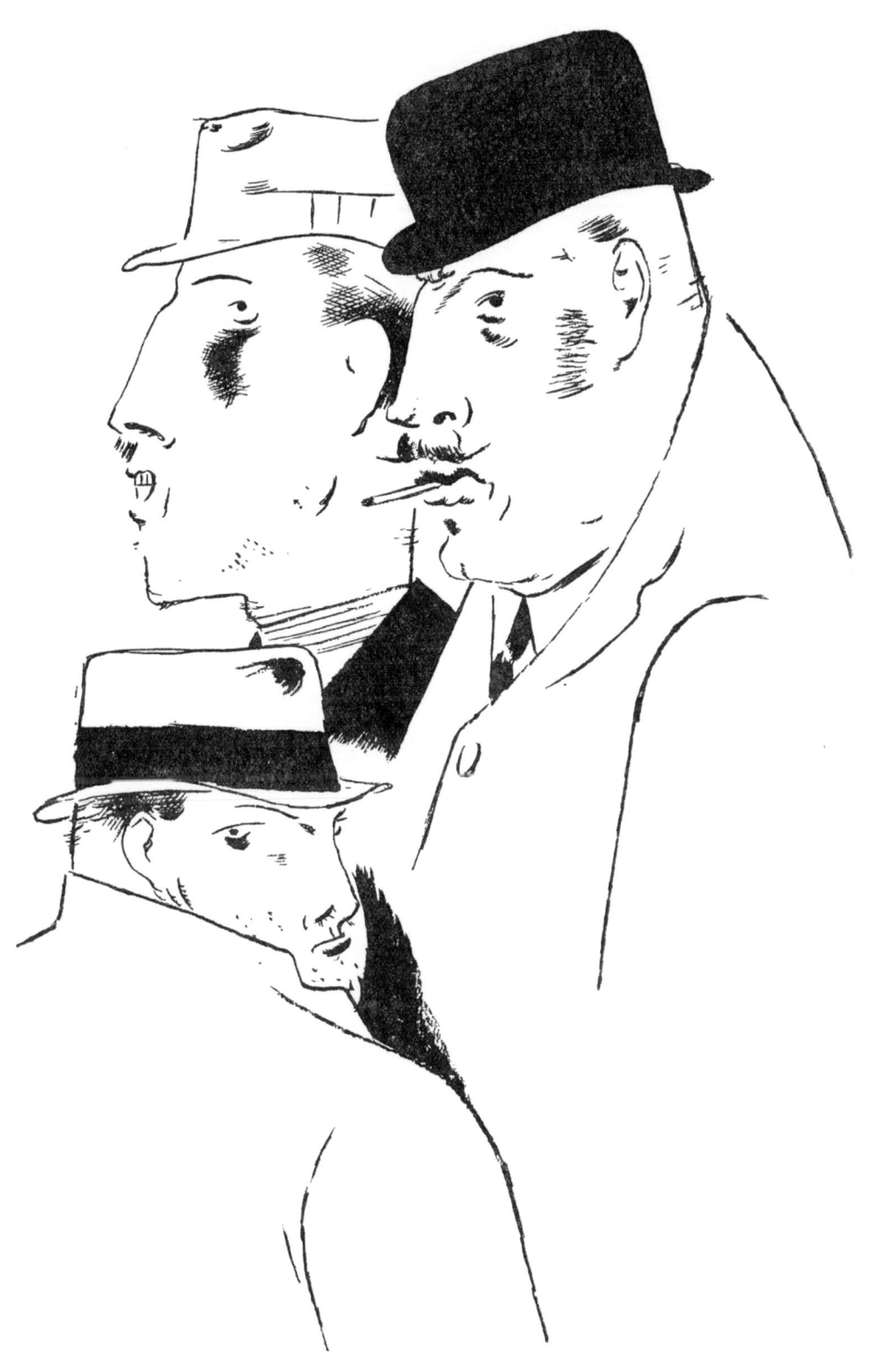

CHARLOTTE STREET

Artists' Congress (AAC) three years later. More immediately, in the depths of the downturn, the very fact of it being staged gave momentum to the notion 'every artist an organized artist'.

The John Reed Club had been founded in October 1929, the month of the stock market crash, with the assistance of staff members of the New York-based communist-aligned cultural magazine *New Masses*; frustrated by the continuing presence of a group of young would-be artists and writers in its offices, the editor had apparently suggested they pursue their destinies elsewhere by forming a club. In New York the JRC had thereafter developed as an independent entity benefiting from arm's-length party support, and it soon became part of a Depression-era radical subculture linking unemployed and barely employed painters, writers, critics, dancers, sculptors, composers, filmmakers and photographers, some of whom took to living communally in 'shock troupes'. But it was not until the spring of 1932, with official unemployment approaching 25 per cent nationally, that John Reed Clubs appeared across the country, forming a network promoting 'proletarian culture'.[35] A national convention that May brought together delegates from Boston, Chicago, Detroit, Hollywood, Newark, New York, Philadelphia, Portland, San Francisco and Seattle, and by the time it reconvened in September 1934 – after a summer of tense and bitter strikes by workers seeking to enforce their rights under Roosevelt's National Industrial Recovery Act – there were thirty John Reed clubs with 1,200 members.[36]

The range of influences and subject matter on display at *The Social Viewpoint in Art* in January 1933 was wide. In the month Hitler became chancellor, its international content included Weimar Expressionist works from George Grosz and Käthe Kollwitz and contributions from Mexican muralists José Clemente Orozco and David Alfaro Siqueiros. America's recent past and present crises – which had precipitated the electoral defeat of the sitting president Herbert Hoover just weeks before – were reflected in images of demonstrations and strikes, lynchings and police actions, alongside works depicting industrial and sweated labour, immigrant life and the daily degradations of unemployment. There were also some highly individual exercises in stylistic repurposing, with Edward Laning, an artist concerned with applying the grand style of muralism to modern American subject matter, displaying *Unlawful Assembly, Union Square*, a depiction in tempera of mounted police breaking up a communist-organized unemployment demonstration on 6 March 1930 – a work that might have given amusement to Cliff Rowe had he seen it.[37] Similarly, Walter Quirt's *The Future Belongs to the Workers*, an oil on gesso panel, described 'a clearly articulated industrial landscape and formalised groupings' reminiscent of quattrocento painting, but injected 'a mythical narrative of rising class consciousness, from the martyrdom of the worker to the mixed racial group rallying round the Communist banner'.[38]

So wide in fact was the range of stylistic conventions on display that it was difficult for critics to discern any commonality of approach even among those seeking to get a political message across, or any clear dividing-line between, as Meyer Schapiro put it in *New Masses*, 'the revolutionary viewpoint on the one hand, and the unclear though sympathetic social viewpoint on the other'. This was despite the fact that well-known artists who 'merely depict the social scene around them', such as the American Regionalist Thomas Hart Benton, had in fact been invited by the JRC – with a degree of Machiavellian pedagogic intent – to demonstrate what revolutionary art was not.[39]

But this still begged the questions of what it was, how mere 'victim art' was to be avoided and that which contributed to the struggle elevated? Answering these questions was not helped by the fact that, as Schapiro observed: 'More than half the objects shown express no revolutionary ideas; and of the rest, only a few re-enact for the worker in simple plastic language the situations of his class.'[40] This perspective in fact foreshadowed Tom Wintringham's reaction on reviewing *The Social Scene* in London: there was a need for committed artists to find ways to get 'inside the class struggle' and engage the working class through building a recognizably realistic record of present struggles 'glorifying their part in building a new social order'.[41]

One observer, Anita Brenner, demurred. Writing in *The Nation* she praised the show's ambition but accused the club's artists of not appreciating that the very forms of modernist painting were in themselves revolutionary devices: 'they cannot adequately and movingly paint or carve their time and place in the technical and emotional terms of another age' – a point akin to Read's reaction on seeing *The Social Scene*, but lacking its waspishness.[42] For her, the exception that proved the rule was probably *Adit, No. 2 or French Factory* by Stuart Davis, or another in a series the ever-experimenting artist had completed after returning from an eleven-month stay in Paris.

For Davis, it was a period of penury as gallery contracts lapsed and patrons reacted to the crash ('I haven't sold anything for so long I forget what it feels like', he wrote to a friend), followed by tragedy. In its aftermath, joining the JRC and helping to initiate its Unemployed Artists Group (UAG) ushered in a period of extraordinary personal activism with far-reaching consequences. But as *The Social Viewpoint in Art* closed these were not foreseeable, and as Davis put it: 'I had no family, no wife, no nothing. I just lived in a small room and so it was proper for me to go in it, and there wasn't anything else for me to do.'[43]

*****

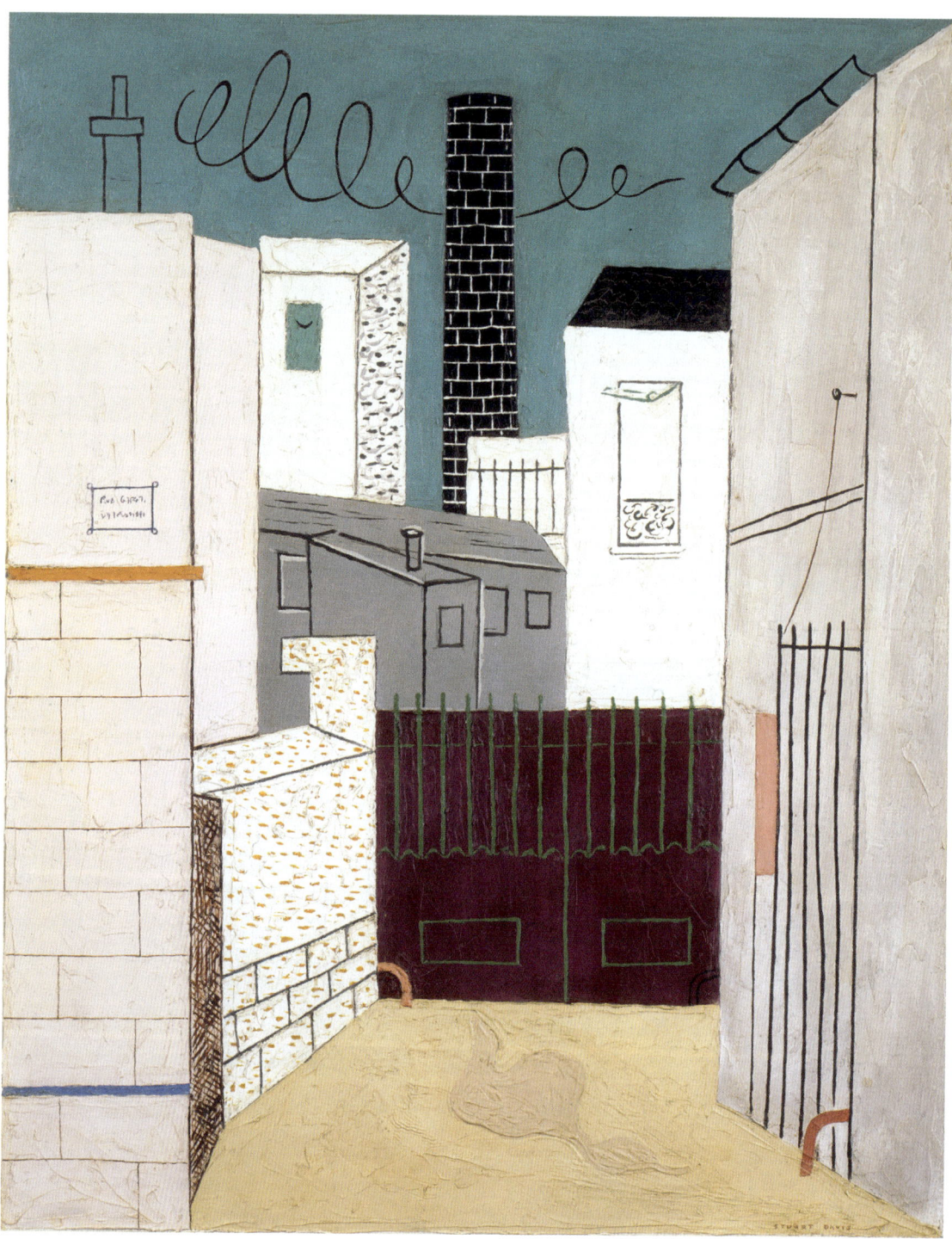

2.12 Stuart Davis, *Adit, No. 2 or French Factory*, oil on canvas, 1928. 73.3 × 60.3 cm (28⅞ × 23¾ in.)

Born in Philadelphia in 1892 to artist parents, Stuart Davis dropped out of his New York high school in 1909 to enrol at art school, where he was taught by Robert Henri. Henri's rejection of academicism and insistence that artistic endeavour must be founded on – and mean something for – the present day were formative for his talented pupil; it was an ambience that fostered a critical sense of social values, encouraging Stuart to find subjects in poor neighbourhoods, to discover ragtime and jazz and to depict 'the dynamics and complexities of modern life with a quick bravura brushwork'.[44] Soon after his twentieth birthday Davis became possibly the youngest participant in the groundbreaking Armory Show, exhibiting five watercolours, but it was the impact of the Europeans there, in particular works by Gauguin, Van Gogh and Matisse, that determined his future. He would long remember it as 'a World's Fair of ideas, a complete bombshell ... it opened up a whole panorama of possibilities that had no counterpart in American art', and that 'it gave me the same excitement I got from the numerical precision of Negro piano players in the Newark saloons. I resolved that I would have to become a "modern" artist. It took an awful long time.'[45]

As an illustrator for socialist magazine *The Masses* from 1912 he gained exposure to politics of the left, producing targeted satire and accepting the desirability of socialism but without any great impetus towards personal activism;[46] experimenting with the techniques of modern art ('the possibility of using colors, shapes that one hadn't regarded as legitimate before') had in fact become his guiding passion. This manifested not only in making thickly textured paintings outdoors in the style of Van Gogh and exploring in parallel a remarkably broad spectrum of approaches but also – more significantly for Davis's destination as perhaps America's most significant abstract realist – in mining the lessons of Cubism and its derivatives, the art of Braque and Picasso. By presenting a single object from various perspectives, juxtaposing different scenes and using an aggregation of symbols, Davis began to look beyond naturalism's search for the complete expression of one phase of an object or location, moving instead towards a personal artistic language that sought to express 'many phases, incongruity, a greater sense of life', and to employ it capturing the sights, sounds and rhythms of the downtowns, the watersides, the fast-moving industrial city he now knew so well.

In 1925, while eking out an existence from commercial illustration, he met Bessie Chosak, fourteen years his junior, the daughter of immigrant Russian musicians. They were soon living together in relative poverty, but in 1927 Stuart began to receive a monthly stipend from gallerists Gertrude Whitney and Juliana Force, the latter purchasing a work from him at a deliberately generous price, enabling the couple to go to Paris where they married before returning after a year away.⁴⁷ Re-entry to New York, however, was not easy and the financial crash four months later compounded difficulties. Over the next two and a half years, Davis completed the series he had begun in France, held exhibitions more admired by peers than patronized by purchasers, and took up part-time teaching as the market seized up.

In spring 1932 John D. Rockefeller's hiring of Diego Rivera to paint a mural in the Radio City building at the under-construction Rockefeller Center sparked loud protests from American artists, and in an attempt to deflect the controversy by stimulating other commissions, the Museum of Modern Art (MoMA) invited sixty-five American artists – Davis included – to exhibit designs for murals on the theme of post-war American life. Rather than defusing controversy, the manoeuvre led to a far greater one: designs submitted by Ben Shahn, Hugo Gellert and William Gropper – three artists who would later join Davis in the American Artists' Congress – variously depicted recognizable establishment figures, including Andrew Mellon, J. P. Morgan and Rockefeller himself, as 'gangster types dependent on troops, cops and hired thugs to protect their loot'. Attempts to exclude the offending works were then bitterly and successfully resisted amid much publicity.⁴⁸ Davis's work, *New York Mural* – though replete with political symbolism – escaped censure and, in one of the exhibition's few positive spin-offs, led to a commission to provide a mural for the men's lounge at Radio City.

While he was developing this mural design, Bessie disappeared. Davis searched for her frantically for two days, eventually finding her desperately ill at her parents' home in Brooklyn Heights. She had gone there after a botched abortion, which she had not told Davis about, and died the same day. Distraught, weeping uncontrollably for weeks and drinking heavily, Davis gave up their apartment and moved into the Chelsea Hotel. Coaxed through the abyss by friends, he completed his mural, exhibited at *The Social Viewpoint in Art* and became active in the Unemployed Artists Group, arguing forcibly that artists as much as any other workers should be included in relief work provisions – a well-timed demand just as the Roosevelt administration's intentions of moving fast to protect the vulnerable during the winter of 1933–34 were becoming clear. By October the UAG had formulated a platform 'to secure the means of existence for art and artists' via the state either paying all artists a living wage or buying their completed work through a federal purchasing programme, supporting permanent and travelling exhibitions in schools, libraries, hospitals and other public buildings.⁴⁹

Driven out of New York by his own lack of funds, Stuart Davis was in Gloucester, Massachusetts, when these demands were presented to

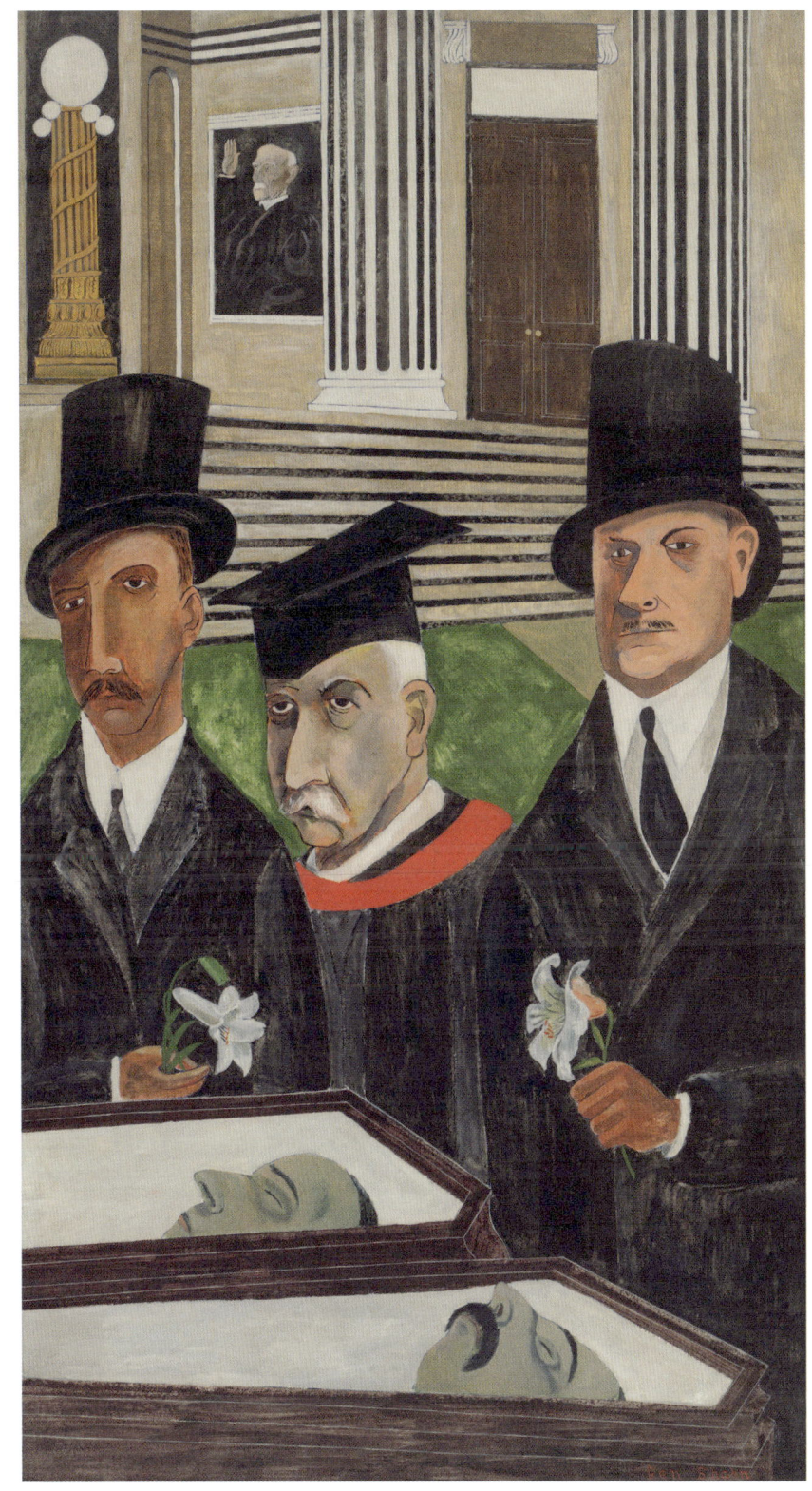

2.13 Ben Shahn, *The Passion of Sacco and Vanzetti*, tempera and gouache on canvas mounted on board, 1931–32. 213.4 × 121.9 cm (84 × 48 in.)

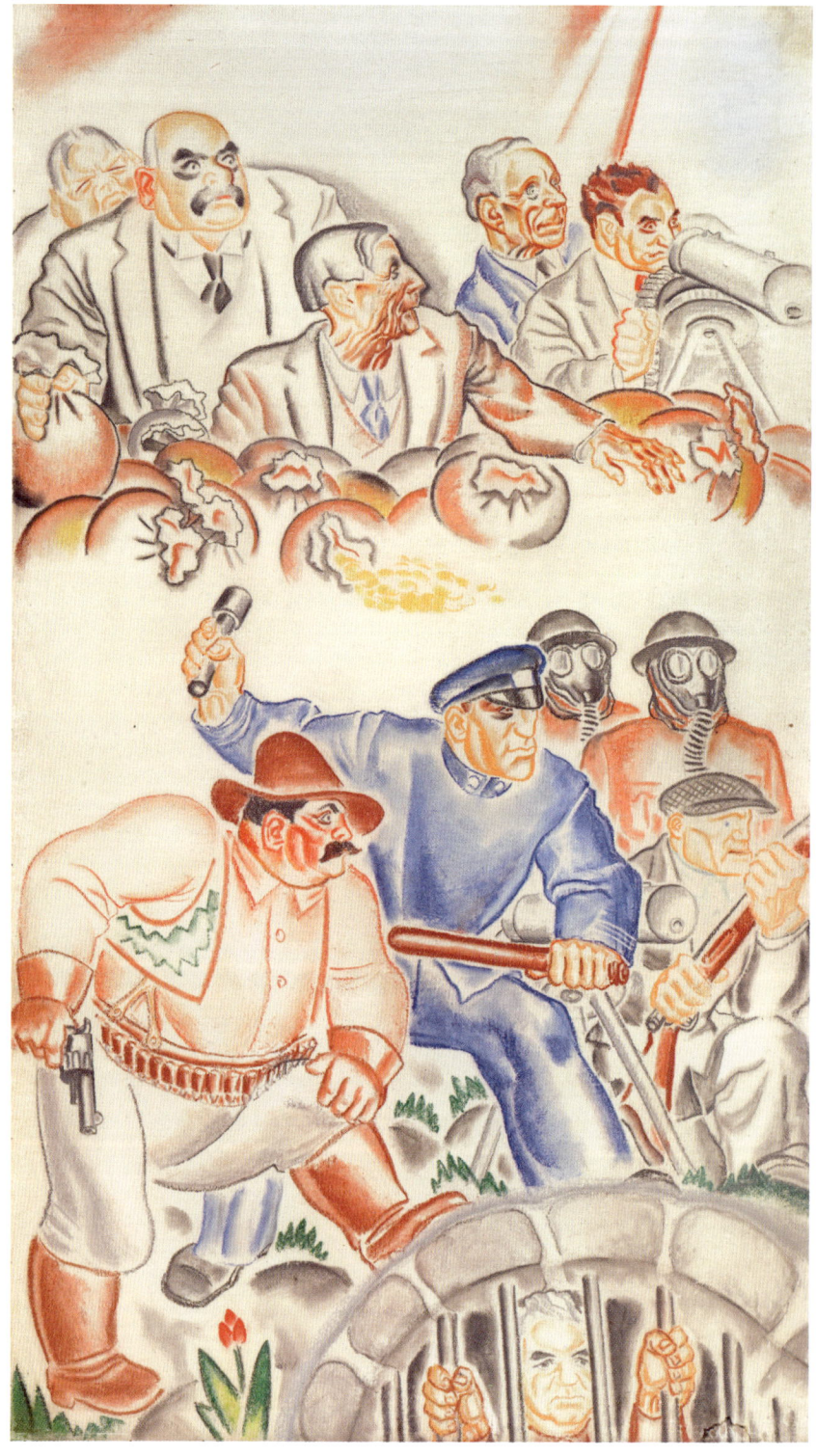

2.14 Hugo Gellert, *Us Fellas Gotta Stick Together or The Last Defence of Capitalism*, chalk on Celotex and plaster, 1932. 215.9 × 125.7 cm (85 × 49½ in.)

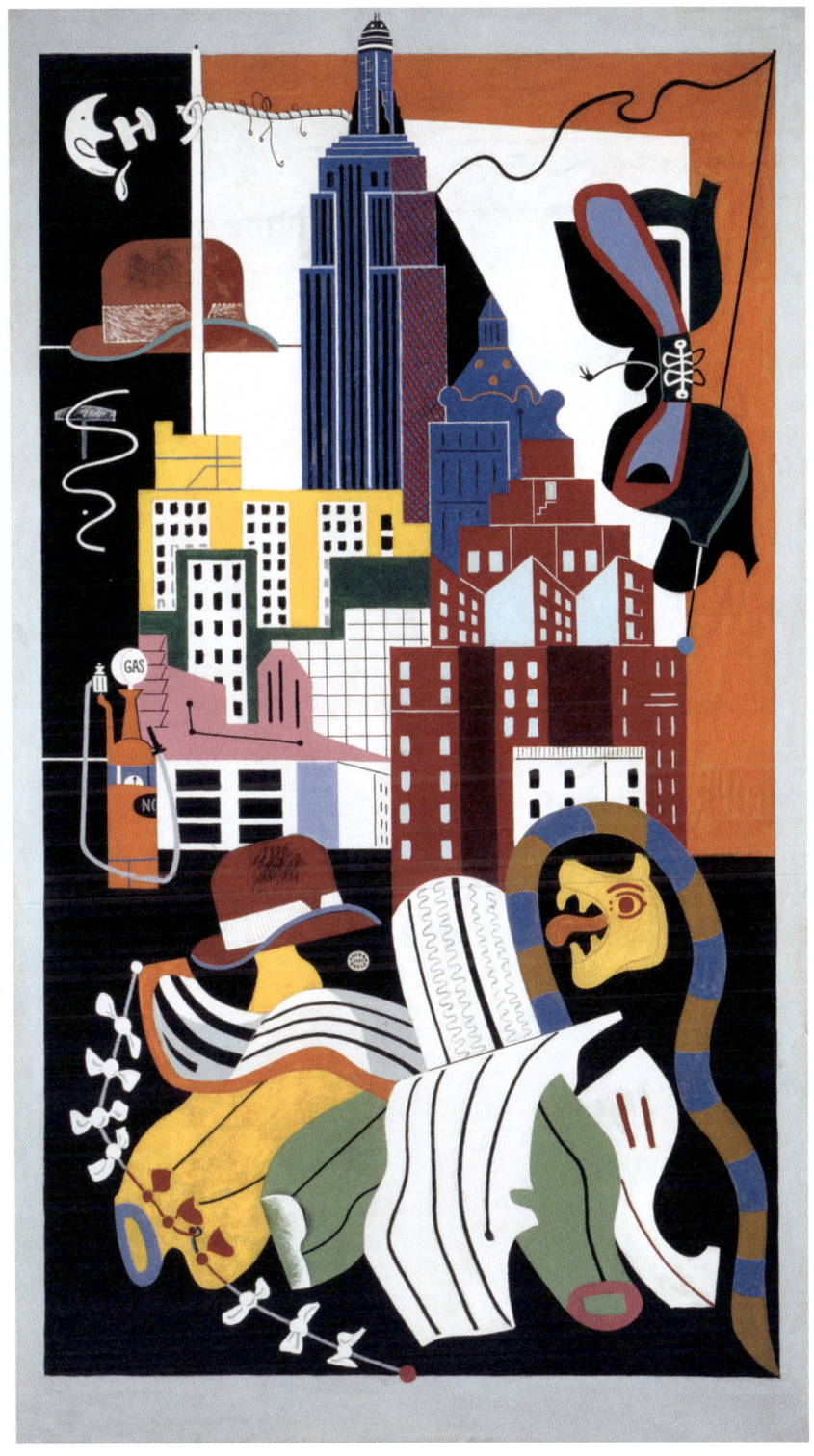

2.15 Stuart Davis, *New York Mural*, oil on canvas, 1932. 213.4 × 121.9 cm (84 × 48 in.)

a federal official in New York, and still there when he heard a radio announcement that a Public Works of Art Project (PWAP) was being formed to provide relief employment and works of art for public buildings. It was a short-term expedient with a massive reach, employing 3,749 artists over the next four months at a cost of $1.3 million, Davis being one of them. 'Amazed that such a thing could exist', he headed back to New York City, enrolled on arrival and moved into a room above Romany Marie's, a favourite bar.[50] From then on, starting almost precisely at the same point in time and for the next seven years, he in New York and Misha Black in London would fulfil very similar roles as key actors promoting unity among artists.[51]

The advent of the PWAP had not gone unnoticed in London, where *The Studio* began its report: 'For the first time in history the Government is recognising not only the existence but also the talent of American Artists', and ended it, 'this is a real step forward and one which it is hoped will be continued.' A precedent had indeed been set, raising possibilities of long-term change in the relationship between artists, the market and the state; in the short term, a focus had been created for pursuit of more permanent New Deal arrangements.[52]

* * * * *

In London no prospect of benign government support for artists was on the horizon, nor had any domestic demands been formulated akin to those of New York's Unemployed Artists Group. National Government rearmament policy was, however, attacked in the AI exhibition's poster section, which also included images of 'the savage heads of European fascism, literally *armed to the teeth*', and its housing policy was unfavourably compared to that of the Soviet Union, in a section described by Wintringham: 'The architects' group of the Artists' International fill a room with a poster-montage contrasting the housing plans and achievements of capitalism and socialism. The material in this is striking if studied; as a poster it is too disconnected.'[53]

In a similar vein, the AI's recruiting leaflet wore its political heart on its sleeve:

> Progressive artists have always been on the side of that class of society which has fought for Social advance. Today in the conflict between the Capitalist class, endeavouring to preserve its power, and the Working class, fighting for world socialism, the artist must be on the side of the Working class. ... Artists the world over are looking with increasing interest to the Soviet Union, where artists are treated as professional

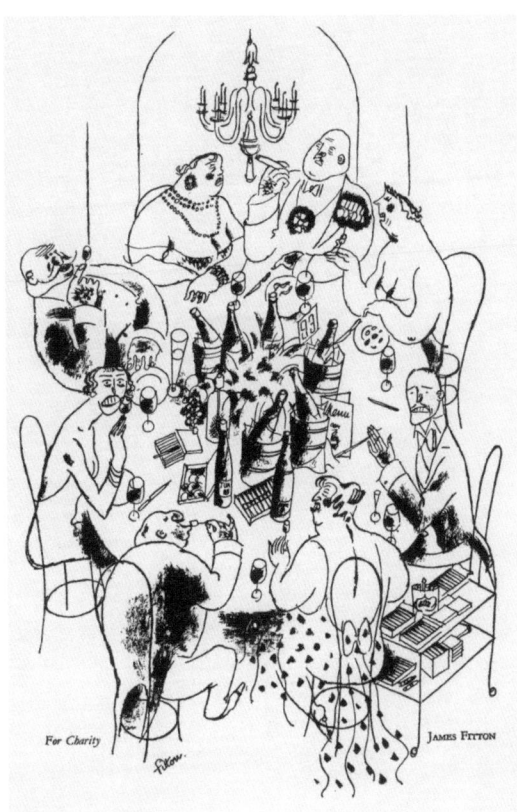 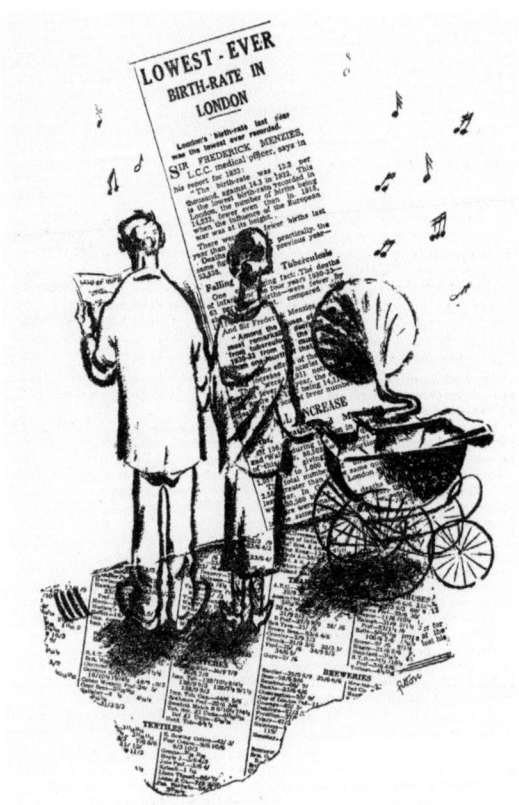

2.16 James Fitton, *For Charity*, line-drawn cartoon in *Left Review*, February 1935. 24.6 × 15.7 cm (9¾ × 6¼ in.). *Left Review*'s foundation coincided with the Charlotte Street exhibition, establishing a growing audience for 'the three Jameses' acerbic social commentary

2.17 James Fitton, *A New Use for Perambulators*, line drawing and collage in *Left Review*, November 1934. 24.6 × 15.7 cm (9¾ × 6¼ in.)

workers of the greatest value to the State. Through their Trade Unions and Co-operatives they take a most effective part in the furtherance of the 1st and 2nd Five Year Plans and the building up of Socialism. Assured of economic security they are free for creative experiment and advance towards a new culture and a new art. Their great travelling exhibitions, journals, clubs and Artists' Homes are world famous.[54]

Such statements, along with criticism of religion in the *AI Bulletin* on a 'pleasing looking bookstall', evidently attracted the attention of G. M. Godden, a Catholic activist dismayed to learn that eight hundred people had visited the exhibition in four days. She concluded that the art on display was merely an excuse for daily propaganda lectures, one being given by 'the Principal of the London Marxist School and another by the principal promoter of opposition to the Incitement to Disaffection Bill; neither of these speakers having the least pretensions to any knowledge of art'.[55] Locating the AI as an auxiliary in 'the Communist attack on Great Britain', she included a denunciation of it in a book she was preparing, noting that a selection of works was indeed being sent to the USSR.

Had Godden had access to the call for contributions to a touring exhibition organized by the Secretariat of the International Bureau of Revolutionary Artists in Moscow, she would have had even better copy.[56] Circulated early in the summer on AI headed paper and signed 'the Committee', it noted that 'paintings, drawings, sculpture etc., will be chosen not only for their revolutionary and proletarian content but also for their aesthetic value', and assured artists that 'technique and treatment are entirely at the will of the artist'. Nevertheless, a list of favoured subjects was suggested, including: 'Strikes, elections, demonstrations, meetings, etc, showing definite working-class activity ... Struggles between workers and reactionary forces. Workers must be shown definitely opposing their enemies ... Unemployed scenes at Labour Exchanges, outside factories, eviction scenes etc. The negative sentiment "Pity the poor down and outs" is not required. The organisational struggles of the unemployed should be the keynote'; landscapes should preferably include 'the life of the agricultural proletariat'. Seeking submissions by the end of August, the committee exhorted 'only by contributing our best work can we begin to solve the question of Proletarian art', flagging a topic that would be much debated, and then sidelined as the popular front formed over the following two years.

Godden would publish her book *The Communist Attack on Great Britain* in early 1935, but more immediately she penned a 1,500-word condemnation of the Artists International's 'Godless Propaganda' for the *Catholic Herald*; headed 'Proletarian Art Comes to England', it provoked an extended riposte a week later from the most prominent Catholic artist then working in Britain. Widely known to Godden's co-religionists since completing his fourteen *Stations of the Cross* in Westminster Cathedral in 1918, Eric Gill had recently become a national celebrity while working on the BBC's Langham Place headquarters, his smocked figure high on a scaffold carving *Prospero and Ariel* a staple of newsreel and mass newspaper reports.[57]

On the morning of Wednesday 17 October Gill had met Charles Holden, London Transport's main station architect, at Leicester Square to discuss a potential commission, before dashing up to Charlotte Street to take in *The Social Scene*, a visit he put to good use in his rebuttal ten days later:

> I visited the exhibition rather expecting to find many anti-God paintings, as I had been told I should do, but in half an hour's walk round, I could see none. All I saw were various works depicting the hardship of the proletariat, the brutality of the police, the display of armed forces against street demonstrators, orators, starving children and slum conditions generally. There were also a few works in the vein of Van Gogh's 'Yellow Chair', that is to say scenes depicting simple workmen and

scenes of working life ... Suppose it to be true that Artists' International is primarily concerned to propagate Communism; even so, there was nothing in the terms under which we exhibited which made it obligatory. And there was nothing to hinder any Catholic artist for showing that he could stand up for social justice as well as any Marxian.[58]

Little or nothing was known at the time of Gill's libertine private life and incestuous and bestial couplings, revelation of which has since rendered him an almost untouchable figure in art history discourse, and in 1934 his public support was significant. Particularly telling was his ridiculing of Godden's outrage that 'speakers denounced the present English social system and the Sedition Bill – subjects familiar to Communist speakers but unexpected in the course of addresses connected with an exhibition of art'. 'Now what, may I ask, is this extraordinary thing called art if it is not propaganda ... what are the sculptures on the medieval cathedrals and in modern churches but propaganda?' Gill enquired. 'What are the effigies of eminent politicians in Westminster Abbey and Parliament Square if they are not propaganda ... For me all art is propaganda and it is high time that modern art became propaganda for social justice instead of propaganda for the flatulent and decadent ideals of bourgeois Capitalism.'[59]

Gill rehearsed the to and fro of his dispute with Godden in *Left Review* in June 1935, shortly before endorsing the prospectus for the AI's next major exhibition, *Artists Against Fascism and War*. This in turn led to pressure on him to recant his political stance, orchestrated by Cardinal Hinsley, the newly appointed Archbishop of Westminster – pressure Gill ignored.[60] Godden, meanwhile, incorporated coverage of subsequent AI exhibitions in a 1938 reissue of her book, concluding: 'The Communist attack on the Cultural Front, in England, neglects no side of cultural life. Literature, Science, Drama, Music, Art, Cinema, Education, every branch of cultural activity is to be utilised as a weapon in the class struggle.'[61]

* * * * *

Tom Wintringham had noted that most drawings and paintings of 'meetings, marches, banners' on display at *The Social Scene* were unsuccessful in that 'they make patterns without showing, in and through these patterns, the strength, endurance, solidity-in-movement of the class force that shapes these demonstrations'. Having ticked this ideological box, he then cited an exception solely based on artistic authenticity: 'Boswell succeeds in his street scenes by the solid, normal, seen individuals that make up his groups, their attitudes, the caps they wear as if they had been born in them. As those who saw the first issue of LEFT REVIEW will realize, the man can draw.'[62] By the time the second issue of *Left Review* appeared, edited by the triumvirate of Montagu Slater, Amabel Williams-Ellis and Tom Wintringham, Boswell had effectively been recruited as the founding unpaid art editor of a monthly that from the first had heavyweight literary and intellectual credentials,[63] but which has long since been principally remembered for the cutting edge of its visual content.

The venture had been conceived in embryo the previous February at a gathering of writers in the upstairs meeting room of a Fitzrovia pub. It was an occasion very akin to the assembly of young artists that had formalized the Artists International in Misha Black's nearby Charlotte Street rooms four months before, with Tom Wintringham, who also had first-hand knowledge of the Soviet Union, playing a similar inspirational role to Cliff Rowe. As Edgell Rickword, already celebrated for editing *The Calendar of Modern Letters* in the 1920s, recalled: 'There were about fifteen of us ... Someone had the idea of founding the Society for the Defence of Culture, as I now think it was rather childishly called ... after the first meeting there was one to launch a society of revolutionary literature and obviously such a society needs an organ. So the organ was started and the society rather faded out. And that's how *Left Review* was born.'[64]

Montagu Slater, co-ordinating editor for the first fifteen issues, had first encountered Boswell crossing Regent's Park carrying an armchair four years earlier, and thereafter the *Morning Post* journalist had been a key link in the artist's recruitment to the party two years later. This led, after his turn away from painting towards graphic art, to Boswell contributing cartoons to the *Daily Worker* as 'Buchan', a practice followed by Fitton who contributed as 'Alpha'. But it was under their own names that Boswell, Fitton and Holland now combined to provide 105 of the 188 images that appeared in *Left Review* over the next three and a half years.[65] As James Holland remembered: 'we were all artists by training and intention, graphic designers by occupation, illustrators and cartoonists by conviction.'

During her stays in Moscow, Pearl Binder was struck by the fact that 'the best Russian cartoonist was a combine composed of three separate artists (all in their twenties), Kupryanov, Krilov and Nikolay Sokolov', writing that 'they all work together on the same cartoons which they sign Kukriniksy. Their cartoons are quite the most devastatingly brilliant I have seen anywhere in the world ... they share a Moscow studio and all do separate individual work as well.' There were elements of 'Kukriniksy' practice in the modus operandi the 'three Jameses' now pursued. As cartoonists their individual output was distinctive, but they clearly directly influenced each other – on occasion playfully borrowing characters from one another in pursuit of the same political quarry – and as the Alpha Group they undertook several special projects collectively.[66]

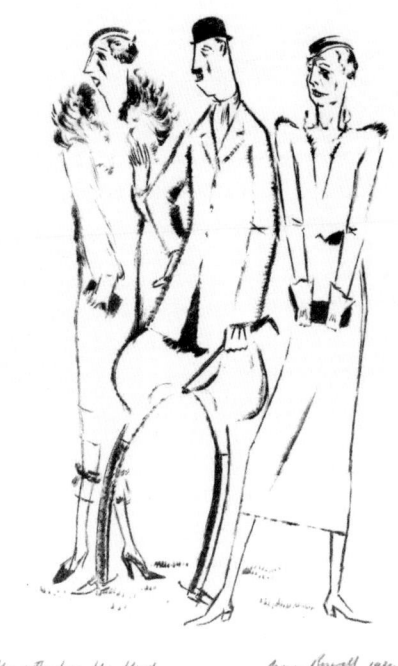
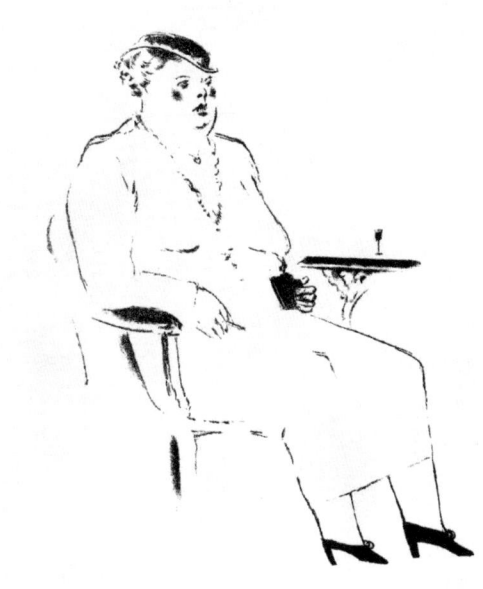

2.18 James Boswell, *You Gotta Have Blue Blood*, line-drawn cartoon in *Left Review*, October 1934. 24.6 × 15.7 cm (9¾ × 6¼ in.)

2.19 James Boswell, *The Lonely Heart*, line-drawn cartoon in *Left Review*, December 1934. 24.6 × 15.7 cm (9¾ × 6¼ in.)

The cartoon that announced Boswell's distinctive style and observant eye to *Left Review*'s readers was *You Gotta Have Blue Blood*, an image that skewers the arrogant disdain exhibited by upper-class 'society' in the face of working-class suffering during the slump – the reality that had so shocked its creator on arrival in London from the more egalitarian ethos of New Zealand.[67] Boswell possessed a book of George Grosz's Weimar-period drawings published in 1930, and in the interval since *Why We Are Marching!* he had been able to absorb the German's adept use of wounding distortion at an exhibition held at the Mayor Gallery in June 1934,[68] an influence which now surfaced in his cartoons, starting with *Hatton Garden Luncheon* in the second issue of *Left Review*. An equally distinctive trait that kept breaking through in parallel, however, was Boswell's deft deployment of line to convey the interior life of his chosen characters, as in *The Lonely Heart*, which appeared in *Left Review*'s third issue but which could equally well have graced a private press edition of Patrick Hamilton's *Midnight Bell* or *The Plains of Cement*.[69]

James Fitton and James Holland opened with equally compelling contributions. Fitton's *A New Use for Perambulators* in issue two uses cartoon and montage to highlight the connection between poverty on the streets, financial crisis and a falling birth rate, while his *For Charity* in issue six offers a rococo, slow-burning take on the hypocrisy of the bourgeoisie at

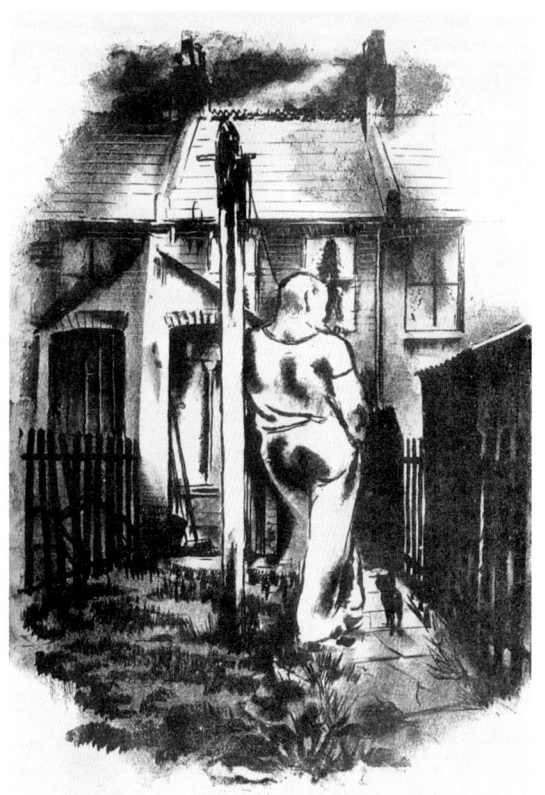
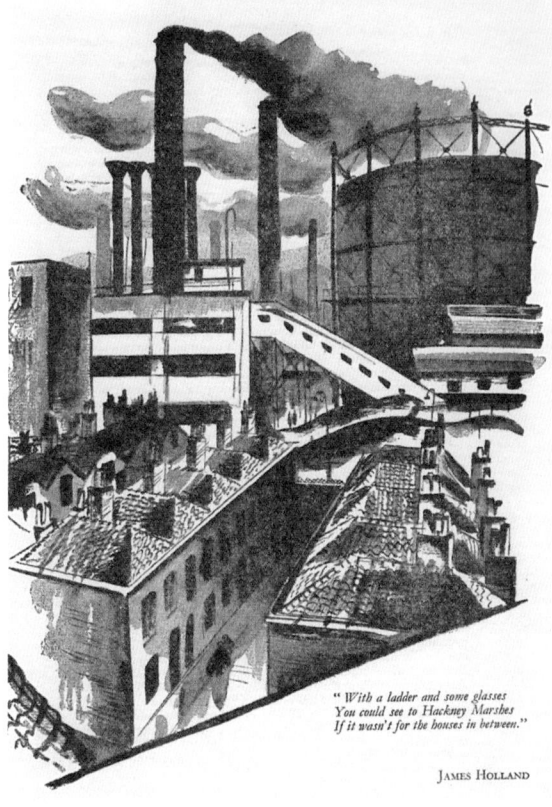

"With a ladder and some glasses
You could see to Hackney Marshes
If it wasn't for the houses in between."

JAMES HOLLAND

2.20 James Holland, *The Sailor's Return*, pen, ink and wash drawing in *Left Review*, March 1935.
24.1 × 15.2 cm
(9½ × 6 in.)

2.21 James Holland, *With a Ladder and Some Glasses*, pen, ink and wash cartoon in *Left Review*, February 1935.
24.6 × 15.7 cm
(9¾ × 6¼ in.)

play in the name of good causes. Holland, meanwhile, would always draw deeply on his waterfront and urban working-class heritage in his painting, and both were evident from the outset in *Left Review*. *With a Ladder and Some Glasses* plays on a music-hall lyric to depict the grim housing and environmental conditions of the East End, and the superb lithograph *The Sailor's Return* is replete with feeling for the existential realities of a deck-hand's shore life.[70]

All three artists took collective aim at the Incitement to Disaffection Bill, a government attempt to extend the law outlawing political engagement with members of the armed forces. In 1925 Tom Wintringham had been imprisoned for sedition under existing legislation, and it was almost certainly he who now penned the appeal for action appearing under a headline set in funereal German Gothic type: 'The first issue of The Left Review comes out during the Parliamentary recess. In the last session the Incitement to Disaffection Bill, a measure which closely affects the freedom of writing and speaking, passed through its committee stage. Before our second number appears it will receive its Third Reading.' The most objectionable aspects of the proposals introduced unlimited powers of search and seizure and criminalized mere possession of any literature that, if seen by an enlisted person, could lead them to question orders, for example to break a strike or fire on civilians. A power grab disguised as a procedural reform, it generated mass support for a campaign co-ordinated by the newly formed Council for Civil Liberties and eventually backed by the mainstream press, which ultimately succeeded in limiting but not eliminating the new powers. *Left Review* was in the van of this effort, with Holland's *Incitement to Disaffection* featuring both Trenchard and Churchill, Boswell's *His Majesty's Servants* echoing Tudor-Hart's *Sedition*, and Fitton's Grosz-like *Twelve Good Men and True* crystallizing anxieties that the people of Britain might 'not have to wait for fascism to take away their liberties as the National Government seems determined to remove them by legislation'.⁷¹

* * * * *

In addition to Boswell's *You Gotta Have Blue Blood* and Wintringham's sedition démarche, *Left Review*'s first issue included *Love Lane, Shadwell*, a lithograph by Pearl Binder, and examples of her East End and theatrical lithographs were simultaneously on display in Charlotte Street at *The Social Scene*.⁷² Binder herself, however, missed seeing the exhibition, having arrived in Leningrad on 25 August. She had travelled via Le Havre

2.22 Pearl Binder, *Russian Railway Journey*, lithograph, 1935. 19 × 31.5 cm (7½ × 12½ in.)

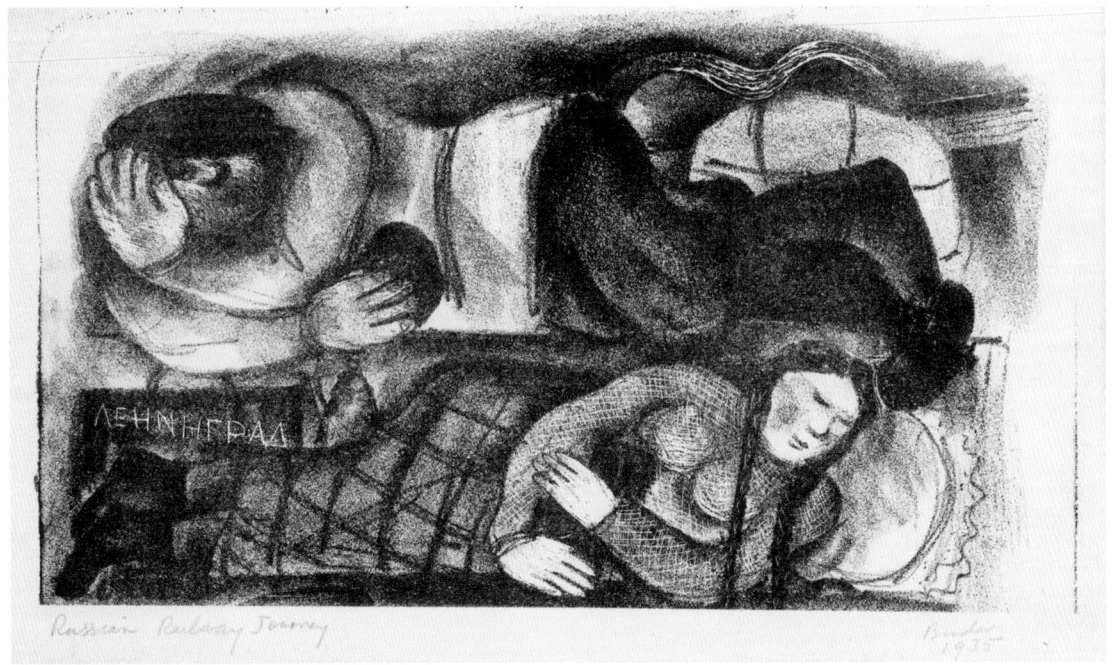

as part of a VOKS-sponsored British delegation en route to a theatre festival in Moscow, and her second visit to the Soviet Union would prove as exhilarating – though slightly more clouded – as the first.

Her diaries reveal the pace of her activity, but also her questioning independence of spirit during three months when she frequently managed to detach herself from her guide to spend time with friends she had made in 1933, such as the US *Daily Worker* cartoonist Fred Ellis and his wife. By 1 September she was in Moscow, noting: 'Great scramble to get tickets for the Red Square Youth Parade but well worth it. The best I have ever seen in my life. Street decoration exceptionally good – enormous oblongs of red bunting over wooden slats (Venetian blind fashion) lettering in plain white.' Four days later, however, she staggered out of bed ill with 'grippe' on the day it had been arranged for her to visit the International Bureau of Revolutionary Artists to convey news of London's Artists International: officials were favourably impressed by the lithographs she had brought with her (subsequently bought by the Museums of Western Art and Fine Art for a combined 800 roubles), but the overall interaction was evidently difficult and laden with advice on future strategy:

1: they stress our getting contact with and drawing in well-known artists
2: that we prepare now for Fascist repression by using different addresses
3: we should establish close contact with colonies and develop these contacts
4: our work amongst the art students is of particular importance as these are the revolutionary artists of the future[73]

This was a package formed at a distance and steeped in the Comintern world-view, and its second point incorporated a significant misreading of the situation in London. Those in Moscow were still processing and reacting to the shattering defeats in Germany in 1933 and Austria in 1934, but the British fascist variant was not a force on the brink of effecting a brutal suppression of the left, and since the BUF's violent Olympia rally that June had been losing establishment and business support.[74] The officials' third point was a faithful reflection of Comintern doctrine at a time when both Britain's hostility to the Soviet Union and its economic dependence on the empire (and difficulties in holding on to India) were ever more apparent; but it advocated activity where distance, ignorance and slight resources would prove almost insuperable barriers.

Consciousness about imperialism and all its works would increase during the coming jubilee year across the AI's almost exclusively white London network, as reflected in some artistic production. But for the rest of the decade, it was the clear and present danger of developments in mainland Europe and the continuing arrival of émigré and refugee artists that was the dominant influence shaping international activity. The AI founders were already making headway in attracting the young and the well-known, but it was clearly not easy to convey the nuances of the situation in London. After her meeting Binder recorded, 'To Ellis's where we had a grand anti-IBRA hate session', also noting that 'Fred says Soviet realism so far not producing anything good – only fumbling'.[75]

Intent on staying longer, Binder managed to gain a visa extension after the delegation's programme finished and attendant hospitality lapsed. Needing money, she was able to pick up at least one broadcast and earn fees for artwork provided to the satirical magazine *Krokodil* and the *Moscow Daily News*, as well as work preparing street decorations for November's celebration of the Revolution. In parallel, right up to her subsequent departure from Leningrad, she was also visiting artists' studios and cultural organizations, noting at a children's literature centre: 'Saw printing shop for kids and learned exciting new process of printing drawings from glass – like lithos only without acid – that I must introduce to the AI. You can get 500 copies easily.'[76]

Shortly after this she contracted influenza, a serious development for someone who had suffered tuberculosis five years before, and arrangements were made for her to recuperate at a health resort in Crimea. This was a time of reflection, and on 11 October she confided to her diary: 'I must do two things which are somehow interrelated for me, 1 – get a divorce from Jack, 2 – join the party.' Multiple sources yield no definitive evidence that Pearl Binder ever did the latter, and indeed a good deal of circumstantial evidence to the contrary. But not long after her return to London, at a party celebrating the publication of *Odd Jobs* – the book she had both written and illustrated – she met Frederick Elwyn-Jones, a radical lawyer defending political prisoners in Austria, who divorce from her first husband would enable her to marry three years later.[77]

5

ON REVOLUTIONARY ART

CONTRIBUTORS

1 HERBERT READ

2 F. D. KLINGENDER

3 ERIC GILL

4 A. L. LLOYD

5 ALICK WEST

PUBLISHED BY WISHART

CHAPTER THREE

SOHO SQUARE

The year 1935 was pivotal for the body that began life as the Artists International British Section fourteen months before. Over the course of the year membership would triple, the group consciously broadening its appeal as a new political era dawned, and its annual exhibition – which opened that November barely a year after the inaugural Charlotte Street show had closed – would marshal the work of 179 artists, including many well-known names, under the banner *Artists Against Fascism and War*.[1]

Held in a three-storey Soho Square townhouse, the exhibition embraced internationalism by including French, Dutch, Polish and Soviet rooms and was accompanied by the publication of a book, *5 on Revolutionary Art*, whose diverse contributions signalled an open-minded pluralism but no retreat from an overtly political stance.[2] The exhibition catalogue also saw the first use of a more inclusive title, announcing that the event had been 'called together by the Artists International Association'. In a similar vein to this transformation from 'AI' to 'AIA', an expression of positive support – 'For Cultural Progress and Expansion, Freedom of Work, Speech and Expression' – now accompanied the militant impulse of its founding intention to forge 'Unity of Artists against Fascism, War and the Suppression of Culture'.[3]

This was a year, probably the last, when it was still possible for many on the left to believe that militant anti-fascism and absolute pacifism were compatible stances, and for many in the centre ground of politics to see no contradiction between opposing totalitarianism and the renunciation of military force in international affairs. The year that opened with Nazi victory in a corrupted plebiscite to determine the future of the Saar Territory,[4] and at its midpoint saw Italy invade Abyssinia – events further underscoring the impotence of the League of Nations – also represented the high-water mark of the inter-war peace and disarmament movement. At an Albert Hall rally on 27 June, it was announced that 11.6 million Britons had voted in the Peace Ballot, organized to demonstrate public support for a British foreign policy based on League of Nations negotiations; it was a result underpinned by the experience of the generations that had lived through, and been forever scarred by, the First World War. Of

3.1 Edward McKnight Kauffer, cover design for *5 on Revolutionary Art*, 1935.
19 × 13 cm (7½ × 5⅛ in.)

3.2 Paul Nash, *Coronilla*, oil on canvas, 1929. 61.2 × 50.8 cm (24⅛ × 20 in.). Exhibited in 1935 as cat. 83 at the AIA's exhibition *Artists Against Fascism and War*

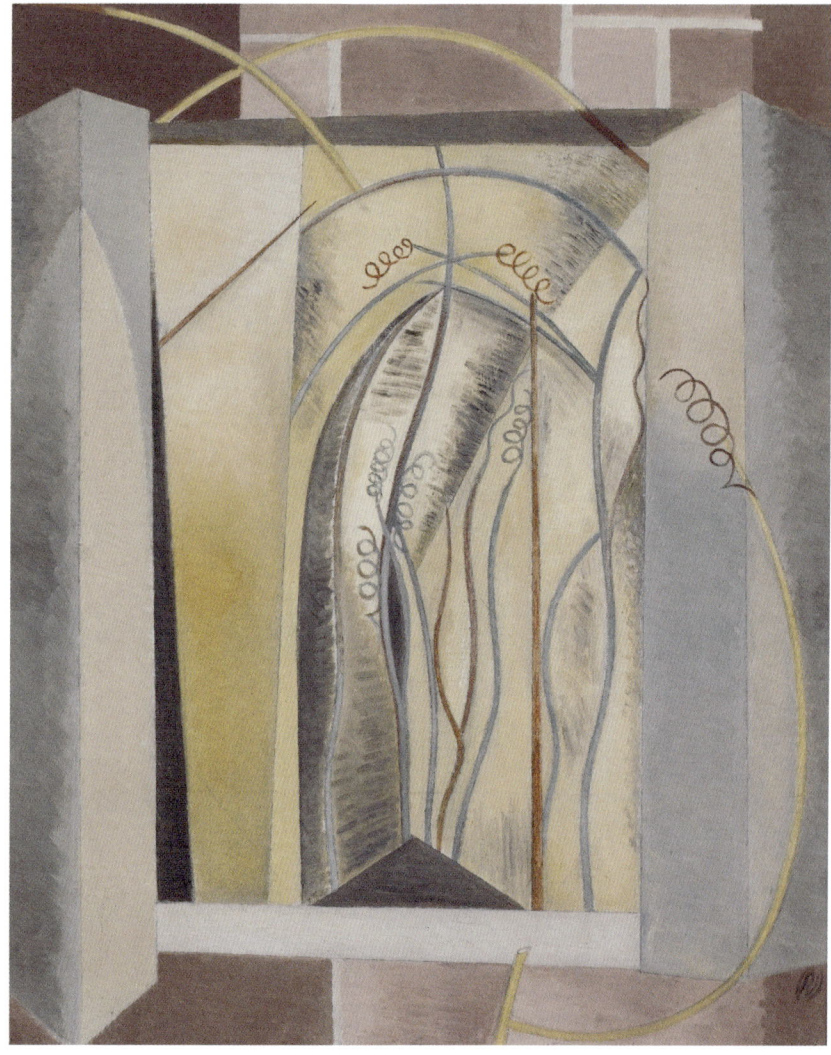

symbolic impact, it could not prevent, the day after the AIA's Soho Square exhibition opened, re-election of a National Government whose actions over the following four years would undermine the residual authority of the League while pursuing an incoherent mix of appeasement and rearmament.

Up to this point, the AI had grown in the main by attracting the generation that had come of age at the time of the financial crash and whose chances of living by art had been curtailed by the Depression, a point well made by artist William Coldstream: 'Through making money much harder to come by, it caused an immense change in our general outlook. One painter I knew lost all his money and had to become a traveller in vacuum cleaners. Everyone began to be interested in economics then in politics. Two very talented painters who had been at the Slade with me gave up painting altogether, one to work for the ILP, the other for the Communist Party. It was no longer the thing to be an artist delighting in isolation.'[5] The urge to combine had not abated: it was still barely possible for many skilled artists to live by their art in January 1935, a period of relative economic revival and renewed prosperity in the metropolis (but not in 'the distressed areas'), and this was giving new impetus to debates about the artist and society, and art and industry.

The position achieved by the AIA by the end of 1935, however, owed as much to its founders' ability to reach upwards generationally as well as outwards politically, as evidenced by the list of the Soho Square exhibition's sponsors, all of whom had been born in the nineteenth century and were of service age during the First World War: 'This exhibition has been called together by the Artists International Association and Eric Gill, Duncan Grant, Augustus John, Laura Knight, Henry Moore, Paul Nash' read the publicity.[6]

The organization's development was also influenced that year by a number of transatlantic journeys – the first of which was a departure. On 14 February 1935 Anna Meblin left Southampton with her eight-month-old son on a Cunard White Star liner, destined for a different life in the United States without Cliff Rowe.[7] Having acted as the AI's secretary for the previous fifteen months, Meblin was replaced by Betty Rea, a member since the early days. Like Rowe and Binder, Rea had also visited Moscow. A sculptor and friend of Henry Moore, who had been one of her teachers when she was at the RCA, Rea was vivacious, mercurial and attractive to both sexes; a good writer and a skilled communicator, the commitment she now brought to alliance-building was set to make a crucial contribution to the AIA's progress, although not without immediate personal cost.

* * * * *

Born in 1904 into a prosperous medical family and christened Elizabeth Marion Bevan, on leaving her exclusive boarding school Betty had been presented at court as a debutante.[8] Shortly after, she began to chart her own course, studying painting at the Regent Street Polytechnic before switching in 1924 to sculpture and the RCA, where she became a good friend of both Peggy Angus and Eric Ravilious.[9] But as Nan Youngman – Betty's future partner of thirty years – recalled, Betty's father Arthur Bevan, although 'probably a good doctor', was habitually choleric, violent-tempered and reactionary, and under pressure to conform Betty became engaged to James Rea, a trainee barrister with establishment connections, at the end of her first year.[10]

The couple married after James qualified in June 1926; Betty left college after two years and their two sons, Nicolas and Julian, were born in 1928 and 1931. But soon after, what had never been an entirely compatible alliance began to fray, not least because of her reaction to the complacency of the opulent society in which they moved during the crisis years. Mutual infidelities followed, most significantly for Betty an affair with the radical Cambridge scientist and polymath J. D. 'Sage' Bernal, with whom she visited the USSR on at least one occasion. Returning after a second visit, having seen the May 1934 International Children's Art Exhibition in Moscow, she published a wide-ranging review of 'Children and Art in Soviet Russia' in *Design Today*, whose editors noted cautiously: 'the vast experiment in social and political design which is going on in one-sixth of the globe cannot be overlooked. Betty Rea ... writes with an enthusiasm, which may offend prejudiced non-communists, but we must risk that because we find the system she presents of great interest.'[11] By now a member of the Communist Party of Great Britain (CPGB), and a participant in its 'Hogarth Group' of artists, she took up the role of AI secretary not long after moving her boys out of the Kensington marital home, leaving behind her cook and parlour maid for a very different lifestyle cooking for herself in a flat in Arundel Gardens, Notting Hill Gate.[12]

Writing in the catalogue of a memorial sculpture exhibition thirty years later, Misha Black recalled Rea's impact: 'She brought to our group a strange quality which acted as a cement to our diversity ... Authority combined with absolute sincerity were Betty's formidable weapons, but they were transmuted by a tender kindness which made all who worked with her the happier for having done so ... In our quasi-political organisation Betty had no enemies, and that endured because we all sensed she had no personal ambition and that the organising and administering which she did so efficiently was a discipline self-imposed by her intelligence and her social conscience.'[13]

The sixth issue of the *AI Bulletin*, dated May 1935, is headed with Rea's name as secretary, at her Arundel Gardens address, and Donia Nachshen's name as treasurer.[14] Its four neatly printed trimmed A5 sides bear less than a thousand words, but the sense of a mass of activity being briskly marshalled is tangible, not least in the announcement:

> The AI has now taken premises at 4 Parton Street, Red Lion Square, WC1. These are small, but within the rent guaranteed by the regional groups and individual members, and will form a basis from which to launch out later to more ambitious schemes. There is a small bar where tea, coffee and sandwiches can be obtained whenever the premises are open, and the nucleus of a library, for which books are urgently

required. On every Saturday from 2.30 p.m. to 11.30 p.m. the bar and library will be open. There will be chess, darts, and, we hope, a wireless set. On every Wednesday at 8 p.m. (commencing May 8th) models will be provided for those who wish to draw and paint. House warming for our new headquarters, Saturday May 4th Members 6d Friends 1/-.[15]

In other events listed for that month, Eric Gill was to speak on Art and Propaganda, but Jacob Burck had not yet arrived from America – talk postponed. On successive Saturdays Alec West's study class on 'The Artist in Society' was to be followed by Francis Klingender's next 'History of Art' talk. Unemployed member artists with time to execute banners and posters were asked to contact C. H. Rowe at 65 Marchmont Street: 'the AI charges a nominal sum to all organisations for which it works, this charge will be paid to any unemployed artists who do this work, less 25 per cent to the central fund.' A political cartoon discussion was to take place on the third Saturday at 6 p.m., while notice of events elsewhere included a concert of recent Soviet music on 1 May, a Committee Against Malnutrition on 16 May, and John Grierson on Advances in Film Production on 12 May.

In a further clear sign of the way the strategic wind was blowing, a section headed 'May Day and the Jubilee' reads:

> This year May Day is of double importance to us in Great Britain. Not only is it a demonstration of solidarity against increasing exploitation ... it is also a protest against the Jubilee celebrations, bidding us to rejoice over a period of our history during which – to mention only two items of these disastrous 25 years – hundreds of thousands of men were killed and millions mutilated in war; and unemployment in Great Britain alone has soared to well over two million. We consider rejoicing out of place, have already issued several thousand posters, stickers, etc as a protest and now call to all members to demonstrate our solidarity of purpose [by] marching in the May Day demonstrations: Meet Mornington Crescent Tube Station at 4 p.m. May 1st. The Labour Party officials have refused to join the United Front demonstration on May 1st, and are calling on their members to march on Sunday May 6th. They think this historical day of strikes and opposition should be changed to Sunday to suit the convenience of the employers. In face, however, of the critical nature of the situation nothing must stand in the way of showing the ruling class the united strength of the opposition ... We therefore urge you also to march in this demonstration on Sunday May 6th.

Sunday 6 May was in fact Silver Jubilee Day itself, with the largest of several parades that month honouring George V as King of the United

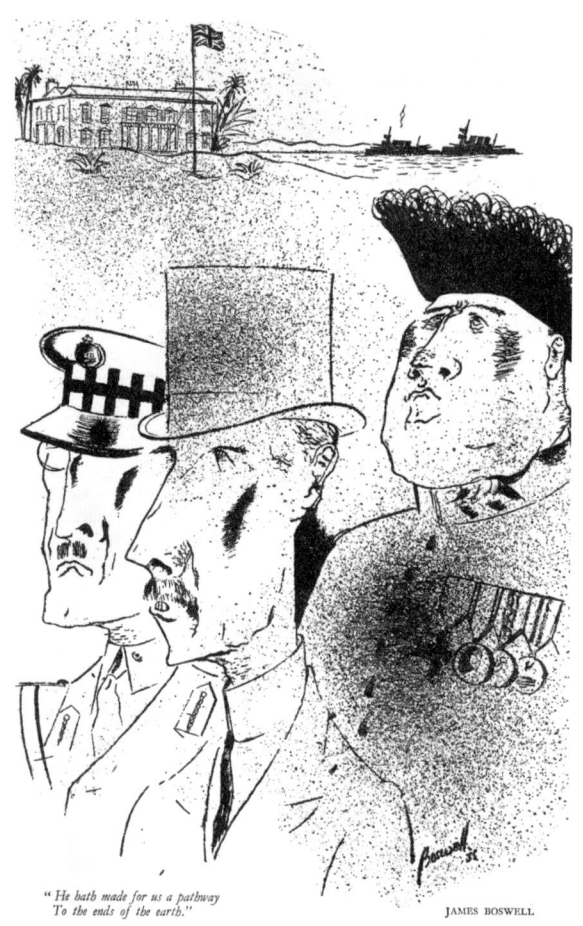

"He hath made for us a pathway
To the ends of the earth."

JAMES BOSWELL

3.3 James Boswell, *He hath made for us a pathway*, ink-drawn cartoon with airbrushed stippling in *Left Review*, May 1935. 24.6 × 15.7 cm (9¾ × 6¼ in.)

3.4 Cliff Rowe, *Jubilee*, poster design for Artists International, 1935. 59.4 × 42 cm (23½ × 16⅝ in.)

Kingdom and Emperor of India, ahead of which *Left Review* carried *He hath made for us a pathway / To the ends of the earth*, a Boswell cartoon depicting three human pillars of the empire with a caption drawn from Rudyard Kipling's 'A Song of the English', and *The tumult and the shouting dies / the captains and the Kings depart*, Holland's depiction of a horse-drawn municipal garbage cart overflowing with bunting and royalist signage, captioned with a verse from the same poet's 'Recessional'.[16] The third cartoon in the May issue was Pearl Binder's *Chalking Squad*, a humorous take on necessary precautions against police apprehension while undertaking protest activity.

The most consequential art produced for the occasion under AI auspices, however, was *Jubilee*, a sensational poster by Cliff Rowe of a crowned royal skeleton above the legend '25 Years of War Hunger Unemployment', which was fly-posted along the processional route. Produced before Parton Street became the AI's official address, it incautiously carried Rea's – 9 Arundel Gardens – a fact soon drawn to the attention of the Metropolitan Police

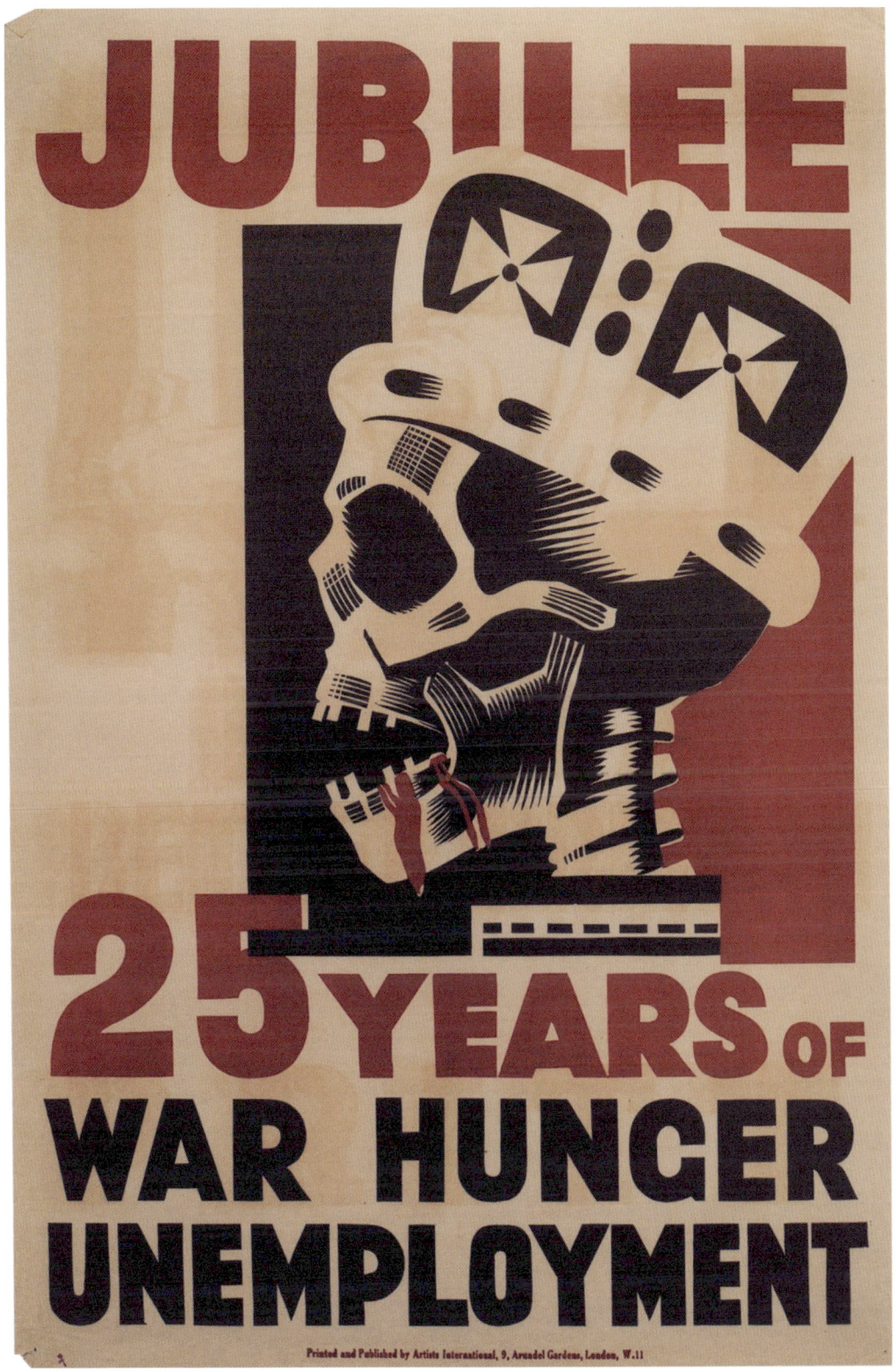

commissioner, Lord Trenchard. Despite requesting retirement, Trenchard had been kept in office by a government nervous about the possibility of extravagant celebrations triggering popular protest; he was also an acquaintance of Arthur Bevan and lost no time in informing him of his daughter's association with the AI. As Nan Youngman recorded: 'Betty received a vituperative letter from her father forbidding her the house, even to visit her mother, cutting off the allowance he had been giving her since she and her husband had parted, and cruelly mocking her about this, saying James at least had had the Dutch courage to leave her. He cut her and her sons out of his will, and she only saw him briefly twice before he died many years later.'[17]

* * * * *

Another transatlantic journey of consequence had occurred the previous summer when Viscount Jack Hastings, son of the 15th Earl of Huntingdon, and Cristina Casati, daughter of an Italian marquis, arrived in London after staying with Frida Kahlo and Diego Rivera in Mexico City. They had been overseas for seven of the last nine years, but during a brief return in 1928–29 Jack had studied at the Slade, getting to know both William Coldstream and Clive Branson, one of the talented artists Coldstream recalled abandoning painting for political activism.

Born into an Indian Army family in 1907, Branson had worked in insurance before overcoming parental opposition to study art and meeting Noreen Browne, a young musician, during a student production at the Scala Theatre. Living in Battersea after their marriage, they played a leading role in efforts to mark the fiftieth anniversary of Karl Marx's death by opening a library and educational facility, a project initiated in March 1933, just as news of Nazi book burning in Berlin was emerging. The first classes at the Marx Memorial Library and Workers' School in Clerkenwell Green had taken place seven months later, while moves to form the AI were under way; following his return and reconnection with Branson, Jack agreed to create a mural in the manner of Diego Rivera for its upstairs lecture room.[18]

Until his mid-twenties, the Eton-educated Hastings – a City stockbroker with Plantagenet forebears whose Mayfair residence, club and tailoring expenses were paid for by his father – had led a predictable existence, troubled only by his own desire to paint and parental disquiet at the 'fast', drug-taking, sexually adventurous set with whom he socialized. Cristina Casati, the woman he had fallen for, could never be the English heiress the family craved, and their marriage and elopement to Australia, followed by two bohemian years in a house on Moorea in the South Pacific,

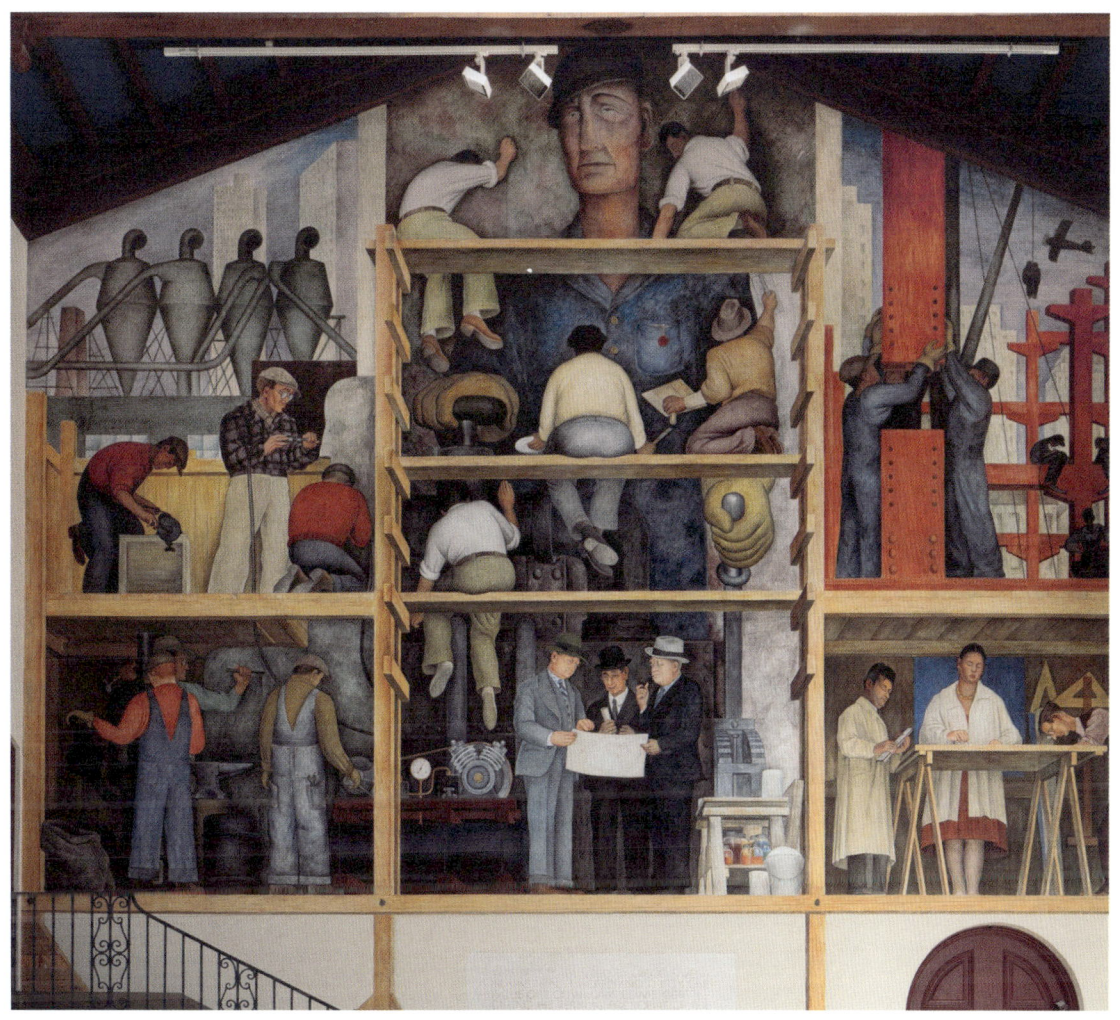

3.5 Diego Rivera, *The Making of a Fresco Showing the Building of a City*, fresco, San Francisco Art Institute (formerly California School of Fine Arts), 1931. 548 × 975.4 cm (215¾ × 377 in.)

had scandalized the society pages before Cristina's pregnancy led to their initial return.[19] En route back from a subsequent, post-Slade, South Pacific sojourn, friends had arranged for Hastings to exhibit in San Francisco, where in October 1931 he engineered a meeting with Diego Rivera, persuading him to let him join the team of assistants working on Rivera's commission for the San Francisco Stock Exchange.

The team was led by Clifford Wight, who oversaw the complex process of layering wet plaster onto wall surfaces and tracing on Rivera's designs during twelve- to eighteen-hour working sessions in which – in true fresco method – paint had to be applied before the plaster dried. Tall and darkly good-looking, Wight, the son of a Swindon railway fitter, had migrated to Canada as a teenager, studied architecture in California, and since the late 1920s had worked as a pupil-assistant of Rivera in Mexico, towards the end of the seven-year period in which Rivera had executed 124 frescoes for the Mexican Secretariat of Education. Wight shared Rivera's revolutionary politics and as he became firm friends with fellow Englishman Hastings, the views of both foreman and master were influential in shaping Jack's outlook. Jack's language skills also made him a trusted interpreter, party to the social traffic, negotiation and political controversy that surrounded Rivera and his work in Depression-era USA.[20] By early 1931, when Rivera embarked on his next major commission, *The Making of a Fresco Showing the Building of a City* at the California School of Fine Arts, such was the triumvirate that he included the figures of both Englishmen in *trompe l'œil* fashion. Thus White, kneeling to draw, and Hastings, holding a plumb line, were memorialized creating the figure of a giant worker in blue overalls adorned with a yellow hammer and sickle; to complete the provocation Rivera included a view of his own posterior front and centre.

By 1932 Hastings had won, somewhat to his surprise, a mural commission for the Hall of Science at the 1933 Chicago World's Fair, but before this was due to commence, Rivera's team was to reassemble in April at the Detroit Institute of Arts, where in its two-storey garden court the Mexican would create one of his most magnificent fresco cycles, *Detroit Industry*, a project funded by Henry Ford's son, Edsel.[21] Ahead of this, Jack and Cristina left California by car for a trans-continental odyssey through the heart of the slump, during which they were shocked to see the poverty and wretchedness of tens of thousands of vagrant families streaming west in search of work, starving at a time – as Hastings later expressed it – when farmers were burning wheat and drowning hogs to keep prices high, millions of gallons of milk were being poured away and shiploads of coffee were being jettisoned at sea. The experience deepened the Hastings' conviction that the very structure of capitalism was irredeemable, and ensured that Jack would return to London 'a near communist'.[22]

Diego's next commission, undertaken while Hastings was in Chicago, was the Rockefeller-funded creation of a mural for the lobby of the fifty-storey RCA building in New York, the award of which had led to protests from unemployed American artists and the unsuccessful attempt by MoMA to deflect criticism by mounting its controversial exhibition of mural designs. Rivera's theme was to be 'man at the crossroads, uncertain but hopeful for a better future', and his initial sketches were viewed favourably. But two months later his 'composition hardened into a dichotomy between a sybaritic, violent capitalist society and a utopic communist one', a design finally rendered unacceptable to the sponsors when Rivera included a portrait of Lenin joining hands with a soldier, an industrial worker and a farmer.[23] On 9 May the largely completed mural was covered up and the artistic team dismissed, and exactly nine months later, on 9 February 1934, while Jack and Cristina were staying with Rivera in Mexico City, the artist learned his work had been destroyed.

Ironically, on the day the mural was first hidden, President Roosevelt received a letter from his patrician painter friend George Biddle, stressing how government funding had allowed Mexican artists 'to produce the greatest national school of mural painting since the Italian Renaissance', and that 'younger artists of America are conscious as they never have been of the social revolution that our country and civilisation are going through,

3.6 Lucienne Bloch, photograph of Diego Rivera's fresco *Man at the Crossroads* at the Rockefeller Center, New York, 1933

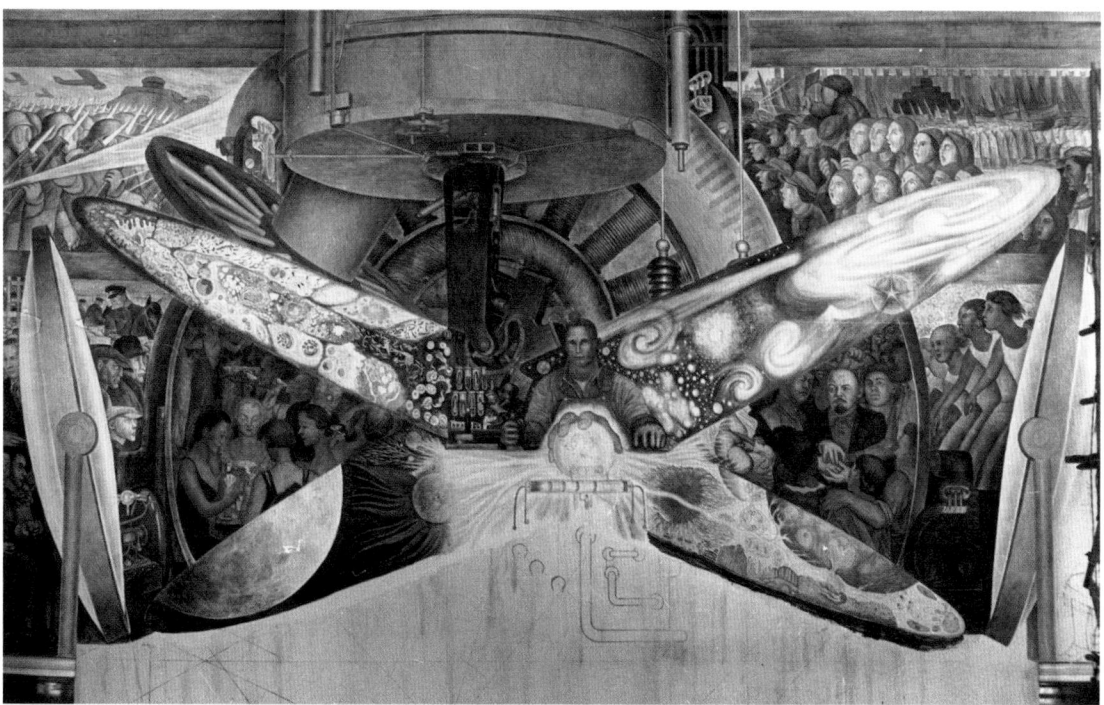

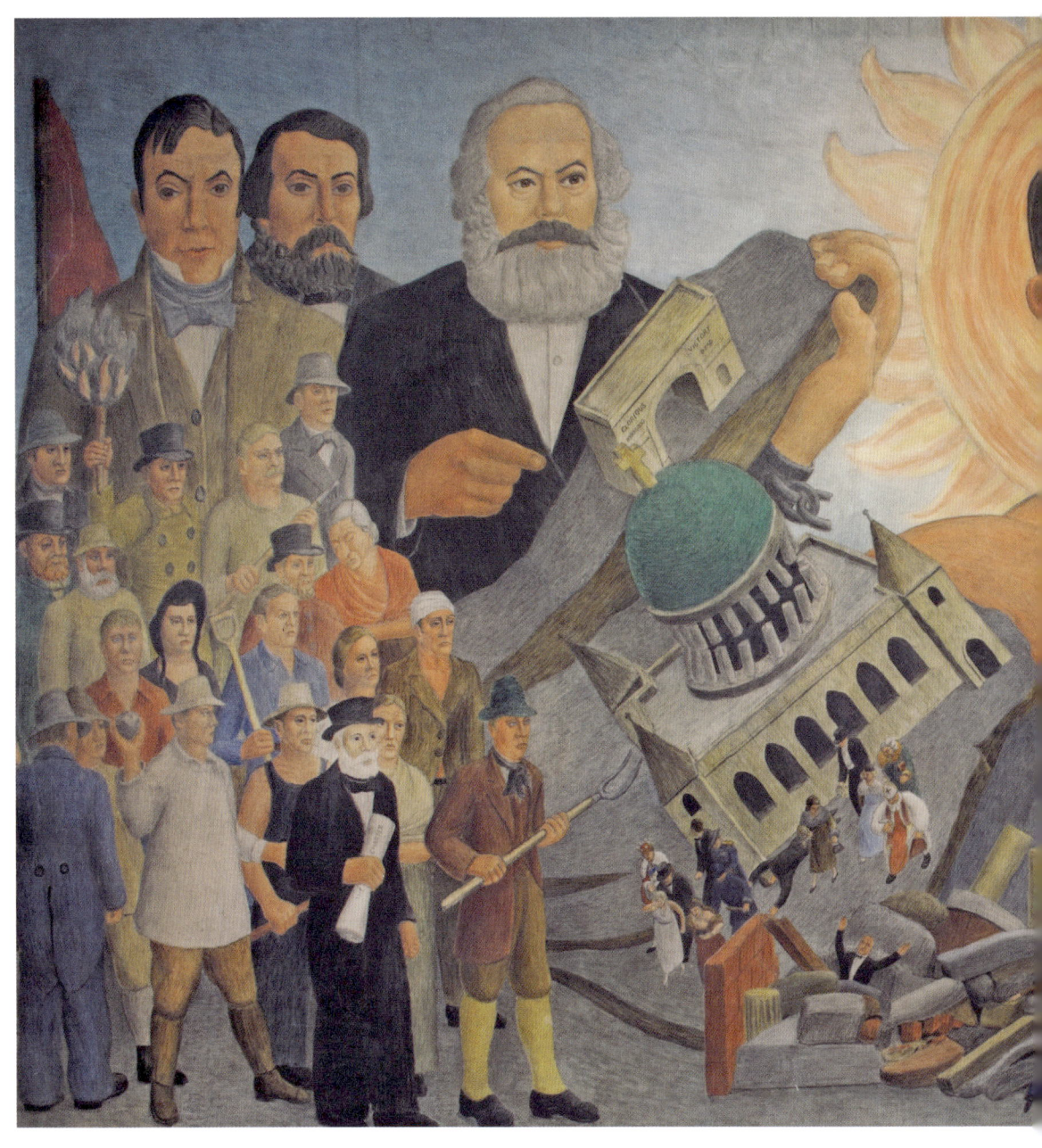

3.7 Jack Hastings, *The Worker of the Future Clearing Away the Chaos of Capitalism*, fresco, 1935. 216 × 460 cm (85⅛ × 181⅛ in.)

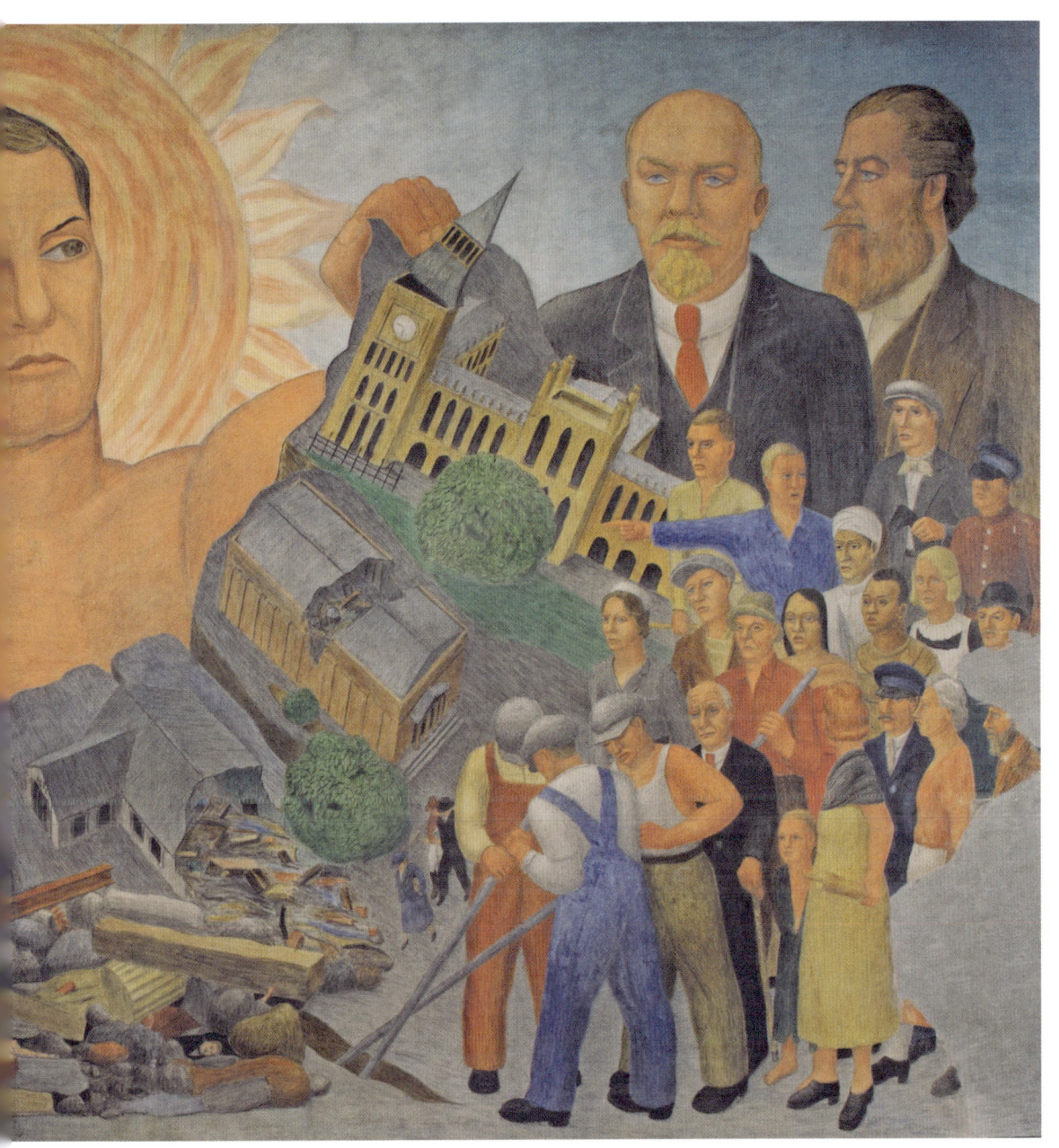

and they would be very eager to express these [ideals] in permanent art form if they were given the government's co-operation'.[24] By the following February, the emergency programme that had given work to Stuart Davis over the winter of 1933–34 was winding down, but in Washington a Fine Arts Section was being established in the Federal Treasury, which over the following nine years would use 1 per cent of project costs to back the creation of 1,116 murals nationwide. In employment terms this would shortly be overshadowed by the Works Progress Administration's Federal Art Project (FAP), part of wider unemployment relief, which at its peak in mid-1936 employed 5,000 artists and, over six years, sponsored 2,500 projects in all manner of community settings. While funding for these activities was a component of the Democrat New Deal, project sponsorship and control was decentralized as hostile political pressures mounted, becoming a recipe for many hard-fought disputes over messages conveyed and artistic freedom. The events at the Rockefeller Center were a harbinger of these future conflicts, but for members of the Artists' Union[25] who protested outside – many of whom had exhibited alongside George Biddle in the second annual John Reed Club exhibition *Hunger, Fascism and War* a month before – they also seemed a present echo of repression already taking place in Europe.[26]

One such conflict over mural content involved Clifford Wight, who had returned to San Francisco where a long-running longshoremen's dispute was about to turn violent. There he joined twenty-six artists employed to decorate the Coit Tower on Telegraph Hill, with its sweeping views of the bay; assigned four floor-to-ceiling panels and lateral spaces above intervening windows, he filled these with 'leaders of California life' – a surveyor, a farmer, a steelworker and a cowboy. Linking decorations centred on the blue eagle emblem of the National Recovery Act, the American dollar and a hammer and sickle, signifying the contending solutions of the New Deal, capitalism and communism to society's crises.[27] In the febrile atmosphere of a general strike in the Pacific Ports, met with lethal force within sight of the tower as Wight painted, right-wing objections to this iconography soon surfaced. After Wight refused to alter his work, he was first supported but then deserted by fellow artists as a press campaign against 'Communist Propaganda' unfolded and the showpiece project stalled.[28] Threatened with deportation he left for London, where in September 1935 he joined Jack at 37a Clerkenwell Green, the Marx Memorial Library and Workers' School, to help create *The Worker of the Future Clearing Away the Chaos of Capitalism*.

Since they last met, Cristina had joined the Communist Party. Jack had not followed suit, but that February he had journeyed to Moscow by train with his old friend Alec Waugh, curious to see 'what the Russian Revolution had given birth to in the way of art'. They arrived via a customs shed with murals depicting new Soviet cities at one end, peasants harvesting and miners digging at the other, for three tightly chaperoned VOKS-organized weeks, during which they 'saw what the system was and how it was meant to work'.[29] Waugh returned convinced he never wished to see a Soviet Britain, Hastings with his belief in the necessity of a socialist alternative to his country's malaise unshaken, but – already influenced by Rivera's admiration for the exiled Leon Trotsky – with reservations about the Soviet leadership, which now surfaced in his omission of Stalin from his Marx House design.

The building and its location were rich in associations: less than a century before, Chartist demonstrations had taken place outside on Clerkenwell Green, and radical crowds had rallied there to greet the Tolpuddle Martyrs on their return from Australia. Sixty years earlier, Marx himself knew the building during the days of the Paris Commune and the Social Democratic Federation, and during exile in 1902 Lenin had edited the Russian-language newspaper *Iskra* there; both men, together with Frederick Engels, Robert Owen and William Morris, were now to figure prominently in Hastings's depiction of an English radical tradition, flanking the revolutionary worker of the future. In an interview with the *Daily Mirror* while work was under way, Jack explained that the central figure overthrowing State, Church and Capitalism was modelled on a Welsh miner; on the left he had depicted the Chartist origins of the labour movement and on the right its present day.[30]

By late October Wight and Hastings, the foreman and the apprentice, had completed a somewhat lumpen homage to Rivera – a work with strong compositional similarities to the destroyed *Man at the Crossroads*, but with none of the master's habitually dynamic visual poetry. It was nevertheless a work that enhanced its host, as the next *Marx House Bulletin* explained:

> If you have not yet been to Marx House this Winter, come and see it. It is a place to be proud of ... Viscount Hastings, because of his interest in Marxism, has painted a magnificent fresco, covering the entire wall at the end of the Lecture hall. Both he and Clifford White [*sic*], who was his assistant and prepared the wall for painting, have voluntarily given nearly two months to the job, commencing work at 7 a.m. each morning and working sometimes until nearly 11 p.m. at night. The Workers' School now possesses a fine and unique work of art.[31]

The claim to uniqueness was not unfounded. No other British mural of the period – including those by Rex Whistler in the Tate Gallery restaurant, Bawden and Ravilious at Morley College, Grant and Bell for Keynes's rooms at King's College, Cambridge, and Stanley Spencer at Burghclere – had been painted in the exacting medium of fresco. But more importantly, as the sole British example of what was under way in the USA, Hastings's work would now trigger critical debate about the merits of overtly political as opposed to whimsical and decorative offerings, along with much AIA interest in the potential of murals as a public art form.

*****

Aside from her administrative impact, Betty Rea played a significant role in crafting and communicating the AI British Section's unfolding strategy during 1935, while helping to shape a platform of ideas with wider appeal. In March Betty's Royal College friend Helen Binyon wrote to her lover Eric Ravilious, 'On Thursday evening Peggy took me firmly to a meeting of the Artists International – the NW group that meets in Belsize Square next door. But I rather think it's my first and last … they apparently meet once a week and discuss what a revolutionary artist is'; but by the end of the year Helen was on the door at the Soho Square exhibition, exhibiting there and reading the collection of essays on revolutionary art which Rea had corralled and edited.[32]

Before she was 'cut off' by her father, Rea could afford to augment stretched organizational finances – something Hastings continued to do regularly for the next half decade, possibly longer – and beyond this she remained connected to artistic and social networks important for both support and building participation. In this her friendship with Henry Moore and close relationship with J. D. Bernal were instrumental, especially in cultivating more positive relationships with the likes of Herbert Read and others in the Mall Studios, Unit One and the broader Hampstead artistic network, and in engaging recently arrived émigrés such as László Moholy-Nagy.[33]

Rea's secretarial duties also involved international communication, and a substantial article she wrote, probably in March, for the Moscow-based journal *International Literature* gave an insight into core AI thinking about the way forward.[34] Cast as a letter from London, it canvassed two areas IBRA officials had focused on in their meeting with Pearl Binder a few months before – attracting the well-known and work among art students – in a way that conveyed both the nuances of the British situation and a sense of momentum. It also delivered a message that here was a body intent on making its own future, unlikely to unquestioningly submit to formulaic prescriptions from afar.[35]

Within two years, efforts to organize artists industrially with a government-facing agenda would become a key focus for the AIA. The seeds of this approach are evident in Rea's exploration of student issues by way of an analysis of the deficiencies of courses devoid of modern methods of production and design, the cultural divorce between art and industry, and the consequences of market failure flowing from low standards of British industrial design: 'Unemployment being high, students everywhere are resenting the lack of proper training, which places them at such a disadvantage in securing what employment there may be. It is only too common that after years of study the student is forced to take employment in some other occupation.'

At the end of the article, under the subheading 'The Left Wing Grows', Rea rehearses the experience of Charlotte Street, where two thousand visitors left 'many interesting criticisms in a book provided' while the mainstream press had 'sent its representatives but remained silent in its

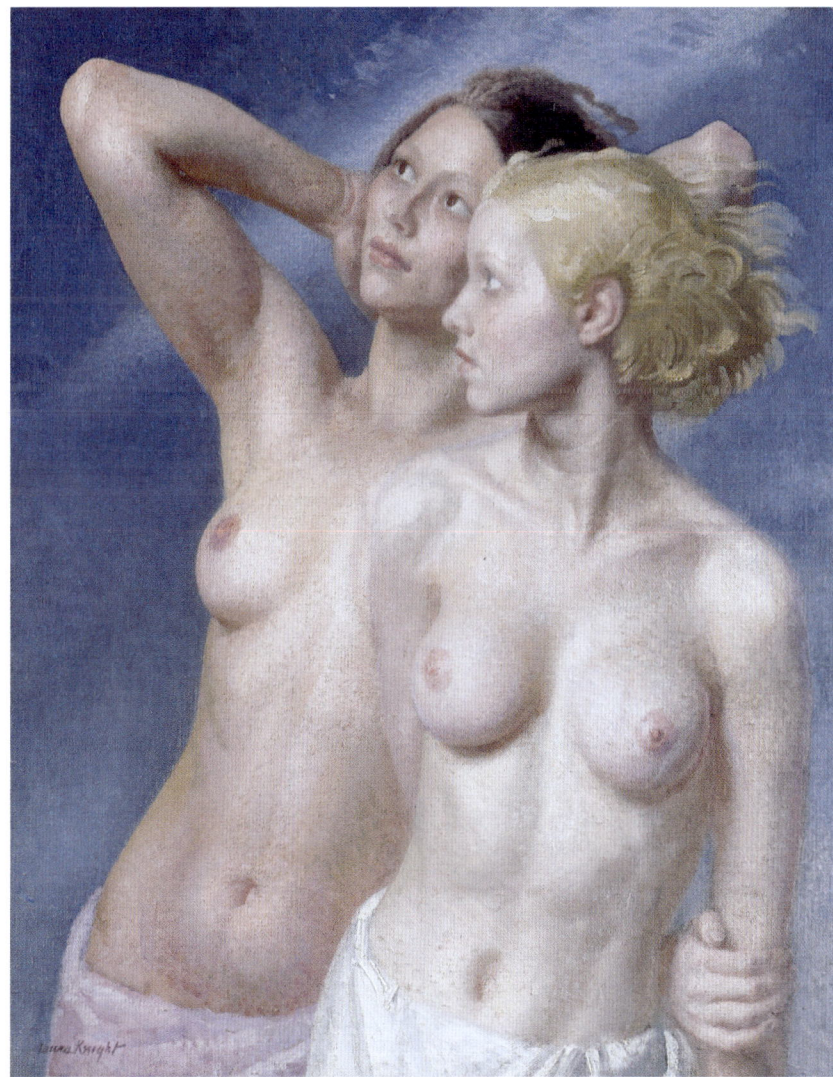

3.8 Laura Knight, *Dawn*, oil on canvas, 1932–33. 75 × 59 cm (29⅝ × 23¼ in.). In 1935 the painting was exhibited at the AIA's exhibition *Artists Against Fascism and War*, cat. 21, before the artist presented it to the Royal Academy as her diploma work on being made a full Academician the following year

SOHO SQUARE

columns'. She adds, however, that England's leading art critic Herbert Read, having delivered 'a severe criticism in the *London Mercury* ... has since accepted an invitation to lecture to our members on Abstract Art'. Before dealing with the aftermath of the AI's first show, Rea articulates the approach being taken to prepare the ground for its successor: she notes that leading RA Augustus John has joined the Council of Civil Liberties; that Dame Laura Knight has signalled her antagonism to war preparations in the papers; that David Low, the famous cartoonist 'very important because of his immense popularity among millions of the workers and intellectuals', has opposed the Sedition Act; and that 'the leaders of Abstract Art' Henry Moore and Paul Nash 'find themselves in opposition to the nationalist jingoism of Fascism'.

Citing a growing mood of dissatisfaction among progressive artists, 'though this finds expression mainly in pacifism', Rea explains: 'In order to test this feeling and to find out how far artists would be prepared to go to support the Artists International in its work against war and Fascism, the committee recently sent out 20 letters to well-known artists, representing definite sections'; a meeting had followed and as a result Duncan Grant, Laura Knight and Ethelbert White had pledged support. It is also clear from Rea's account, though expressed in coded form, that David Low and James Laver were positive as well but did not want their employers – *Evening Standard* proprietor Lord Beaverbrook and the civil service respectively – to be provoked by use of their names. Four other unnamed artists gave clear indications of their sympathy but 'were not convinced as to organised or political action', with much of the meeting 'clarifying the issues of war and Fascism without any practical conclusions being reached'. Nevertheless, it was clear to the AI committee that 'a carefully formulated manifesto, protest or broad action' would gain wider support, and on this basis the May *AI Bulletin* announced:

> AUTUMN EXHIBITION (preliminary notice)
> Plans are being formulated for the holding of an exhibition at the beginning of October. It will include work of every type sent in by artists in sympathy with the aims of the AI as a protest against Fascism and War. The invitation to exhibit will be issued under the name of the AI and a board of artists of national reputation.

Although the Seventh World Congress of the Comintern was still several months away from definitively abandoning the 'class against class' stance of its so-called Third Period by endorsing pursuit of a 'popular front' of communist and non-communist forces, AI party members in London were front-running its decision-making, both stylistically and

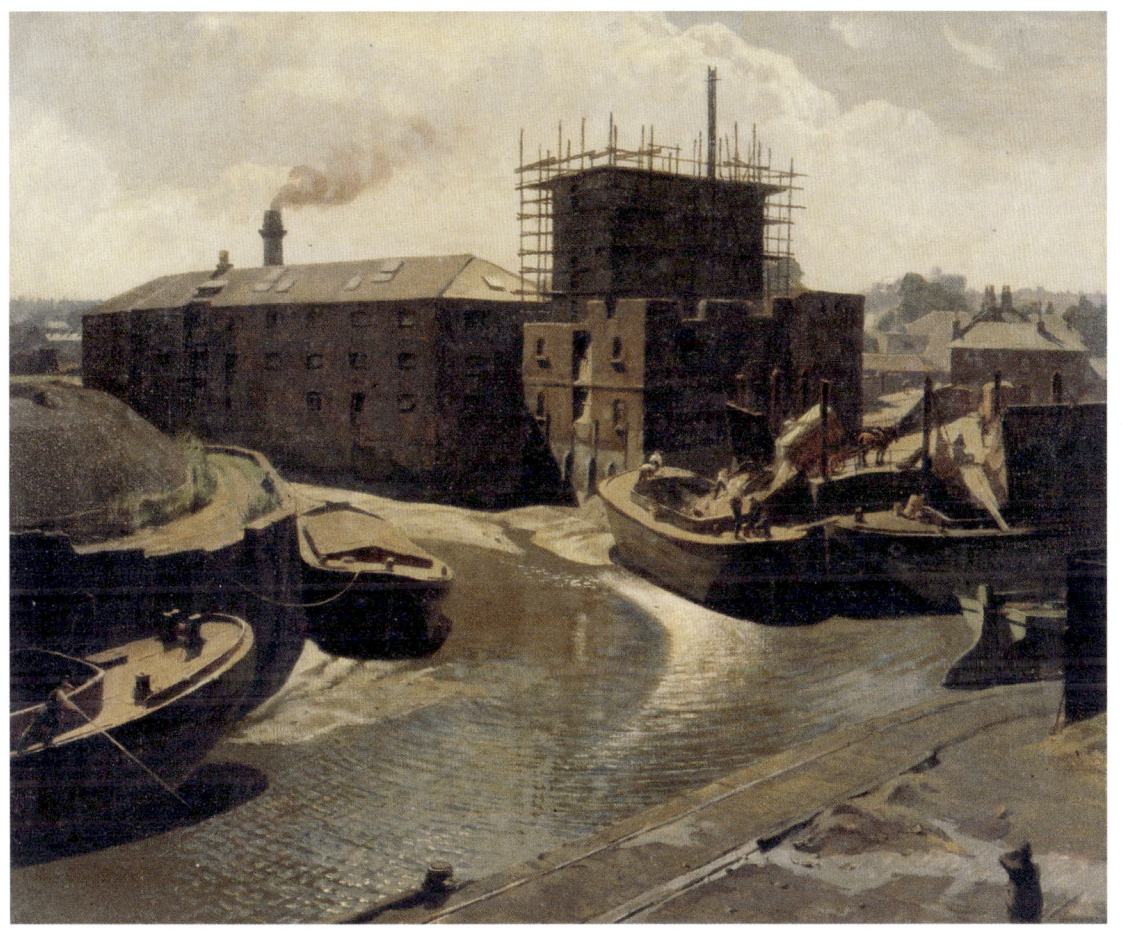

3.9 James Bateman, *Thames Wharf*, oil on canvas, 1929–30. 56 × 71 cm (22⅛ × 28 in.); cat. 70 at the AIA's exhibition *Artists Against Fascism and War*. A future member of the AIA Advisory Council, Bateman was one of the more traditional artists to join in 1935

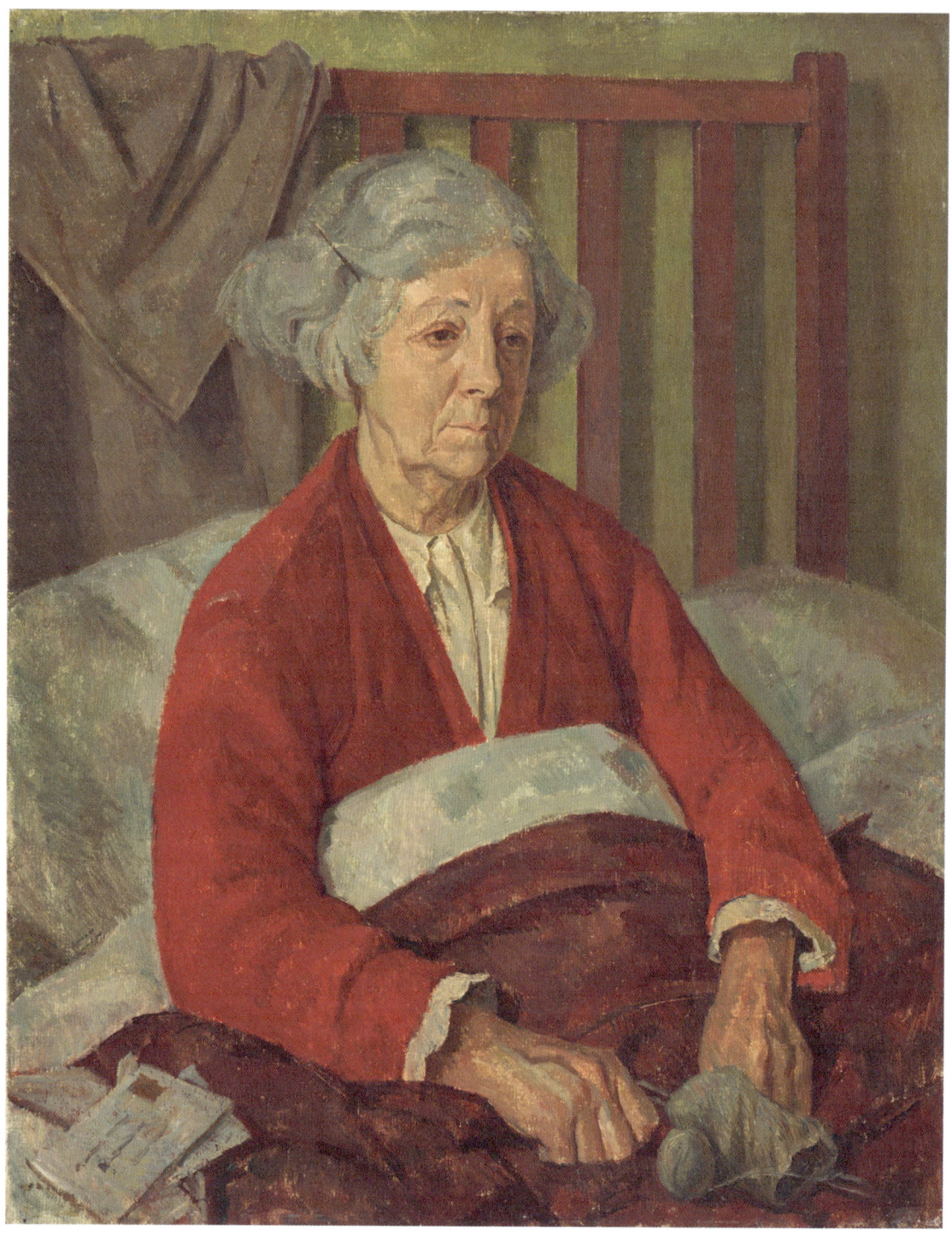

3.10 Percy Horton, *The Invalid*, oil on canvas, 1934. 50.8 × 40.6 cm (20 × 16 in.)

politically.³⁶ In June it was announced that an organizational committee for the exhibition had been formed, consisting of Misha Black, Percy Horton, A. L. Lloyd, Robert Medley, Noel Musgrave and Helen Wilson as secretary, 'with preliminary work proceeding'.³⁷

* * * * *

Arthur Lancaster Lloyd – Bert to his friends – was at this stage something of a Jack of all trades, yet to find the route to radio broadcasting on the path to becoming arguably the most influential figure in England's post-war folk music revival.³⁸ Currently manager of Foyles's foreign book department, he was the only person who had been present at founding meetings of both the AI and *Left Review*, a reflection of his omnivorous networking since returning from Australia in 1930 and the formidable drive with which he had educated himself during years of remote manual labour in the bush. Now living back in Islington, where he was born in 1908, he had been sent out at the age of sixteen as a British Legion charity case after his family had been devastated by tuberculosis arriving by way of the trenches. His self-directed bunkhouse learning, supported by books from a Sydney circulating library and a facility to 'collect languages like postage stamps', had traversed classicism and modernism in art and literature, music and philosophy; and by the time he returned – walking cheerfully into the Finsbury Park second-hand bookshop kept by A. L. Morton, future author of the classic *The People's History of England* – he was able to hold his own with anyone from the educated elite.³⁹

Lloyd had collected songs in the outback and, on occasion, drawn and painted. Morton, struck by his power to convey 'a remarkable sense of the strangeness of that strange land', bought a painting of wild stallions in a stony desert, and the first issue of *Left Review* had carried 'The Red Steer', Lloyd's short story about wranglers 'running the red steer' across the land of exploitative employers by setting bush-fires after unjust lay-offs. By the time Lloyd joined the organizing committee for the AI's autumn exhibition he was contributing to the Parton Street lecture series, assembling the material which would appear in essay form as 'Modern Art and Modern Society' in *5 on Revolutionary Art*. Allying himself with the more practised intellectual Francis Klingender's position that art was a reflection of society's economic base, and obscure experimental art a product of bourgeois crisis, Lloyd nevertheless cautioned against 'earnest sectarians' imagining 'they need only be Marxists to be able to effectively criticise any damn thing … to be able to pass a valuable opinion on della Francesca or Freud, they need to know a lot about art or psychoanalysis as well as Marxism'. Present developments in abstraction and Surrealism might be symptomatic of capitalist decline, but the revolutionary artist of the future needed to build on the work of 'great modern artists such as Gris, Picasso, Helion and Henry Moore'.[40]

A defence of abstract art was also central to Herbert Read's opening essay reproducing his talk to the AI; without retreating from his contention that abstract art forms were inherently revolutionary, and that revolutionary art was more than the depiction of flags, demonstrations and machinery, this had clearly been a far more even-tempered affair. His engagement was a welcome success at a time when Rea was concluding: 'The future of art hangs on the future of civilisation. It is time that artists began to think what sort of future they want, and what they can do to get it.'[41]

* * * * *

For those organizing the Soho Square exhibition, fascism's threat to both peace and artistic freedom was now palpable, with Italy's aggression in Abyssinia the focal point of anxieties about militarism and the potential for war and the situation in Germany stoking fears about totalitarian repression of expression. June's *AI Bulletin* announced: 'The Central London group of the AI is planning a group exhibit on "Fascism and Culture". They plan to divide the subject into various sub-sections (i.e. Education, Dress and Propaganda, Science, Art, Women etc). The suggestion is that each individual member of the group should carry out a work on one of these subjects in any medium.'[42]

At a time when Conservative press coverage was equivocating between fawning admiration for the Führer's economic policies and occasional muted condemnation of Nazi 'anti-Semitic excess', direct AI knowledge of events in Germany was being reinforced by the arrival of émigré artists. Walter Gropius, architect and former Bauhaus director, had moved to London in December 1934 for economic reasons after his concerted attempts at accommodation with the Nazi regime had faltered. In 1933 he had joined the Reich Chamber of Culture but failed to win the commission for the new Reichsbank, a Nazi landmark project; a German nationalist, he would ensure that he kept in good standing with the regime, even seeking Joseph Goebbels's approval for his appointment to the Harvard Graduate School of Design in 1937.[43] While in London Gropius, despite enjoying celebrity status among progressive designers, refused to endorse the anti-fascist cause, unlike fellow Bauhauslers Peter László Peri, who had turned to sculpture from architecture after his arrival in 1933,[44] and the Hungarian László Moholy-Nagy, who had run the Bauhaus foundation course prior to 1928. Moholy-Nagy was an exponent of painting, photography, film and modernist graphic design; under Gestapo surveillance for

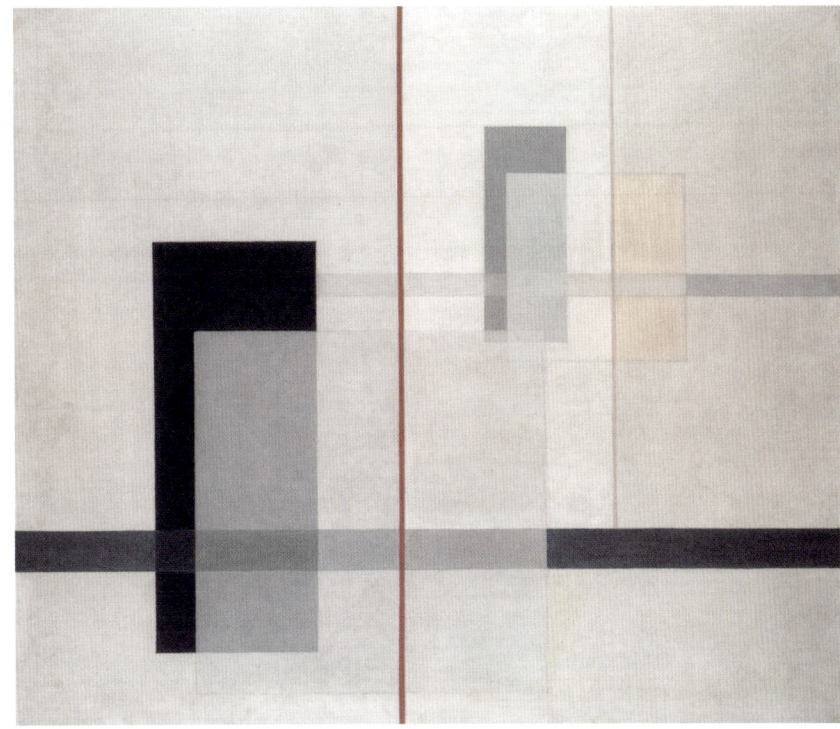

3.11 László Moholy-Nagy, *K VII*, oil on canvas, 1922. 115.3 × 135.9 cm (45½ × 53⅜ in.). *K VIII* was exhibited as cat. 81 at the AIA's exhibition *Artists Against Fascism and War*

his refusal to be censored, he moved to London permanently in May 1935, exhibiting two works – aluminium *AI2* (1926) and oil painting *K VIII* (1923) – at the Soho Square exhibition six months later.⁴⁵

Systematic persecution of Jews and those with Jewish connections in the arts had been under way across Germany for two and a half years, but – despite the purging of 'Jew art' from public collections – for much of this time the regime's attitude to modern art as a whole had been unclear, and Hitler's pronouncements variable. On the Führer's Day of Culture in September 1933 he had denounced Expressionism and abstraction, saying 'under no circumstances must the representatives of decadence become the voices of the future. This is our state, not theirs, we will not be soiled'. But a year later at Nuremberg he had attacked practitioners of *völkisch* 'blood and soil' alternatives as 'backward-lookers who imagine they can impose on the National-Socialist revolution, as a binding heritage for the future, a "Teutonic Art" sprung from the fuzzy world of their own romantic conceptions' – a pronouncement that gave hope to those who believed an accommodation between German fascism and modernism might still be possible.⁴⁶

By autumn 1935, however, the debate was effectively over; Kenneth Clark, recently appointed director of London's National Gallery, noted matter-of-factly: 'In Germany the gallery directors who showed sympathy with abstract art have been dismissed on the charge of *Kulturbolshevismus*.'[47] As the AI issued a call for contributions to its own exhibition, *Die Schreckenskammer der Kunst* ('The Chamber of Horrors of Art') opened in Dresden, leaving little doubt about fascism's threat to artistic freedom. A precursor to the blockbuster *Entartete Kunst* or 'Degenerate Art' exhibition of 1937, it featured artists nominated by Hitler for inclusion in an 'exhibition of disgrace', among them Otto Dix, George Grosz, Kurt Schwitters and Bauhausler Paul Klee, now an unwell man living in Switzerland having been fired from his teaching job in Düsseldorf.

There was now a sizeable expatriate community of German political exiles in Paris, where Fred Uhlman, a thirty-four-year-old lawyer who had defended socialists against political charges in Stuttgart, was on the cusp of breaking through as a painter.[48] Escaping in March 1933 after receiving the message 'Paris is very beautiful *now*' from a judge who knew his arrest to be imminent, once there Uhlman found his qualifications of no use; he had struggled as a writer, a journalist and an aquarium keeper before turning to painting as a respite from the emptiness of exile. In the final Weimar years he had faced violence from both fascists and communists on the streets, and as a result would never be able to bring himself to trust the latter. Now an autodidact painter, his participation in three group shows in distinguished company at the Galerie Le Niveau was beginning to secure him a living.[49]

Pearl Binder was in Paris that June for the First International Congress of Writers for the Defence of Culture at the nearby Salle de la Mutualité. She was there as part of an English delegation that included E. M. Forster, Aldous Huxley and Herbert Read, and her drawing of the author and prominent communist André Gide, as well as his opening address, appeared in *Left Review*'s report: 'That culture is threatened, the intellectual pauperisation of certain countries tells us only too dismally ... we all feel ourselves more or less menaced ... I think we should start from this idea, that the culture we want to defend is the sum of the particular cultures of each country, that this culture is our common heritage, is common to all of us and is international.' Gide was known as an uncritical friend of the Soviet Union, a position that Forster, who followed him on to the podium, disassociated himself from, to reported applause: 'You have guessed I am not a communist: perhaps I should be if I were younger and braver, because in Communism I see hope. I know that its intentions are good, although I think bad many of the acts resulting from those intentions. You may have guessed that I am not a fascist – fascism does evil that evil may come of it.' But yearning for unity was in the air, and Paul Vaillant-Couturier – most recently a Moscow-based Comintern official and a founder member of the AEAR – replied: 'The great virtue of this liberal and radical congress, which will never close its gates in the name of sectarian vanity, is that it can secure the adherence of men of the talent, standing and influence of Mr E. M. Forster: this could not be achieved by purely partisan grouping.'[50]

These instincts were shared by Percy Horton, Misha Black and Bert Lloyd on the Soho Square organizing committee. On his return they asked Huxley to provide an introduction for their catalogue, and did not demur when his text echoed Forster's sentiments: 'The work in this exhibition is being shown as a protest against Fascism and War. Personally, I should have preferred to "Fascism" the more general term "dictatorship", for I am convinced that, however admirable the ends proposed by the dictators, any form of dictatorship is intrinsically bad. Good ends never justify bad means for the simple reason that, in the process of being used, the bad means change the good ends.'[51] It was a stance that allowed the Artists International, in the act of rebranding as the Artists International Association, to attract support from many who might have shied away, those more conscious than ever of fascism's threat but who would not have endorsed pursuit of a Soviet Britain.

As Rea divined, securing Laura Knight, Augustus John, Paul Nash, Henry Moore and Duncan Grant as sponsors encouraged participation from their contemporaries also born in the previous century, including

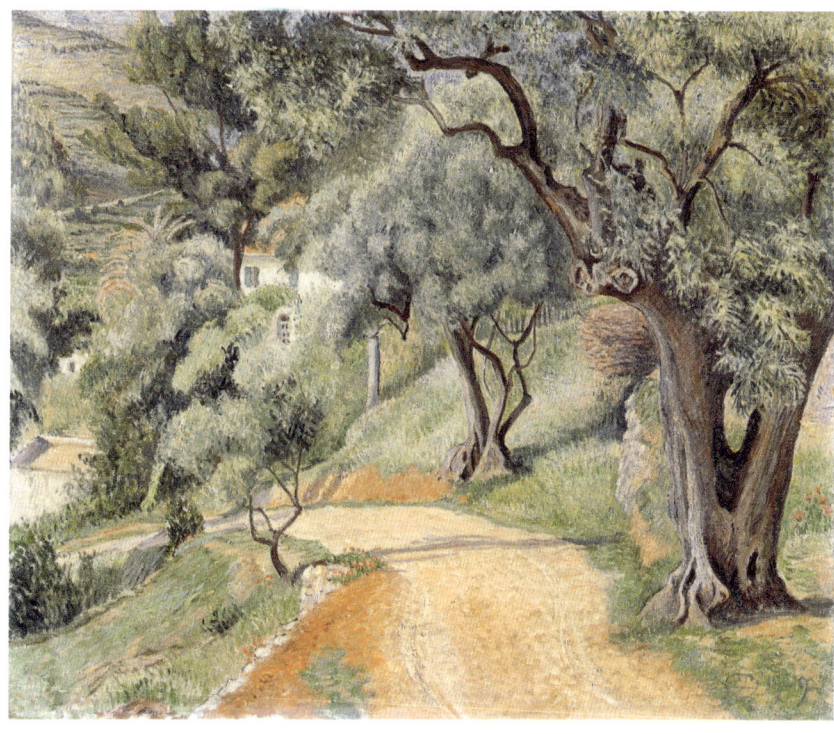

3.12 Lucien Pissarro, *Chemin de l'Hubac, Toulon*, oil on canvas, 1929. 54.5 × 65.5 cm (21½ × 25⅞ in.). For the young founders of the AIA, Pissarro was a living link to both the Camden Town Group and the École de Paris. He exhibited at every major AIA event from 1935 until two months before his death in 1944

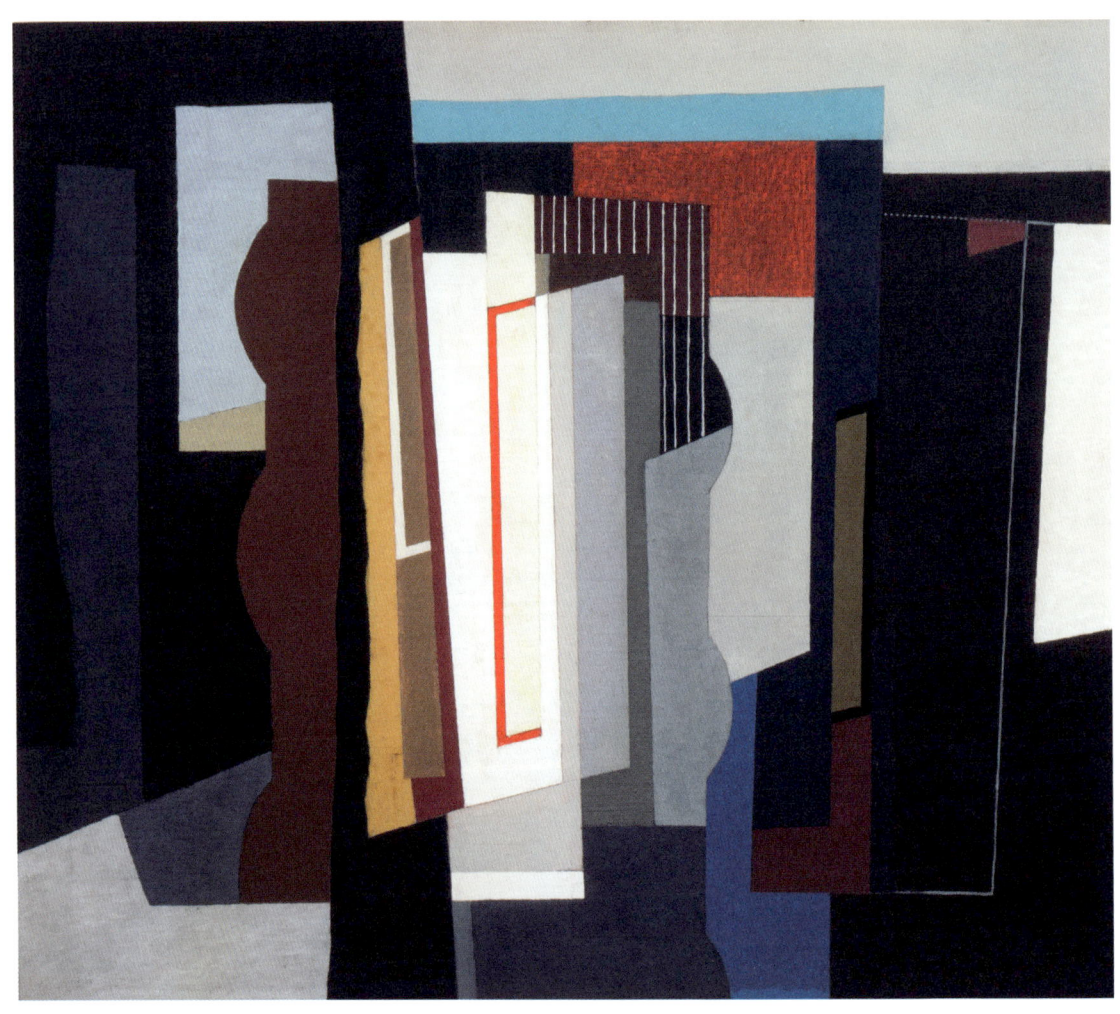

3.13 John Piper, *Abstract 1*, oil on canvas, 1935. 91.7 × 106.5 cm (36⅛ × 42 in.). This may be the work exhibited as *Painting 1935*, cat. 86, at the AIA's exhibition *Artists Against Fascism and War*

Muirhead Bone, Frank Dobson, Eric Kennington, Charles Cundall and Adrian Allinson, and indeed their elders such as Lucien Pissarro and Ethel Walker, both born in the 1860s.[52] By doing so, the initiative reached into established Camden Town, London Group and New English Art Club networks, and also tapped family connections, with Paul Nash bringing brother John on board, Laura Knight her husband Harold, and Muirhead Bone his son Stephen and daughter-in-law Mary Adshead, along with others in the Hampstead circle such as Richard Carline. Soho Square also saw participation from Elizabeth Watson – a friend of Quentin Bell – Nan Youngman, Ruskin Spear and Maurice de Sausmarez, members of a younger generation who, like Carline, would become AIA activists in its aftermath.

Personal connection brought in individuals such as Barbara Hepworth and others from the Unit One and Seven and Five Society networks in which, as Clark put it, 'each group is like a little dissenting sect, sure of salvation while all the rest of the world is damned'.[53] When he wrote this Clark probably had in mind Ben Nicholson, the poster child of artistic sectarianism, and it was Nicholson's presence, and that of artists such as John Tunnard, John Piper and Eileen Agar, which gave rise to Montagu Slater's perceptive quip that 'those whom art-politics have put asunder, an exhibition against war and fascism has joined together. It is an excellent achievement.'[54]

It was indeed an achievement, not least in the scale of international representation, with Ossip Zadkine, André Lhote, François Desnoyer, Jean Marchand and Fernand Léger among thirty-three named French participants in an exhibition visited by six thousand people at threepence a time over two weeks. When a similar transnational exercise had been planned to accompany the Writers' Congress in Paris, it was cancelled for lack of suitable space;[55] the three storeys of 28 Soho Square, fitted out and redecorated for the event, could not accommodate everything that over six hundred artists sent in. Nevertheless, it was sufficient to accommodate a very broad artistic church indeed – and therein, perhaps, lay the one aspect in which the event fell short of its organizers' original hope that a large proportion would be 'work dealing more directly with the social conditions and struggles of today'.[56]

Examples of such directly political art were scattered throughout, including Pearl Binder's lithograph *Down the Mine, South Wales* and Edith Tudor-Hart's seven photographs of life in the Rhondda Valley, products of a joint expedition earlier in the year. Titles of artworks such as Charles Cundall's *Durham Miners' Gala*, Cliff Rowe's *Canvassing with the Daily Worker*, Peggy Angus's *Poison Gas* and Peter László Peri's *Against War and Fascism* suggest conscientious responses to the original brief, although

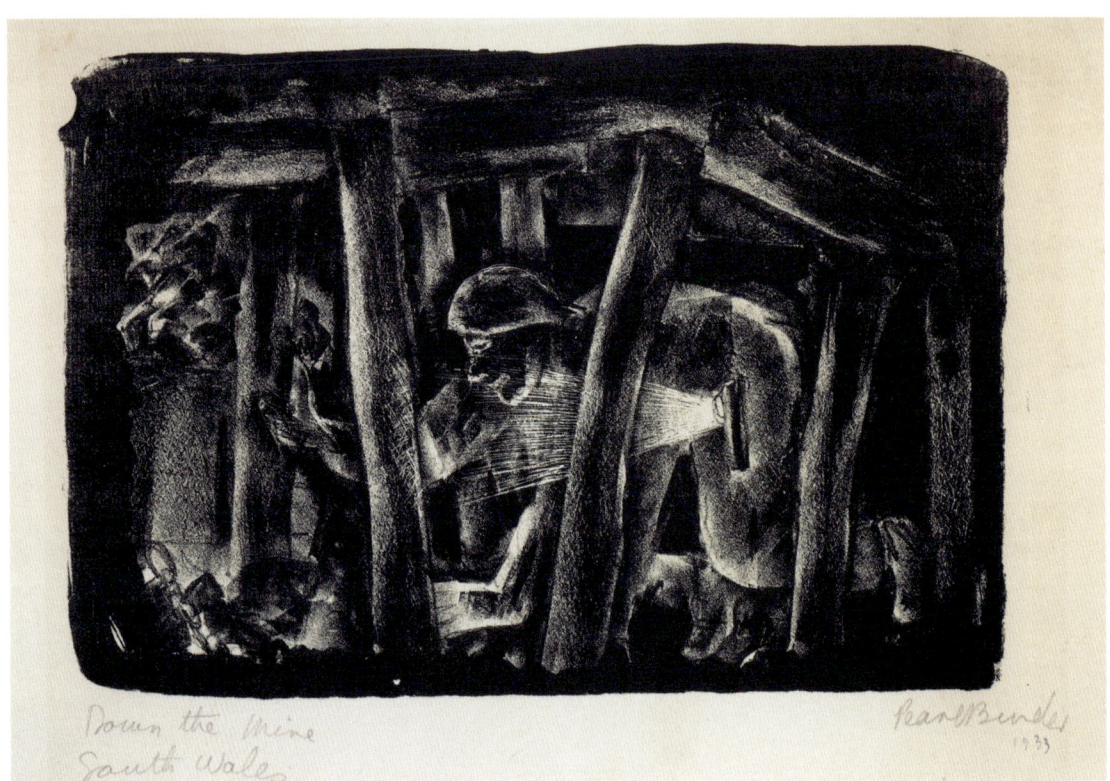

3.14 Pearl Binder, *Down the Mine, South Wales*, lithograph, 1935. 19 × 28.3 cm (7½ × 11¼ in.); from the same series as *South Wales Tubercular Miner*

Slater detected 'too much cerebration' and 'grey matter' and not enough colourful vitality among these more political offerings. His review of a show he dubbed 'a cross between a demonstration and a national gallery' did not mention Boswell's lithograph *Empire Builders* but, coming at the end of the Silver Jubilee year in which the artist had taken up employment in Asiatic Petroleum's publicity department, it must surely have been among the standout works of this type. What had fallen by the wayside, however, was the intention of central London AI members to create a group exhibit on 'Fascism and Culture', an omission now more than covered off by linking the AIA exhibition to another, brought from Cambridge and mounted in parallel next door at 27 Soho Square.

One visitor to no. 28 was an anonymous representative of the *Catholic Herald*, whose review 'Nazi Brutality Pilloried' carried news that 'a German artist, who remains anonymous, shows a series of startling drawings illustrating life in a German concentration camp. He was imprisoned in Borgemoor camp. Surely such bestiality and savage brutality have never been portrayed before. Yet these drawings only corroborate the reports that have been circulating.'[57] Noting that the exhibition was organized by the AIA 'in association with certain artists who are not members', the piece then gave a roll-call of the well-known, confining criticism to supercilious asides about Augustus John's 'fine portrait of King Feisal (surely an absolute ruler?)', France being 'represented by several names which certainly are not French' and, in a sole reference to Russia, there being 'more humour in the names of the Soviet artists than in their work'. Generally respectful, it was a far cry from the denunciation of 'godless propaganda' the paper had carried twelve months before.

* * * * *

About the time the Soho Square exhibition was first mooted, Virginia Woolf wrote to her twenty-four-year-old nephew Quentin Bell: 'By the

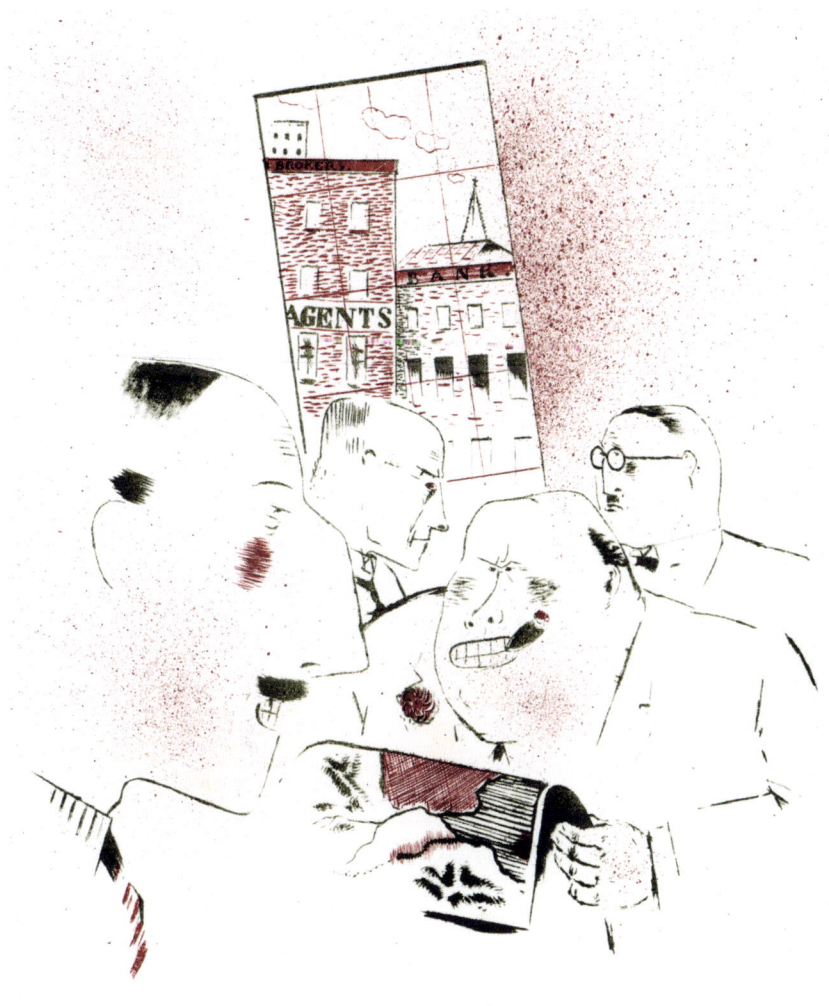

3.15 James Boswell, *Empire Builders*, lithograph, 1935. 39 × 25 cm (15⅜ × 9⅞ in.)

SOHO SQUARE

way I have just bought a picture of yours – a collage, as you call it, I think it is very lovely ... Lord Ivor tells me the other Fascist exhibition has been proved to be a Communist plot; and I'm to have my five pounds back.'[58] Woolf did not mention that a dispute stirred up by Clive Bell, Quentin's father, had caused this turn of events, but she was clearly aware that her younger nephew was already involved in the AI, a connection almost certainly facilitated by occupation, on his own account, of a studio adjacent to James Holland's in the 8 Fitzroy Street nest of artists. Within two years Quentin would be elected to the AIA Central Committee and chairing the education commission preparing for the 1937 Artists' Congress – his political engagement, and by 1939 that of his half-sister Angelica, Duncan Grant's daughter, the polar opposite of his father's unpleasantly reactionary elitism.[59]

Virginia Woolf also knew that her other nephew, Julian, had been active in the anti-war movement while at Cambridge and had relished the confrontations with jingoist hearties during Armistice Week 1933 that had galvanized student politics there.[60] In November 1933 Julian had helped to organize a *No More War* exhibition, an assemblage of photographs, documents and posters, with Cliff Rowe providing a cover for an explanatory guide and Misha Black designing and mounting the displays, a photograph of which had then appeared alongside the AI's first statement of aims in *International Literature*.[61] A second iteration of the exhibition with expanded anti-fascist content had been staged in Cambridge in November 1934, intended to tour to other towns and cities, and it was evidently in support of this that Woolf had joined a fundraising committee, an effort now partially derailed by Clive Bell who, after receiving a request for support via his sister-in-law, wrote 'one of his absurd pompous letters' to its chairman, Lord Ivor Spencer-Churchill. As a consequence, just before Woolf was due to dine with Henry Moore, Herbert Read and others, 'Mr Blunt came round, & I had to explain, & then to write a letter, which brings blood to my head & takes time'.[62] Anthony Blunt had returned from overseas study the previous year 'an ordinary Cambridge intellectual – an art for art's sake type with no interest in politics and even an active disbelief that the arts – in which I was genuinely interested – had any connection with active life or politics at all'.[63] As an art critic writing in the *Spectator*, Blunt had hitherto been a staunch defender of the Bloomsbury line, but this was now changing with his engagement in the anti-fascist exhibition, a stepping stone to advocacy of politically engaged art in both AIA circles and more widely.[64]

Of service age during the First World War, Clive Bell had been an articulate pacifist but not an 'absolutist' objector to the conflict; unlike Percy Horton and other working-class opponents of conscription, who had either

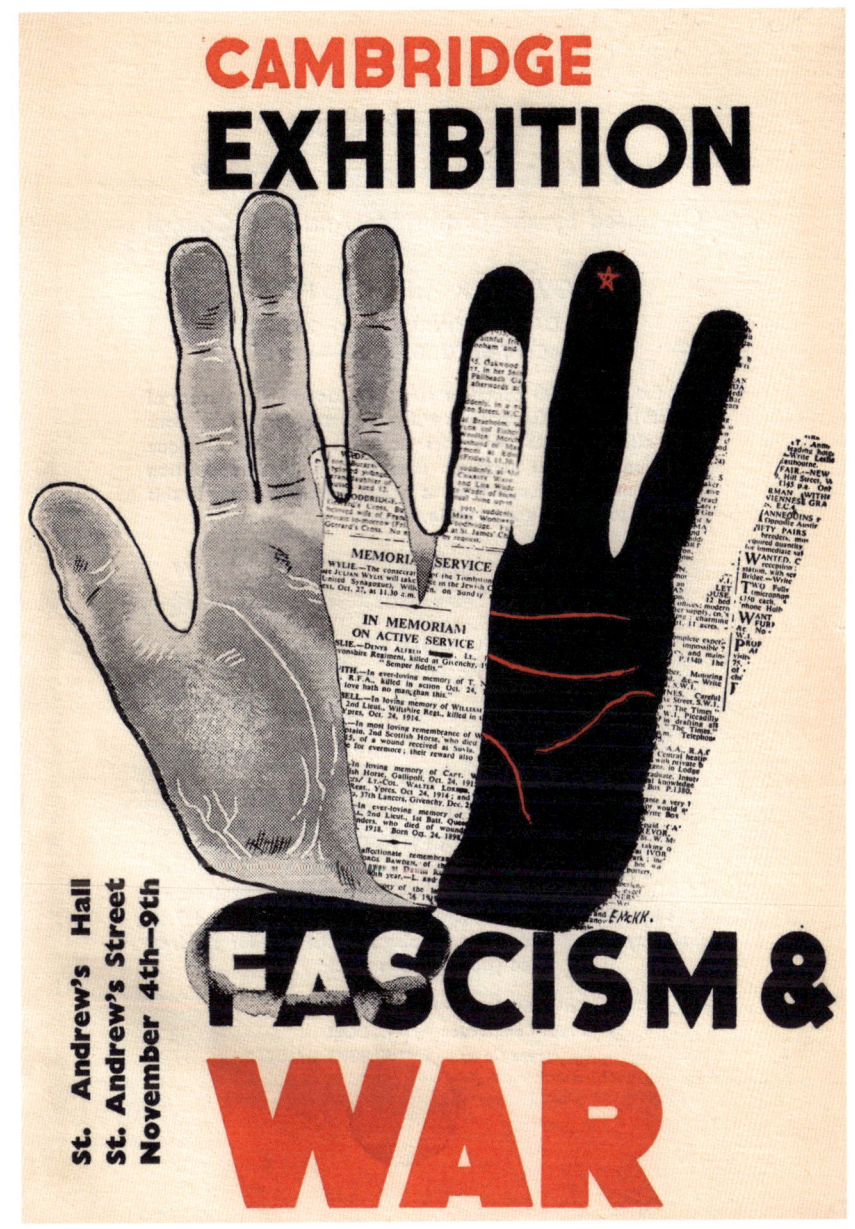

3.16 Edward McKnight Kauffer, cover design for *Cambridge Exhibition Against War and Fascism*, 1935. 21 × 14.8 cm (8⅜ × 5⅞ in.)

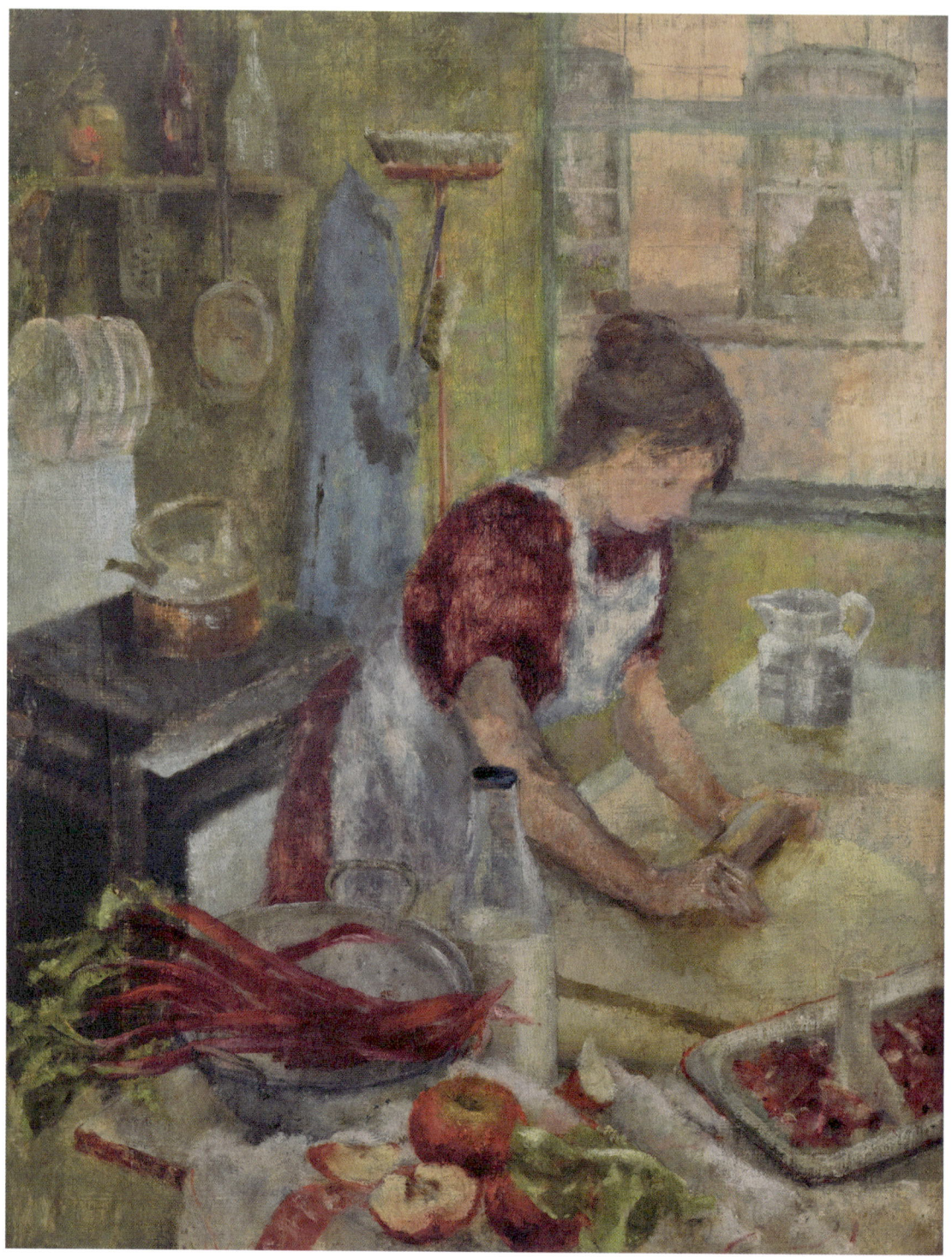

3.17 Margaret Fitton, *Rhubarb Pie*, oil on canvas, mid-1930s. 70 × 54 cm (27⅝ × 21⅜ in.); Slade-trained Fitton's accomplished works were a constant feature of AIA exhibitions, attracting both popular approval and critical acclaim

risked or lost their lives in prison, Bell had been among the well-connected able to navigate the tribunal system to good effect. Grants of exemption to perform agricultural labour had led Vanessa Bell to acquire a lease of Charleston farmhouse in 1916 in order to facilitate this in Duncan Grant and David Garnett's case, while Bell was able to live at Garsington Manor from August 1916, undertaking 'work of national importance' in the form of farm work in the afternoons, claiming his hostess Lady Ottoline Morrell insisted he would be 'a traitor to civilisation ... if I didn't write all the morning'.[65] A principal anxiety for Bell during this period was ensuring that his father, a tribunal member in Gloucestershire inclined to condemn conscientious objectors as cowards and shirkers, did not get to know of his status because 'it would be fatal to everything – it would probably lead to a rupture with the family and the loss of all our prospects ... it is worth taking some trouble to preserve our lien on the Bell millions'.[66]

Though now styling himself a religiously observant landed aristocrat as the owner of Cleeve House at Seend, Bell senior had accumulated these millions as joint owner of one of the most exploitative coal-mining operations in the Rhondda Valley, where the vicious greed of the Cambrian cartel had led to the Tonypandy riots in 1910.[67] It was trust income derived from profits extracted by the miners of Cynon Valley and Merthyr Vale that had supported his son as an aesthete in the early Bloomsbury years, and which created the pool of capital that in the inter-war years was a principal support – well shepherded by Keynes's financial advice and far exceeding any earned income from art – for Charleston's experiment in living.[68] Protecting these benefits led to an elaborate charade when Angelica was born on Christmas Day 1918 and Clive hurried to East Sussex so that letters to the family misleading them about the baby's paternity would bear the correct postmark.

Unlike Virginia and Leonard Woolf, and the coalition that formed behind and succeeded in financing the Soho Square exhibitions, Clive Bell did not believe that political liberty was necessary for art to flourish, pointing out that in the golden age of Athens the liberty of some 25,000 citizens was 'supported by the compulsory labours of some four hundred thousand slaves'; it was a perspective that coloured his 1928 book *Civilisation*, which argued that modern civilization required the existence of a leisured class, and a leisured class required the existence 'of slaves – of people, I mean, who give some part of their surplus time and energy to support others'.[69] The assumption that his discriminating sensibility rendered him part of a civilizing elite worthy of unconditional support led Bell to have an insouciant attitude to the rise of fascism; for him the attempted coup in Paris while he was there in February 1934 was a 'rumpus', and he raised no objection in Rome when his mistress Mary Baker, an admirer of Mussolini, donated her Cartier ring to be melted down in support of the invasion of Abyssinia.[70] For Julian Bell, who departed for a teaching post in Wuhan in August 1935 as a new version of the anti-war exhibition was in preparation, the times were indelibly marked by 'unemployment, economic crisis, nascent fascism, and approaching war'; for his father these were surface phenomena, less important than timeless aesthetic truths and the maintenance of conditions whereby 'a small but potent core of highly civilised individuals' might thrive – something he could imagine happening under a variety of political systems.

After being shown in Cambridge, where David Low lent a set of cartoons, the third version of *No More War*, now dubbed *The Cambridge Exhibition Against War and Fascism*, opened simultaneously with the AIA show. James Boswell contributed artwork to its display on the Reichstag fire and Edward McKnight Kauffer a cover for the explanatory guide, which detailed sections on fascism's rise in Italy and Germany; 'semi-fascism' in Austria and Spain; 'Embryo Fascism – Can Fascism Come to Britain?'; fascism and culture; and the anti-fascist movement. Graphic documentary evidence shocked those who visited, and together with the art next door, it was both a powerful recruiting sergeant and a turning point. Looking back more than two decades later, Betty Rea recalled 'we were struggling with the apathy of the profession until the Soho Square exhibition in 1935', but the AIA strategy for organizing in stark times now had a degree of momentum.[71]

* * * * *

Five days after *Artists Against Fascism and War* closed, Pearl Binder visited the International Association of Revolutionary Writers in Moscow. Two days earlier, she had arrived in the Soviet Union for a third time, bringing news of management changes at *Left Review*, copies of recent issues and the newly published *5 on Revolutionary Art*, plus a copy of the exhibition catalogue with Huxley's introduction.[72]

The year 1935 had been a momentous one for Binder. *Odd Jobs*, combining lithography and her writing about people in Whitechapel, East End industries and London's theatreland, had been published to acclaim.[73] After returning from the Writers' Congress, she and Edith had explored the mining districts of South Wales, where Alex Tudor-Hart was facing an uphill battle with the British Medical Association to establish a community medical practice. And now, at year's close, she was embarking on a project to document two decades of revolution through lithographic portraits and unvarnished personal histories. But most importantly the year had seen the blossoming of her relationship with Frederick Elwyn-Jones, who recalled the launch party for *Odd Jobs* as their first meeting and a summer house party in France as the genesis of their love affair; in due course he would become her husband, the father of her three children, an East End MP, a Labour Lord Chancellor and her companion of fifty-four years.

Elwyn-Jones had been born in 1909 in Llanelli, his grandfather a displaced agricultural labourer driven to seek industrial employment, his father a steelworker left without any company pension after forty years of service. It was a poor but remarkable family; three children won their way to university – to Cambridge in Frederick's case, where he became president of the union in 1931, before moving to London and studying for the bar. In his last vacation he had tutored the son of an industrialist in Cologne, experiencing a first chilling encounter with fascist demagogy. A protégé of well-known radical D. N. Pritt KC, Elwyn-Jones had been selected by Ernest Bevin, chairman of the joint council of the Labour Party and the Trades Union Congress, to travel to Vienna in aid of trade unionists imprisoned after the Dollfuss coup. Consequently, when he met Pearl, he already knew much of the terrible realities that had driven Edith Tudor-Hart into exile and her father to suicide.

Pearl's Moscow meeting with M. S. Veleskayan of the Revolutionary Writers' Association was not easy. The Russian delegation at the Paris Writers' Congress had been less than impressed when forbidden to read out an eighty-four-page manifesto, and Aldous Huxley's preference for opposing 'dictatorship' rather than fascism was immediately noted and disapproved – as was her blunt explanation that 'cautious Marxism' was now the sensible strategy in the British environment. Challenged on this, she pushed back that the timing of the recent publication by Victor Gollancz of D. S. Mirsky's *The Intelligentsia of Great Britain*, which ripped into figures such as Woolf and Forster as 'theoreticians of the passive dividend-drawing and consuming section of the bourgeoisie ... extremely intrigued by their own minutest inner experience', had required hard work to dispel the impression made.[74] 'It caused a sensation but this sensation is negative', said Binder.[75]

The Russian minute of this conversation reads as a harbinger of conflicts to come, as Stalin's foreign policy imperatives and the instincts of progressive artists in the West diverged in the year ahead, a year which would also see much debate in London about whether visual artists' fascination with their inner experience could ever have political significance. It was not, however, an encounter that deflected Binder from her task. By the time Elwyn-Jones flew to Moscow to meet her the following April – and Jack Hastings began painting a mantelpiece mural at D. N. Pritt's house to welcome her back[76] – she had collected the life stories and images which Gollancz would publish as *Misha and Masha* five months after the Spanish Civil War had begun.

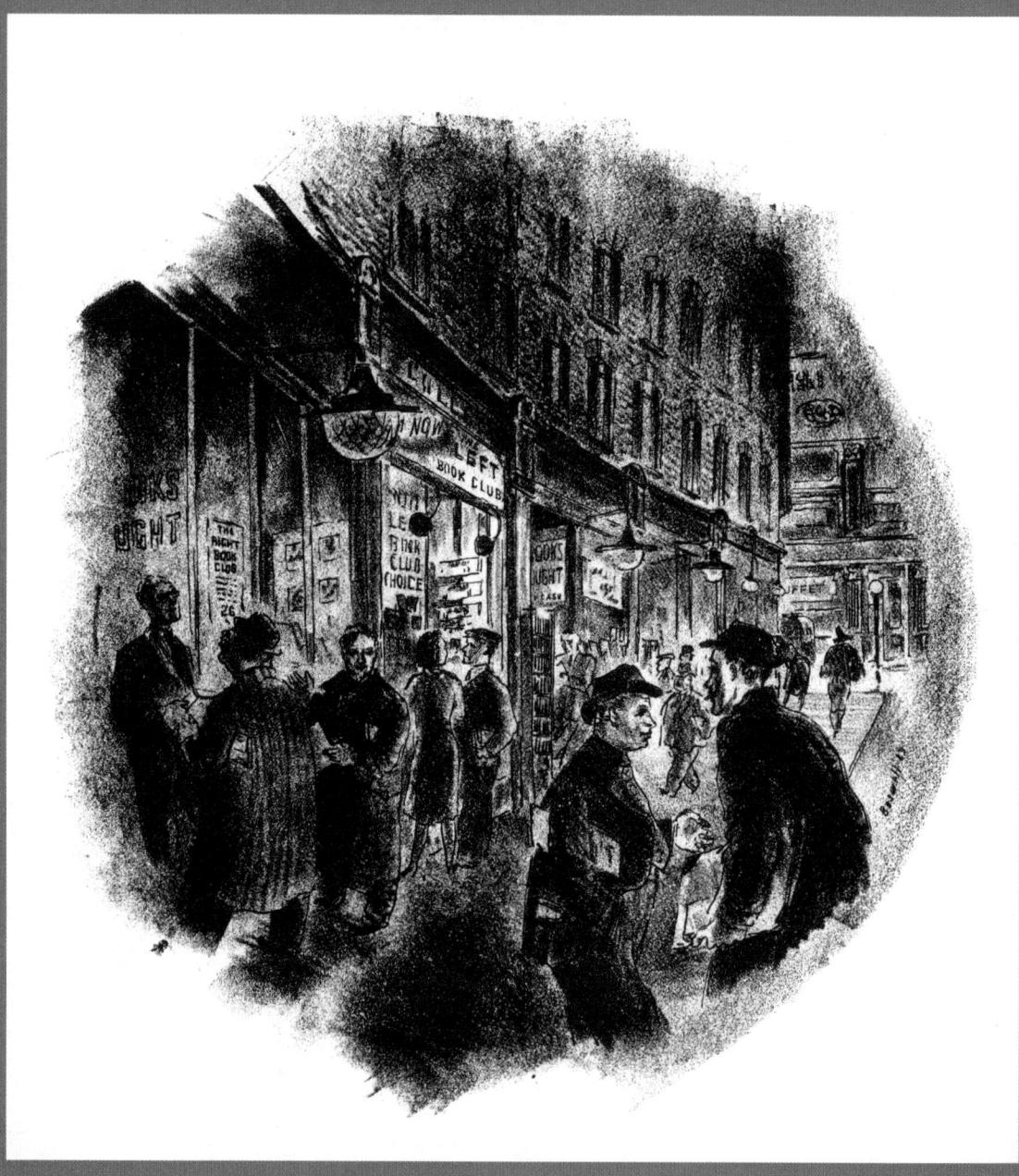

CHAPTER FOUR

CHARING CROSS ROAD

While *Artists Against Fascism and War* was open in Soho Square, news reached London from New York that 114 artists had signed a 'call' convening an 'American Artists' Congress'. It took place at Manhattan Town Hall on 14 February 1936, and by way of preparation Artists' Union members were already holding a fundraising exhibition at the American Contemporary Art Gallery at 54 West 8th Street.[1]

Co-ordinated by Stuart Davis and six months in the making, the 'Call to all artists, of recognized standing in their profession' appeared in an October issue of *New Masses*, a journal available at two London bookshops well known to Betty Rea – Collet's at 66 Charing Cross Road and David Archer's bookshop on the ground floor of the AIA office and clubroom building at 4 Parton Street.[2]

As well as stocking political literature, Archer published experimental poetry and in the fateful year of 1936 supported the landmark French-inspired International Surrealist Exhibition which opened in London on 11 June, barely a week after the Popular Front won power amid a massive strike wave in Paris. By year-end, as a consequence of the military uprising that took place in Spain's garrison towns on 17 July, Collet's bookshop would become one link in a clandestine chain conveying volunteers from Britain's distressed areas to Republican Spain – a cause which would soon preoccupy many artists in both London and New York.[3]

During 1935, expansion of employment on US federal arts programmes had been the focal point for the Artists' Union, precipitating a stream of contention concerning terms and conditions, in the face of which the union had become known both for its creative use of picketing and sit-ins and for its willingness to lend imaginative support to others. In parallel with action on economic matters, a New York Artists' Committee of Action – formed in the wake of the Rockefeller Center debacle – was vigilant in its defence of professional freedoms while calling for the creation of a municipally funded artist-controlled city gallery.

4.1 James Boswell, *The Street*, one of six lithographs created for the New York World's Fair, 1939. 21 × 19.3 cm (8⅜ × 7⅝ in.). Here the artist depicts himself, at centre, outside Collet's Bookshop talking to James Holland on the right, observed by James Fitton to the left; Collet's premises housed *Left Review*'s initial office

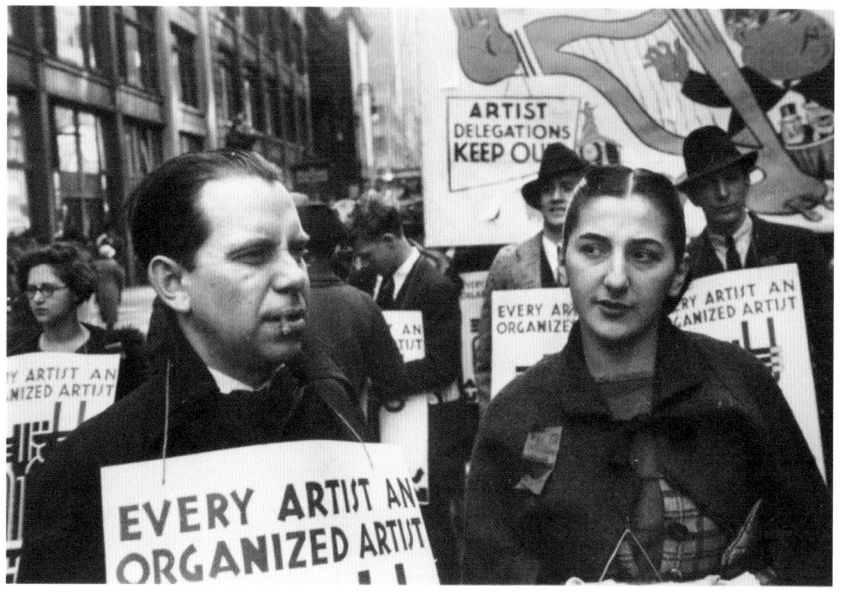

4.2 Ben Shahn, *Stuart Davis and Roselle Springer at the May Day Parade, New York*, 1934

Davis, together with Roselle Springer – with whom he now found a love akin to that he had known with Bessie – was active in all these areas, devoting much time to his role as editor-in-chief of *Art Front*, the spikily brilliant broadsheet jointly sponsored by the Committee of Action and the Artists' Union.[4] Although originating from networks dominated by social realists, Davis developed *Art Front* into a forum of vital debate for the left, creating a dialogue between social realists, Surrealists, Expressionists and abstract artists while vocalizing trenchant militancy on matters of common political and professional concern at home and abroad. He contributed to this dialogue directly, publishing a favourable review of Salvador Dalí's art (immediately rebutted by two further contributors the following month)[5] and also a searing indictment of the Municipal Art Commission for rejecting – in an event reminiscent of the Coit Tower controversy[6] – a mural developed by Ben Shahn and Lou Block for Rikers Island Penitentiary.[7]

Davis's stylistically ecumenical, politically attuned instincts made him a natural choice as organizing secretary when an American Artists' Congress was first mooted in May 1935, following the American Writers' Congress which had just taken place.[8] Seeking to win over those the John Reed Clubs had failed to recruit during its 'proletkult' days, Alexander Trachtenberg of the Communist Party USA advocated formation of a new broadly based organization. This reflected the changing strategy of a Soviet leadership convinced that war with Germany was now inevitable, fearful that Western nations might support Hitler, and prepared to prioritize the fight against fascism over the struggle for a Soviet USA. In the realm of cultural work

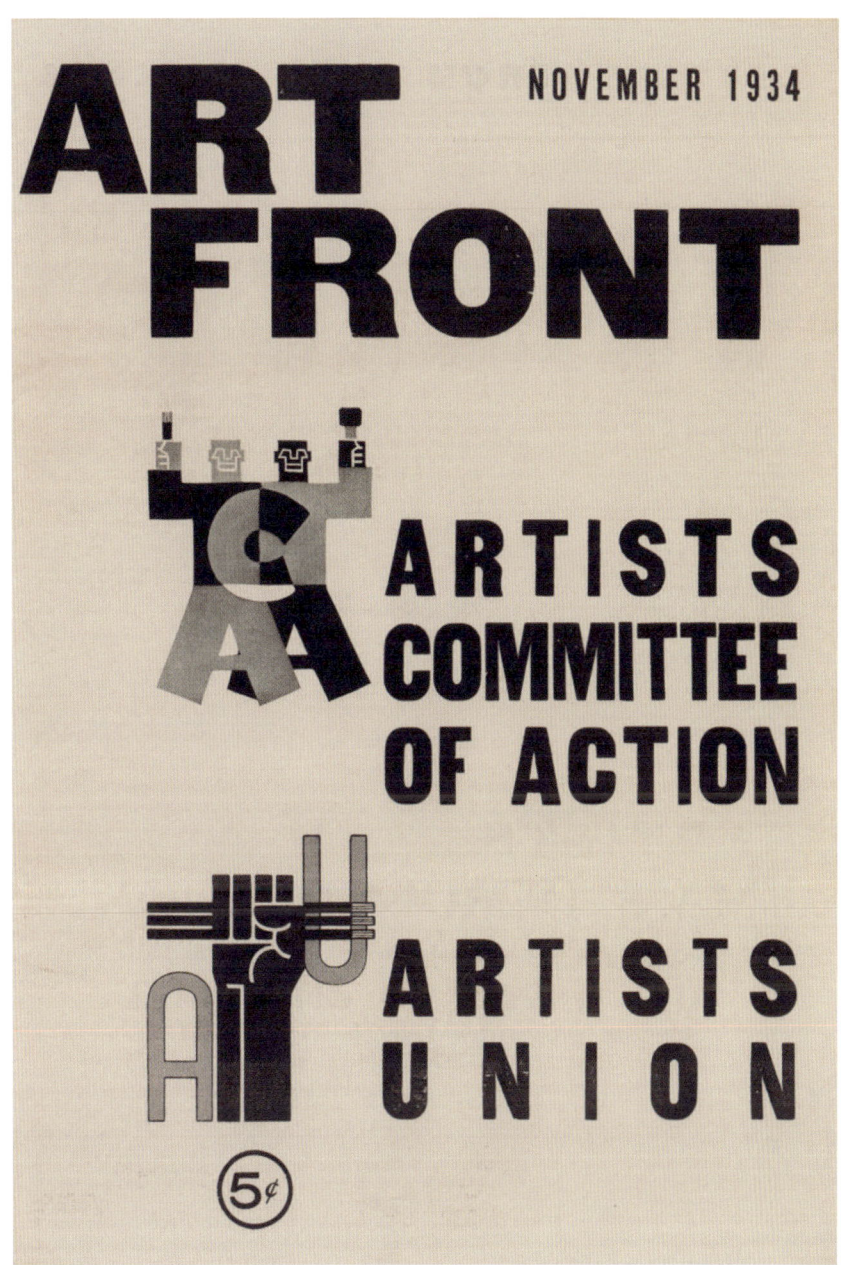

4.3 Unknown artist, cover design for *Art Front*, November 1934. 41 × 28 cm (16¼ × 11⅛ in.)

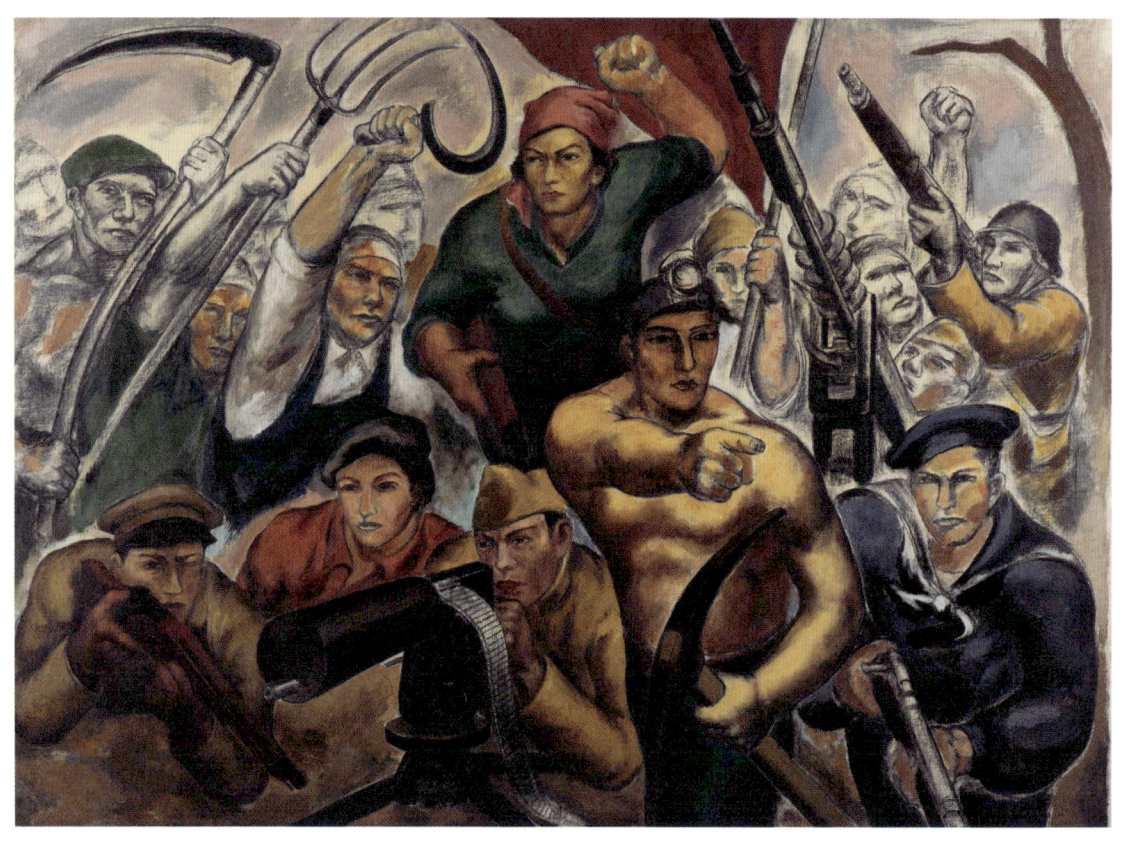

4.4 Eitaro Ishigaki,
*Soldiers of the People's
Front – Zero Hour*,
oil on canvas, *c.* 1936.
148.6 × 207 cm
(58⅝ × 81½ in.)

in the democracies, this meant elevating coalition-building above generation of a distinctively proletarian culture.

It was a stance Davis, not a party member, embraced at a meeting in painter Eitaro Ishigaki's studio on 18 May after receiving assurances that any new organization could function democratically and develop independently – a position that held during the highly participative process of crafting both the call and the congress agenda. In a manner similar to AI activity in London, this gradually broadened out from a core group including Shahn to attract well-known artists of many persuasions, as Davis became one of a number of strong voices linking conditions at home to the threat of fascism and war from abroad: 'We are confronted with the high probability of a world cataclysm, threatening creative workers with barbarous destruction ... Within this country, not only is the great body of American artists harassed by economic insecurity, but they have just cause for alarm in the rapidly increasing attacks upon the liberty of honest artistic expression.'[9]

Once published, the call met with an extraordinary response, and by the time the congress opened on 14 February 1936 over four hundred artists 'of recognized standing' were publicly backing proposals for an ongoing organization. Articulated in moderate language scrubbed of sectarian association, its draft objectives were:

1. to unite artists of all esthetic tendencies to enable them to attain common cultural objectives
2. to establish closer relationships between the artist and the people and extend the influence of art as a force of enlightenment
3. to advocate and uphold permanent Governmental support for the advancement of American art
4. to support other organized groups on issues of mutual interest in an effort to develop and maintain conditions favourable to art and human existence
5. to oppose all reactionary attempts to curtail democratic rights and freedom of expression
6. to oppose war and prevent the establishment of conditions that are conducive to the destruction of culture and detrimental to the progress of mankind

The agenda spoke to the fears and hopes of the moment, and such was the momentum that the congress was restructured into a public opening session at the Town Hall, followed by two member-only days at the New School for Social Research, an institution already functioning as an intellectual safe house for refugees from Europe. Suitably enough, it was

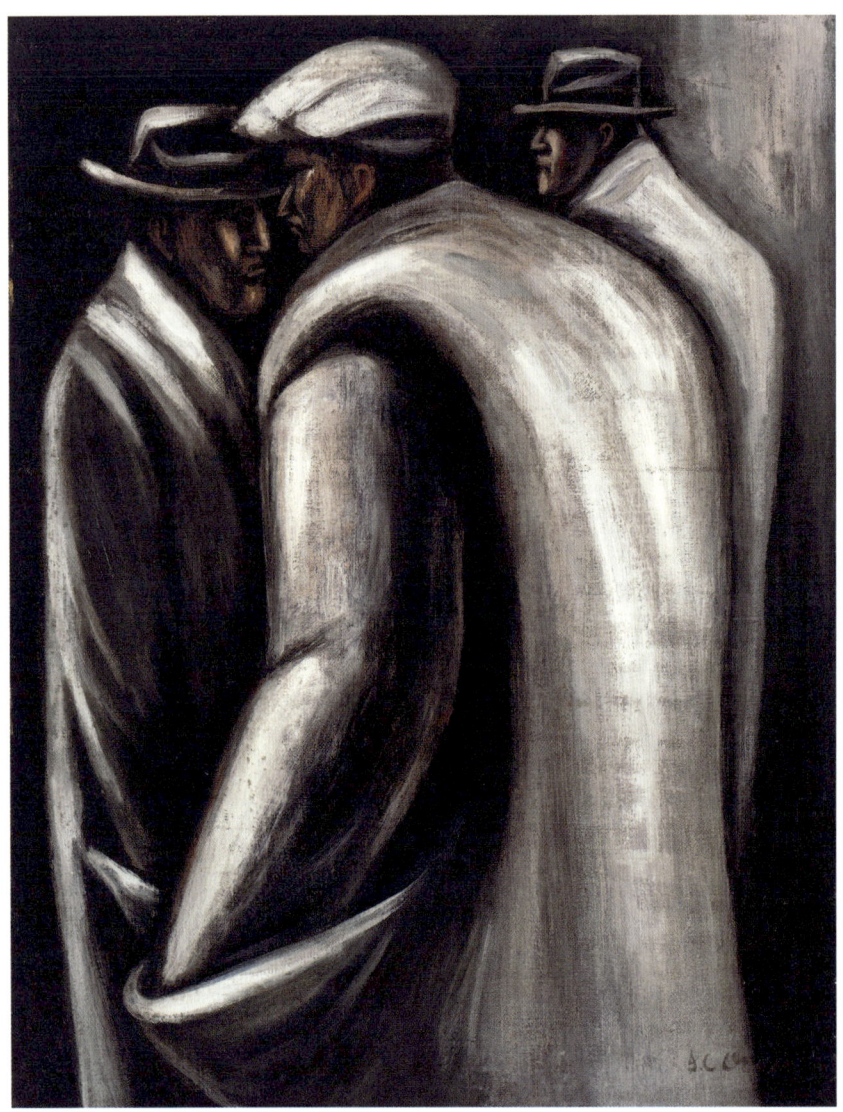

4.5 José Clemente Orozco, *The Unemployed*, oil on canvas, c. 1929. 65 × 51.4 cm (25⅝ × 20¼ in.)

4.6 David Alfaro Siqueiros, *Peasant Mother (Madre Campesina)*, oil on canvas, 1924. 220 × 175 cm (86⅝ × 69 in.)

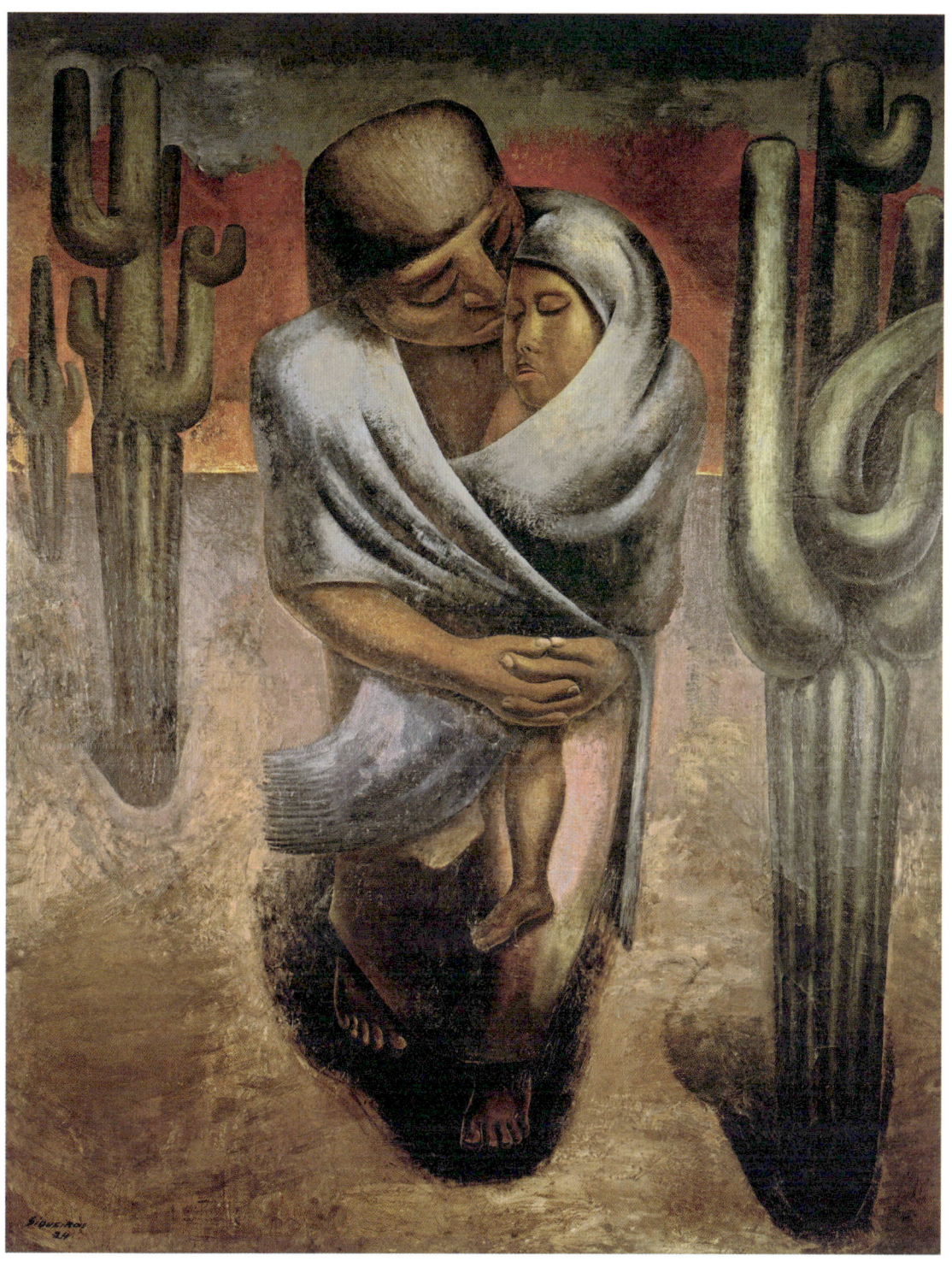

4.7 Unknown photographer, *American Artists' Congress in Session*, 1936

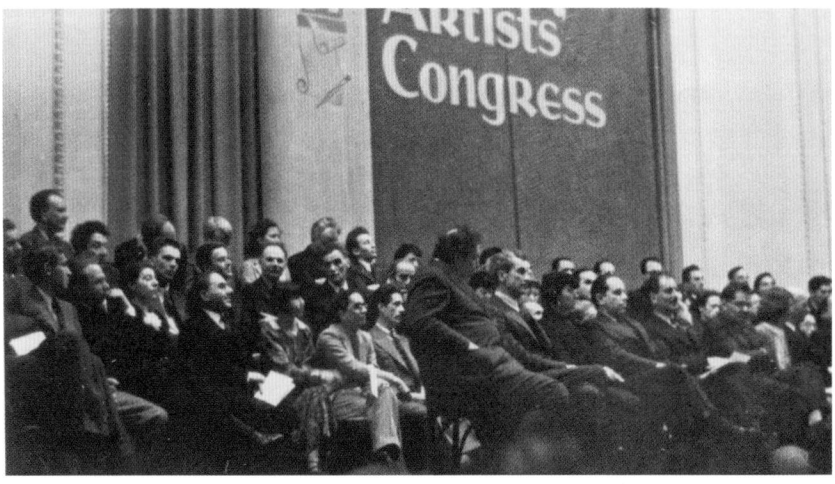

where José Clemente Orozco, a congress speaker alongside fellow Mexican muralist David Alfaro Siqueiros, had decorated four dining-room walls with *A Call for Revolution and Universal Brotherhood* five years earlier.[10]

As the date of the congress approached, thrice-weekly meetings gave way to daily 'jam sessions' finalizing a diverse programme with thirty-four speakers;[11] among them was the artist Max Weber, later voted in as national chairman after the closing session of 360 members endorsed the creation of a permanent organization.[12]

Asked to talk on 'The Artist, His Audience and Outlook', Weber's address to the first closed session was challenging, dissecting the relative isolation of his audience and their lack of reach in contemporary culture, where variety and sex magazines were 'Novacain in the struggle and agony of daily existence of the great multitude' and where the gallery world was one of 'chameleon cleverness' and hair-splitting introversion. Excoriating the narcissism of small differences, he urged: 'we must first eschew the *isms* and *ists*, the maze of movements, theories and cults prefixed so often by the monosyllables *pre*, *sur*, *post* and *neo*', because 'art for its own sake is doomed to suffocation and extinction' while only an engaged art could meet the 'great and impending danger of fascism':

> World culture and art are in a very critical condition, and it seems to me that this era calls for a new aggressive and independent art which should serve as a dominant educational force ... an art for all – for men and women who toil and create real wonder and [the] wealth of modern times, and live and hope by the sweat of their brow. Their dreams, their environment, their happiness should be our human concern and artistic inspiration.

Weber's was a clarion call for art realistic in form and grounded in daily life, not simply limited to 'scenes of back-breaking labor, poverty, disease, and ill treatment of racial minorities' triggering outrage, but one that also 'inspired with ideas of new possibilities'.[13]

After 500 were turned away from the sold-out opening, 1,500 people heard Lewis Mumford's opening address relaying fraternal greetings received from the Artists International Association of London.[14] Over two days proceedings unfolded in an atmosphere bordering on euphoria; for George Biddle, whose influence with Roosevelt had proved so consequential three years before, the congress was simply 'the most significant

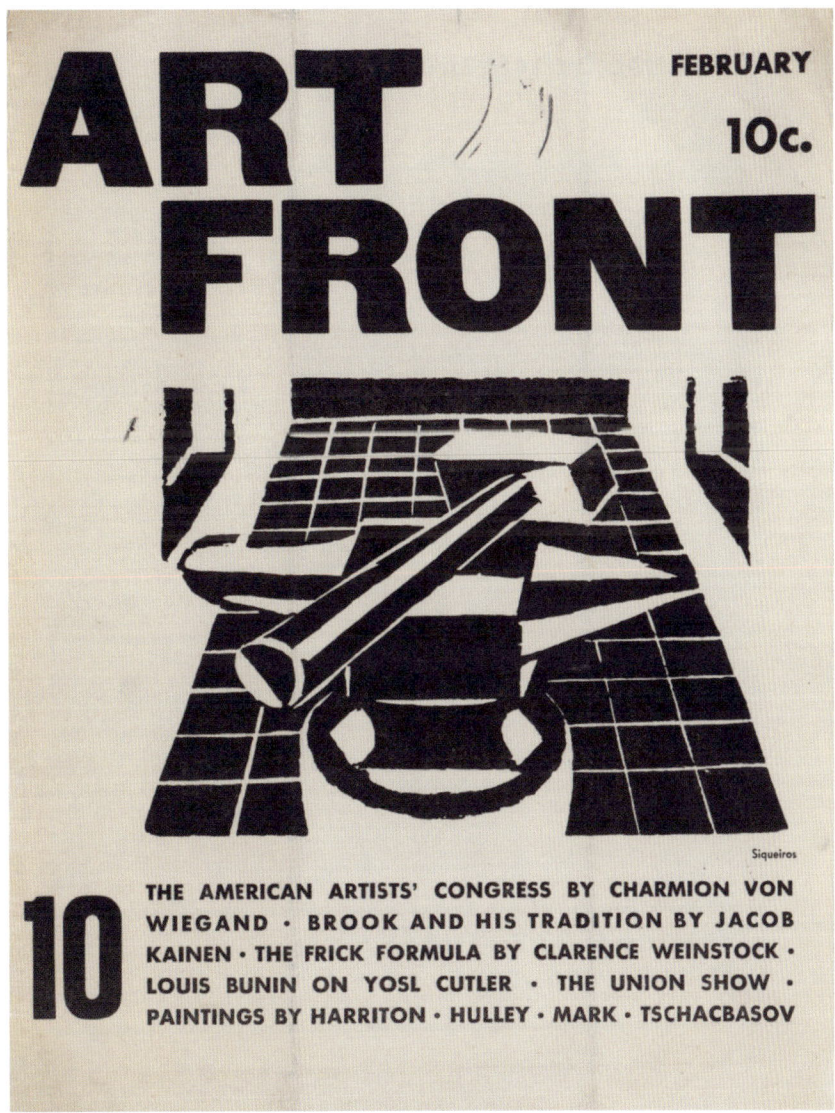

4.8 David Alfaro Siqueiros, cover design for *Art Front*, February 1936. 30 × 23 cm (11⅞ × 9⅛ in.)

event in our art world since the Armory show of 1913'. Closing the last session, Davis, now national executive secretary-elect, drew both cheers and laughter: 'All I can say is that the artists who inaugurated this Congress are gratified with the results of their labor ... it is beyond anything we expected. When we first started we talked about fifty artists.'[15]

* * * * *

News of the congress was not slow to enthuse AIA circles in London, where Percy Horton devoted two-thirds of the next *Bulletin* to its proceedings: 'Name follows name of almost every well-known artist representing every school of painting in America ... what impresses one most is the comprehensive and business-like agenda of the four sessions, and the concrete way in which the subjects were thrashed out by speaker after speaker and the way they stressed the point that what they were doing was part of a world-wide movement of artists, including in England such men as Augustus John and Eric Gill.' Summarizing key contributions, he concluded: 'from this report there emerges a similarity of aim and actual method of work between the American Congress and the Artists International Association, which, to us, is encouraging and stimulating to a very high degree.'[16]

Writing under the pseudonym 'Toros', Horton then sought to broadcast the implications of the congress more widely in *Left Review*: 'It looks as if the years 1935 and 1936 will be remembered by artists as a period of awakening – a period during which they began to turn from their wranglings about aesthetics to face a common danger.'[17] The success of the Soho Square exhibition was, as Toros remarked, 'still fresh in the memory'. It had brought increased membership but also left practical and aesthetic questions in its wake, about where and how efforts to organize should be concentrated and what style or styles of art should be used to promote the anti-fascist, pro-peace agenda.

In the USA a division of labour now existed, with New York at its epicentre; the Artists' Congress, having engaged many well-known figures who it could call on for support, would now function as the political wing of a progressive alliance, tolerant in terms of aesthetic credos but internationally alert and vigilant in its nationwide defence of cultural freedoms and advocacy of public art. At the same time the Artists' Union, its membership base fed by the scale of Federal Art Project spending, was in action as the industrial wing focused on artists' livelihoods; and as the Roosevelt administration, anticipating economic recovery, made its first moves towards moderating New Deal employment schemes in late 1936, it was able to mount a militant defence of threatened projects.[18]

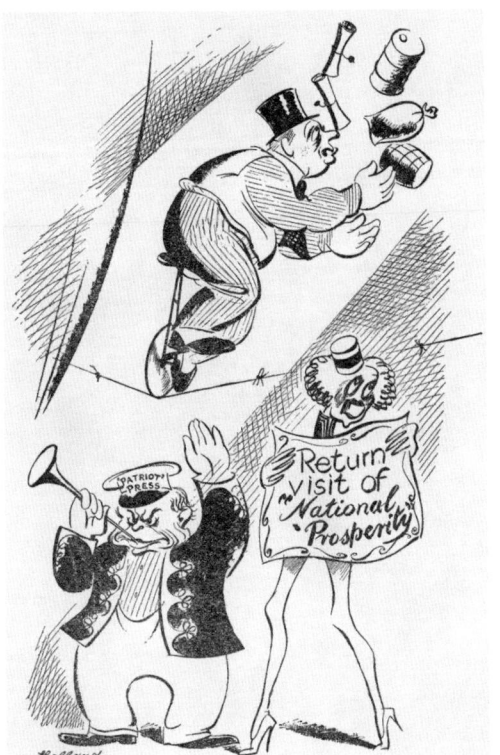
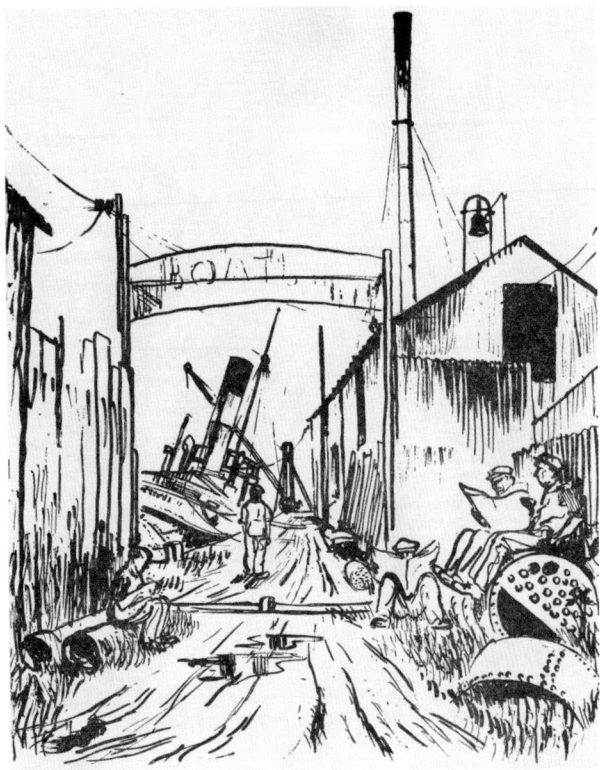

4.9 James Holland, *Happy Days*, line-drawn cartoon in *Left Review*, March 1936. 24.6 × 14.4 cm (9¾ × 5¾ in.)

4.10 James Holland, *Our Heritage, The Sea*, line drawing in *Left Review*, May 1935. 24.6 × 16.5 cm (9¾ × 6½ in.)

In Britain, however, no such framework existed. Armaments spending, growing consumer industries around London and car manufacture in the Midlands lent some credence to National Government claims of an upturn being under way – satirised by James Holland's *Happy Days* in *Left Review* that March – but the country's distressed areas were still just that, and the month of October would see marchers from Jarrow, the 'town that was murdered', on the tramp to London. Schemes like the Federal Art Project remained an alien concept: less well-endowed than their US counterparts, museums and public institutions seldom purchased the work of living artists, while commercial galleries, the gatekeepers to constrained private patronage, could only offer unpredictable support to a small minority, with part-time teaching and the often fruitless search for illustration work an essential strategy for aspirant fine artists without independent means.

The nearest equivalent to US government-backed demand arose via bodies such as the Empire Marketing Board, the London Passenger Transport Board and the General Post Office, where publicity executives alive to emerging communication techniques and sympathetic to modernism provided a London-centric source of work, as did a number of conglomerates including Shell-Mex. But in aggregate this was modest in scale, and as of

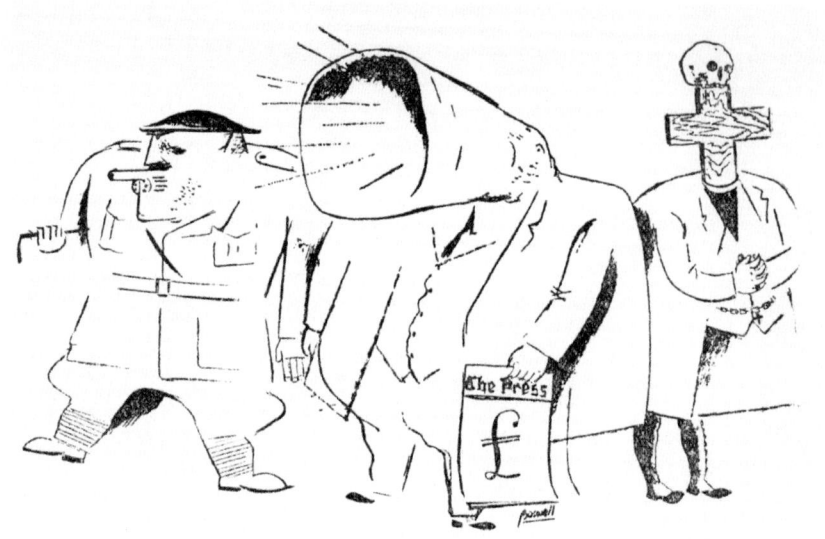

4.11 James Boswell, *Church, Press and Army*, line-drawn cartoon in *Left Review*, February 1935. 14.6 × 24.6 cm (5¾ × 9¾ in.)

1936 an estimated 60,000 commercial artists and designers of all stripes, including fine artists seeking paid employment either through the studio system or as self-employed jobbing art workers, faced a highly fragmented market fitfully responsive to anaemic economic recovery.[19]

Misha Black, in particular, was alive to this. In April he published the article 'An Equity for Artists?' in *Left Review*, analysing barriers to realizing the widespread demand 'every artist an organized artist' and using the occasion of a joint survey by the Society of Industrial Artists and the Society of Artists in Commerce, backed by the AIA, to promote a code of practice for freelance industrial design, concluding 'the next move is to organise the employed commercial artists … [and] the sweated pottery and textile designers'. Wearing his AIA chairman's hat, Black – a strong advocate of team-working in his own commercial practice – now called for all 'artists, lay-out men, copy-writers and others engaged in Publicity who agree that Peace Propaganda must now be undertaken on constructive and practical lines to assist in developing a Production Group to handle such campaigns'.[20]

One hundred and twenty invites were sent out, and half that number – including sympathetic advertising executives from Siviter's, Vernon's, J. Walter Thompson and the *New York Herald Tribune* – were present at an inaugural meeting in Euston Road on 25 June. Chaired by James Holland, with Black, Fitton, Boswell and James Lucas also there, it set up a committee of nine to oversee a ramping up of AIA capacity just a few weeks before the outbreak of the Spanish Civil War.[21]

Reflecting on this period of campaigning over forty years later, Holland wrote: 'I think that some of our collective successes came from the circumstances that many of us were employed in advertising ... and the techniques for selling soap or petrol to a not-very-interested public are not so different from those needed to put across a political and social message.' Although still painting and exhibiting through the AIA and the London Group, for several years Holland's main source of income had come from freelancing, chiefly through a small agency which inherited the Shell account from an American conglomerate where he had observed the duplicity at play in capturing celebrity tobacco endorsements.

In a similar vein, after abandoning easel painting in favour of activism and deploying his satirical talent for free, James Boswell had kept afloat financially through book illustration and casual graphic design; but in mid-1936, about to become a father, he applied for a position with Holland's contact Jack Beddington, and a fortnight after his daughter was born started as a full-time art director with the Asiatic Petroleum Company, a Shell subsidiary. Not unaware of the irony, for the next four years he would combine AIA activity, work for the *Daily Worker* and *Left Review* and drawing and painting urban working-class life at weekends with a full-time role offering close observation of the City types and capitalist manoeuvres he had skewered in *Empire Builders*.

With regular but slight teaching income from the Central, James Fitton – who now lived with his wife Margaret at Pond Cottages in Dulwich Village, next to Percy and Lydia Horton – had been the first to turn away from the 'superficially attractive slavery' of freelancing where 'any free time one gets is spent touting ... worrying where the next job is coming from and whether the rent can be paid'.[22] An offer of three days a week from Vernon's Advertising, accepted 'with some show of reluctance that belied my feeling of relief', was the beginning of five decades with an enterprise that expanded as one of London's most successful agencies in the 1930s with Fitton as art director. Apart from the London Passenger Transport Board and the General Post Office, and notwithstanding his *Daily Worker* cartoons as 'Alpha', his clients included major corporates such as Boots, Cornhill Insurance and the Abbey National Building Society.[23]

Left Review, formally the organ of the Writers International, had made the 'Three Jameses' a known entity, and when after six months of publication a contributors' conference was held, its visual content was applauded amid mixed reviews for its written material. The three Jameses plus Pearl Binder were duly elected to its committee, and as the Soho Square exhibition closed Martin Lawrence was promoting a 1936 'Three Jameses' desk diary, presenting twenty-five drawings as 'a triple alliance against the Absurdities

4.12 James Fitton/Alpha Group, *It's Up to Us*, cover design, 1935. 20.8 × 18 cm (8¼ × 7⅛ in.)

4.13 James Fitton/Alpha Group, *Army Medical*, montage, *It's Up to Us*, 1935. 20.8 × 18 cm (8¼ × 7⅛ in.)

4.14 James Fitton/Alpha Group, *Hitler and Mussolini*, design for double-page spread, *It's Up to Us*, 1935. 20.8 × 36 cm (8¼ × 14¼ in.)

and Hypocrisies of the Existing Scheme of Things'.[24] Providing a platform for worker writers was an explicit *Left Review* aim that now extended to its artwork, as Cliff Rowe co-ordinated AIA drawing classes focusing on 'the requirements of working for reproduction [which] should be of particular interest to worker artists who have sent work to *Left Review*'.[25]

The desk diary was a niche offering for the converted ('the cartoon you meant to keep'), but the next joint venture, *It's Up to Us*, was planned on a different scale with an ambitious objective: to mobilize mass opinion against rearmament and hostility to the Soviet Union and in favour of collective security and the creation of a popular front, nationally and internationally. A thirty-two-page pamphlet printed in black and reddish-brown on white, 'Designed and carried out by the Alpha Group', its forthcoming publication was announced in *Left Review*'s editorial for June: 'It puts you in a mood for planning, this early summer weather … Well it was like that in June 1914. Then the lovely summer weather was blacked out, plans smashed, people driven apart … If that is not to happen again, it is quite literally up to each one of us. Hence the title of our pamphlet. We want it sold in tens of thousands all over the country, we want it taken into the villages, the isolated farms. The towns can be worked by organisations, this is the job for the ramblers.'[26]

The 'Alpha Group' branding, echoing Fitton's *Daily Worker* alias, reflected his lead role in a joint enterprise six months in the preparation and – given the militancy of its denunciations and the three Jameses' employment situation – a shared caution. After returning from his latest mission in aid of political prisoners in Austria, Frederick Elwyn-Jones had written to Pearl Binder, three months into her longest stay in Russia: 'Jim showed me some stuff for the book. It really is superb and grand propaganda.'[27] The artwork in question was a mixture of photomontage, line drawing, quotations, highly varied typography and fourteen double-page 'infographic' spreads, several too busy and fact-laden to be effective, but striking in overall narrative impact.

Up with the pace of events, its back cover celebrated: 'In France the People's Front has been elected to office by huge majorities on a programme of Peace abroad, and at home Make the Rich Pay.' With a print run of 50,000 ordered, July's *Left Review* carried a full-page announcement of imminent publication: 'It will sell at sight. This can become a classic of Peace Propaganda.'[28] But by the time distribution began three weeks later, so had the Nationalist uprising in Spain, triggering events which would eventually drown all assumptions that peace by pact and negotiation – that peace without war – was still possible.

* * * * *

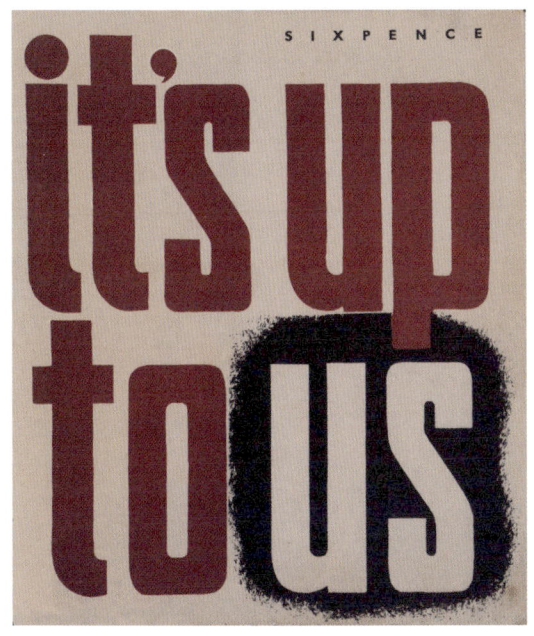
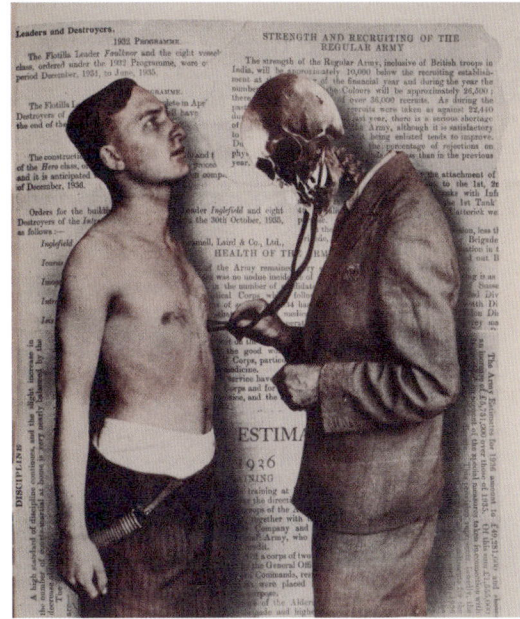
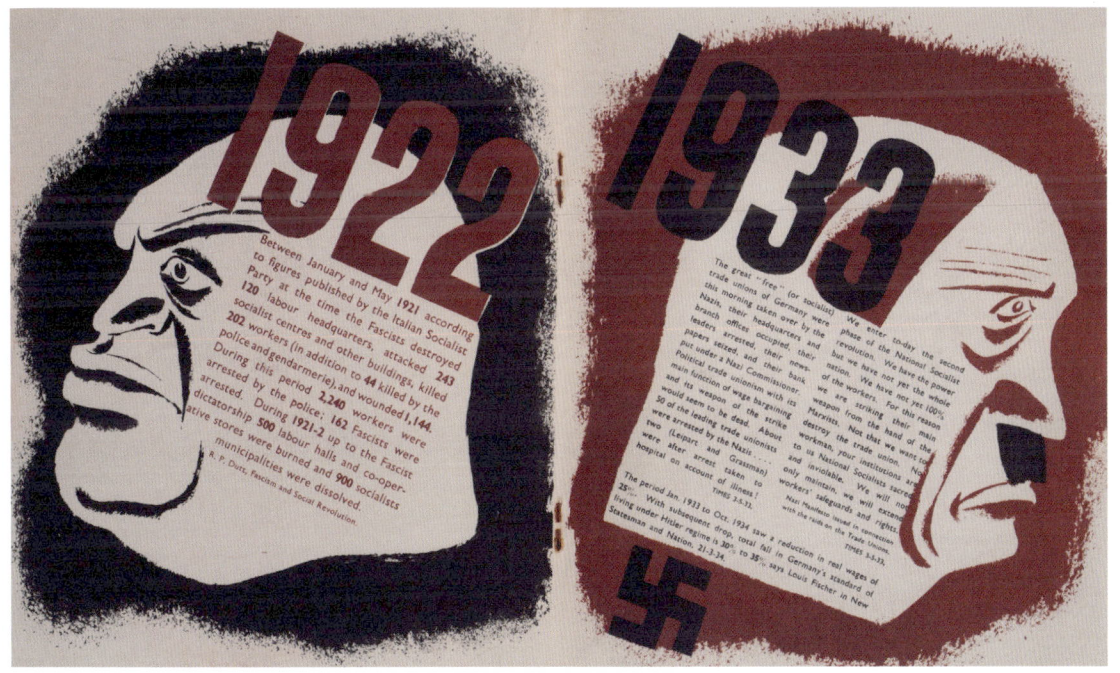

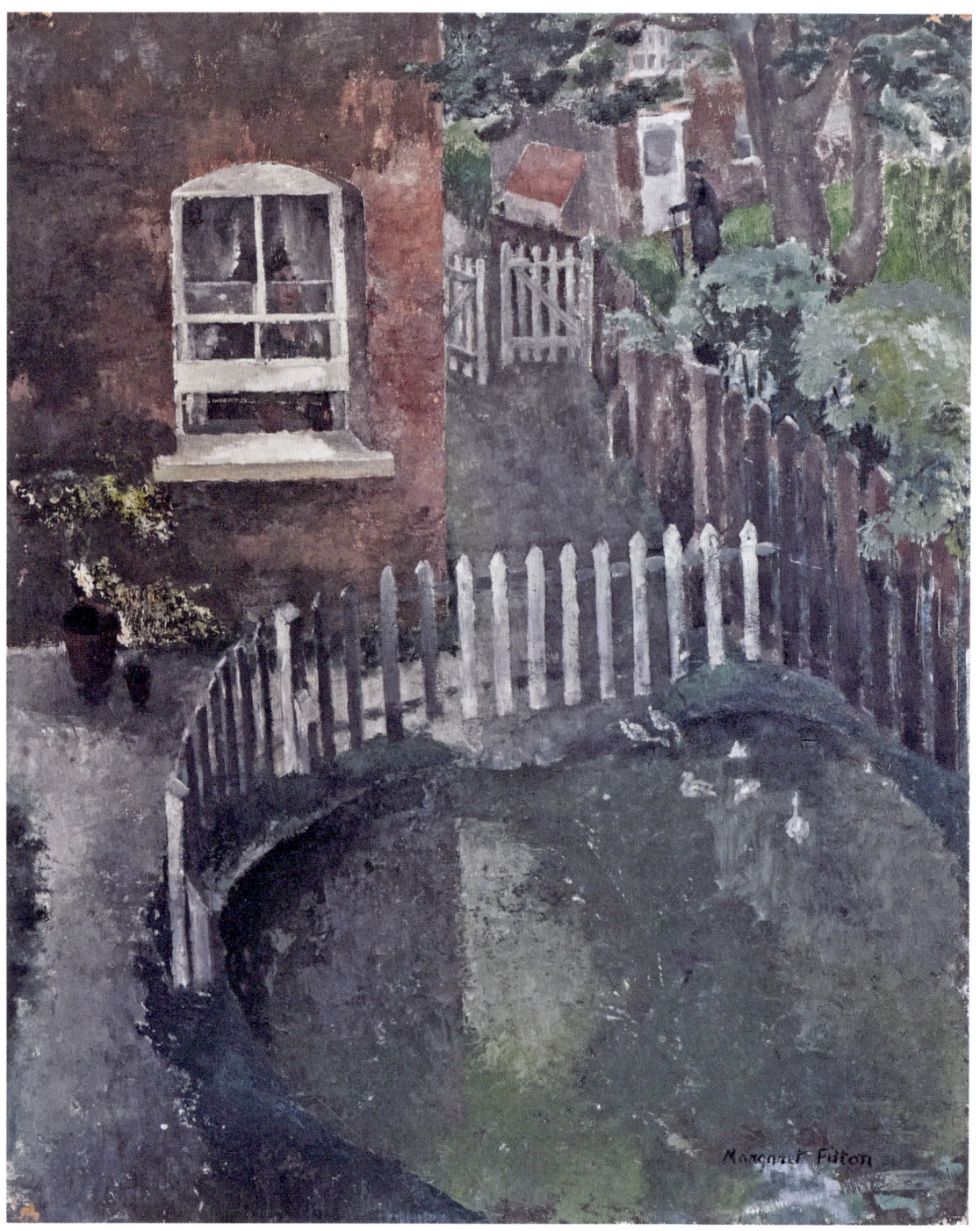

4.15 Margaret Fitton, *Duck Pond, Dulwich*, oil on canvas, mid-1930s. 78 × 64 cm (30¾ × 25¼ in.). A view of the back garden at Pond Cottages, the Fitton home visited by Elwyn-Jones; this painting was displayed at the AIA's Grosvenor Square exhibition in 1937, cat. 140

In parallel with these projects, early 1936 witnessed continuing debate about what both socialist art and cultural freedom should look like – questions publication of *5 on Revolutionary Art* had articulated but not resolved. Huxley's catalogue sally voicing opposition to 'dictatorship' rather than simple 'fascism' had not only disconcerted Pearl Binder's interlocutor in Moscow but had clearly hit a mark in London's liberal artistic circles as well.[29] Awareness of Nazi repression of free expression and co-option of approved styles in preparation for the Berlin Olympics was growing, but so too was a perception that Moscow's hostility to modernist 'formalism' and insistence on anodyne 'Socialist Realism' undermined claims about the benign situation of artists in the Soviet Union. In January, judging that these were issues better ventilated than dodged, the AIA announced a twelve-week talk series, 'Arts and the Dictators', where 'one of the chief aims of the discussion will be to answer the current view that the position of arts under "dictators", whether they are from the Left or the Right, is identical'.[30]

On both the aesthetic and the organizational front, however, a more serious challenge was brewing for those radical in politics but conservative in their preference for communicable social realist content. In May it was announced that the AIA would convene a debate at the Conway Hall, where Anthony Blunt and 'several well-known artists' would speak 'on the occasion of the forthcoming Surrealist Exhibition'. Potentially divisive, the exhibition was an event that could not be ignored, particularly as Henry Moore and Paul Nash, two of the most prominent sponsors of *Artists Against Fascism and War*, plus Herbert Read – who a few months before had provided the opening contribution of the AIA's own book of essays – were now all identifiable players in a rising tide of enthusiasm.[31]

Works by Max Ernst, Giorgio de Chirico, Joan Miró and Jean Arp had occasionally appeared in London commercial galleries in previous years, and surveys of Surrealist art and literature were available both at Anton Zwemmer's Charing Cross Road bookshop and gallery, four doors down from Collet's, and at David Archer's shop below the AIA office, while across the road at no. 1 Parton Street, Roger Roughton was in the habit of editing the Surrealist journal *Contemporary Poetry and Prose* at a table in the Arts Café. But prior to Roland Penrose's 1935 arrival from Paris, Surrealist art remained the province of a very small circle of enthusiasts. When Zwemmer's exhibited Salvador Dalí's work in late 1934 – as an example of art based on 'a vertiginous descent into the unconscious', acknowledging 'the omnipotence of the dream' in revealing 'what lies behind the facade of reality' – it was readily dismissed by Kenneth Clark in the *New Statesman* as 'vulgar trash intended to take in the would-be smart and up-to-date', while Anthony Blunt in the *Spectator* observed that Dalí's projection of

CHARING CROSS ROAD

sexual disturbances was 'so personal that even those to whom the matter is sympathetic will find satisfaction hard to obtain'.[32]

Before settling in Hampstead, where he promptly connected with Moore, Nash and Read, Penrose had spent years based in Paris, initially studying art and then buying it after receiving a substantial inheritance.[33] During that time he travelled widely and got to know Georges Braque, André Breton, Max Ernst, Paul Éluard, Pablo Picasso, Ossip Zadkine, Jean Hélion, Man Ray and André Lhote; he had worked with Robert Bresson on his first film and had a part in *L'Age d'Or*, Buñuel's second film – in short he not only lived through the period when Surrealism erupted as a cultural force, but also knew all its key players. The spark that now led to the organization of an International Surrealist Exhibition in London had been struck in Paris in late 1933 when twenty-two-year-old David Gascoyne exclaimed to Penrose 'Why do we know nothing of this in England?!' A published experimental novelist, Gascoyne would return the next year to research *A Short Survey of Surrealism* and, the year after it appeared, join the organizing committee Penrose convened at his house in Downshire Hill in April 1936.[34]

Moore, Nash, Read and Edward McKnight Kauffer were now all party to an effort to which Éluard and Breton in France, E. L. T. Mesens in Belgium and leading Surrealists in Europe were recruited – a cross-channel liaison ensuring that the exhibition of 392 paintings, sculptures, drawings, 'collages', photographs and objects brought together at the New Burlington Galleries in early June was both staggeringly varied in scope and truly international, with artists from fifteen countries participating. Mesens, a close friend of René Magritte, insisted that chronological conventions and harmonized groupings should be abandoned in favour of accentuating clashes of colour, size, medium and content to produce 'by shock tactics, the maximum of excitement' – an approach which produced walls in 'an unusual state of unrest', with incongruous adjacencies seeking to add new dimensions to images and objects on display. Penrose later recalled the show coming together at a moment of 'dazed confidence' in London, a momentary zeitgeist probably reinforced by the arrival of participants from Paris, where over two hundred factory occupations and a seismic wave of strikes were under way; with May's elections having produced a Popular Front majority in France, on 5 June – six days before the exhibition opened – Léon Blum's left-wing coalition came to power.[35]

When the exhibition opened on a Thursday afternoon, 'behind the back of the Royal Academy, in a heat wave' lift-only access to the third-floor gallery generated a pedestrian tailback, then a traffic jam.[36] The promoters had played a canny game publicizing the event, heightening expectations with rumours of a short run and absurd happenings in the run-up, with

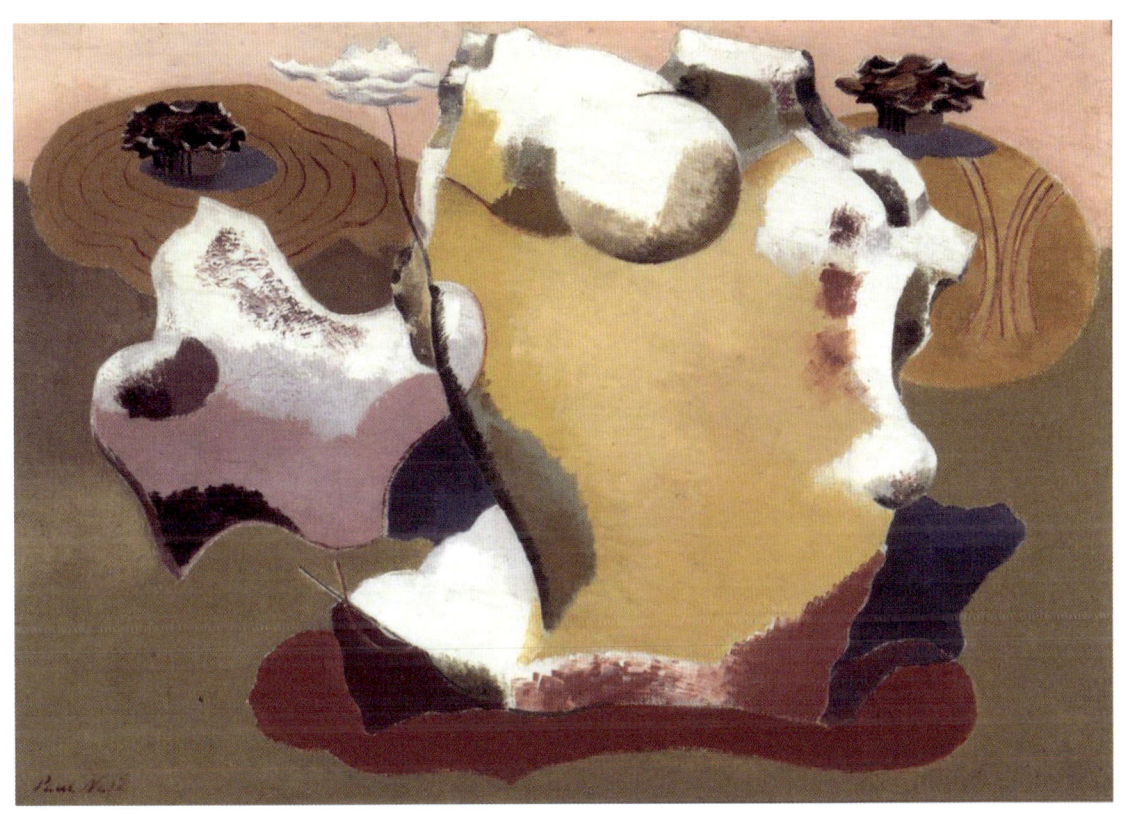

4.16 Paul Nash, *Landscape of the Megaliths*, oil on canvas, 1934. 49.5 × 73.2 cm (19½ × 28⅞ in.)

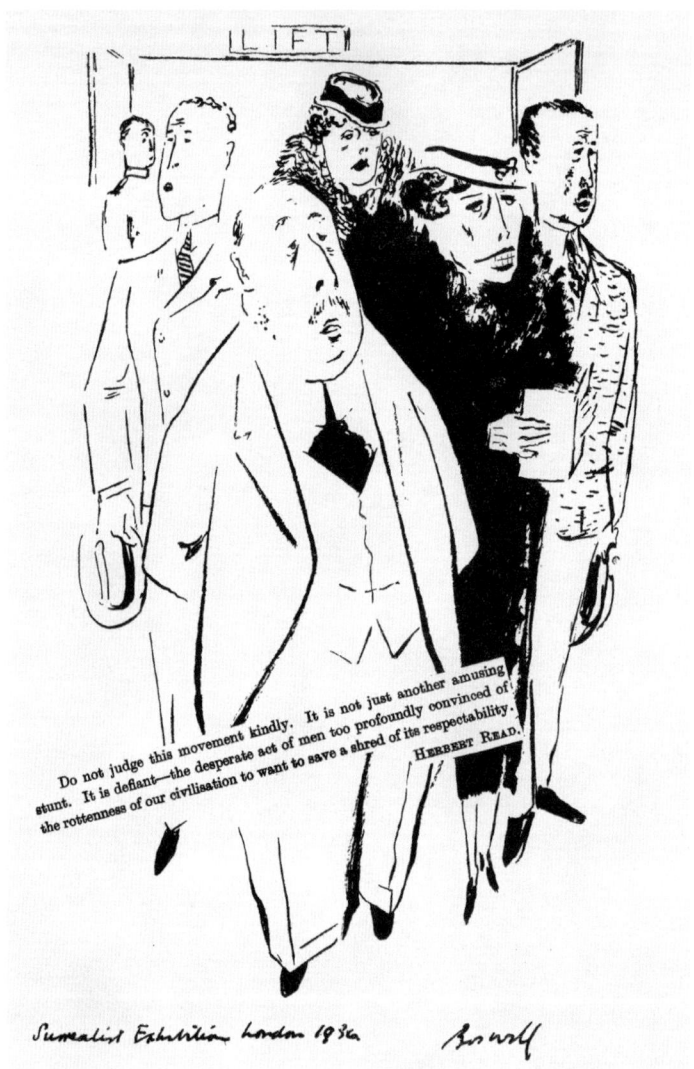

4.17 James Boswell, *Surrealist Exhibition London 1936*, in *Left Review*, July 1936. 24.6 × 15.7 cm (9¾ × 6¼ in.)

Salvador Dalí playing the role of prankster-in-chief on the day. An estimated 1,150 visitors crowded in to hear Breton open the proceedings in French and to be 'in turn, shocked, infuriated, amused and stimulated' by the work of artists including de Chirico, Magritte, Picasso, Ernst, Man Ray, Yves Tanguy, Constantin Brancusi, Marcel Duchamp, Paul Klee, Alberto Giacometti, Edward Burra, Julian Trevelyan, Nash and Moore.

Although critical reaction to the exhibition's bewildering iconoclasm generally ranged from dismissal to damnation, this helped cement its status as an amusing *succès de scandale*, drawing in a paying public averaging a thousand a day over twenty-four days. Its progenitors, however, were not above taking themselves seriously, as evidenced by the famous photo of nine men in ties standing behind five demurely seated women, an institutional portrait with not a sniff of cultural upheaval in the air, an image completely untouched by the spirit of Dada.

In his opening address, Breton had identified Surrealism, Dada's successor, without irony, as 'an international organism with the potential to become the absolute core of a world consciousness', a launch pad for global enlightenment, revolutionary in its disruptive potential. Read, in the first flush of a later qualified embrace, had hailed the arrival of a movement 'more Marxist than the Marxians', outstripping social realism by introducing a truly dialectic approach whereby collapsing bourgeois culture, confronted by imagination accessing the unconscious, would produce a socially and politically consequential Surrealist synthesis. Meanwhile Paul Nash, while preserving a degree of personal distance, identified Surrealism as 'not just another art movement, but a state of being and behaviour', informed by the 'poetry of ideas' in its engagement with 'that which is beyond what seems to be real'.[37]

Such claims triggered dismissive irritation in private among the AIA core; for Percy Horton 'it was damned cheek of André Breton and others to pose as Marxists',[38] and the following January A. L. Lloyd would publicly summarize the case for the prosecution: 'if Surrealism were revolutionary, it could be of use. But Surrealism is not revolutionary, because its lyricism is socially irresponsible. It does not lead fantasy into action of real social significance. Surrealism is a particularly subtle form of fake revolution.'[39] But during the summer months, when Paul Nash could observe that 'the magnetism of its name is now constant in current speech', tactical engagement with Surrealism was essential.

The AIA's Conway Hall debate was the initial forum for such engagement, with both Read and Blunt speaking, as well as Peter László Peri.[40] Unsurprisingly no consensus emerged, and subsequently selected contributions were gathered together in an AIA supplement stapled into July's *Left Review*, next to a brilliantly deflating James Boswell cartoon set in the Grosvenor Galleries, which in a sense stole the show while it was still on. Depicting five besuited and be-furred visitors emerging from the lift into their first moments of bewilderment, the cartoon carried a stylistic device borrowed from James Holland – namely a statement pasted slant-wise across the image, in this case an extract from Read's catalogue introduction, rendering its self-regarding pretentiousness laughable: 'Do not judge this movement kindly. It is not just another amusing stunt. It is defiant – the desperate act of men too profoundly convinced of the rottenness of our civilisation to want to save a shred of its respectability.'

Notwithstanding this lampoon, the *AIA Bulletin* for August reported: 'The meeting on Surrealism was a great success. The Surrealists came and

4.18 Joan Miró, *Maternity*, oil on canvas, 1924. 92 × 73 cm (36¼ × 28¾ in.). One of the five Miró works displayed at the New Burlington Galleries in 1936

spoke, and opposing points of view were made. The hall was crowded and many people turned away. Whatever any of us finally think about this movement, we have all been stimulated into inquiring and arguing about it, and have enjoyed the discussion to which it has given rise.'[41] It proved to be an important note to strike, because distant events were about to challenge all politically aware artists, sidelining theoretical disputation.

The Barcelona-born artist Joan Miró had been present for Breton's opening address, travelling to London for the first time from Paris, his base of fifteen years, which had been punctuated with frequent returns to the southern Catalan town of Mont-roig. One of the least explicitly political of the Surrealists, he was nonetheless an early adherent, signing Breton's Surrealist Manifesto in 1924. For Breton, Miró the painter was 'the most surrealist of us all', having absorbed and moved beyond the lessons of Fauvism and Cubism to reify the secret life of objects in reimagined visual territories, before 'assassinating' Dutch golden age masterworks in a Surrealist idiom.[42] Prime examples of both – *Le Carnaval d'Arlequin* of 1924–25 and *Dutch Interior I* of 1928 – were among five Miró works in the Surrealism show; two months earlier his work had featured in Nicolete Gray's *Abstract and Concrete* exhibition at London's Lefevre Galleries, making him – along with Moore and Nash – one of a handful of artists straddling the abstract/Constructivist versus Surrealist divide opening up in Britain that summer.

Earlier in the year Miró had been in Barcelona collaborating with his friend the architect Josep Lluís Sert when the Frente Popular won a national majority and declared an amnesty for political prisoners, soon followed by the reconvening of the self-governing Catalan Generalitat. He had witnessed anarchist actions directed at Church and bourgeoisie and political assassinations by the right, and now, shortly after his return from London to Mont-roig, the military moved against the elected government, led by the generals Franco in Morocco, Mola in the north and Goded in Mallorca, his wife's home. Within weeks exploding political violence had claimed his brother-in-law's life, and by October Miró had left Spain once again. In the French capital the next spring he would create the Surrealist lithograph *Aidez Espagne*, featuring a Catalan peasant, huge fist raised; and then at the Paris Exposition Internationale, working from a staircase scaffold in the Republican government pavilion designed by Sert and Luis Lacasa, he would paint *The Reaper*, a five-metre-high fresco of a peasant wielding a sickle, while on the floor below his compatriot Picasso was installing his massive oil painting *Guernica*.

* * * * *

CHAPTER FOUR

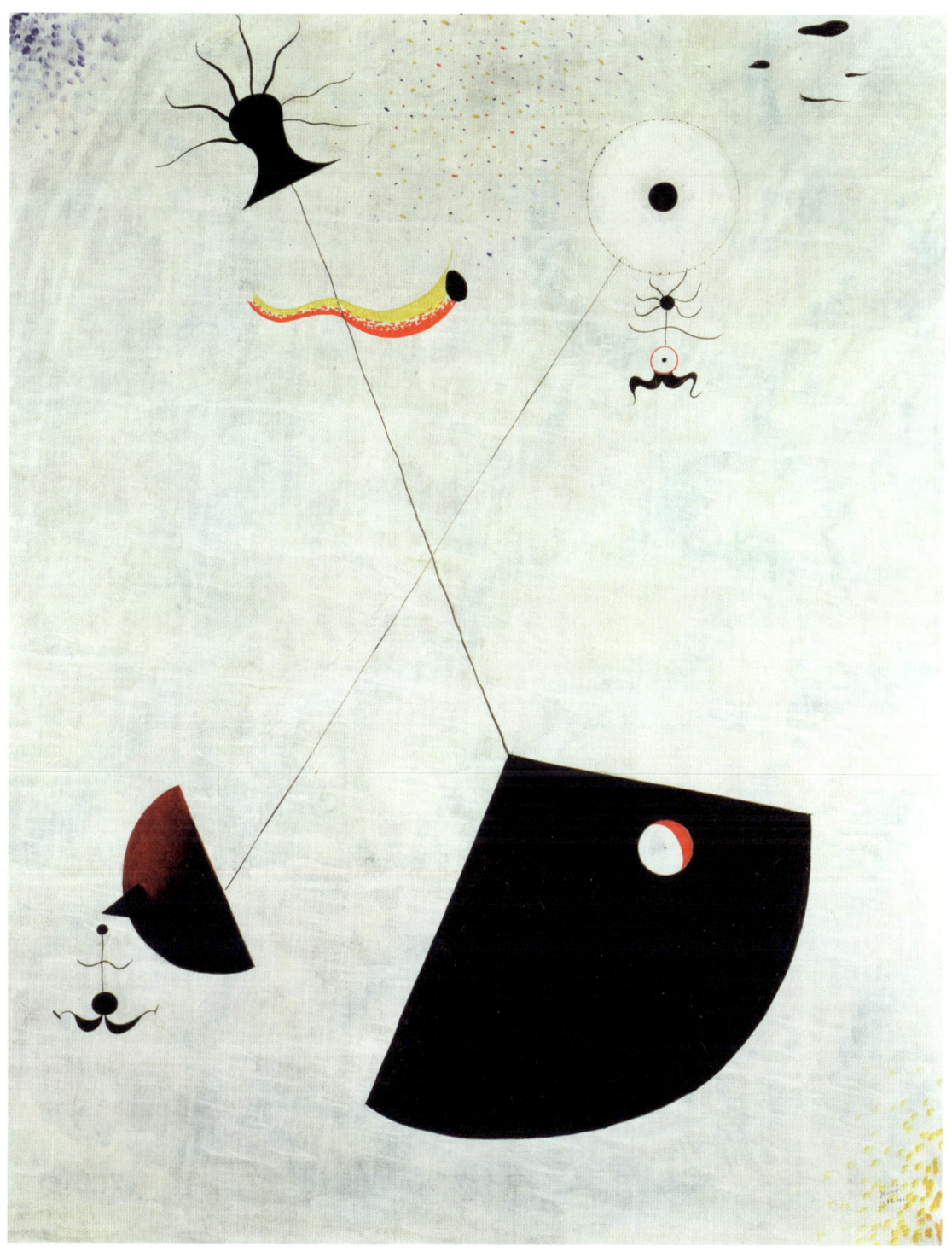

Eight days into the Surrealist exhibition in London, the International Association of Writers for the Defence of Culture, founded at the Paris Writers' Congress the previous summer, convened at the Friends Meeting House in Euston Road. Pearl Binder was present once again as both writer and artist, having just returned from her six months in Russia; this time she sketched H. G. Wells, but not André Gide, who had hastened to Maxim Gorky's deathbed in Moscow – a journey immediately preceding the first show trials which led to Gide writing *Retour de l'USSR*, published in Paris that November. In it he recanted his previously unqualified communist enthusiasms and sounded alarm about Stalinist authoritarianism, to the dismay of those already looking to Russia as the principal external supporter of the beleaguered Spanish Republic.[43] In London that June, however, Binder was working on her own highly original and nuanced book on the state of the Soviet Union, eight lithographed portraits and the extended life stories published as *Misha and Masha* the same November. For Ralph Fox, who that summer had analysed the tumultuous events of June 1936 in *France Faces the Future*, Binder gave 'a truer picture of Socialist Life than is to be found in the work of scores of "investigators" into social and economic development. We hear a great deal about the new man and new woman but so far nobody has succeeded in describing them for us. It is this bold task that Pearl Binder has undertaken, and successfully.'[44] This review was written a few days before Fox left London to join the International Brigade but, by the time it appeared, he had died on the Córdoba front in the disastrous engagement which also saw the poet and student activist John Cornford cut down the day after his twenty-first birthday.[45]

Shortly after the London conference, Binder and Elwyn-Jones travelled to Athens, ostensibly as tourists but in fact on one of several missions Frederick undertook that year in aid of trade union prisoners in Germany, Greece, Hungary and Romania.[46] Much in love, they had committed themselves to each other before she left for Russia, pledging since to forgo the pleasurable distractions of other relationships and to sink any political differences between their Labour and communist 'tribe allegiances' in a personal version of 'Le Front Uni'.[47] For Elwyn-Jones, seeking to establish himself as a fee-earning junior barrister before pursuing Parliamentary selection for the Labour Party, staying 'with my feet well in Transport House' was important, and the prospect of his future wife selling the *Daily Worker* in front of their house and going on 'chalking squads' was potentially threatening. He urged that she could do the most good politically through creative work as an artist, a position from which she did not demur, contemplating at various points projects with Edith Tudor-Hart, James Fitton and – before he left for Spain – Ralph Fox, while also pursuing a range of journalism, freelance illustration and some broadcasting.[48]

Another frontier crossing of long-term significance for the AIA network had taken place that spring, when Fred Uhlman, after failing to sell any paintings at a solo show at Galerie Le Niveau, left Paris by train on 1 April bound for Tossa del Mar on the Catalan coast. A fishing village much favoured by painters and exiles for its climate and cheap living, it was where the erstwhile Surrealist André Masson had a house, as did Uhlman's friend Zügel, an abstract painter from Stuttgart who had invited him to stay.[49] Four weeks later, encountering in a bar two young English women who had arrived in a Lagonda en route to Barcelona, he danced with twenty-four-year-old Diana Croft and they talked at length in both French and German about the political situation in Germany. It may well have been that night he learned she had defied her parents to join a welcome rally for hunger marchers in London. When she left two days later, he was reduced to writing postcards to every Thomas Cook office in Spain asking to hear from her again; picking up his card in Toledo, she reciprocated.

Witnessing anarchists burning the contents of the local church in late July, Uhlman realized a social revolution was in the making. He briefly contemplated joining the International Brigade reportedly under formation in Barcelona, but lack of a permit to travel prevented him accepting a lift with a passing journalist. Four days later he got a place on a northbound train to Marseilles and from there rang Diana in London, meeting her in Paris at the Gare Saint-Lazare before arriving in England on 3 September. Shortly after, a cousin of Diana's mother spotted her 'with a little Jew in Kew Gardens', which gave rise to a tea party at which the second daughter of Sir Henry Page Croft informed her horrified parent she intended to marry.

Page Croft was the Conservative MP for Bournemouth, an ardent imperialist and former chairman of the Tariff Reform League, who lauded English control over 'backward races' and advocated permanent political union for the empire. In 1926 he had raised a volunteer force in Bedfordshire to oppose the general strike, and he was someone for whom the National Government's sham neutrality facilitating the dictators' covert assistance to rebel Spain was not enough. As a leader of Conservative MPs caucusing as the Friends of National Spain, he pressed for recognition of the nationalist Burgos-based regime, maintaining Franco was 'a gallant Christian gentleman' and that all reports of summary executions in Nationalist Spain and German and Italian complicity in the terror bombing of civilians were 'flimsy'; in his crusade against 'red anarchy' El Caudillo, the Spanish Führer, had always proceeded 'with the greatest humanity that war permits' – small wonder that the Movimiento Nacional regarded Croft as a prime propaganda asset.[50]

Diana's humanity was of a different stripe, which boarding school from age seven and finishing schools in Paris and Florence had failed to eradicate.

Defying family tactics intended to derail a marriage regarded as 'social suicide', she and Fred wed in November. Although speaking no English and knowing little of English culture, he was beginning to make contacts, having met the painter Julian Trevelyan – 'an extraordinary-looking person in corduroy trousers and a red waist coat' – at a party given by Naomi Mitchison in Chiswick.[51] Diana had previously trained as a secretary and worked in a hospital, despite enjoying independent income from her grandfather's family trust and 'having a little more money than a real Socialist should possess'.[52] This helped sustain a partnership of skill, belief and circumstance that would see Uhlman continuing to paint, and within two years the couple's Hampstead home in Downshire Hill would become the birthplace of the Free German League of Culture and the Artists' Refugee Committee, Diana's activism thereafter leading her to join the AIA Central Committee.

A Spanish border crossing of more immediate consequence, whose outcome would provide both an emotional and an organizational focus for AIA activity during the following months, had taken place while Uhlman was still in Tossa del Mar. Travelling down the coast with the communist journalist Edith Bone, after witnessing women's groups march in the Paris May Day celebrations, thirty-two-year-old Felicia Browne arrived in Barcelona just before the Nationalist coup broke cover in Spanish Morocco – and was there as violence spread on 19 July when mainland garrisons joined the revolt and disparate militias rushed to defend the Republic.

Both artist and activist, Browne had been born into 'a well-upholstered family household' to parents who would shortly separate but who had nevertheless supported her during six years of intermittent study at the Slade.[53] There Henry Tonks was the presiding influence, and Browne's prowess in drawing both animals and working people came to the fore. Small in stature, tough, talkative, bespectacled and habitually dressed in black, she cut a distinctive, even mysterious figure according to her Slade contemporary Nan Youngman, amid more conventionally beautiful women friends such as fellow student Elizabeth Watson; and her nearby room in Euston Square was a gathering place for friends, including teenagers Wystan Auden and William Coldstream. Interested in studying sculpture, Browne had moved to Berlin in 1928, pursuing metalwork and stone carving, relishing 'communal life with fellow craftsmen', using her own means to support some of them, witnessing the violent rise of Nazi insurgency in Germany and travelling to Czechoslovakia, Hungary and Russia. After her return to England, she split her time between a wooden shed studio in Billericay and a room in Percy Street, Fitzrovia, joining the Communist Party in 1932 and, prior to her journey to Spain, working as a waitress intent on unionizing her fellow catering workers.[54]

By this time her friend Elizabeth Watson had returned from her own extended stay in Paris, where she had become friends with Quentin Bell while studying painting at the Académie Moderne; back in London Watson had moved into 10 Fitzroy Street, next door to the building where Quentin, his mother, Duncan Grant and James Holland all still had rooms and studios. It was to this address that Browne's last letters to her friend Watson, who took on the role of AIA secretary in May 1936, were directed – from which a sense of how accidental the fateful choices were that Browne made during the last weeks of her life has been gleaned.

Much would be made in the following year of words she had written to Watson before leaving. Watson had evidently challenged her about her faltering artistic activity, to which Browne replied:

> If painting and sculpture were more valid and more urgent to me than the earthquake which is happening in the revolution, or if these two were reconciled so that the demands of one didn't conflict (in time, even, and concentration) with the demands of the other, I should paint and make sculpture. Do you honestly think that any sort of Party job is an escape, for me? Perhaps you do. I have let you think that, cursing myself for not being able to paint, for being a paralysed fool ... I think the first and true reason is actual conditions in the world today which stop one from painting when there are other things to be done like this trade union stuff and the AI. Other reasons personal not possible to discuss, obscure.

As has been forensically analysed by the historian Tom Buchanan, the idea that Felicia Browne had made some definitive and irrevocable choice between art and politics is erroneous: 'in Spain she not only continued to sketch, producing some of her best work, but also to see the world with an artist's eye.'[55]

Her arrival in Barcelona coincided with the build-up to the People's Olympiad, the democratic sporting riposte to the International Olympic Committee's collaboration with Hitler in Berlin. Its parallel in the art world was the exhibition *The Olympics under Dictatorship*, about to take place in Amsterdam with 300 works from 150 artists, including works by Nevinson, Peri, Rea, Pissarro, Dismorr, Simon, de Sausmarez, Watson, Weight and Rowe among a contribution of twenty-two sent by the AIA.[56] Like the Soho Square show it also contained documentation, cartoons (including Low's), photographs and drawings illustrating Nazi repression and manipulation of education, science, theatre, literature, film and music.

Six thousand athletes had registered to take part in the Barcelona Games, but with borders closing and the city falling under the control of

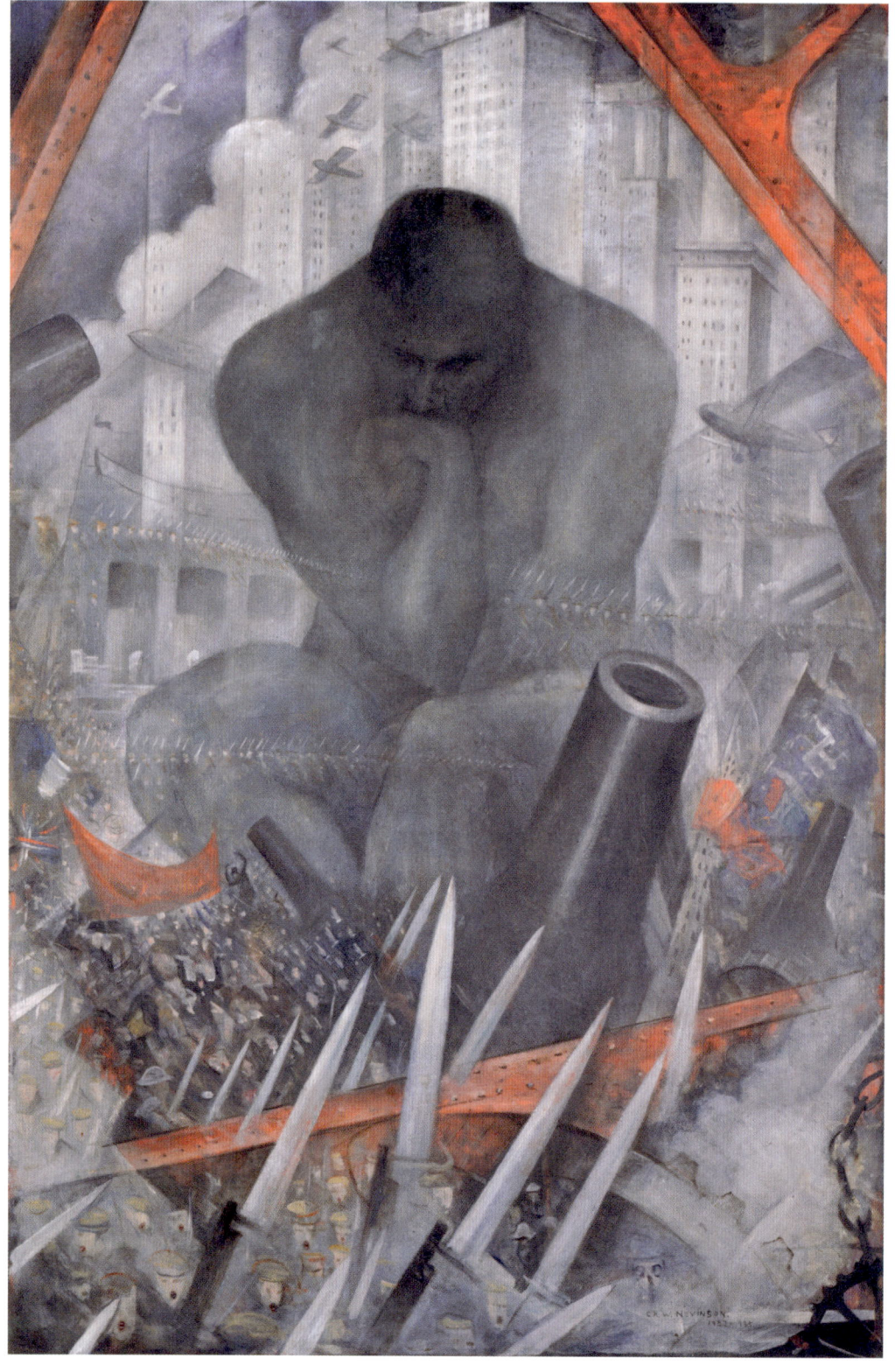

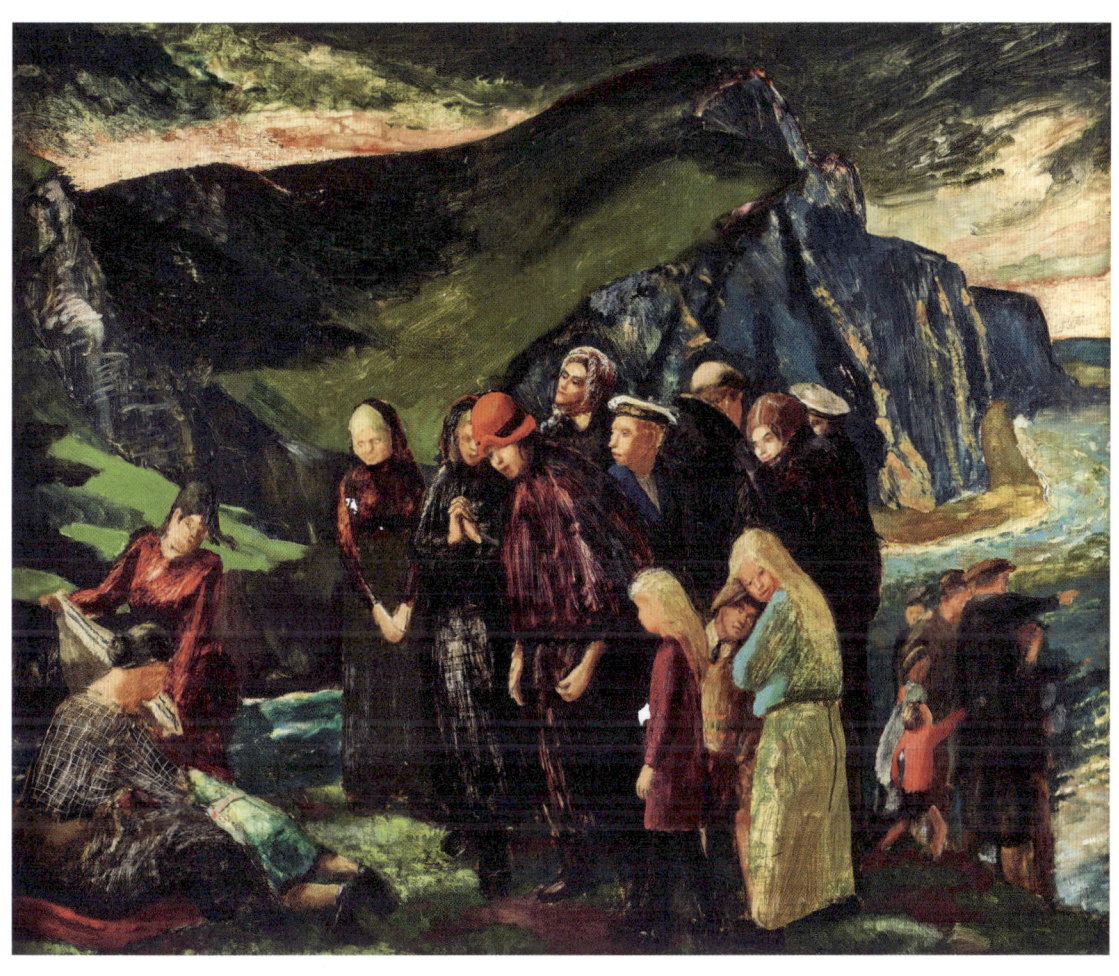

4.19 C. R. W. Nevinson, *The Twentieth Century*, oil on canvas, early 1930s. 183.7 × 122.5 cm (72⅜ × 48¼ in.)

4.20 Carel Weight, *La Symphonie Tragique*, oil on canvas, 1936. 99 × 122 cm (39 × 48⅛ in.)

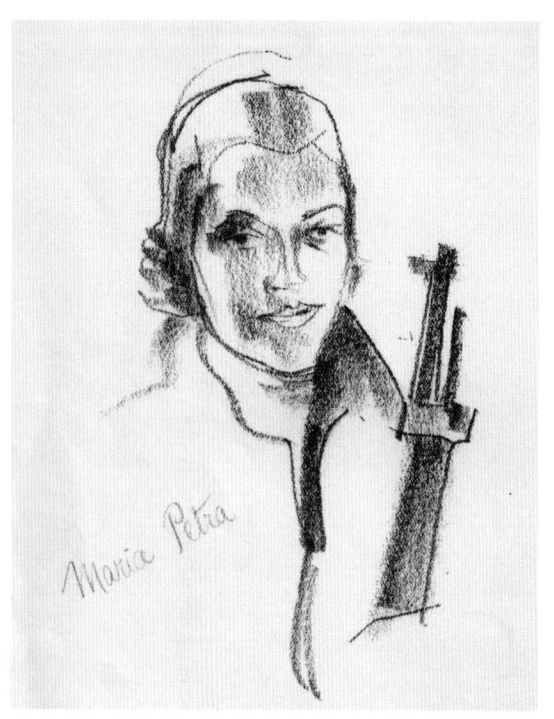
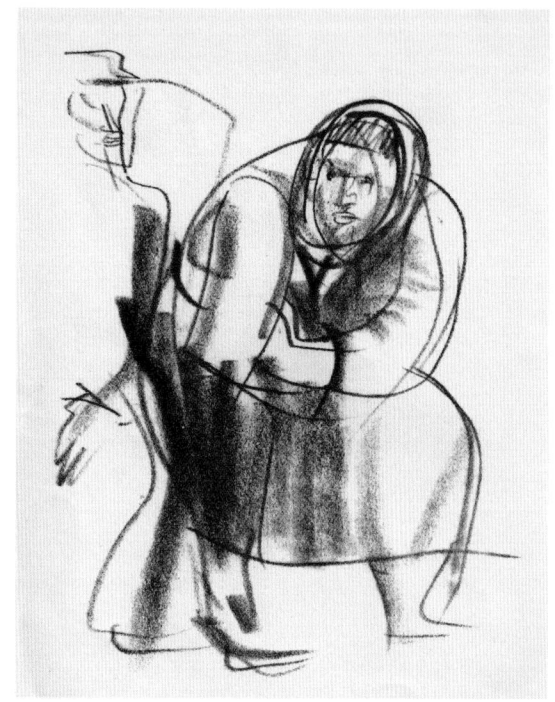
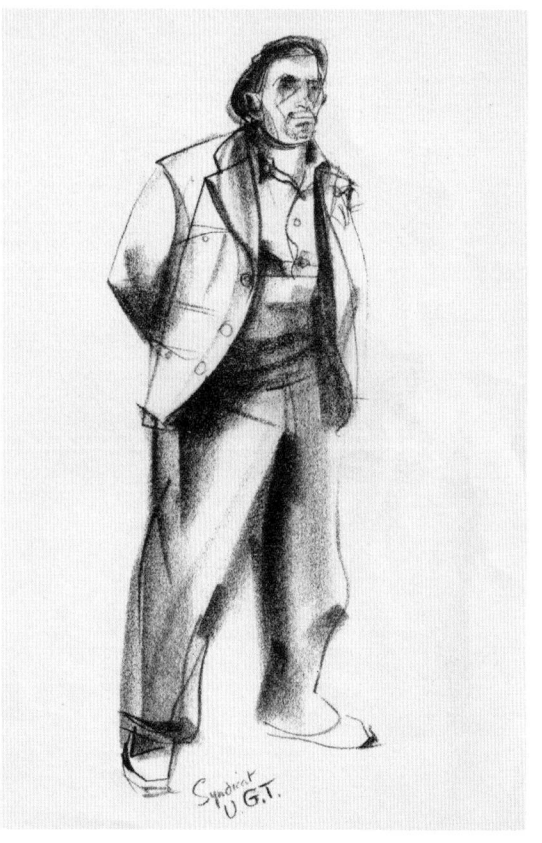
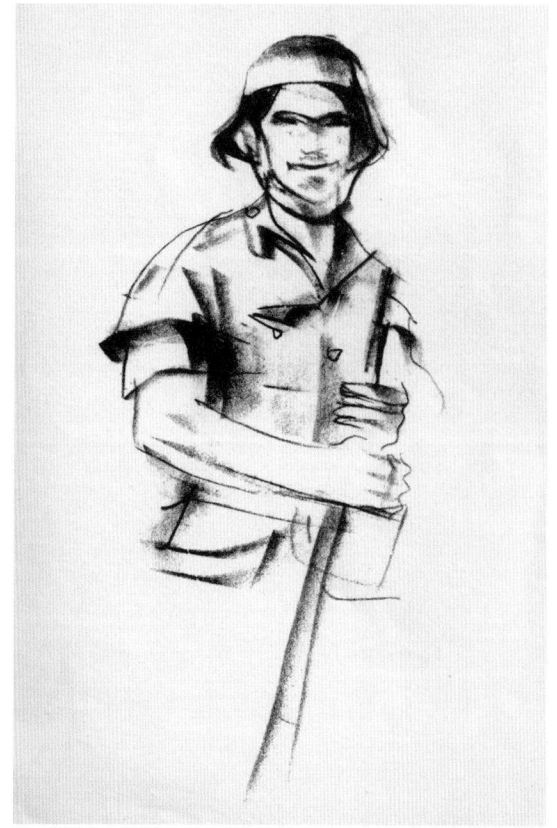

militia groups, the event was hastily cancelled; and Browne found herself alone as Bone and the *Daily Worker* reporter Claud Cockburn left to report developments on the Aragon front. In the following days Browne 'contemplated a range of options including escape into the countryside, pursuing her own journalism, joining the militia and relief work'; in the event she travelled west towards the fighting at Saragossa, but frustrated in this she decided to make for the Pyrenees with its possibilities for sketching, which as she let Watson know 'had been my original intention in coming here'.[57] However, soon after turning north, she was detained for interrogation as a potential spy and taken to the Casa del Pueblo in Lérida, where she sketched her captors.

Returning to Barcelona after being exonerated, and now convinced there was 'no prospect of exploring, painting, or getting anywhere beyond this monstrous city', she applied to work with the Socorro Rojo (Red Aid) but was not needed; following that her days were spent drawing, 'doing it up with black ink' in case the *Daily Worker* might take her work. On 3 August she enrolled in the communist militia and two weeks later, barely equipped and little trained, she was at Tardienta, eight kilometres from the porous Aragon front. On 22 August she volunteered for a raid across no man's land to plant explosives on the railway supplying rebel-held Saragossa; that evening, after a hike of twelve kilometres the party of ten succeeded in their objective, but were surprised by Nationalists whose fire hit an Italian volunteer, whereupon, in the words of a survivor: 'Felicia wanted to bring first aid to the wounded comrade. When she reached him, the Fascists directed their united fire against the two of them. With several wounds in the breast and one in the back, Felicia, our brave fighter in the cause of Freedom, sank dead to the ground.' Both bodies had to be abandoned, but a sketchbook 'full of first-rate studies of the militia' was among the personal possessions recovered, and three weeks later Tom Wintringham, future commander of the British Battalion of the International Brigade, despatched it from Barcelona, suggesting the AIA auction it to raise money for Spain.[58]

*****

Nan Youngman recalled sitting on a Cornish cliff while the 1935 Peace Ballot campaign had been under way, saying 'I don't know anything about politics and I don't care (though I had always voted labour) I went on to say that the only thing I was sure of was that I was a pacifist. It seemed so simple then.'[59] Over the eight years since leaving the Slade she had painted, exhibited with Lucy Wertheim's Twenties Group and the London Group, and – absorbing the influence of Marion Richardson

4.21–4.24 Felicia Browne, Drawings of Republican militia and supporters, crayon, 1936. Each 24.8 × 18 cm (9⅞ × 7⅛ in.)

at the London Day Training College – had become an inspiring part-time art teacher. Holding that pupils' artwork should spring from self-expression unconstrained by mimicry of academicism, she had organized a revelatory exhibition of children's art in Burlington Gardens five years before, an event which stimulated new fields of enquiry for a visiting Herbert Read. Travelling to New York with material from the show, she had discovered the denim jeans and blue cotton shirts which had since become her trademark.

But this August bank holiday weekend, eating lunch on a Cornish beach after a solitary swim, she glanced at the *News Chronicle*: 'suddenly my eye was on the statement that Felicia had been killed. I shouted NO, and my hand went down, trying to blot it out … at last I realised I was living in history.' Returning to London, Nan went 'to see Elizabeth Watson, who had loved Felicia … She had many drawings by Felicia in her studio in Charlotte Street – drawings in Prague and of her fellow soldiers in Spain. The AIA was to mount a memorial exhibition of these and I found myself involved in the preparations.' On a subsequent day the studio door was opened by Betty Rea: 'She was there for the same purpose as I. Betty was on the way out to buy some Heinz sandwich spread for the boys' tea, she said her two sons were upstairs with Elizabeth. Betty was 32, I was 30. She was about my height with curly brown soft hair, eyebrows like two little wings over blue rather-heavy lidded eyes. Her top lip echoed the small wing shape.' Youngman had now met the woman who 'had more vitality' than anyone she ever knew, a 'good warm friend, lover, teacher' who was to be her partner for thirty years, and at the same time she began a period of intense activism centred on the AIA.[60]

For those who had known her, Felicia's death was a visceral connection to the news from Spain, but the sense of a dark corner irrevocably turned was shared far more widely. 'Our thoughts and consciences were turned to Spain', Julian Trevelyan wrote: 'Until the Spanish Civil War started in 1936, there was an air of gentle frivolity about our life in London. True, the Hitler terror had begun, and refugees were pouring into England. Moreover it was clear from Abyssinia and Japan that war and violence were to be the order of the day. We were vaguely uneasy, but also determined to forget about it when we wanted.'[61] Scion of a Bloomsbury-connected academic family network, Trevelyan had studied English at Cambridge garbed in 'large black felt hats such as I imagined artists wore [as] I bicycled through the streets in carpet slippers'; Roger Fry was duly consulted on how best to prepare for life as an artist and predictably advised study in Paris. There Trevelyan, like Bell and Watson, attended the Académie Moderne, before learning to etch at Stanley William Hayter's Atelier 17, gaining entry to a network including Miró, Ernst, Giacometti and on occasion Picasso. After

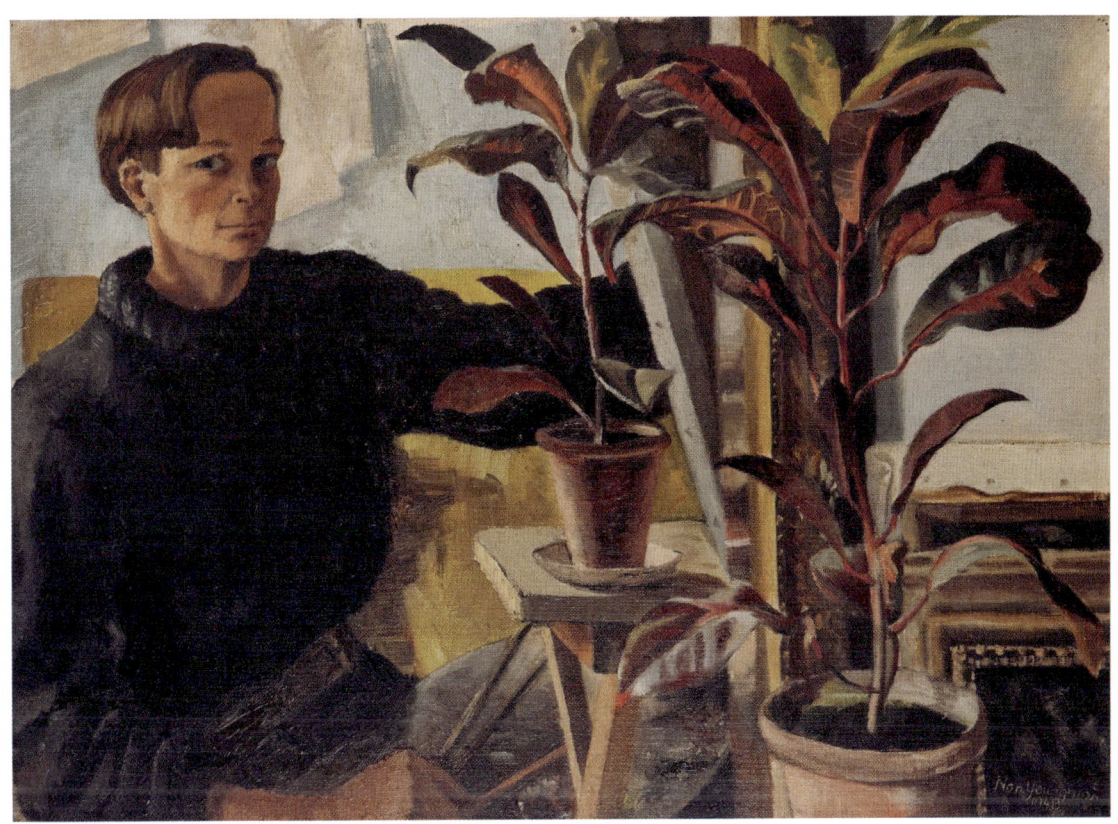

4.25 Nan Youngman, *Self-portrait*, oil on canvas, 1954. 49.5 × 69.5 cm (19½ × 27⅜ in.)

travels in Eastern Europe, he had returned to London in 1935 and was thus both on hand and well connected with Paris Surrealism as Penrose began organizing the international exhibition, which he had just participated in when civil war broke out. By November the London Surrealist Group had issued a trenchant, clear-eyed 'Declaration on Spain' through their house journal, Roger Roughton's *Contemporary Poetry and Prose*, calling 'for the ban on arms exports to the Republic to be lifted. We accuse our National Government of duplicity and anti-democratic intrigue, and call upon it to make the only possible reparation ARMS FOR THE PEOPLE OF SPAIN.'[62]

The eleven signatories to this manifesto – which contrasted the Nationalist murder of Spanish poet Federico García Lorca with the Republican government's appointment of Picasso as director of the Prado – included Nash, Moore and Read as the group put itself in the vanguard of articulating a chilling reality. At the time of *It's Up to Us*, belief in the potential of collective security and League of Nations negotiations as viable responses to Mussolini's aggression in Abyssinia and Hitler's reoccupation of the Rhineland had seemed just about tenable. However, a new era had now dawned with the non-intervention agreement – sustained by a Conservative cabinet including at least six supporters of Franco[63] – and during it international agreements would be shaped to appease dictators at the expense of democrats by those who preferred fascism to socialism. The 'Declaration' was a démarche within the artistic network that meant A. L. Lloyd – even as he was unfavourably comparing the 'fake revolutionary' nature of their art with Socialist Realism in the pages of *Left Review* – had to acknowledge that the London Surrealists had their response right.[64]

On 15 October, less than two months after her death, the AIA's memorial exhibition of Felicia Browne's drawings was opened by Jack Hastings in a vacant club hired for the occasion in Frith Street, Soho. Elizabeth Watson had shown Felicia's work to Duncan Grant, who wrote: 'I do not think I should have ever thought of them as sculptor's drawings had you not told me. They are so alive, but they exist on their own merit ... even the slightest express such a tense awareness of character ... something deeply felt is expressed in a way that is quickly comprehended ... she seems to have been gradually extracting from her drawing a wonderfully flexible and personal language.'[65] Critics praised the exhibition based on artistic merit alone, evidence of 'great gifts used with integrity', a matter of ineffable sadness given that the artist herself had both lacked confidence in her own varied talents and gained but scant recognition while alive – realities acknowledged in an anonymous and insightful appreciation, possibly written by Ralph Fox, which prefaced *Drawings by Felicia Browne*, published in parallel with the exhibition by Lawrence & Wishart 'with all profits to Spanish Medical Aid'.[66] Writing in the first issue of an expanded AIA *Artists' News-Sheet*, its editor Percy Horton applauded 'brilliant characterisation achieved with the utmost sureness and economy ... Here was an artist who escaped from the studio and the posed model and got near to the heart of life – especially the life of the common people.'[67]

One hundred and seventy of the 257 drawings were sold in two weeks with £150 profit cleared for Spanish Medical Aid, which had been formed less than a month after the military revolt with Cristina Hastings as joint-treasurer, sending out twenty-five doctors, nurses and support staff eight days later.[68] Appeals at an Albert Hall rally led the AIA to return to Frith Street in December with *Artists Help Spain*, an exhibition of donated works including John, Epstein, Paul Nash, Lucien Pissarro, Gill, Grant, Vanessa Bell, Ben Nicholson, Moholy-Nagy, Ethelbert White, Ravilious and Bawden. Barnett Freedman acted as auctioneer on opening night and £260 was raised in all, enabling despatch of a lorry loaded with medical supplies to the British Battalion of the International Brigade four weeks later.

Vanessa Bell experienced Browne's death as both a warning and a harbinger. 'I am really glad you are not in Europe now', she wrote to her son

Julian in China. 'We had a visit from Eliz. Watson in London who came to ask me & Duncan to help with a preface to a catalogue of drawings by her friend Felicia Browne who has been killed fighting in Spain ... which does seem a terrible waste of someone gifted as she evidently was ... I am glad my dear that I don't have to reconcile myself to you rushing off to Spain. I think though, if it were necessary I could find plenty of arguments against your doing so – but I wonder if they'd prevail?'[69] At this point though she can have had little notion that the consequence of her fears and his desire to fight, after 'so many arguments', would be his enrolment six months later as an ambulance driver with Spanish Medical Aid.

*****

October's *Left Review* carried two of Browne's Spanish sketches as a preview of the memorial exhibition, along with an article by the Alpha Group on 'Artists and the People's Front'. Noting that 'the old fear that organisation is the death of individual ability is disappearing', it referred back to the AIA's formation of a group to handle propaganda 'with the efficiency of an advertising agency' and its ability to offer 'expert assistance and advice to those parties and organisations of the Left, whose programmes *must* include the overshadowing questions of Peace and War'.[70]

As they looked to Spain, there was now a palpable sense for many visual artists that 'their struggle, should they fail, will certainly be ours tomorrow', and nearer home the threat to cultural freedom was highlighted when Jacob Epstein works were attacked with carbolic acid, blue paint and swastika insignias at the London Passenger Transport Board offices and in Hyde Park. Internationally, the Berlin Olympics, with its courtship of establishment figures sympathetic to the 'New Germany', had just burnished a respectable face for fascism, its anti-Semitism and savage repression of political freedom discreetly closeted for the occasion; but in London the mask was about to slip as at least 2,500 Blackshirts, protected by over 6,000 police, attempted to strut their stuff through London's East End, resulting in what would become known as the Battle of Cable Street.

In his eyewitness account of Sunday 4 October 1936, published with five drawings from his sketchbook, James Boswell wrote: 'I nearly fell over the first barricade as I came out of Back Church Lane. There it was, a big yellow lorry, bang across the street and piles of boxes and lengths of timber, broken glass all over the cobbles in front of it ... Down the street another bustling crowd is building a barricade of paving stones. They are levered up with cow-bars and lengths of iron piping and dragged across the street until there is a four-foot-high-barrier. Children come from the houses dragging old junk – a bedstead, a few old picture frames and

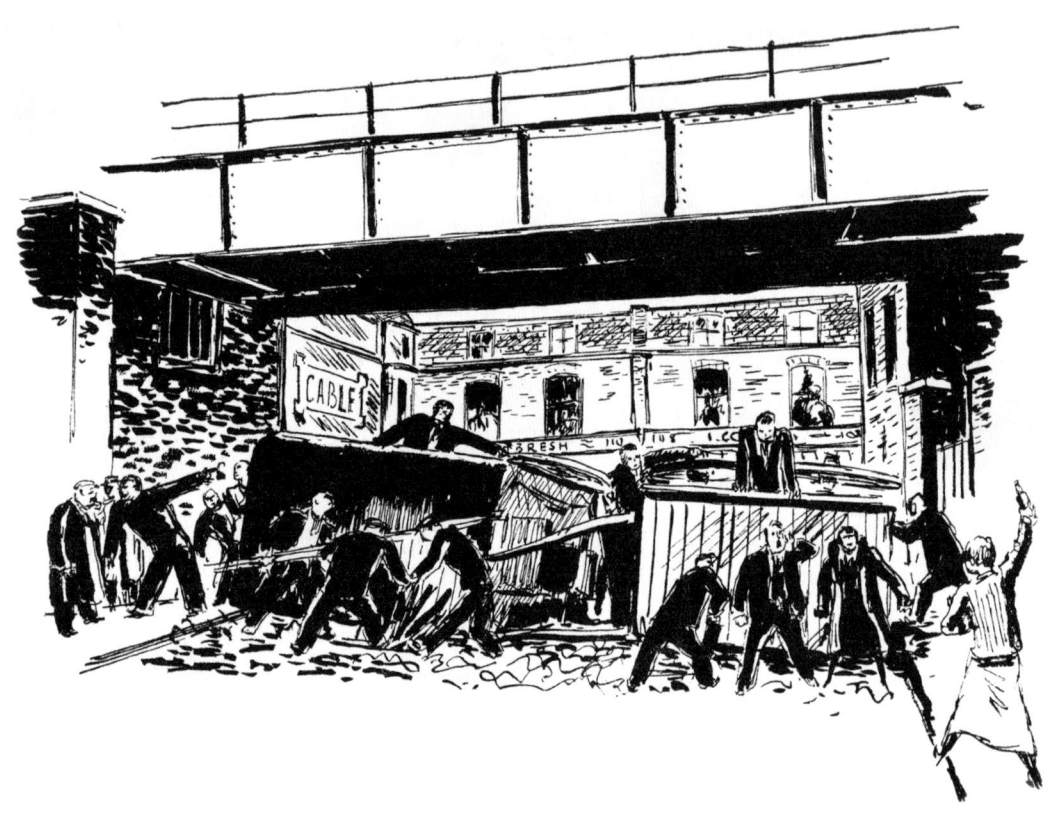

packing cases. The whole is covered with a huge rubbish heap and out of that sticks a great bunch of chrysanthemums – a little faded perhaps, but very jaunty.'

He had travelled to the area on the Underground with Montagu Slater, shadowing a crowd of fascists as they assembled under police guard in Royal Mint Street. Heading east, he lost touch with Slater near Leman Street as mounted police charged the crowd; he sketched an arrest, catching the likenesses of 'hard-faced bigshots in peak caps', and saw policemen 'wrestling with a young boy. His face is streaming with blood, and behind them an inspector jumps about, truncheon raised, trying to get in a blow. The boy is shouting "unity, unity, unity, unity" ... a little way down the street I stopped and began to scribble again. Behind a barricade was a tight mass of people. Just over the barricade – it was the yellow lorry – a solid mass of police were marching towards us. Looking down the slope into the oblique sunlight, you could see in the air a dancing mass of sticks and stones. The people of Cable Street were fighting for the freedom of their street.' Escaping after a police charge, he had evidently recovered his breath by the time he reached the Minories, where a lone policeman, deceived by

4.26 James Boswell, *Leman Street Barricade*, pen and ink line drawing, 1936. 30.5 × 38.1 cm (12 × 15 in.)

his clean collar, indicated his way to the Underground with a 'Second on the left, sir'. Soon after, he heard 'the crash and roll of drums' as 'Mosley's private army marched dejectedly westward'.[71]

Next morning, the Jarrow March departed Northumberland headed for London; but by the time it arrived on the last day of October, BUF thugs had returned to smash up Jewish shops in Mile End Road.

*****

A week before Cable Street, tributes to Felicia Browne opened the AIA's annual meeting at the Friends Meeting House, together with a declaration that 'only when every eligible artist is a member can the AIA realise its aims'. Business reports indicated that over five hundred members had been recruited, after which Cliff Rowe rose to explain the Central Committee's proposal to convene the first British Artists' Congress the following March 'to deal with every problem, economic, political and aesthetic, facing the artist in present-day social conditions'.[72] The plan was to stage a parallel exhibition uniting all aesthetic tendencies and in the run-up to launch a newspaper-style *Artists' News-Sheet*, 'lively and interesting ... so that every progressive artist and art student will wish to take it regularly'. As the next *Bulletin* reported, many prominent figures had pledged their support but 'in the meantime there is loads of work to do. You can help if you will. Write to C. H. Rowe, 42 Devonshire Street, WC1.'[73]

Indefatigable in tasks ranging from organizing worker art classes to improving publication distribution, Cliff Rowe was an exemplar of how Communist Party members, numbering perhaps a tenth of the AIA membership, exercised a guiding influence through the sheer velocity of their commitment. But he was also the only party member on the AI committee who had lived for a sustained period in Moscow and who could contextualize from personal experience the news that sixteen prominent figures, including veteran Bolsheviks Zinoviev and Kamenev, had been arrested, tried, convicted and executed for forming a 'Trotskyite terrorist organization'. Although initially defended as fair by legal figures on the London left, the show trials occurring between August 1936 and July 1937 would steadily add to existing doubts and dissension, creating strengthening headwinds for other popular front activity. Ahead of this, Rowe – in a similar signalling of private unease as his *Lenin and the Peasants* at the time of the Ukrainian famine – had already created *The Fried Fish Shop*, an extraordinary and highly political roman à clef in paint.

Sometime after Anna Meblin left for the USA, Rowe had moved into rooms at 42 Devonshire Street, a short thoroughfare running north–south

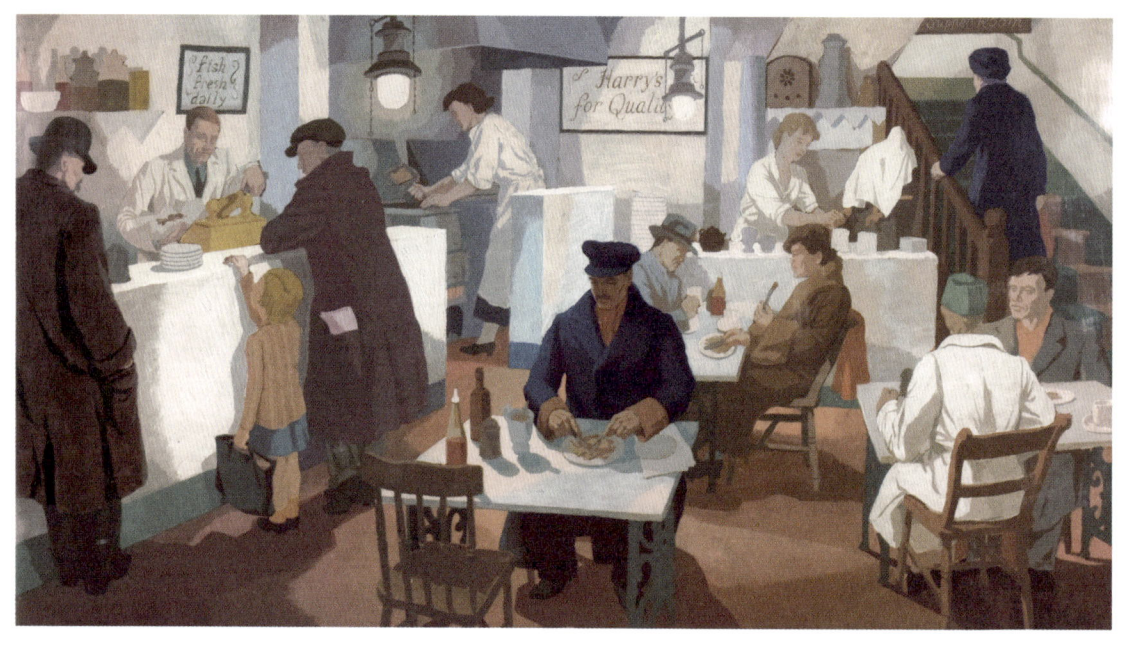

4.27 Cliff Rowe, *The Fried Fish Shop*, oil on panel, 1936. 59.5 × 112.8 cm (23½ × 44½ in.)

between Theobalds Road and Queen Square.[74] Formerly a brushmakers and furniture store, the ground floor now housed Schiavetti's fried fish shop, the setting for a painting that is ostensibly a piece of socially realistic reportage but whose significance as political allegory has been deciphered in the present era by the artist's son-in-law Joe Thornberry. Painted early in 1936, *The Fried Fish Shop* was acquired in late June by Leicester Museum and Art Gallery, almost certainly at the prompting of its assistant curator A. C. Sewter, who Herbert Read – sending in his review of Nikolaus Pevsner's *Pioneers of the Modern Movement* for the new-style *Artists' News-Sheet* – recommended to Percy Horton as a contributor 'who has the right point of view and is very competent'.[75]

The key to the painting's allegory lies in the shop legend 'Harry's for Quality', along with a recognizable Harry Pollitt, the CPGB general secretary, as proprietor behind the main counter and his long-time assistant Kay Beauchamp busy in the background. Pollitt's efforts serving a figure akin to Horton's *Unemployed Man* are watched closely by the equally recognizable bowler-hatted detective from Tudor-Hart's *Sedition*. The restaurant is brightly lit, and at its centre – dining in dark shadow opposite an empty chair – is Joseph Stalin. Beyond his left shoulder Clive Branson, a future volunteer in Spain, eats with his wife Noreen; benefactors of Marx House, they were prominent in the political scene linking party and AIA.

From a table on the right Cliff Rowe scrutinizes Stalin; his companion in white, back turned, is possibly his former lover Anna. Elizabeth Watson, Meblin's successor but two as AIA secretary, busies herself behind a counter in front of a shrouded urn, while a woman in black ascends the stairs, departing life below. Had the painting been created later in 1936 this figure could have been taken as representing Felicia Browne, but that spring Rowe might have had in mind the courageous and not long deceased activist Clara Zetkin. Like Stalin, she too had visited London in the early years of the century, returning to Moscow while Rowe was there, but held very different ideas to Stalin's about the appropriate relationship between freedom, art and politics.[76]

UNITY OF ARTISTS

1937 EXHIBITION AND ARTISTS' CONGRESS

The exhibition of drawing, painting and sculpture in support of Peace, Democracy and Cultural Development will be held at 41 Grosvenor Square, W.1. from 14th April to 5th May. Hours: 10-30 a.m. to 8-30 p.m. daily, including Sundays. Admission 6d. and unemployed free

---

The First British Artists' Congress will be held at 41 Grosvenor Square, W.1, on 23rd, 24th and 25th April. A public meeting will be held at Conway Hall, 23rd April at 8 p.m.

Tickets for the professional sessions on 24th and 25th April for painting, sculpture, industrial design, education, etc., are obtainable from the Congress Secretary, 18 Greville Rd., N.W.4

Supporters of the Exhibition and Congress:
S. R. BADMIN
JOHN BANTING
JAMES BATEMAN
VANESSA BELL
STEPHEN BONE
SERGE CHERMAYEFF
PROF. W. G. CONSTABLE
RAYMOND COXON
JACOB EPSTEIN
JAMES FITTON
GORDON FORSYTH
ERIC GILL
EDNA GINESI
STEPHEN GOODEN
DUNCAN GRANT
MILNER GRAY
VISCOUNT HASTINGS
BARBARA HEPWORTH
GERTRUDE HERMES
BLAIR HUGHES-STANTON
E. McKNIGHT KAUFFER
J. MAYNARD KEYNES
CLARE LEIGHTON
DAVID LOW
JOHN MANSBRIDGE
ROBERT MEDLEY
INNES MEO
HENRY MOORE
PAUL NASH
L. MOHOLY NAGY
BEN NICHOLSON
AGNES MILLER PARKER
MARESCO PEARCE
DOD PROCTER
ERIC RAVILIOUS
HERBERT READ
FRANK RUTTER
SIR MICHAEL SADLER
HOWARD WADMAN
EDWARD WADSWORTH
ETHELBERT WHITE

THE EXHIBITION AND CONGRESS ARE ORGANISED BY THE ARTISTS' INTERNATIONAL ASSOCIATION, 10 FITZROY STREET, W.1

PRINTED IN ENGLAND AT THE KYNOCH PRESS, BIRMINGHAM.

CHAPTER FIVE

GROSVENOR SQUARE

At some point in January 1937 Cliff Rowe, Misha Black, Betty Rea and Percy Horton agreed to postpone the opening of that year's AIA exhibition until 14 April, to convene the first British Artists' Congress on the second weekend of a four-week exhibition run, and to take a short-term lease on a cavernous four-storey mansion in the heart of plutocratic Mayfair.

With previous occupants including the late 10th Earl of Chesterfield and the Dowager Lady Nunburnholme, the rococo gilt-and-marble splendour of 41 Grosvenor Square was at first glance an odd choice. However, its vast formal rooms were big enough to debate 'every problem, economic, political and aesthetic, facing the artist' and numerous enough to allow separate displays of Abstract and Surrealist art, as well as five mixed 'galleries' of Impressionist, Post-Impressionist, realist and more academic work.

It was already clear that the call for exhibits was eliciting a massive response – in the event some 1,500 works were submitted and more than 730 were eventually displayed[1] – and the venue was clearly sufficiently capacious for a physical demonstration of the AIA's aim to unite all aesthetic tendencies behind a progressive agenda of 'Peace, Democracy and Cultural Development'. The servants' quarters in the attic were set aside for two elements reflecting more explicitly political AIA activity: an exhibition of worker art evidencing proletarian cultural credentials and a room displaying posters and campaigning broadsheets from France, Holland, Spain and the USA alongside the domestic output of the AIA's own Peace Publicity Bureau.

The intention was to repeat the approach that had worked well for the 1935 Soho Square exhibition *Artists Against Fascism and War*, when celebrity endorsement had lent credibility and enabled a West End presence; but this time, buoyed by increasing membership, the démarche would be to the physical heart of the establishment, the Duke of Westminster's Grosvenor Estate, and the roll-call of supporters reflected an enhanced ambition to shape public policy. To this end, economist John Maynard Keynes, W. G. Constable, director of the Courtauld Institute, Sir Michael Sadler, vice-chancellor of Leeds University, and the political cartoonist of the hour David Low were among early additions to the list of congress

5.1 Unknown artist, *Unity of Artists – 1937 Exhibition and Congress*, poster design, c. 1936. 76.2 × 50.7 cm (30 × 20 in.)

supporters. So too was Victor Gollancz, who had launched the rapidly growing Left Book Club the previous April and who, together with Jack Hastings and a handful of others, now underwrote the not inconsiderable sum of £450 (equivalent to about £26,000 in the mid-2020s) required to lease the mansion and run the event.[2]

For an organization founded by impecunious painters and illustrators forty months earlier, it was an audacious double-headed initiative, with the process of gathering and selecting work, producing a catalogue, publicizing the event, running previews and staffing the show perhaps the lesser of two exacting challenges. To meet it, separate juries were formed to sift different styles of art, with Henry Moore, Roland Penrose and Paul Nash selecting 118 works from 11 countries for the Surrealist display; Edward Wadsworth participating in curating the Abstract section, involving prominent contributions from Barbara Hepworth, Ben Nicholson and John Piper along with international figures such as Kandinsky, Léger, Ozenfant and Hélion; and Percy Horton and James Laver, both deeply involved with the Working Men's College in Camden Town, co-ordinating 'Working Men's Groups', whose thirty-seven contributions included nine from the Ashington Group, soon to be known as the Pitmen Painters.[3] Beyond this, the desire to bring together as many artists as possible under the AIA banner led to acceptance of work from a further five hundred artists, the sheer weight of exhibits spilling out of available rooms to be hung in corridors, on staircases and along ornamental balustrades.

In parallel with the assembly of the show ran the sensitive task of crafting a policy agenda to engage support from the broadest possible swathe of opinion. Despite the tenor of the times internationally, the decision was taken to give the congress a strong domestic and professional focus. The push for 'the unity of a broad front' was to centre on economic issues, stressing the progressive potential of reform for artists, industry, government and the public realm. This, it was hoped, would bring into the fold other artists' groups – such as the New English Art Club, the London Group and specialist professional societies – as congress sponsors and potential participants in a cultural popular front.

By January 'Professional Commissions' had been established on painting, sculpture and engraving, teaching, students and industrial and commercial art; their task was to develop practical recommendations based on a broad understanding of all relevant issues and a critical reading of the recent slew of government reports that had highlighted problems without securing solutions. It was a process that Quentin Bell and Nan Youngman became involved in after being elected chair and secretary of the group respectively; dealing with art education, Youngman recalled confiding in Bell that, 'I didn't know what a Minute was. He said he didn't know

5.2 Otto Freundlich, *Komposition*, pastel on paper, c. 1935–37. 53.2 × 37.5 cm (21 × 14⅞ in.). The artist was one of nine prominent international contributors to the ground floor Abstract gallery at 41 Grosvenor Square

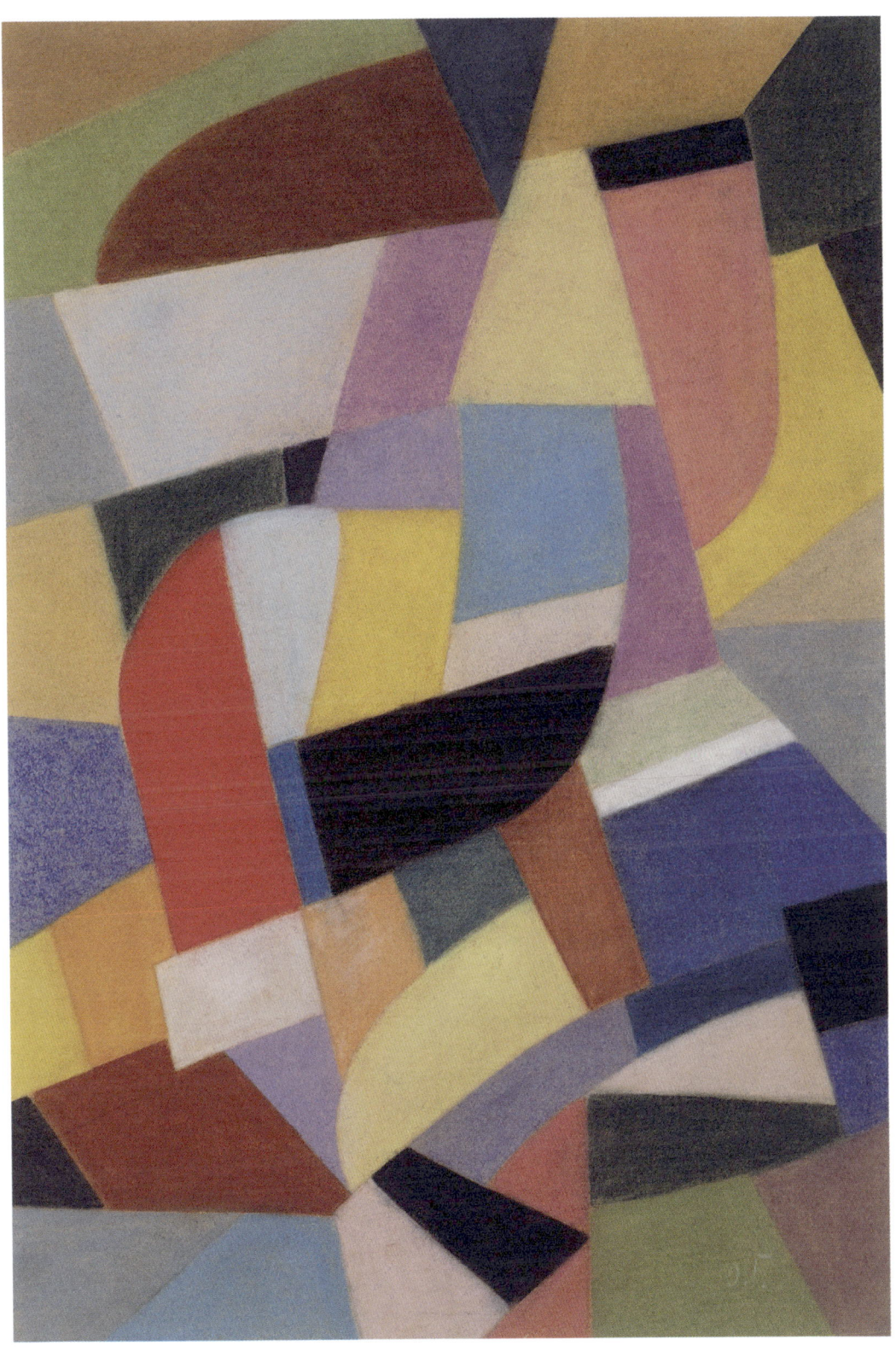

GROSVENOR SQUARE

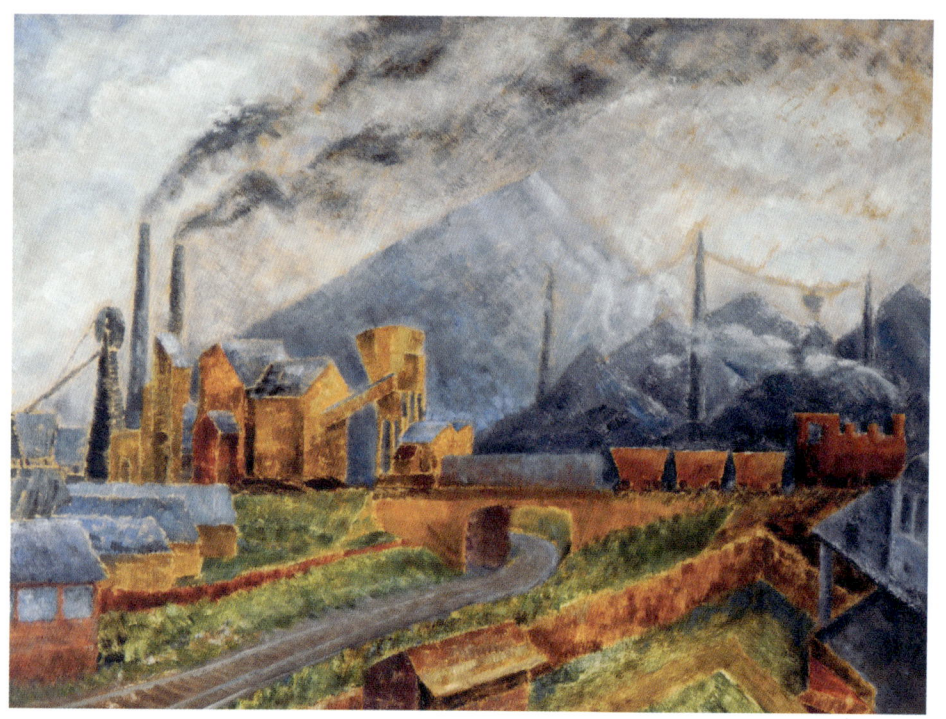

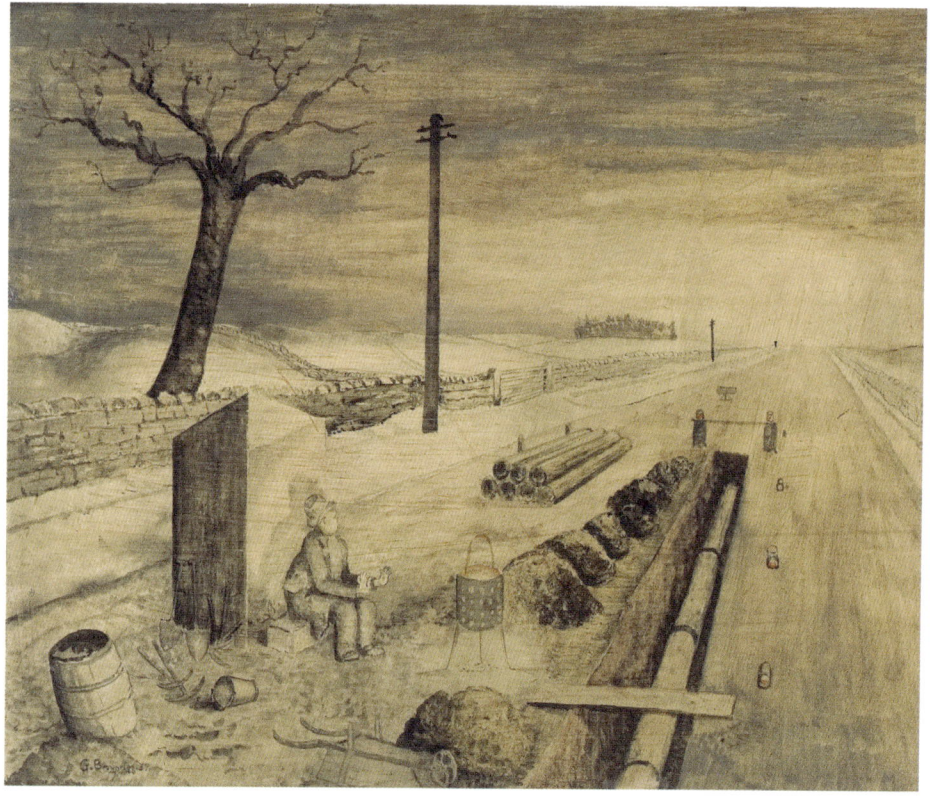

5.3 Harry Wilson, *Ashington Colliery, Northumberland*, oil on paper, *c.* 1936. 37 × 51.5 cm (14⅝ × 20⅛ in.)

5.4 George Brownrigg, *Dawn*, Walpamur household gloss on plywood, 1937. 50.5 × 60.5 cm (20 × 23⅞ in.). Brownrigg and Wilson were two of the seven 'Pitmen Painters' who exhibited at Grosvenor Square

5.5 Ethel Walker, *Vanessa*, oil on canvas, 1937. 61 × 50.8 cm (24⅛ × 20 in.); cat. 130 at the AIA Grosvenor Square exhibition

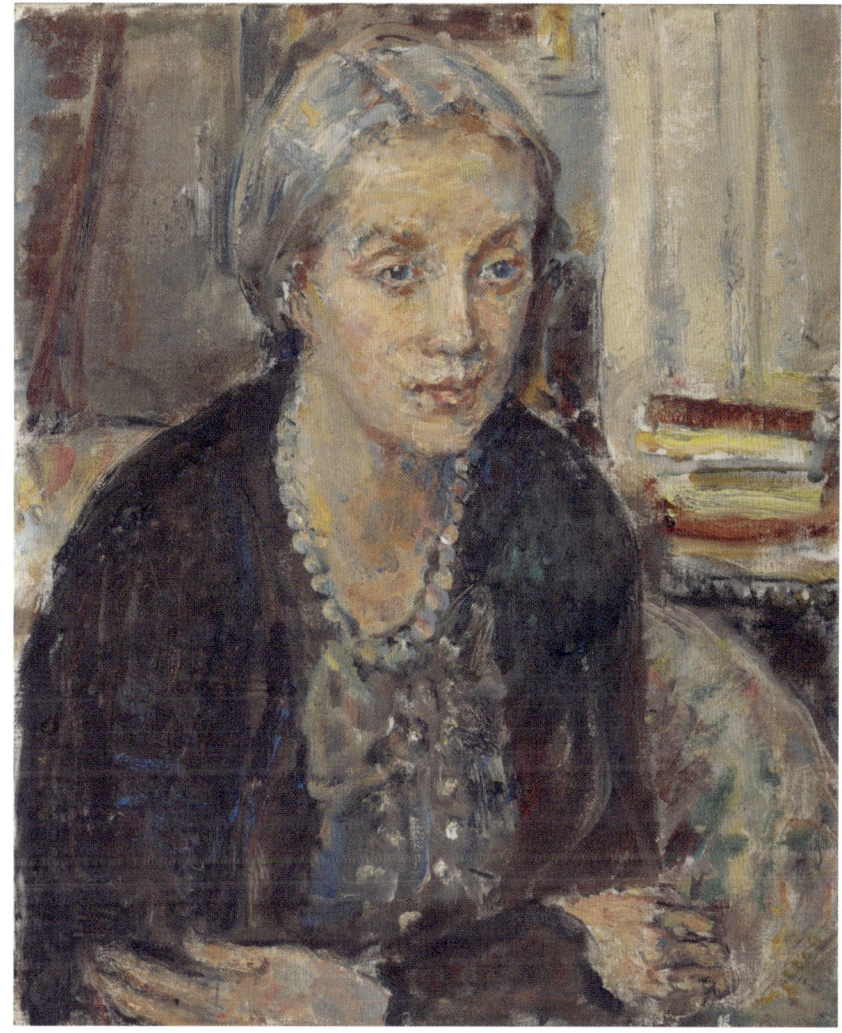

either. Cliff Rowe (a Communist painter) was the most experienced and I learned much from him.'[4]

By April the fourth issue of the new-style *Artists' News-Sheet* was carrying fresh endorsements from Frank Rutter, Ethel Walker, Charles Cundall, Herbert Read, Clare Leighton and James Bateman, and 109 wide-ranging draft recommendations had emerged from the commissions.[5] Reading them more than eighty years later, many stand out as compellingly practical forerunners of initiatives that would eventually take their place as part of post-war British art policy.[6]

* * * * *

The *Artists' News-Sheet* which announced that a Conway Hall public meeting on 'The Relation of Art to the State and the Public' would open the congress also carried a letter of fraternal greetings from the American Artists' Union. Addressed to Joan Rhoades, Congress Secretary, it was signed by Clarence Weinstock, Stuart Davis's successor as journal editor, and opened: 'The editors of "Art Front", official organ of the Artists' Union of the United States, greet the British Artists' Congress in the name of the organised anti-fascist artists of the United States.'[7] The AU's two thousand-plus members were said to be keen to receive a detailed report of proceedings in London, which *Art Front* would publish on arrival.

Soon after taking up his position as national secretary of the American Artists' Congress the previous spring, Stuart Davis had helped organize *Against War and Fascism*, an exhibition of cartoons, drawings and prints at New York's New School. This responded to events in Manchuria and Abyssinia under the rubric:

> American millions, they look at the photographs of fighting in Asia and Africa, of marching soldiers in many lands and war ships in many seas. But they do not see the war that will soon be calling for them … They see and hate the cruelties, the repressions, of Fascism in Europe. They say 'It can't happen here – we won't let it.' Yet in many communities their basic liberties are now being taken from them while they are being whipped to a blind frenzy of hate against the 'reds'. It is the high duty of artists to make these blind millions see and understand.[8]

As a three-week Manhattan event with an international focus, this AAC exhibition, like its Soho Square counterpart, was always destined for limited cut-through, something the congress now sought to address with a nationwide initiative, even as the Artists' Union was engaged in protracted action to fend off mooted cuts to the Federal Art Project.

In October 1936, while the AIA's Felicia Browne exhibition was open in Frith Street, the AAC had held its own fundraiser 'To Aid Democracy in Spain',[9] but its next venture was far more ambitious: to hold a mirror up to American society through an exhibition of accessibly priced duplicate prints created by one hundred different artists opening simultaneously in thirty cities. Selected by a jury operating an innovative blind tally system, the prints making up *America Today* were also published in book form, prefaced by explanations of the media involved and commentary laying claim to socially engaged realism in the tradition of Dürer, Rembrandt, Goya, Hogarth and Daumier.[10]

Depicting scenes of the Depression, of quotidian working-class family life, of lynching and police brutality, of black culture, urban and class

5.6 Anton Refregier, *American Artists Congress Exhibition*, poster, 1937. 55.9 × 33 cm (22 × 13 in.). The first of four AAC annual membership exhibitions took place in New York in the same month as the AIA British Artists' Congress and Exhibition in London

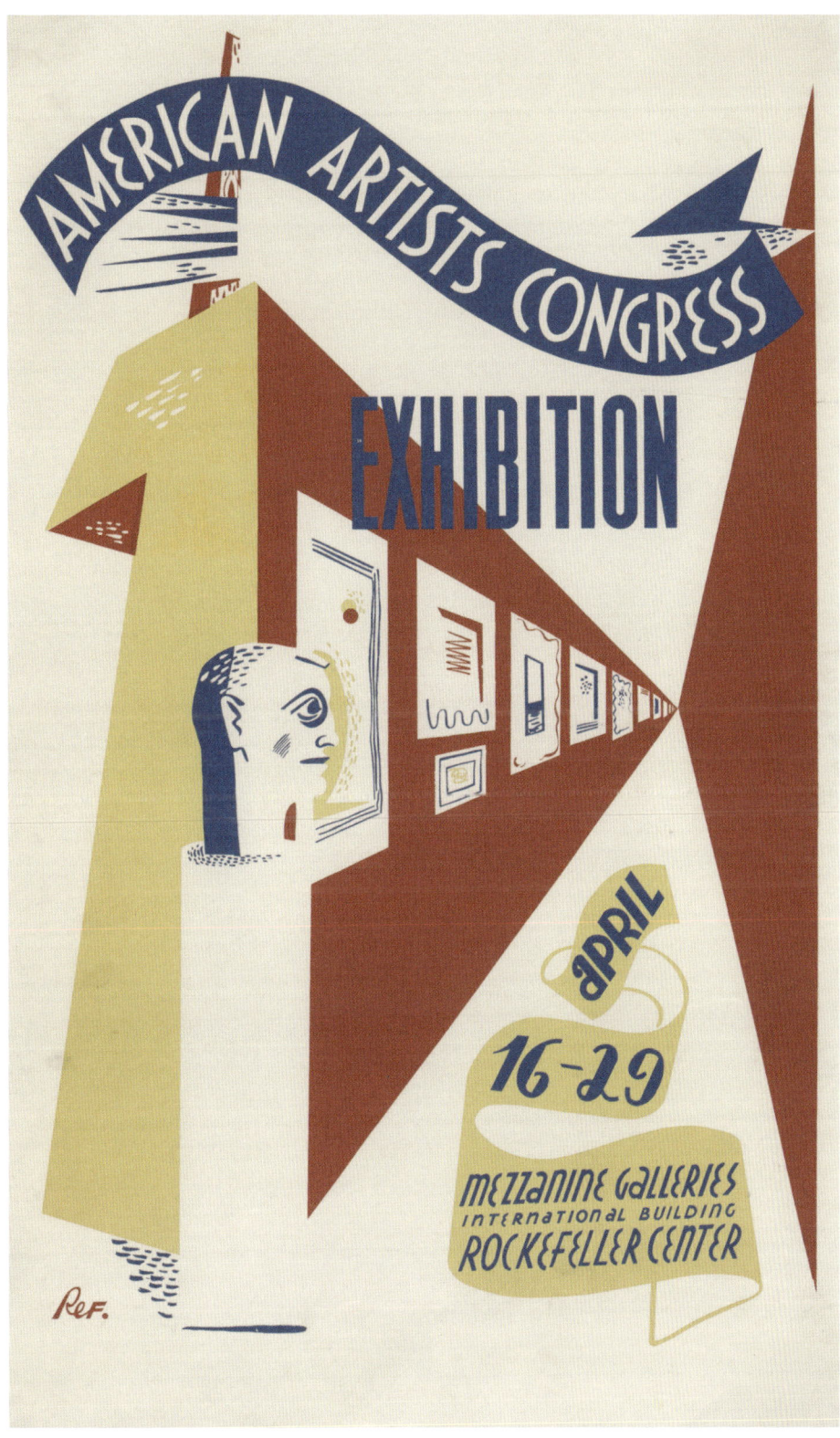

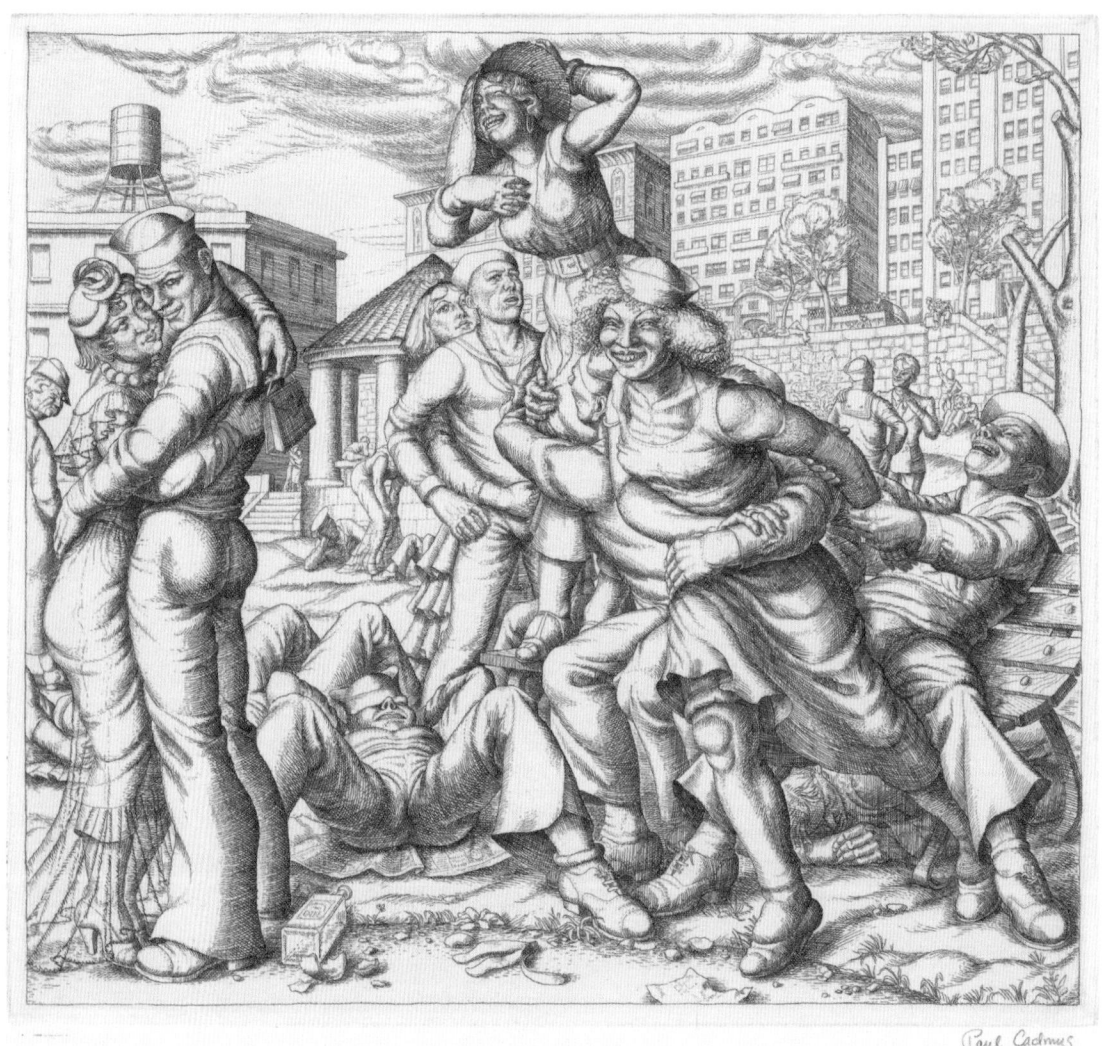

5.7 Paul Cadmus, *Shore Leave*, etching, 1935. 25.4 × 28.3 cm (10 × 11⅛ in.)

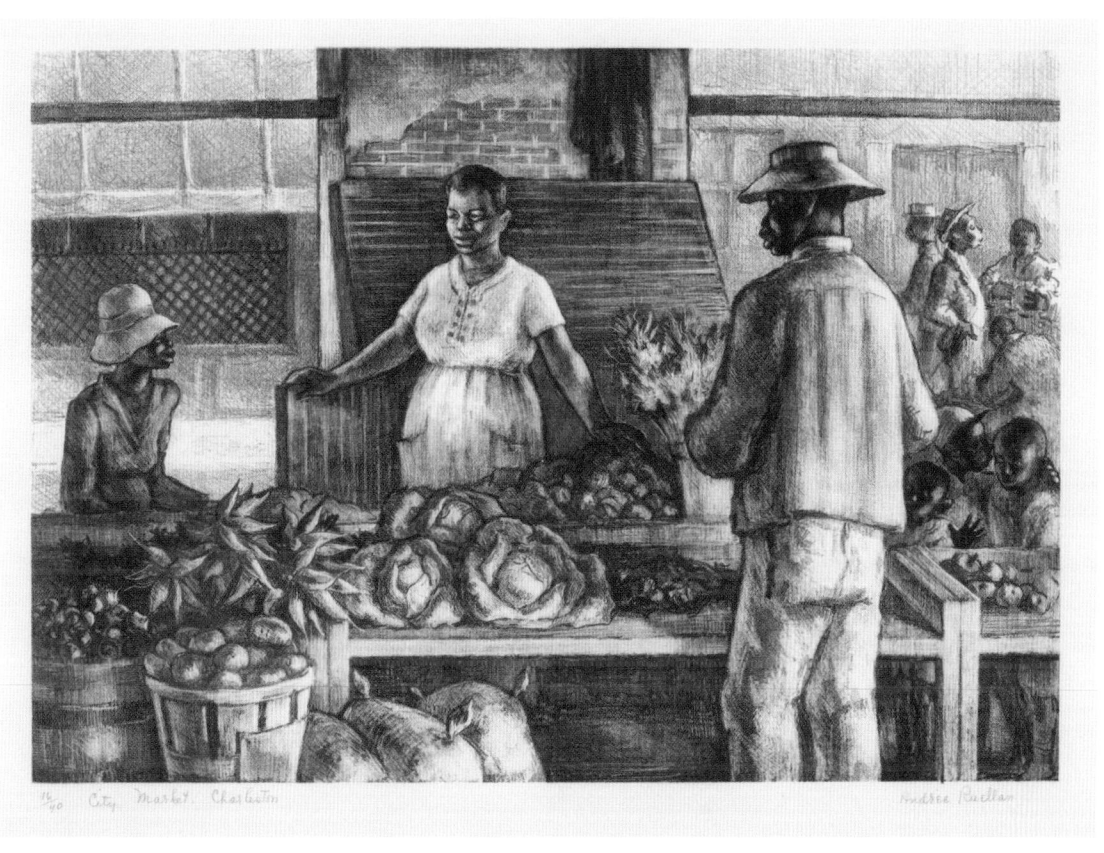

5.8 Andrée Ruellan,
City Market, Charleston,
lithograph, *c.* 1936.
22.5 × 32.7 cm
(8⅞ × 12⅞ in.)

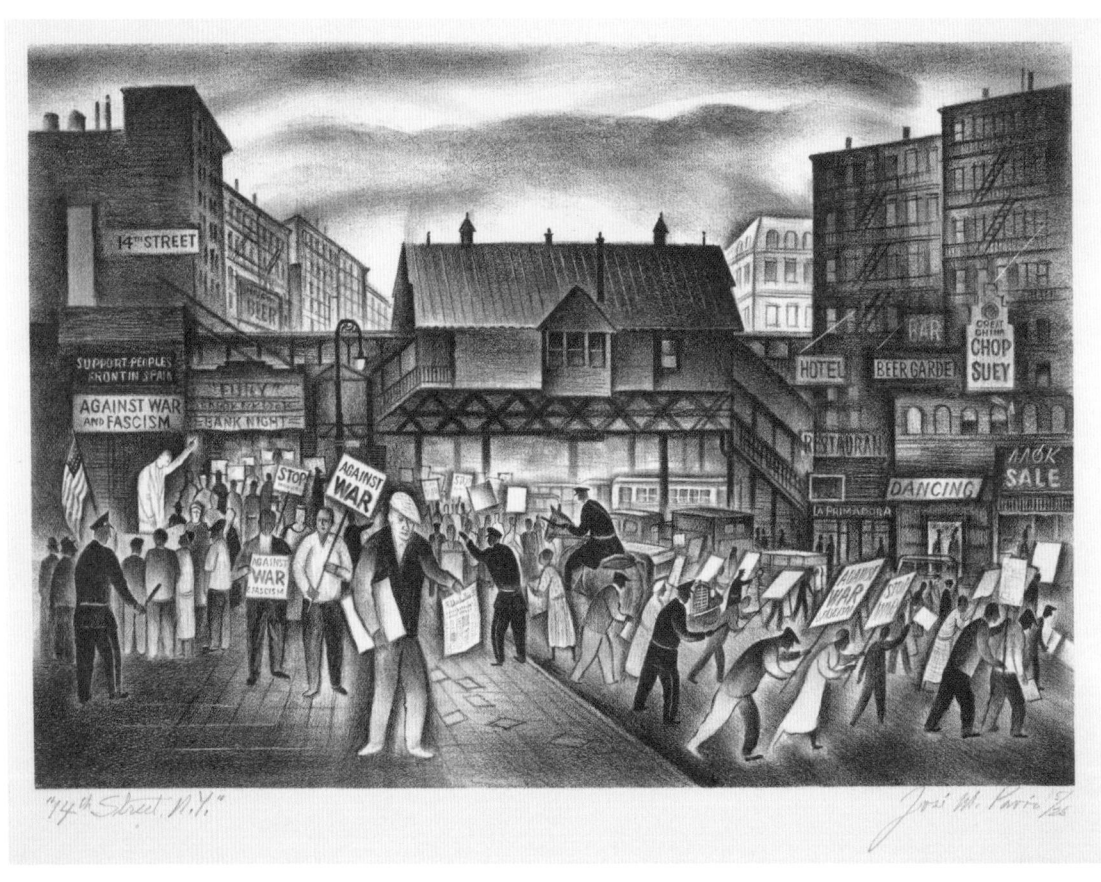

5.9 José M. Pavón,
14th Street,
lithograph, *c.* 1936.
23.8 × 34.5 cm
(9⅜ × 13⅝ in.)

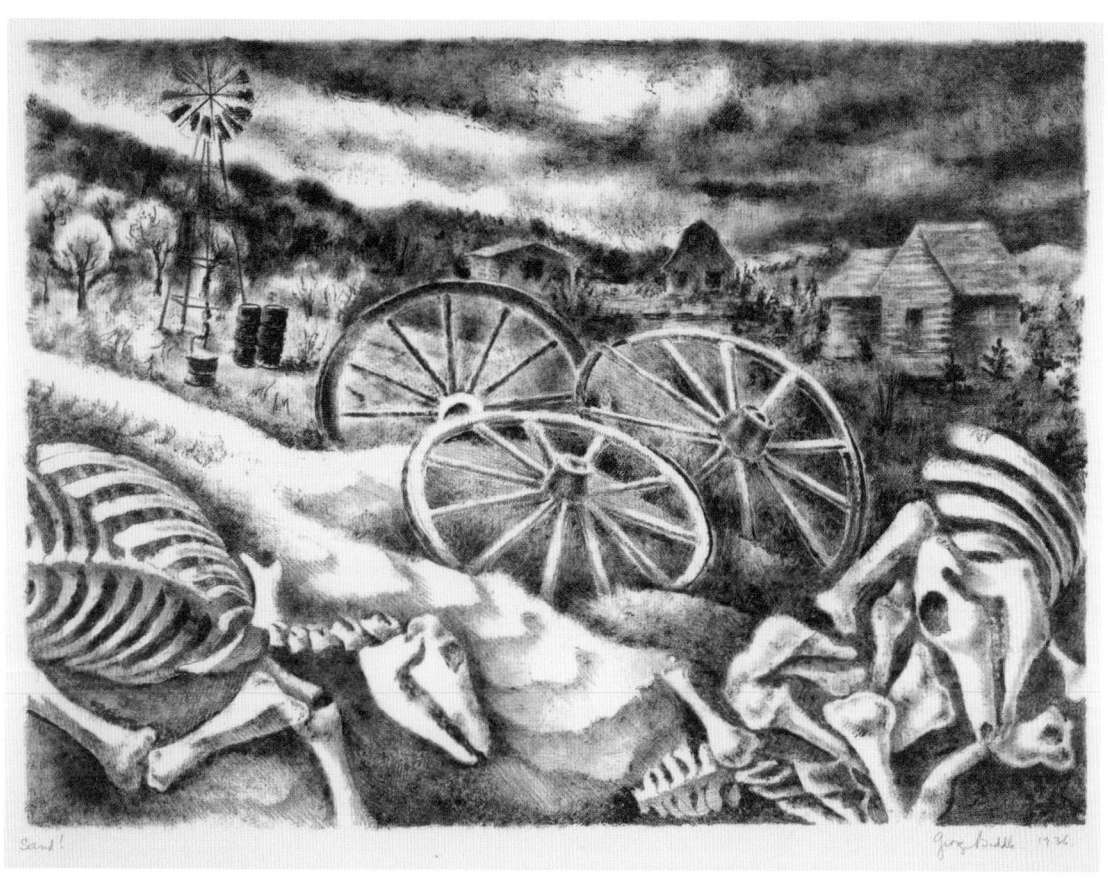

5.10 George Biddle,
Sand!,
lithograph, 1936.
25.1 × 35 cm
(10 × 13⅞ in.)

division, it was an extraordinary conspectus of American life assembled in the belief that 'the present divorce of user and producer, encouraged and fostered by middlemen, for whom there is a specious respect, is an unhealthy and constricting condition'. Just as murals were favoured over easel paintings for their public reach and social purpose, the AAC now moved to promote modestly priced unlimited edition prints for the 'possibilities inherent in this medium for humor, tragedy, satire, and full bodied depiction of life [and] to reach a public comparable in size to the book and motion picture'.[11] It was an example that would in due course cross the Atlantic and help to inspire the AIA's Everyman Prints series as contacts between the two organizations increased.

Despite similarities in outlook and activity – the AAC was holding a 'First Annual Member Exhibition' in New York and seven other cities as Grosvenor Square opened – the existence of the Federal Art Project as a mass employer, and its vast attendant output of murals and graphic art, helped create a climate of industrial militancy quite different to the reality prevailing in Britain. As the etcher and AAC executive committee member Ralph Pearson wrote in the preface to *America Today*: 'Art is taken out of the studio, the gallery and the art museum and put to work in the homes and public buildings of everyday. The artist ceases to be an ornament of the pink-tea, a playboy companion of the dilettante patron, a remote hero with a famous name. He becomes, instead, a workman among workers. He paints murals on a scaffold of planks and ladders. He prints his etchings, lithographs or woodblocks with hands which know ink and rollers ... He works. He produces.'[12]

On 30 November 1936, while addressing a rally of 1,200 members protesting against threatened cuts, Boris Gorelick, AU organizer and close colleague of Pearson and Davis, raised the demand that rather than being discarded as the economy revived, the FAP should become a permanent feature of American society, adding 'from now on, we are on the offensive'.[13] The next day over four hundred members attended a demonstration outside the FAP's Fifth Avenue offices demanding a moratorium on planned firings; when over half gained entry and began a peaceful sit-in, police responded with brutality, wounding 12 demonstrators and forcing 219 into eleven 'paddy wagons'. Paul Block, a sculptor and spokesman for the action, was among those most severely beaten.

Arraigned in two mass sittings two days later, those arrested were convicted of disorderly conduct and received suspended sentences, but the publicity was such that Mayor La Guardia ordered that arrest of AU protesters should cease unless they were violent or destroying property. It was one episode in a season of militancy that succeeded in forestalling lay-offs for six months.[14] After his arrest the lithographer and muralist Joseph Vogel was charged and convicted as 'Che Zan', one of several famous artistic identities assumed for court purposes; shortly after he left for Spain, as did Paul Block.

Shell-shocked on the Córdoba front, Vogel provided illustrations for the newspaper *Volunteer for Liberty* while recuperating at Albacete, before being repatriated to the USA in September 1937. Paul Block served with the Abraham Lincoln Brigade's Third Company, assuming command during the Battle of Belchite; severely wounded soon after, he died in a field hospital on 7 September 1937.

* * * * *

Left Review's report of the congress, shared with the editors of *Art Front*, noted that while the preparatory commissions focused on professional and internal problems, questions of national and international culture excited the liveliest response. At the crowded Conway Hall opening night, gathering 'distinguished critics, artists and representatives of sympathetic bodies assured the Congress of their good will and interest. Among the foreign delegates, a representative of the German artists exiled in Paris had an especially cordial welcome. Before the end of the meeting messages of solidarity were sent to Spanish artists through their organisation.'[15] The congress platform espoused a positive vision of 'Cultural Progress', and

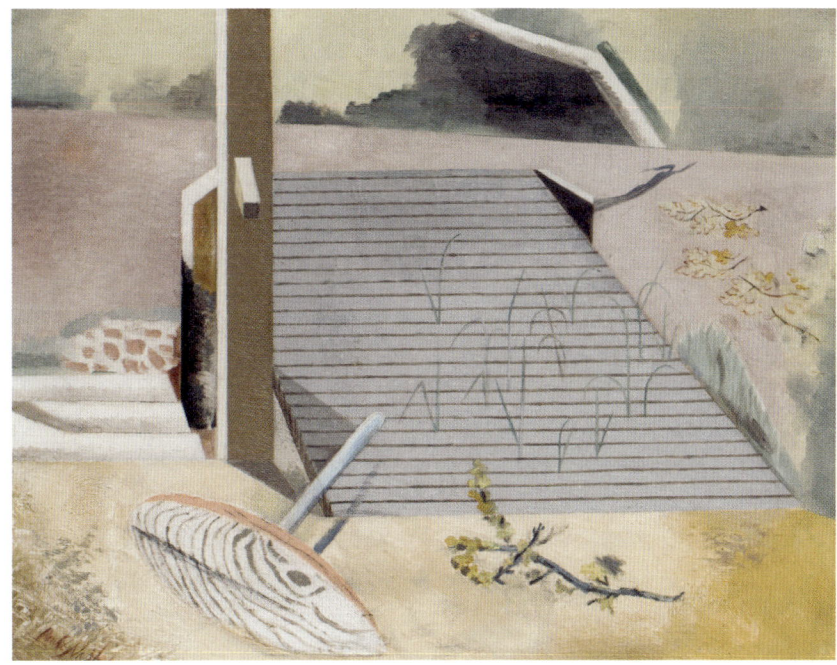

5.11 Paul Nash, *The Archer Overthrown*, oil on canvas, 1931–38. 69 × 89.5 cm (27¼ × 35¼ in.). Subsequently altered by Nash, this work was displayed in its original form as cat. 211 in the Surrealist section at Grosvenor Square, together with Nash's *The Archer*, cat. 203

recommendations were circulated detailing how British government at all levels, educators and industry could assist its realization; but it was suppression of cultural freedom in Germany and fear for its survival in Spain that coloured many of the weekend's debates.

Jack Hastings, presiding over the opening evening's proceedings, had visited Republican Spain the previous September as part of a delegation including Labour MPs and Isabel Brown, the founder of Spanish Medical Aid.[16] Social revolution in the immediate aftermath of the military rebellion had seen the destruction of 150 churches and damage and loss to thousands more, as well as the seizure of private mansions and their opulent contents, provoking a propaganda war in which the right-wing press in Britain, fed by Nationalist sources, had condemned 'red barbarians' as destroyers of Spain's artistic heritage.[17] Returning with evidence that Germany and Italy were arming the rebels in defiance of the non-intervention agreement, Hastings had also been able to attest that loyalist authorities had moved rapidly to control the situation through the work of a junta for the Confiscation and Protection of Artistic Treasures, now part of the Education Ministry.

In the same month, the Republic had bolstered its cultural bona fides internationally by appointing Pablo Picasso Honorary Director of the Prado, but in November indiscriminate Nationalist bombing of besieged Madrid had forced evacuation of its collection to Valencia. Organized by Picasso's friend the poet José Bergamín, it was a dangerous night-time exercise during which the camouflaged van carrying Goya's *The Second of May* and *The Third of May* crashed, necessitating repairs in transit for the iconic masterworks depicting Madrid's 1808 revolt against French occupation.[18] As the Nationalist siege intensified, Hastings back in London made clear his own commitment to the Republican cause with a portable mural depicting Spanish government militia on the march. Painted with a spray gun on aluminium panel – a technique pioneered by Siqueiros which Hastings had used at the Chicago World's Fair – it was one of three works in the medium included in his solo show at the Lefevre that December, now known only from its reproduction in the following month's AIA *Artists' News-Sheet*.[19]

Roland Penrose was another platform speaker who had investigated developments in Spain at first hand, in his case during a six-week tour the previous autumn facilitated by Catalonia's Generalitat, which took in Barcelona, Gerona, Lérida and Valencia. Staying at Mougins, near Cannes, with Picasso and friends when reports of destruction during the anarchist rising first arrived, he had returned to London, taken out temporary membership of the Independent Labour Party, the British affiliate of POUM,[20] and in company with David Gascoyne rendezvoused with art publisher

Christian Zervos, another Mougins habitué, in Barcelona. He was still there in late November to witness the funeral of Buenaventura Durruti, leader of the largest anarchist column and hero of the early anti-fascist victories, who had been killed during the Battle of Madrid. Despite Durruti's position that 'the only church that illuminates is a burning church', Zervos and Penrose authored a report concluding that less than 2 per cent of Catalonia's artistic patrimony had been lost, while a much greater volume of previously unknown unseen art was now in public hands.[21] Penrose felt he had witnessed the confused, at times disturbing, birth pangs of a new society, and returned convinced that – in spite of the shockingly misguided non-intervention policy orchestrated by Britain – democracy and the Republic 'would and must survive in Spain'.[22]

It was a faith that events were sorely testing by April 1937, and a commitment to the Republican cause which led Penrose, working with Moore and Nash to craft the Surrealist presence at Grosvenor Square, to add his signature to the most political publication accompanying the exhibition.[23] *We Ask Your Attention*, a broadsheet whose black text on yellow, overprinted with a vivid red Moore motif, delivered a trenchant analysis of how, under the guise of non-intervention, Britain rulers had become de facto allies of fascism. By contrast, the preface to the exhibition catalogue, in line with the AIA's broad church and alliance-building objectives, mentioned neither Germany nor Spain and had confined itself to an endorsement of pluralism

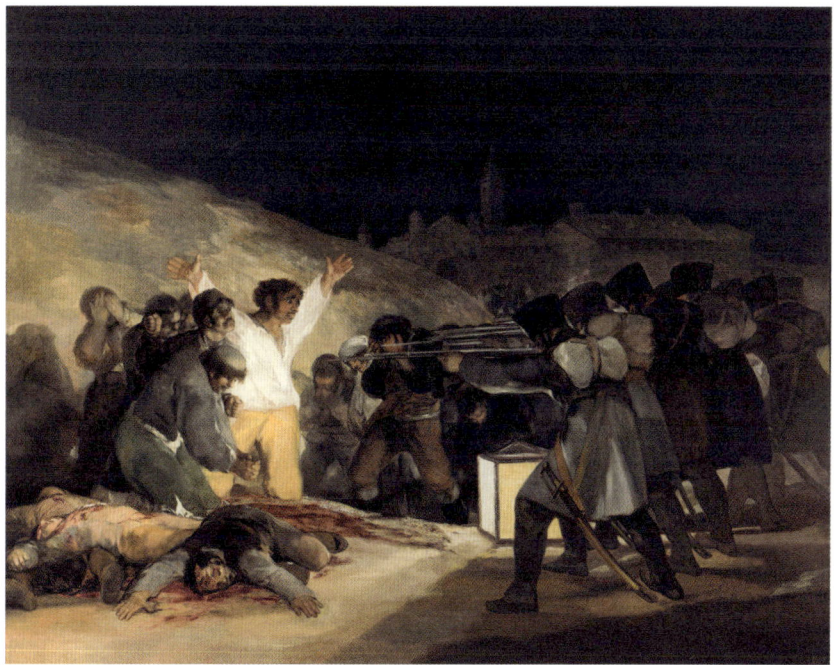

5.12 Francisco de Goya, *The Third of May, 1808*, oil on canvas, 1814. 260 × 340 cm (102⅜ × 133⅞ in.)

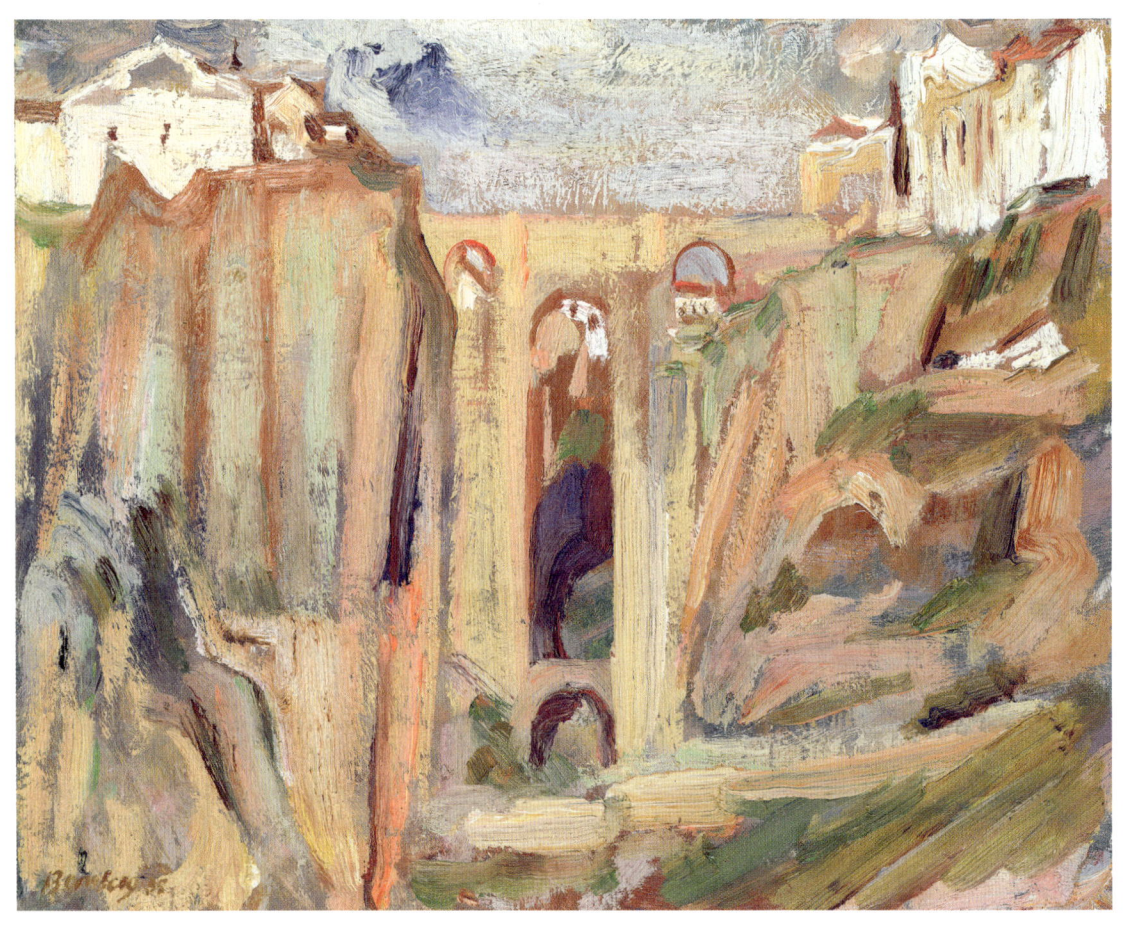

5.13 David Bomberg, *Ronda Bridge*, oil on panel, 1935. 31 × 41 cm (12¼ × 16¼ in.)

and a generalized appeal for artists to organize under the banner 'For Peace, Democracy, for Cultural Progress'.[24] But the Surrealist Group's broadsheet pulled no punches in denouncing the National Government's harassment and criminalization of International Brigade volunteers and in calling for a united front of direct action against the National Government's 'fascism of deceit', combining this with a Surrealist challenge to bourgeois susceptibilities: 'The Revolution which we can bring about must have as its objective the DEVELOPMENT of CONSCIOUSNESS and the WIDER SATISFACTION OF DESIRE ... INTERVENE AS POETS, ARTISTS AND INTELLECTUALS BY VIOLENT OR SUBTLE SUBVERSION AND BY STIMULATING DESIRE'. It was a performative flourish that enabled the visiting critic of the Catholic *Universe* to denounce the AIA and all its works as a manifestation of 'the bitter fruit of subversive ideas' recently cited by the Pope in an anti-communist encyclical.[25]

David Bomberg was another with personal connections to Spain who now became a strong advocate of progressive artists combining – and in so doing unwittingly exposed how difficult it would be for the AIA to formalize organizational alliances. Unlike his friend Pearl Binder, with whom he addressed the International Bureau of Revolutionary Artists in 1933, Bomberg had returned from his sole visit to the Soviet Union disillusioned about the state of art and society there, his brief period of active communism ended.[26] In 1934, penniless and neglected in London, he returned to Spain, where he had painted at Toledo five years before; this time he and his wife moved between Santander, Cuenca and Ronda, then finally to Linares in the Asturian mountains where they witnessed the aftermath of the Franco-led bloodletting that had put down that year's miners' strike.[27] Premonitions of conflict to come then led Bomberg to return to England where, rejoining the London Group after a lapse of fourteen years, he exhibited two Ronda paintings at its November 1936 exhibition.[28]

The show became a target for Professor Rudolf Hellwag, a Nazi operative charged with engineering a propaganda coup by staging a British contemporary art exhibition in Berlin. Circulating promises of generous expenses and likely sales, Hellwag had already been feted by the Royal Academy and the art establishment, including the eminent Sir John Lavery, who, although sending work to 41 Grosvenor Square, was naive enough to opine that the German proposal had 'nothing to do with politics. It is purely and simply an invitation by German artists to British artists.'[29] Lavery was replying to Jacob Epstein's public denunciation of the initiative following an offer from the German Embassy to transport the entire London Group exhibition to Berlin 'with the exception of works that cannot be accepted for political reasons' – a formula embracing the work of

Jewish artists Bomberg, Hans Feibusch, Mark Gertler, Bernard Meninsky and Edward Wolfe. Duncan Grant, Ethelbert White (another congress sponsor) and James Fitton were among the non-Jewish group members who led a fierce opposition and secured rejection of the proposal – a move praised in the January 1937 AIA *Artists' News-Sheet*, which also reported that Goebbels had just issued an edict banning 'non-factual' art criticism in Germany.

Immediately after this Bomberg, acting independently, submitted a motion to the London Group AGM that 'members be prohibited from exhibiting with reactionary groups', that the London Group should 'consolidate with the AIA and the Surrealist Groups in their support of Anti-Fascism in politics and art', that funds should be given to Spanish Medical Aid, and that 'Honorary membership [should] be extended to certain left-wing poets and writers'.[30] All his suggestions were rejected, and April's issue of the *Artists' News-Sheet*, in a portent of difficulties to come, carried a letter clarifying that 'refusal to participate in the exhibition has no political significance whatsoever, and it cannot be too strongly emphasised that the aims of the London Group are purely artistic and that it has no political ties. I am, Sir, yours etc, R. P. Bedford, Chairman, London Group.'

* * * * *

5.14 Barbara Hepworth, *Ball, Plane and Hole*, teak on oak base, 1936. 21 × 61.1 × 30.5 cm (8⅜ × 24⅛ × 12⅛ in.). This work may have been displayed as cat. 91 at the AIA Grosvenor Square exhibition, one of four works contributed by Hepworth

5.15 Henry Moore, *Reclining Figure*, elm, 1935–36. 48.3 × 93.3 × 44.4 cm (19 × 36¾ × 17½ in.). This work may have been displayed as cat. 300 at the AIA Grosvenor Square exhibition

On 10 April 1937 the *Evening Standard* ran a preview beginning: 'In an empty house in Grosvenor Square a committee of artists is at work selecting from among 1500 entries from all over the world', and by the time the exhibition opened four days later a deft promotional strategy had already garnered nationwide attention far surpassing any previous AIA activity. To stimulate notices a photograph of the Surrealist selection committee of Nash, Moore and Penrose at work had been circulated two days previously to the provincial press, together with lists of locally connected participants – alerting, for example, the *Western Mail* that 'Mr John Tunnard of Ruan Major' would be participating, and enabling titles across Yorkshire and the north to link Barbara Hepworth, Edna Ginesi and Raymond Coxon with detailed descriptions of the Ashington Group's oeuvre and the news that a work by twelve-year-old unknown Hazel Owen of Bedale would hang next to Picasso's *Harlequin*.[31]

A private view attended by five hundred on 13 April provided good copy for columnists ('beards and plucked eyebrows could not be numbered'), but also generated some serious reporting of Herbert Read's appeal, delivered standing on a trestle table, for 'professional solidarity' among artists to raise their economic status, defend essential freedoms and recast the

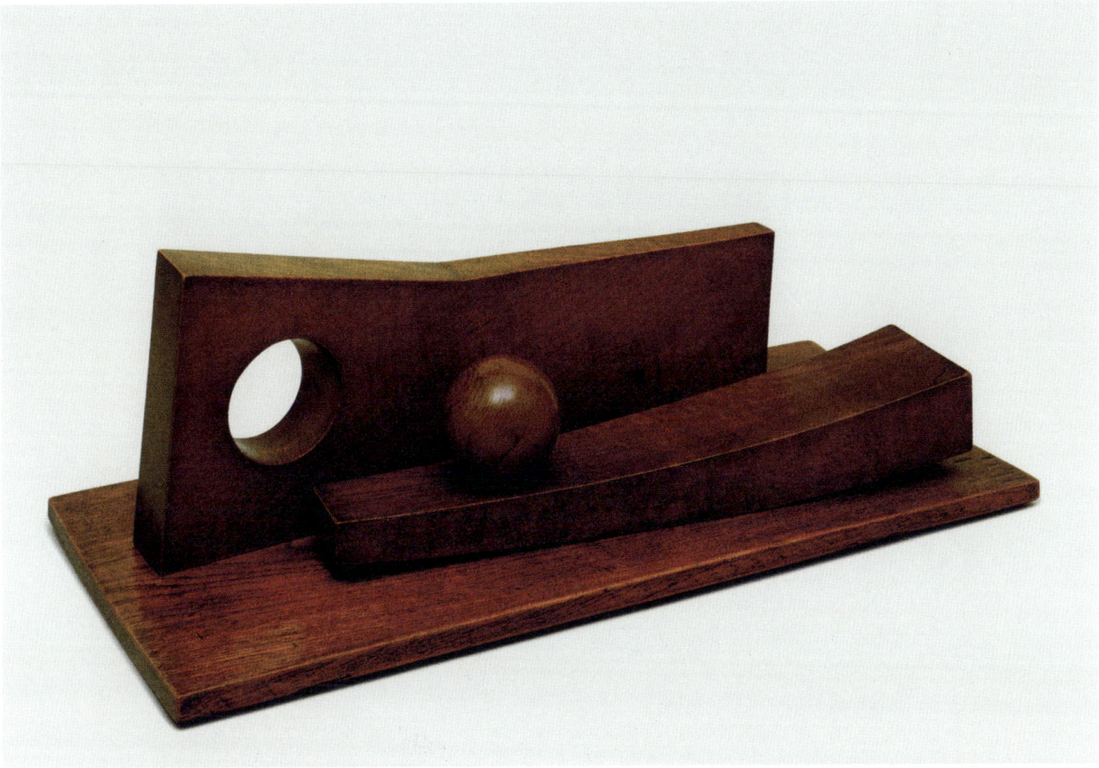

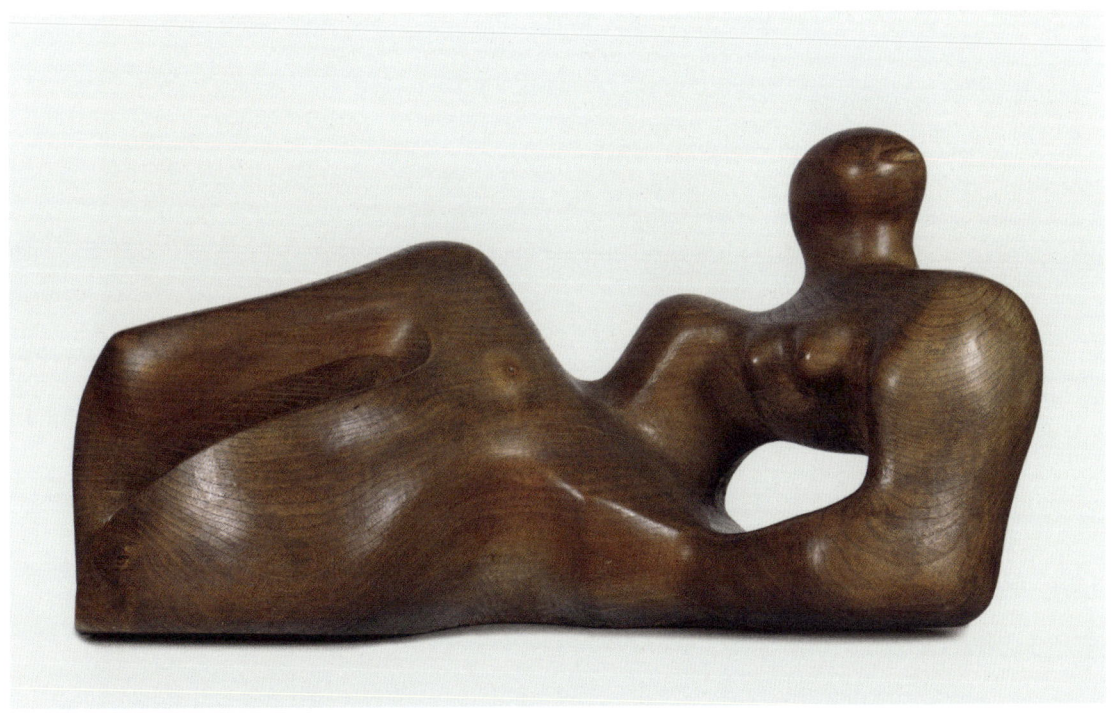

GROSVENOR SQUARE 183

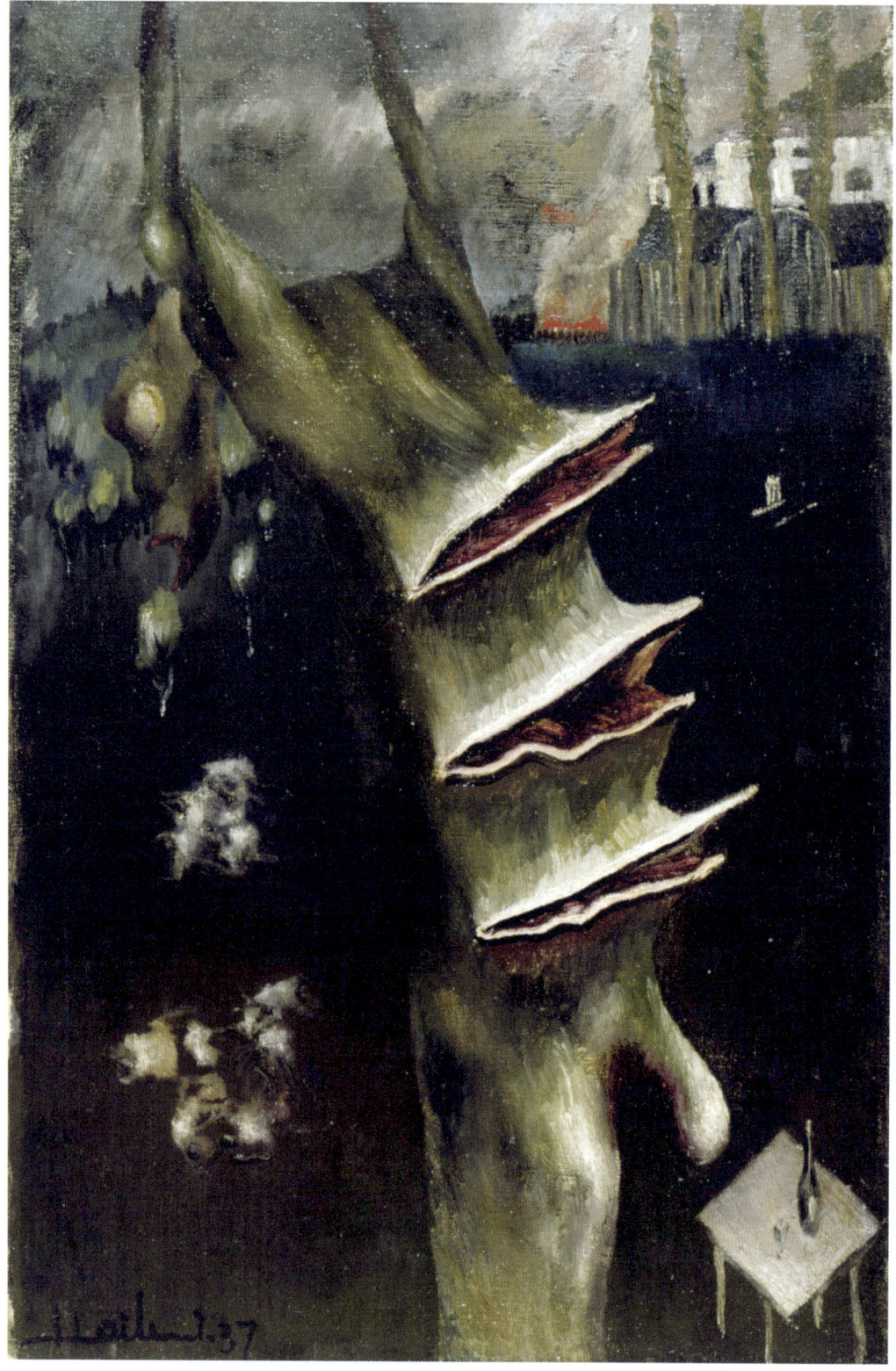

relationship between art and industry. The case was articulated at length in a letter to *The Times* the following day, signed by Cliff Rowe as 'Chairman, Organising Committee, First British Artists' Congress', and followed up elsewhere with a widely reproduced letter of support from Epstein, Grant, McKnight Kauffer, Moholy-Nagy and Paul Nash.

Most of the many reviews that appeared in the following days ranged from neutrally analytic to broadly positive.[32] Many stressed the scale and variety of the exhibition, quite a few specifically applauded the Abstract gallery and, according to taste, they picked out artists or works, with roll-calls of the well-known sitting alongside credits for the unknown, such as 'a painting done on a packing case cover by a postman'.[33] In the *Observer* Jan Gordon noted the exhibition was 'quite difficult to see, containing as it does over six hundred pictures elbowing one another from the ground floor to the attics of an inappropriate London mansion', but recommended two visits: 'The first for exploration and selection. The second for evaluation and enjoyment.'[34]

About a third of the reviews were marked by predictable partisanship, some supportive but the most consequential politically hostile. For the *Daily Worker* it was simply 'London's Best Art Show'; for *Time and Tide* it was 'alive from end to end'; for the *News Chronicle* its 'new and remarkable pictures' by 'nearly all the interesting British artists one can think of' would 'Stagger Art Lovers'; a full-page spread of images in *Reynolds Illustrated News* was headed 'The Pompous Royal Academy is Forestalled For Once', and a second report headlined 'Mass Attack on Mars – Artists to Knock Glory Out of War'.

A diametrically opposed view appeared in the Northcliffe Newspapers' *Sunday Dispatch* three days before the opening, penned by a 'special correspondent' who had attended the press day. Headlined 'RED GALLERY OF HORRORS Insulting Union Jack', it reproduced three Surrealist paintings, one of which incorporated adjacent Soviet and British flags as minor background detail, enabling the opening: 'I have just seen a private view of an art exhibition which will disgust many art lovers and offend patriots.' Citing James Fitton's adaptation of Kitchener's image as a skull in the Peace Publicity Display, the report noted 'Posters in different languages attack our rearmament programme, and the profits of the firms who are engaged on it'.[35] In a similar vein the *Daily Mail* complained in bold type that the exhibition's 'promotion of peace and liberty of action for artists conceals a strong attempt to attack one political creed, Fascism, and to defend another, Communism'.[36]

Shortly after the opening, officials of the Grosvenor Estate, asserting rights as 'the superior lessor', visited the exhibition unannounced. Its owner, the Duke of Westminster, reputedly the richest man in Britain,

5.16 Sam Haile, *Non-Payment of Taxes, Congo, Christian Era*, oil on canvas, 1937. 75.9 × 51.1 cm (30 × 20⅛ in.); cat. 233 at the AIA Grosvenor Square exhibition and one its most politically and emotionally challenging works

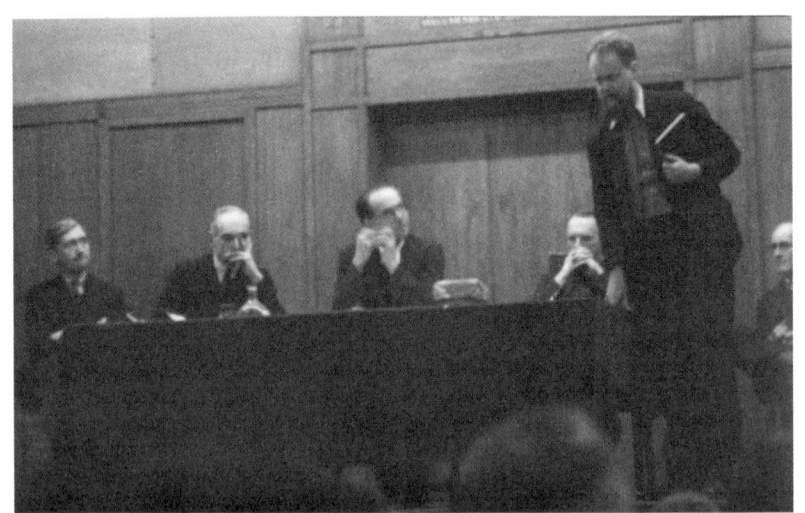

5.17 Unknown photographer, Plenary Session at the British Artists' Congress; l to r: Herbert Read, Director of the Courtauld W. G. Constable, Misha Black, Jack Hastings, Quentin Bell – delivering Education Commission report – and Ronald Kidd, founder of NCCL, April 1937

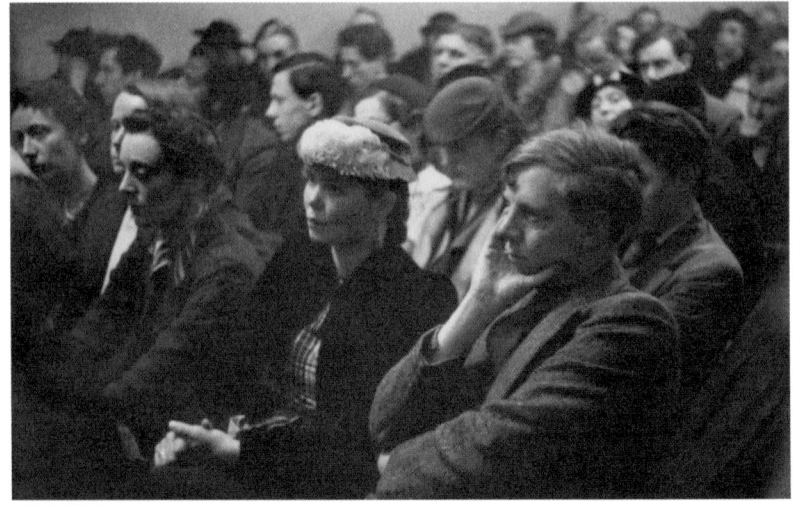

5.18 Unknown photographer, Participants at Plenary Session; r to l: James Fitton, Margaret Fitton, Elizabeth Watson and, partially obscured, Nan Youngman, April 1937

5.19 Unknown photographer, James Boswell addressing the British Artists' Congress, April 1937

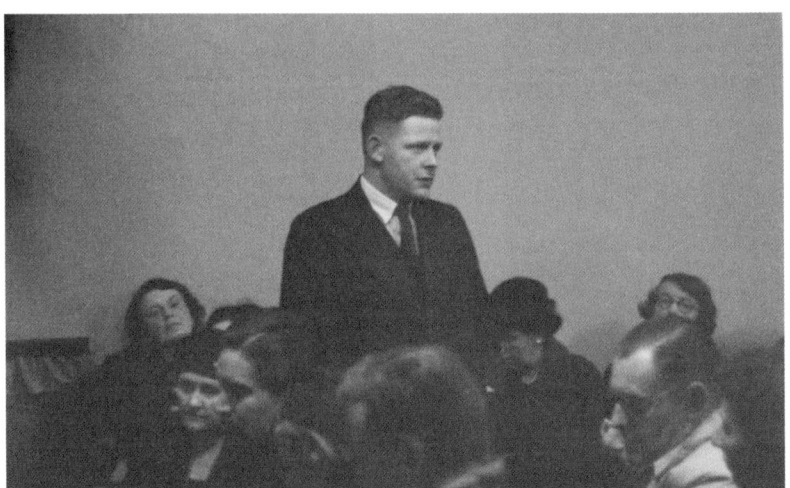

was moving steadily to the right politically in the mid-1930s; reactionary and rabidly anti-Semitic, on the eve of war he would become a council member of The Link, a pro-Nazi, pro-appeasement organization, where he sat as a colleague of Diana Uhlman's aunt, Lady Pearson of Canterbury, a former BUF Parliamentary candidate.[37] Two days before the weekend of meetings constituting the congress was due to begin, Grosvenor Estate officials used a condition in the short-term lease to forbid it from being held at 41 Grosvenor Square, the advertised venue.

Forced to relocate, the congress dance took place that Saturday night at a venue in Baker Street; the congress sessions were moved to Red Lion Square but, as Conway Hall was unavailable the following Tuesday, a public meeting David Low was to chair on 'Artists and Politics' had to be postponed. In Mayfair the Duke's agents removed two offending peace posters, but the exhibition remained open. Misha Black was careful not to be publicly drawn on the motivation behind the widely reported ban, but an anonymous organizer did comment: 'In my opinion we made a mistake from the first in going to Grosvenor Square ... we have put our heads in the lion's mouth and the jaws have closed.'[38]

On the following weekend the *Sunday Dispatch*'s headline read 'Red Artists Propaganda Foiled' as it claimed credit for helping to defeat an attempt to spread communism in London; but by the time the paper appeared an event was being reported which would give a new and terrible resonance to the display of Peace Publicity which it had found so offensive.

* * * * *

The final session of the congress drew to a close early on the evening of Sunday 25 April 1937, having endorsed the need for an ongoing trade union-style organization. Twenty hours later a British naval officer was standing on the deck of HMS *Hood* as it patrolled the Basque coast, preventing, in the name of 'non-intervention', British merchant ships from supplying democratic Spain; just before three o'clock he observed 'an endless stream of planes, clearly marked with the black saltire cross' approaching across the Bay of Biscay, sights set on the mouth of the Mundaca River.[39]

For the next three hours, waves of aircraft dropped a lethal combination of splinter and incendiary bombs on Gernika, fulfilling an operation originally devised as a birthday present for Hitler.[40] Carefully calibrated to maximize loss of human life, the destruction of the historic Basque town was to be a demonstration of new technology and 'total war': those not burnt to death or crushed by falling buildings were strafed trying to escape. A factory of military significance was left unscathed on the outskirts, but the ancient town was turned into a fireball, killing as many as possible by saturation bombing.[41]

In the months that followed, Nationalist apologists, including Henry Page Croft in England, would promote the big lie that the Basques had destroyed their own spiritual capital as part of a scorched earth retreat, but more truthful reporting was generally believed.[42] In Grosvenor Square posters carried images of children killed by bombs during the siege of Madrid, but a majority of the public now quickly understood that what had befallen Gernika was of a different order; and that with it, methods previously used by the British in distant parts of Africa and Asia, by the French in North Africa, and most recently by the Italians in Abyssinia, had arrived in mainland Europe, but on an industrial scale at the behest of the dictators.

In Paris the following Saturday, as Popular Front rallies marked May Day, Picasso made the first of sixty-seven preparatory sketches for his painting *Guernica*, and six weeks later the finished canvas – 3.5 metres high by 7.8 metres wide (11½ × 25½ ft) – would be transported to the Spanish Pavilion at the Paris International Exposition.[43] In early January, shortly after completing some savagely satirical etchings for Spanish Refugee Relief, he had been visited in his Rue de la Boétie apartment by a Republican delegation including the newly returned José Bergamín (who had overseen the Prado evacuation), Josep Lluís Sert and Luis Lacasa (the architects appointed to design the pavilion), the poet Max Aub (a leading member of Spain's Alliance of Anti-Fascist Intellectuals for the Defence of Culture) and José Renau (the Director General of Fine Arts, himself an accomplished loyalist poster designer).[44]

They came at the request of a government newly determined to mount a presence at the International Exposition as a demonstration of the Republic's humanity, rich culture and resilience, aware that procuring a major mural by Picasso would be of 'equivalent value in propaganda terms of a victory at the front'.[45] After a brief hesitation, Picasso had accepted the assignment and, in the three months since, visited the pavilion site, rented a massive loft space on the Rue des Grands-Augustins (which would later become his retreat during the German occupation) and received and stretched a vast canvas. However, he had not begun work or conceived a design – that is until emerging reports of Gernika's destruction propelled him into an intense, obsessive process of creation in which his personal iconography was to achieve extraordinary universal symbolism.

Some three weeks later, barely a fortnight after the AIA exhibition they had helped to mount closed in London, Henry Moore and Roland Penrose rendezvoused in Paris with Picasso, Éluard, Breton, Giacometti and Max Ernst for a lunchtime reunion of seven key participants from the previous

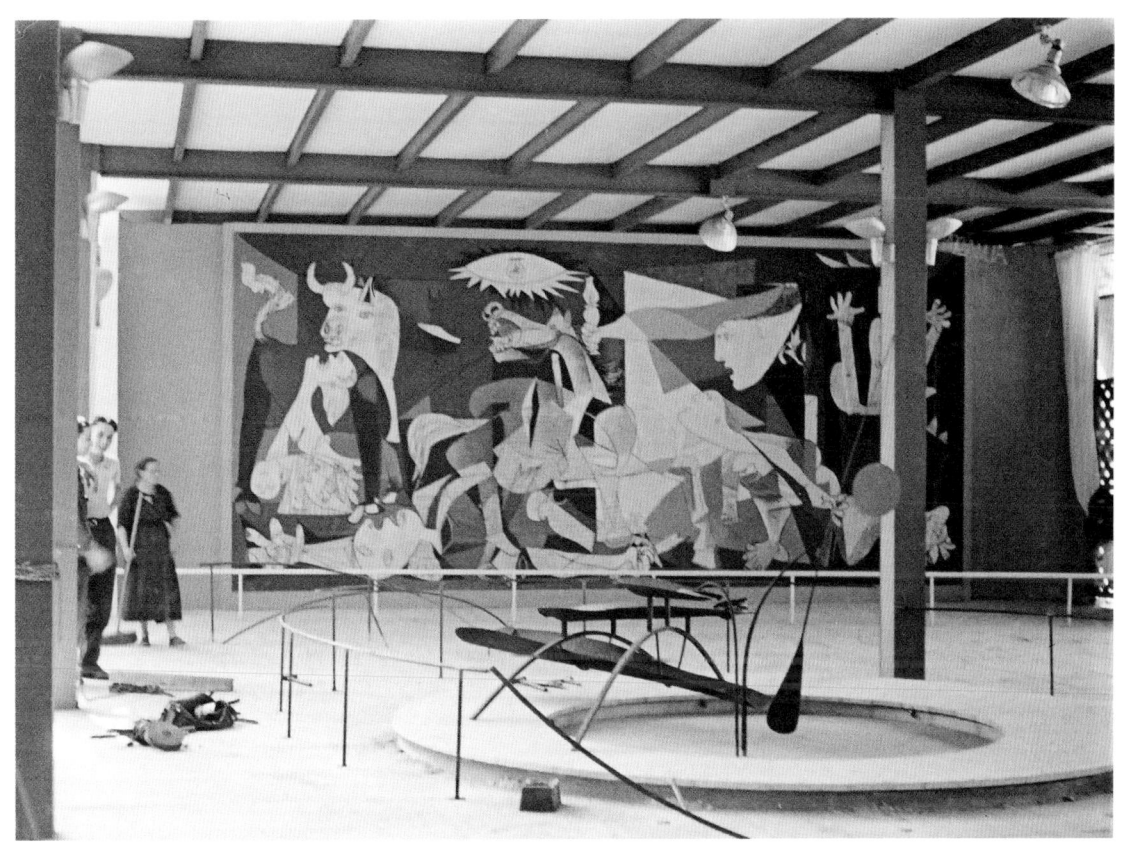

5.20 José Lino
Vaamonde Valencia,
photograph of Picasso's
Guernica in situ at
Spanish Pavilion, 1937

year's International Surrealist Exhibition. 'It was all tremendously lively and exciting and we all trooped off to the studio, and I think even Picasso was excited by our visit', Moore recalled, 'but I remember him lightening the whole mood of the thing, as he loved to do. *Guernica* was still a long way from finished. It was like a cartoon just laid in black and grey, and he could have coloured it as he coloured the sketches. Anyway, you know the woman who comes running out of the little cabin on the right with one hand held in front of her? Well, Picasso told us there was something missing there, and he went and fetched a roll of paper and stuck it in the woman's hand, as much as to say that she had been caught in the bathroom when the bombs came.' Penrose recalled Picasso concluding, 'That shows clearly enough the commonest and most primitive effect of fear'.[46]

Two other AIA visitors to Picasso's studio during these days, also fresh from their work on the congress, were Elizabeth Watson and Quentin Bell, accompanied on the first occasion by Duncan Grant and Vanessa Bell, who had been supporters of the event but not so centrally involved. Vanessa had farewelled her elder son Julian as he departed from Newhaven on 7 June driving an ambulance for Spanish Medical Aid, and fear for his fate was possibly in her mind as she reacted 'C'est un peu terrible' on seeing Picasso's work in progress.[47] Watson and Bell were charged with eliciting Picasso's support for a 'Spain and Culture' rally at the Albert Hall to raise funds for the upkeep of four thousand children who, as Basque resistance crumbled, had been evacuated from Bilbao aboard the *Habana* and arrived in Southampton on 23 May. As Quentin recalled, it was Watson who secured a promise from Picasso that he would attend in person, a prospect which then generated rapid ticket sales in London, where the rally was being organized by the National Joint Committee for Spanish Relief with significant AIA input.[48] Picasso donated a drawing to be auctioned and sent another for use on the programme cover, but when 24 June arrived – having finished *Guernica* a fortnight before, after which the great canvas was being unpicked, rolled up and delivered to the Spanish Pavilion – he was nowhere to be found. Fortunately for Bell, the last plane for London had already left the newly opened Le Bourget airport when Watson suggested he should be the one to fly back and apologize on behalf of an absent star attraction to a packed Albert Hall.

Picasso – expected to speak after the Duchess of Atholl had opened proceedings – was not the only absentee; Heinrich Mann at no. 3 on the programme was also a no-show. But both absentees were more than compensated for by the unexpected entry of the actor and singer Paul Robeson who, scheduled to broadcast from Moscow, had flown to London after being informed this might be frustrated by the British authorities. Declaring with sonorous beauty that 'artists must take sides, choosing between freedom and slavery', he linked the struggle for black rights 'denied in every country save one' to the worldwide fight against capitalist oppression, and urged the hall: 'May your inspiring message reach every man, woman and child who stands for freedom and justice. For the liberation of Spain from the oppression of fascist reactionaries is not a private matter of the Spaniards but the common cause of all advanced and progressive humanity.' Although Picasso's drawing *Weeping Woman* sold for a slightly disappointing £80, the night raised £1,500 (around £86,000 at mid-2020s prices) and inspired several significant future initiatives.[49]

One attendee so inspired, whose engagement with the AIA would deepen, was twenty-eight-year-old William Townsend, his hands smarting from constant applause. For seven years since leaving the Slade, he had eked out a living from occasional exhibits, even rarer sales of watercolours and hard-won book illustration jobs, while remaining close to student friends Claude Rogers, Geoffrey Tibble and Rodrigo Moynihan. An acute observer of national and international politics, and an expressive diarist unable to afford life in London, his journals record his energetic activism through the Workers' Educational Association in support of the Peace Ballot, and with the local labour movement while living at his parents' home at Bridge, near Canterbury, during the middle years of the decade.[50] Townsend had exhibited a watercolour at Soho Square's *Artists Against Fascism and War* and, after some administrative confusion, had three of four works submitted hung at Grosvenor Square; but six experimental abstractions by his friends Moynihan and Tibble were, according to the *New Statesman*, 'banished to the bannisters' after being denied space in the core display replete with Nicholsons and Pipers, because they were 'the only school of abstract painting in England which does not derive entirely from the continent'.[51]

Visiting with Tibble, Townsend concluded: 'The Grosvenor Square show is monstrous, every painter is there but the effect is depressing beyond words. There are many too many pictures in an effort to include a great number of artists rather than maintain a very high level; not only too many pictures, so all drown together, but much too great a proportion of trash. Geoff and I even ran through some of the rooms.' At the congress itself his observations were prescient, noting that plenty of resolutions were passed, 'some pious but some perhaps useful', and 'a permanent Congress to be set up ... instructed first to study the possibility of a trade union for artists. The keen politicians who were there and whose concern was more nearly Trade Unions than artists have not seen all the difficulties of such an affair, but they are determined to have one; and it may be of some value, but ... there is not a reasonable qualification one can think of for membership and without that it will lack authority in just those spheres where it would need it.'[52]

On hearing Robeson, however, he experienced a different sense of engagement:

> Tonight one felt that even in the awful present, where the forces of the past and of the future overlap, and both so much that the present itself seems to have no claim to a place, the dark and negative power had been banished already. I felt happy to have had the chance to be in the centre of the conflict instead of hovering coldly at the circumference, with so much less hope.[53]

* * * * *

Five days after the *Habana* docked at Southampton, Stanley Baldwin had resigned as Britain's prime minister, leaving advocates of appeasement in the ascendant; the incorporation of Austria into the German Reich still lay nine months in the future, but the forces that would lead to Chamberlain and Daladier's betrayal of Czechoslovakia at Munich six months after that were already in play. At the same time, in summer 1937 past hopes that collective security might prevent descent into another European Great War had not yet been extinguished.

The Peace Ballot of 1935 had been followed in September 1936 by a World Peace Congress at Brussels, where forty International Peace Campaign (IPC) national committees endorsed the sanctity of treaty obligations, disarmament and League of Nations action 'to remedy conditions which might lead to war'.[54] After Brussels an Artists' Peace Campaign had been formed, and it was in its service that Misha Black, Elizabeth Watson, Betty Rea, Nan Youngman and James Holland now travelled to Paris to decorate two spaces in an unofficial IPC Peace Pavilion, funded by local Popular Front sources and erected outside the main Trocadero Exposition entrance.[55] Surviving photographs show the AIA contingent at work on a massive graphic designed by Holland, incorporating 'a diagrammatic mural – almost a flow chart' linking all the group's work together for peace. In one of a number of sabotage attempts, the wooden scaffolding was set on fire, but Youngman, commuting back to teach in London, could not interest Fleet Street in the story; Holland, however, published two sketches in *Left Review*, one, *Comment on Guernica*, showing construction workers hauling down the Nazi flag, the other of a construction workers' *Midday Meeting* debating a one-day strike against fascism and war.[56]

The Exposition Internationale des Arts et Techniques was notionally an apolitical celebration of technology and industrial design's contribution to modern life, its Palace of Discovery intended to be a surviving legacy; but in actuality the World Fair's grounds were a politically charged arena,

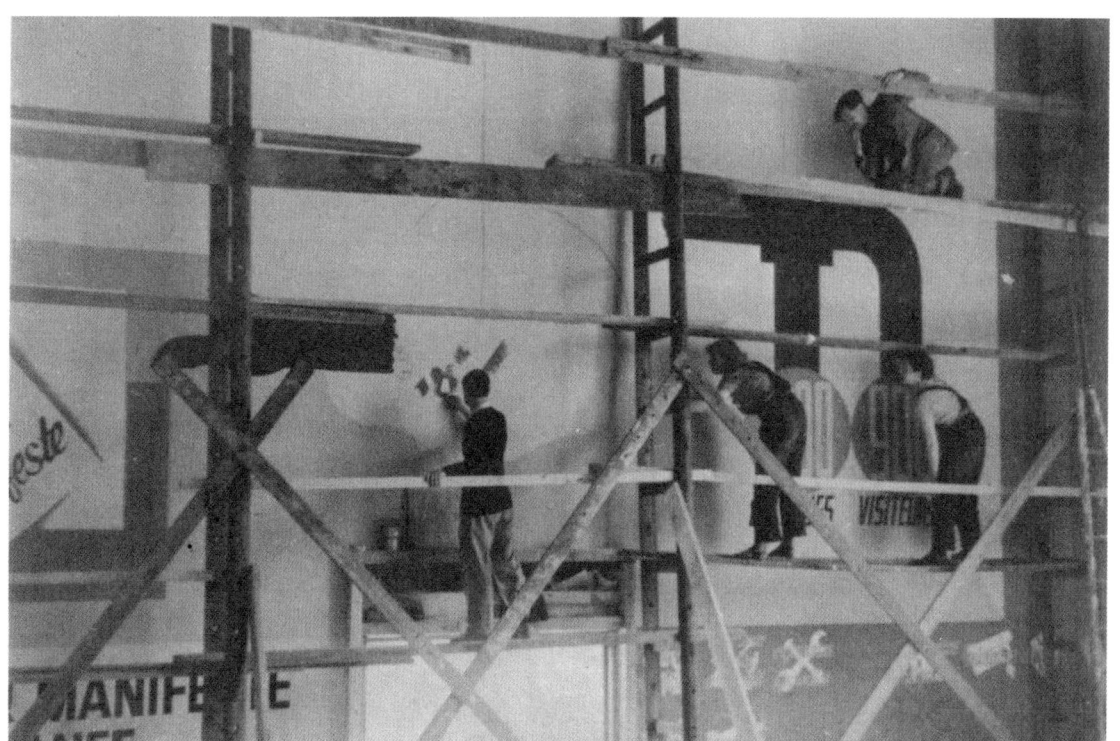

5.21 Unknown photographer, AIA members working on Peace Pavilion, Paris Expo, May 1937; the contingent includes James Holland and, below, r to l, Elizabeth Watson and Nan Youngman

with national pavilions projecting 'ill-concealed desire to vindicate the present map of Europe – or the urgency of remodelling it'.[57] Albert Speer, jockeying to become the Third Reich's architectural supremo, had deployed espionage to obtain early possession of plans detailing the Soviet Pavilion's height; this ensured a giant eagle, swastika in its talons, was poised atop Germany's tall polished stone neo-classical edifice, appearing ready to swoop down on the pavilion opposite and dismember its two advancing workers signifying the alliance of Soviet industry and agriculture.[58]

The German and Soviet pavilions were among the minority completed in time for the official opening, and it was not until 12 July, eight weeks later, that the Spanish Pavilion designed by Sert and Lacasa opened. Adjacent to it, on the same side of the main axis as Germany's, was the Polish Pavilion, separating the Republic's presence from the power bent on its destruction; and immediately behind it lay the Pontifical Pavilion, celebrating an institution whose Spanish archbishops were complicit in summary mass executions and steadfast in denying eyewitness accounts of their own priests as to what had occurred at Gernika. A week after *Guernica* went on public display, on 19 July the Nazi *Degenerate Art* exhibition opened in the Hofgarten in Munich, and in line with its agenda the German-language guide to the Paris Expo denounced Picasso's painting as 'a hodgepodge of body parts that any four-year-old could have painted'.⁵⁹

Lacasa had worked in Dresden's planning department during the Weimar years, and the design he and Sert developed as a demonstration of the Spanish Republic's achievements in social welfare, education and the arts drew on the flair and functionality of the Bauhaus design ethic. Eschewing stone and brick for prefabricated elements to speed construction and making generous use of window space for lightness, it used exterior photomontages to project its cause – protest against Nationalist military rebellion – and a limited colour palette with surfaces painted red, white or, in certain sections constructed with cement fibreboards, left raw. Rising from an open ground-floor performance space, with *Guernica* to one side, a walkway delivered visitors to a top-lit second floor, where they were introduced both to Spain's applied arts and industries and also to the anguish of the civil war through drawings, paintings, posters and photomontages, including one depicting the transport of El Greco's *The Holy Trinity* from the Prado to Valencia, along with tributes to the poet Lorca and others who had already perished. Descending the internal staircase, past Miró's *Catalan Peasant* mural, visitors then encountered a narrative depicting the Republic's progressive reforms using information boards, posters and social realist and avant-garde artworks, before descending once again into the space occupied by *Guernica*, where for four months the Republic's resilience was celebrated daily through music, theatre and film.

When the Exposition closed in late November, the pavilion was dismantled and nearly all its contents, including Miró's mural, were subsequently lost after being transported back to Spain where – with Valencia threatened by the Nationalists – the government was once again preparing to relocate, this time to Barcelona. However, *Guernica* was demounted, re-rolled and returned to Picasso's studio on the Rue des Grands-Augustins, to be stored ahead of future use in support of the beleaguered Republic.

* * * * *

Recalling his reaction to *Guernica* on first entering the Spanish Pavilion, many years later Anthony Blunt wrote: 'I was very much moved by it, but I was horrified by it from a theoretical point of view. I wrote an article in *The Spectator* saying that this was not the right way to communicate a great human and revolutionary tragedy.'⁶⁰

Already a man of masks – he had met his Soviet handler for the first time eight months before – fifteen years later he would come to hail Picasso's work as 'the last great painting in the European tradition', but in 1937 such a notion flew in the face of his advocacy of, indeed his yearning for, a social realism which could connect artist and society in a time of crisis. This gap between thought and feeling clearly chafed, and seeking to deny it he provoked controversy, plus a long-running dispute with Herbert Read. During it, Blunt's hyperbole castigated Picasso's etchings *The Dream and Lie of Franco* ('there is something pathetic in the sight of a talented artist struggling to cope with a problem outside his powers') and belittled *Guernica* as 'the private brainstorm' of an artist who had seemed 'a giant' but was now 'unfrocked' as a 'pygmy' having spent too long in the 'Holy of Holies of Art'.[61]

In the realm of theory, Blunt conceded that Surrealism, with which he associated Picasso's efforts, was at least superior to abstract art, which 'sought to avoid saying anything about the world', but he still saw it as the 'last refinement of a dead tradition', marginally useful in assaulting the certainties of decadent bourgeois society, but primarily appealing 'to those whose minds are clogged in a love of the obscure and the unusual'.[62] Once the controversy had subsided, Blunt returned in more measured fashion to his pavilion experience, citing Diego Rivera's frescoes as having driven up attendance at the Detroit Institute of Arts a hundredfold, as they were met with:

> great interest and approval by the people for whom and about whom they were painted, that is to say, for the people working in the industries in Detroit. That is very different from the reaction shown in Paris to the Picasso painting, also a subject of general interest. People came and were interested in the idea of a painting representing Guernica, but when they looked at it they were baffled and, as far as I could see, most people could make nothing of it and went away disappointed.[63]

Similar preoccupations had surfaced in Blunt's *Spectator* review of Grosvenor Square. Having saluted the congress as the most important event of the British art year 'because it shows that at last artists in this country are realising the old methods of organisation that controlled the arts are no longer adequate to present conditions', he welcomed the exhibition's diversity, noting that abstract painters and 'superrealists' each filled impressive rooms: 'But scattered among the other exhibits are the elements of what is beginning to be called the New Realism, that is to say the work of artists who wish to express with maximum clarity their progressive view of life.' Margaret Fitton, Nan Youngman, Robert Medley and Peter László Peri were among the half-dozen contributors picked out for special mention, before he concluded: 'Let us only hope that artists such as these will get together and organise themselves as efficiently as the abstract painters or the superrealists, so that at the next exhibition of this kind they may be able to appear as a definite group with a clear programme.'[64]

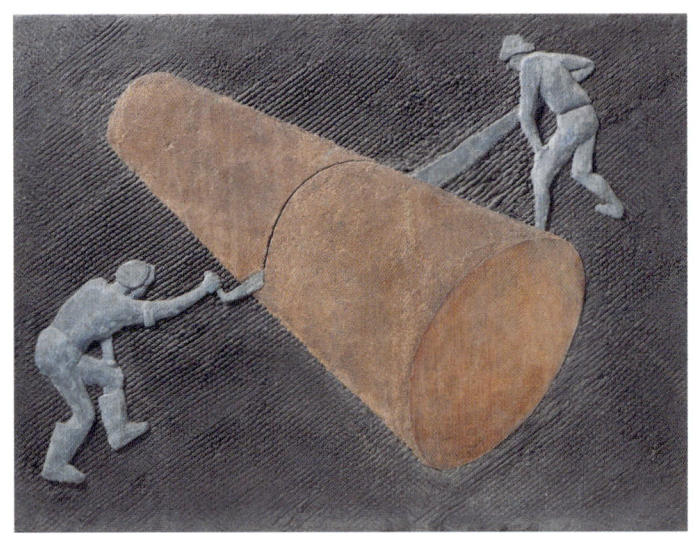

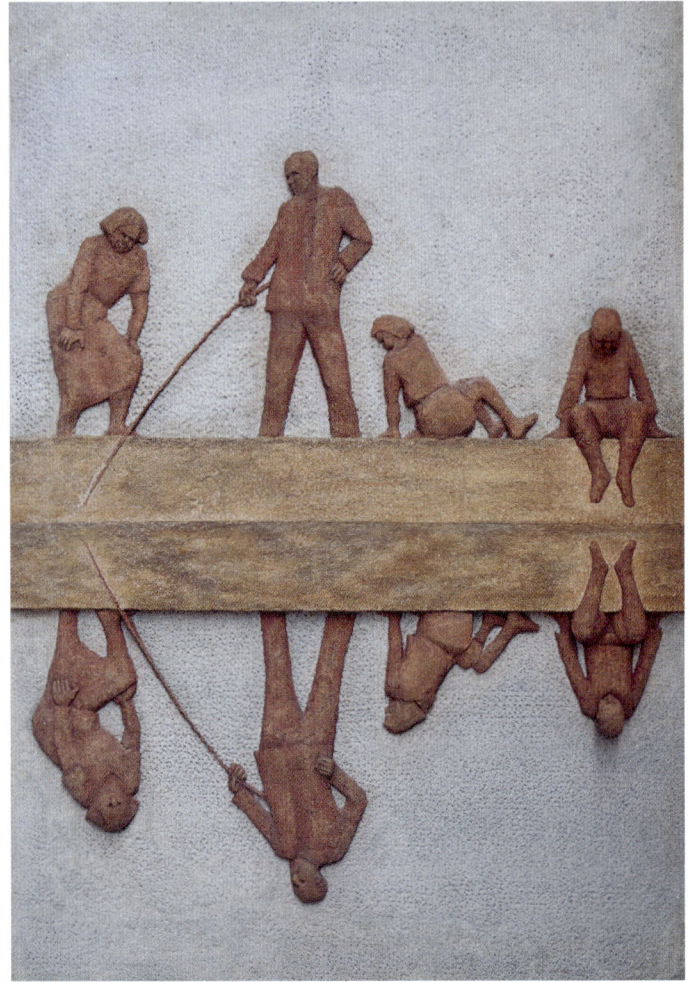

5.22 Peter László Peri, *Sawing*, pigmented concrete, 1937. 55 × 85 × 17 cm (21¾ × 33½ × 6¾ in.)

5.23 Peter László Peri, *Fishing*, pigmented concrete, 1938. 102 × 71 × 4 cm (40¼ × 28 × 1⅝ in.)

5.24 Peter László Peri, *Chess*, pigmented concrete, 1938. 71 × 93 × 13 cm (28 × 36⅝ × 5⅛ in.)

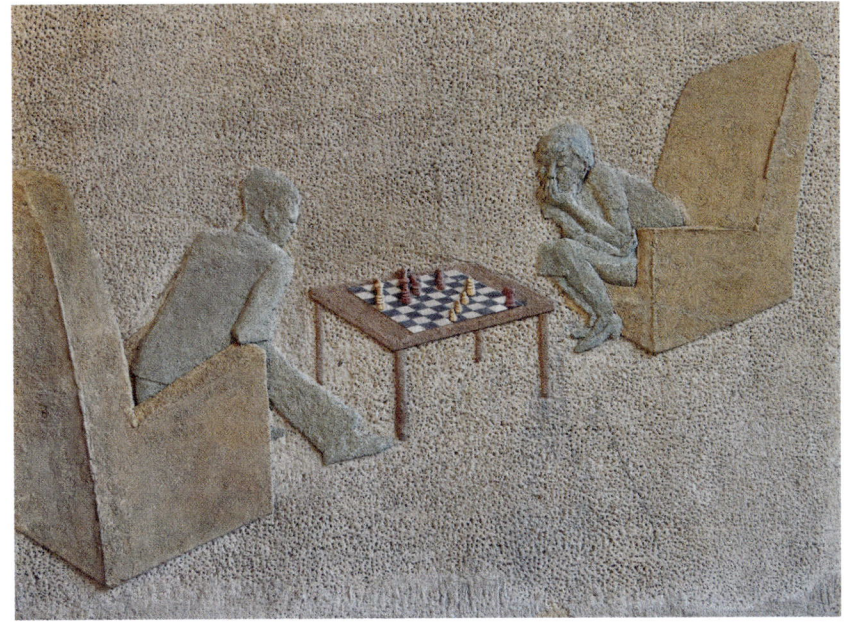

In 'The Realism Quarrel', a *Left Review* article published the same month, Blunt cited sculptor Peri as 'an artist now operating in the great tradition of Daumier, Courbet, and early van Gogh', who had already shown how a training in abstract art could be of use in a realism basing itself on 'the ordinary life of the people in the streets and parks of London'.[65] A Jewish political refugee from his native Hungary, and a communist who had studied at the Bauhaus before being forced to escape Nazi Berlin with his activist English wife and their child, Peri had been in London since 1933. An early, if rather isolated, member of the AIA, in 1928 he had turned from constructivist design to figurative sculpture of working scenes and everyday life, modelled in concrete rather than carved in marble or cast in bronze. It was an art form that Blunt loyally championed in the face of highbrow disdain, seeing potential for it to take its place 'as a part of architecture, as part of a public activity', and writing the catalogue foreword for Peri's solo show *The New Realism in Sculpture*, which opened in Cambridge during the congress. This was itself a forerunner of *London Life in Concrete*, an AIA-organized London exhibition of Peri's work in Soho Square in June 1938.[66]

Another, very different AIA activist was twenty-three-year-old Ewan Phillips, now a third-year student at the Courtauld Institute, where Blunt was supervising his MA thesis on 'English Expressionism from Blake to Beardsley'. Phillips's mother had modelled for Jacob Epstein and Augustus John; his father, of Dutch Jewish descent, ran a gallery in Duke Street,

GROSVENOR SQUARE

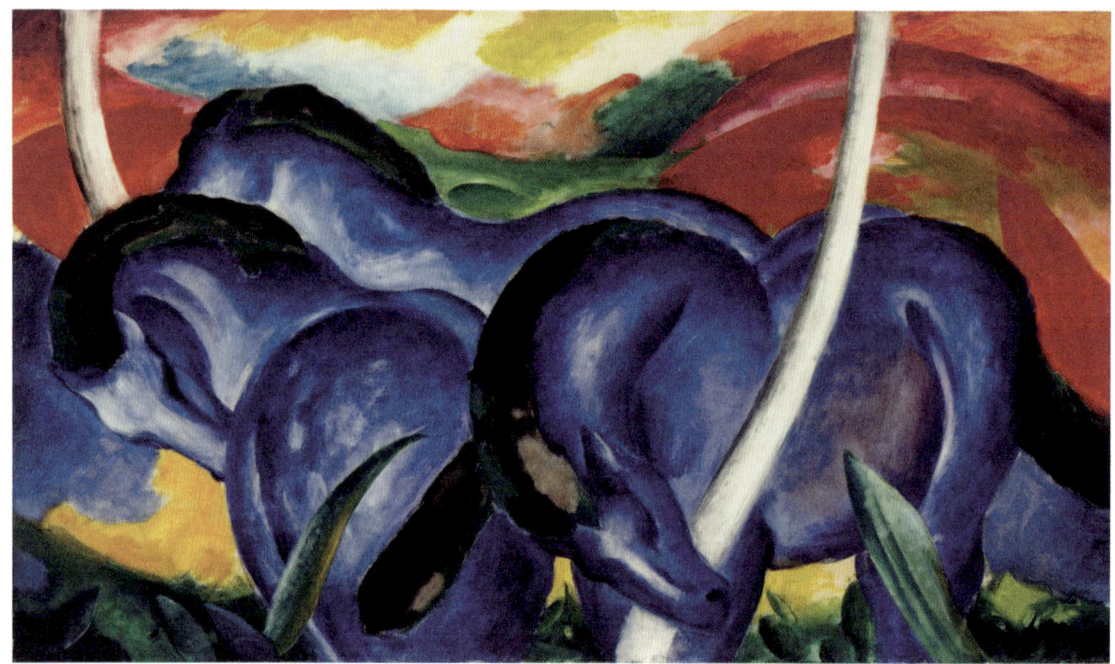

5.25 Franz Marc, *Blue Horses*, oil on canvas, 1911. 105.7 × 181.1 cm (41⅝ × 71⅜ in.)

and strong Continental connections meant the family home in Crediton Hill, Hampstead, became an early staging-post for German and Austrian refugees. While a student at Goldsmiths art school, Phillips had been arrested, beaten by police and fined for protesting the Reichstag fire, and later the same year he became one of the first thirty-two members of the AI.[67] At Goldsmiths he met painting student Betsy Blake, with whom he had travelled cheaply and extensively in Europe, and by late 1937 their first child was on the way. Not long after his son's birth, Phillips would begin developing 'Portraits for Spain', a new AIA fundraising initiative.

A linguist who spoke French, Spanish and some Italian and German, Phillips was modest, personable and energetic, and in due course would serve as secretary of the Spanish section of the Artists' Refugee Committee while an AIA Central Committee member in 1938–39. As well as gallery experience in his father's business, in May 1936 he had also curated a trail-blazing adult education exhibition of modern art at Sawston in Cambridgeshire. This background made Phillips a natural choice as a curatorial assistant when the AIA decided to support the organization of the *Exhibition of 20th Century German Art* at the New Burlington Galleries in June 1938. A direct riposte to the vilification embodied in the 1937 *Degenerate Art* show that was touring the Reich, the exhibition brought together the work of fifty-seven artists, both living and dead, in London. Spearheaded by Irmgard Burchard and backed by a clutch of well-known supporters of the previous year's

Artists' Congress,[68] it used 269 works to dramatize the narrative of contemporary German Expressionism and its Post-Impressionist, Cubist and Surrealist antecedents in the Novembergruppe, Die Brücke and Der Blaue Reiter, accompanied by a Pelican Special paperback and its own music and lecture programme.[69] Seventeen participants were still in Germany, their works stripped from public collections while they suffered various levels of prohibition and exclusion (twenty-three were already exiles in London and Paris, five elsewhere), and a disclaimer made clear their work was shown without seeking the artists' consent.[70]

Launched using Franz Marc's *Blue Horses* as its signature image, the exhibition brought an unfamiliar artistic story to London. Hitler helped to publicize it by denouncing the eleven-week run as 'another attempt by the enemies of Nazi Germany to belittle National Socialist cultural achievements' – and in the same speech, which instantly became the subject of an AIA handbill, the Führer advised any modern artist who had not already done so 'to leave Germany immediately'.[71]

* * * * *

Fifteen-year-old Lucian Freud, born in Berlin but already five years a Londoner, was one visitor to the New Burlington Galleries that summer who would draw on the psychological force of Expressionism over the decades ahead. The influences on display were very different from the more cerebral abstract and Surrealist experimentalism evident at Grosvenor Square and, while resonating with intensity in darkening times, their impact would over time permeate the diverse figurative practice of a rising generation. But in the shorter term a different sensibility was coming to the fore in London's art scene, giving sustenance to Blunt's hopes that a communicable new realism might emerge as an organized force at the next major AIA exhibition.

Five months before the *Exhibition of 20th Century German Art* opened, Claude Rogers, Graham Bell, William Coldstream and Victor Pasmore had moved the atelier-style art school they had started in Fitzroy Street the previous autumn round the corner into a larger space on the top floor of 314 Euston Road, commercial premises with a funfair at street level and an industrial lift giving access to a former car showroom above. The location would soon become synonymous with a school of painting whose thirty-something principals were all to varying degrees in retreat from what they saw as a cul-de-sac of abstraction,[72] while seeking idioms that 'might make painting more accessible to more people'.[73] To this end their practice as both artists and teachers placed observation rather than any particular stylistic convention at the centre of explorations of the material

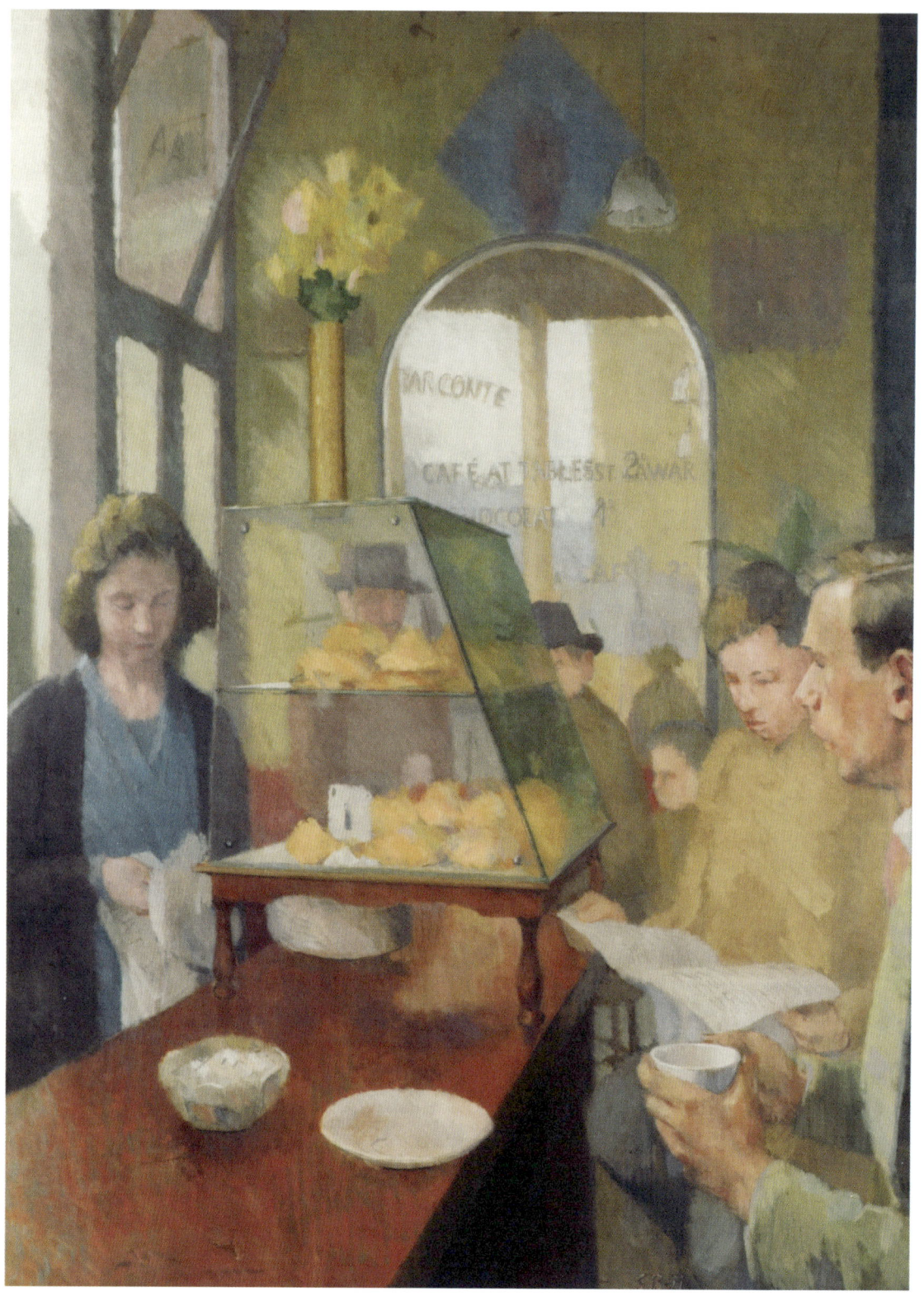

world in paint. Subsidized by Kenneth Clark and bolstered by a cohort of better known 'visitors', including Augustus John, Vanessa Bell, Duncan Grant and John Nash, it was sufficiently successful as a venture to set William Coldstream and Graham Bell (no relation of Quentin) free from their previous dependence on filmmaking and journalism respectively, for Victor Pasmore to move on from a decade of employment in the London County Council Public Health Department, and for Claude Rogers to prioritize painting over teaching at Raynes Park School.[74]

As Coldstream reflected just before the doors first opened: 'The slump had made me aware of social problems, and I became convinced that art ought to be directed to a wider public; whereas all ideas which I had learnt to regard as *artistically* revolutionary ran in the opposite direction. It seemed to me that the broken communications between the artist and the public should be built up again and that this probably implied a movement towards realism.'[75] For Coldstream, who had almost completely abandoned painting mid-decade, portraiture was the central focus of renewed effort, and when two months later Graham Bell published 'Escape from Escapism', his own survey of a London Group show at which Coldstream had just hung a much-praised portrait of W. H. Auden, he noted an increase in portraiture as 'the first sign of the new objectivity'. More broadly, he judged 'purely subjective art is in decline', 'abstract works ... have lost their pre-eminence', and that Surrealism was even less in evidence: 'The escapist art forms diminish as the conditions which gave rise to them change. The main body of the London Group is objective in content, more or less subjective in treatment.'[76]

The focus on recording the material which united the Euston Roaders turning towards a form of 'New Realism' did not mean they saw themselves as proponents of social realism, as previously advocated in Comintern circles where subject selection and handling was praiseworthy if it made manifest class struggle and the forces of history. For Coldstream, realism rooted in observing the texture of real-world phenomena would always incorporate an element of subjectivity, for it was 'not a scientific record [but] a record of fact enlarged and modified by one's reaction to it, and the most realistic painting can be nothing like reality'.[77] It was a point echoed in *Left Review* by Graham Bell, who welcomed the decline of 'the non-intelligible code' of 'extreme subjectivism', but nevertheless cautioned: 'In the creation of a work of art, there are infinite possibilities of emphasis and selection.'[78]

These views made Bell and Coldstream obvious invitees when the AIA felt impelled to organize a member debate on the rival claims of realism and Surrealism at the Group Theatre Rooms in early March 1938.[79] The immediate trigger was the sectarian tone of an anonymous report in that January's *AIA Bulletin* covering the second American Artists' Congress and

5.26 Graham Bell, *The Café*, oil on canvas, 1937–38. 122 × 92 cm (48⅛ × 36¼ in.)

its accompanying *Exhibition in Defense of World Democracy: Dedicated to the Peoples of Spain and China*;[80] unable to attend, Picasso had contributed a paper on 'The Defence of Culture in Spain' to the New York congress and lithographs to the exhibition. Stylistically heterogeneous, the exhibition had attracted predictable criticism from purist social realists, duly echoed in the *AIA Bulletin*, which opined that: 'the bad influence of Expressionism, Surrealism, Futurism and Abstraction are still too much in evidence. This applies even to the new etchings by Picasso presented to the exhibition, *The Dream and Lie of General Franco*; they are as fantastic and far less comprehensible than Goya's work in denunciation of war.'[81] This attracted a threat of resignation from the London Surrealist Group, and a hasty apology in the February *Bulletin*.[82]

The debate itself was evidently a somewhat inchoate affair, which pitted a combative Bell and a more nuanced Coldstream as advocates of new realism, in alliance with the more single-mindedly socialist Peri, against Julian Trevelyan, Humphrey Jennings and Roland Penrose, the latter contingent stealing a march by arriving with two paintings by Picasso and Miró as silent witnesses. Coldstream, in arguing the need for art's accessibility, was nevertheless at pains to acknowledge that Picasso was indeed a greater artist than any contemporary realist, a point of becoming modesty referenced by Anthony Blunt in a *Spectator* review of a Euston Road School exhibition the same month: 'To the system of shocks, incongruities, obscurities, with which the Superrealists work, Coldstream opposes, above all, the quality of honesty. In art, as in morals, honesty is often not exciting at first sight. But the test comes not at the first, but at the fiftieth hour; and it is not obvious which will look duller then – a Picasso or a Coldstream.'[83] Herbert Read, writing in the *London Bulletin* from the opposite perspective, was snide: 'We have tried to remember anything contributed to the debate by Graham Bell and William Coldstream ... but there is only the stammer and the sweat ... the camera and Courbet. Actually our English Realists are not the tough guys they ought to be but the effete and bastard offspring of the Bloomsbury school of needlework.'[84]

More tellingly, eight weeks later Coldstream, Bell, Humphrey Jennings[85] and Trevelyan were all working together in Bolton as a group of artists assembled across the stylistic divide as part of Mass Observation's 'Worktown' programme. An independent initiative recording working-class life and opinion with a strong anthropological element, it included a component creating art based on the locality and gathering local reactions to the resulting images, and as such was designed to test communication between artists and their public in a distinctly innovative way. Working together, initially on the roof of Bolton's municipal Mere Hall, then in its streets, Bell and Coldstream produced some remarkable townscapes ('squalorscapes' in Bell's

5.27 Julian Trevelyan, *Bolton*, pencil, watercolour and collage, 1937. 38.5 × 57 cm (15¼ × 22½ in.)

5.28 Graham Bell, *Thomasson Park, Bolton*, oil on canvas, 1938. 50.8 × 61 cm (20 × 24 in.)

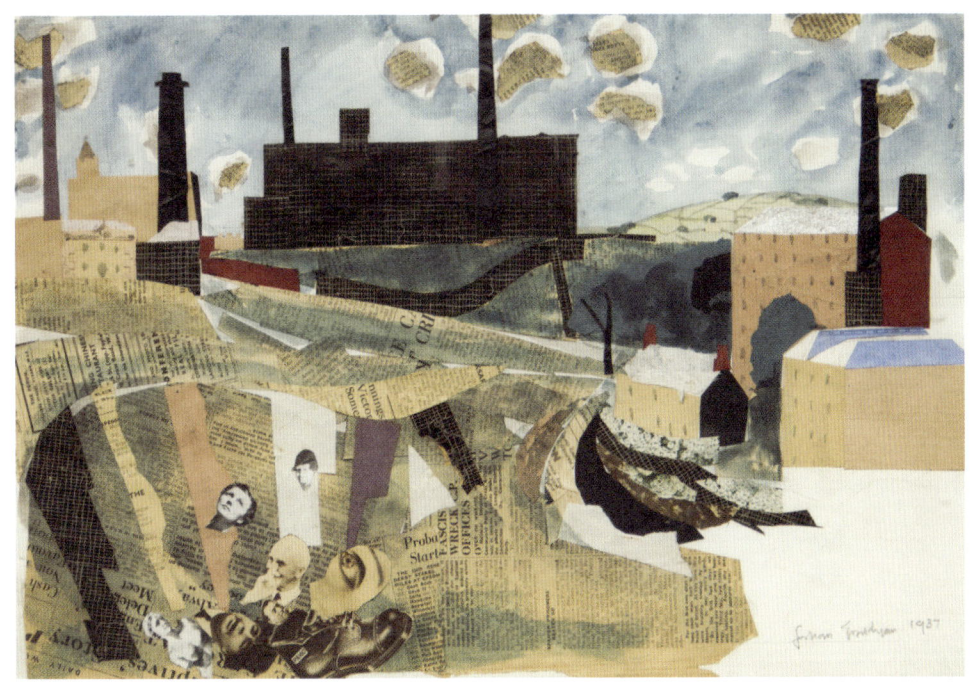

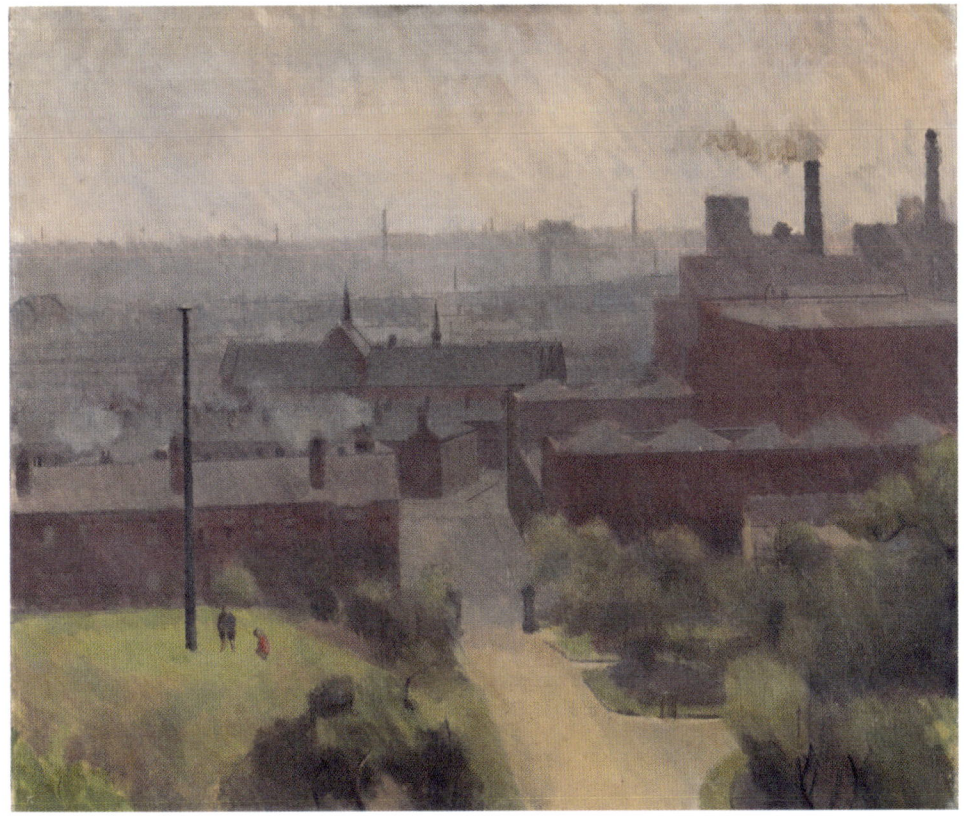

GROSVENOR SQUARE

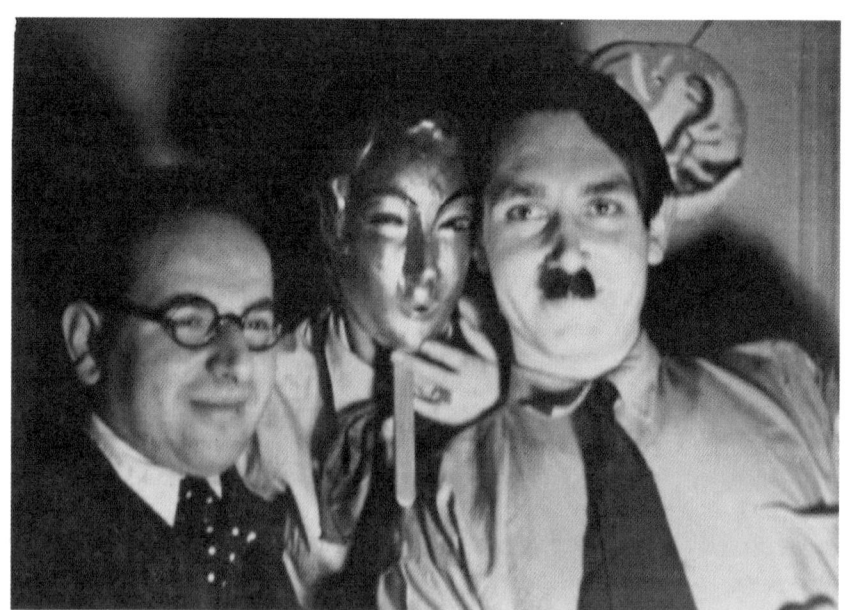

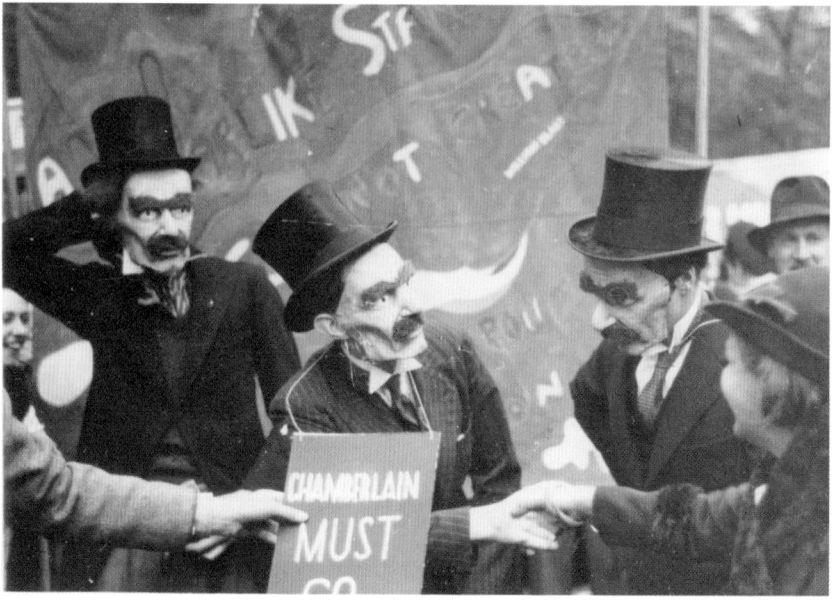

5.29 Unknown photographer, Misha Black and designer Leo Wyatt as Hitler, Cliff Rowe's Halloween Party, 1937

5.30 Unknown photographer, Surrealist Chamberlains at the May Day March, 1938

phrase), as did Julian Trevelyan in a very different idiom before he returned to London to take part in the May Day parade.[86]

Fifteen days earlier, the fascist offensive on the Aragon front had cut Republican Spain in two as Nationalist troops reached the sea at Vinaròs. For many in the politically aware AIA network – which prepared banners and placards and mobilized over two hundred artists to add to the labour movement and thousands who marched that day – it was the logical consequence of Conservative foreign policy and the moment that foretold democracy's defeat. Four years later, George Orwell would recall: 'In the most mean, cowardly, hypocritical way the British ruling class did all they could to hand Spain over to Franco and the Nazis. Why? Because they were pro-Fascist, was the obvious answer [but] whether the British ruling class are wicked or merely stupid is one of the most difficult questions of our time.'[87] Watching an anti-appeasement demonstration, Page Croft, Franco's principal apologist at Westminster, could only see 'a very ugly crowd overwhelmingly foreign in appearance', but it was a shared revulsion at events in Europe that was now reinforcing unity among the artists who had exhibited at Grosvenor Square a year before, and one that once again rendered the niceties of aesthetic dispute a second order issue.[88]

On May Day Trevelyan took his place on the Embankment as one of four masked and top-hatted Chamberlains leading the Surrealist contingent as it demanded 'Arms for Spain' and the prime minister's resignation. After contributing a papier mâché horse's head to a display that included a skeleton hung in a giant birdcage and speakers broadcasting 'The Internationale', Trevelyan remembered: 'It was a day of cold east wind and I was soon hoarse with shouting, but on the whole I think we added something effective to the cortege.'[89]

Five months later, on the evening of 30 September 1938, Chamberlain's flight from Munich landed at Heston Aerodrome; having agreed to the dismemberment of Czechoslovakia, he arrived back in London to declare 'Peace for our Time'. Earlier that afternoon a ship docked at Tilbury carrying *Guernica* in its hold, and four days later Picasso's painting went on display, together with sixty-seven of his preparatory drawings, at the New Burlington Galleries.[90]

*****

The fifteen months that had elapsed between the first British Artists' Congress and the Munich crisis had not been easy ones for the AIA either organizationally or strategically. As Townsend sensed, the basis for a broad trade union among artists was elusive, as were hopes that merger between existing artists' organizations such as the Society of Industrial

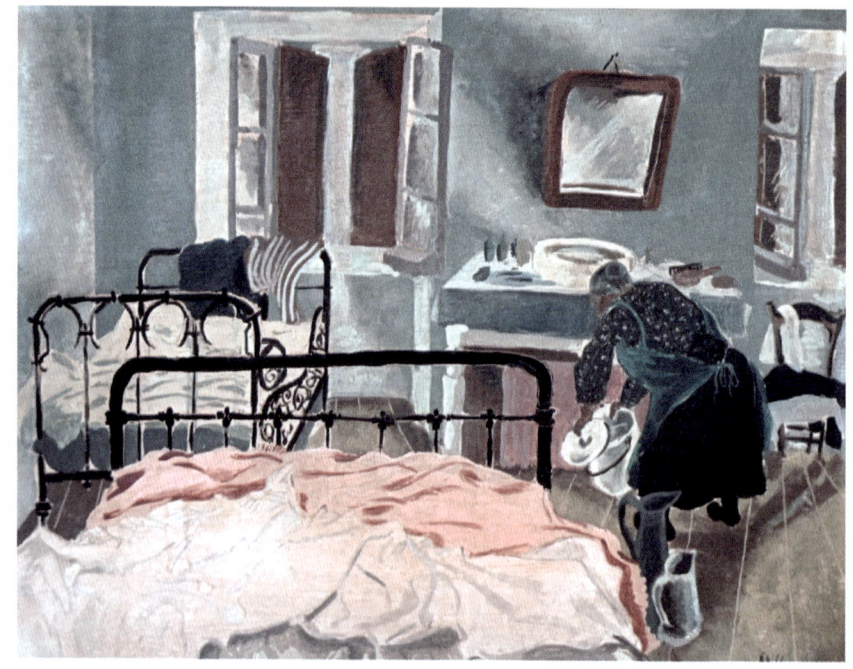

5.31 Edith Simon, *Isle de Ré Bed*, gouache on board, 1938. 30 × 36 cm (11⅞ × 14¼ in.)

Artists and the London Group might be readily forthcoming. AIA membership numbers were growing, vitality abounded with fundraising cabarets, socials and a brilliantly enjoyable July holiday on the Île de Ré which attracted a cluster of key players;[91] but scale and the times brought challenges in terms of resourcing communications, seed-funding a growing list of initiatives, trying to sustain AIA groups in major cities and build them 'in the provinces', and – above all – in evolving a structure to bridge potential political tensions.

At the second American Artists' Congress held on 17 December 1937, Philip Evergood, a friend of the London-based painter Richard Carline since their Slade days in the early 1920s, now president of the New York Artists' Union, had been able to announce affiliation to the Congress of Industrial Organizations as Local 60 of the United Office and Professional Workers of America.[92] Radical in terms of calling for anti-lynching legislation and the freeing of imprisoned labour leaders, and in its denunciation of German and Italian intervention in Spain and Japan's invasion of China, the New York congress was nevertheless addressed by public officials and could advertise Mayor La Guardia as speaking. This was a reflection of the critical mass of activity under way as part of the Federal Art Project, which even as it came under increasing Republican attack in Washington was still providing a material platform for nationwide organization of artists and a model for art's incorporation into the civic realm.

No such conditions existed in Britain, either in terms of government demand or the trade union movement, where key institutions were under the sway of leaders such as Walter Citrine and Ernest Bevin, who remained hostile to 'Red-tainted' popular front initiatives. In these pre-war years, the British state – notwithstanding great power status and control of colonies on which the sun never set – in fact made a negligible contribution to the employment of artists, generating little demand beyond teaching and almost none via public acquisition of work by living artists. Fine artists remained dependent on the uncertain favours of the economically anaemic gallery and connoisseurship nexus; and as James Boswell noted in his book *The Artist's Dilemma*, most commercial artists and graphic designers faced insecurity and exploitation in a highly fragmented studio system, the high-end opportunities generated by corporates such as Shell-Mex or public bodies such as the London Passenger Transport Board being few and far between.[93]

These realities were evident as Herbert Read wrote to Paul Nash at the end of January 1938 noting 'during the last week or so I have been approached by three people with schemes for the salvation of art in England'. He relayed that the AIA wanted him to 'formally identify' with them, and that one of the approaches had been from the painter Norman Dawson, proposing an Artists Co-operative 'very much on the lines of your scheme, but full of confused ideas and political red-herrings'.[94] In only a slight rewriting of history, Read continued: 'I have always advocated that the AIA should drop its spurious internationalism and turn itself into a trade union for all grades and creeds of practicing artists. I made a speech to that effect at the Congress they held last year. Dawson's scheme is largely inspired by the dissatisfaction with the AIA which he says is in the hands of communists and commercial artists.' He noted Dawson would desist if the AIA would 'broaden its basis and become democratic and representative', and Read himself felt that what artists needed was a single organization 'parallel to the Society of Authors or the British Medical Association' with any political positions, if necessary, 'determined by the majority'.

For five years, extraordinary growth had indeed been disproportionately powered by the dedication of those either in the Communist Party or very close to it – 'fellow travellers' to use the favoured phrase of detractors. Continuous voluntary effort by Misha Black, Cliff Rowe, Betty Rea, Percy Horton, James Boswell and others among the founders – and the pivotal role of an annually endorsed Central Committee guiding more diverse sub-committees – had ensured the original vision of politicized international co-operation among artists had not been lost. But now news of the Moscow trials and events in Spain – George Orwell's *Homage to Catalonia* was published in April 1938 – were heightening suspicions of Soviet motivations,

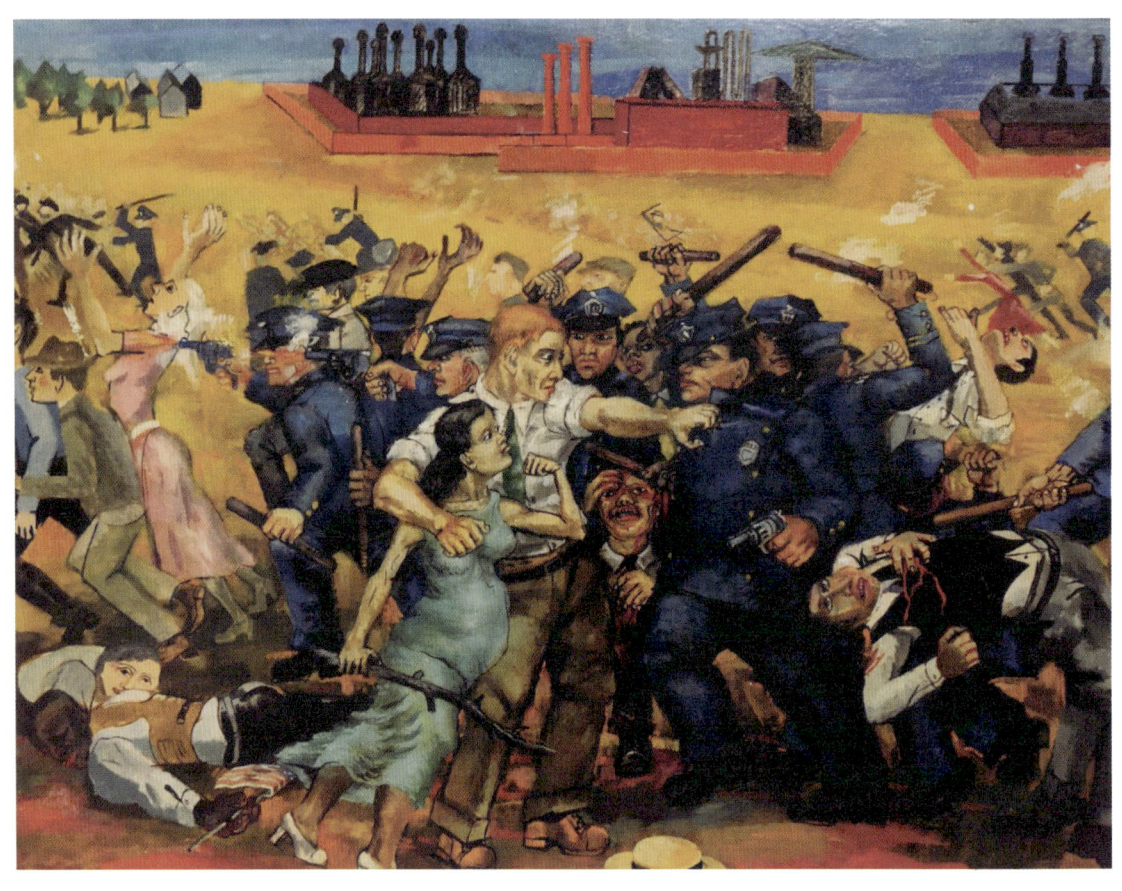

5.32 Philip Evergood, *American Tragedy*, oil on canvas, 1937. 74.9 × 100.3 cm (29½ × 39½ in.)

threatening schism. And we can now see that these tensions would have been explosive had the chillingly precise parallels between contemporary Nazi and Stalinist repression of artistic freedoms – for example the extermination of 'degenerate' Ukrainian Boichukists under the Russification policy – been known in London at the time of the *Exhibition of 20th Century German Art*.[95]

Those who had created the AIA had no desire to abandon 'spurious internationalism' – indeed they saw it as more urgent than ever. At the same time, unity amid political and aesthetic diversity had to be preserved, and the means adopted was to formalize a constitution which enshrined ultimate accountability to the membership, reinforced checks and balances, and retained organizational agility. In the period since the Artists' Congress, realizing 'An Equity for Artists' via merger with other organizations and affiliation to the Trades Union Congress had proved impossible, but this did not prevent an extremely detailed constitution being put to and adopted by the AIA's Conway Hall AGM on 28 October, four weeks after Munich.

At that meeting – which formalized tiers of membership including provision for associates and student members, financial controls and voting arrangements – a new sixteen-person Central Committee was elected, once again chaired by Black. Its membership included Nan Youngman, Betty Rea, Elizabeth Watson, Cliff Rowe and James Holland who had served before, members already central to significant activities such as Walter Durac Barnett, Helen Binyon and Ewan Phillips, and new adherents including Graham Bell and William Coldstream. The constitution also created an Advisory Council on which, despite his correspondence with Read, Paul Nash agreed to serve.

At the meeting Richard Carline rose to introduce an initiative for 1939 – working with the American Artists' Congress to bring a major exhibition of progressive Mexican and American art to Britain. The first step was to form a working group and, in the prevailing spirit of pluralism, those who agreed to serve included Klingender and Blunt, Ewan Phillips, Miriam Gabo and – ironically – Norman Dawson.[96]

At the London Gallery the previous year Dawson had attracted notoriety with his exhibit *British Diplomacy*, a tiny angler hooked to a large fish stuck with a syringe and pegged to a wooden board.[97] In the interim Dawson had maintained his aversion to communist influence, but as the dark consequences of the surrender to fascism at Munich took hold, so too did a desperate desire – for him and many others – to once again demonstrate 'the Unity of Artists for Peace, Democracy and Cultural Development'.

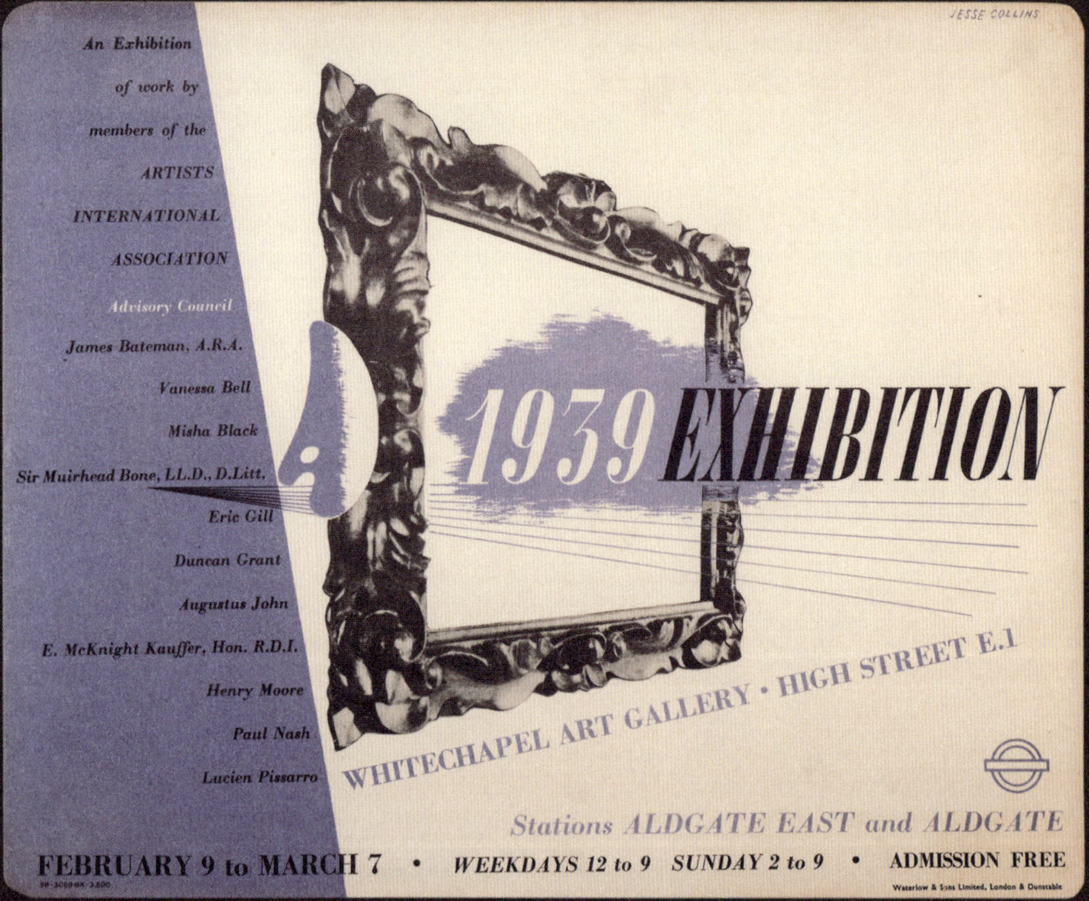

JESSE COLLINS

An Exhibition of work by members of the ARTISTS INTERNATIONAL ASSOCIATION

Advisory Council

James Bateman, A.R.A.

Vanessa Bell

Misha Black

Sir Muirhead Bone, LL.D., D.Litt.

Eric Gill

Duncan Grant

Augustus John

E. McKnight Kauffer, Hon. R.D.I.

Henry Moore

Paul Nash

Lucien Pissarro

1939 EXHIBITION

WHITECHAPEL ART GALLERY · HIGH STREET E.1

Stations ALDGATE EAST and ALDGATE

FEBRUARY 9 to MARCH 7 · WEEKDAYS 12 to 9 SUNDAY 2 to 9 · ADMISSION FREE

Waterlow & Sons Limited, London & Dunstable

CHAPTER SIX

WHITECHAPEL HIGH STREET

The AIA Central Committee which convened on the first evening of November 1938 at Misha Black's Belsize Park home would gather twenty-three times before war was declared ten months later.[1]

Black chaired all but three sessions, only absent during a trip – itself useful for AIA business – working on the British Pavilion at the New York World's Fair.[2] Now a leading light in the Industrial Design Partnership, his project management acumen and collaborative instincts would become central to an array of initiatives as an inexorable darkening swept the European scene.

Betty Rea became vice-chair and Nan Youngman – now her partner – accepted the key task of leading the Exhibitions Committee, where Elizabeth Watson, Graham Bell and William Coldstream were joined by six others, including commercial artist William Scroggie, set designer Stella Burford and Surrealists Sam Haile and F. E. McWilliam.[3] Seventeen months after Grosvenor Square closed, the Whitechapel Art Gallery had been booked for a members' exhibition on 9 February 1939. How much and what style of political content to include was under debate and an immediate priority was to set up selection committees for each section.

The decision to swap Mayfair for the East End was part of a push to 'bring aesthetically good work, with some social and political meaning' to new areas and a wider public.[4] Just before Whitechapel, a quarter of a mile away at Toynbee Hall an AIA travelling exhibition of 'lithographs, woodcuts, etc' aimed at trade union branches, co-ops and working men's clubs was going to open.[5] Called *Britain Today*, its next stop would be Edinburgh, and following Whitechapel a members' travelling exhibition of one hundred paintings was to begin a tour of fifteen municipal art galleries at Southport.[6]

That night Pat Carpenter, an eighteen-year-old student at Chelsea, agreed to organize the Students Committee and Feodora Leontinoff, a philosophy graduate, the Lectures Committee. Helen Binyon took on social events and fundraisers with Olga Mitkevitch, another new member.

6.1 Jesse Collins, *AIA Annual Exhibition Whitechapel Art Gallery*, poster design, 1939. 25.5 × 31.8 cm (10⅛ × 12⅝ in.)

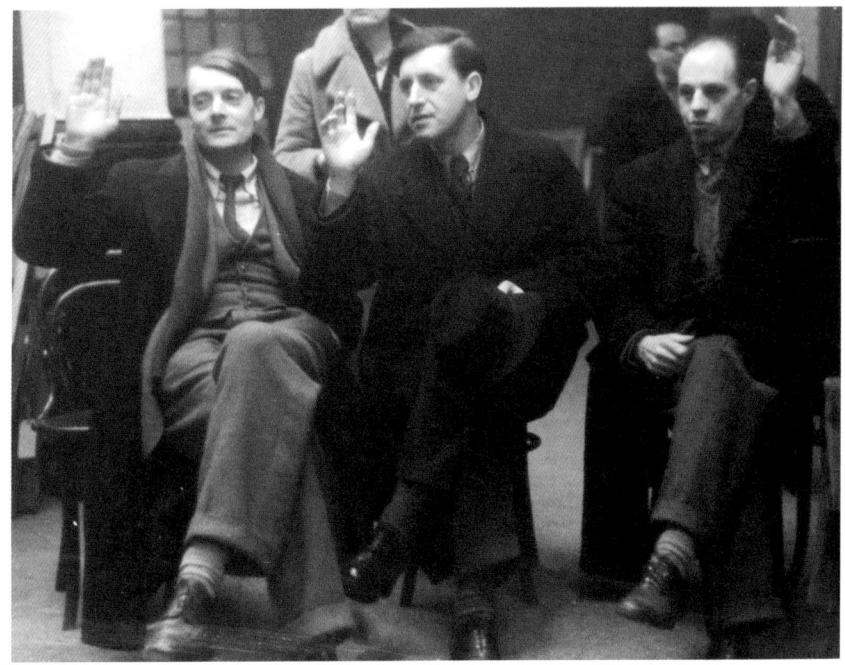

6.2 Unknown photographer, *All in Favour*; Eric Ravilious, Percy Horton and Edward Bawden acting as a selection committee, Whitechapel Art Gallery, 1 February; Misha Black can be seen in the background behind Bawden

Cliff Rowe was nominated to chair the Production Committee, overseeing material for allied organizations, demonstrations and events, and James Holland to edit the *Bulletin*, with Jesse Collins – an IDP colleague of Black's – assisting both. Holland also agreed to manage the Voluntary Printing Unit, where possibilities of producing an in-house print series were under discussion.[7]

Quentin Bell was asked to join Rea and Black 'in developing an International Bureau to keep contact with artists' organisations similar to the AIA in some 15 countries'. Ewan Phillips was confirmed as delegate to the Artists' Peace Campaign and to co-ordinate solidarity activities, including 'Portraits for Spain'. It was clear that the need to support a rising number of refugees was going to stretch resources, and a new treasurer was yet to be identified; but there was no shortage of potential volunteers for other roles, both newly arrived and from the old guard, as Percy Horton, Priscilla Thornycroft, Julian Trevelyan, James Lucas, Stanley Badmin, Stephen Bone and William Townsend assumed subcommittee positions.

Even as approaching global conflict strained spirits and twisted lives, it was the onset of a period fecund with achievement, but one which would terminate in a crisis requiring every iota of Black's diplomacy to hold the AIA together.

* * * * *

A fortnight before on 19 October, Oskar Kokoschka, accompanied by Olda Palkovská, had been overcome with relief on being cleared through Croydon Aerodrome with three months' leave to remain.⁸ After Chamberlain's capitulation at Munich, as Hitler's intention to occupy Prague after annexing Sudetenland became clear, twenty-three-year-old Olda, Kokoschka's mistress during four years of Czech exile, had queued daily to obtain exit visas and two scarce tickets. At departure Kokoschka was allowed to leave with £5 and one small painting.

Earlier that spring, as *20th Century German Art* was under preparation in London, Kokoschka had appealed to Augustus John and Herbert Read, observing that 'an artist who does not possess an English, American or French passport these days is outside the protection of the law … because your Lords have generously made the Nazis a present of my homeland Austria'.⁹ The Anschluss had swelled the flow of writers, artists and musicians escaping the Reich for Prague, where Kokoschka, reacting to the destruction of his work in Germany, had already painted *Self-Portrait of a Degenerate Artist*. Apolitical in the past, after experiencing these events as a British-condoned betrayal of democracy in Central Europe the work of his second exile would centre on searing allegories of a world in flames as seen from an English sanctuary.

A week after Kokoschka's arrival, the last meeting of the outgoing AIA Central Committee had decided to appeal for members to offer 'temporary hospitality to the large number of refugees who were arriving in England in the next week or so' and that Betty Rea would write to a Prague artists' organization to ask 'what way can the AIA assist their artists'. By the second meeting of the new committee on 8 November no reply had arrived, but discussions were under way with Stephen Bone and Roland Penrose, who had received a letter from the painter Josef Čapek asking for urgent assistance to obtain visas and work permits. The following night was *Kristallnacht*, a German Reich-wide pogrom of unparalleled ferocity which added menace to urgency, and at the following meeting a broad appeal to the profession was agreed. The Central Committee decided the London Group and the Royal Academy should be asked to join a bespoke artists' body working with the British Committee for Refugees. To further this, prospective AIA Advisory Council members would be asked to individually endorse the appeal.¹⁰

A week later Stephen Bone tabled a list of nineteen artists in great danger in Prague and Ewan Phillips reported that the scheme to send food hampers to artists in Spain was being postponed due to the urgency of assisting Czech refugees. Seven names were added to a list of individuals asked to work with Rea, Bone and Penrose, including Jack Hastings and the German-speaking Mrs Uhlman. Within two weeks Diana Uhlman had become secretary to

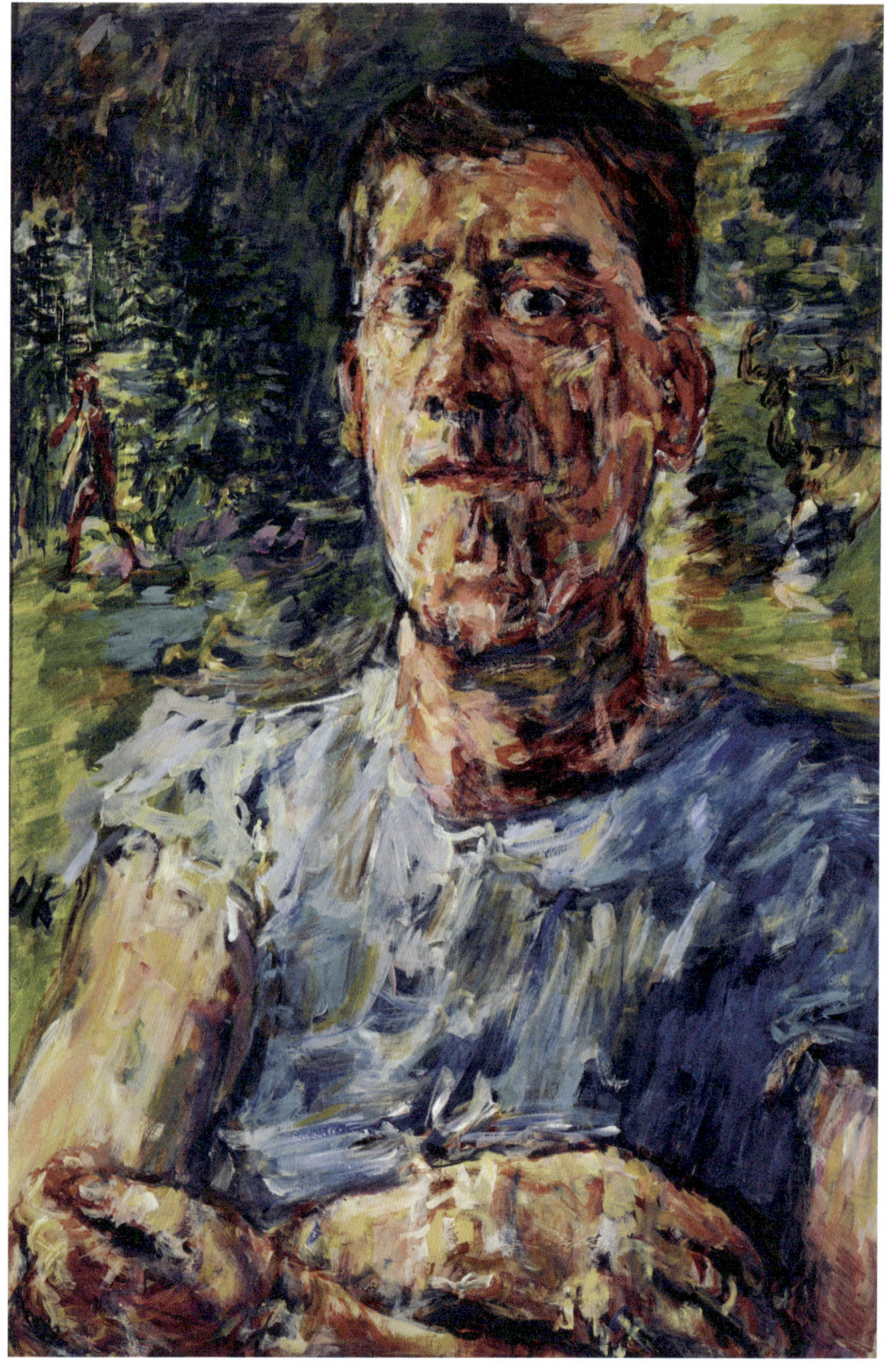

the emerging Artists' Refugee Committee based at her and Fred's recently acquired house in Downshire Hill, Hampstead, and shortly after Rea was able to report on 'the satisfactory progress of the Refugee Committee'. Over the next eighteen months, before internment of her husband as an enemy alien and the birth of her first child, Diana's energy and skill were crucial, as indeed they would be during two decades of AIA work to come.

On 23 November Olda wrote in her diary, 'Evening at Uhlman. Founding of the *Freie Kunstlerbund*'. At another evening session a month later a working committee was formalized.[11] Made up of the social democrat Fred Uhlman, exiled writer Hans Flesch, the recently arrived and exhausted Communist Party member John Heartfield and unaligned humanist Oskar Kokoschka, it worked towards a public launch of the Free German League of Culture (FGLC) in March 1939.[12] In the Dresden of 1920, Heartfield and Kokoschka had engaged in bitter dispute in the aftermath of the Kapp putsch, but now the reality of exile and the urgency of resisting fascism was uniting them.[13]

*****

For two years since Felicia Browne's death, the Spanish Republic had been the nucleus of democratic hope, the object of fundraising initiatives and acts of solidarity, but now attention was rapidly shifting towards what could be done to secure survival for victims of its impending defeat.

As Kokoschka flew to London, the *Guernica* exhibition at Burlington Galleries was under way and in Barcelona 305 British volunteers were taking part in a farewell parade for the International Brigades, their withdrawal part of a forlorn diplomatic gamble to build pressure for German and Italian disengagement. From London, Roland Penrose wrote disconsolately to Picasso that only 3,000 had visited the West End gallery, the Munich crisis having engendered 'a drained-out feeling of collective lethargy'.[14] Soon after, however, there was a more energetic incarnation when selections of Picasso's preliminary drawings attracted enormous interest in Oxford and Leeds.

As the Central Committee met at Nan Youngman's on 7 December, the Brigade survivors were arriving at Victoria Station after crossing the Channel to Newhaven. Met by Major Clement Attlee, leader of the Labour opposition, they were bussed to the London Co-operative Society's headquarters in Stepney prior to a dinner honouring the more than five hundred Brigaders who had died, the *AIA Bulletin* then in circulation carrying notice of a Dependants' Aid Fund with a £50,000 target.[15]

Alongside studio parties for Spanish Medical Aid and selling exhibitions in supporters' houses, 'Portraits for Spain' was the most significant

6.3 Oskar Kokoschka, *Self-Portrait of a Degenerate Artist*, oil on canvas, 1937. 110 × 85 cm (43⅜ × 33½ in.)

AIA fundraiser in 1938, signing up 118 members offering work at their usual fees to donors. In July Eric Ravilious – passing up the opportunity to paint Dame Adelaide Livingstone's dachshund – was an early contributor when Lord Farringdon, one of Jack Hastings's closest friends from the 1920s, paid ten guineas for a watercolour of his country house Buscot Park, at the time hosting a Basque children's camp.[16] 'Portraits for Spain' had already raised £570 (around £33,000 at mid-2020s prices) when just after New Year Ewan Phillips received a cheque for 500 guineas from George Cadbury for a portrait by Augustus John, the fee being paid ahead of his father sitting 'due to the urgency of the Spanish need' and on condition that no publicity attached to family or confectionery company.[17]

Need had already led Spanish Relief to launch a nationwide campaign of 'Foodships for Spain', the first leaving Glasgow in late October with others following from Merseyside, Tyneside, the Humber and London, where collection of £5,700 enabled despatch of the *Clonlara* on 29 December. Intended for Barcelona it had to be diverted to Valencia, and the day before it arrived the fall of Tarragona to the Nationalists sparked the beginnings of a mass exodus from Catalonia to France as civilians and ex-combatants fled, pushed by fear in the dying weeks of a lost war.[18] Over 400,000 refugees crossed the border in bitter winter weather; under the French Socialist prime minister Blum they might have received a humane welcome, but under his successor Daladier concentration camps awaited; 100,000 would be herded into the one at Argelès-sur-Mer alone. Funds from the 'Portraits for Spain' scheme, originally launched to resupply the AIA ambulance, were now required for other purposes, and soon after Mark Gertler, Muirhead Bone and Henry Moore represented the AIA at an all-London meeting, efforts began to reach thirty-five artists already known to be in the camps.[19]

In the new year Picasso's drawings were reunited with *Guernica* at Whitechapel for a fifteen-day exhibition opened by Attlee and supported by the Labour Party and the AIA, with Jack Hastings acting as financial guarantor. Held in aid of Stepney Trades Council's 'million pennies' foodship appeal, it attracted 15,000 visitors in the first week, and a remarkable sight was 'the serried ranks of working men's boots' left at the painting's base, the alternative price of admission being a pair 'in a fit state to be sent to the Spanish front'.[20]

On 4 February a second ship left the Port of London after a campaign supported by nine London MPs, seventeen Borough Mayors and Herbert Morrison, chairman of the London County Council (LCC), a body which now provided twenty-two hoardings to the AIA in support of the continuing campaign. With Picasso's great mural already moved for display in an unused Manchester car showroom and the AIA's member exhibition at Whitechapel a week into its four-week run, Betty Rea briefed the Central

6.4 Norman King, Clement Attlee opening the *Guernica* fundraising exhibition at Whitechapel, January 1939

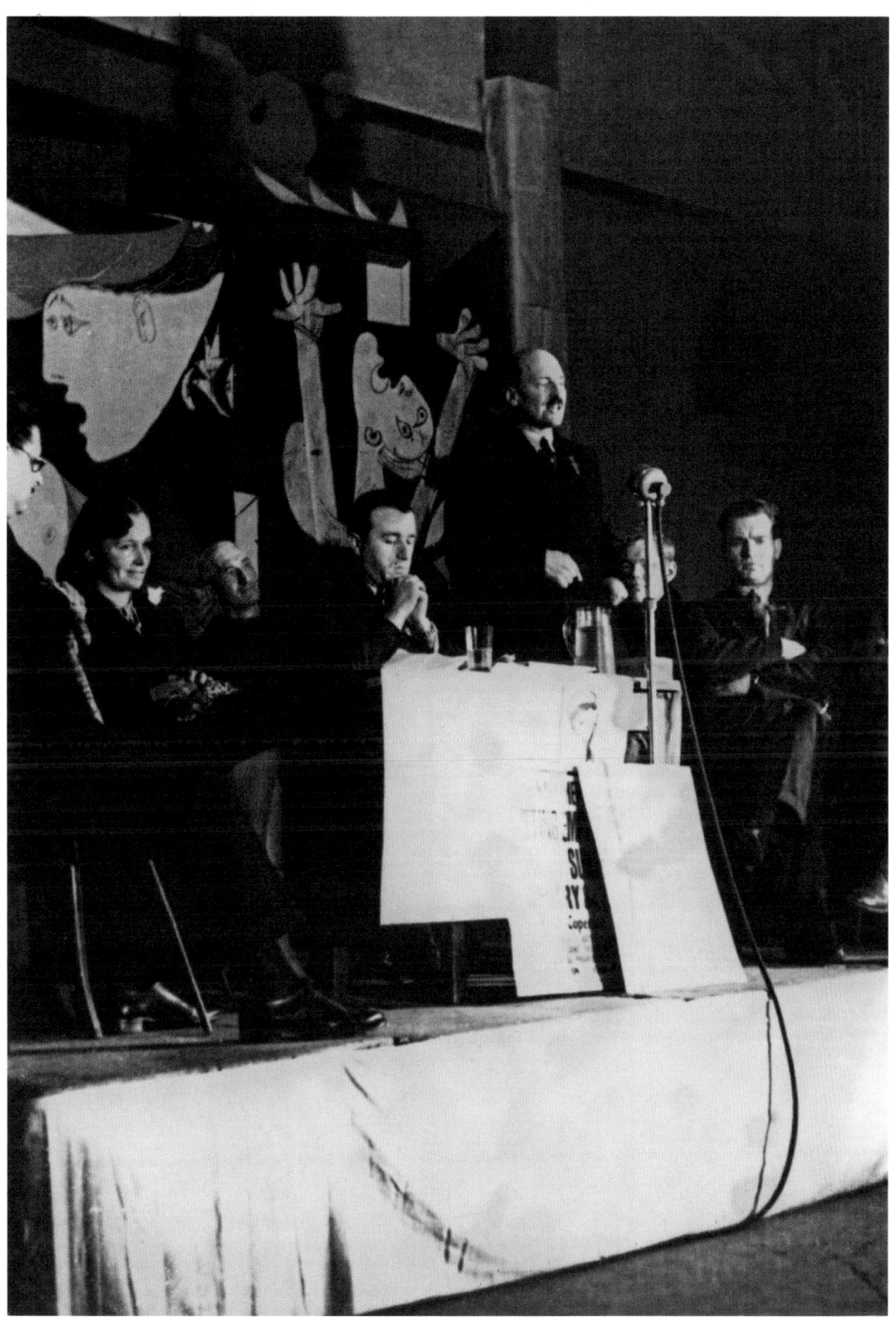

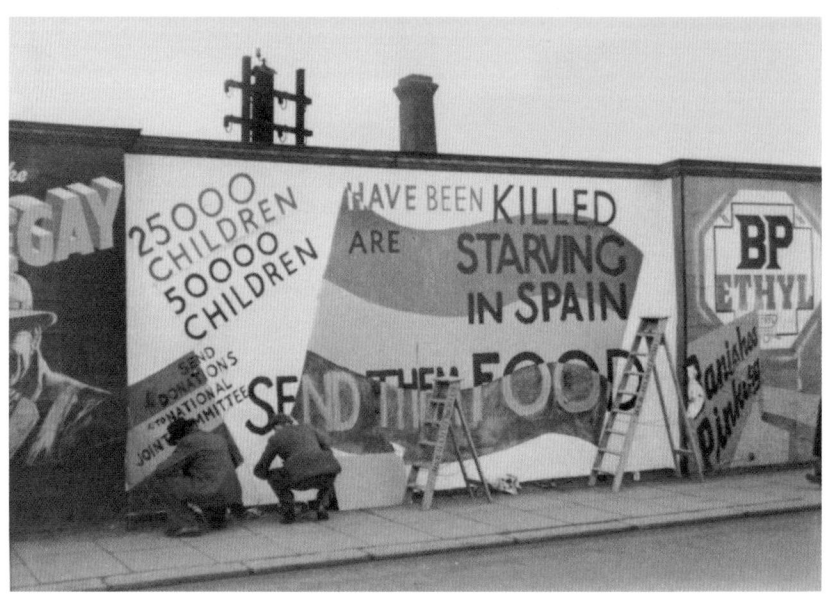

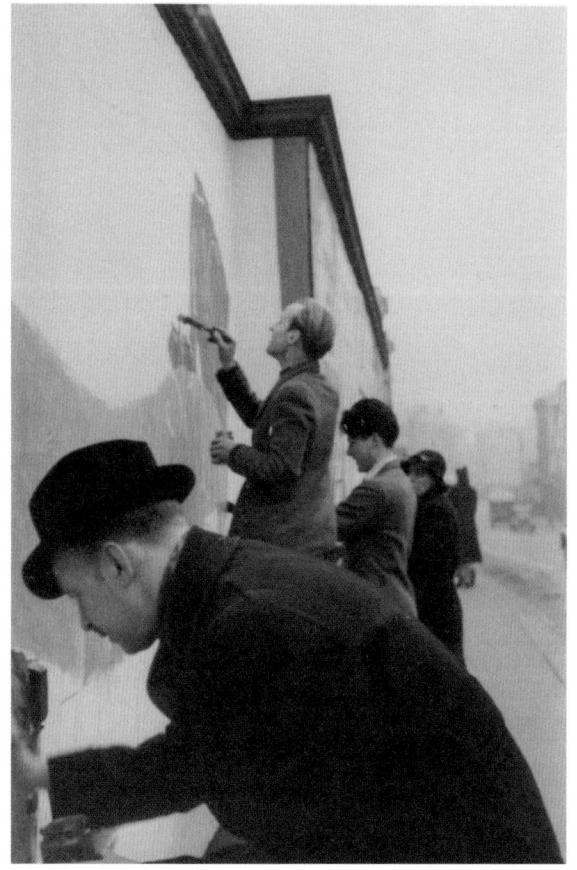

6.5 Unknown photographer, AIA billboards reflecting the shift from a call for arms to food aid to be supplied to Republican Spain, February 1939

6.6 Unknown photographer, Ceri Richards, Sam Haile and colleagues working on a campaign billboard, February 1939

Committee that eight hoardings were to be 'painted live' by teams of artists, the rest used for posters, adding that those already developing schemes should be made aware of recent developments in Spain; Barcelona had fallen on 26 January.

On Saturday 18 February the *Daily Herald* reported: 'ninety men and women, artists and students, set out to paint London red, and every other colour yesterday. Some are still painting.'[21] It narrated how passers-by saw 'Send Food to Spain Now, Save 50,000 children' appear in Bouverie Street, and how in South Kensington Cliff Rowe, Edith Simon, Roy Laurier and Alex Koolman worked into the night painting columns of troops winding out of sight behind a foreground of refugees, highlighting Angelica Bell's starving child beside an empty plate in Vauxhall and Sam Haile and Ceri Richards blazoning 'Send them Food' across a giant Spanish flag outside West Brompton tube station. Extensive press publicity was amplified by the cinema newsreels, and the March *News-Sheet* welcomed 'the interested and sympathetic crowds' who had watched it happen, decrying the subsequent defacing of several sites with fascist graffiti.

* * * * *

The AIA's *Unity of Artists for Peace, Democracy and Cultural Development* at Whitechapel has gone down in history as 'the exhibition opened by the man in the street' – as indeed it was, although only after protracted efforts to find a better known figure.[22] Initial suggestions included asking Anthony Eden, who had resigned as Foreign Secretary in protest at Chamberlain's appeasement of Italy, J. B. Priestley, H. G. Wells or Kenneth Clark; Herbert Morrison had been approached, but the LCC leader evidently declined to appear in the gallery quite so hard on Attlee's heels. Instead at the appointed hour Nan Youngman, accompanied by a press photographer, apprehended 'a small man in a cap with a fag and an unemployed look' on Whitechapel High Street, persuading him to step inside and declare the exhibition open.[23] Jesse Collins's exhibition poster, meanwhile, happily made use of 'names', listing eleven members of the newly minted AIA Advisory Council, the absentee being David Low, whose acceptance had arrived too late for the press work.[24]

As Youngman recalled: 'The show was didactic, in that it was arranged in kinds – abstract, figurative, surrealist, etc. We even laid on artists to speak for each section'; a party of teachers she was taking round quizzed a painter, probably Julian Trevelyan, about his works, eliciting the explanation 'that was done under the influence of a South American drug'.[25] In all 297 works by 165 members were included, with a notable contribution from women exhibitors: of those identifiable by gender, 74 were female,

84 male. As at Grosvenor Square, both abstract and Surrealist sections incorporated leading figures, but this time within a tighter selection; thus Ben Nicholson, Barbara Hepworth, Jessica Dismorr and the Irish painter Mainie Jellett figured among eleven contributors to the Abstract gallery, and Paul Nash, Henry Moore, Julian Trevelyan, Sam Haile, Ceri Richards, Eileen Agar, Ithell Colquhoun, Edith Rimmington, John Banting and F. E. McWilliam among the twenty-four Surrealists. In addition to Moore and Hepworth there was a strong presence of sculpture, with Betty Rea, Gertrude Hermes, Frank Dobson, Peter László Peri and Tisa Hess contributing thirteen pieces.[26] Four – *Group*, *Friends*, *Toil* and *Lovers* – were by Hess who, born into Prussian nobility as Elisabeth von der Schulenburg, had left Germany for East Anglia and joined the AIA in 1936; she then spent the next two years teaching at the Spennymoor Settlement in County Durham, 'promoting the artwork of miners, employed and unemployed alike, in the Northeastern coalfield'.[27] A Central Committee member the previous year, she was now working on the American exhibition and preparations for May Day.

Although he left to work in Dublin the day after it opened, Graham Bell had a major influence on the Whitechapel show: as conduit for the Euston Road School's 'new realism' (the show's most striking artistic departure); as author of the catalogue preface and that for its follow-on tour; and as instigator of its most political element – a series of visual transliterations from Goya, marking with uncanny timeliness the passing of the Republic and the horrors and cruelties then under way.[28] His voice is also discernible in the unsigned foreword, declaring: 'In the last 50 years, particularly those who paint pictures or do sculpture have through no fault of their own become isolated from the greater part of society which supports them … In this show the artists have gone to some trouble to make their work available to as large a public as possible … Artists believe they could still be useful. They are trying to find out how.' Unsurprisingly the exhibition included notable work from Bell's key collaborators William Coldstream, Claude Rogers and Victor Pasmore.

Over the five days following the fall of Barcelona, Bell, Pasmore, Lawrence Gowing and Rodrigo Moynihan had created a series of protest banners referencing Goya painted on cheesecloth purchased through East End Communist Party contacts.[29] Their use two weeks later at an 'Arms for Spain' rally in Trafalgar Square was evidently disorganized and ineffective, the iconography more appropriate to a peace rally than the demand articulated, leading Cliff Rowe to point out that the Production Committee should have been consulted.[30] But a more substantial contribution graced Whitechapel in the form of seven canvases, hung separately but variously listed as 'after Goya': Bell's own *Bury Them and Be Silent*, Moynihan's

6.7 Ben Nicholson, *Composition, 1933*, oil and pencil on board, 1933. 47.7 × 45.7 cm (18⅞ × 18 in.). This is probably the work Nicholson exhibited at Whitechapel as cat. 149

6.8 Jessica Dismorr, *Superimposed Forms*, oil on gesso prepared board, 1938. 46 × 61 cm (18⅛ × 24⅛ in.); cat. 152 at Whitechapel

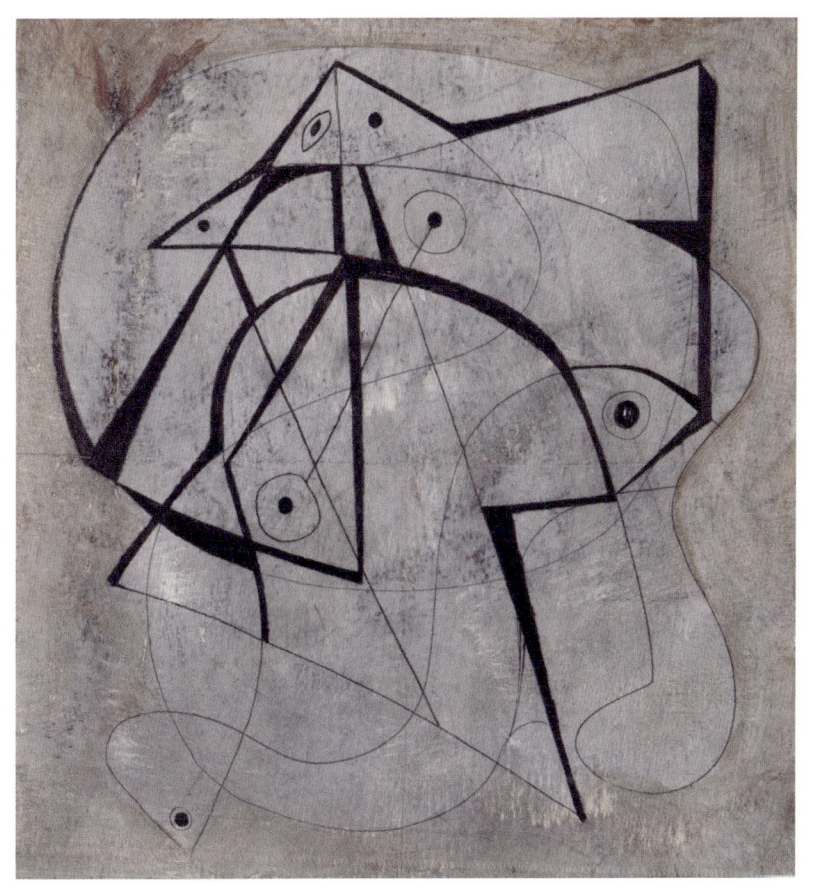

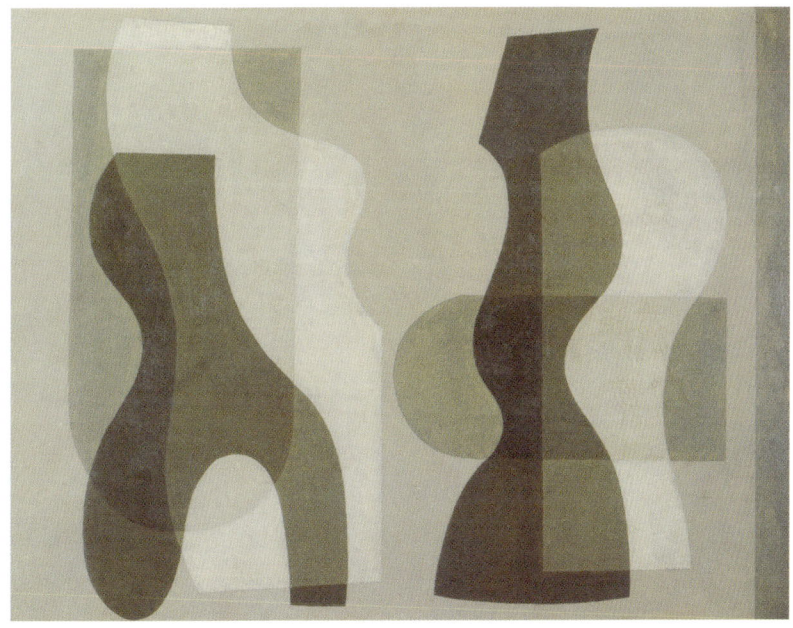

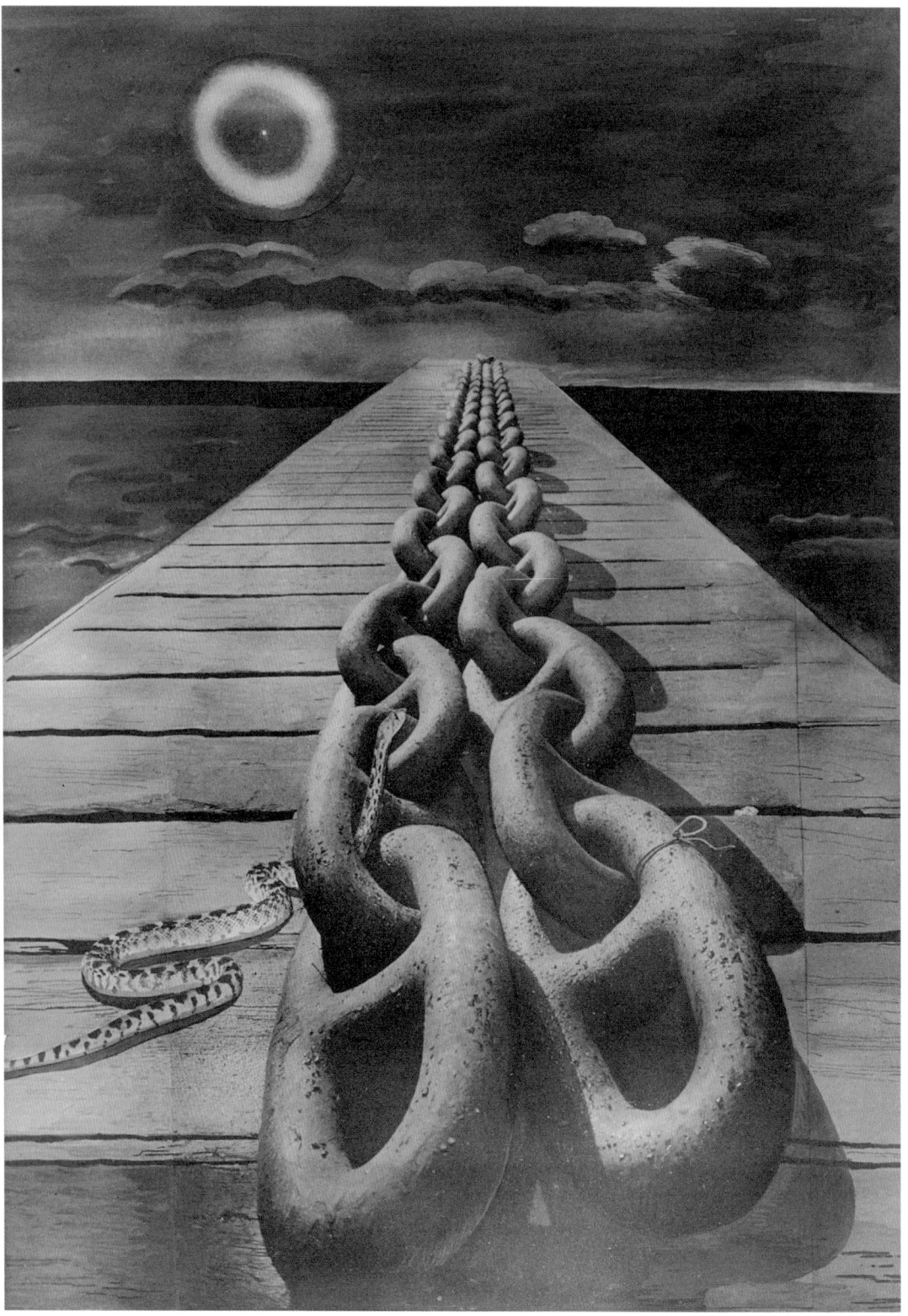

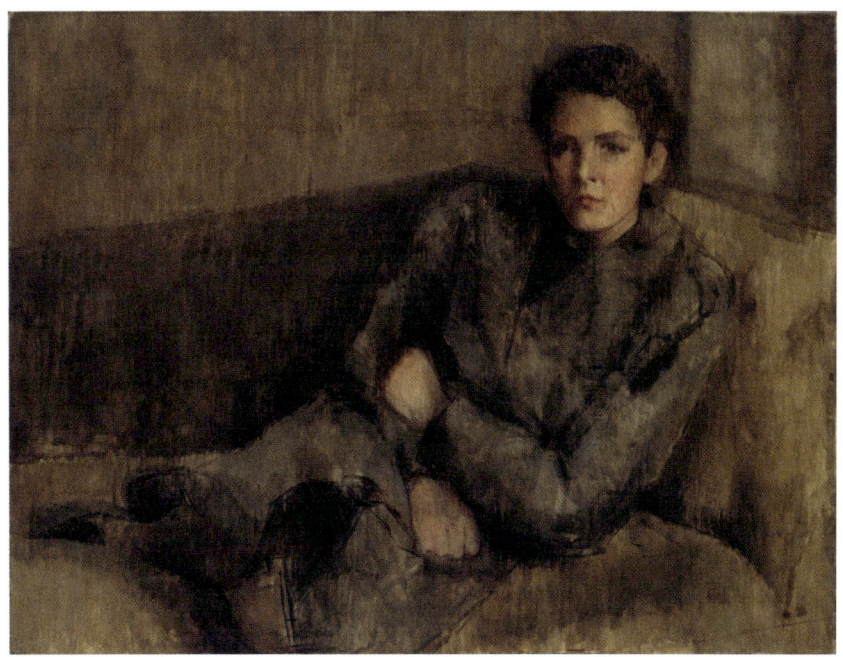

Pursuers Have No Mercy, Gowing's *Non Combatants*, Pasmore's *It Cannot Be Long Now*, Duncan Grant's *After Goya* and Carel Weight's *Transcription of Goya's Unhappy Mother*. Together with Helen Binyon's *Puppets for Spain* and Peter László Peri's sculpture *Spain* – a mother and daughter looking skywards at approaching bombers – these made up the most elegiac and at once the most political vein of the exhibition. As for the banners, they helped decorate the dance hall at the concluding social on 7 March.

An estimated 40,000 people had visited over four weeks, many voting for their favourite works: in descending order, the top seven were by William Coldstream, Stephen Bone, John Nash, Stanley Badmin, Frank Dobson, Patricia Preece and Cliff Rowe. The instincts of the Exhibitions Committee in terms of venue and the selection committees in terms of the hang had been rewarded. After agreeing letters of thanks, the Central Committee immediately booked the Whitechapel for the 1940 members' show and suggested using it as the venue for the American exhibition.[31]

6.9 Edith Rimmington, *Family Tree*, photographic collage, 1937. 35 × 25 cm (13⅞ × 9⅞ in.). Rimmington exhibited three collages at Whitechapel

6.10 William Coldstream, *Inez Spender*, oil on canvas, 1937–38. 77 × 101.8 cm (30⅜ × 40⅛ in.); cat. 35 at Whitechapel, voted best picture by the visiting public

* * * * *

With contributors on hand to provide explanations and talks such as 'They know what they like – Criticisms of the Present Exhibition', Whitechapel reflected the desire for a new dynamic between artist and public, a mission now furthered beyond the metropolis with *Travelling Exhibition No. 1* and

Britain Today. The former sought to take contemporary but conventional easel art and sculpture to provincial locations starved of it, and the latter to leverage artists' prints as an affordable and accessible way of reaching a mass audience.

The previous autumn the AIA had come together with the Lithographers' Union and the anti-fascist vigilance body For Intellectual Liberty to create a Voluntary Printing Unit equipped with a miniature high-speed offset press.[32] With James Holland and Jesse Collins on its executive committee, thoughts now turned to how its capacity could be used to produce lithographs at affordable prices, the ambition being to replicate what the sixpenny paperback had recently done for writers. Partly inspired by Robert Wellington's 1937–38 venture Contemporary Lithographs (an artistic success but a commercial failure), along with an awareness of mass print output achieved by the Graphic Arts Division of the US Federal Art Project, development of a 'prints scheme' was now endorsed, the intention being to test the market with reproductions of works by Winifred Nicholson, Augustus John, Laura Knight, Richard Eurich, John Nash and James Fitton. In the event the economics of short runs defeated this, the first of a number of false starts in which a variable supply of skilled volunteers also played a part. But by mid-summer 1939 a tentative model for an 'Everyman Prints' series was emerging, with marketing through department stores being explored and forty or so zinc plates distributed to members for the creation of original works.

The other major project in development tapped transatlantic inspiration more directly. Richard Carline had been an official war artist in the Great War and was part of a Hampstead artistic nexus that included Gertler, Penrose, Sir Muirhead Bone and his son Stephen. He had engaged with the AIA from 1935, facilitating contacts with anti-fascists in Holland and France; but this deepened in 1938 after he visited a joint Artists' Union/American Artists' Congress exhibition in New York and was galvanized by the socially conscious art on display, feeling it would be 'an eye-opener for British artists and absolutely in line with what the AIA wished to do themselves'.[33] Through Philip Evergood, a friend from his Slade days, Carline opened discussions with Harry Gottlieb of the AU and Stuart Davis, now AAC president. After further visits to New York by himself and Misha Black, the AIA working group in London was soon examining a list of 187 potential contributors for an exhibition of 500 works, plans for a linked Penguin Special and a provincial tour.

There was now every possibility of mounting a blockbuster exhibition, although Mexico City's commitment to a different European tour had scuppered this component. The passage of time had also rendered redundant opening at Whitechapel in July, and after tortuous negotiation with gallery management the dates shifted to 10 April–5 June 1940. With financial details between the AIA in London and the AU/AAC in New York already negotiated, a relieved Misha Black wrote to Gottlieb on 12 June stressing that the Federal Art Project, then under attack, would engender enormous interest and that all works produced under it would be clearly marked as such.[34] The only negative development was the forced resignation of Tisa Hess after receiving a Home Office warning that her permission to stay in Britain precluded political activity.[35]

As if in rehearsal of oncoming events, the AIA Central Committee frequently debated public policy that impinged on the economic prospects of artists, a focus since the 1937 Artists' Congress; thus Ron Horton, Percy's brother and a member of the CP Hogarth group of artists, advised on the implications for art teachers of the Spens Report on secondary education and Rowe on display opportunities that might arise from the Markham Report on museums. But from spring to summer 1939 one issue became dominant – the stance to be taken towards military conscription.[36] An initial position that voluntary Air Raid Precaution (ARP) service 'adhering to democratic principles' might be acceptable but that 'service which came within the scope of the military machine' could not be considered 'under the present Govt. policy' delivered more questions than answers, exposing divisions between pacifist beliefs and peace campaigning on the one hand and those primarily concerned to confront fascism and appeasement's dereliction on the other. Multiple redrafts and consultation with the Advisory Council followed (David Low commenting that the body had no point if its advice was not sought at the outset), as did accommodation of militant student voices and a general meeting prior to a rewrite by Rea ahead of an intended autumn pronouncement.

It was the strangest of summers, combining ennui, personal difficulties and snatched moments of escape with lingering hope that diplomacy might yet forestall global conflict. A memorandum on a proposed photography exhibition presented to the Exhibitions Committee began: 'The people of this country will shortly be asked to record their votes in a General Election. The election will almost certainly be run on a wave of militant patriotism. If there is a Russian pact it will undoubtedly be the main plank in the Conservative platform, only to be ignored in favour of appeasement once the Munichers are assured of another run of power. The purpose of the exhibition is to remind people as forcibly as possible of their democratic rights [and] the appalling position to which we have been brought by ten years of blundering and moral bankruptcy.'[37] In late June Mark Gertler, who defying slender means and depression had recently donated generously to AIA refugee relief, gassed himself in his Highgate studio, seized by fears of war and anti-Semitism.[38] In July Tisa Hess, having attended her father's funeral in Germany, was denied re-entry and forced to return to the Nazi domain.[39]

At the penultimate meeting before the August break, Beryl Sinclair reported receiving a phone call from J. N. Duddington, secretary at the Whitechapel, informing her that his committee had decided against letting the gallery to the AIA during 1940, having 'sufficient ideas of its own to fill up all the dates'.[40] The news was received 'with no little astonishment', but it soon emerged that the chairman of the gallery trustees, Lord Balneil MP, had vetoed the AIA as a 'red organisation'. Soon after, a *Time* review of the Left Book Club's new title *Tory MP* cited Balneil – related by blood or marriage to a dozen other Conservative MPs – as typical of those who 'give Prime Minister Chamberlain his majority, crisis after crisis'.[41] Meanwhile, efforts to reverse the decision were left in the hands of Black and Sinclair, and a campaign for Tisa's re-entry was agreed, both issues to be taken up in mid-September after a month's pause, with meetings called only in an emergency.

* * * * *

The news from Moscow which would create first disbelief, then chasms of division among friends and comrades, reached London over the airwaves within the hour on 23 August; it was soon followed by a black-and-white image of Stalin smiling as he oversaw Ribbentrop and Molotov signing the Nazi-Soviet non-aggression pact.

Had this shock wave hit the year before, key AIA members would have had the opportunity of reacting together during a group holiday on the Île de Ré. But summer 1939 was a season of more diverse journeys, a proffered repeat at Concarneau in Brittany apparently attracting few takers.[42] Nan Youngman and Betty Rea, in France with Betty's sons and friends who thought it a Russian masterstroke 'that meant there would be no war', nevertheless hurried back across the Channel, but Sam Haile – opposing any compromise with militarism – crossed the border to Switzerland, determined to avoid conscription as indications mounted that a German invasion of Poland was imminent.[43]

At 1.30 p.m. on Thursday 31 August the Central Committee members who were in London met at 4 Bedford Square, the offices of the Industrial Design Partnership.[44] There they agreed a statement to members, beginning: 'We had planned to distribute today the September issue of the *AIA Bulletin*. This contained details of our plans for the autumn – new exhibitions, the cheap prints scheme, and other activities to which we had looked forward with pleasurable anticipation ... Unfortunately the Munich agreement of last Autumn has brought the results prophesied by ourselves and all those who were not deceived by Mr Chamberlain's talk of lasting peace. We feel therefore that temporarily we must hold up our plans and reconsider our general position.' One thousand unsparing words of analysis dissected how Britain's failure to negotiate in good faith had confirmed Moscow's judgment that Russia was vulnerable because Britain's government was no more serious now in resisting Hitler than 'it had been in its avowed guarantee of Czechoslovakian independence'. After noting that Moscow's démarche had undermined the basis of the anti-Comintern pact binding 'fascist and semi-fascist states' together, the statement called for a British government 'sincere in its desire for a lasting democratic peace', before concluding 'we in Britain must on no account retreat from our pledge to Poland'.[45]

Mimeographed on Friday 1 September, the day German troops crossed into Poland, this reached most London members that day or the next, but only arrived in some hands after Chamberlain's broadcast on the morning of 3 September declaring that Britain was at war with Germany.

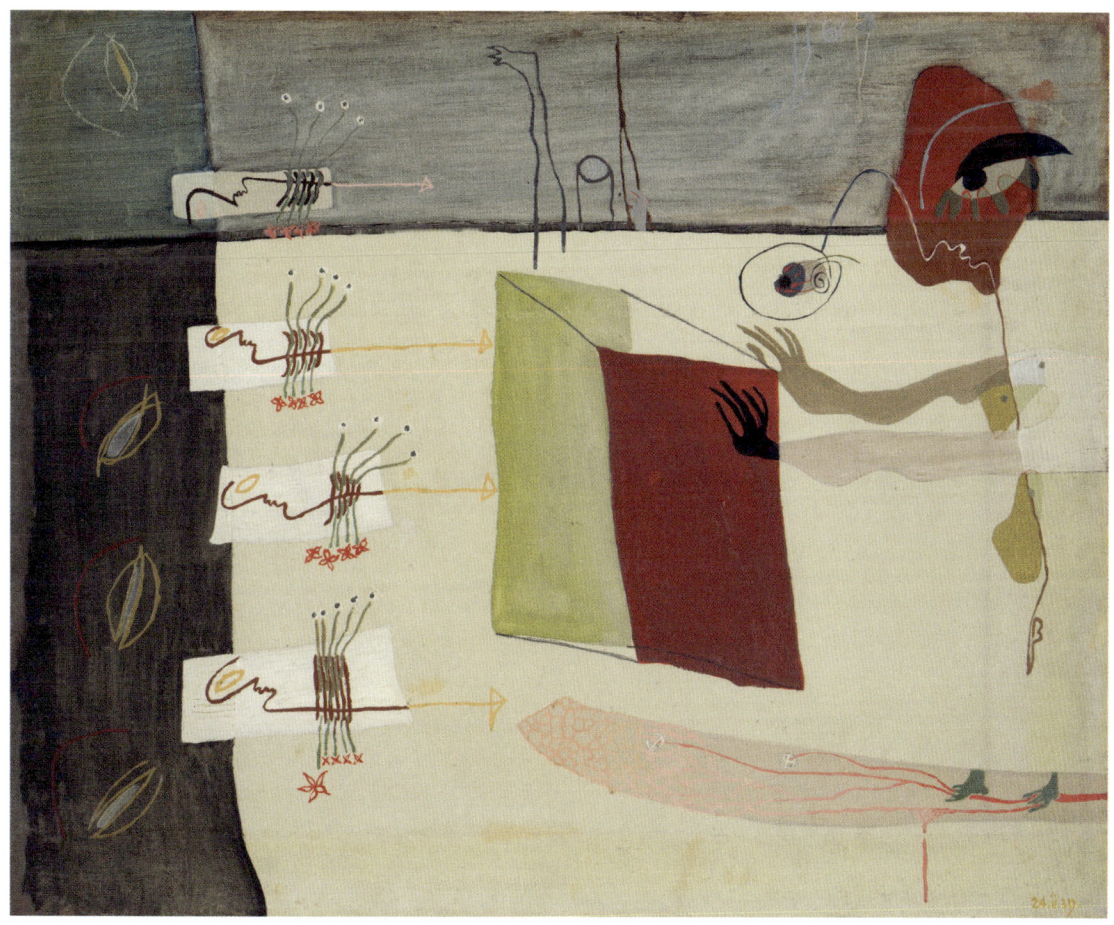

6.11 Sam Haile, *Surgical Ward*, oil on canvas, 1939. 61 × 76.2 cm (24⅛ × 30 in.). A work from the same series as *Then Lie there Precious White Psychiatrist* which was exhibited at Whitechapel, cat. 136

With events accelerating, conscription coming into force, children being evacuated, an exodus from London for fear of bombing and public galleries and art schools closing, a nucleus of the Central Committee met on 5 September, deciding to suspend weekly meetings, pause activity and keep in contact via Black and Rea. Issued four days later, *Emergency Bulletin No. 2* gave members information on how to apply for camouflage and propaganda work and proposed the committee should stay in office until the end of November, 'by which time it may be possible to see more clearly what the situation is likely to be in this country'.[46]

But by the time a printed *Emergency Bulletin No. 3* was despatched less than a month later, AIA activity had radically changed gear, partly in response to controversy but largely through an intense effort to redefine strategy and tactics for a time of war. As its preamble related: 'Immediately it was seen that, at least temporarily, it was possible to continue working from London, the AIA Central Committee was recalled and action was taken to try and improve the disastrous position in which many artists found themselves at the outbreak of hostilities. The Central Committee has been meeting twice each week, the sub-committees have been augmented, and a certain amount of progress has been made.'

The first item of business after the recall was news that Edward McKnight Kauffer and Eric Gill had resigned from the Advisory Council in opposition to the stance taken, subsequently agreeing to hold off only until the AGM; letters of protest had also been received from David Low and others variously critiquing support for 'Stalin and the present Communist Party', compromise with a 'war to save Imperialism in the interests of the ruling-class', and naive thinking that 'war-like means could bring about peaceable ends'.[47] To meet the evident danger of division the committee began preparations for an AGM, setting the date so as to allow time for postal voting, a new departure; at the same time, over two weeks and five meetings, Black, Rea, Rowe, Phillips and Horton developed a 'political statement' which appeared in the *Bulletin* headlined 'The Wider Issues'. Designed to forestall matters, it reported the criticisms made, but did not retreat from the notion that the Soviet stance had been 'a genuine peace policy' and that collective security had collapsed in Europe 'largely due, we believe, to the lack of co-operation of our own Government'. Instead, it declared: 'We are willing to support this war only so long as it remains a genuine war to defeat Nazism, free Europe from the constant threat of aggression, and bring a greater degree of democracy and freedom to the world.' In closing it suggested the Association now had two tasks – to 'assure that the talent of those artists who wish to help win the war is not wasted' and 'to see that the culture of the country is not annihilated during the period of hostilities'.

It was hoped this would be acceptable to most; but within days a second political earthquake hit which would strain unity beyond measure over the next twenty months. Before Chamberlain's broadcast, Harry Pollitt, general secretary of the CPGB, had called the impending conflict 'a just war which should be supported by the whole working-class and all friends of democracy in Britain'; 'to stand aside', he added, 'to contribute only revolutionary-sounding phrases while the Fascist beasts ride roughshod over Europe would be a betrayal of everything our forebears have fought for'.[48] But on 11 October Pollitt – who believed that in a defeated Britain 'the Nazi Party and the Gestapo will outlaw every atom of working-class organisation' – was ousted and replaced by Rajani Palme Dutt, an upholder of the newly proclaimed Comintern line that the war was a struggle between imperialists which revolutionaries should thwart rather than support. It was a volte-face that heightened the risk of an AIA split.

* * * * *

Even after five weeks, however, the claim that progress was being made on things that mattered to artists in war time was not unfounded.

When the Central Committee reconvened, demand for the services of artists of all types – fine and commercial, employed and freelance – was in freefall. Wholesale lay-offs and job cancellations were already besetting the country's estimated 3,000 commercial artists, London's galleries, schools and institutions were indefinitely closed, and it now emerged names already on a Ministry of Labour camouflage and propaganda register outstripped potential requirements by ten to one.[49] In response, a subgroup including Ewan Phillips, Elizabeth Watson, the painter Walter Durac Barnett, Percy Horton and Nan Youngman were deputed to develop an agenda 'to further productive employment of artists during the war period' and Black to co-ordinate lobbying of government departments.[50] Within weeks an AIA survey showed 73 per cent of 1,426 respondents had either lost jobs or commissions since hostilities began.[51]

By 19 September a letter from Sir Kenneth Clark had arrived regretting the art school closures and making suggestions which were referred to the Productive Employment Committee, whose draft report drew on previous AIA experience of travelling shows, visual propaganda and information campaigns. When the 'government draft' was read out by Percy Horton a week later, an appendix on the Federal Art Project was added, and another on portable exhibitions as 'a medium for Health, ARP and Emergency instruction'. Similar moves were afoot within the Society of Industrial Artists (SIA), where Black's IDP colleague Milner Gray was secretary. Both men now met with Clark who indicated full support for the AIA agenda, including 'organisation of artists to chronicle conditions at the war fronts and the changing life of the country'; travelling exhibitions to serve the reception areas; itinerant artists to provide classes for evacuees; employment of artists to decorate barracks, hospitals, canteens and ARP shelters; the setting up of design research units for specific industries; and the reopening of the National Galleries for displays of contemporary work.[52]

Appointed director of the National Gallery in 1934 at the age of thirty-one, Clark was both well-networked and well-off, telling his visitors he was considering providing his Portland Place townhouse for use as a war-time artists' club and suggesting that the AIA convene 'a meeting of delegates from the more progressive art societies' to consider their proposals. In the past he had been chary of involvement, neither associating himself with the 1937 congress nor agreeing to appear at the Albert Hall *Spain and Culture* event, after being warned off from 'any expression of political opinion' as a 'Government servant'.[53] But now, having overseen evacuation of the national collection to Wales, and on the point of an unlikely recruitment to the burgeoning Ministry of Information as director of its film division, Clark was contemplating campaigning for artists to be employed with Treasury funds 'to make a record of the war in all its aspects'; four weeks later he published his suggestions in *The Listener*. Before this, however, three days after meeting with Black and Gray, he wrote to Humbert Wolfe, deputy secretary at the Ministry of Labour: 'the situation of artists is so serious that I have been wondering if it would not be desirable for the Government to take some action; rather a wider application than mere employment of artists for camouflage and propaganda. I have in mind something like the federal scheme for artists carried out in America during the last five years, though ours would no doubt have to be on a less ambitious scale.'[54]

A meeting of delegates from twenty-two artists' societies took place on 2 November in the empty National Gallery. Chaired by Clark, it called for the formation of a Central Institute of Art and Design (CAID) as a clearing house for artistic endeavour during the war effort and to 'enable opinion to be concentrated in such a way as to greatly increase the possibility of effective action'; articulated by Horton, the AIA view that the Central Institute of Art and Design (CIAD) should be government-supported but controlled by affiliates was endorsed. In the same week an AIA–SIA Artists' Unemployment Advisory Committee placed a memorandum before a new internal committee of the Ministry of Labour which was 'favourably received'; this marked the first step in a lengthy and uneven diffusion of AIA project ideas across the government network. Clark meanwhile had secured agreement that a War Artists Advisory Committee (WAAC) would form under the aegis of the Ministry of Information to begin appointment of official war artists attached to the fighting services.

When the AIA AGM opened early on the afternoon of Saturday 2 December, the outgoing Central Committee could demonstrate to the 54 out of 756 members who attended in person that its lobbying was furthering the goal – elusive since the 1937 congress – of bringing artists' bodies into closer alignment; they could point to practical moves to help members, such as the provision of free legal advice and exhibiting activity, initiated in calmer times, still under way.[55] The threat of political division, however, was palpable – not least because Sam Haile, from his Swiss exile, had submitted a motion that the AIA should refuse any co-operation with the National Government which had been in place since the rise to power of the Nazi Party. Voices in the hall then rehearsed how the men of Munich had crippled the League of Nations by their actions during the Manchurian and Abyssinian crises, aided fascism in Spain, given the defences of Czechoslovakia to Hitler, made war inevitable by refusing to join an effective peace bloc, and supported Hitler for as long as they believed he would fight against the USSR, all of which 'made the British Government equally responsible for the war'.[56]

It was a challenge Black now met head-on with a deft personal statement:

> Our job, as I see it, is to try and ensure that artists are not allowed to starve, and that culture is not annihilated during the progress of the war. To this end we should put all our efforts and resources behind schemes which your new Committee will doubtless evolve, and to building the Central Institute of Art and Design into a body with power and influence, able to speak and act on the major issues for all the artists in this country ...
>
> As far as the wider political sphere is concerned, you will have seen from the correspondence in the last Bulletin, that there has been considerable discussion regarding the first two statements your Committee issued immediately after the outbreak of war. I personally feel we made a grave error in issuing those statements without first obtaining the opinion of our members. I think our basic aims must remain completely unaltered, i.e. the Unity of artists for peace, democracy and cultural development: but I cannot believe that we shall be best serving the cause of peace or democracy or culture by splitting our membership on political issues which are now troubling all of us and about which very few of us have, I imagine, really made up our minds ...
>
> Some of us favour an immediate armistice without any prior conditions being laid down, some think that Nazi consent to an independent Czechoslovakia and Poland are essential conditions to be agreed before

an armistice. Some are against artists taking any part in this war on the grounds that, in their opinion it is a purely imperialist war – others oppose artists helping because of their pacifist convictions, while on the other hand some of our members can see no alternative but to go forward with the war ...

I believe I am speaking for the majority of the retiring Central Committee when I say so, that *as an Association*, we should proceed with a definite programme to help artists and keep culture alive ... We should make every effort to retain the degree of unity among artists that we have built up during the past six years, and later, when the world situation is clearer, we may see a moment when we can collectively, with the wholehearted support of all our members, add what influence we may have towards bringing about a peace we pray may be more stable than that of 1918.

This appeal ensured rejection of Haile's motion by fifty-four votes to two. A blind ballot of Central Committee members had already selected Cliff Rowe, James Holland and Black himself to stand for a further year and results from postal voting confirmed re-election for those of Black's peers who had stood. However, the churn of war meant that lithographer Henry Holzer, Olga Mitkevitch, Nan Youngman and Betty Rea were among those stepping down, with Cliff Rowe replacing Rea as vice-chairman. With unity preserved, Carel Weight, Percy Horton, Priscilla Thornycroft – a former CC member who as a Slade student had designed brilliant Spanish Aid posters – Freda Nichols and the painter Lowes Luard now took their places. Within weeks, however, the hitherto uncontentious prints scheme had opened up a new divide.

* * * * *

6.12 Walter Durac Barnett, *Bread and Circuses*, Everyman lithograph no. 3, 1939–40. 22.8 × 33.5 cm (9 × 13¼ in.)

6.13 Elizabeth Spurr, *Washing Day*, Everyman lithograph no. 46, 1939–40. 33.5 × 22.8 cm (13¼ × 9 in.)

The intention had been to enhance the Voluntary Printing Unit by training up others to work the machinery, but this now looked unlikely with a key man from the Lithographers' Union unavailable;[57] seven overseas bookings for prints scheme exhibits had already been secured and a Russian request for two more sets was received in October. James Holland felt every effort should be made to circulate the series in neutral countries, but the twenty-plus plates received exclusively carried images of Britain at peace, lacking topicality, which might also now limit their appeal at home. The attraction of 'making it possible for anyone who can afford a shilling to own an original work of art' remained strong: originality would stem from artists having 'drawn on the metal plate from which are pulled the prints', pricing 'comparable with a Penguin Book' from editions only

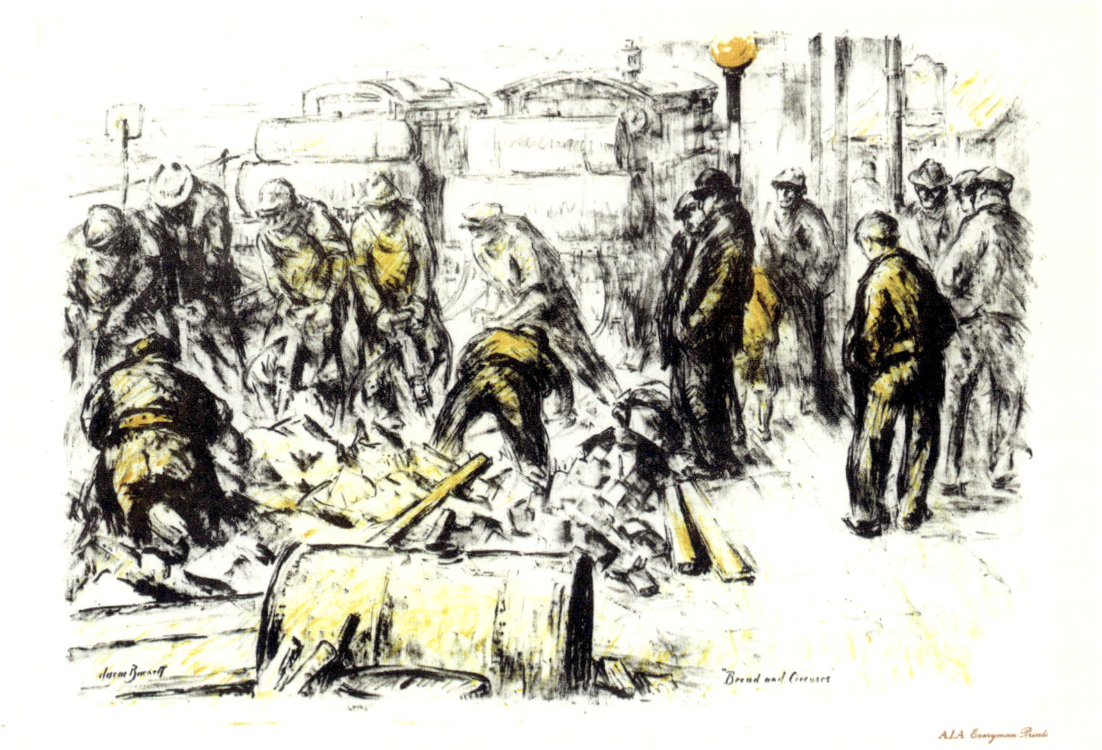

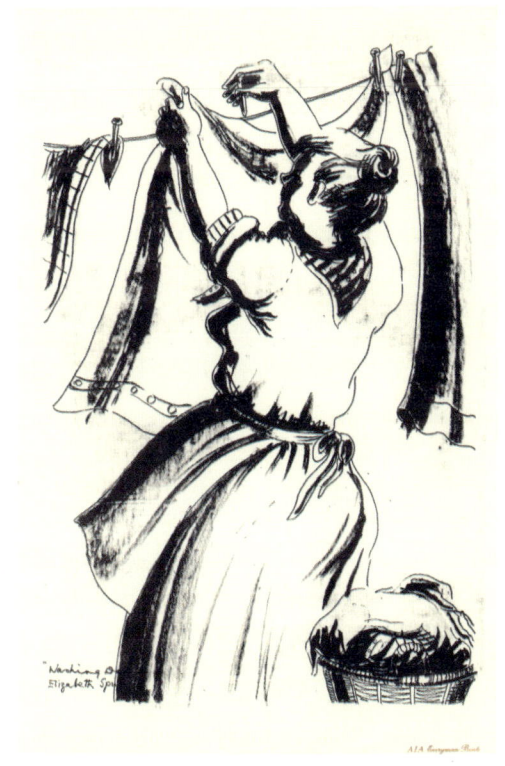

WHITECHAPEL HIGH STREET

limited by the life of the plate. But it was now recognized that the scheme would have to be reorganized on 'an entirely new footing', adding new images by invitation and marketed much more effectively – after which 'a reasonable profit for the artists and some financial gain for the AIA' might follow.[58]

With no venue booked for a members' show, success was now judged essential, and Beryl Sinclair, Percy Horton and Edmond Kapp formed the nucleus of a group which, with an external printer, brought Everyman Prints to fruition in time for a high-profile launch at the Picture Hire Gallery in Brook Street, London, on 30 January 1940.[59] Those contributing new work included Vanessa Bell and Pearl Binder with evacuation scenes, the three Jameses with variations on conscripts observed ('Candidates for Glory' in Boswell's phrase), and a dozen others providing barrage balloon and shelter subjects, images of domesticity in the blackout, of the changing urban landscape and of a bombsite rescue. Added as counterpoints to the leisured social observations gathered the previous summer, this delivered fifty-two works from forty-three printmakers to form a remarkable conspectus of Britain's transition from fragile peace to the uncertain 'phoney war' period into which the series was now launched. Outliers included Cliff Rowe's depiction of bureaucratic injustice in an Unemployment Assistance Board office (which would not have been out of place in the hunger march cartoons of 1934) and Carel Weight's *Blockade*, an almost biblical Expressionist rendition of civilian – possibly Basque – suffering.[60]

At the opening Kenneth Clark praised the exhibition's 'representation of the passing scene', observing that 'the price of the print has enabled the artist to become a little less high hat in the choice of subjects'. His instinct that it would prove popular was accurate: 3,000 prints, priced at 1/- monochrome, 1/6 for two-colours, were sold in three weeks; within a month showings in Bristol, Durham, Chichester, Luton, Winchester, mid-Rhondda and Bromley were taking place, Heal's had announced an exhibition and Marks and Spencer a four-week store trial. To manage this, Everyman Prints Limited was incorporated, making a first distribution of £58 to artists in July after 4,291 prints had been sold; but activity was already slowing as invasion fears mounted and the paper shortage led to regulations restricting fine printing for retail. This jeopardized plans for a second series on which a selection committee including Vanessa Bell, Gwen Raverat and Stanley Badmin was already working.[61]

Worse still, exhibition overseas had become controversial. Two days before the 1939 AGM, the Soviet invasion of Finland had begun, confirming Stalin's malevolence to Stephen Bone, an Everyman contributor, who wrote protesting the intended tour to Russia. Attempting to hold the line, the Policy Committee replied that paid-up bookings should be honoured but asked Bone to pen an open letter, to be printed alongside one from a defender of the Soviet action as a way of testing the waters. Dripping with sarcasm, Bone's response was reproduced in the March 1940 *Bulletin*, ending: 'what I want to know boys, is this: the AIA protested against wops in Abyssinia and Japs in China and Hitler almost everywhere, because that was aggression: but the AIA won't protest against Russians in Finland because that's not aggression, it's something else. Have I got this correct? ... Because, if so, I'm not sure I can go much further on this bus.'[62] Photographer Douglas Glass's contribution argued in sober tones that it was indeed something else, a necessary pre-emptive to General Mannerheim's reactionary Finnish White Guard movement. This sparked a flood of further correspondence, with 30 letters received in a fortnight, dividing into two piles that split 17–13 in favour of Bone's position. Continuing pressure led to an AIA-organized public debate at Conway Hall on 20 March, by which time it had already been agreed that 'for the time being exhibition should be restricted to Great Britain and Northern Ireland'.[63]

* * * * *

In January 1940 the Free German League of Culture, born of discussions round the Uhlman kitchen table, had secured premises at 36a Upper Park Road, Kilburn, six doors down from Misha and Rivka Black.[64] There two rooms housed its mission to unite Reich refugees behind an 'anti-Nazi, Anti-Fascist, non-party, refugee organisation' dedicated to preserving democratic culture, advancing solidarity among refugees, and building a bridge between exiles and their host community. On the first floor a large reception room served for concerts and exhibitions, a smaller ground floor one as library, club room and office. With a membership of 1,300 – divided into writers', musicians', artists', actors' and scientists' sections – this enabled twenty-eight events of 'astonishing cultural diversity' to take place in April 1940, the month before mass internment of 'enemy aliens' began, by which time the artists' section had 117 members.[65]

Fred Uhlman and the sculptor Paul Hamann, a friend of Ewan Phillips since his arrival in 1936, were leading figures in the artists' section, organizing a *First Group Exhibition of German, Austrian, Czechoslovakian Painters and Sculptors* in June 1939 after Uhlman approached Mayfair gallerist Lucy Wertheim.[66] Curated by Hamann it comprised forty-seven works by twenty-nine artists, nearly all of whom had only recently found refuge in Britain.[67] Although many were being helped by the Czech Refugee Trust Fund and the Artists' Refugee Committee (which with Stephen Bone as secretary raised £1,700 for direct assistance activity),[68] this was a cohort of artists almost totally unknown in London, suffering extreme dislocation and poverty, and not yet involved in AIA activities such as the Whitechapel exhibition or Everyman Prints; as such, the well-reviewed exhibition was a crucial first step in combatting collective isolation.

Oskar Kokoschka, despite Continental fame and having lived in London in 1926, was not immune. Although reporting 'Everything goes swimmingly with the help of people at the top' on arrival, an invitation to take tea next day with Tate director John Rothenstein merely yielded a request to donate a painting, not an offer to purchase one.[69] Early financial support came not from establishment contacts like Clark, offering 'vague promises of help' out of a 'desire not to offend', but from £100 lent by Eric Körner, another refugee, and two portrait commissions from Diana Uhlman's brother Michael Green, one of which – of their sister Posy – was exhibited at the Wertheim show.[70]

Such support only sustained a frugal life in London, and in early August 1939 Oskar and Olda, disillusioned with the metropolis, moved to the harbour village of Polperro in Cornwall, remaining there until France fell nine months later. It was a period of illness for Kokoschka, but he completed two significant paintings based on the location before regulations forbidding foreign nationals' coastal residence forced a return to London. In *Private Property* he peopled a harbour view with allegorical action, with a knitter transmuted into a greedy cat as she eyes both a scampering mouse

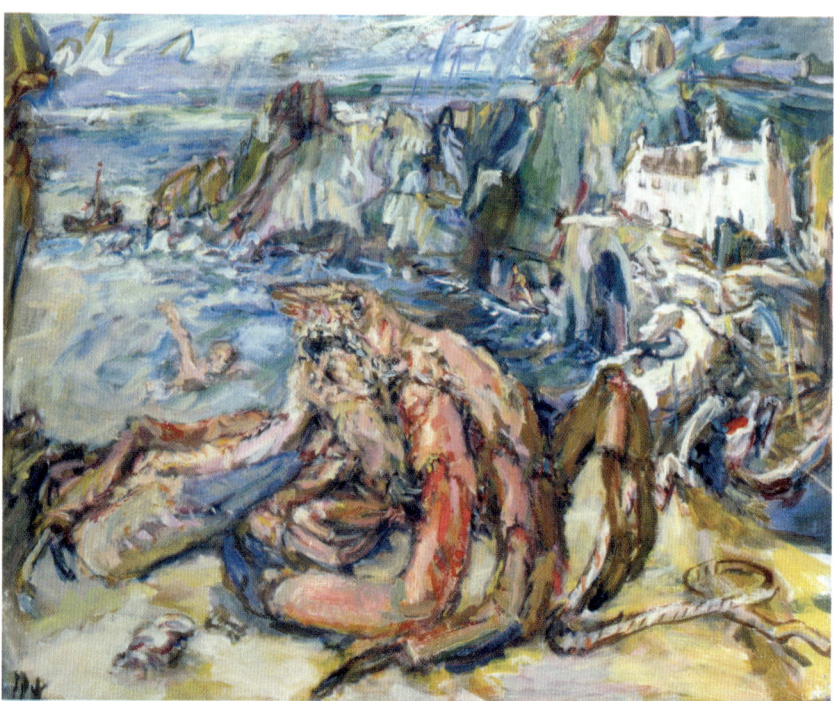

6.14 Oskar Kokoschka, *The Crab*, oil on canvas, 1939–40. 63.4 × 76.2 cm (25 × 30 in.)

6.15 Hellmuth Weissenborn, *View from Internment Camp, Douglas, Isle of Man*, watercolour and pencil, 1940. 17.8 × 23 cm (7⅛ × 9⅛ in.)

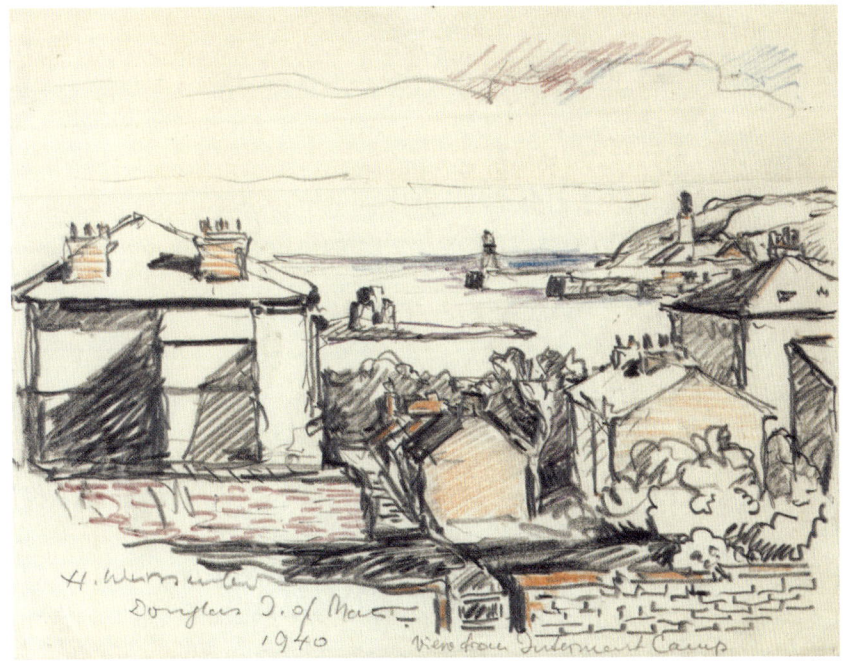

and a pile of dead fish. In *The Crab*, eventually purchased by the Tate in 1982, Kokoschka depicted himself as a swimmer pursued by a malevolent giant mollusc representing Chamberlain. Alternatively titled *Hospitality* it was a work speaking to the emotions of both political and racial refugees as incarceration loomed.

MI5 had argued for internment of all enemy nationals at the outbreak of hostilities irrespective of background, but lost out to a three-tiered Home Office review system; this led to 569 Category A 'enemy aliens' being detained by the end of 1939, roughly 5,000 Category B individuals being subjected to some restrictions on movement and reporting requirements, and 64,000 Category C cases being left at unrestricted liberty. In a rolling process between early April and late June, however, as Norway, Belgium, Holland and France were conquered, the newly installed prime minister Winston Churchill – acting on instincts to 'collar the lot' – sanctioned a programme that saw 29,000 arrested. These included Uhlman, Hamann and a majority of the FGLC artists' section, although Kokoschka was spared by virtue of previously acquired Czech citizenship. Ill-prepared and under-resourced at a time of extreme crisis, the sweep generated abuses, with very poor conditions in transit facilities, lack of capacity in hastily constructed camps on the Isle of Man and attempts to export detainees to both Australia and Canada. By the time the *Arandora Star* was sunk on 2 July 1940, with the loss of 650 detainee lives, opinion was moving strongly against indiscriminate internment, and shortly after a government white paper outlined categories under which those interned could apply for release. At this point the Artists' Refugee Committee secured a specific release criteria for anti-Nazi artists, providing information that led to ninety individuals being released over the following year. It was a slow and uncertain process during which the AIA sent art supplies to those on the Isle of Man, cabled the American Artists' Congress to organize support for those sent to Canada, and kept up pressure for internment of aliens to become 'the exception rather than the rule'.[71] Such moves were the first step in a process of collaboration that would eventually lead to all members of the FGLC artists' section becoming AIA members – and in the more immediate term, as the Blitz began, for the organizers of the October 1940 AIA members' exhibition to set aside a special section for the work of exiled artists.

*****

Just before he departed for New York the previous spring, Misha Black had suggested that the next annual show should be themed *The Face of Britain*, 'on the lines of, but more comprehensive than, the British Pavilion at the World's Fair'. Although the favoured venue was now in doubt, he had worked up the idea during summer 1939 and, as war interposed, was ready to solicit contributions from both fine and commercial artists.[72]

It was 14 May 1940, however, before the Central Committee returned in very different circumstances to the detailed task of organizing a major members' exhibition. That evening Black alerted his colleagues that a new chairman might be required at short notice, as despite having lived in Britain since early childhood he was technically an alien, and the gathering hysteria about 'fifth columnists' – plus the assumption that Russians, post-pact, were a particular threat – meant he might be detained himself.[73] Five weeks later, just after Dunkirk, the committee chose Rowe to take over if required, and a cull of AIA files was under way to frustrate Gestapo reprisal activity in the wake of expected invasion. In late July Black stepped down from the post he had held for nearly eight years, and for the next six months Cliff Rowe took over as chairman and Elizabeth Watson as deputy. In the interim, an arrangement to hire the Royal British Artists Gallery in Suffolk Street, Mayfair, for three weeks in September had been agreed; conceived as the Battle of Britain was erupting over southern skies, the exhibition would open as the Battle of London began.

Rationalizing slightly, the July *Bulletin* explained that a West End gallery had been favoured over Whitechapel in order to maximize sales in dire times, but that this did not mean 'that the Association has in any way changed its policy of endeavouring to establish contact between the artist and a public wider than the one which normally visits exhibitions': a second travelling exhibition would be organized to tour provincial towns and other London districts in its aftermath. Exhibitions Committee efforts during the phoney war period had indeed ensured that both *Britain Today* – at Pontypool, its ninth location, when hostilities began – and the first travelling exhibition, which was at Brighton, had continued to tour. After visiting Northampton, Carlisle, Hereford and Lincoln earlier in the year, the travelling exhibition was seen by 30,000 people at Bradford in August 1940.[74]

AIA lobbying efforts were now also having modest success at one remove: as delegates to the CIAD, Beryl Sinclair and Cliff Rowe were pushing for schemes generating demand for living artists; the War Artists Advisory Committee was expanding its armed service activity with Treasury funds; and after considering the original submission on the Federal Art Project, the Ministry of Labour edged in its direction by securing philanthropic funding to employ twenty artists for four months on an initial tranche of a Recording Britain initiative.[75] But this left many artists bereft of chances to exhibit, a gap organizers Carel Weight, Lowes Luard, Kenneth Rowntree and Graham Bell now sought to fill, with Leonard

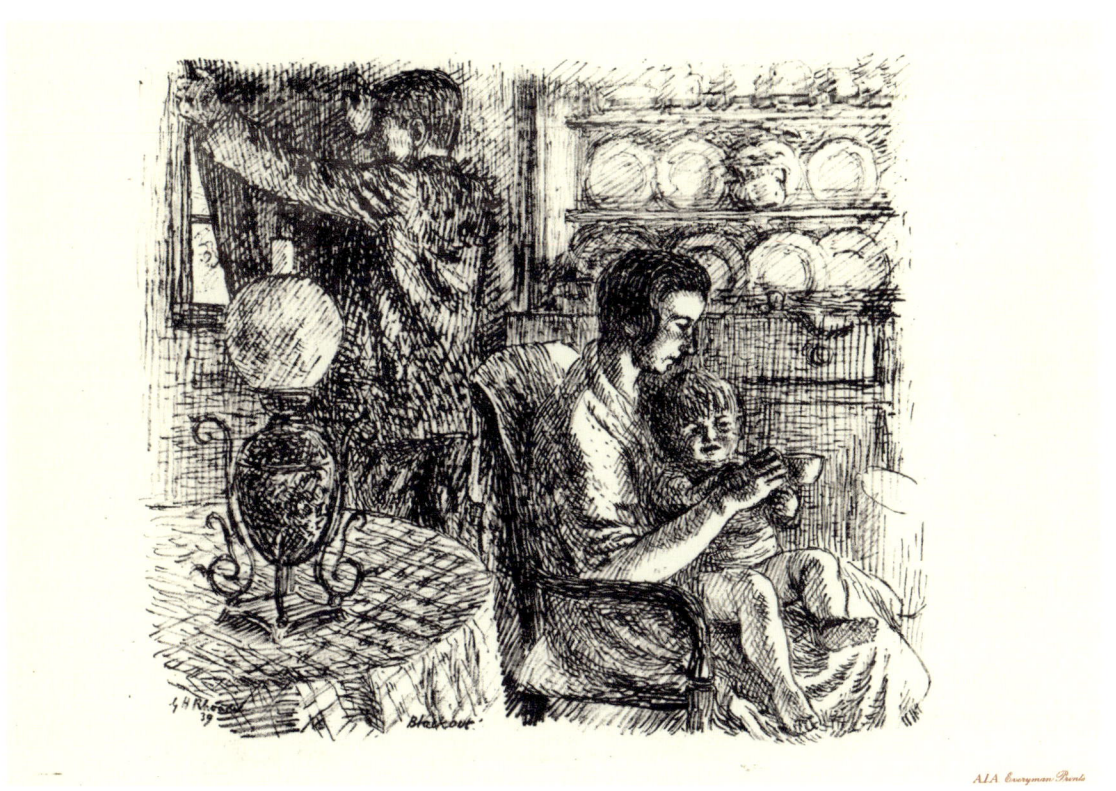

6.16 Geoffrey Rhoades, *Blackout*, Everyman lithograph no. 40, 1939–40. 22.8 × 33.5 cm (9 × 13¼ in.)

Greaves, a twenty-two-year-old former Chelsea student, acting as exhibition secretary. Through minimizing hanging fees and abolishing them for refugee artists, eschewing notions of a theme in favour of stylistic diversity, and allowing three works per artist to be submitted to the jury, they sought to 'enable members to show that, in spite of the difficulties of war conditions, in spite of many of our members being in the forces, engaged on other war duties, or evacuated, artists are still continuing to paint, draw and carve, so that at least one aspect of the cultural life of the country shall not be extinguished during this critical period'.[76]

The event nearly did not happen: the opening had been set for 13 September, but at 5 p.m. on Saturday 7 September the Blitz began with an attack on the East End at five in the afternoon, which lasted for eleven hours as waves of bombers set the docks ablaze, the first of seventy-six consecutive nights (bar one) of continuous raids. Sometime in the first week Leonard Greaves's house and studio in Redcliffe Road, Chelsea, was destroyed, leading to his resignation at a time when 280 works had been gathered in; two incendiary bombs then crashed through the gallery roof, setting its parquet flooring alight, damaging some paintings and forcing a week's delay. Working through dangers, Weight, Sinclair and Rowntree, with Jesse Collins acting as replacement secretary, nevertheless managed to hang the show.

Publicity for the AIA's progressive agenda seemed certain when J. B. Priestley, whose weekly 'Postscripts' were being broadcast each Sunday after the BBC news, agreed to speak at the formal opening. His was the pre-eminent and most emollient voice articulating a spreading popular conviction that there could be no turning back to pre-war conditions, as on 21 July, when an estimated one in three of the adult population heard him conclude: 'Now the war because it demands a huge collective effort, is compelling us to change not only our ordinary, social and economic habits, but also our habits of thought. We're actually changing over from the property view to the sense of community, which simply means that we realise we are all in the same boat. But, and this is the point, that boat can serve not only as our defence against Nazi aggression, but as an ark in which we can finally land in a better world.' Such 'leftish' sentiments were already leading to concerted Conservative pressure on the BBC, which resulted in Priestley being taken off the air in October.[77]

The afternoon of 25 September was without a daylight raid, and a crowd of over two hundred had gathered at the RBA gallery, when a message arrived that Priestley could not appear – leaving John Rothenstein to stand in and congratulate the AIA for its achievement, a view repeated across a remarkable spread of press reviews in the days that followed.[78] *The Times* praised the event's 'fidelity', observing that 'such a title as *Isle of Man,*

6.17 Unknown designer, 1940 Exhibition private view card, 1940. 12.6 × 15.3 cm (5 × 6⅛ in.)

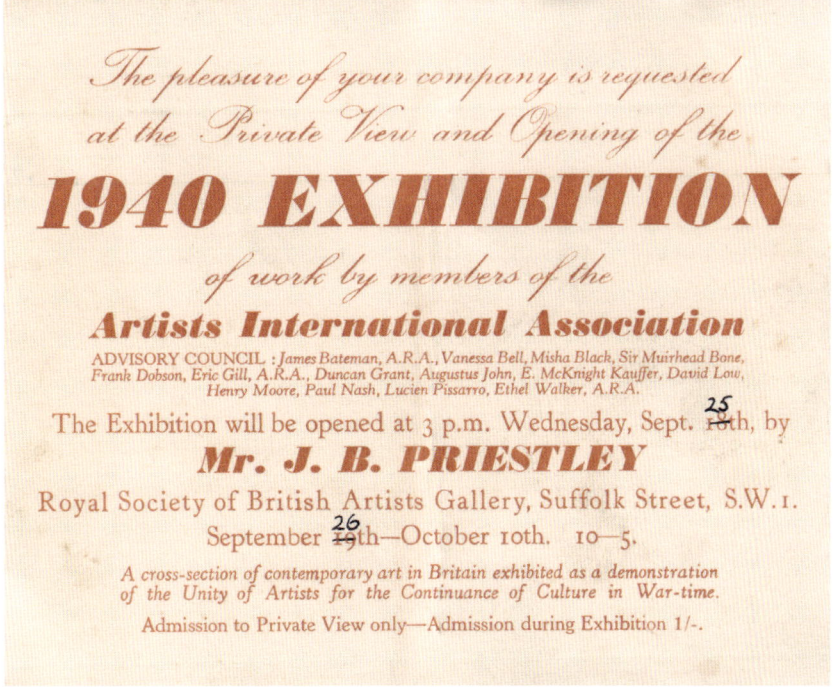

Douglas: *View from Internment Camp* proves that the inexplicable instinct to paint is altogether inextinguishable'. The FGLC's *Freie Deutsche Kultur* announced it had been able to include about fifty works, despite a majority of its artists still being behind the wire.[79] When the AIA's own *Bulletin* appeared in November it noted 'many of our more eminent members were unable to send in work and none of the Advisory Council exhibited. The younger and less well-known artists were thus the backbone.'[80] This imbalance was, however, addressed before *Travelling Exhibition No. 2* opened at Liverpool's Walker Art Gallery in February 1941. Six of the Advisory Council had added works to a selected eighty from Suffolk Street, and for good measure Kenneth Clark, Anthony Blunt and the Courtauld had leavened the mix by lending paintings by Matisse, Bonnard, Marchand, Derain, Sickert, Stanley Spencer, Sutherland, Moore and Ardizzone.[81]

*****

In November 1940 Helen Mary Petter took over the role of AIA secretary from Phyllis Terry after she too was 'compelled by circumstances' to resign during the Blitz. On 7 February Petter wrote from her Portman Square apartment to Percy Horton who was teaching in Ambleside, Cumbria, at the evacuated Royal College of Art. Her purpose was firstly to inform him that – following the death of Eric Gill and Edward McKnight Kauffer's departure for New York – he, Kokoschka and Blunt were being nominated as Advisory Council members in the forthcoming postal ballot, which would also elect the 1941/42 Central Committee; second, she wanted to know if Ambleside was a possible destination for the travelling exhibition.[82]

Horton was one of 269 members known to have relocated to remote locations by that point, and in passing Petter also mentioned that during his absence from London the Central Committee had been 'much absorbed in argument about the People's Convention'. It is a piece of correspondence attesting to the two areas of difficulty which beset the AIA to the point of threatening its survival between the autumn of 1940 and summer 1941: the first logistical and organizational, the second divisively political.

Mobilization and the move towards a planned war economy involved constant relocation – Horton's was but one of 80 million civilian changes of address recorded during the conflict – as well as the absence of hitherto key AIA activists. The same Central Committee meeting that chose Rowe to succeed Black if required also learned that Ewan Phillips, now in Army Intelligence Recruitment, would shortly be unavailable, and co-opted Petter, Elizabeth Spurr, Kenneth Rowntree and Betsy Blake as members pending the next ballot.[83] Of the first thirty-one appointments under the Official War Artists' scheme, more than twenty were active AIA members, and as the scheme expanded it added a further element of dispersal; Edward Bawden, for example, who left Southampton for the Middle East in July 1940, would not return until spring 1943. From the first both Rowe and Black had been acutely aware that a large number of AIA members would also be absorbed into the military through conscription. In some cases this led to new nuclei of activity, as in camouflage operations at Leamington Spa where Trevor Tennant was an effective organizer, but more often than not it led to their isolation, so from mid-1940 initiatives to keep in touch with forces members, to supply materials and to gather in examples of their art became part and parcel of extraordinary voluntary efforts to sustain the AIA as a force.[84]

More immediately the build-up to the People's Convention of January 1941 threatened the uneasy political truce holding in AIA circles – where Central Committee opinion ranged from Rowe's belief that the organization 'should avoid activities of a pro-war nature ... opposing anti-democratic measures as far as possible' to Lowes Luard's that 'the Association should support the present Government in its prosecution of the war'.[85] Organized by the Communist Party and supported by a miscellany of fragmentary peace and labour movement bodies, the convention process was accompanied by denunciation of Labour figures such as Attlee,

6.18 Lionel Maurice de Sausmarez, *A Garden – God Wot!*, Everyman lithograph no. 43, 1939–40. 40 × 23.5 cm (15¾ × 9⅜ in.)

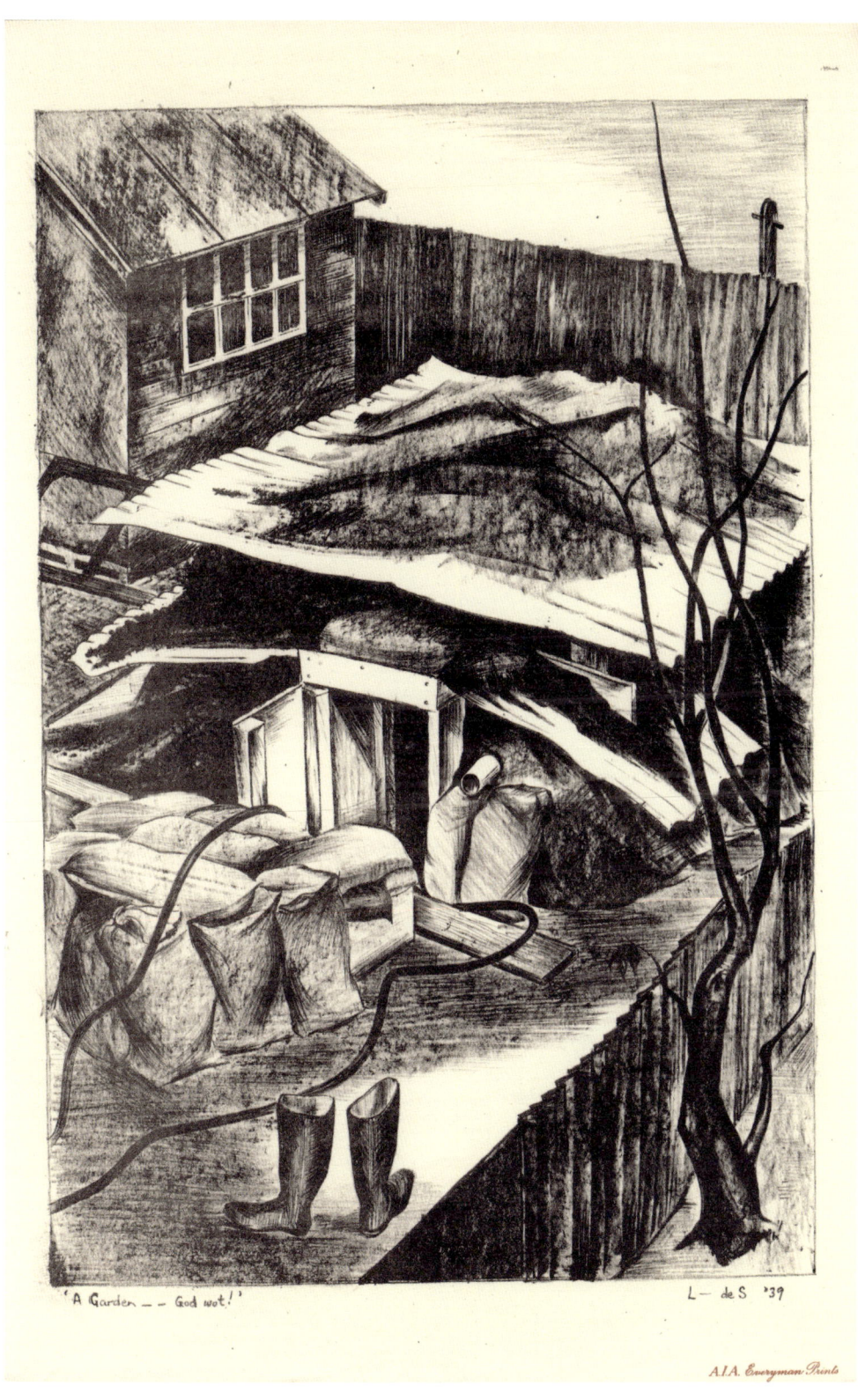

WHITECHAPEL HIGH STREET

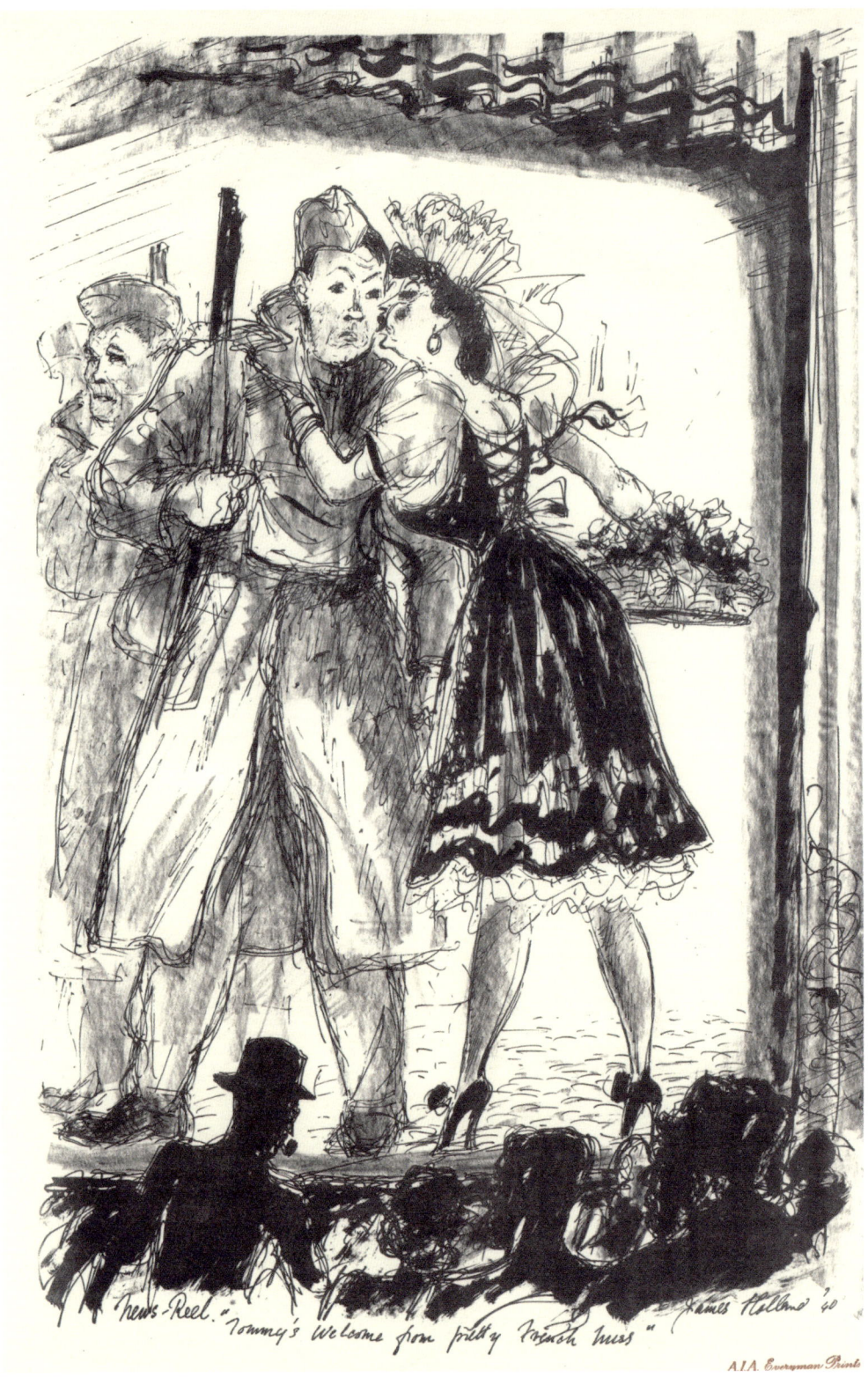

6.19 James Holland, *Newsreel*, Everyman lithograph no. 26, 1939–40. 40 × 23.5 cm (15¾ × 9⅜ in.)

Bevin and Morrison who had joined the coalition, demands for eviction of the 'men of Munich' from Whitehall, and calls for installation of a 'People's Government' to pursue equality of sacrifice at home and renewed friendship with the USSR abroad to secure a 'People's Peace'. It was an agenda opposed by those who believed such campaigning mid-conflict could only increase the likelihood of Nazi victory, and hence the destruction of all political and cultural freedom. Victor Gollancz crystallized this position in his book *The Betrayal of the Left*, a passionate refutation of Communist Party 'revolutionary defeatism' from October 1939 to January 1941, which included a contribution from George Orwell.

Nevertheless, when the convention took place at a central London hotel on 12 January, it attracted 2,234 'delegates', many relatively young, and earned a surprisingly balanced press – a response that led Morrison, using emergency powers lest the momentum increase, to suppress the *Daily Worker* five days later.[86] Freedom of speech had always been championed by the AIA, but these events created organizational jeopardy in the form of a request to participate in the convention, a move a divided Central Committee felt unable to make.[87] On airing its dilemma with the Advisory Council, it received six largely negative replies which, when reprinted in the *Bulletin*, elicited sixteen member letters supportive of allying with the convention, eighteen opposed. After sending an observer rather than a delegate, the Central Committee agreed that 'the AIA will not take any action, but will be prepared to consider any specific issue raised by the Convention Committee over which our membership may be in more general agreement'.[88]

It was an awkward attempt to paper over debilitating division, but one rendered suddenly irrelevant on 22 June 1941 as news of Operation Barbarossa broke in London. Pausing by some railings in St James's Square that evening, Yvonne Kapp – a known communist who had been dismissed from her position with the Czech Refugee Trust after the Nazi-Soviet Pact, and then systematically excluded from employment for over a year and a half – heard Churchill's rousing tones rising from a basement radio: after Hitler's attack on the Soviet Union, Russia was now Britain's ally, to be supported at all costs.[89] By the time an Anglo-Soviet Pact of Mutual Assistance was signed in Moscow twelve days later, new confidence was already energizing AIA spirits in London, the *Bulletin* reporting: 'Your Central Committee has sent the following message to the Union of Soviet Artists in Moscow: Greetings to Artists of Soviet Union withstanding fascist attack on civilisation. We welcome all possible co-operation in the common task.'[90]

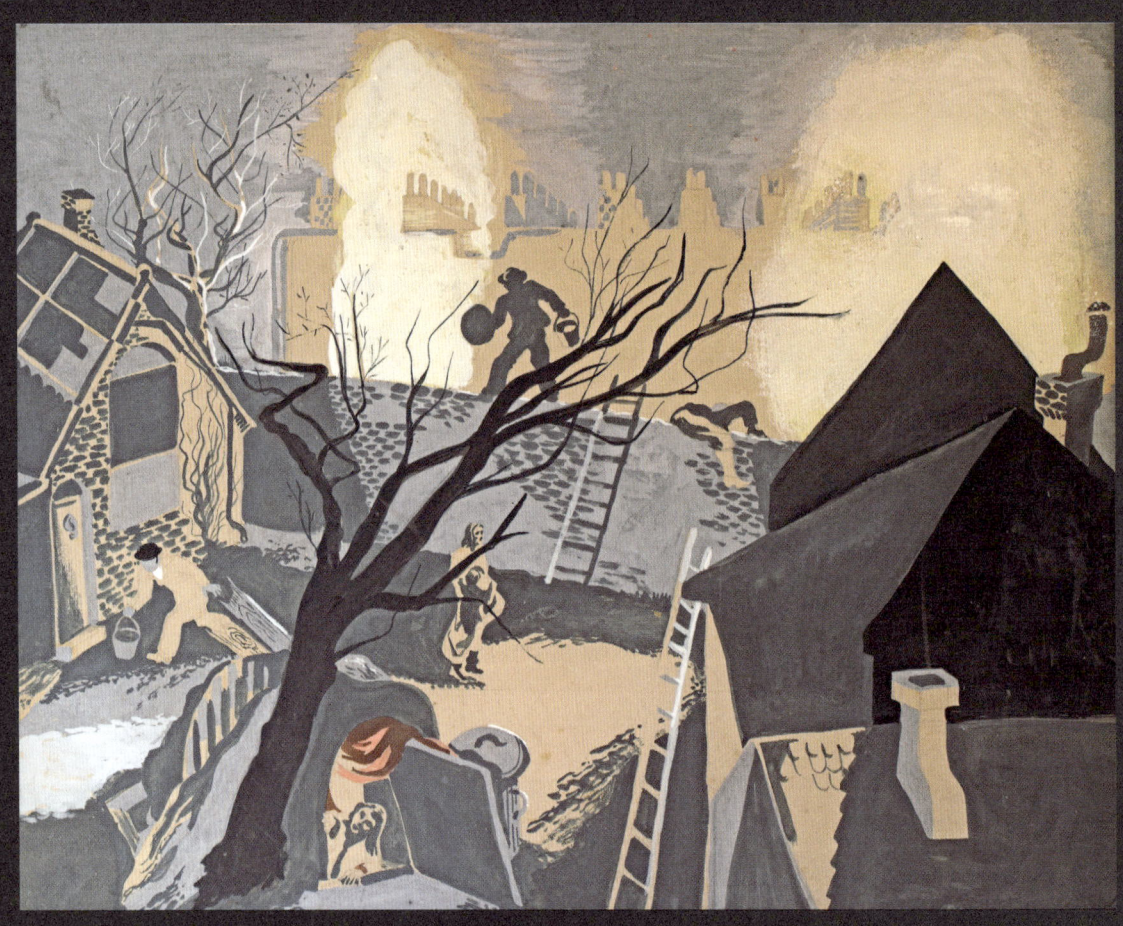

CHAPTER SEVEN

CAMDEN STREET AND SENATE HOUSE

Three weeks after Hitler launched the blitzkrieg designed to destroy the Soviet Union, Percy Horton, teaching at the evacuated Royal College of Art at Ambleside in the Lake District, received a handwritten note on AIA letterhead from Priscilla Thornycroft. Requesting a reply to her address at 3 Camden Studios, 28a Camden Street, NW1, she asked if Horton could help with an exhibition of war paintings the AIA would be mounting in the booking hall at Charing Cross Station that September.[1] She hoped a weekend escape from his northern exile might coincide with the selection meeting at Morris Kestelman's place in Belsize Park.[2]

It did, and Horton's catalogue essay for an event subsequently seen by 120,000 people over four weeks noted: 'the totalitarian war of today has brought the actual experience of warfare to far more people in this country than the war of 1914–18 and artists have had as full a share in it as other folk. Many of them have been bombed, many of them are in war services and among those who are not there are few who have not been shaken up in some degree by the war.' He highlighted that the exhibition, held in an Underground station rather than a gallery in line with AIA desires to popularize art, differed from the Official War Artists' exhibitions at the National Gallery across Trafalgar Square in being an 'undress' event of work by exhibitors mainly engaged in actual war service, creating uncommissioned pieces in their spare time. The exhibition posed the question 'What is meant by "painting the war"?' In Horton's view, it surely required from the artist 'deep sympathies and the power to express and communicate human ideas' rather than perfunctory sketches of bombed buildings or traditional landscapes with an unobtrusive barrage balloon somewhere in the sky.[3]

Thornycroft's Camden Street address was well known to Horton; before travelling north, he had been attending AIA Central Committee meetings there, and ten years earlier he had rented one of its nine Victorian artisan studios while teaching down the street at Crowndale Road Working Men's College by night and tutoring at the RCA in South Kensington by day. In 1935 his brother Ron had taken on no. 7 while he used no. 3, and after

7.1 Edith Simon, *Incendiary Bombs, Old Camden Studios*, gouache on paper, 1942. 40.6 × 61 cm (16 × 24 in.)

247

7.2 Carel Weight, *It Happened to Us!*, oil on canvas, 1941. 72 × 102 cm (28⅜ × 40¼ in.)

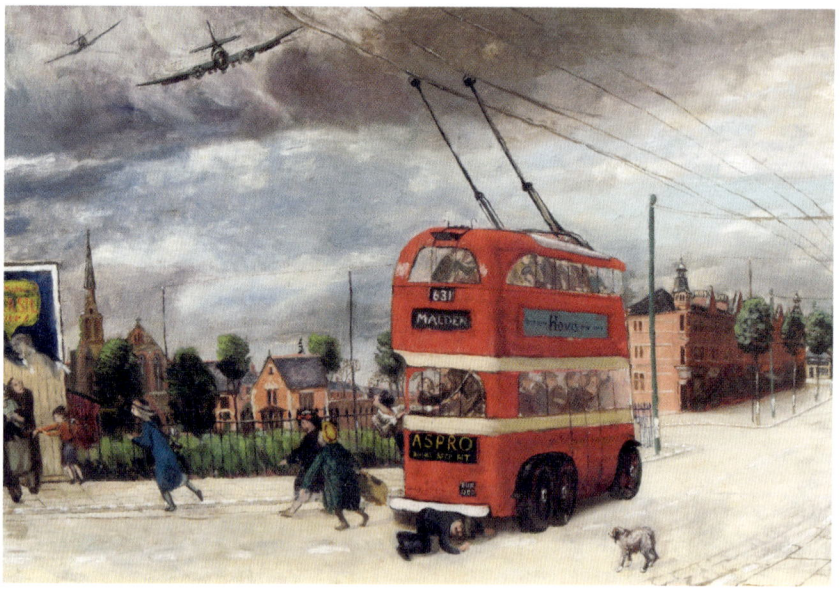

moving to Pond Cottages in Dulwich and becoming a neighbour of the Fittons, Percy had sublet his studio to Peggy Angus; their mutual friend Eric Ravilious had used it in 1936, he and many others happily ignoring the prohibition on sleeping on the premises.

In late 1937 or early 1938 Peter László Peri, needing space to create larger work for his exhibition *London Life in Concrete*, had moved into nos 1 and 2 – and since then, as the phoney war had turned into the Blitz, the two studio terraces facing inwards across an enclosed courtyard garden had become a veritable hive of AIA activism. Cliff Rowe, Edith Simon and Alex Koolman (like Peri, all founder AIA members in 1933) were often there, and by the time Thornycroft penned her letter, Carel Weight, re-elected to the Central Committee that February, had arrived with his partner Helen Roeder, leaving behind a one-room apartment shared by five in Notting Hill.[4]

Weight and Roeder had become lovers while studying at Goldsmiths in 1931; he had subsequently pursued his painting while teaching at Beckenham Art College, while she had worked assisting Misha Black and Milner Gray at the Industrial Design Partnership. Now she was working as secretary to the Artists' Refugee Committee, co-ordinating the lobbying that was securing gradual release of 'enemy alien' artists and designers from internment, among them F. H. K. Henrion, a fellow IDP colleague. Weight was now working in Civil Defence, painting as occasion allowed after the War Artists Advisory Committee listed him as an artist from whom work might be acquired; that July, however, when he submitted

It Happened to Us!, depicting passengers fleeing a suburban trolleybus about to be strafed by a German raider, it was declined with the suggestion that the recent escape of a zebra from London zoo during an air raid might be a more acceptable example of panic. For many Londoners, however, the rejected work was a highlight of the Charing Cross show two months later.[5]

Peter László Peri had secured citizenship in 1939, so avoiding internment, and in 1941 both he and Cliff Rowe were serving in the same St Pancras unit of the Light Rescue Service. Their night-time activity aiding the bombed provided motifs for new departures in their art, long depot hours the opportunity to develop them. For Peri this meant a turn from his distinctive concrete sculptures and larger friezes, now less feasible to produce and market, towards smaller pieces and etchings capturing the spiritual darkness and human tragedy of war; for Rowe it involved new observation of familiar urban territory even as he sustained his involvement with the People's Convention, the campaign against the *Daily Worker* ban and his role as replacement AIA chairman.[6]

In the lead-up to war, after painting *The Fried Fish Shop* Rowe had combined party work, including campaigning for deep shelters, in

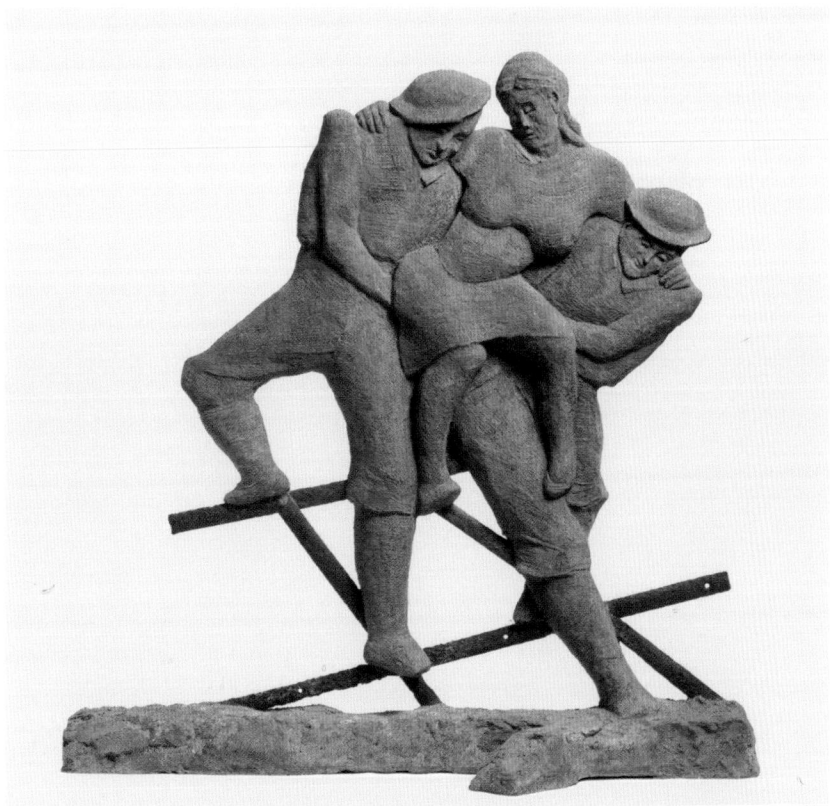

7.3 Peter László Peri, *The Rescue Men*, concrete and steel, c. 1940.
86 × 86 × 24 cm
(33⅞ × 33⅞ × 9½ in.)

the St Pancras and Kentish Town area with painting the life of its working-class streets. In mid-April 1941 the first of his three war-time applications to the WAAC had been turned down, in all probability as a result of MI5 intervention, but he was successful in obtaining a permit to paint in the St Pancras marshalling yards.[7] Here his daytime activity yielded a significant series of watercolours and drawings of the industrial war work women were undertaking, while his night service provided the subject matter for paintings and lithographs such as *Stretcher Party*, *The Raid*, *Moonlight Incident*, *Next Morning* and *The Call-out*. This last was his contribution to Charing Cross, where it hung with two works by Elizabeth Watson derived from her own harrowing experience as an ambulance driver in the City; while watching emaciated children from the slums departing from London as war was declared, she had decided that artists must now be combatants, not solely commentators in the fight for a better world. As her understated memoir records, this led her to be marked by horror during the heaviest raids, even as she maintained her AIA commitments as Rowe's deputy.[8]

Four James Boswell works hung at Charing Cross, three of which (*Depot Barber Shop*, *Fatigue Party* and *Three Volunteers – You, You and You*) reflected his recent conscription as a private in the Royal Army Medical Corps; the fourth (*The Night the Sergeant Copped It*) probably related to the months before his February call-up, when he too had been working in Civil Defence, fire-watching during the destruction unfolding in inner north London.[9] Living a couple of miles away from Camden Studios in Parliament Hill, it was territory Boswell knew intimately which had previously fed his turn towards graphic social reportage. Beginning at Cable Street, this had deepened after the spring 1938 demise of *Left Review*, which removed one source of relentless appetite for Boswell's political cartooning, although he continued to supply the *Daily Worker* and other labour movement clients as 'Buchan'. This left more space, even allowing for his continuing role at Shell, for creation of works such as the lithographs still touring as part of the AIA's *Britain Today* exhibition.[10]

Like Rowe, Boswell was a member of the Committee of Arts and Entertainment Professionals supporting the People's Convention; and just before his call-up both were part of a working group (together with John Banting, who would shortly join the AIA Central Committee) preparing for the appearance of *Our Time* – the replacement *Left Review* for a new era.[11] The activist poet, novelist and last *Left Review* editor Randall Swingler was a prime mover in this, but it was in the pages of *Poetry and the People*, the magazine Swingler had developed as an interim step, that Boswell made an important and challenging critical contribution just prior to becoming a soldier.

7.4 Cliff Rowe, *Woman Cleaning, St Pancras Yards*, pencil, oil and wash on board, 1940. 46.1 × 72.1 cm (18¼ × 28½ in.)

7.5 Cliff Rowe, *The Call-out*, colour lithograph, c. 1941. 38 × 53.2 cm (15 × 21 in.)

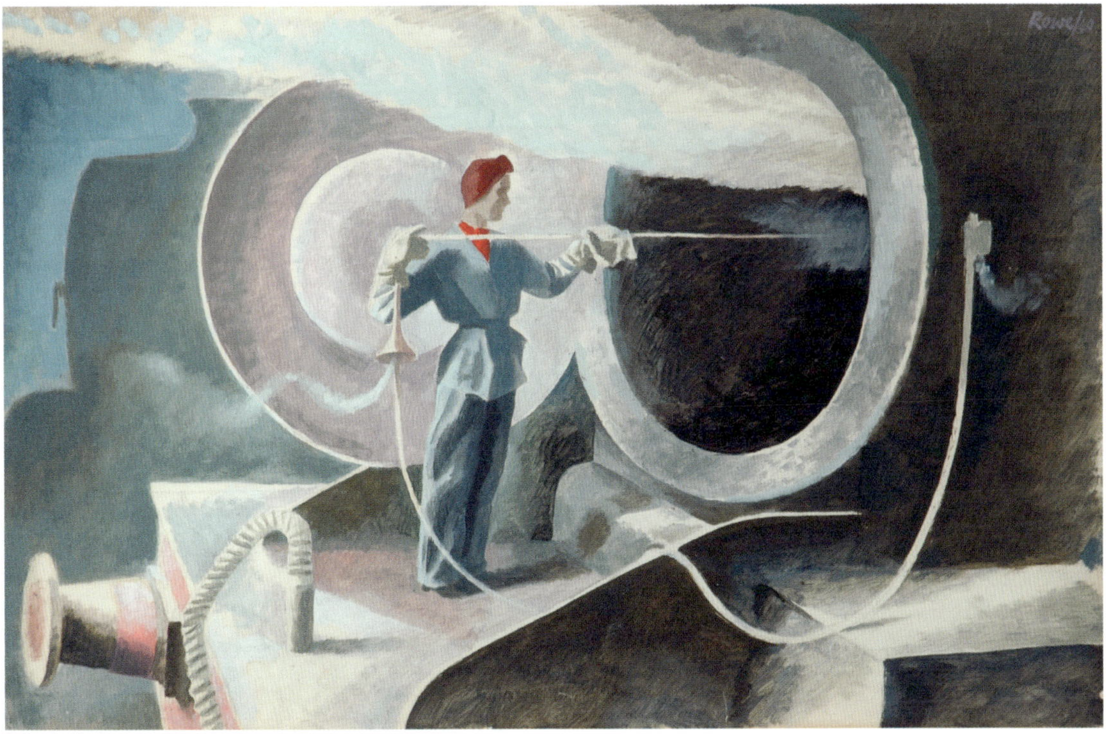

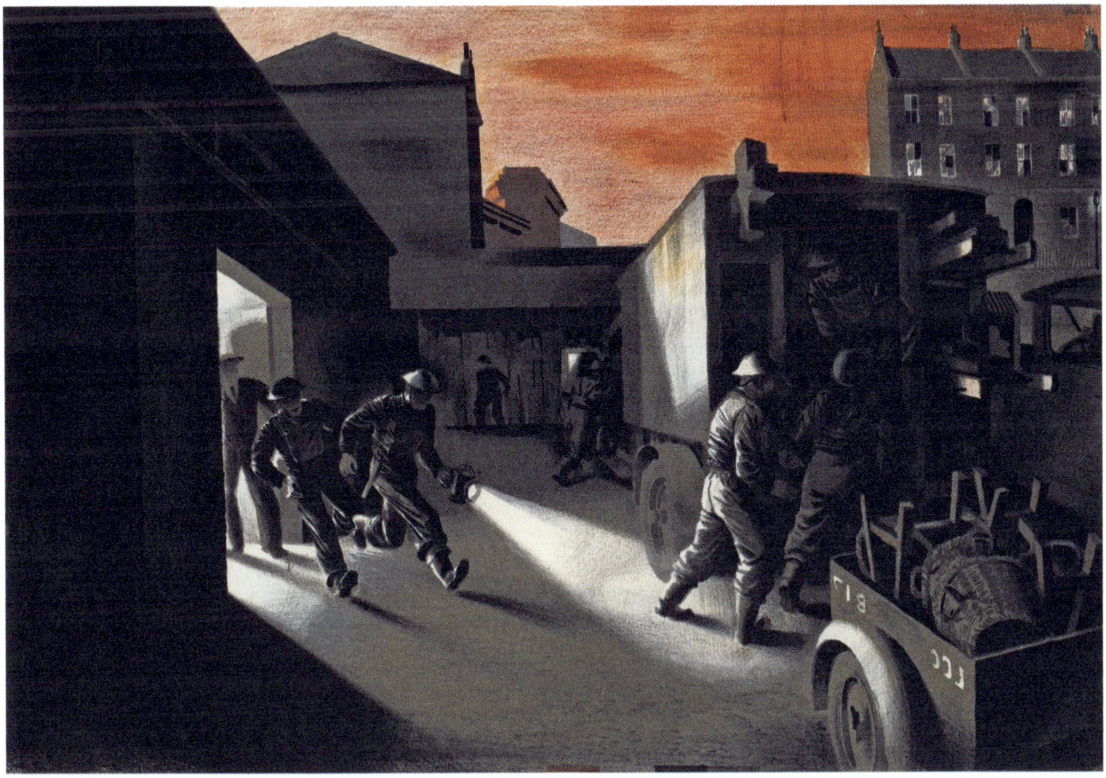

CAMDEN STREET AND SENATE HOUSE

Under the heading 'WANTED A GOYA by Buchan', Boswell reviewed three 1940 exhibitions – the London Surrealists at Zwemmer's, the Euston Roaders at the Leicester Gallery and the official war artists at the National Gallery – posing the same basic question as Horton, but in excoriating terms. Searching for 'the reactions of a sensitive and imaginative section of the community to the greatest crisis civilisation has yet experienced', he concluded 'these artists are either unable or unwilling to deal with such problems'. Kinder to the Surrealists in acknowledging a previous, now lost, liberating influence, and to the 'dull and spiritless' realists for at least trying 'to give us human beings', he was scathing about the officially endorsed offerings as coming from 'a generation of artists who have carefully trained themselves to eliminate human beings and human emotions from their work [and] are hardly likely to produce anything that will give rise to awkward questions'.

In Boswell's thinking 'the neat antiseptic formulae of South Kensington' had during the last years of peace delivered:

> a sort of birthday-cake realism done with clever touches of the brush and a studied insistence on the odd and the queer. Those quaint little villas and broken-down cottages and farmyards and jolly heaps of scrap iron, when we get the icing off them, are nothing more than the detritus of our social system, and these painters have chosen the task of making it look pretty. Put into uniform and sent around to see the war, they can find no reason to alter their point of view and just as they found the

7.6 AIA exhibition in Charing Cross booking hall, 1941

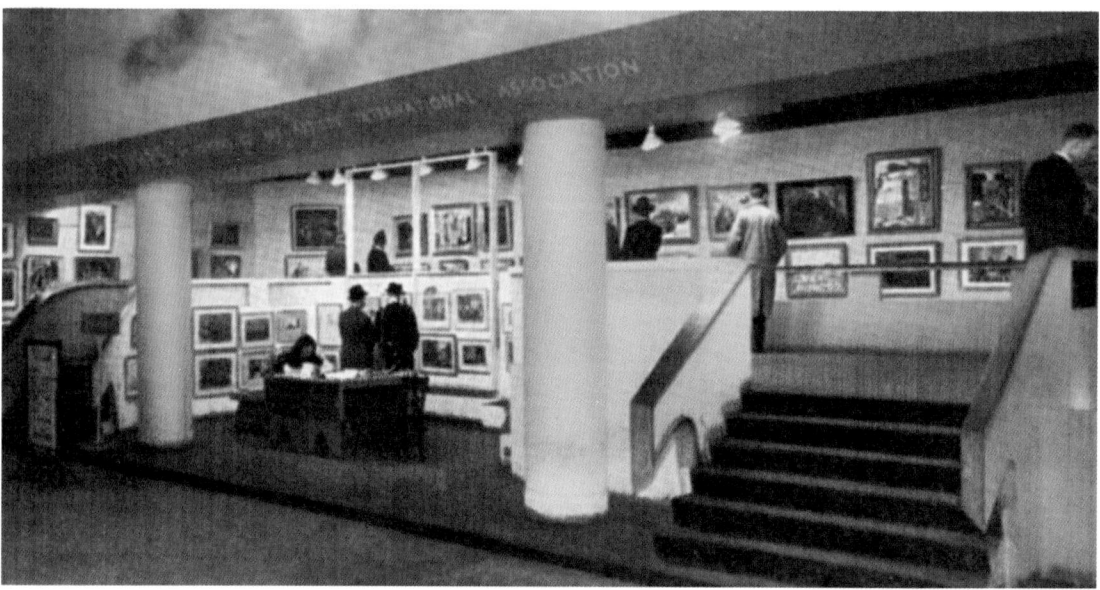

waste of human labour a rather whimsical affair they find the waste of human life is only an opportunity for a further exercise of their little trick. And so they lend themselves willingly to the greater deception.[12]

In seeking to demolish false satisfaction enveloping the art scene, with his clarion reference Goya, Boswell also foreshadowed one of the most singular acts of creation that would mark the darkest years of the war, namely his own coming visual odyssey. In addition, he provided a militant allusion to two dilemmas that would shape AIA efforts over the next two years.

Use of the exhibition space at Charing Cross, although part of the London Passenger Transport Board estate, came courtesy of the Ministry of Information (MOI), an arm of government now drawing many into a system that for so long had self-evidently failed to resist fascism, prevent war or promote democratic cultural development. Having consistently opposed national conservatism's status quo, and argued for a new relationship between the artist and society, how could the AIA now take advantage of many of their number being 'both in and against the state' during its coalition successor? And what could comrades in art, or indeed artistic production, actually do during a people's war to secure a better future?[13]

* * * * *

Up in Ambleside, both Horton and fellow RCA staffer Gilbert Spencer had joined the Grasmere Home Guard in early 1941. Writing to his brother Ron, now an evacuated teacher in Staffordshire, Horton observed: 'It looks as if the regular troops will be used for imperial defence and the Home Guards will be the main-stay for this country.'[14] It was a major departure for Horton, who at the age of eighteen had endured extreme cruelty for his absolute refusal to don uniform in a futile bloodletting unleashed by capitalism and imperialism. But it was not the result of any middle-aged rightward drift – rather he felt, with the poet Cecil Day-Lewis, 'It is the logic of our times/ No subject for immortal verse/ That we who lived by honest dreams/ Defend the bad against the worse'.[15] Still conservative in art, Horton remained steadfastly radical in politics, convinced – like Pollitt – that global fascism was at this moment a more pressing enemy than the native ruling class.

By the end of 1941, 3.8 million people were in the armed forces, a quadrupling of peacetime levels, more than 3 million were active in Civil Defence and some 4 million workers were employed in industries and services restructured to meet war-time needs – and the recruitment net party to this government-directed tide of change had been cast wide.[16] Nazi policy had brought much professional talent to British shores; tarred with suspicion, notwithstanding being racial and political refugees, and interned as 'enemy aliens' long past the point at which it was clear 'fifth column' activity had played no military role in Hitler's European conquests, a significant number of such refugees were now incorporated into the war effort on release.[17] In parallel, numbers of domestic radicals previously subject to MI5 sanction as 'premature anti-fascists' were cleared for employment in the public realm as – even prior to Russia's emergence as Britain's ally – national survival now took precedence over combatting the 'Red Menace'. Thus Misha Black, shadow of internment removed, was able to resume the role of chairman at the AIA AGM held at the Chantecler restaurant in Frith Street on 22 March 1941 – by which time he had also been brought into the Ministry of Information as part of an urgent restructuring of its displays and exhibitions division, an operational base he would inhabit to great effect for nearly four years.[18]

The ministry had been having a bad war. Set up in London University's newly completed Senate House, from which administrators and the Institute of Education had decamped, and saddled with shifting amorphous responsibilities for monitoring civilian 'morale', controlling news flow, overseas propaganda and public information, it had promptly acquired the moniker 'Ministry of Muddle' in Parliament and that of 'Ministry of Misinformation' among the journalists and broadcasters it censored. Staffed at inception by an astonishingly inappropriate old boy network of former civil servants, museum curators and clerical and military retirees with little relevant experience (Kenneth Clark believed he was requested to direct its film department because he was thought to 'know about pictures'), its patronizing communication skills led to the early, quickly scrapped poster campaign '*Your* Courage, *Your* Cheerfulness, *Your* Resolution will bring *Us* Victory'.[19]

Three ministers and several directors-general had been run through by the time Brendan Bracken, a Churchill confidant, arrived as minister in July 1941, as well as numerous senior executives including Lord Reith and Frank Pick, previously publicity and design supremo of the London Passenger Transport Board, who departed during a period Evelyn Waugh would shortly satirize in his novel *Put Out More Flags*. Three months into his four-month tenure in November 1940, however, Pick had laid the foundation of future success by recruiting Milner Gray, Black's senior partner at IDP, to a leading role in the production division, which embraced publications, displays and exhibitions, and James Holland was also now employed there. Lacking citizenship, Black was ineligible for conventional civil service appointment, but rolling consultancies now supported prolific output from himself, Henrion and James Fitton among others, as the MOI exhibitions and displays function began to establish a track record of innovation delivering the MOI's own outputs and servicing bodies such as the Ministries of Food, Home Security and War Transport.

When the results of the AIA postal ballot were declared after lunch at the Chantecler, some familiar names were lacking as only those able to attend regular London meetings had been eligible to stand, so thanks were due to key absentees carried away through the churn of war. Apart from Ewan Phillips, both Hortons and Boswell, these included Helen Binyon, now an Admiralty cartographer in Bath;[20] Graham Bell and William Coldstream, who had enlisted during the previous year;[21] Nan Youngman and Betty Rea, now in Huntingdon teaching, Youngman at her relocated Highbury school and Rea working with children from care homes now scattered throughout the fenlands; Trevor Tennant in the Camouflage Directorate at Leamington Spa; Julian Trevelyan in the Royal Engineers as a camoufleur, where he was finding his fellow officers negative and pompous;[22] and Phyllis Terry, who after moving young children out of London had relinquished her secretarial duties to Mary Petter.[23]

A core cadre of the most experienced remained – Black, Rowe, Holland, Watson – and alongside them Beryl Sinclair, Stanley Badmin, Jesse Collins, Carel Weight, Priscilla Thornycroft and Lowes Luard, all of whom had been highly active since Munich. Painters Russell Reeve and Kenneth Rowntree[24] had been co-opted to vacancies the previous year and they were now joined by Helen Roeder, the potter Charlotte Bawden, art teacher Mildred Lockyer and painters Paul Gillet, Mary Wykeham – Trevelyan's wife – and David Caplan. Caplan's 'Davy' cartoons could no longer appear in the banned *Daily Worker* but his modernist design skills provided the cover for *Gabriel Peri*, editor William Rust's tribute to the foreign editor of the French newspaper *L'Humanité*, executed in Paris on 15 December 1941.[25]

Another notable arrival at the Central Committee table was John Banting, who had exhibited with the AIA as a Surrealist since Grosvenor Square, and whose 'Their Time' tailpiece cartoons in the first seven issues of *Our Time*, which he co-edited, were reprising something of the visual class animus of early *Left Review*. He too was now employed within the Ministry of Information as an art director working on documentaries for its Strand Films operation.

Hard graft and some personal loans meant the AIA had made progress in cutting its debts, but as Black resumed his chairman's role the challenge of delivering significant activity and of keeping in touch with – and collecting subscriptions from – a dispersed membership, now reduced by a quarter at 613, remained prodigious.[26] But while past political controversies still lingered, an impressive collective determination to work the system harder through the CIAD and the MOI, to strengthen the organization and mount diverse events in less likely places, to develop a progressive forum for debate about art in war and to promote new alliances among artists was taking root.

*****

The Charing Cross Underground exhibition was not the first mounted by the AIA in public property that year. On the last day of April Sir John Foley, Permanent Secretary for Shipping and Economic Warfare, officiated when an exhibition of seventy-one works by forty-nine invited members was opened in the ministry's canteen. A month later the ubiquitous Kenneth Clark was on hand with an opening speech when the show transferred to the Senate House canteen.[27]

Organized as a forerunner to other travelling exhibitions in government offices, factory canteens and communal feeding centres, it was furnished with a cyclostyled catalogue bearing a puckishly challenging preface by the veteran *Observer* art critic, painter and AIA member Jan Gordon. 'There are two ways of looking at pictures', he explained; 'pick out the ones you like and say "Pooh!" to the rest ... or ask "Now why don't I like this?" For that purpose this exhibition in a canteen is fortunately placed. In an everyday gallery to stay pondering over a picture you don't agree with is not always easy. Here you can pick your table and have your lunch or tea at it.'[28] At the AGM Gordon had argued that art schools were wasting their time training artists while not training the public: 'Each art school should be made the cultural centre of its own district. Each art master ... could be more or less in control of the whole district surrounding his school and the public could be visited by him and given lectures at the art school.' Co-operation with music, drama, sports groups and municipalities should all, he argued, form part of a drive for popular artistic appreciation: 'The public do not buy pictures because they do not understand pictures and they do not understand pictures because artists do not teach them to do so.'[29]

In colloquial spirit his preface took readers through the most directly accessible works – pointing out 'the character' in Rowe's lithographed heads of Auxiliary Fire Service men,[30] 'the ambience of Elizabeth Watson's *Bombed in the City*', the 'comedy of Carel Weight's *Allegro Strepitoso*' – before assaying Keith Baynes's abstract harbour scene *Concarneau*, where boats lacked sharp definition because the painter deliberately 'wanted to insist on an emotional colour effect', and George Downs's *Cycle Race* based on 'the chaotic feelings of a cyclist, all out, at the end of a race'. 'With that as a clue have a go at some of the others of its kind', Jan urged viewers of an exhibition including Surrealist works by Ithell Colquhoun and Julian Trevelyan.

Catalogue titles suggest war subjects were in a minority (as they would not be at Charing Cross four months later), but a confronting exception to

7.7 Géza Szóbel, *Execution of Hostages*, drawing in pen and ink with airbrush stippling, c. 1941. 15.7 × 20.5 cm (6¼ × 8⅛ in.)

7.8 Géza Szóbel, *Back to the Dark Ages*, drawing in pen and ink with airbrush stippling, c. 1941. 15.7 × 20.5 cm (6¼ × 8⅛ in.)

7.9 Géza Szóbel, *Jewish Procession*, drawing in pen and ink with airbrush stippling, c. 1941. 15.7 × 20.5 cm (6¼ × 8⅛ in.)

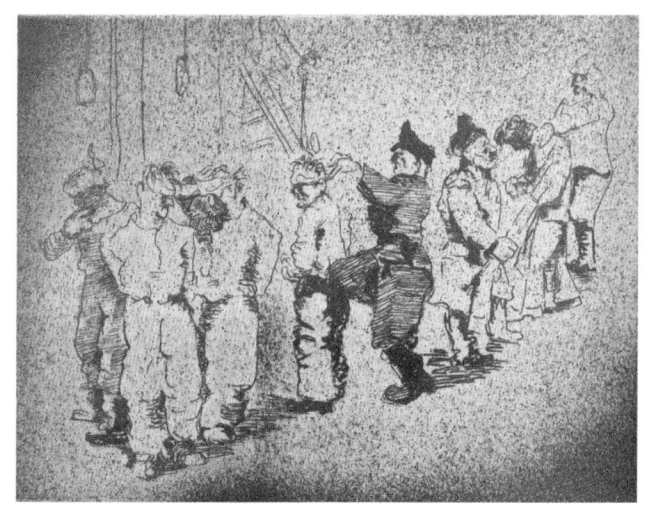

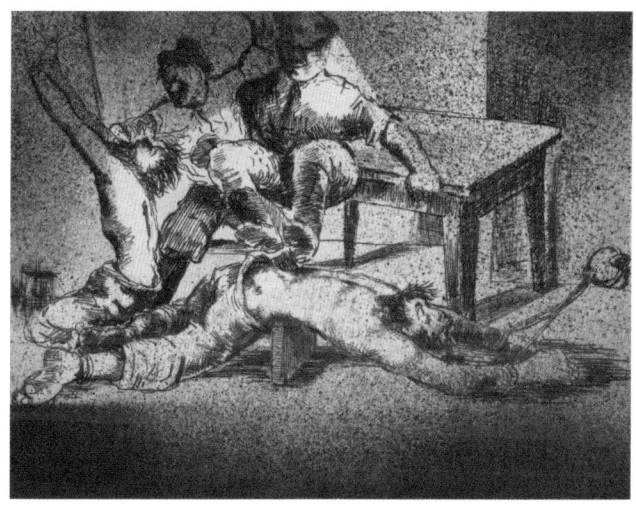

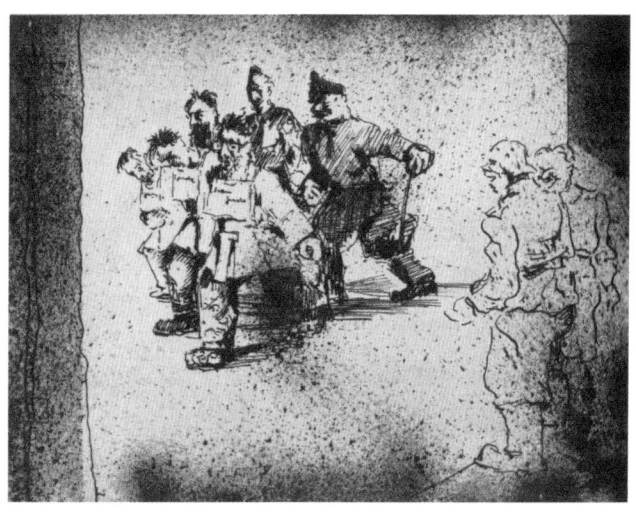

CAMDEN STREET AND SENATE HOUSE

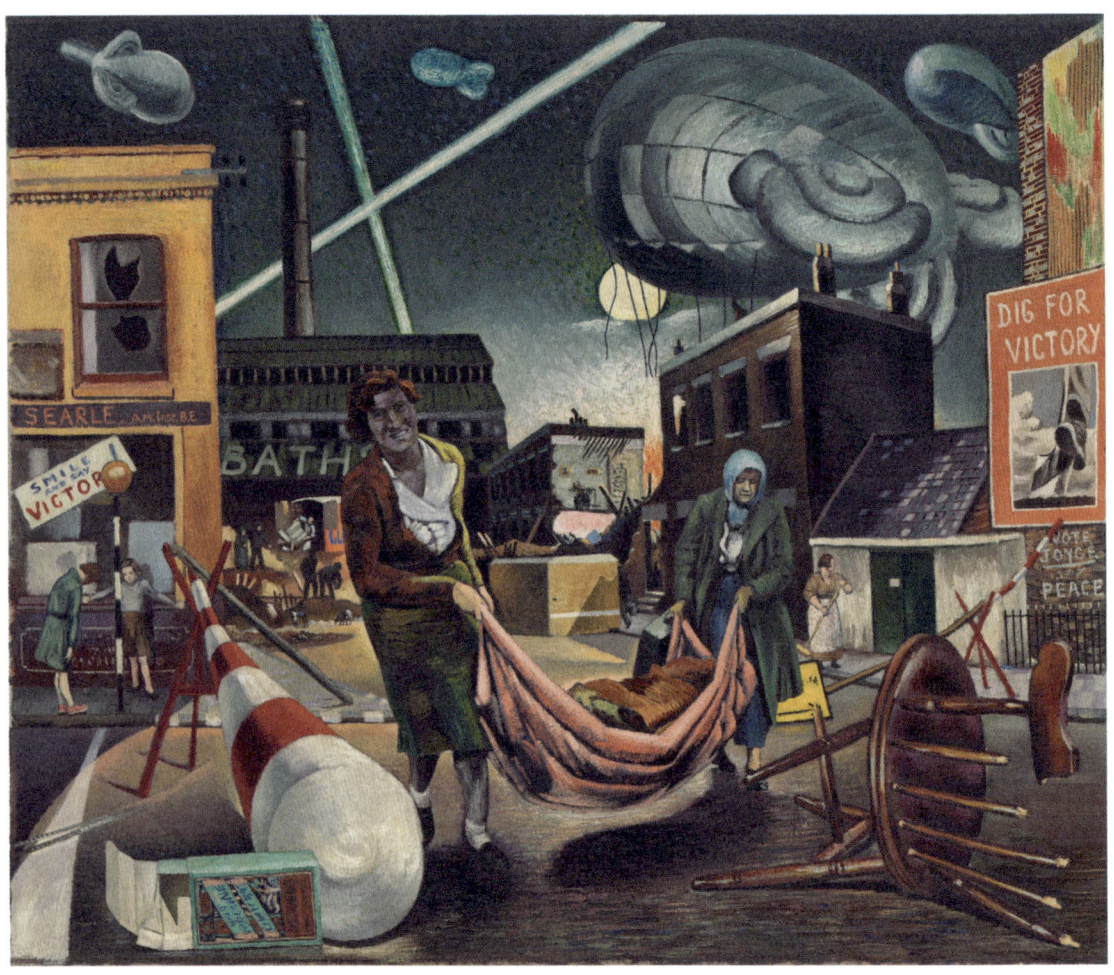

7.10 Clive Branson, *Bombed: Women and Searchlights*, oil on canvas, 1940. 50.9 × 61.2 cm (20⅛ × 24⅛ in.)

this was the inclusion of three works by Géza Szóbel: *Refugiés*, *La Route Nationale 13 Juin* and *Poste de Mitrailleuses*. A recent escapee from Vichy France, thirty-seven-year-old Szóbel had moved from Prague to Paris in 1927, studied with Léger and developed a semi-abstract oeuvre fusing 'diverse aspects of French modernism, such as fauvism, orphism, surrealism, and cubism'. In 1939 he had joined the Free Czech forces, fought during the French collapse in 1940 and reached Britain the following year 'after many painful experiences', where 'this adherent of the artistic vanguard laid aside his usual style, and began to paint reality as he had seen and experienced it'.[31] 'This I have seen ...' had been Goya's certification to *Disasters of War*, and Szóbel was now working on a series of forty-one images which drew to ferocious effect on his own journey, exile testimonies of torture and execution and Goya's style to create a sustained expression of the pain, evil and cruelty he knew to be unfolding in occupied Europe.

In four sections titled 'The New Order', 'The Third Front', 'Blitzkrieg' and 'Concentration Camps' they were exhibited at the Czechoslovak Institute in July 1942, and simultaneously reproduced as *Civilisation*, a black-clad Penguin paperback. In the introduction Jan Stránský, assistant to the Czech prime minister in exile, wrote: 'The object of these drawings is not to make you shudder with horror – their object is to make you clench your fists and hit back. All of us pursued the easier path when we refused to see ... But all that we would not believe has come true ... something unspeakably evil has come upon us.'[32]

War's reality closer to home resulted in another notable inclusion, a painting displayed in the canteen under the title *Bombed*, now in the Tate collection as *Bombed: Women and Searchlights*. Its creator, Clive Branson, had largely abandoned painting for political activism in the mid-1930s and had not exhibited with the AIA since *The Social Scene* in 1934. A recruiter for the International Brigade, he himself had enlisted and left for Spain in January 1938 after his role in London led to Special Branch surveillance; at the battle of Calaceite three months later he was captured by Nationalists. After incarceration in a disused monastery near Burgos, he was transferred to Palencia, where he obtained art materials sufficient for a return to drawing, sketching fellow prisoners, and to oil painting, depicting the Italian-run camp and the landscape beyond on scrap canvas. Released in late 1938, he returned to London, becoming prominent in the campaign for deep shelters; by now he had rediscovered both métier and motivation as an artist (and developed as a poet), completing a series of highly accomplished canvases portraying working-class life and politics in Battersea. *Bombed* spoke directly to both during London's Blitz; but by the time it was shown, Branson had departed civilian life once again and was confronting incipient depression in barracks on Salisbury Plain, a conscript trainee in the Royal Armoured Corps, closely monitored as politically unreliable. In due course he would become a skilled and popular tank commander and be sent to India, the land of his birth; but he would never see civvy street again.

*****

While *Bombed* was on show in the Senate House canteen, Oskar Kokoschka spoke at the opening of *Refugee Artists and their British Friends*, an exhibition of 102 works – mainly drawings and watercolours but including 27 sculptures – that opened on 19 July at 36 Upper Park Road. Initially confined to the rear, the Free German League of Culture had gathered sufficient funds and pledges of voluntary labour to take over the entirety of the dilapidated dwelling the previous December. It now housed a café, library and exhibition space, and had just hosted a four-day fiftieth birthday display of John Heartfield's work – an MI5 informant duly recording the German exile's introductory talk extolling the revolutionary potential of photomontage.[33] As a president of the FGLC and newly elected member of the AIA Advisory Council Kokoschka was perfectly placed to foster co-operation between the two and, although refugee artists outnumbered their friends when the show opened on 19 July, he had succeeded in attracting work from fellow council members Vanessa Bell and Duncan Grant, as well as from Beryl Sinclair, Richard Carline and Carel Weight.[34]

In April Olda and Oskar had married in an air raid shelter doubling as the temporary home of Hampstead registry office, and while grateful for their English sanctuary, he in particular remained charged with anger about the betrayal of Czechoslovakia, an emotion which now surfaced in his political allegory *The Red Egg*. An oil painting replete with a yelling Hitler, a gross Mussolini, a moth-eaten, sterling-tailed British lion sitting on a podium of books labelled 'Pace Munich' and a sly French cat, its central action is the flight of the about-to-be-devoured Czechoslovak fowl leaving its eponymous red egg at the table while Prague burns in the background. Reflecting the realpolitik of great power betrayal, and drawing on Eastern European folk symbols as well as James Gillray's 1805 Napoleonic-era satirical print *The Plum-pudding in Danger*, it was an Expressionist allegory of the European conflict prior to Operation Barbarossa – but a powerfully raw and wilfully gnomic one.[35]

In early September the couple travelled to Port William in south-west Scotland as guests of Emil Körner, the exiled economist who had helped them on arrival; it was the first of almost annual visits over the next five years, from which they returned at the end of October just as a further AIA/FGLC co-operative effort was reaching fruition. The *AIA and FGLC Exhibition of Sculpture and Drawings* gathered together twenty-six drawings and sixty-nine three-dimensional exhibits from sculptors and potters, the latter including six sets of work by Bernard Leach. Its catalogue carried a reflective introduction by Herbert Read lamenting that sculpture suffered as a 'memorial art' in peace and was neglected to the point of making its practice impossible in war, two-thirds of the exhibits being by artists 'uprooted, deprived of their studios, their materials, their very tools'. Read praised both the linking of 'the art of cut stone or wood, the art of cut clay and the art of thrown clay' as three-dimensional arts and the exploration of the Gothic tradition's contribution to modernism – citing Peter László Peri's works *Tube Scene* and *Road Worker* and Willi Soukop's terracotta forms as examples of realist and abstract breaks with that tradition. Visiting as reviewer for the *AIA Bulletin*, the potter John Cole (who would join the Central Committee at the next election) wished the indigenous contribution had been stronger but came away feeling 'intensely pleased' by its rich internationalism; as the next AIA annual review reported it had evidenced the value of refugee artists' 'future contribution to the development of British art'.[36]

The modest response to the AIA member appeal for participation partly reflected the number no longer in a position to produce new work, but was also a matter of timing: the Charing Cross exhibition the month before had been heavily promoted as a signature event requiring war-related, recently created work from members. However, it also reflected the fact that wider possibilities for artists to exhibit in London had not collapsed as expected – rather the reverse had happened. The bombing of London was now less intense, encouraging those galleries that had remained intact to stage new shows; and the push for continuing opportunities – which had fed through as early as 1939 to enormous non-juried Red Cross United Artists' exhibitions involving twenty-five artistic societies at the Royal Academy – was also now spawning further, more focused opportunities. The product of the Recording Britain scheme, including drawings by AIA members, was placed on display in the National Gallery in summer 1941 and the two succeeding years; transatlantic philanthropy in the form of a grant from the Harkness Foundation also led to the opening of the first *Civil Defence Artists* exhibition at the Cooling Galleries in New Bond Street on 8 October 1941. Supported by Clark, Matthew Smith and Eric Newton and promoted by the AIA, this was the first of eleven successive shows organized over eighteen months, during which over two thousand works from five hundred civil defence artists (including professionals like Rowe, 'Sunday painters' and amateurs in the ranks) were shown; £1,800 of sales were generated and a separate *Fireman Artists* show at the Cooling led on to further iterations at the Royal Academy and a tour to the USA.[37]

What also began to be noticed around this time, both in London and 'the provinces', was a strengthening of popular interest in art, evidenced in unprecedented attendance levels whenever and wherever it could be accessed; employment levels, wages and savings had risen, but there were far fewer if any consumer goods in the shops, less food in the restaurants, and swathes of peacetime leisure activities such as professional sport simply no longer operated. These were the material factors, but there also seems to have been an existential one at play, at least among many inclined to be interested: life had never been so uncertain, so potentially ephemeral and, amid personal danger, was being lived with a hitherto unknown intensity. This had ramifications for many relationships in flux, and potentially for that between the artist and society as both tried to discern the pattern of the future, the possibilities of reconstruction from present ruin.

Even set against the interest garnered by other events, the AIA Charing Cross exhibition was an unprecedented success; the Underground booking hall display space had not always attracted attentive footfall,[38] but this time it did, necessitating reprints of the twopenny catalogue. There, in addition to the questions posed in Horton's 'Artists and the War', Francis Klingender analysed 'Our Tradition'. Linking 'the first triumphs' of democratic war art in the French Revolution, Goya's 'immortal record' of his country's resistance to 'imperial aggression', Daumier's 'grand cartoons' of 1870 and the 'heartening revival of artistic activity and of public interest in art' in a Britain where freedom was under threat, he concluded: 'The common struggle against fascist aggression has bridged the gap which has for so long divided the interests of the artists from those of the people at large. From it both have drawn a new vitality.'

Sixty members took part, including two recently released from internment: Walter Nessler displayed *Destruction*, *Devastated Area* and *Age of Chaos*, and F. H. K. Henrion a single still life – but it was Henrion who had the greatest individual impact of anyone as designer of the overall display, a treatment that put the space on the map and led to him being commissioned by the Ministry of Food to produce 'Off the Ration' there the following spring. Subtitled 'Grow More Food and Save Ships', it brought modernist design, live animals and fruit and vegetables to the booking hall to encourage pig-, poultry-, rabbit- and allotment-keeping, and subsequently toured nationally in modular form.

Of all the 'enemy aliens' Henrion had had the swiftest transition from 'the IOM to the MOI', recalling later: 'the sudden change was absolutely surrealist ... an episode in a bad dream.'[39] A week after release from the Isle of Man he was en route to an aerodrome in a military car with a Ministry of Information camera to photograph planes for use in a montaged RAF recruiting poster. Before his arrest he had designed a celebrated image combatting phoney war alarm about the security of Post Office savings, and it was to the business of public information that he now returned. Employed like Misha Black as a consultant, this also enabled Henrion to carry out weekend work for private clients from a studio in Chelsea, but – soon after the attack on Pearl Harbor on 7 December 1941 – such was the demand for his work that he was splitting fifteen-hour weekdays between the MOI and the USA Office of War Information; having cycled to Senate House in the morning, he and his bicycle would be collected by Packard to service his Mayfair-based American client during the afternoon.[40] In early 1943 his consequent familiarity with Roosevelt's war aims would feed into *For Liberty*, the most extraordinary of all AIA war-time exhibitions, staged as the imprint of Britain's transatlantic alliance became ever more evident on London's streets. But more immediately, it was Russia's fate that preoccupied both artists and populace, and its revived appeal that troubled others working at Senate House.

* * * * *

Pearl Binder did not show any work at Charing Cross, but during its run she broadcast *English Artist in Moscow*, subsequently published in *The Listener* on 6 November illustrated with a Kukrynisky cartoon linking resistance to Hitler with Napoleon's 1812 defeat before Moscow. In it she revisited her earlier experiences, expressing an admiration for Soviet experimentation that would have been unacceptable on the BBC airwaves a few months before. Since her marriage to Frederick Elwyn-Jones in 1937, Pearl had avoided overt party-aligned activity while he pursued his anti-fascist work and sought selection as a Labour candidate, a route that eventually led to his election as Member of Parliament for Plaistow in 1945. In the interim Pearl had worked in advertising, given birth to a daughter in 1938, and undertaken the first TV fashion broadcasts from Alexandra Palace. It was some time since her work on *Misha and Masha* of 1936 but now, amid a popular wave of Russophilia, she illustrated *Russian Families*, a children's picture book.[41]

That autumn Russia suffered astounding losses of personnel and equipment, and many thousands of square kilometres were turned into racial killing fields as the SS followed the advancing front; by September Leningrad was encircled – not long after Nazis were at the gates of Moscow. In government circles there was initially little confidence in Soviet military capacity and the fear was that Hitler, having disposed of his ideological enemy to the east, would soon be able to hurl vast forces into an invasion that had been forestalled in 1940 but might indeed materialize in 1942. In hope of at least delaying this, commitments were made to supply Stalin with military aid by Arctic convoy, an undertaking getting under way just as the BBC's nightly news reports began to sharpen public admiration of Red Army resistance. This in turn allowed those on the left, particularly those that had supported the People's Convention, to take the initiative in organizing well-supported Anglo-Soviet Friendship Weeks throughout the country, grass-roots activities now matched by officially sanctioned ones such as 'Tanks for Russia Week'.

From Leek in Staffordshire, Ron Horton wrote to Percy, enclosing a sketch of shopfronts turned into an Aid to Russia exhibition by a local committee which raised £1,000 (around £43,000 in mid-2020s prices).[42] Notice of a more metropolitan variant was announced on the last page of December's *AIA Bulletin*: a folio of engravings for sale at 2 guineas with contributions from 'Augustus John, Julian Trevelyan, John Buckland-Wright,

7.11 Julian Trevelyan, *Camouflage*, engraving contributed to *Salvo for Russia*, 1942. 17.5 × 23.2 cm (7 × 9¼ in.)

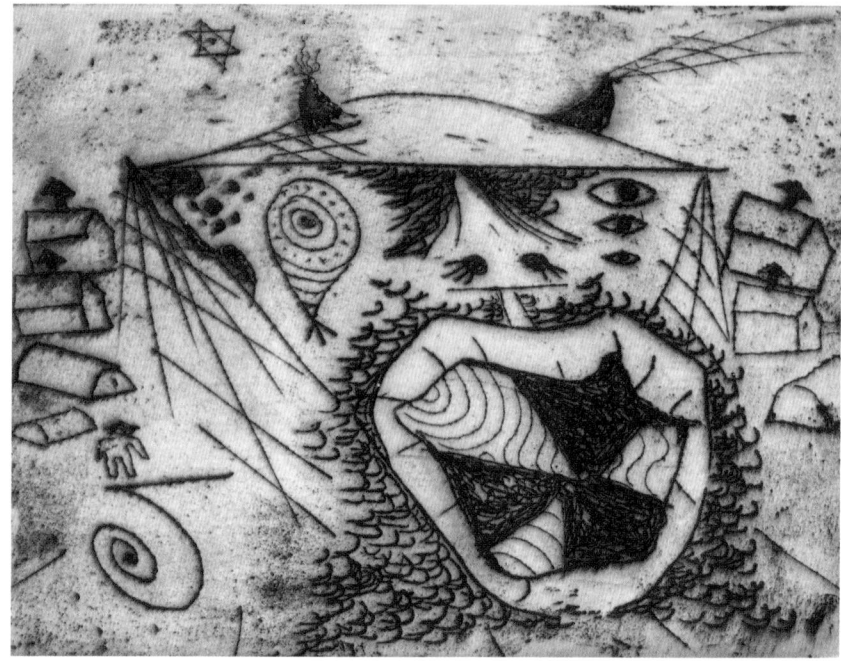

Geza Szóbel, Ithell Colquhoun, Graham Sutherland and others'. By the time *Salvo for Russia* appeared in the new year, Augustus and Graham had fallen by the wayside, replaced by John Piper, John Banting and Roland Penrose; Julian Trevelyan's image playing subtle tricks with his experience as a camouflage officer in North Africa was perhaps the most striking of an intriguing series.[43]

By then those monitoring national morale in Senate House were getting consistent reports of Russian success acting as an antidote to bad news from elsewhere: 'Thank God for Russia is a frequent expression of the very deep and fervent feeling for that country which permeates wide sections of the public.'[44] For many this was accompanied by a perception that the government was less than wholehearted in its support of a former political foe, a suspicion reinforced when Colonel Moore-Brabazon, Churchill's Minister of Aircraft Production, was caught opining that Russia and Germany – 'our two chief enemies' – should be allowed to destroy themselves at Stalingrad.[45]

Moore-Brabazon was dismissed, but there was no escaping that Russian success was beginning to pose an acute dilemma for the forces of national conservatism. The Soviet Union, the only European power to have thwarted Hitler's armies in battle, was now the existing order's essential ally in a life-and-death national struggle; moreover the resilience of the Red Army, and war-time Russian leadership, presented an unavoidable contrast to British failures in France, Norway, Crete, Malaya, and most recently at Singapore. Yet for two decades those in power had been denouncing the Soviet system as inefficient, morally degenerate and incapable of matching capitalist democracy; unfolding events were powerfully suggesting otherwise, even as a reluctant British government was being forced to utilize state control for public ends on an unprecedented scale.

Whitehall's expedient response combined securing a tacit understanding with Moscow that in exchange for expanded military support there would be no attempt to influence Britain's internal politics or advance the communist cause domestically. This was accompanied by a campaign – generated from within the Soviet affairs section of the Ministry of Information – to 'steal the thunder' of the left by elevating official celebration of the Anglo-Soviet alliance to new heights while moving to canalize activists' local campaigns into safely apolitical channels endorsed in mayoral parlours. Thus the booking hall at Charing Cross and other venues nationwide soon played host to displays fronted by portraits of Churchill and Stalin extolling Russia's tsarist-era culture and its patriotic fight to defend native soil while carefully avoiding anything that might

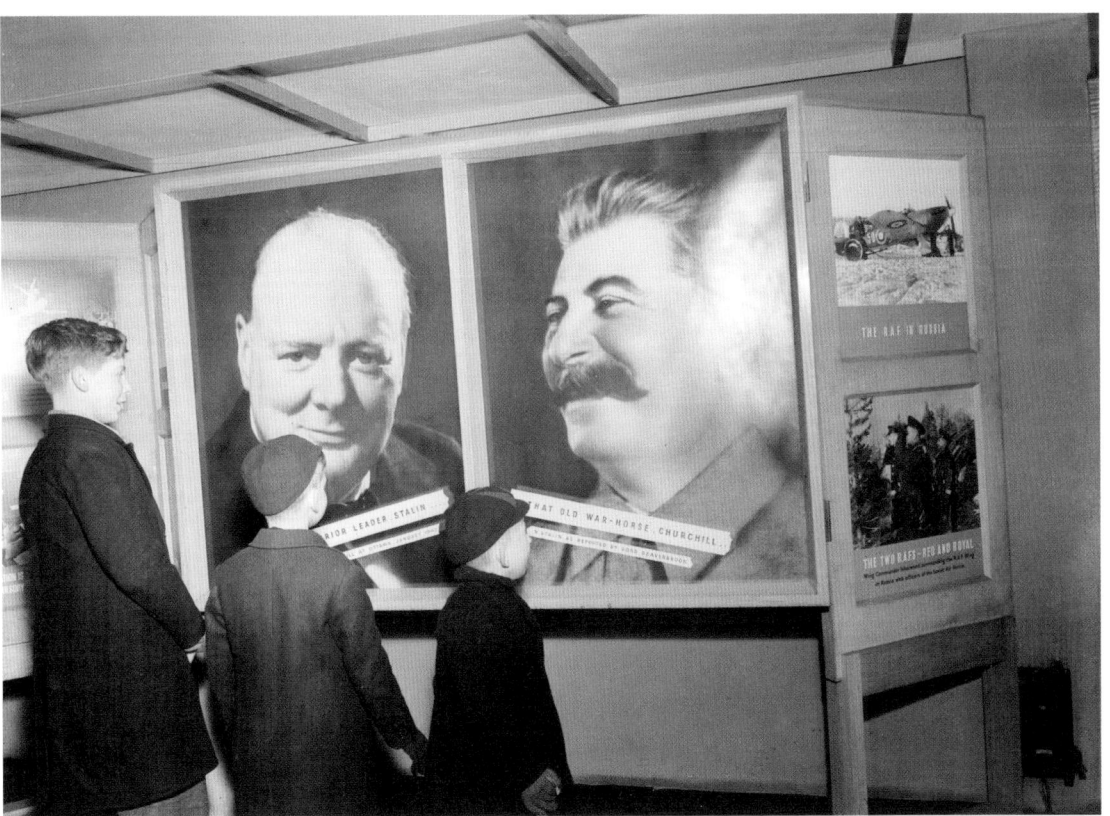

7.12 Ministry of Information photographer, *Comrades in Arms, Pictures of the Soviet Union at War*, Charing Cross, 1942

7.13 F. H. K. Henrion, *Artists Aid Russia Exhibition*, lithographed poster, 1942. 63.9 × 49 cm (25¼ × 19⅜ in.)

popularize Soviet-era social progress. This vein of propaganda, pursued with vigour by MOI Regional Information Officers, would culminate on 21 February 1943 in celebrations marking the twenty-fifth anniversary of the Red Army, during which the political establishment joined an Albert Hall rally featuring massed choirs and readings by John Gielgud and Laurence Olivier. But before this a significant holding move was the installation of Clementine Churchill, the prime minister's wife, as titular head of a national charitable fund.

During mid-summer 1942 core AIA members and leading supporters were involved in two 'Aid to Russia' selling exhibitions of very different scale and orientation. The smaller one, comprising sixty-eight items from thirty-five artists, was opened on 4 June by Mme Maisky, wife of the Soviet ambassador, at 3 Willow Road, Hampstead, the strikingly modernist home of architect Ernő Goldfinger. Sponsored by his union, the AIA-affiliated Association of Architects, Surveyors and Technical Assistants (AASTA), its proceeds were destined for the National Council of Labour's Aid to Russia Fund. A cyclostyled catalogue, adorned with a single red star applied by hand, carried 'Art Too is a Weapon', an introduction from AASTA president Colin Penn, arguing that workers in design, construction and decoration were integral to building society's future and shared with all artists the knowledge that 'if culture is to develop, flourish and become part of the life of the people, it is necessary first that Fascism be destroyed'. The roll-call of donated and displayed items, over half for sale, was extraordinary, including works by Picasso, Léger, Klee, Masson, Miró, Moore, Ozenfant, Arp, Downs, Paul Nash, Nicholson, Hepworth, Hodgkins, Schwitters, Kernn-Larsen, Penrose, Piper, Rousseau, Agar, Banting, Craxton, Michael Rothenstein, Tunnard, Trevelyan, Wickham and Augustus John.[46] Lectures on Soviet architecture, cinema and music ran next door at 1 Willow Road and, fittingly enough, on 22 June, the evening after it finished, the BBC broadcast the second ever performance of Shostakovich's Symphony No. 7, begun nine months before while he was serving as a firefighter during the siege of Leningrad.

By then Henrion had completed a poster and catalogue design for the exhibition *Artists Aid Russia*, which Mme Maisky was also called on to open eight days later at Hertford House, Manchester Square, the home of the Wallace Collection. Utilizing the interplay between a painter's red palette, the Soviet hammer and sickle insignia and William Blake's lines about the sword that sung a song of death but could not make the sickle yield, they advertised the exhibition as having been organized 'on behalf of Mrs Winston Churchill's Aid to Russia Fund'; at this 595 artists were exhibiting 897 works under the auspices of the Central Institute of Art and Design and an organizing committee including Beryl Sinclair.

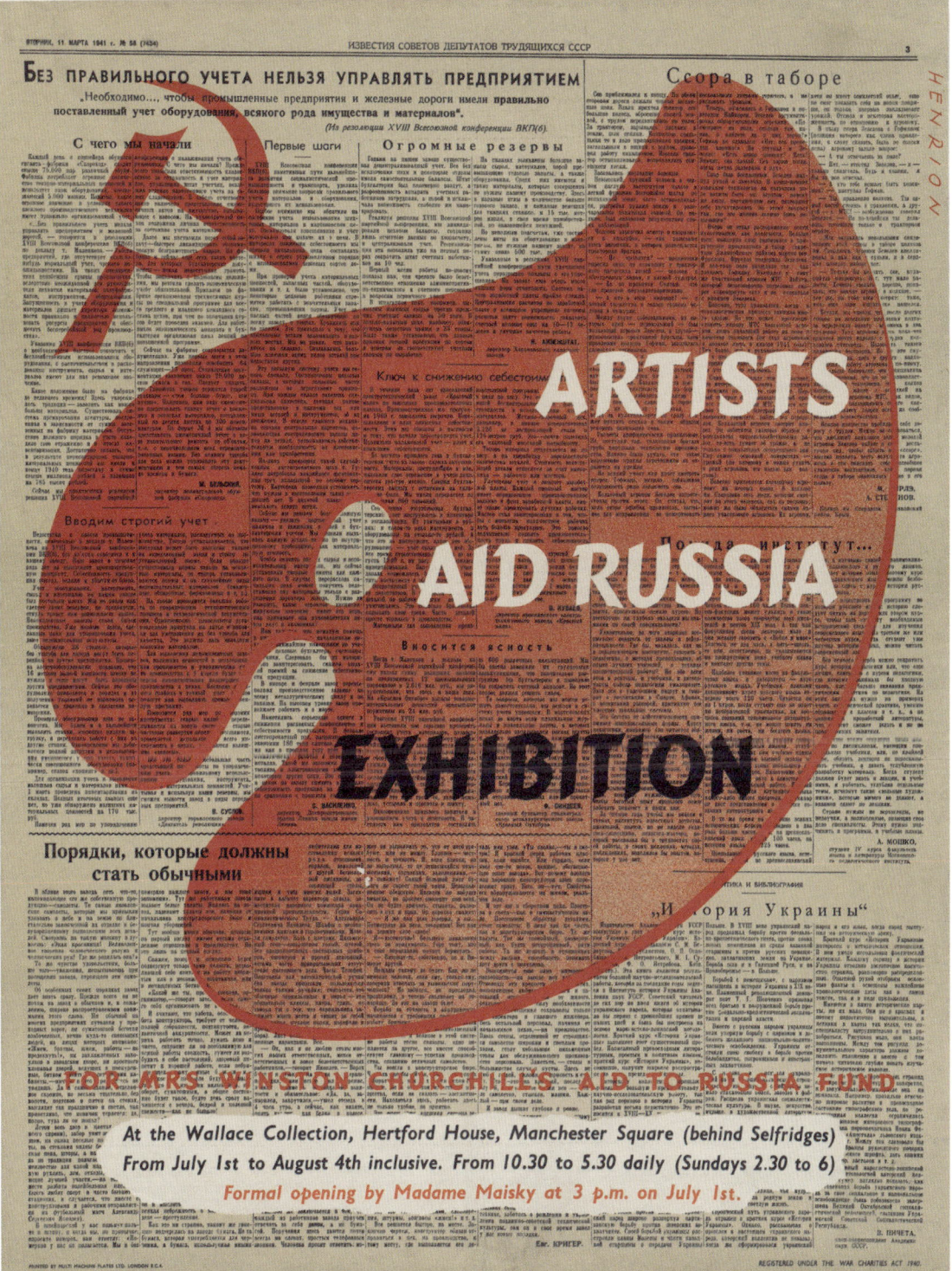

7.14 Peter László Peri, *Nazi Photographing Hanged Couple*, ink and watercolour on paper, 1940–44. 43.5 × 44.5 cm (17¼ × 17⅝ in.). Peri only discovered after the war that his four brothers had all perished during the Holocaust

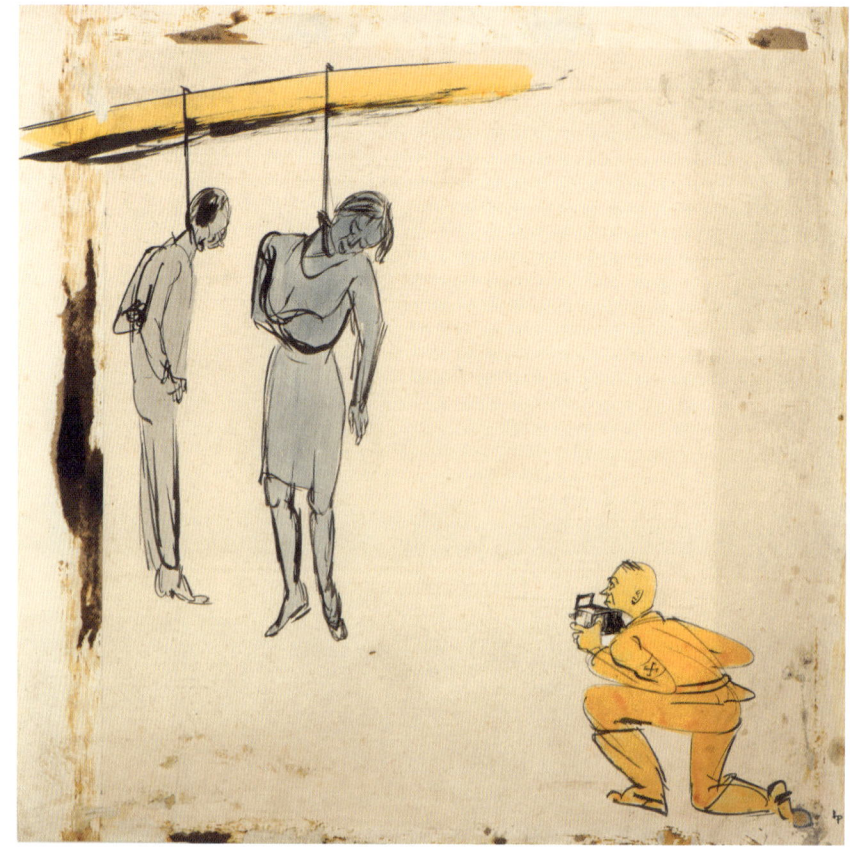

The CIAD had previously rejected the idea of organizing all-comer shows like the annual Red Cross United Artists' exhibitions at Burlington House,[47] but now its twenty-three affiliated artists' societies combined willingly in the Downing Street-endorsed venture and, by happenstance of alphabetical order, the AIA led the list of sponsors. These included exhibiting bodies the London Group and the New English Art Club, along with a myriad of societies – Miniature Painters, Muralists and Marine Artists, the Pastel Society, the Wood Engravers and the Royal British Colonial Society of Artists.

Although largely lost among a crowded hang, there were contributions from a majority of the AIA Advisory Council and current Central Committee members.[48] Pearl Binder also exhibited, as did Helen Binyon, about to return from Bath to a job in the Senate House photographic section. Rea and Youngman sent in from Huntingdon, Peri and Rowe from Camden Studios, and both James and Margaret Fitton contributed, as did Private James Boswell, now en route to Iraq.

* * * * *

Five months earlier, on Saturday 21 February, Slater's restaurant in Brompton Road had been the venue for the AIA AGM and 1942–43 election; Cliff Rowe, Elizabeth Watson and John Banting were among those not re-nominating, but Ewan Phillips returned and F. H. K. Henrion was elected for the first time, along with Jan Gordon, Helen Lowenthal and Helena Clark.[49] Misha Black was confirmed as chair, James Holland as deputy and Mary Petter as secretary. As before the tides of war had carried some away, with a greater number now serving overseas, but the gathering was well attended, and significant in agreeing to adopt the AIA's 'new programme' – an ambitious move to expand activities as a platform not merely for survival but to generate momentum for artists 'to organise themselves as propagandists'. Building up resources to secure club rooms and a gallery and working capital for publishing and co-operative retailing of artists' materials was also in prospect.

The AIA's 1937 aspirations to organize artists as trade unionists had faltered pre-war as negotiations with other bodies had become clouded by political division and bogged down in sectional interests. Since then, the AIA had helped create an institutional ecosystem, with the CIAD at its centre and government as its target, aimed at furthering continued employment of artists in war time; but the CIAD was now offering individual membership and was therefore a de facto competitor requiring the AIA to sharpen its unique appeal. The meeting heard how the finances were in reasonable shape after indebtedness had been reduced from profits made on the two travelling exhibitions, but that implementation of the proposed new programme would require a staffed office and an increased annual subscription. For full professional members this was set at £1 7s. 6d., with a lesser amount asked from professional members not opting for welfare benefits, associate members and students. Full members now gained access to new services: legal advice on copyright, collection of professional debts, reduced insurance premiums, reduced agents' fees, credit checks on clients, advice on war work and national service, advice on hardship payments for Armed Forces dependants, help with storing and exhibiting work if away, and 'general advice on all matters affecting artists as technicians'.[50]

As the meeting took place, the 1942 members' exhibition was two weeks into a three-week run at the Royal Society of British Artists Galleries in Suffolk Street. Unlike Charing Cross the previous autumn, this was a general show without an overarching narrative but with 261 exhibits including many notable works; to the surprise of many, amid shortages of other consumer goods, a 20 per cent commission on sales ensured it made a profit.[51] The one notable innovation was an option, in line with Jan Gordon's instincts, for artists to provide one hundred words of accompanying explanatory text – a departure dismissed by *The Times* with 'surely it's a painter's business to express himself in paint'.[52] Kenneth Clark, speaking once again at an AIA opening, used this occasion to praise the organization for making artists 'more conscious of the world of political ideas', recalling the banners painted to 'show sympathy with the Spanish Government during the Spanish Civil War'. He commended it as a trail-blazer in challenging 'the faulty relationship of artist to society' by 'holding exhibitions in unlikely places' and producing works of art at affordable prices. But he added: 'No society of artists could carry these experiments far enough unaided by the State.' In Clark's view there had to be exhibitions not only at Charing Cross but at Swindon and Crewe and all important railway centres. Initiatives like Everyman Prints would be better off with official support.

The necessity of continuing debate among artists and between artists and the public had been part of the compromise war-time mission Misha Black had promoted during the first crisis of the conflict; this now took the form of a series of AIA lectures on art and society held in the National Gallery 'by courtesy of the Trustees' on eight successive Sundays. Headlined 'The Purpose of Art Today', it opened with lectures on painting by Lord Methuen, sculpture by Frank Dobson and design by Black himself. Maxwell Fry – a recent AIA recruit – followed on architecture, Nan Youngman on teaching, and Eric Newton on criticism, before Francis Klingender lectured on art history, with Clark himself concluding the series with a talk on patronage – a further opportunity to air the case for expanded state support for the arts.

Klingender's talk covered ideas that would inform his widely read book *Marxism and Modern Art* the following year, and having recently written 'Our Tradition' for the Charing Cross catalogue, his presence in the line-up began a period of close involvement with the AIA, during which he became the prime mover in organizing a new AIA centre in Charlotte Street. Before this he had been working as a temporary scientific officer at the Ministry of Home Security's Princes Risborough research unit, studying bomb damage and its impact on Birmingham and Hull, but his employment had been terminated, probably as a result of MI5 intervention.[53] Now in a relationship with Millicent Rose, one of Blunt's Courtauld students, he was living in her Downshire Hill flat a few doors down from the Uhlmans and working on *Russia: Britain's Ally, 1812–1942*. A lively work comparing British and Russian political caricature and propaganda in the Napoleonic era with that in the present conflict, the book reproduced images Lord Beaverbrook, visiting as Minister of Supply, had brought back from Moscow, as well as Cliff Rowe's *Stretcher Party* lithograph and Boswell's drawing *The Night the Sergeant Copped It*, first seen at Charing Cross.

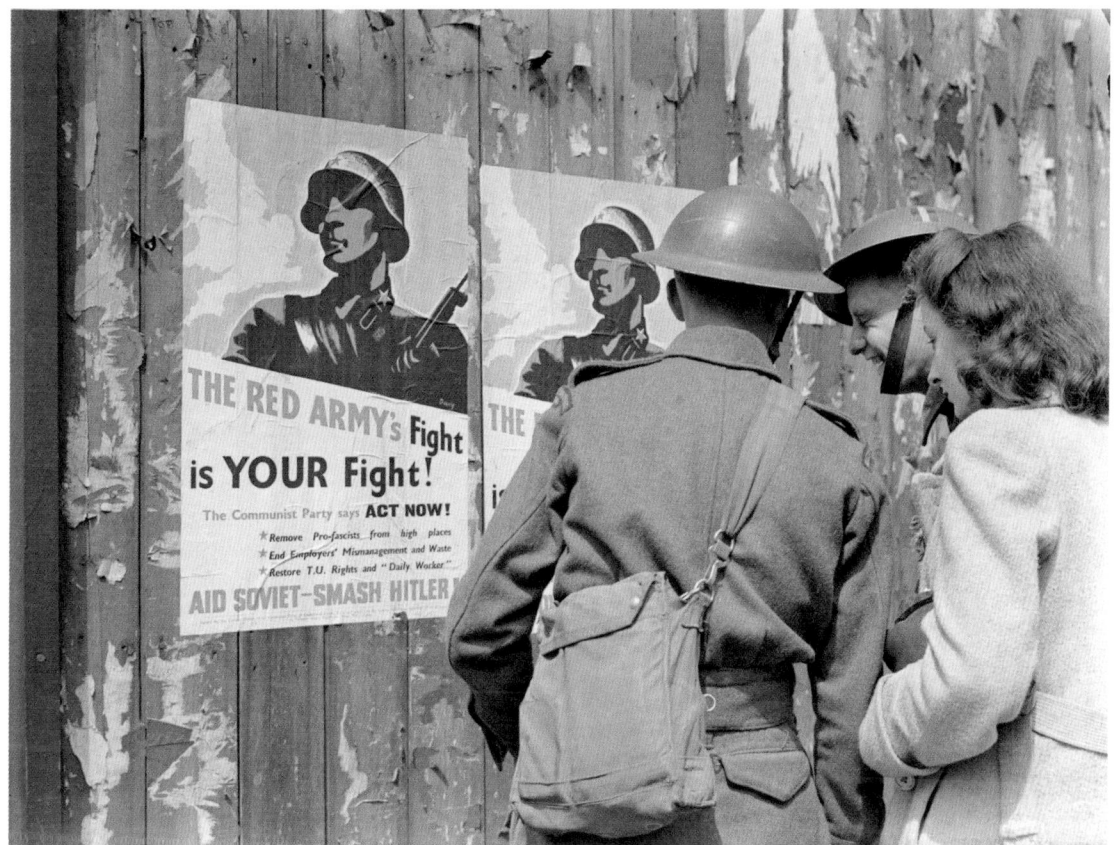

7.15 Ministry of Information photographer, *The Red Army's Fight is Your Fight!*, 1941; an image evidencing the Communist Party's push for immediate opening of a second front in the fight against Hitler's Germany

Just before its publication, the largest political demonstration of the war occurred when 43,000 rallied in Trafalgar Square demanding 'Second Front Now'. It was a call chalked on inner urban walls nationwide, and more formally echoed in Ambassador Maisky's introduction to Klingender's book, dated 18 August 1942: 'no second front has so far been opened, which makes the burden of the present war still heavier for my people than was the case in 1812. However the second front is bound to come, with the promise to take off some of the burden from the shoulders of the USSR. The sooner this happens the earlier will Hitler's power be broken, and the smaller will be the price we must pay for liberation of the peoples from the fascist yoke.'[54]

*****

'Have you not got a single general in that army who can win battles? Have none of them any ideas?', Winston Churchill demanded of General Sir Alan Brooke, Chief of the Imperial General Staff, at a meeting of the War

Cabinet in mid-1942.⁵⁵ As Taylor Downing has analysed, Britain's war-time prime minister thought the army's senior officer cadre lived in a narrow-minded world obsessed with rank and privilege, its leaders unwilling to engage with new ideas and technologies or to act strategically outside the safety of inherited routines, their immediate subordinates only fit to serve – in Harold Macmillan's doubly revealing phrase – as 'secretaries of golf clubs'.⁵⁶ Class differences also meant that many line commanders were incapable of communicating naturally with those they led. This was the army culture, including a 'calculated process of breaking down the recruit's spirit', into which 7392959 Pte Boswell was conscripted in January 1941 and which, from a very different vantage point than the Cabinet table, he began to record in his sketchbooks.⁵⁷

After induction at Boyce Barracks in Hampshire, Boswell had been posted back to London for six months' training at the Army School of Radiography at Millbank. During this time he filled an album with delicate anatomical drawings that might have been created in the Renaissance, but in two others he had begun to depict the brutishness of modern service life. While billeted at home in London he was still in close touch with AIA activity, and writing in the Charing Cross catalogue Horton commented: 'James Boswell's racy commentaries on life in the army are in the English tradition that goes back through Rowlandson to Hogarth.'⁵⁸ Boswell also sent work into the War Artists Advisory Committee at Senate House. Later he became sure his known politics had debarred him from a salaried commission, but he was placed on a list of artists from whom work might be purchased, and the WAAC Army representative undertook to write to the commander of his unit requesting he be given occasional facilities and permission to work.⁵⁹

This proved beneficial shortly after, when Boswell was sent to Peebles in Scotland as a trainee radiographer allocated to the 49th General Hospital, as he made clear to Jan Gordon, who was compiling an AIA report on the situation of artists in the forces: 'I think I have been luckier than most ... because the kind of work I do doesn't need a lot of equipment or space. (That is if you skip lithographs.) I use the X-ray department in the hospital as a studio in the evening and at weekends.'⁶⁰ As a result of the WAAC intervention he was excused training for a day a week over the next six months, allowing his art to develop strongly in two distinct dimensions.

The first included portraits of fellow soldiers and led on to a series of naturalistic, grimly atmospheric, reportage drawings in pen, ink and watercolour. These depict life in the ranks with fatigues undertaken at all hours and in all weathers, plus the rituals of Nissen hut social life, and in parallel the hospital world of medical orderlies, nurses and submissive

7.16 James Boswell, *Bringing in a Casualty at Night*, ink, watercolour and chalk on paper, 1941. 34 × 45 cm (13½ × 17¾ in.)

7.17 James Boswell, *Taking Details from Casualty*, pencil ink and wash on paper, 1941. 20.7 × 25.7 cm (8¼ × 10⅛ in.)

7.18 James Boswell, *Steinmann Pin Going In*, pencil ink and wash on paper, 1941. 20.7 × 25.7 cm (8¼ × 10⅛ in.)

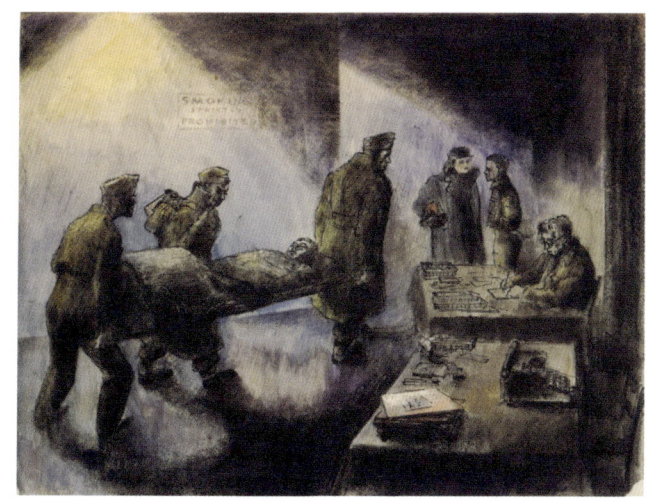
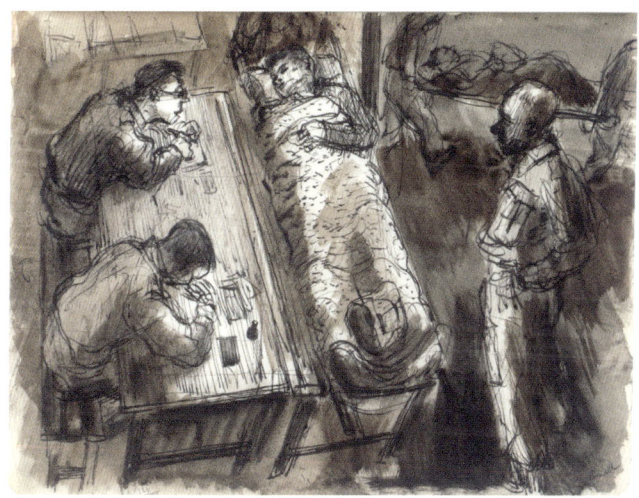
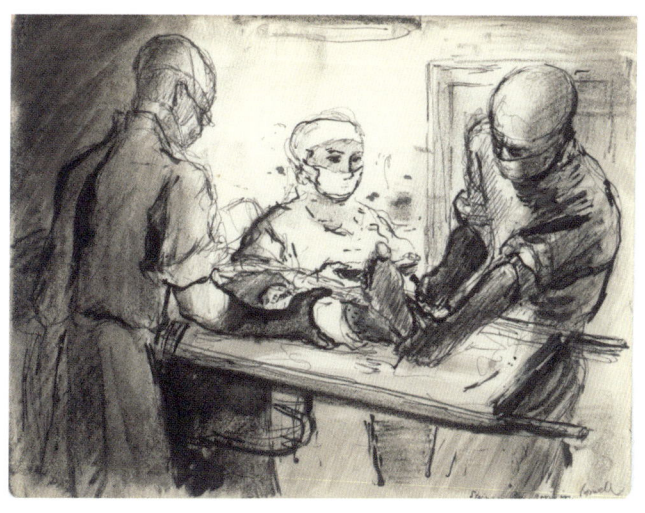

CAMDEN STREET AND SENATE HOUSE

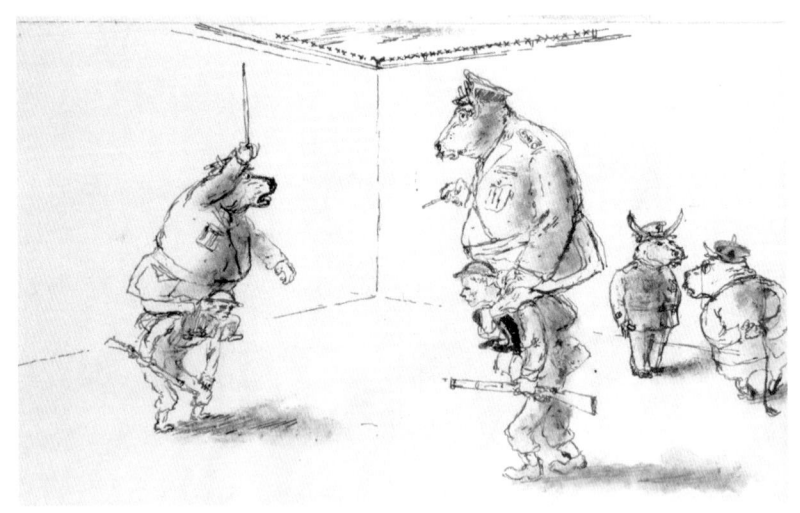

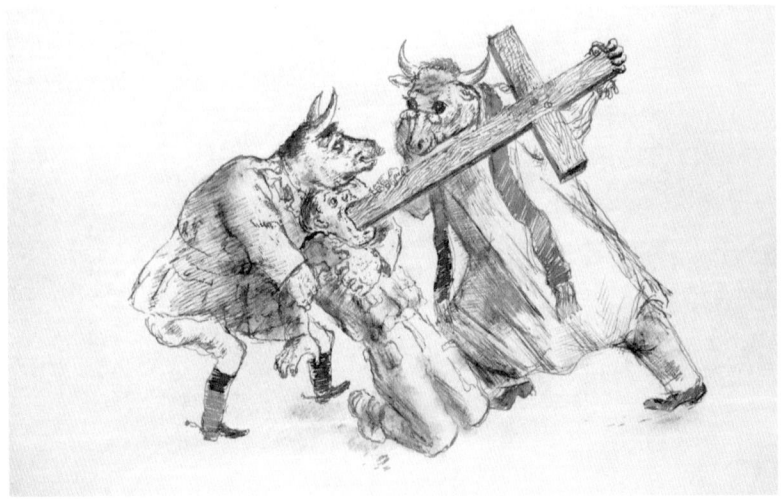

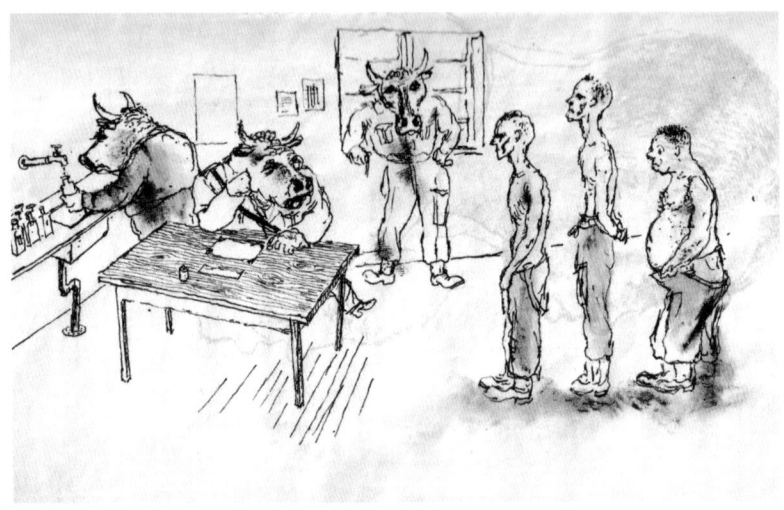

7.19–7.25 James Boswell, untitled images from the 'Bull' sketchbook, pen and ink, Iraq, 1941–42. Each 15.4 × 23.2 cm or 23.2 × 15.4 cm (6⅛ × 9¼ in.)

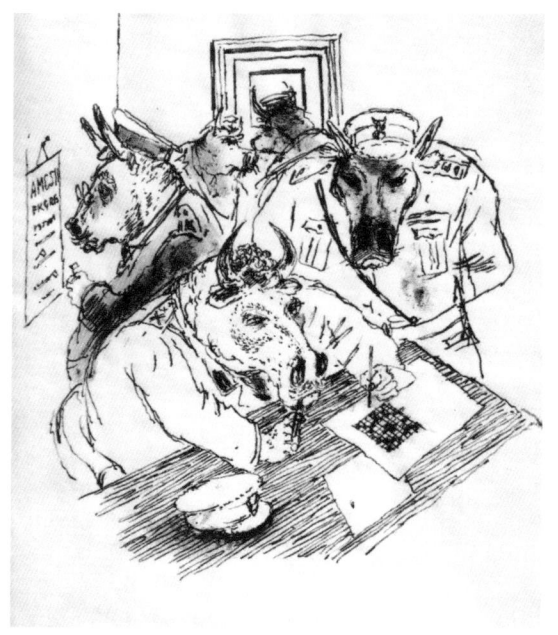
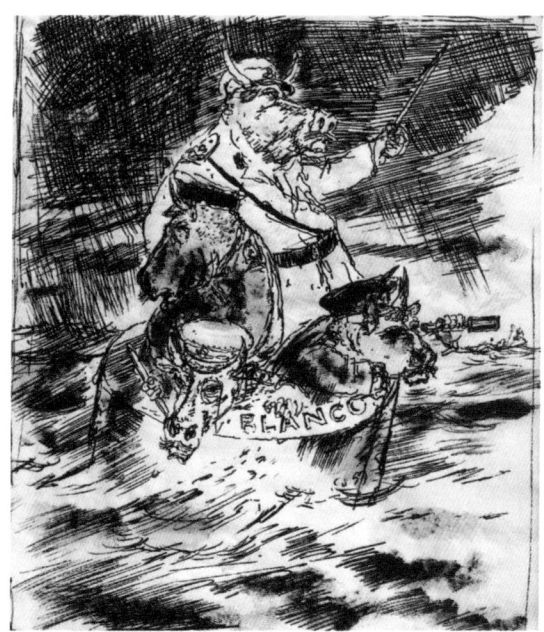
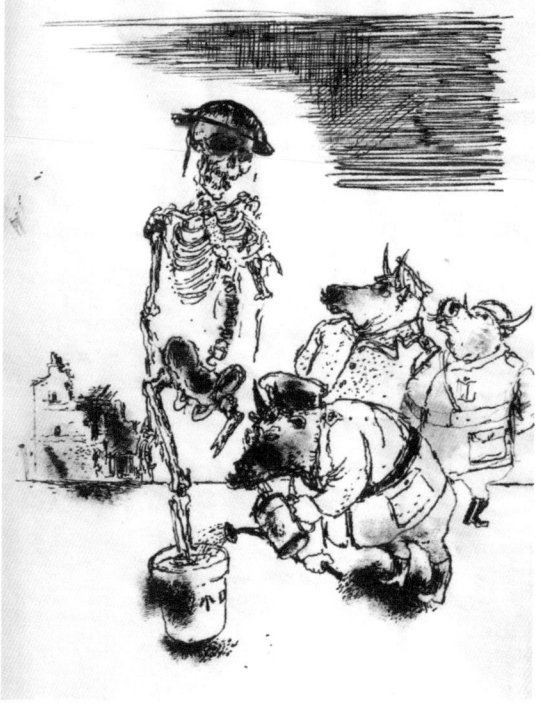
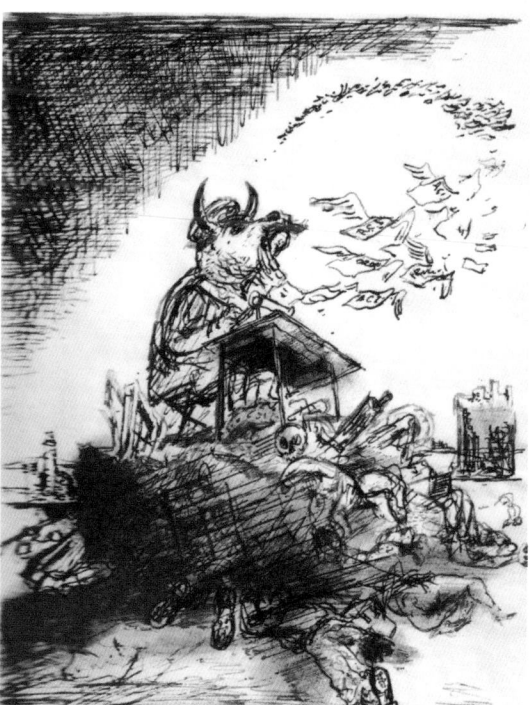

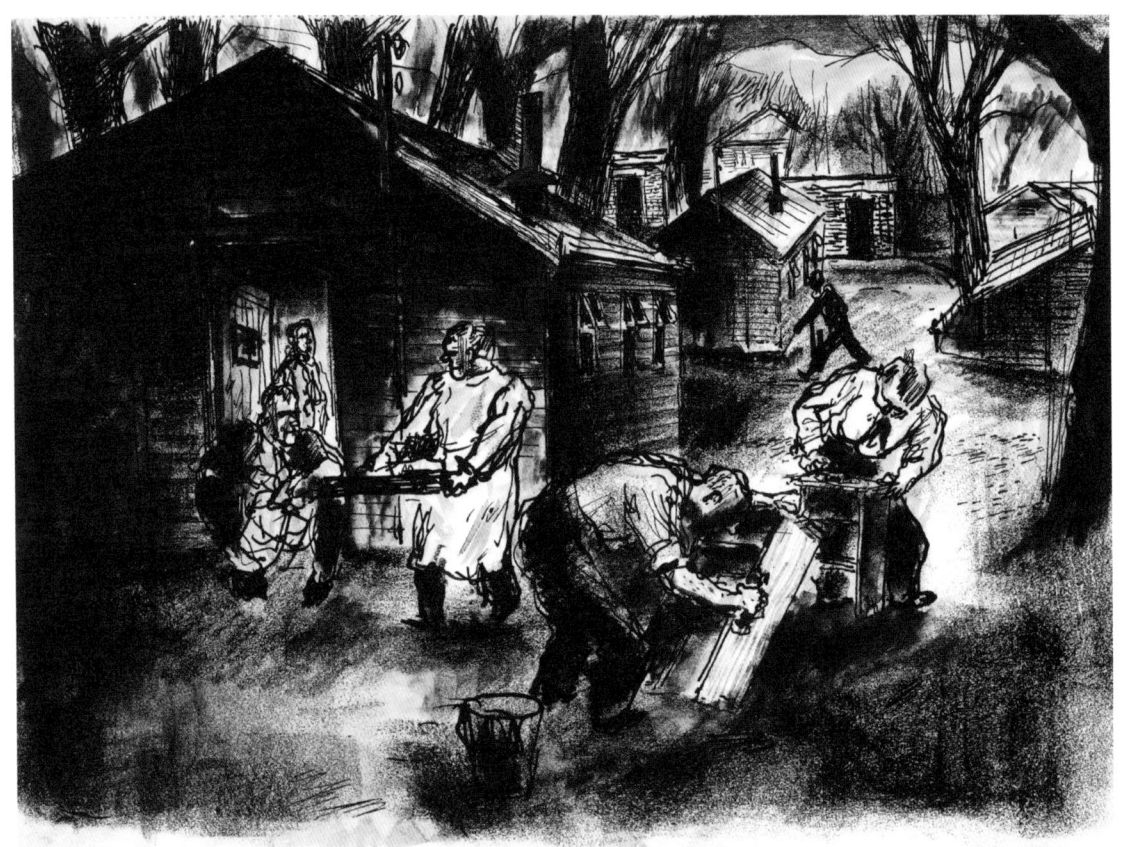

7.26 James Boswell, untitled image from the 'Bull' sketchbook, pen and ink, Iraq, 1941–42. 20.7 × 25.7 cm (8¼ × 10⅛ in.)

patients, filing forward in a chiaroscuro of sharply observed unfolding incident. The former made no attempt at the picturesque, and the latter could scarcely be further removed from the anodyne, unpeopled war art that had failed to impress Boswell at the National Gallery.

These naturalistic scenes convey feeling, occasionally a certain sardonic humour, but the second emerging dimension of Boswell's work was charged with an altogether more acerbic force, reminiscent of his earliest drawings for *Left Review*, as with an outsider's eye he scraped bare the oppressive relationship between the British Army's officer class and its soldiery. His intention was 'to extract the dream reality, to evoke the unreality of the soldier's life' and in order to do this he now created a series of ink drawings dramatizing a unique personal bestiary.[61] Here bemedalled bovine generals ride on the back of human underlings and tend soldier-skeleton pot plants with a watering can; horned staff officers play 'battleships' in the mess, while others set to sea on a raft of 'blanco'. A bull in uniform sits typing athwart a Calvary of mangled bodies as endless memoranda initialled Army Council of Instruction fly skyward, and another violently restrains a private as a cassocked bull priest rams a crucifix down his throat.

David Low, well known to Boswell through the AIA, had long since propelled Colonel Blimp into popular consciousness through his strip cartoon; an archetype of English reaction, 'Blimps' had now become popular shorthand for all obtuse appeasers who had instinctively favoured fascism abroad over the possibilities of socialism at home. Even now earnest discussions were taking place in the Ministry of Information about the possibility of suppressing Michael Powell and Emeric Pressburger's film *The Life and Death of Colonel Blimp* lest it reinforce the public view of certain types of army officer that Churchill himself privately held.[62]

But compared with such satire, Boswell's is a scatological vision in which trace elements of Grosz, Holbein's *Dance of Death*, Picasso's *Guernica* and Goya's *Disasters* seem to combine as 'bullshit' threatens to drown common soldiers in excrement. 'Load of old bull' was service slang which may have initially sparked the central visual conceit, but Boswell's knowledge of the classics evidently also put him in mind of the bull in the Rape of Europa myth.[63] The 1941–42 sketchbook in which he began to develop the series is indeed entitled 'Bull', but its successor, which he carried into the desert, is inscribed 'Europa', and in its pages the mythological narrative he was creating develops an ever darker hue.

After eighteen days' embarkation leave, during which he briefly resumed drawing in Camden Town and the West End, Boswell left London bound for the Middle East via the Cape in mid-April 1942. He would be away for twenty months and absent when the most politically innovative AIA exhibition of the war took place. He had already shown his latest work to Montagu Slater, now Head of Scripts in the Ministry of Information film production section, and it may well have been at his Senate House desk that Slater finalized a profile of Boswell, picking out nine images as illustrations, four of them from 'Bull'. After reviewing their eventful friendship and Boswell's progress since the day Slater had encountered him carrying a rocking chair through Regent's Park, he wrote: 'for my part I should like to print all three notebooks en bloc. Those we have printed introduce an issue of *Our Time* which is largely made up of contributions from the Army. They give us a picture not only of their subjects, but of the Good Soldier Boswell.'[64]

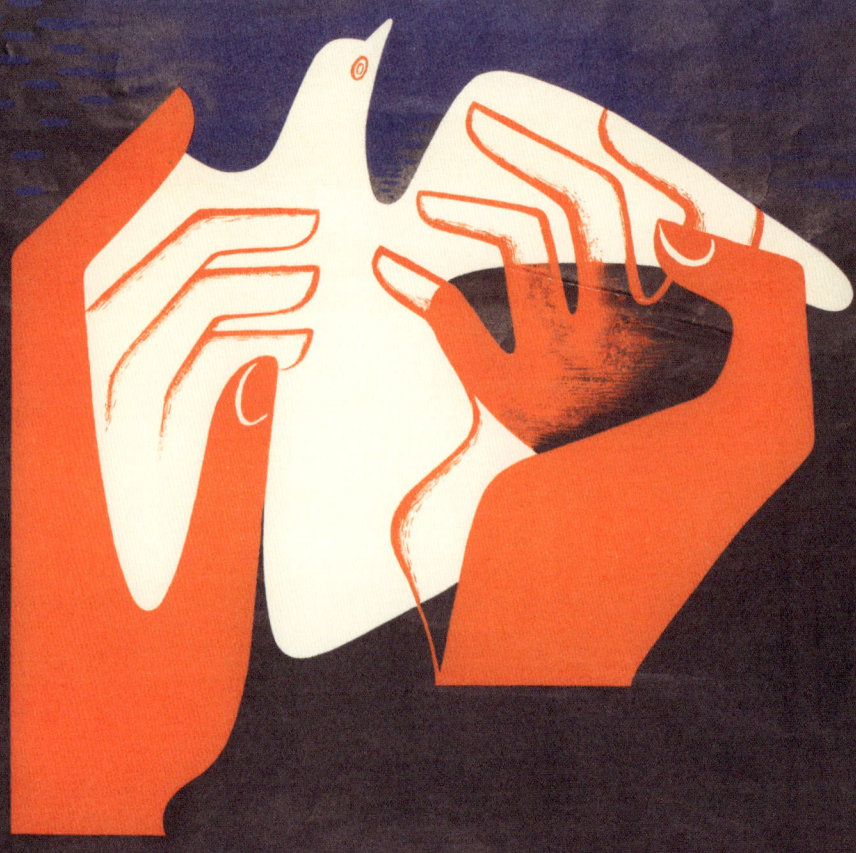

CHAPTER EIGHT

HOLLES STREET

Soldier Boswell's experience had convinced him that 'bulls' in the military hierarchy prevented artists from playing a full part in the fight against fascism because 'the function and purpose of propaganda in the British Army is as little understood in 1942 as the function and purpose of a Panzer Division in 1939'.[1] His departing message after witnessing disillusionment and brutalism in the ranks was that the AIA, with its record in the anti-fascist fight, should now campaign for the democratization of the services to raise motivation and hasten victory. Boswell would return to a role in the Army Bureau of Current Affairs (ABCA) and activity influencing the climate of opinion as 1945 approached, but before this eighteen months of isolation would test his optimism.

The new programme envisaged AIA members campaigning for their ideals and led that July to the announcement of an agenda for the next annual exhibition to 'create a new propaganda form hitherto unknown in this country', to which end painters and sculptors were to work in collaboration with copywriters and 'lay out men'. The aim was to demonstrate the contribution artists could make towards 'successful prosecution of the war and constructive peace' by bringing home 'the full significance of defeat', inspiring people by recording their 'heroism and suffering' and showing 'the possibilities which could spring from an imaginative peace, and how these possibilities could be developed'.[2]

The Exhibitions Committee envisaged that at the show's heart – room 1 in the original outline – would be twelve to twenty specially commissioned large panels or murals on three themes: 'This will happen if we lose the war', 'This is what we are fighting for' and 'This is how we are fighting'. The room was to be planned by specialist exhibition designers as a coherent whole, 'a propaganda exhibition in which paintings (instead of photographs) and display devices are the basic elements', and a writer would be asked to compose 'simple titles' for each picture 'on the lines of Goya's titles under his *Disasters of War*'. Room 2 would show paintings submitted by AIA members on the same themes, but in two set sizes hung on mobile display panels 'suitable for erection in railway stations, underground stations, factory canteens etc', and potentially framed 'in

8.1 F. H. K. Henrion, *For Liberty*, poster design, 1943. 74 × 48.5 cm (29¼ × 19⅛ in.)

a special sawdust/concrete material' which the committee was evaluating. Room 3 would contain other work by members who 'do not wish to paint either to specified subjects or sizes' but would demonstrate 'the other uses of art in war-time, the provision of aesthetic refreshment and inspiration' and foreshadow the work that mobile screen exhibitions could carry 'when victory is finally achieved'. A section was to be set aside for original poster designs and other printed matter, and it was hoped the exhibition would open in 1942 at a venue yet to be announced on 'approximately September 23rd'. Calling on all AIA members to treat the exhibition as a priority, the *Bulletin* added 'if you start at once you have nearly three months in which to produce work for one of the most interesting and important experiments we have yet tried'.

Misha Black was the prime initiator of these proposals, developing them in collaboration with colleagues in Russell Square House, home of the expanded MOI displays and exhibitions division, a base within walking distance of Senate House but handily separate. Three years before, in the dying days of Europe's peace, he had returned from the New York World's Fair inspired by the artistic fruits of Roosevelt's New Deal and the pragmatic idealism of Mayor La Guardia;[3] in very different circumstances he was now revisiting his previous aspiration that the AIA's next major event would by design be a thematically unified, politically challenging one. There were two main impediments: the likely cost and finding a suitable venue.

In the face of Central Committee concerns that mounting a highly produced, large-scale free exhibition would destabilize AIA finances, Black did two things: he gave an undertaking, amounting to a personal financial guarantee, that the exhibition could be staged 'without call on the AIA general fund';[4] and he then set about working his network of contacts to access sponsorship and assistance in kind. Harris and Sheldon were suppliers of commercial display equipment who Black knew from pre-war IDP commissions and the current MOI programme of public information under way nationwide,[5] and the company now agreed to work on the fit-out for cost price less £100; in parallel the *News Chronicle* agreed to generous sponsorship.[6] But an appropriate venue proved elusive and only in November 1942 was 'a grand site' secured: the exhibition was now to be held in the new year at the canteen shelter erected where department store John Lewis's West Building had stood in Oxford Street.[7]

Two years earlier, on the night of 18 September 1940, as the AIA's annual exhibition was being hung in Suffolk Street, an incendiary oil bomb had exploded on the top floor of John Lewis's West House, starting fires which reduced its five storeys to a carcass of rubble; the flames leapt across Holles Street to the store's East House and burned there for a further day and a half before being extinguished, only to erupt again six days later. Two hundred people, a mix of retail workers and the blitzed homeless, were sheltering in the former basement canteen that night and all escaped, but three firemen died as further incendiaries and high-explosive bombs fell. Leaving the BBC five days later George Orwell saw the late afternoon sun glittering on innumerable glass fragments along Oxford Street and 'a pile of plaster dress models, very pink and realistic, looking so like a pile of corpses'; for fellow journalist Kingsley Martin the landmark building's pillared carcass now looked like 'the ruins of a Greek temple'.[8]

Enemy action had created a site of unique appeal, located on one of London's premier thoroughfares, quite unlike any gallery or available public building. Combining adaptable outdoor space amid surviving girders and stanchions with indoor space of a rebuilt and enlarged basement shelter to the rear, it would host the Ministry of Information's extensive 1943 Army exhibition *Equipment of a Division* – but only after the AIA had demonstrated its viability for such a large-scale event. Associated with a progressive employee-profit-sharing enterprise, the flagship store's ruins were a compelling place for the AIA to pose the question 'What are we fighting for?' at the heart of Britain's war-time capital.

* * * * *

In a Lord Mayor's luncheon speech at the Mansion House that November, Churchill declared: 'We mean to hold our own. I have not become the King's First Minister in order to preside over the liquidation of the British Empire.'[9] In his mind, holding one's own meant above all resisting Indian independence abroad and, domestically, ensuring that war victory was achieved without any major upheaval in the existing social order.

Churchill's speech was in part a corrective aimed at National Conservative diehards, such as Fred Uhlman's father-in-law Henry Page Croft, now a war minister in the House of Lords, who feared the prime minister had conceded too much in signing Roosevelt's Atlantic Charter the year before.[10] This faction bridled at the colonial implications of the charter's clause asserting the right of people of every race to choose their own government, and noted that its vision for a post-war world embraced not only free trade (rather than imperial preference) but also improved labour conditions, social security and economic advancement for all.[11] The charter was at one with the American president's State of the Union Address, which had defined the USA's global ambitions in terms of every individual's human right to 'Four Freedoms': freedom of speech and religion and freedom from fear and want. Addressing Congress, Roosevelt had also outlined six goals which with little translation could be read as a crisp summary of the policies favoured by conservatism's political opponents in Britain: the ending of special privileges for the few; equality of opportunity for the many; jobs for those who could work; security for those who needed it; preservation of civil liberties; and a fair sharing of the fruits of scientific progress to raise living standards.

From the outset of the coalition government, Churchill had insisted that military victory was the only war aim, suppressing demands for a statement of post-war goals with the objection 'precise aims would be compromising, whereas vague principles would disappoint'; he conceded that existential conflict necessitated unprecedented government direction of national resources, but believed that such means to victory could be rendered redundant in peacetime.[12] The Labour Party leader Clement Attlee, however, within weeks of joining the coalition in summer 1940, was recorded not unsympathetically by Harold Nicolson, a junior Tory minister at the MOI, as believing 'we should put before the country a definite pronouncement on Government policy for the future. The Germans are fighting a revolutionary war for very definite objectives. We are fighting a conservative war and our objects are purely negative. We must put forward a positive and revolutionary aim admitting that the old order has collapsed and asking people to fight for the new order.'[13]

A National War Aims Committee set up in Whitehall that autumn was mandated 'to consider means of perpetuating the national unity achieved in this country during the war through a social and economic structure designed to secure equality of opportunity and service among all classes of the community'. Although sidelined within the corridors of power, it was in fact 'the first of an unbroken relay of committees, each of which handed on the baton of reconstruction to the next'. The widespread destruction caused by the bombing of Britain's cities was by 1941 posing the question of the form physical reconstruction might take and the social possibilities that might follow – a process with which the AIA engaged in November 1941 via the CIAD by submitting to ministers a 'Memorandum on Artists in Post-War Reconstruction'.[14] Although somewhat subterranean, the process of debate within government, gradually gathering pace, was by now disproportionately influenced by Labour members of the coalition; and by autumn 1942 the rudiments of much post-war policy in relation to economic management, housing, education, town planning, health and welfare were beginning to be laid down.

On 2 December, as AIA discussions about configuring the Holles Street site were getting under way, this process erupted into public consciousness with the publication of the Beveridge Report, its advocacy of 'freedom from want' a direct echo of Roosevelt's terminology. With its call for a comprehensive system of social security and a national health service, the recommendations would become a key dividing-line when electoral politics returned, but more immediately the popular reception of Beveridge's detailed recommendations was extraordinary: 635,000 copies of the report were eventually sold and polling soon showed 86 per cent in favour of the proposals, triggering a Conservative reaction. On 21 December an Army Bureau of Current Affairs pamphlet summarizing Beveridge was withdrawn two days after publication, its distribution to troops provoking a second attempt on Churchill's part to close its publisher down.[15]

As Christmas 1942 approached, the third and most deprived of the war, it was just about possible to believe that a better post-war world might

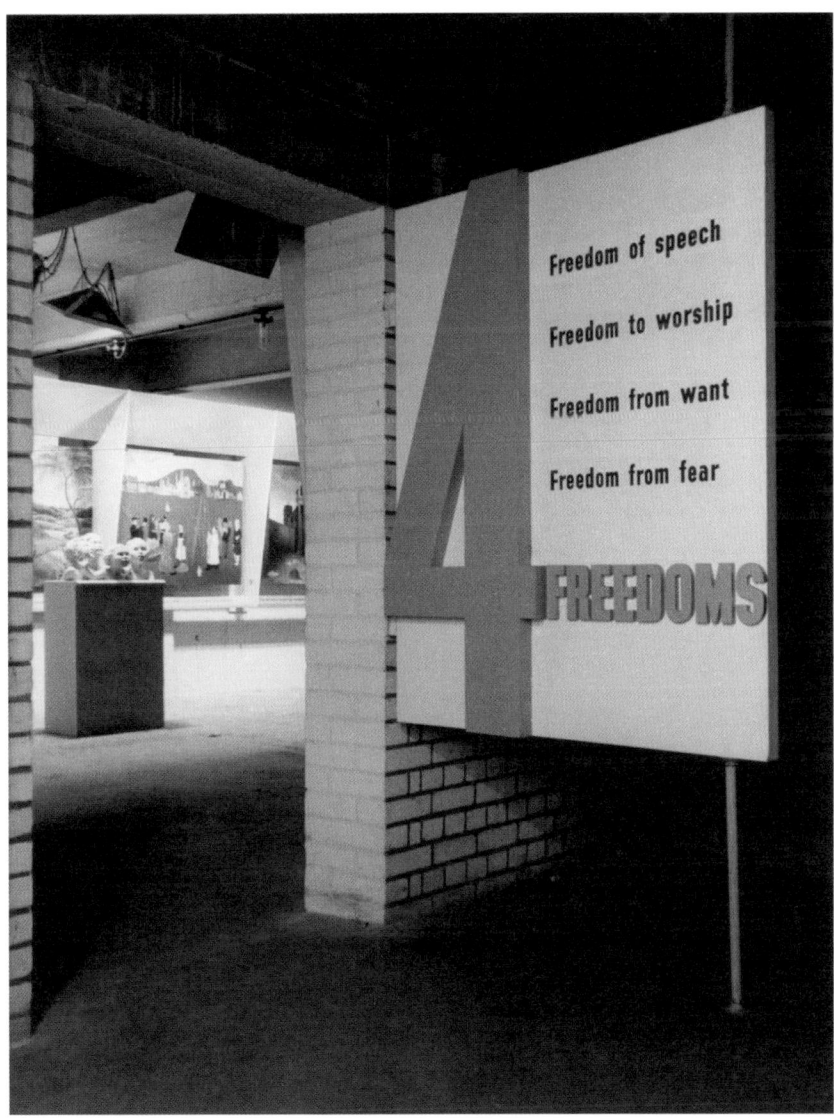

8.2 Ministry of Information photographer, Entrance to room 4 of the *For Liberty* exhibition, installation shots, March 1943

arrive. After being premiered elsewhere, on 9 August Shostakovich's Leningrad Symphony had been performed in the besieged city for which it was named, musicians called back from their front-line posts to perform. At Stalingrad five months of heroic fighting at terrible cost had stopped Hitler's forces at the Volga, while in November news arrived of Rommel's defeat at El-Alamein, the first British victory after a year of seemingly unending defeats and reversals. In the same month Operation Torch, the Anglo-American invasion of Algeria and Morocco, provided a first intimation that the transatlantic allies would indeed create a second front in Europe.

It was amid this stream of events that, having secured the John Lewis site, the sixteen-strong AIA Exhibitions Committee refined its proposal, deciding that the invited artists whose work would form the show's centrepiece would now be asked to take Roosevelt's 'Four Freedoms' as their motif.[16] 'This is how we are fighting', 'This will happen here unless...' and 'This is what we are fighting for' would now be used as themes for hanging other submissions. To make the package work, 'For Liberty' was adopted in place of the previous working title 'For Freedom' and became the brief for the Technical Committee of Misha Black, Ronald Dickens, F. H. K. Henrion and Peter Ray, all colleagues at Russell Square House. Finally, it was decided to simplify matters by mounting a parallel AIA exhibition elsewhere dealing solely with 'Poster Design in War Time Britain'.[17]

* * * * *

The sun climbed quickly up the sky, spreading an eye-searing heat that drove us all to shelter before midday. We made our beds and put up our nets to keep off the flies, and then we lay and sweated like rashers in a frying pan ... the sun became a butter coloured disc, shadows disappeared, colour died. Dust seeped steadily through us, [and] with a gentle interminable pressure, wore our tempers to a thin fragile membrane of sense ... Month after month, in one place or another, the wide curving circle of sand circumscribed our lives, setting a pattern for their monotony and helplessness. The future and the past became remote but infinitely desirable as we learnt to live on our own resources, making the best we could of the present.[18]

For Boswell, making the best of the present involved creating two largely distinct bodies of work while in the Iraqi desert and the Euphrates valley. One was a visual record of outpost life, part of a scattered army holding operation to secure oil reserves and the Middle Eastern supply route to Russia, the other a more private, surreal take on his growing

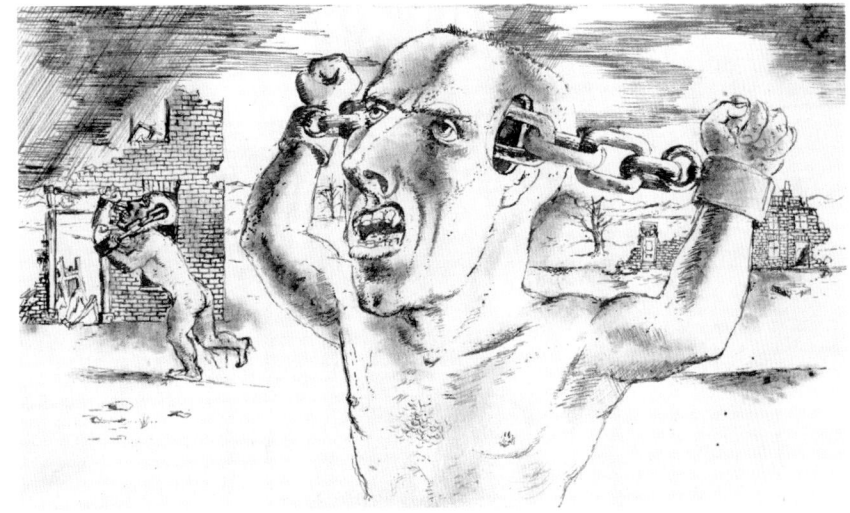

8.3 James Boswell, *The Mind in Chains*, from the 'Europa' sketchbook, 1942–43. 15.4 × 23.2 cm (6⅛ × 9¼ in.)

disturbance, bordering at times on despair, at 'the undercurrent of fear and distrust among men'. In his own words, this second body of work, created in small sketchbooks, was a conscious attempt 'to eliminate the incidental' while evoking 'the unreality of the soldier's life', and included a run of images evoking mental constriction and anguish. One image echoes the book title *The Mind in Chains*, a 1937 collection of Marxist cultural essays, while another depicts a soldier in terror of the skies, immured in a vertical barbed wire cage. These give way to a dozen equally distressing images evoking an allegory of Eros and Thanatos, in which a skeletal horned warrior looks down on a naked woman as he thrusts a sword up into her ribs, a scarecrow reveals itself to be a scaffold of corpses, and at the apparent climax a woman riding a bull flees a burning city.[19]

In the desert Boswell, a man of distinct mental strengths, evidently sublimated a degree of psychological distress into his art, but he was by no means the only one among the AIA's scattered membership to live through such experiences. After serving in the Royal Engineers, first as an instructor at home and then as a captain in the Western Desert in 1942, Julian Trevelyan was now in the process of being discharged for 'psychoneurosis',[20] and a little over a year after he was drafted, Claude Rogers was sent to Southport Emergency Hospital for a psychiatric evaluation which would lead to his discharge in June 1943.[21]

Because of the practical and psychological difficulties of working while serving, these private odysseys often left little artistic trace; enlistment as a gunner in 1941, for example, not only cast William Coldstream into deep depression but also temporarily destroyed his confidence in his artistic capabilities. One consequence was that the viewpoints of direct military

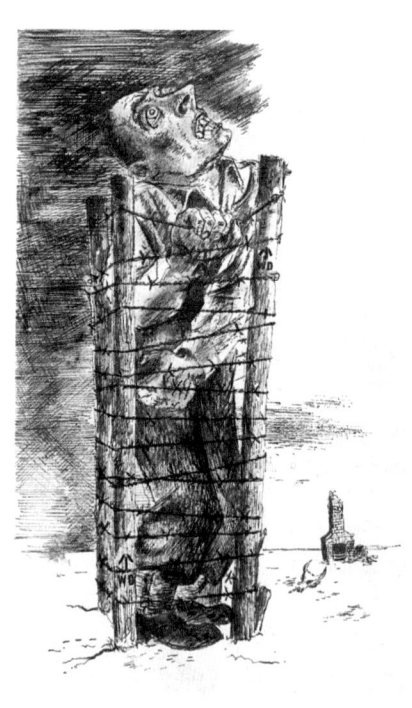
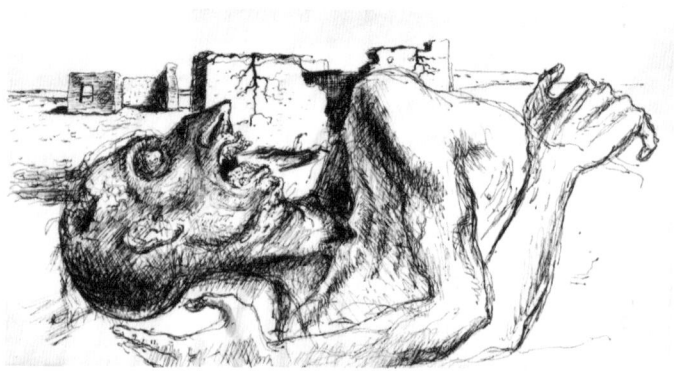
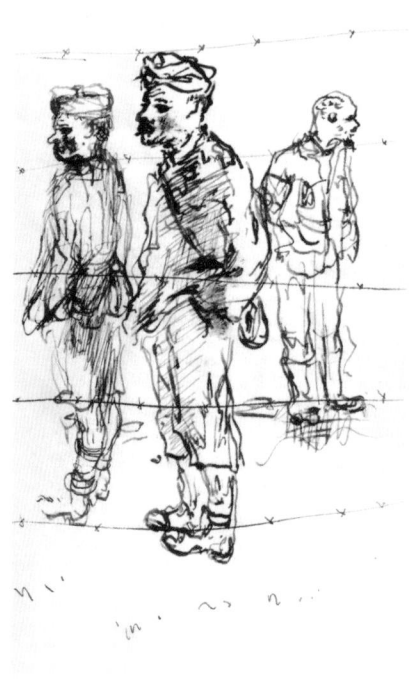
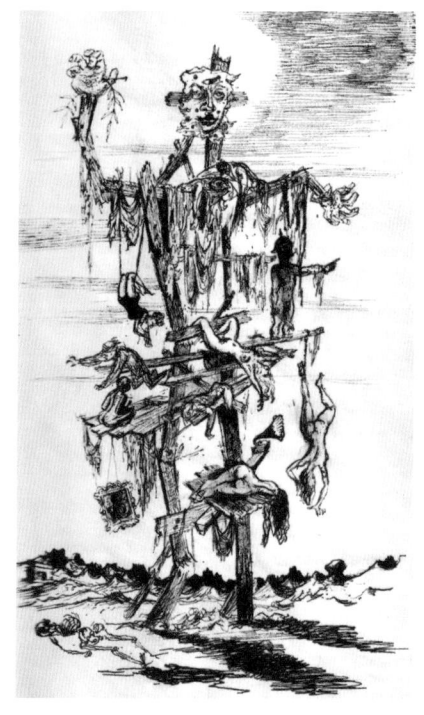

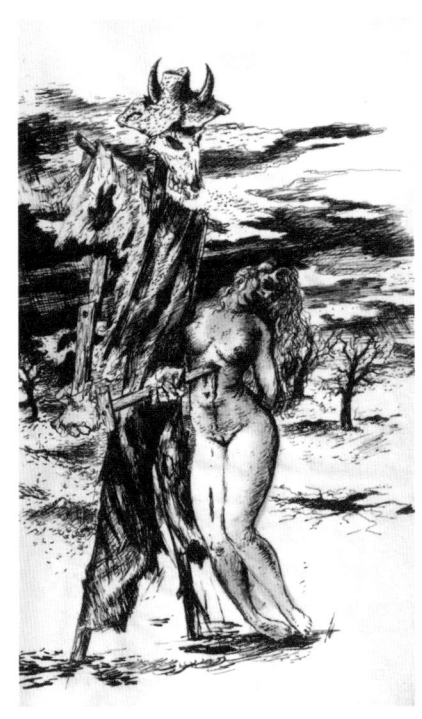
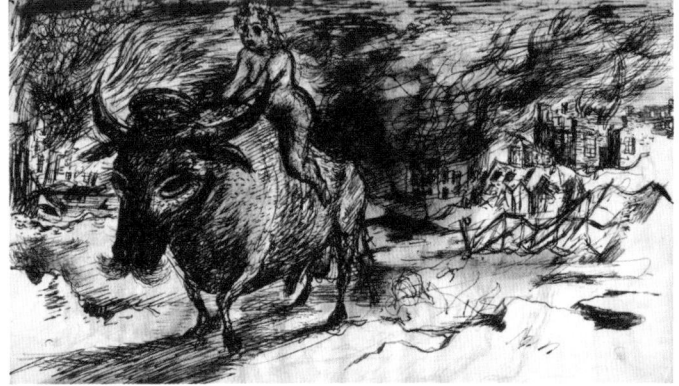
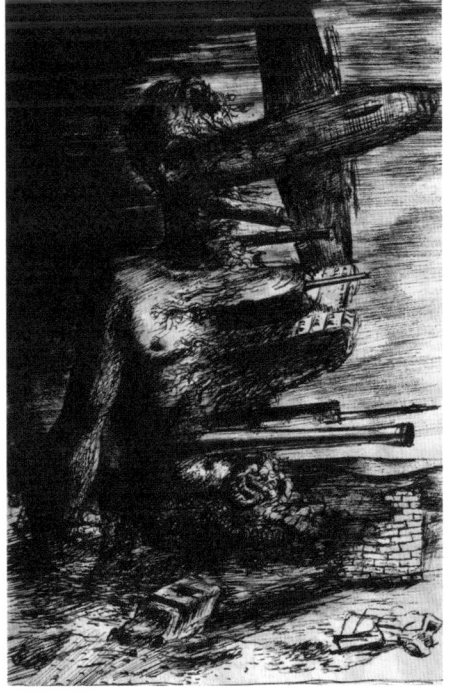

8.4–8.10 James Boswell, untitled images from the 'Europa' sketchbook, Iraq, Middle East and North Africa, 1942–43. Each 23.2 × 15.4 cm or 15.4 × 23.2 cm (9¼ × 6⅛ in.)

participants – an important existential element of the exhibition's theme 'This is how we are fighting' – would be largely absent from *For Liberty*, even if the shadow of war's traumas was not. Boswell's experience did figure in the form of two pre-embarkation works – *Crewe 2 a.m.* and *A Corner of the NAAFI* – displayed among the prints and drawings selection in the Holles Street shelter, but it would not be until mid-1944, at its newly inaugurated Charlotte Street Centre, that the AIA would be able to arrange *On Duty in the Desert*, an exhibition of Boswell's watercolour drawings depicting 'scenes of uneventful, unprivileged, service life'. Even then, his extraordinary 'Europa' series, the climacteric follow-on from 'Bull', would remain unseen by the public for many years.

The position of the minority of AIA members who became official war artists was more usually that of temporary outside observers, less oppressed by military disciplines but not immune from war-time hardships. Eric Ravilious was one for whom 'cheerfulness kept breaking through' and who in a curious way had relished rather than regretted the opportunities of military travel. Assigned to the Admiralty, he made several voyages to the Arctic Circle during the disastrous Norwegian campaign, producing luminous images of vessels either sunk or in action. Four of these had formed one of the most striking elements of the initial Official War Artists exhibition at the National Gallery in June 1940, but their aesthetic resonance was in a sense ambushed by circumstance as the national situation dramatically deteriorated in the six weeks between their creation and display. Looking at them Kenneth Clark initially felt they trembled on the brink of affectation, and as he wrote his review 'Wanted a Goya', Boswell may well have had them in mind when taking aim at the elimination of human beings and human emotions from war art. But such was the lethal lottery of war that the September 1942 *AIA Bulletin* which announced progress under the new programme also carried the news that Eric Ravilious, 'one of our original members', had just been reported missing off Iceland. It was a devastating personal blow for friends, including his former lover Helen Binyon, who was back in the AIA London orbit and about to take on the organization of studio socials and the basement shelter party that would accompany *For Liberty*.[22]

* * * * *

We should not underestimate the stamina and commitment that was required from the key activists during war time to sustain the AIA as a voluntary organization pursuing the principle 'every artist an organized artist' while also managing – with slight material resources but a good deal of networking and ingenuity – to mount an expanding programme of activity. The November 1942 *Bulletin* which informed members that a site had been found also announced that a second series of six AIA lectures would run in parallel at the National Gallery on Sundays at 3 p.m.; that an *Artists Aid China* exhibition modelled on the recent Russia fundraiser would soon open at Hertford House; and that a second AIA/CEMA (Council for the Encouragement of Music and the Arts) travelling exhibition for factory canteens would pay hiring fees annually and a share of sales as they occurred.

Lowes Luard took over organization of the lectures from Ewan Phillips, who wrote to him from his Intelligence Corps recruiting office a few days before John Rothenstein, Director and Keeper of the Tate Gallery, was due to give an introductory overview on 'Artists and War': 'Before he was at the Tate he was Director of Leeds or Sheffield Gallery (I forget which) ... he has been responsible for a greatly improved acquisition policy (*vide* recent exhibition of new acquisitions of the Tate at the National Gallery). The Tate itself has been bombed and will take several years to repair.'[23] Anthony Blunt – now based in MI5 and passing withheld but crucial decrypted intelligence on German troop movements to Britain's Soviet ally – gave the second lecture, on art in the Napoleonic era, linking Goya and Blake. James Laver, Keeper of Paintings at the V&A – and Horton's associate at the Working Men's College – gave the third, on the war of 1870 as a prelude to Impressionism; and Luard himself had to step in at short notice to cover the Great War era for fellow Central Committee member Jan Gordon, who was seriously ill. This gave Luard the chance, however, to stress a point he felt Rothenstein had missed: that much of the best war art created in modern conflict was by artists who actually fought. Feliks Topolski, now an AIA member, gave the fifth in the series on 'Contemporary Comment and Caricature', and Philip Hendy, formerly of the Wallace Collection, now at Leeds and Clark's future successor at the National Gallery, concluded with 'The Artist in this War and Future Developments' – a talk whose detail is lost but which included the artist's potential role in reconstruction, a topic clearly aligned with the *For Liberty* agenda.[24]

The second AIA travelling exhibition of the war had returned to London in July 1942 having been on show in Liverpool, Derby, Doncaster, Aberdeen, Cambridge, Swansea, Lincoln and Harrogate. That month CEMA, the only state-supported organizer of tours, requested the AIA Exhibitions Committee to collect work from members for a British Institute of Adult Education (BIAE) exhibition tour of large factory canteens. The result was *Pictures to Live With*, featuring eighty-three works from sixty-seven members, including Duncan Grant, Vanessa Bell, Paul Nash, Laurence ('L. S.') Lowry, James and Margaret Fitton, Ithell Colquhoun and Fred Uhlman. Horton's catalogue introduction noted that even in Moscow and Leningrad arts continued while 'the enemy was hammering at the gates' and defined 'the chief reason' for an exhibition in a canteen: 'in a democracy art should be for the people ... And when the people cannot, for one reason or another, come to art – art should come to them.'[25] A notable inclusion was the oil painting *The First Siren*, a streetscape with figures sent in from Huntingdon by Nan Youngman. It was based on a moment early in the Blitz when she had glanced out of Betty Rea's first floor in Primrose Hill during a daylight raid and seen men at the corner looking skywards, a child fleeing and a woman with a pram running for the shelter. At Dewsbury, a businessman asked visiting schoolchildren to vote for their favourite picture, and when Youngman's was chosen he bought it for their school.[26]

As this travelling show was launched, Beryl Sinclair's Exhibitions Committee began assembling a second AIA/BIAE show of forty-five works to tour local authority-run British Restaurants. In parallel, by the time *For Liberty* opened in mid-March, leaving aside fourteen invitees already provided with canvases, ninety-three AIA members – equally split between men and women – had responded to the appeal to send in work.[27] In total 175 separate items were listed in the *For Liberty* catalogue, meaning that in spring 1943 upwards of 350 member works were being exhibited as a result of AIA initiatives that can be evidenced in detail. To this figure we should add a further 152 works by 48 graphic artists that went on display in Knightsbridge that same month in another AIA-organized event – one in its way every bit as significant in its demonstration of what was changing in Britain, and what might change, as a consequence of the people's war.

*****

Before the war nine out of ten posters had, as Eric Newton now observed, been commissioned by private companies as 'salesmen', and their creation had more often than not made graphic artists complicit in a confidence trick: 'A's Beer is Best!', 'Take this!', 'Possess that!', 'Come here!' and life will be transformed. In Newton's view – expressed in the Knightsbridge catalogue – market competition had not generated excellence but a deplorable 'aesthetic degradation', as publicity agents assumed that 'the man in the street' would not 'buy a tube of toothpaste or purchase a tennis racquet unless a sickeningly realistic poster of a pretty girl invited him to do so'.[28] A few bodies, such as the London Passenger Transport Board and Shell-Mex, had risen above this, but even then contradictions had often existed between image and ulterior purpose; they were now in retreat as 'fierce concentration on the idea' took precedence:

> The war has involved us all in a new set of urgencies, in the midst of which industrial competition has almost ceased to count. It is no longer a question of inducing us to buy things. (More often it is a question of inducing us *not* to buy things.) We have to acquire a new set of habits. Our fundamental attitudes to life have to be changed, and changed quickly ... New and revolutionary modes of behaviour have to be imposed on us and the poster artist is the modern propagandist's most potent agent.

As if to underline Newton's point, the first venue for the AIA touring show *Poster Design in War-time Britain* was Harrods Ltd, but only one of the 152 posters on display in the apogee of luxury retailing had been produced for a private client – a magazine promotion for *Time and Tide* – while 96 had been produced for campaigns run by central government ministries, a majority of the rest for other public bodies. A further component comprised fourteen posters created for exile authorities including the Polish Army Press Bureau, the Fighting French Information Service and the Czechoslovak Information Service. These had been produced over the previous seventeen months, during which the Harrods exhibition area had played host to nine events depicting 'The Life and Culture of Our Allies', six of them occupied European countries.[29]

Henrion was involved in the January 1942 Harrods display 'Our Ally: the USA' on behalf of the United States Office of War Information, and so was well-versed in the projection of Roosevelt's war-time leadership, making him the knowledgeable voice at the AIA Central Committee table when the decision to adopt the 'Four Freedoms' theme was taken. He had by now pioneered combinations of flat expanses of lithographed colour, black-and-white photomontage and crisp typography for posters promoting the MOI's own travelling exhibitions on tanks and RAF war photos and for campaigns for the Ministry of Home Security, the General Post Office and the Ministry of Agriculture – ten examples of which were at Harrods. Looking back four decades later he remembered the urgency of these assignments and the commonality of purpose – 'there wasn't the usual client reaction couldn't the circle be round, the red be green etc' – and judged them the most satisfying of his career: 'there was a kind of involvement whether it was poison gas or the Merchant Navy which you can't have with margarine or cigarettes or whatever ... you felt there was an importance that you hardly ever feel nowadays – it was good.'[30]

The artist whose work arguably made the greatest impact in the show was Abram Games, who shared the same political instincts as Henrion, but differed aesthetically in preferring the airbrush and drawn image to the photograph as a key tool for achieving 'Maximum Meaning, Minimum

Means'. Established as a freelance poster artist of ingenuity and originality before the conflict, Games had been conscripted as an infantry private in 1940 and then plucked from the ranks when the War Office discovered a desperate need for visual communication; seizing his opportunity he had generated all manner of instructional posters from matters medical to technical and outward-facing recruitment images.[31] He had produced already well-known 'Grow Your Own Food' posters linking dinner table and allotment, as well as the celebrated 'Blonde Bombshell' Auxiliary Territorial Service recruitment poster which had proven too much for puritans in Parliament. But much of Games's work – like that of others produced for specialist situations in the forces or the factories – had not been seen before by the general public, including key posters produced for the Army Bureau of Current Affairs.

'Your Britain – Fight for it Now' had been an ABCA series since 1940, when fellow exhibitor Frank Newbould had produced an image of a shepherd and his sheepdog on the South Downs with Belle Tout lighthouse in the distance, another of an idyllic village green with pub and church, and a third of Salisbury Cathedral as seen by Constable. Games had more recently produced three posters under the same 'Your Britain' rubric, taking the themes of housing, education and health – contrasting deprivation and dire social need with modern LCC public housing in Ladbroke Grove designed by AIA member Maxwell Fry, the pioneering Impington Village College in Cambridgeshire, and Berthold Lubetkin's Finsbury Health Centre, a beacon of progress when it opened in 1938. The contrast between Newbould's railway advertising art repurposed to patriotic ends and Games's strikingly modernist clash of dark and light was both ideological and visual, because it made manifest two contending political visions. One spoke to national conservatism's war aims of preserving the traditional social order, blind to its oppressions, while the other determined that the future would not circle back to the past, acutely conscious of both realities endured in the 1930s and the potential for progressive change. It was his brilliant rendition of the contrast between these last two factors that gave Games's series its emotional force, with an impact which led to the poster on health – the one with 'the boy with rickets' – to be denounced by Churchill as 'disgraceful libel and distorted propaganda'.[32]

What was striking to Harrods visitors was the freshness on display – Sir William Crawford, a leader of the pre-war advertising industry, thought it the best exhibition he had ever attended – and also some of its political content. Alongside the 130 posters produced for official bodies were Henrion's own poster for the AIA *For Liberty* exhibition, another for the International Brigade Association, one for the Soviet Embassy, another for the Society for Cultural Relations with the USSR, and six produced

8.11 Frank Newbould, *Your Britain – Fight for it Now*, poster design, 1940. 51.3 × 75.1 cm (20¼ × 29⅝ in.)

8.12 Abram Games, *Your Britain – Fight for it Now*, poster design, 1942. 50.4 × 74.5 cm (19⅞ × 29⅜ in.)

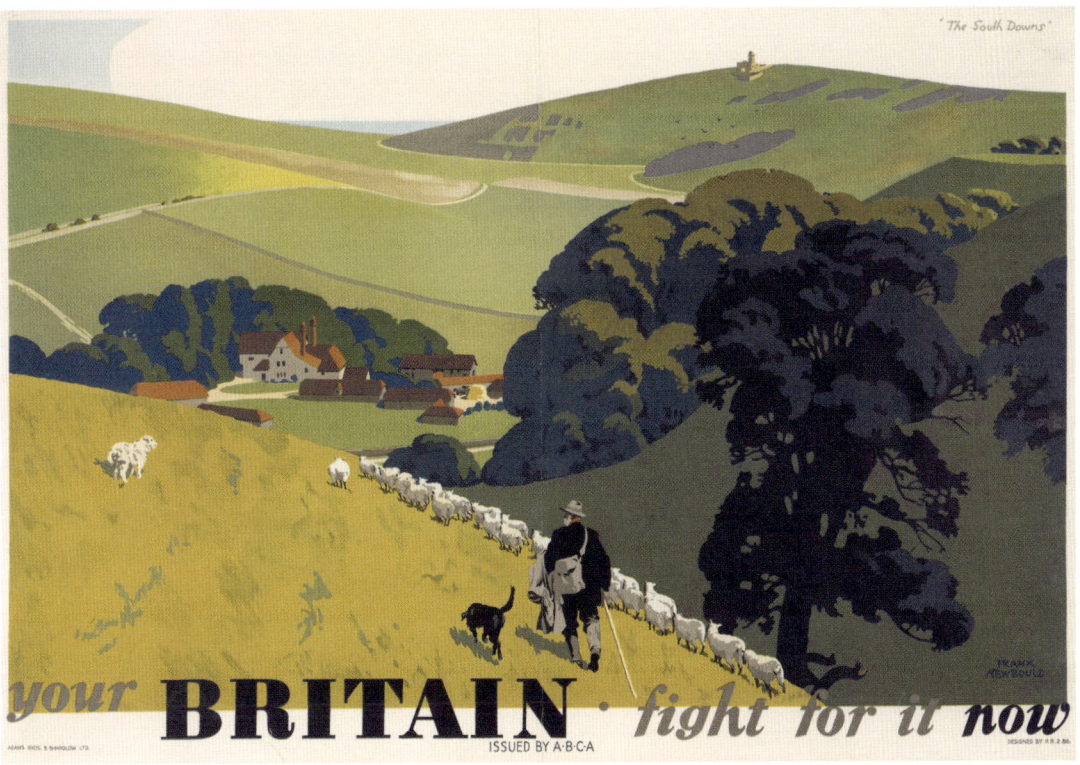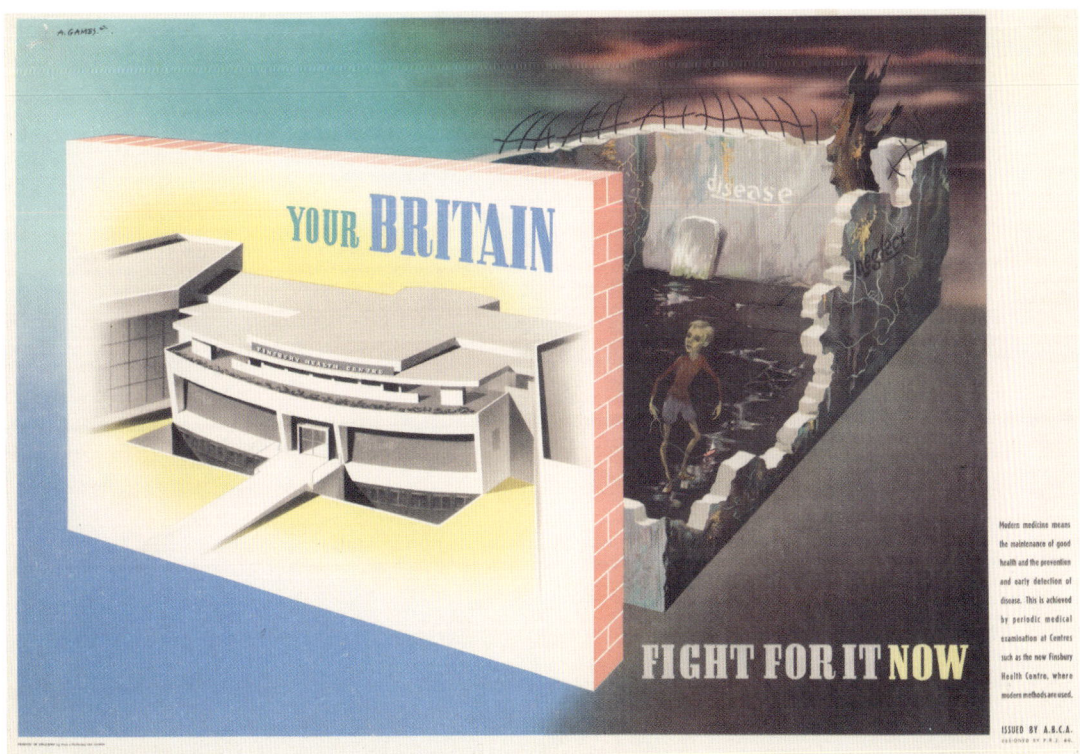

by the Communist Party. While the suspension of electoral politics had rendered the coalition partners mute mid-conflict, this was not so for the party, which was using poster art in its campaign to raise production to support military aid to the Soviet Union and to call for a second front. David Caplan as 'Davy' had contributed four of these posters and another by K. G. Chapman took as its theme the opening lines of Gabriel Peri's letter: 'The prison chaplain has just informed me that I am going to be shot in a few moments as a hostage ....' Amid so many violent deaths in occupied Europe, and intimations of the scale of the holocaust unfolding to the east, Peri – previously a leader of the popular front – had now become an icon of anti-fascist resistance.

*****

In early December 1942 Misha Black, the initiating impresario of *For Liberty*, had written to Paul Nash in Oxford seeking his participation in 'the most interesting experiment which the AIA or any other body of artists has launched for some considerable time': 'On the blitzed site of John Lewis in Oxford Street a large shelter has been built, the fore part abutting on to the main street has still standing some half-ruined walls,

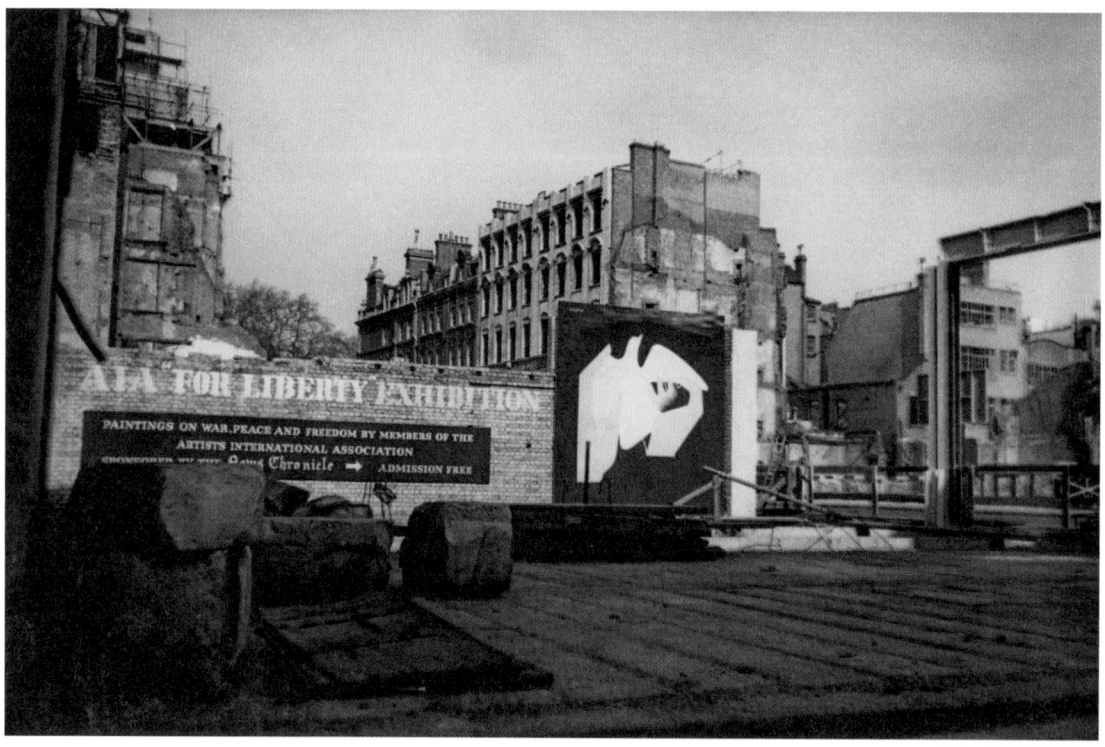

8.13 Ministry of Information photographer, *For Liberty* signage on Oxford Street, March 1943

etc. which we propose to transform into a kind of large Dramatic open-air display, advertising the exhibition housed in the shelter behind. The shelter itself is being transformed by designers and architects so as to form a fitting background.' He asked the Advisory Council member to paint a personal interpretation of the 'Four Freedoms', to take its place as one of 'some twelve commissioned works' in this 'special architectural setting' at the heart of an exhibition 'so situated as to make it possible for large numbers of the general public to visit'; 'we would, of course, supply the canvas', he added.[33]

It was not a good time for Nash – he had been an advocate for the 'power of pictorial art as a means of propaganda' but was now beset with chronic illness – and the stamped addressed envelope included to encourage a speedy response lay in his file of AIA papers for the remaining three and a half years of his life.[34] In late January, however, Nash telephoned Beryl Sinclair, chair of the Exhibitions Committee, apologizing for being unable to provide a panel himself because an infected thumb was preventing him working, but evidently hoping to make the selection session on 23 February to review the large number of works sent in by other members. The spirit was evidently willing, but it is doubtful if Nash was actually present during preparations for the delayed opening on 13 March, and for the first time since its foundation a major AIA show did not feature one of his new or existing works. Fourteen other paintings created over the previous six weeks had, however, been received as a result of Black's efforts asking for work in a 5 by 4 foot (1.5 × 1.2 m) format.

On-site production now lay in the hands of the Technical Committee, with Henrion in charge of creating an overall visual identity and making the most of the dramatic possibilities of the location, elements of which had already 'been brightly coloured by the London Fire Brigade like a Graham Sutherland painting in orange, yellow and blue'.[35] This treatment was extended to direct the attention of a street 'teeming with people and soldiers on leave' to four soaring, overlapping 'Doves of Freedom' standing out against a blackened wall (the same imagery was carried over into press advertising and the exhibition poster), while lettering running along a side wall announced the AIA's free exhibition of paintings on 'War, Peace and Freedom' in the buildings behind. An exhibition booth was created by Ronald Dickens, who also laid out room 3 with eleven member works in a display 'This is how we are fighting', another eleven for 'This will happen here unless …' and fifteen representing 'This is what we are fighting for'. Installation photos indicate that Hans Feibusch's *Resurrection*, showing the wonder and ecstasy of four robed figures, while catalogued as being in room 4, was a late inclusion here; when Feibusch's finished work arrived it emerged he had rotated the canvas to work in portrait rather

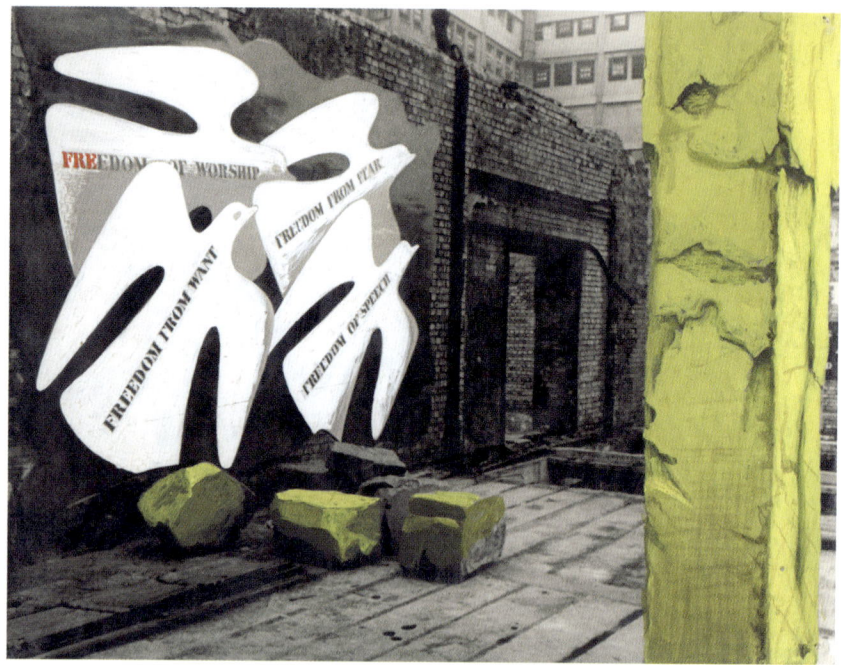

8.14 Ministry of Information photographer, Henrion's Freedom Doves, March 1943

than landscape format, thus rendering its intended placing in Peter Ray's display units impractical.

Room 4 was intended as the emotional heart – a 'cavern' in one formulation, 'a brightly lit labyrinth' in another – of 'an exhibition with a new meaning and a new purpose', a form of imaginative propaganda 'differing from poster art in the same way as poetry and songs differ from written propaganda'.[36] In putting it together another immediate problem that had to be faced was that Augustus John, ignoring matters of detail, had sent in a previously completed, almost ecclesiastical work – *The Return of the Fisherman*, 'a cartoon for a decoration' – in an 11 by 8 foot (3.4 × 2.4 m) format.[37] Physically this was accommodated by creating a niche akin to a side chapel in an apse, but its subject matter was also somewhat tangential to the 'Four Freedoms' theme, although not to a point made in the catalogue's 'foreword by the AIA'. There it was argued that prior to the alienation of the modern market, and the emergence of mutually unsatisfactory relationship between private patrons and isolated artists absorbed in experiments beyond public understanding, artists had served as socially engaged propagandists through church art, as 'people were taught to believe in Christianity and to live as Christians, now through art of the kind exhibited here, people may learn to have a belief in civilisation and may be stimulated to fight for it'. In Jan Gordon's reading, John's work had an unfinished demeanour and showed 'a bulky man, vaguely like

8.15 Ministry of Information photographer, View of room 4, installation shot, March 1943, showing, l to r, partial view of *Freedom of Worship* by Kenneth Rowntree, *The Death of Gabriel Peri* by Pat Carpenter, *The Return of the Fisherman* by Augustus John, *The Land of Ears* by Carel Weight, and a partial view of Cliff Rowe's *Freedom of Speech*; Betty Rea's *New World* is displayed on a plinth, left foreground

a self-portrait, posing about halfway along an irregular frieze of regular John figures against a tenuous Galway background'. Nevertheless, its symbolism of salvation from peril could at a stretch be attached to the *For Liberty* theme and John's celebrity spoke for its inclusion; its onward sale would indeed make a significant contribution to rescuing the event's finances.[38]

The other commissioned works were all carried out under great time pressure, and given that personal interpretation was requested, it is probable that there was little or no discussion between contributors, notwithstanding the ambition to make a collective 'socially conscious' statement. There may have been some prior allocation to ensure that all Roosevelt's four freedoms were covered, but both differences in style and approaches to the ideas being presented meant that many of the works, once brought together, made 'strange frame fellows'. Thus Edward Le Bas's *Bathers on the Serpentine* and Beryl Sinclair's *Air, Light, Land and Water* – a park scene with children playing and sailing dinghies on water beyond – were straightforwardly naturalistic visions of what peace might bring in terms of personal freedom, expressed in the artists' expected styles. By contrast Matvyn Wright's *Fear Motive*, now known only from a black-and-white photograph, was evidently a major departure from his usual idiom.[39]

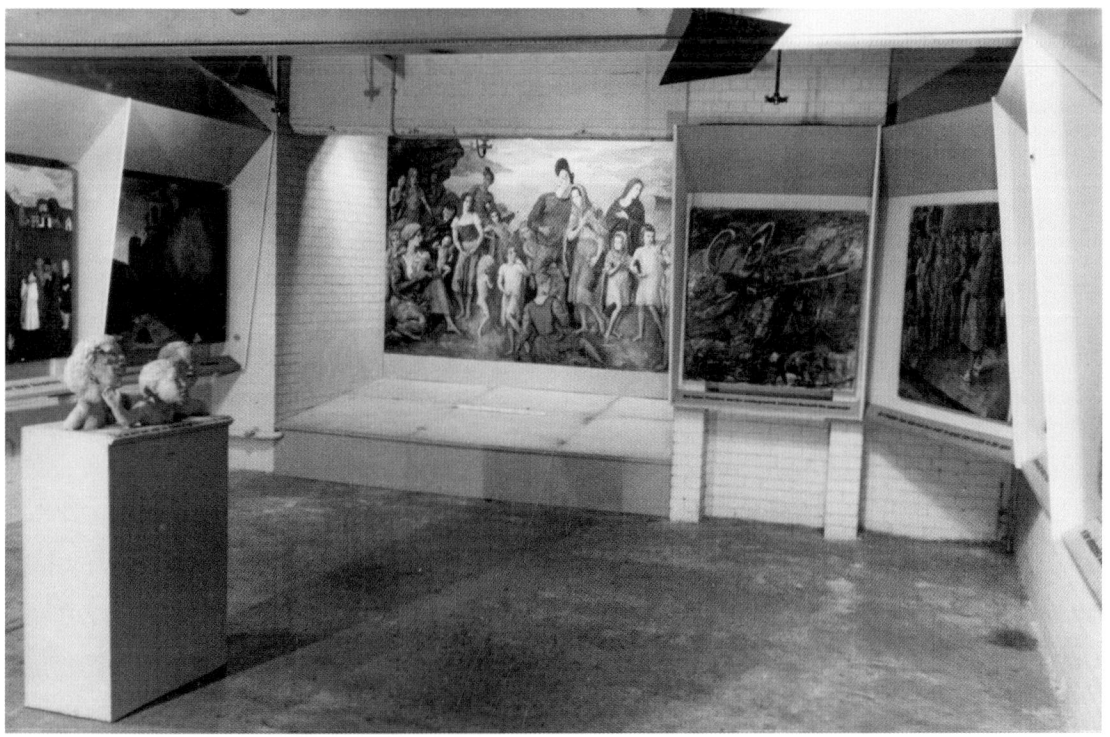

HOLLES STREET

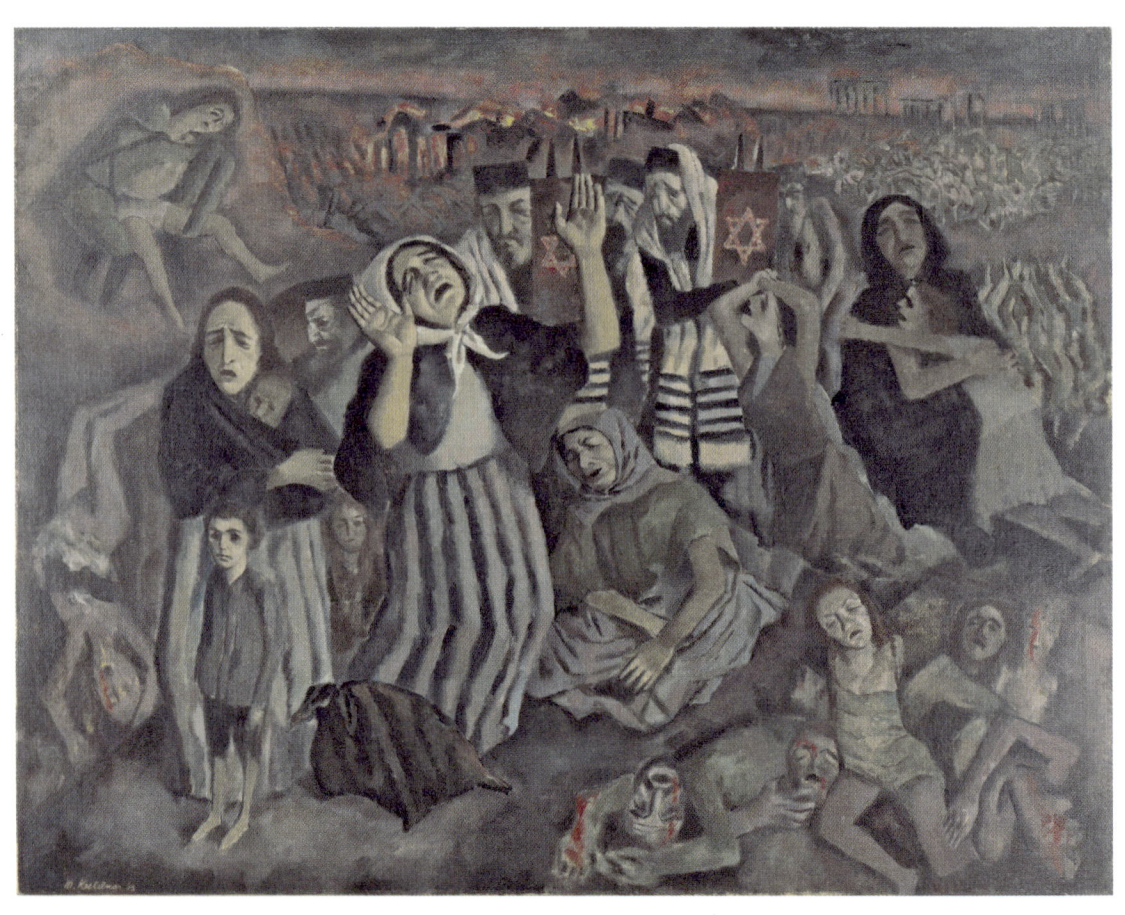

8.16 Morris Kestelman, *Lama Sabachthani? (Why have you forsaken me?)*, oil on canvas, 1943. 117 × 153 cm (46⅛ × 60¼ in.)

Wright served in the Auxiliary Fire Service and his experience of London under aerial siege had fed directly into portraits of his fellow firemen, an action scene of four firemen on a city roof training a hose on a conflagration below, and a fine work of a descending parachute bomb silhouetted against the Thames skyline in the seconds before its blast; showing affinity with Euston Road 'new realism', these led to him being granted a short-term war artist contract.[40] *Fear Motive*, however, was a major stylistic departure using a mix of Cubo-Surrealism, depicting a clawed apparition rising up in domination over a cowering populace. This was probably hung near Morris Kestelman's *Lama Sabachthani (Why have you forsaken me?)*, a figurative work of great emotional force showing the children of Israel as modern refugees crying aloud in the wilderness – in Gordon's view 'perhaps the most complete fusion of motive, expression and compositional device' in the exhibition.[41]

Wright's and Kestelman's paintings worked as visual contradictions of the ideal being propagandized, while Kenneth Rowntree's *Freedom of Worship* was nuanced in a different vein; with a folksy humorous naivety it signified pluralism in a parade of religious buildings seen across verdant open space, but this open territory is itself being busily measured off by plenipotentiaries of different creeds, suggesting freedom of religion might have its downsides. Rowntree's irony was gentle, however, compared with Kokoschka's selection of *What We Are Fighting For* as the title of his Expressionist howl of rage at the perpetrators of global conflict which hung opposite.

Carel Weight's *The Land of Ears* was another painting which evidently represented freedom (in this case of speech) through its antithesis – and one also distinguished from his recent work by experimentation. In it diminutive modern citizens traversed pathways across a pitted medieval landscape reminiscent of Breughel and Bosch – and the central conceit may indeed have been inspired by the blade-wielding disembodied ears pierced by an arrow in the right-hand 'hellscape' panel of Bosch's *Garden of Earthly Delights*; for this is a land overshadowed by giant ears, huge floating balloons of surveillance 'waiting to catch false evidence and rumours to the encouragement of the informer'.[42]

Conversely Cliff Rowe's realistic contribution focused on freedom of speech through a trenchant depiction of it being exercised. It centred on a young woman in a belted coat at a microphone, seen in profile, addressing a mostly male factory-gate meeting, a chalked 'Lift the Ban on the *Daily Worker*' partially visible behind. Rowe had depicted a similar scene in a watercolour drawing which can be dated to September 1942 as it incorporated a newspaper placard also indicating 'Ban Lifted'.[43] That version was more broadly framed as a streetscape, the speaker in back view and

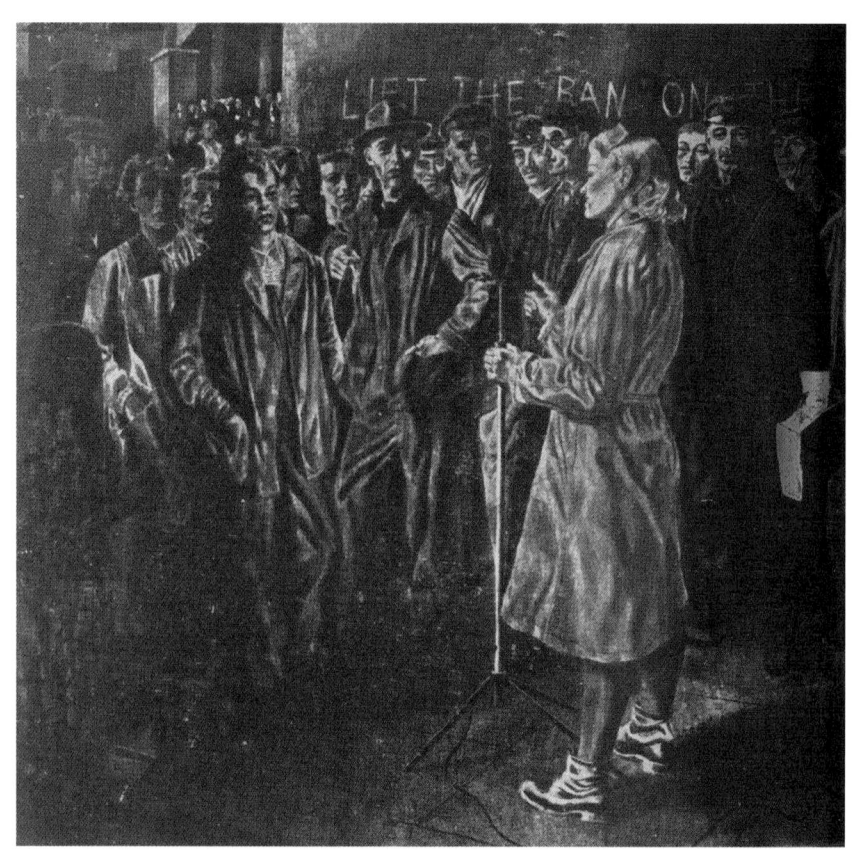

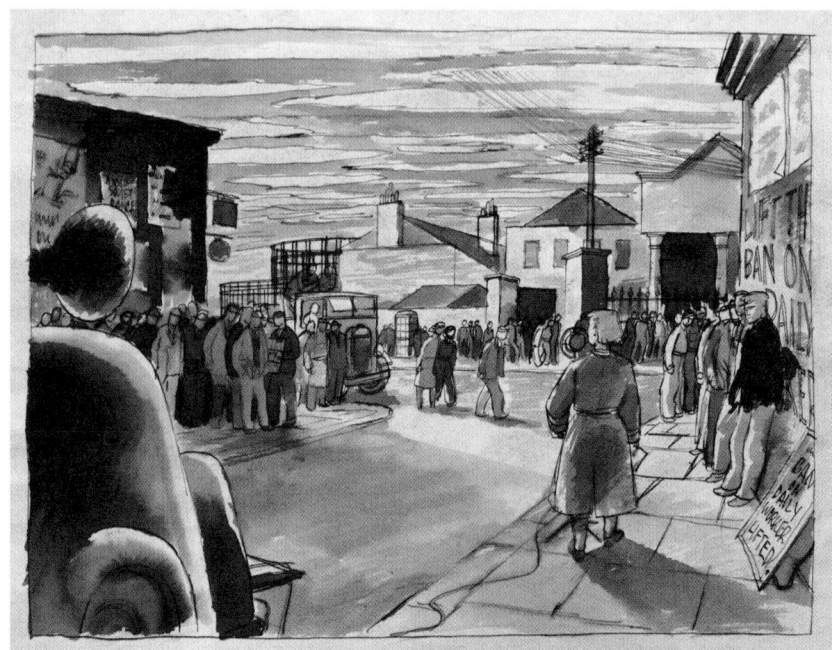

8.17 Photograph published in *Our Time*, May 1943, of Cliff Rowe's oil on canvas painting *Freedom of Speech*, 1943

8.18 Cliff Rowe, *Factory Gate Meeting*, pen and ink and wash, c. 1942. 21 × 27 cm (8⅜ × 10¾ in.)

the microphone connected by cable to a speaker cab to the left. In the new oil, however, Rowe sought greater intensity, emphasizing the crowd's engagement and the speaker's articulate confidence, and to realize this he required a model. The person who reluctantly fulfilled the role was Doris Collins, Rowe's future wife and partner for forty years. Born into a working-class family enduring hard times, animated by a deep antipathy to injustice, Collins was working at the Carreras factory in Kentish Town when they first met. As shop steward for the Tobacco Workers' Union, she had helped organize a demonstration demanding that management open up the factory shelter to the local population.[44]

Rowe's message was straightforward – freedom had to be fought for – and his painting was hung near to an equally political but more complex work: Oskar Kokoschka's *What We Are Fighting For*. Commissioned to paint a portrait of the Soviet ambassador Ivan Maisky (who was present as *For Liberty* opened),[45] Kokoschka had donated his £1,000 fee to the Stalingrad Hospital Fund with the stipulation that the money be used to treat both Russian and German wounded, a reflection of his overriding humanism; he had also been a prime backer of *Allies Inside Germany*, an enormously successful Free German League of Culture exhibition documenting anti-Nazi resistance, which had held an extended run in an empty Regent Street shop premises

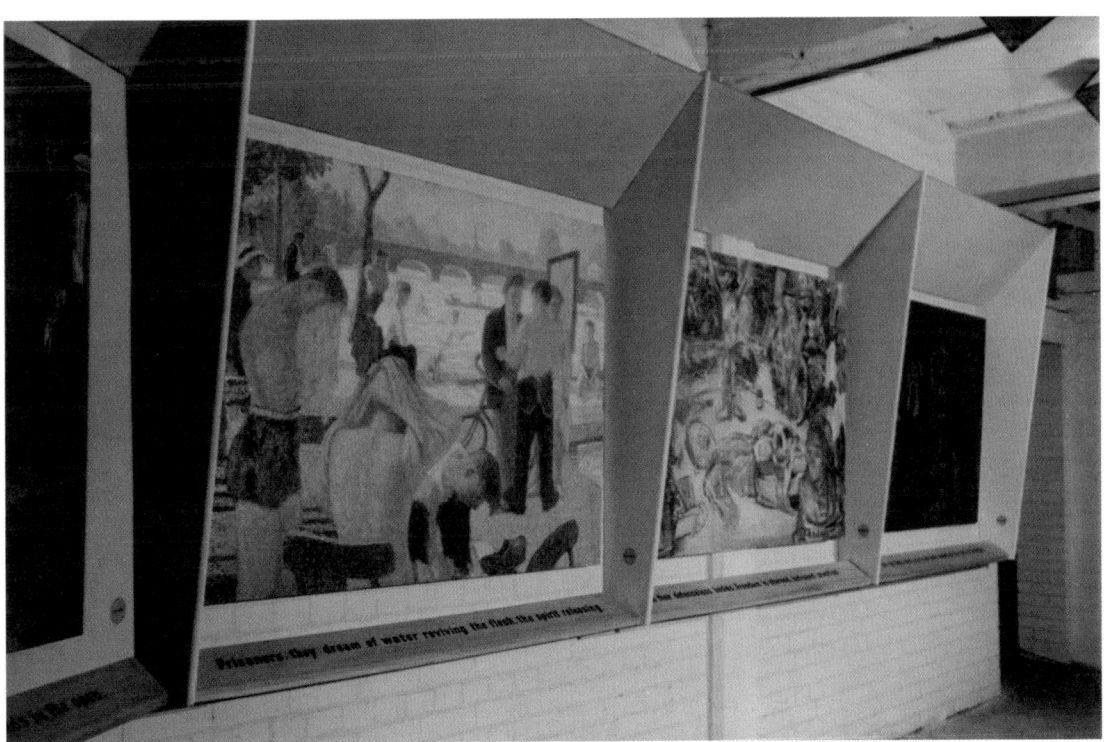

8.19 Ministry of Information photographer, View of room 4, installation shot, March 1943, showing, l to r, a glimpse of *Freedom of Speech* by Cliff Rowe, *Bathers on the Serpentine* by Edward Le Bas, *What We Are Fighting For* by Oskar Kokoschka, and, unlit, *Lama Sabachtani?* by Morris Kestelman

the previous summer.⁴⁶ Passionate humanist partisanship could also be read in the urgent brushwork of the painting he now produced as a crushing denunciation of great power nationalism and war's progenitors, a tour de force excellently captured in Robert Radford's description:

> The central figure is an emaciated woman, prone and close to death; her child fondles a rat as its pet. Behind her is placed a figure in the posture of crucifixion who is branded with the figures 'PJ' – Perish Judea. A fantastic war machine on the left feeds on a constant diet of bones while spewing out bullets in return, at the same time as delivering mechanised Nazi salutes and embracing a globe of the world picked out with flags of Nationalist aggression. The collaborative guilt of Church and Capital in furthering war is pointed to by such figures as the overweight bishop dropping his penny in the Red Cross box, and by identifiable representations of the German industrialist Schacht and Montagu Norman, a governor of the Bank of England …⁴⁷

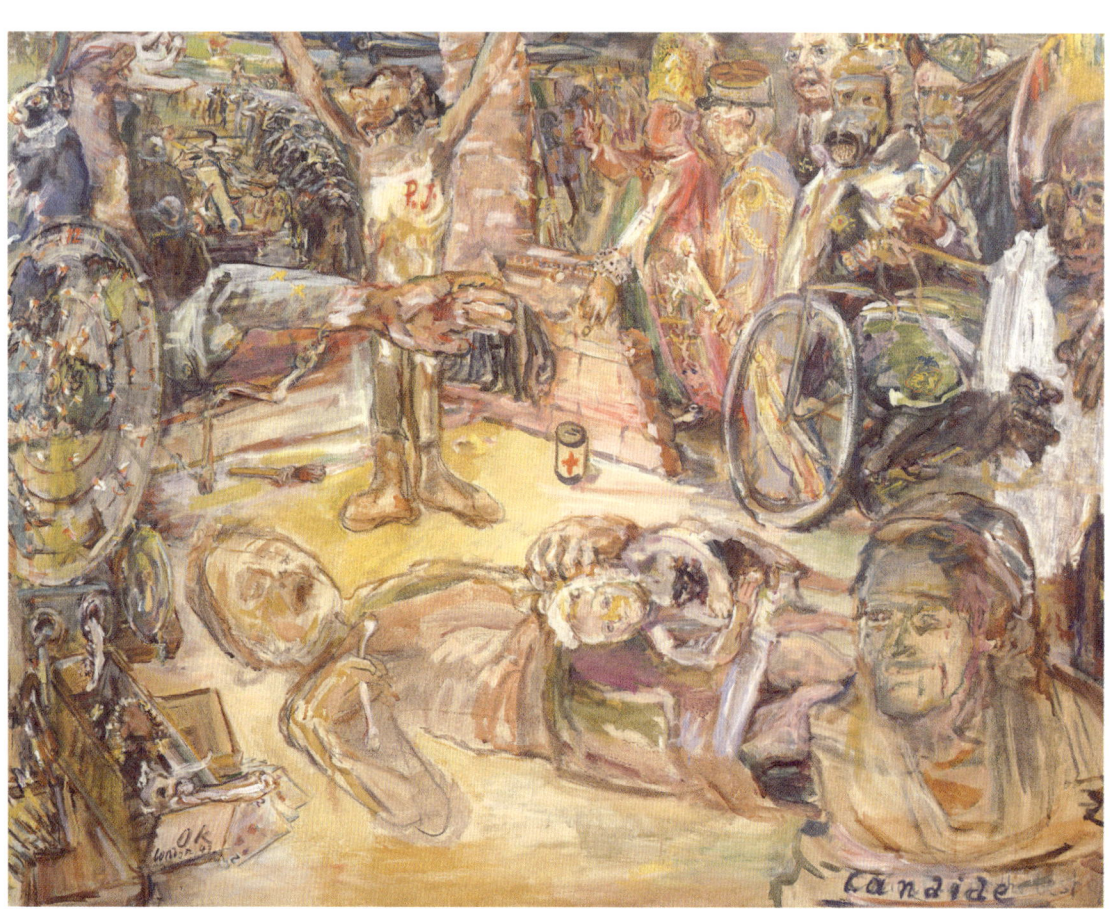

8.20 Oskar Kokoschka, *What We Are Fighting For*, oil on canvas, 1943. 116.5 × 152 cm (45⅞ × 59⅞ in.)

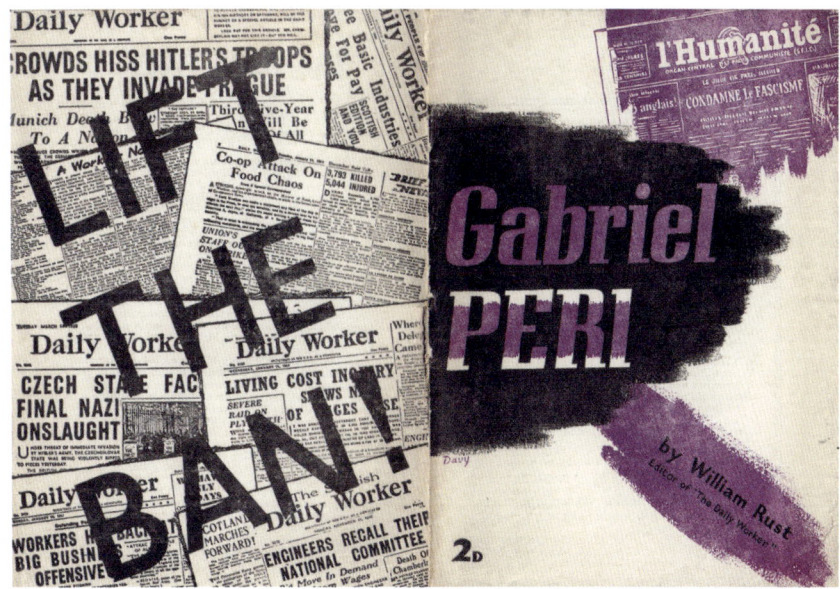

8.21 David Caplan, *Gabriel Peri*, cover design for William Rust's pamphlet, 1942. 19 × 25.2 cm (7½ × 10 in.)

The presence of a farmer cultivating his fields, the figure of Gandhi – whose leadership of Indian resistance to British imperialism Kokoschka admired – and the Enlightenment in the form of a bust of Voltaire can be read as optimistic elements amid the enveloping malevolence. But taken as a whole there is no mistaking the artist's critique of the ruling order: immediately prior to the war 'PJ' had been a favoured signifier of the pro-Nazi Anglo-German Fellowship and The Link in their opposition to a 'Judaeo-Bolshevik conspiracy'. Montagu Norman was close to Hjalmar Schacht, who had served as Hitler's Minister of Economics, and both were members of the Fellowship and officers of the Bank for International Settlements; Norman's role in authorizing Nazi acquisition of Czechoslovakia's gold reserves after the occupation of Prague would have made him a particularly culpable member of the British establishment in Kokoschka's eyes. Post-exhibition it was Kokoschka's ambition to raise a further £1,000 by selling the painting in the USA to assist the escape of Jews from Hungary and to publicize the seeming indifference of Allied governments, including Britain's, to their fate.

For some visitors to the shelter's back room, Kokoschka's allegorical Expressionism was too gnomic to be effective as propaganda, for others too 'kaleidoscopic in colour, chaotic in composition'.[48] But there could be no such objection to Patrick Carpenter's *Death of Gabriel Peri* hanging opposite, a work whose combination of plain draughtsmanship and sombre palette so powerfully conveyed the tragic fact of Peri's execution in the towered fastness of Paris's Fort Mont-Valérien. Scattered pages on

8.22 Pat Carpenter, *The Death of Gabriel Peri*, oil on canvas, 1943. 116.6 × 152.4 cm (46 × 60 in.)

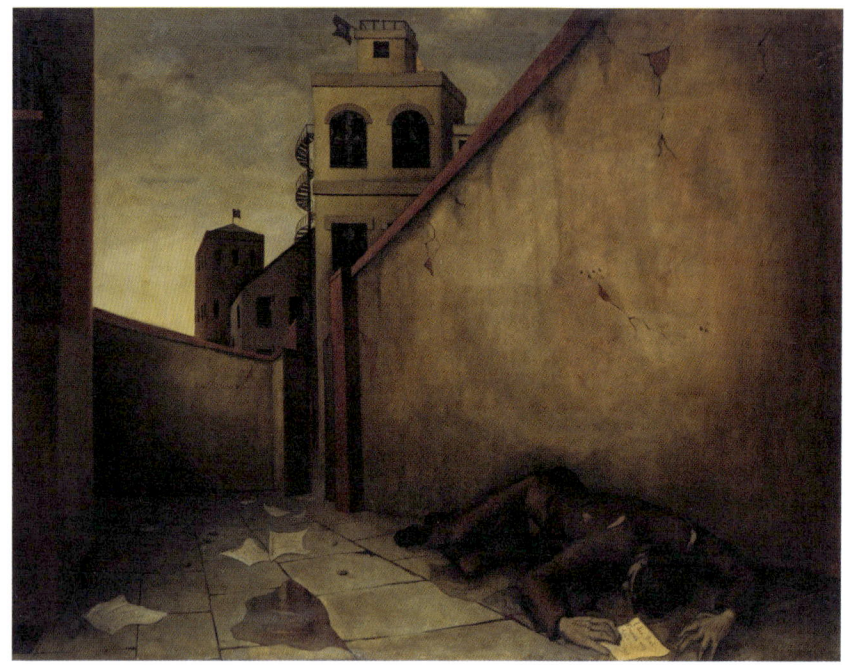

the stones beside Peri's corpse signified his role as journalist, including his underground editing of *L'Humanité* until his arrest in April 1941, and the note in his hands stood for his farewell words affirming his enduring political faith that communism would 'prepare the way for the radiant dawn'.[49] Private Carpenter had previously written to the *AIA Bulletin* about the potential for those living life in the ranks to create valuable art if given half a chance: 'I personally find it impossible to do more than sketch, however, and I believe that is the experience of most other artists on active service; the main difficulties are keeping one's painting equipment in a barrack room and getting a little quiet and privacy.'[50] But somehow over six weeks he managed to create the painting which arrived in Oxford Street as one of fourteen personal interpretations of the 'Four Freedoms' – thirteen of them works on canvas of uniform dimensions, but great stylistic diversity.

* * * * *

By the last week in February, Henrion had approached Cecil Day-Lewis and the poet became the fifth man in the Ministry of Information rendering significant assistance to AIA efforts to create 'propaganda of the imagination'. It had always been the intention to engage a writer to provide captions, but given the heterogeneous harvest of commissioned works, some way of linking them as a whole had now become even more desirable.

Day-Lewis had been recruited as an editor in the publications division in April 1941 and exempted from service as a Signal Corps conscript. Earlier in the war his known communism had led to an MI5 ban on his broadcasting for the BBC, but the erstwhile militant editor of *The Mind in Chains* had in fact already distanced himself from the party in public after the Moscow trials and privately finally broken with it over its support for Russia's invasion of Finland.[51] Accepted into the Senate House operation he became part of a team creating 'a new kind of documentary book, the popular illustrated documentary, to meet the needs of the time', which produced over forty titles such as *The Battle of Britain*, *Ocean Front*, *Bomber Command*, *Ark Royal* and *The Campaign in Burma*, some of which Henrion had designed.

After viewing the assembled artwork, Day-Lewis went on to write a twelve-line poem – a short-form sonnet – which appeared in the catalogue dated 12 March 1943, the day before the exhibition opened, but which was evidently available in time to furnish single-line captions for eleven of the fourteen paintings in room 4, as well as its sole piece of sculpture:

> *The cry for help, each cry is an open wound on the body of Freedom:*
> *In their defenceless bodies, Freedom is starved, betrayed, crucified:*
> *Prisoners, they dream of water reviving the flesh, the spirit releasing.*
> *But Freedom lives wherever men meet to speak their minds in the open.*
> *But Listen! Freedom works underground, volcanic beneath the oppressor.*
> *But one man's blood, for Freedom shed, can shake the towers of tyrants.*
> *Men of all lands, all faiths, start NOW to lay your hope's foundations,*
> *To design a world that shall tremble no more to the tread of gathering armies,*
> *A world where the rat-toothed nightmare of want shall gnaw man's breast no longer.*
> *So shall our time reveal long vistas of calm, of natural growth,*
> *A pattern mysterious yet lucid, for Love is the focal point of the pattern;*
> *And our heirs shall unfold, like a cluster of apple blossom, in a fine tomorrow.*

In an event conceived as a collective effort, it drew praise as work 'done to a purpose', and forty years later Henrion observed 'it seems corny now, but it was very successful'.[52] Part of its impact clearly lay in adept referencing of imagery from strong paintings – Kestelman's tragic lament, Rowe's and Weight's on freedom of speech and revolt, Carpenter's depiction of one man's fate, Kokoschka's crucified humanity – but another element was its projection of hope for the future – 'to design a world' – and its progression towards a redemptive denouement. In doing this the last lines provided the titling for two key works, John Tunnard's *Focal Point* and Betty Rea's *New World?*

A conscientious objector, Tunnard was working as a coastguard on the Lizard peninsula. As an AIA member, he had been exhibiting works of abstraction influenced by both Constructivism and Surrealism since the 1937 Grosvenor Square exhibition. Often imbued with a sense of both the natural and the technological, and composed of highly textured forms suggesting both architecture and metamorphosis, they spoke to future possibilities and a teleological view of progress, represented in this case by a red sphere at the vanishing point of a precise design.

Betty Rea was still in Huntingdon, teaching children evacuated from children's homes and living with Nan Youngman as they looked after Rea's own sons and the three children of friends whose mother had suddenly died. Rea had not been involved in the organization of *For Liberty* and had done little of her own work for a while, only returning substantially to sculpture with the piece exhibited: a group of four life-sized heads, tilted

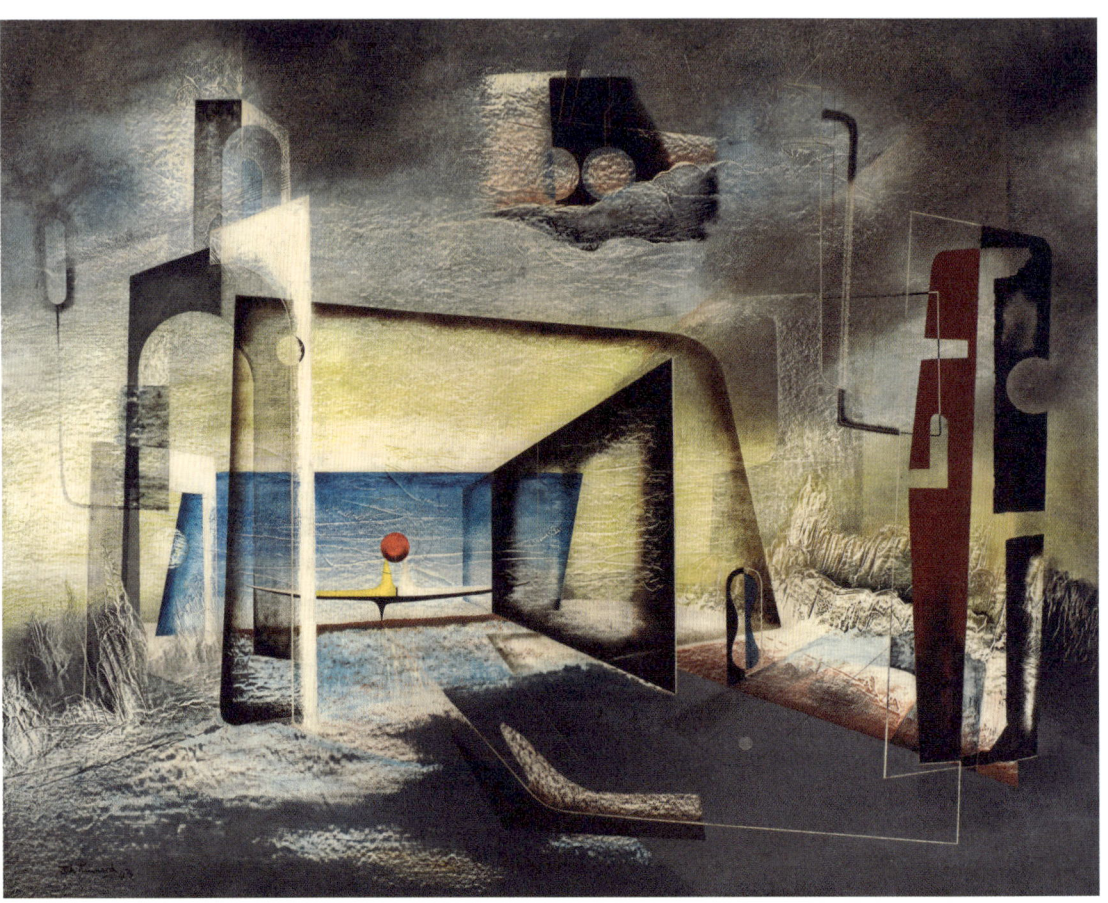

8.23 John Tunnard, *Focal Point*, oil on board, 1943. 121 × 152 cm (47¾ × 59⅞ in.)

8.24 Betty Rea, *New World?*, terracotta, 1943. Dimensions unknown

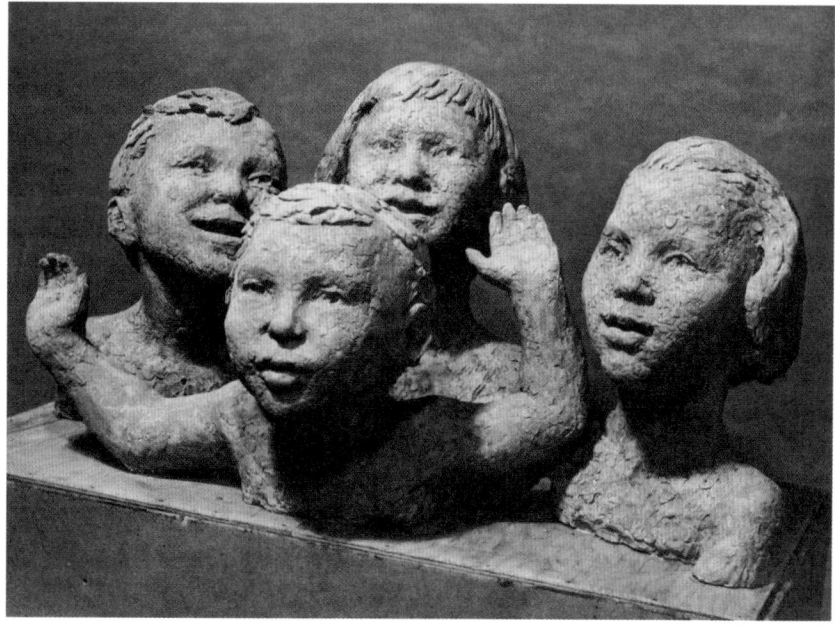

upwards, expectant and questioning. It was to this evocation of the young people Rea was teaching that the poet attached his final line: 'And our heirs shall unfold like a cluster of apple blossom in a fine tomorrow.' 'This embarrasses me now, but we liked it then', Nan Youngman wrote after Rea's death – and to those in the know at the time, it must have seemed fitting that the final piece of the sequence was by someone who had been so central to the AIA's growth since 1935.[53] For many of the thousands who paused to contemplate it – after being enticed in from the street, at one of many knife-edge moments of the war – it must indeed have encapsulated hope.

* * * * *

It was something of a coup to entice Brendan Bracken, Minister for Information and Churchill's confidant, to open *For Liberty*. The other speaker was Gerald Barry, editor of the *News Chronicle*, whose introduction made clear the newspaper's alliance with the AIA was motivated by two aims: making a contribution to securing victory and 'to help in laying the right foundation for the peace'. The paper had noted 'the swift debasement of cultural values' during the Munich years, but looked to co-operation between 'newspaper and artist' as a force in creating the 'enduring civilisation' of tomorrow.

The exhibition as a whole had been put together by designers and painters attuned to future possibilities for artists to play a significant role in

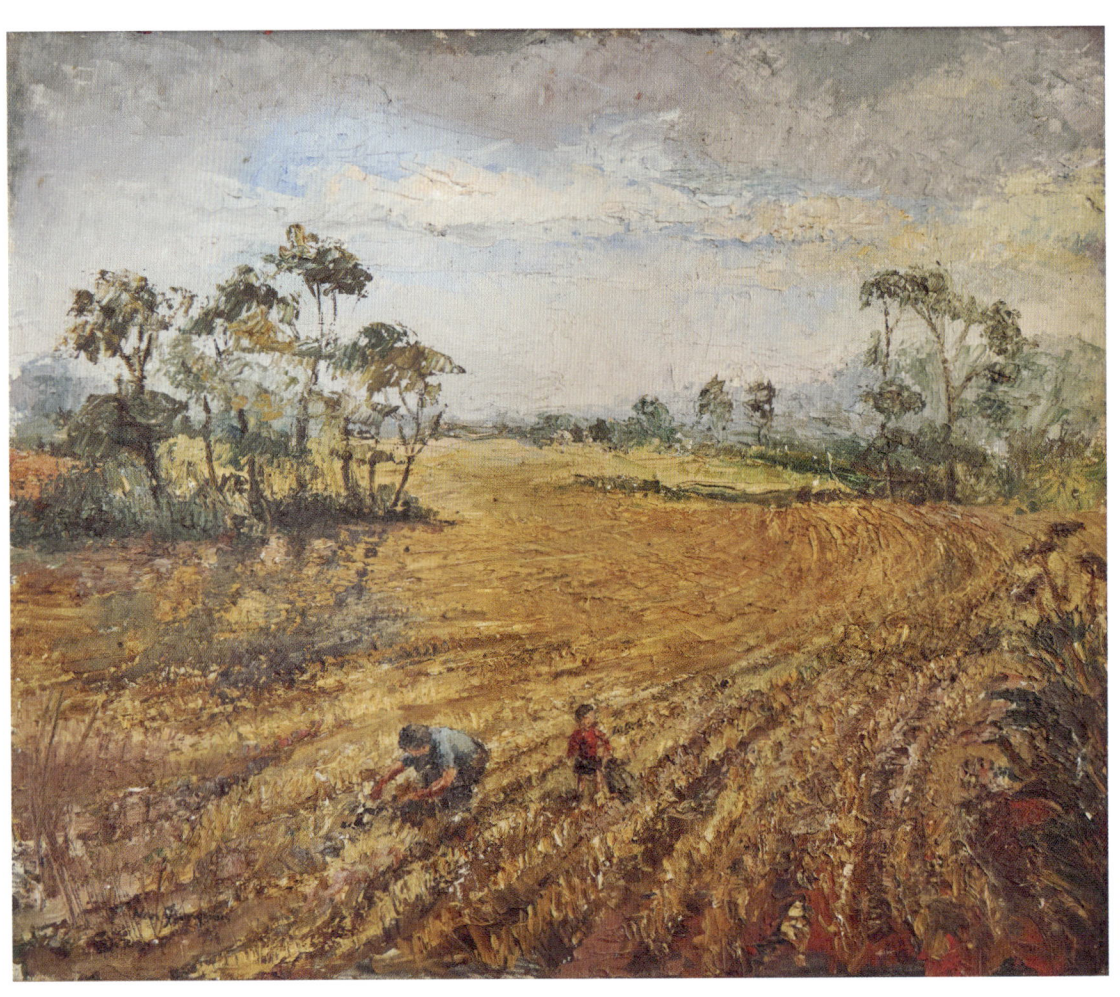

8.25 Nan Youngman, *Gleaning at Godmanchester*, oil on canvas, 1944. 57 × 67 cm (22⅜ × 26⅜ in.). Youngman displayed two paintings, *Harvest 1942* and *Harvest Field*, at the *For Liberty* exhibition

the reconstruction that would surely follow the conflict; and the method of its staging was seen as something of a dress rehearsal of this yet-to-be-specified potential in 'working to a theme and arranging the works in such a way that they become part of a whole scheme and not separate units. We hope to develop this new technique in the future.' As a token of intent, *For Liberty* included two works by 'Members of Artists and Designers Collective, Leamington Spa', the first 'Designs for murals in a workers' hostel. Theme: Holidays at Home', the second 'Canteen of a workers' hostel. Theme: Agriculture'.[54]

By 1943 the exigencies of mobilization for war production had necessitated the creation of many such hostels and even more British Restaurants sponsored by the Ministry of Food and local authorities in civic spaces and at industrial sites. Over two thousand such restaurants were open, increasing at a rate of ten a week, a model of mass provision meeting new social needs – specifically the displaced civilian proletariat's requirement for a midday meal – and creating, in Eric Newton's words, venues where 'people sit down in a receptive mood, once they have wormed their way along with the queue and secured a seat. They look forward to a half hour of relative enjoyment. When they look up from their plates, they are ready to take in pleasant decoration.'[55] Perhaps a hundred such places had been improved by art students and the ministry had appointed AIA member Clive Gardiner as art adviser, but Newton argued that resources – perhaps in the form of a farthing on every meal – would be needed. Murals, as an art form, had long been favoured by the AIA and its push for a national scheme would become a priority in 1944, but collectivist urges were not to all members' tastes; John Piper, whose work would shortly feature in a British Restaurant at Merton, felt there was far too much 'theorising about the past and future of co-operative art in the AIA catalogue' and that competent painting was 'a single-handed and single-minded job, even for an unusually capable human being'.[56]

When it came to tally up more than forty reviews, the *Bulletin* reported Piper's commentary in the *Spectator* as one of three that were hostile, with that by Raymond Mortimer in the *New Statesman* being almost vituperative.[57] Under the title 'Leave the Chap Alone', Mortimer dismissed the fraternization of 'Abstract, Royal Academic, surrealist, and impressionist paintings' and the organizers' 'catalogue jabber' of 'silly and shop-soiled pronouncements': 'It is impossible to view without dismay the prospect of these uninspired persons being employed to cover walls with the formulation and expression of "ideas"', he declaimed, adding for good measure that 'the multiplication of art-schools has impelled far too many people who could otherwise be useful to become professional painters'.[58]

Mortimer's article, decrying engagement between art and politics in terms reminiscent of Clive Bell, provided a useful signposting of arguments yet to come in Britain during the last two years of war and the broken Cold War peace that would follow. But they were probably not ones that troubled those gathering in the Holles Street shelter on 11 April for a celebration party.[59] For, as the *Bulletin*'s round-up noted, negativity had been confined to the highbrow journals; the enthusiastic endorsements had appeared in publications for the people. Reaching fellow citizens had always been one of two key priorities for the AIA, the other being pursuit of united action by as many progressive artists as possible, notwithstanding differences of style.

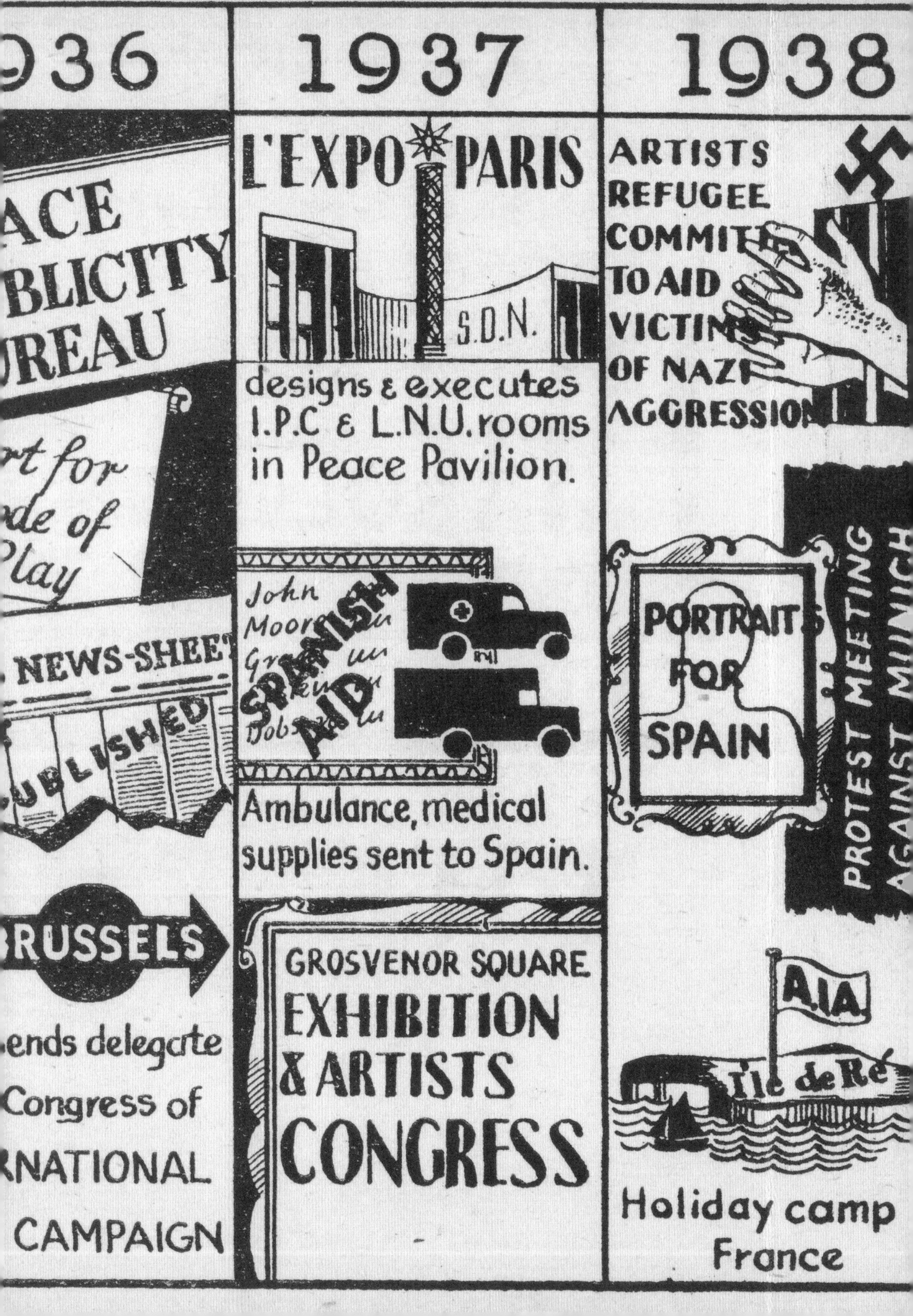

1936 | 1937 | 1938

1936
- PEACE PUBLICITY BUREAU
- ...rt for ...de of ...Play
- NEWS-SHEET PUBLISHED
- BRUSSELS — sends delegate Congress of ...RNATIONAL CAMPAIGN

1937
- L'EXPO PARIS — S.D.N. designs & executes I.P.C. & L.N.U. rooms in Peace Pavilion.
- SPANISH AID — John Moore... Gr... ...Jobs... Ambulance, medical supplies sent to Spain.
- GROSVENOR SQUARE EXHIBITION & ARTISTS CONGRESS

1938
- ARTISTS REFUGEE COMMITTEE TO AID VICTIMS OF NAZI AGGRESSION
- PORTRAITS FOR SPAIN
- PROTEST MEETING AGAINST MUNICH
- AIA — Ile de Ré — Holiday camp France

AFTERWORD

Three weeks later, on May Day 1943, some fifty people were in attendance when the AIA AGM was held at the Art Workers' Guild in Queen Square. A new Central Committee was elected and Misha Black, now thirty-two, was once again confirmed as chairman, James Holland as deputy.

It was just over a decade since Cliff Rowe had written from Moscow urging creation of an artists' organization against fascism and war, barely nine and a half years since the first candle-lit meeting in Little Earl Street had determined to try. James Fitton, Margaret Fitton, Francis Klingender, Peter László Peri and Cliff Rowe were probably among the other early members present. James Boswell was still overseas, and Pearl Binder was probably not there: she now had three small children and Elwyn Jones was stationed at Portsmouth; he would soon embark as a forces' lawyer for North Africa, then Italy, return to be elected MP for West Ham and thereafter serve as a prosecutor at Nuremberg.

The meeting heard that the finances were now in good enough shape to sustain expanding activity, including a new push to build up AIA regional groups, greater co-operation with the Society of Industrial Artists and that for Education in Art, joint work with the National Council for Civil Liberties, further approaches to the Trades Union Congress and a drive to recruit film and theatre workers. It was reported that fifty-seven new members had joined in the previous eight weeks: the leading designer Ashley Havinden and the painters Marie-Louise von Motesiczky and Michael Ayrton were among the established, recently arrived and young who had signed up. Apart from the forward agenda of lectures and exhibitions, plans for the *Bulletin* and for socials, the meeting agreed a programme for new international activity working with exiled artists. Another forthcoming initiative was a Hogarth Group exhibition on English caricature in a rented shop which would soon become the AIA's Charlotte Street Centre, programming a considerable range of soldier art, including that of returned 'Good Soldier' Boswell.[1]

As Black recalled, the AI had been formed at a time when there was an expectation that if enough people of goodwill combined, the drift to fascism and war could be avoided, and as James Fitton modestly observed, 'We

9.1 AIA timeline from a 1943 *Bulletin*, detail

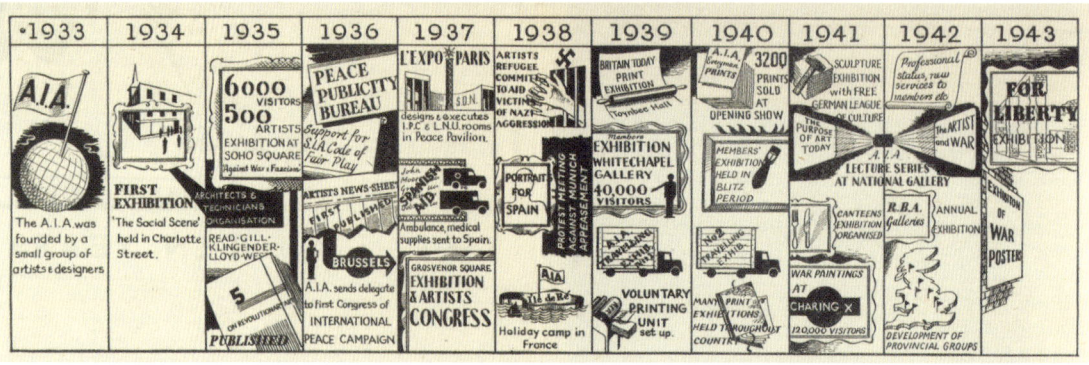

9.2 AIA timeline from a 1943 *Bulletin*. 13.5 × 40.6 cm (5¼ × 16 in.)

didn't prevent the war, but perhaps we served as the bell on the fire engine'.² In the attempt the AIA strategy of reaching upwards generationally and outwards in terms of artistic credo had built a visual art component for the British popular front, the first British Artists' Congress had articulated an agenda of cultural reform that would help shape the future, and – against the odds – the AIA had successfully navigated successive political crises that threatened to pull its progressive constituency apart.

The story of the AIA is a neglected one in the annals of mid-twentieth-century British art history, despite biographical and archival evidence that attests to participation at one time or another of a clear majority of the country's leading artists in its collective endeavours. In this author's view, this is partly due to an apolitical bias that colours so much monographic writing in a cultural era where art is an asset class and competitive individualism – and the banal pursuit of celebrity – thrives largely unquestioned. But it is also due to a misreading of the evidence, which has meant that even sympathetic analyses of the AIA have concluded that with war came irrelevance, radicalism betrayed and a precipitate decline into being just another exhibiting society.³ By 1943 the experience of operating in and around the state while retaining a campaigning vision was sufficient to ensure that, in myriad ways, the principal players would remain influential – and the AIA itself consequential – as new existential realities overtook artists and contesting visions of post-war Britain were put into play. The network they had sustained during the fight against National Socialism abroad would shortly play an honourable part in the eclipse of national conservatism at home.

ABBREVIATIONS

ORGANIZATIONAL BODIES

AAC American Artists' Congress
AASTA Association of Architects, Surveyors and Technical Assistants
ABCA Army Bureau of Current Affairs
AC AIA Advisory Council
AEAR Association des Écrivains et Artistes Révolutionnaires
AI Artists International
AIA Artists International Association
ARC Artists' Refugee Committee
AU Artists' Union
BIAE British Institute of Adult Education
BUF British Union of Fascists
CC AIA Central Committee
CEMA Council for the Encouragement of Music and the Arts
CIAD Central Institute of Art and Design
Comintern Communist International
CP Communist Party
CPGB Communist Party of Great Britain
DRU Design Research Unit
FAP Federal Art Project
FGLC Free German League of Culture
IBRA International Bureau of Revolutionary Artists
IDP Industrial Design Partnership
ILP Independent Labour Party
IPC International Peace Campaign
JRC John Reed Clubs
LAA London Artists' Association
LCC London County Council
LG London Group
LSE London School of Economics
MOI Ministry of Information
MoMA Museum of Modern Art, New York
NCCL National Council of Civil Liberties
NEAC New English Art Club
NUWM National Unemployed Workers' Movement
PWAP Public Works of Art Project
RA Royal Academy
RCA Royal College of Art
SCR Society for Cultural Relations
SIA Society of Industrial Artists
SWE Society of Wood Engravers
UAG Unemployed Artists Group
VOKS All-Union Society for Cultural Relations with Foreign Countries
WAAC War Artists Advisory Committee
WPA Works Progress Administration

INDIVIDUALS

PA Peggy Angus
EA Edward Ardizzone
EB Edward Bawden
GB Graham Bell
JBe Julian Bell
QB Quentin Bell
VB Vanessa Bell
PB Pearl Binder
HB Helen Binyon
MB Misha Black
AB Anthony Blunt
JB James Boswell
CB Clive Branson
NB Noreen Branson
FB Felicia Browne
DC David Caplan
RC Richard Carline
KC Kenneth Clark
WC William Coldstream
SD Stuart Davis
FEJ Frederick Elwyn-Jones
JE Jacob Epstein
HF Hans Feibusch
JF James Fitton
MF Margaret Fitton
EG Eric Gill
JG Jan Gordon
DG Duncan Grant
MG Milner Gray
SH Sam Haile
FHKH F. H. K. Henrion
BH Barbara Hepworth
JH James Holland
PH Percy Horton
RH Ron Horton
AJ Augustus John
EMK Edward McKnight Kauffer
MK Morris Kestelman
FK Francis Klingender
OK Oscar Kokoschka
CL Clare Leighton
AL A. L. Lloyd
DL David Low
LL Lowes Luard
HM Henry Moore
PN Paul Nash
VP Victor Pasmore
RP Roland Penrose
PLP Peter László Peri
EP Ewan Phillips
ER Eric Ravilious
BR Betty Rea
HR Herbert Read
CR Cliff Rowe
KR Kenneth Rowntree
ES Edith Simon
BS Beryl Sinclair
MS Montagu Slater
WT William Townsend
JT Julian Trevelyan
ETH Edith Tudor-Hart
FU Fred Uhlman
EW Elizabeth Watson
EWa Ethel Walker
CW Carel Weight
TW Tom Wintringham
VW Virginia Woolf
NY Nan Youngman

ARCHIVES

BL British Library
ESRO East Sussex Record Office
IWM Imperial War Museum
MML Marx Memorial Library
NA National Archives
NG National Gallery Archive
RGASPI Russian State Archive of Socio-Political History
TGA Tate Archive

NOTES

**CHAPTER 1:
SEVEN DIALS**

1 For biographical details of MB and other key artists and activists, see Biographies (pp. 336–44). JB remembered MB's rooms as being on Little Earl Street, part of present-day Earlham Street that ran west from Seven Dials; Morris and Radford 1983, p. 10.
2 See Blake 1984, pp. 15–17. MB met Lucy Rossetti, a great-niece of Dante Gabriel Rossetti, on a shop window-dressing course; after setting up Studio Z together, they designed bookplates, letter headings, display stands and a bedside table before illness forced Rossetti to give up.
3 May Tilney Miles (1897–1977) had qualified as a Doctor of Medicine, subsequently practising in Wandsworth; after returning from Russia, she worked as medical officer for the General Post Office.
4 International Labour Defence, or MOPR after its Russian initials, was originally known as International Class War Prisoners Aid and was organized by Willi Münzenberg on behalf of the Comintern. Its mission was legal defence of communist and left-wing prisoners, politically persecuted strikers and unemployed militants; for Münzenberg see McMeekin 2003.
5 Harry Pollitt (1890–1960) was General Secretary of CPGB from July 1929 to September 1939 and from July 1941 until his death in June 1960.
6 Extract from intercepted letter from ROWE, Moscow, to Misha BLACK, London. Copied from minute sheet of NA P.F.40214 Black Misha, placed in the MI5 surveillance file WINCOTT (E.5587.T). CR was not a member of CPGB before going to Russia but joined after returning; MB is believed to have joined before CR, although in post-war interviews he avoided referring to his membership.
7 References to the existence of the file on MB are found in NA KV/2/3729 BECKER, Violet Winifred; the file confirms that the General Post Office was sent instructions on 12 October 1932 initiating interception of MB's post.
8 MB interviewed by Robert Radford, TGA TAV 668/1974.
9 For MB's early ambitions to become a painter and working experience in designing posters and trade-show stands see Blake 1984, pp. 13–15.
10 Rowe arrived at the RCA in the same intake as ER, EB, PA and HB, all of whom would become AIA colleagues. It was compulsory for both painters and designers to study architecture for the first term and CR's report read: 'Influenced by extreme schools of Modern Painting. Anxious to modify architectural styles without the necessary knowledge. Distinctly bored with the whole subject which is nevertheless an excellent discipline for him', RCA Student Record file. CR had been granted a Surrey County Council exhibition of £40, but this was not enough to exist on for a year and it seems he was concerned about depleting his aunt's resources to access unsympathetic teaching; the file records CR's employment as 'advertising artist' at Business Builders in 1920–21, and this may have been another point of contact with Dunlop, who was working in advertising to support his painting.
11 In his book *Art*, Clive Bell argued: 'The starting point for all systems of aesthetics must be the personal experience of a particular emotion; the objects that provoke this emotion we call works of art [and] this emotion is called the aesthetic emotion; and if we can discover some quality common to all the objects that provoke it, we shall have solved what I take to be the central problem of aesthetics ... Only one answer seems possible: significant form'; C. Bell 1914, p. 6. At this point Bell was yet to publish his deeply reactionary defence of cultural elitism *Civilisation* (C. Bell 1928, discussed on p. 121.
12 The group included musicians, poets and sculptors as well as painters. The young poet and coming actress Peggy Ashcroft was a participant; George Bernard Shaw, Sybil Thorndike and Aldous Huxley were occasional visitors.
13 'Emotionism', *The Times*, 23 January 1928, p. 10. EWa was also cited positively: in 1940, the same year she was made an Associate of the Royal Academy, EWa accepted an invitation to join the AIA Advisory Council at a time when CR was a member of the AIA Central Committee; see AIA minute book in TGA Kestelman, uncatalogued, entry for 4 March 1940. See also 'Emotionist Drawings', *The Times*, 4 April 1928, p. 12.
14 *The Times*, 15 December 1930. CR was also selected by the gallerist Lucy Wertheim as a member of her Twenties Group of young artists; see Wertheim 2022, pp. 94–95. This group also included CB, NY, WT, Edna Ginesi, VP, BH and Roger Hilton, all of whom would also become engaged in AIA activities in subsequent years.
15 Morris and Radford 1983, p. 9.
16 NA KV2/1059 Jack Cohen: on 7 November 1931 Special Branch recorded Jack Cohen, the Communist Party's publications manager, leaving a dwelling occupied by 'an artist named Hooper Rowe'; CR had used the name Clifford Hooper Rowe in his painting career up to this point, as well as C. H. Rowe, which became his more usual titling from then onwards.

17 Ereira 1981, pp. 155–56. The Invergordon mutiny broke out on Tuesday 15 September 1931; on Thursday 18 and Friday 19 September there were major withdrawals of gold from the Bank of England, nullifying the beneficial impact of recently negotiated foreign loans. Prime Minister Ramsay MacDonald was informed that there was no alternative to abandoning the gold standard on the Friday evening and on Sunday 20 September a Treasury press release announced the move to the markets.
18 Morris and Radford 1983, p. 8.
19 VW became a vice-president while her husband Leonard Woolf was serving on the founding executive committee in 1924; she retained the role up to her death in 1941. PB supported its activity by fundraising and giving talks on Soviet art, and served on its executive committee in 1935–36; see SCR annual reports held in the Society for Co-operation in Russian & Soviet Studies Library, Brixton, London.
20 May Tilney Miles was the defendant to her husband John Miles's 1932 petition for divorce, co respondent Hooper Rowe, NA J 77/3039/3693.
21 Morris and Radford 1983, p. 9; CR is recorded as having visited VOKS in Moscow on 14 June 1932 and is believed to have commenced at the Co-operative Publishing Society soon after.
22 *Izvestia* review of the exhibition, quoted in *Advertising as Art: British Posters of the Late 19th and Early 20th Centuries*, Pushkin Museum, Moscow, 2020, pp. 195–97. This also states that while in Moscow CR 'worked in the art propaganda department of IZOGIZ, side by side with the Soviet poster artists. As part of the Isobrigade, Rowe participated in the preparation for the anniversary of the Great October Socialist Revolution and the design of the festive demonstration column'; while not subsequently referred to by CR, this is plausible in that the Foreign Workers' Publishing Co-operative and IZOGIZ (the State Publishing House of Fine Art) had a close working relationship.
23 Morris and Radford 1983, p. 8: 'I thought that this was a great idea and that there should be similar organisations of artists in all countries and wrote to Misha Black.' *15 Years of the Workers' and Peasants Army* opened at the Central Park of Culture and Leisure in June 1933.
24 In 2019 the painting was identified as being in the National Gallery of Ukraine, Lviv; the details of its travels after 1933 are unclear, but in 1965 it was transferred to Lviv for 'permanent storage' by the Directorate of Art Exhibitions and Panoramas in Moscow.
25 Hannington 1936, pp. 256–57.
26 Eastman 1934, pp. 3–13. The Communist International (Comintern), also known as the Third International, was an international organization founded in 1919 that advocated world communism; it was led and controlled by the Communist Party of the Soviet Union.
27 Eastman 1934, pp. 16–17.
28 *Advertising as Art*, cat. 482; I am indebted to Nina Klose for her translation.
29 PB is known to have visited the Soviet Union in 1933, 1934 and 1935–36. 'English Artist in Moscow', *The Listener*, 6 November 1941, pp. 627 and 635, carried the transcript of a recent Home Service talk by PB beginning 'I went to Russia for the first time a few years ago. I was taking a collection of my drawings to an exhibition in Moscow' and describes in detail the circumstances surrounding her exhibition at the Museum of Modern Western Art in Moscow, her July 1933 meeting with the sculptor and museum director Professor Ternovets, and her subsequent work for the satirical magazine *Krokodil*. The broadcast would appear to have conflated events from her 1933 and 1934 visits, but on this basis it would seem that Lindey 2018, p. 18, is mistaken in stating that 'Pearl Binder (b. 1904) visited the USSR several times in the 1920s and 1930s, working as an illustrator for eighteen months in 1929–30'. PB worked as an illustrator in Paris at the earlier time.
30 See Egbert 1970, p. 499, and Rickaby 1978, p. 154. Both authors had direct communication with CR while researching the origins of the AI/AIA and report on this meeting; PB's 1933 diary (privately held) mentions meeting Mrs Rowe.
31 *The Listener*, 6 November 1941, p. 627.
32 Autobiographical notes, privately held in PB family archive.
33 *The Studio*, April 1925, p. 221; the review by 'HBG', in which he cautioned her against *saeva indignation* (savage indignation) was illustrated with a PB drawing, *More Unpleasant People*.
34 PB's first illustrated books in this satiric vein were *Bed and Breakfast*, written by Coralie Hobson (1926), and *All Children Must be Paid For* by Lancelot de Giberne Sieveking (1927). PB lived with her first husband, the anthropologist Jack Driberg, between 1928 and 1930, illustrating his *People of the Small Arrow* and becoming a close friend of anthropologist Bronislaw Malinowski and his wife Elsie, to whom she dedicated *Odd Jobs*.
35 Thomas Burke, *The Real East End*, Constable & Co, 1932; Binder 1935.
36 JF took over from Hartrick's short-lived successor Gerald Spencer Pryse in autumn 1933. Hartrick's letter recommended JF as 'one of the ablest young lithographers in the country'; see Sheeran 1986, pp. 6–7.
37 JF's father took up the role in 1920, with JF following the family south in 1925, having been made redundant by textile merchants in Manchester; JF senior had been blacklisted by employers for activity with the United Machine Workers Union. For many years, he could only find distant night-shift employment under an assumed name; unpublished JF memoir, privately held.

38 JF's exhibited works in 1930, as listed in Wilcox 1995, pp. 77–78: LG, *Sitting Down to it* (cat. 105); NEAC, *Cinerarias* (cat. 214); RA, *Books and Beer* (cat. 665). In 1931 his work was included in *XVII Artists: 2nd Exhibition* and three works (*Landscape, Kent, Riverside* and *Chelsea Figures*, cats 191, 204 and 742 respectively) were hung at the RA, as was *Church Landscape* (cat. 418) in 1933.

39 JF memoir, p. 96, describes how at the time he was lodging at 11 Downing Street, the residence of his father's friend J. R. Clynes, the Labour Home Secretary; 'chatting to Mrs Clynes, I told her the story of meeting Mr Terakopov and having my poster accepted. She seemed very pleased for me but at the same time excessively relieved about something'; under surveillance by Scotland Yard his movements had been monitored and reported back to Downing Street.

40 On 15 July 1927 the workers of Vienna rose in revolt, taking both socialist and communist leaders by surprise. After the rising, the Heimwehr, a semi-fascist military organization, gained ground across Austria; see Borkenau 1938, p. 333.

41 Morris and Radford 1983, p. 10.

42 ES, 'Eye Witness', talk commissioned by the Scottish Arts Council, Edinburgh, 1984; transcript available at TGA TVA 357B, p. 5.

43 *The Listener*, 6 November 1941, p. 635.

44 For PA in Russia see Trant 2004, pp. 49–56.

45 VOKS foreign visitor daybook, 16 July 1933, State Archive of the Russian Federation, F.5283, Op.8, 174.1.5; on her return PB wrote 'Russian Children's Books', *The Studio*, June 1934, pp. 309–13.

46 See 'Artist Life in Russia', *The Studio*, March 1934, pp. 111–13, for an interesting contemporary survey of conditions by an anonymous author.

47 See Jankowski 2020, pp. 115ff., for the failure of the World Disarmament Conference, and pp. 335ff. for failure of the London Economic Conference.

48 Morris and Radford 1983, p. 10.

49 Sal Shuel, 'James Boswell (warts and all) 1906–1971', pp. 6–9, MS privately held in Boswell family archive.

50 JH, quoted in 'Two Jameses – Holland and Boswell Meet', *James Holland, 20th Century Artist* (blog), 1 May 2011, https://plantagenetconsulting.typepad.co.uk/james_holland_20th_centur/, accessed 9 August 2024. This blog, produced by Holland's daughter Jane, is an invaluable resource of information regarding his life and work.

51 MS, 'Private James Boswell', *Our Time*, March 1942, pp. 11–15.

52 JB, autobiographical letter of 1969, quoted in Roth 1977, p. 4.

53 Michael Middleton, 'James Boswell: A Familiar Stranger', *The Studio*, February 1962, p. 49.

54 See Skidelsky 1992, p. 243; Spalding 1983, pp. 245–47. Keynes persuaded Samuel Courtauld and two other businessmen, Hindley Smith and L. H. Myers, to join him in securing the members a guaranteed income of £150 a year. The LAA held its first show at the Leicester Galleries in April 1926. The original seven members were all in some way connected with the Bloomsbury aesthetic: Grant, VB, Roger Fry, Keith Baynes, Frank Dobson, Freddie Porter, Bernard Adeney. As a result of its early success (by 1929 income of £22,000 had been generated by sale of seven hundred works), Paul Nash, Douglas Davidson, William Roberts, Edward Wolfe and Christopher Wood joined. Keynes's altruism had an unhappy ending after Grant, in financial difficulty in 1931, was refused an advance on guaranteed income and he, VB and Baynes entered into conflicting arrangements with the dealers Agnews and Lefevre. The slump and mismanagement thereafter took their toll and the LAA was wound up in 1933, but not before others – including HM, WC, VP, Ivon Hitchens, William Roberts and Claude Rogers – had benefited from its existence.

55 Both exhibited with the LG in June 1927 and January and October 1929; see Wilcox 1995. Other significant members of the AI/AIA who exhibited with the LG during the 1930s included EA, PA, PH, MK, BR, CR, NY, EW, BS, CW, SH, WT and JT.

56 Roth 1977, p. 4; this was not a selection that would have been hung at the LG but may well have appeared at the LAA.

57 JB, autobiographical letter, 1969, quoted in Roth 1977, p. 4.

58 JH, quoted in 'Two Jameses – Holland and Boswell Meet'.

59 JH, quoted in 'Remembering the Royal Dockyard at Chatham', *James Holland, 20th Century Artist* (blog), 24 May 2011.

60 The visiting New Zealander was the artist and photographer Eric Lee-Johnson; Roth 1977, p. 4, quoting Eric McCormick, *Eric Lee-Johnson*, Hamilton, 1956.

61 JB's first book cover design was commissioned by Chatto & Windus for the novel *Solemn Boy* by Hector Bolitho, another Aucklander. Between 1932 and 1935 JB provided fifteen covers for Boriswood, a progressive publishing house which published sixty-one titles but folded after publication of James Hanley's novel *Boy* led in 1931 to a prosecution for indecency four years later. JB also provided six covers for a spread of other publishers during this time; H. G. Wells, J. B. Priestley, A. A. Milne and E. M. Forster were among the NCCL supporters who campaigned in Boriswood's defence, *Manchester Guardian*, 26 March 1935, p. 18.

62 'Advertising in the Thirties', *James Holland, 20th Century Artist* (blog), 12 May 2011; Robert Radford, 'To Disable the Enemy: The Graphic Art of the three Jameses', in Croft 1998, p. 32.

63 JH, 'The Three James's', *James Holland, 20th Century Artist* (blog), 4 June 2011.

64 Shuel, 'James Boswell', p. 13.
65 Quoted in Alfred Durus, 'English Revolutionary Graphic Artists', *International Literature*, 1936, p. 110.
66 Although MB would later describe it as 'effectively a young man's organisation' (TGA TAV 668 1974), the women present included ES, PB, PA, MF and Betty Soars, JB's young wife who was a student at Central; these were soon to be joined by BR and CL.
67 Milner Gray and brothers Charles and Henry Bassett established the Bassett-Gray Group of Artists and Writers as a multidisciplinary design house in 1934 after studying together at Goldsmiths in the 1920s; Gray helped found the Society of Industrial Artists in 1930. In 1935 Bassett-Gray became the Industrial Design Partnership, where MB was a leading figure while acting as AIA chairman.
68 TGA TAV 668 1974.
69 For a thoughtful analysis of MB's qualities of leadership and organization see introduction to Avril Blake (ed.), *The Black Papers on Design*, Pergamon Press, 1982.
70 The possible exception to this would have been CB who, turning away from painting at this time in favour of political activism, was using his inheritance to play a major role in founding the Marx Memorial Library and Workers' School in Clerkenwell Green.
71 TGA TAV 668 1974.
72 ES, TGA TVA 357B, p. 6.
73 Read 1938, p. 13. Publication of *Art Now* in October 1933 was followed by *Unit One* in April 1934; in the former, Read located Nazi denunciation of Kulturbolschewismus (cultural Bolshevism) and the persecution of artists as rooted in 'a monstrous illogicality' identifying modernism in art with communism in politics.
74 *The Times*, 12 June 1933; *The Listener*, 5 July 1933, pp. 14–16.
75 After opening in April 1934 the exhibition subsequently toured to Manchester, Hanley, Derby, Swansea and Belfast. Frances Hodgkins was an early resignee, being replaced by Tristram Hillier. Douglas Cooper, an outspoken and rich twenty-two-year-old art collector, had opened the Mayor Gallery in Cork Street in April 1933 with twenty-six-year-old Freddie Mayor, the son of a Cambridge family with Bloomsbury connections: 'With its clean, white, functionalist premises and pictures by artists hitherto unseen in London – Joan Miró and Paul Klee among them – it quickly became perhaps the most influential modern gallery in London'; Carter 2001, p. 95.
76 Of these, twenty-seven can be identified as CR, MB, BR, JB, JH, JF, HF, MF, ES, FK, EA, EP, PB, PA, PH, RH, PLP, AL, John Davison, James Lucas, S. E. Weaver, Bill Woolfe, Phyllis Ladyman, Reg Turner, Anna Meblin, Reg Bartlett.
77 Friend 2017, p. 83.
78 Pooke 2007; for FK's life and work see this trail-blazing study.
79 ES, TGA TVA 357B, p. 1.
80 In autumn 1935 the styling originally adopted by the group, Artists International British Section, would be superseded by the organizational name Artists International Association, or AIA, see p. 89.
81 Jasper Rowe was born on 13 June 1934 at the Royal Northern Hospital in north London, Anna Rowe registering the birth while she and CR were resident at 65 Marchmont Street, Holborn.
82 Morris and Radford 1983, p. 10.

CHAPTER 2: CHARLOTTE STREET

1 Hannington 1936, pp. 254ff.
2 Trenchard had served in the cavalry in India, the Boer War and as the leader of punitive expeditions in Nigeria. Learning to fly in 1913, he subsequently commanded both the Royal Flying Corps and the Royal Air Force, retiring in 1930 to become a director of the Goodyear Tire and Rubber Company. An advocate for terrorizing native populations through air power, in 1920 he suggested to Churchill that the RAF could be used to suppress 'industrial disturbances, or risings' in the United Kingdom, but Churchill forbade further reference to the proposal; see David Omissi, *Air Power and Colonial Control: The Royal Air Force 1919–1939*, Manchester University Press, 1990. Ramsay MacDonald, concerned about police loyalty in the aftermath of pay cuts, recruited Trenchard as a hard-line commissioner in October 1931.
3 Hayburn 1972, pp. 638–43; Ronald Kidd in *Civil Liberty*, no. 2, Autumn 1937. On 3 February 1934 the producers of *Empire News Bulletin* and *Universal Talking News* wrote to Trenchard assuring him they would comply with his request to avoid covering the hunger march.
4 The AI's *Why We Are Marching!* included an introduction analysing the government proposals and further typescript inserts throughout the pamphlet bringing out different aspects of the proposed regulations.
5 Branson 1985, p. 76.
6 See Griffiths 1980 for an analysis of this vein of political thinking in Britain.
7 The Gestetner works had opened in Tottenham Hale in 1906 and by the late 1920s its duplicators had become a staple of office administration.
8 The majority of the cartoons are unsigned, but the collection would seem to include work by seven or eight hands including JB, JF, JH, CR, EA and Roy Laurier.
9 'Hurrah for the Blackshirts', *Daily Mail*, 15 January 1934, p. 10.
10 J. A. Barlow to the NUWM National Congress and March Council, February 1934, repr. in Hannington 1936, p. 286.
11 Kidd 1940, p. 145.
12 'Hunger Marchers in London, Vigilance for Civil Liberty', *Manchester Guardian*, 24 February 1934, p. 6; the other signatories were Lascelles Abercrombie, Ambrose Applebee, G. H. Bing, Dudley Collard, A. P. Herbert, Harold Laski, Evelyn Sharp Nevinson, Henry W.

Nevinson and D. N. Pritt. Radford 1987, p. 37, also cites AJ as one of the early instigators of the NCCL.

13 Kershaw 2015, pp. 236ff. The AEAR was founded by communist and communist-sympathizing writers in March 1932 as the French section of the International Union of Revolutionary Writers, established as a Comintern entity in 1930. Leading figures included Paul Vaillant-Couturier, Léon Moussinac, Charles Vildrac and Francis Jourdain. Originally the task of the organization was to promote Soviet art and culture, but later, under the direction of Vaillant-Couturier, members of the AEAR mobilized against war and fascism in much the same way as the AIA.

14 In Bordeaux a reported 100,000 demonstrated and large demonstrations also took place in all major provincial cities; see Danos and Gibelin 1986, p. 34.

15 PA to ER, 16 February 1934, in Ullmann 2008, p. 141. On the night of 12/13 February 1934 Austrian government forces, aided by fascist auxiliaries, shelled the Karl-Marx-Hof, a model complex of 1,400 workers' flats at Heiligenstadt, capturing it after a subsequent assault lasting from dawn to midday; *The Times*, 14 February 1934, p. 12.

16 ETH (née Suschitzky; 1908–1973); see Forbes 2013 for a series of illuminating essays and the detail of ETH's time in Vienna and early years in London.

17 ETH (as Edith Suschitzky) published an article, 'Whitechapel: London's Elendsviertel', in *Der Kuckuck*, 29 March 1931; Forbes 2013, p. 18, note 27.

18 ETH's work appeared in *The Listener*, 29 November, 13 December 1933; 10 January, 16 May, 13 June 1934; 2 January 1935. For surveillance of ETH by the Security Service see NA KV2/1012–14.

19 *Left Review*, vol. I, no. 6, March 1935, p. 191.

20 Herbert Read, 'Art – Picasso and the Marxists', *London Mercury*, December 1934, pp. 95–96.

An unsigned article had appeared in the mimeographed *Marx House Bulletin* for Winter 1934 and similarly observed: 'Another particular feature was the remarkable photographs by Miss Tudor-Hart which proved there can be revolutionary photography.' 64 Charlotte Street was (and is) situated on the north-east corner of the junction of Tottenham Street and Charlotte Street, opposite what was then the Scala Cinema on the south-east corner; the building's stone signage 'Hogarth Studios' evidences previous artistic uses.

21 *The Listener*, 16 May 1934, p. 820; BBC correspondent Stephen Heald's report 'Austria in Transition' was broadcast from Vienna on 10 May 1934.

22 Whitford 1986, p. 171.

23 Binyon 1983, p. 67.

24 On 29 August 1934 ER's wife Tirzah Garwood, while staying at Furlongs with ER, noted in her diary 'Peggy's pictures for Artists International'.

25 JB entry by John Saville in Joyce M. Bellamy and John Saville (eds), *Dictionary of Labour Biography, Volume 3*, Macmillan, 1976, pp. 14–15.

26 Artists International Special Notice, TGA 771/1/3; this is EB's copy annotated by PB. After Moscow the exhibition was to tour the capital cities of Ukraine, White Russia, the Caucasian and Middle Asian Republics and Leningrad; the nternational Bureau of Revolutionary Artists' request appears to have been the initial spur that led to the idea of holding *The Social Scene* in the first place: 'The Committee of the AI hope to receive enough work of sufficient quality to justify holding an exhibition in London prior to sending the work to Moscow.'

27 Announcement on inside back cover of *Left Review*, vol. I, no. I, October 1934. Douglas Goldring in *The Studio*, December 1934, p. 307, quoted the catalogue foreword as making the AI's standpoint clear: 'We must say plainly, therefore, that the Artists' International supports the Marxist position that the character of all art is the outcome of the character of the mode of material production of its period ... To-day, when the capitalist system and the socialist are fighting for world survival, we feel that the place of the artist is on the side of the working class against the capitalist class. In this struggle we use our abilities as an expression and as a weapon, making our first steps towards the new socialist art.'

28 Recruiting leaflet, 1934, signed by Anna Meblin as AI secretary, private collection.

29 The lecture on civil liberties was given by Ronald Kidd; Robin Page Arnot, first director of the Marx Memorial Library and Workers' School, was the speaker on Revolutionary Proletarian Art, while FK presented on Marxist Art History. Page Arnot (1890–1986), a conscientious objector in the First World War, was a founding member of the CPGB, a member of its central committee 1927–37, co-founder of *Labour Monthly*, and an advocate of close co-operation between the party and the broader labour movement. TW described the Workers Film and Photo League camera club display as 'mainly of incidents of the movement'; the League also exhibited at the 1935 Soho Square exhibition *Artists Against Fascism and War* but not apparently as a body with the AIA thereafter.

30 Berthoud 1987, p. 144.

31 *The Studio*, December 1934, p. 307.

32 T. H. Wintringham, 'Artists' International', *Left Review*, vol. I, no. 2, November 1934, p. 40.

33 Herbert Read, 'Art – Picasso and the Marxists', *London Mercury*, December 1934, pp. 95–96.

34 See Hemingway 2002, especially pp. 51–59, for an authoritative discussion of this exhibition.

35 Hemingway 2002, pp. 20–24.

36 Denning 1996, pp. 205–12.

37 Hemingway 2002, p. 55, comments that it is 'an accomplished painting, but the precisely calculated

style makes it less emotionally immediate' and it does indeed lack the sense of chaotic vitality and fierce struggle of CR's painting.
38 Hemingway 2002, p. 56.
39 In Benton's case, according to Hemingway 2002, p. 52, this meant 'picturesque Americana' paintings of a train wreck, cowboys, African Americans shooting crap and cotton-picking.
40 Meyer Schapiro (writing as John Kwait), 'John Reed Art Club Exhibition', *New Masses*, vol. 8, no. 7, February 1933, pp. 26–27.
41 Meyer Schapiro speaking at a symposium held on 10 February 1933, quoted in Hemingway 2002, p. 59.
42 Anita Brenner, 'Revolution in Art', *The Nation*, 18 March 1933, p. 268, quoted in Hemingway 2002, p. 58.
43 SD to Hazel Foulke, 13 January 1932, quoted in Cooper and Haskell 2016, pp. 171–72.
44 Cooper and Haskell 2016, p. 2.
45 Cooper and Haskell 2016, p. 152, quoting SD in Rudi Blesh, *Stuart Davis*, Grove Press, 1960.
46 Patterson 2020, p. 39, cites SD's illustrations in *The Masses*, *The Liberator* and *New Masses* as evidence of him having been 'involved in socialist politics for decades'; however, this involvement was more attitudinal than organizational prior to his joining the JRC in 1933 and effectively becoming a full-time activist in succeeding years.
47 SD guessed Force felt sorry for him as the only artist in the Whitney Studio Club 'who hadn't been to France and she thought it would be good for me. I didn't ask her for the money but I accepted it gratefully and was on the next boat over ... it was a very profitable experience'; transcript of SD broadcast from 1953, quoted in Cooper and Haskell 2016, p. 166.
48 For an enlightening analysis of the exhibition and the surrounding controversies, see Patterson 2020, ch. 1, 'We Capture the Walls'.
49 Hemingway 2002, p. 85. The first appearance of the AU was at a meeting of unemployed artists at the New School for Social Research on 27 October 1933, arranged by Audrey MacMahon of the College Art Association. Thus, the AI in London and AU in New York were formed within weeks, if not days, of each other. The AU later claimed its lobbying of the executive director of the New York State Emergency Relief Administration had been directly instrumental in the setting up of the PWAP, although Hemingway 2002 thinks this unlikely; see 'The Artist's Struggle for Relief', *Art Front*, no. 1, November 1934.
50 Cooper and Haskell 2016, p. 173.
51 SD resigned from AAC on 5 April 1940 as a consequence of the splits occasioned by the Russo-Finnish Winter War, as controversial in the USA as it was in the UK; see p. 234. MB did not resign from the AIA, but temporarily ceased to be chairman a few months later when it seemed possible he would be interned as an enemy alien.
52 The Public Works of Art Project, headed by Edward Bruce, was set up in December 1933 with a grant to the Treasury Department to employ artists on the embellishment of public buildings; 'Art in America', *The Studio*, April 1934, p. 221.
53 *Left Review*, vol. 1, no. 2, November 1934, p. 41; *Marx House Bulletin*, Winter 1934, n.p.
54 Recruiting leaflet, 1934, private collection.
55 Godden 1935, p. 80. G. M. Godden, 'Proletarian Art Comes to England, Godless Propaganda at an Exhibition in London', *Catholic Herald*, 27 October 1934, p. 9. EG letter, *Catholic Herald*, 3 November 1934, p. 9. BR, *International Literature*, no. 4, 1935, p. 102, reported an attendance of over two thousand.
56 TGA 771/1/3.
57 MacCarthy 1989, pp. 245–48.
58 *Catholic Herald*, 3 November 1934, p. 11. EG made a diary note that he wrote this on 27 October 1934 (TGA TAM 70), the same day as Godden's article appeared.
59 *Left Review*, vol. 1, no. 9, June 1935, pp. 341–42.
60 MacCarthy 1989, pp. 274–75.
61 Godden 1935, rev. edn 1938, p. 97.
62 *Left Review*, vol. 1, no. 2, November 1934, p. 40.
63 Writers who contributed to the first twelve issues of *Left Review* included: W. H. Auden, Phyllis Bentley, C. Day-Lewis, Lewis Grassic Gibbon, James Hanley, Winifred Holtby, Langston Hughes, Storm Jameson, John Lehmann, Naomi Mitchison, J. B. Priestley, Siegfried Sassoon, George Bernard Shaw, Stephen Spender and Stefan Zweig. In April 1936 JH was cited as being *Left Review*'s Art Editor; *Left Review*, vol. 2, no. 7, April 1936, p. 352.
64 See John Lucas, 'An Interview with Edgell Rickword', *Renaissance and Modern Studies*, vol. 10, 1976, p. 6. Rickword recalled the attendance as being 'about fifteen of us, Hugh MacDiarmid, I think, Bert Lloyd, Ralph Fox, Amabel Williams-Ellis, Tom Wintringham and others'. This would make AL the only known attendee at both the AI and *Left Review* founding meetings. In April 1934 the Writers International, in an intermediate step towards the launch of *Left Review*, published the journal *Viewpoint* with a claim to stand for 'militant Communism and for individualism and metaphysics in the arts'; see Radford in Croft 1998, p. 34.
65 Of the 188 images, JB contributed 41, JH 44, JF 20 and PB 12; the remaining 71 were provided by 43 other artists.
66 The first example of this occurred with JF's *Esprit de Corps* (*Left Review*, vol. 1, no. 3, December 1934), where the jodhpur-wearing white colonial confronting two tribesmen seems to have been conceived as the son of the male figure in JB's *You Gotta Have Blue Blood* two issues prior; for joint projects see in particular the Alpha Group's *It's Up to Us*, discussed on p. 138.
67 The penetrating, slightly aghast eye of an outsider is evident in much of JB's creation of class archetypes

in his *Left Review* work of 1934–38. In 1990 Jimmy Friel, who came south from Glasgow to work as 'Gabriel' on the *Daily Worker*, expressed a similar perspective: 'I stayed seething at all those bloody Baldwin's, and platitudes over the radio ... the fatuous newsreels and I just wanted to hit out at them. I saw the Hunger Marchers on the streets, and on the cinema screens there were the Bright Young Things, pushing prams down Mayfair to some fancy dress party, or the wealthy at grouse shoots or Baldwin and Chamberlain invoking the national family "all in it together" ... I don't know why there wasn't a bloody revolution'; see Radford in Croft 1998, p. 30, citing Peter Mellini, 'Gabriel's Message', *History Today*, February 1990, pp. 46–52.
68 Reviewed by Douglas Goldring in *The Studio*, July 1934, pp. 154–55. Grosz was by now in the USA; having accepted an invitation to teach at the Arts Student League of New York in 1932, on returning to Germany he had carefully prepared his escape from Berlin with his wife on 12 January 1933, a fortnight before Hitler came to power. *The Social Viewpoint in Art* included four works by Grosz.
69 Hamilton's *The Plains of Cement* was published in 1934, the third novel in the trilogy subsequently known as *Twenty Thousand Streets Under the Sky*; the first, *The Midnight Bell*, which revolved around life in a Kings Cross pub, was first published in 1928.
70 *Left Review*, vol. 1, no. 5, February 1935, p. 153, and vol. 1, no. 6, March 1935, p. 192.
71 See Thom Young, *Incitement to Disaffection*, Cobden Trust, 1976, p. 67. JH in *Left Review*, vol. 1, no. 4, January 1935, p. 115; JB in vol. 1, no. 6, March 1935, p. 226; vol. 1, no. 9, June 1935, p. 363. TW's leading article in vol. 1, no. 1, October 1934, concluded: 'The LEFT REVIEW calls on all its readers and all its contributors to join in the fight against the Sedition Bill, and incites them to maximum disaffection with the authors of its proposals.'
72 PB contributed sixteen lithographs and fourteen pen drawings to Philip Godfrey, *Back Stage: A Survey of Contemporary English Theatre from Behind the Scenes*, Harrap, 1933.
73 I am extremely grateful to the fashion historian Professor Emerita Lou Taylor, PB's younger daughter, for making available PB's 1930s travel diaries held in the family collection for this study.
74 At the Olympia meeting of 7 June 1934, fascist stewards used extreme violence against protestors and the resulting publicity led to the withdrawal of endorsement from the *Daily Mail* and other right-wing Tory press publications, a turning point at which the 'respectable phase' of BUF activity came to an end.
75 PB diary, 5 September 1934.
76 PB diary, 6 November 1934. PB visited Yakov Meksin (1886–1943), a teacher and poet who had opened a Museum of Children's Books in Leningrad in 1934. In 1937 he was arrested and the museum closed down, its collection of 70,000 books dispersed; he died in prison in 1943.
77 Elwyn-Jones 1983, p. 47.

CHAPTER 3:
SOHO SQUARE

1 TGA 9610/1/14.
2 AIA 1935.
3 In extant documentation, this formulation first appears on the masthead of *AI Bulletin*, July/August 1935, TGA 8524/20.
4 In the plebiscite held on 13 January 1935, 90 per cent of those voting supported return of the Saar Basin – a League of Nations Mandated Territory since 1919 – to Germany; the poll was accompanied by widespread intimidation of non-Nazi voters.
5 WC, 'How I Paint', *The Listener*, 15 September 1937, p. 570.
6 This listing, which appeared prominently on the front cover of the exhibition catalogue, was previously used on the sending-in card issued in July 1935, TGA 7043/4/1.
7 Register of Alien Passengers Embarking at Port of Southampton, *Olympic* Cunard White Star, for 14 February 1935, NA, departing passenger lists.
8 HB, an RCA contemporary of BR, was also presented at court; see Friend 2017, p. 33, note 48.
9 Ullmann 2008, p. 166.
10 NY memoir, pp. 137–41, TGA 20029/5/1.
11 *Design Today*, November 1934, pp. 415–19. The same edition carried a substantial feature on the MARS (Modern Architectural Research) exhibition at Olympia, the content of which had a significant overlap with the housing section of the AI's *Social Scene* exhibition in Charlotte Street.
12 The Hogarth Group was the artists' faction within the CPGB, and as the AIA expanded it functioned as an informal group within the broader coalition being assembled. Its name was adopted in homage to William Hogarth, who was seen as an exemplar of a socially conscious British artist. As well as BR, the group's known members included Christopher Cornford, Pat Carpenter, Norman Weaver, Roy Laurier, Lawrence Gowing, Reg Turner, NY, JH, Priscilla Thornycroft, CR, James Lucas, RH, PH, Carel Weight, Patrick Gieth, William Reed and Albert Patterson.
13 MB, in *Betty Rea: Sculpture*, memorial exhibition catalogue, June 1965, unpaginated, private collection.
14 PH archive, ESRO.
15 By taking second-floor premises at 4 Parton Street, a short narrow thoroughfare running from the north-west corner of Red Lion Square to the junction of Theobald's Road and Southampton Row, the AI had located itself in a cluster of alternative activities with Meg's café at its heart; much frequented by Central School students, the café was where Betty Soars, JB's future

wife, was waitressing when he met her. The Parton Street Bookshop, run by David Archer and specializing in 'Left novels, Poetry, criticism, Marxist, literature, Education etc', occupied the ground floor of number 4. Esmond Romilly's *Out of Bounds: Against Reaction in Public Schools* had been distributed from its basement and the Workers' Theatre Movement was headquartered there; the progressive publisher Ernest Wishart held the lease of number 2, and when he merged with the CP publisher Martin Lawrence, Lawrence & Wishart was located there, as was *Left Review* from early 1936. The Conway Hall, scene of many public meetings, was just around the corner in Red Lion Square itself.

16 *Left Review*, vol. 1, no. 8, May 1935, pp. 320 and 305 respectively.

17 NY memoir, p. 137, TGA 20029/5/1.

18 In early 1933 a commemoration committee was set up as the fiftieth anniversary of Marx's death approached. A conference of 190 labour movement delegates spanning trade unions, the CP, the ILP and Labour Party branches took place at Conway Hall on 11 March 1933 as the burning of books was underway in Germany, and the motion passed declared that the best memorial would be a Marxist library, workers' school and educational centre. Over the following six months substantial funds were collected, with CB and NB making a major contribution both financially and organizationally. At a second conference on 22 October 1933 the decision was taken to open at 37a Clerkenwell Green, where the first classes took place on 30 October; see Rothstein 1966, ch. 5.

19 Hastings 2014, pp. 116ff., for circumstances of his meeting with Rivera, and the book as a whole, from which these summary details are sourced, for his intriguing story.

20 Wight had visited the Soviet Union, in all probability accompanying Rivera to Moscow in 1927–28 as an invited guest on the occasion of the ten-year anniversary celebrations of the October Revolution.

21 For further analysis see also Alison McClean, 'England's Rivera: The Lost Murals of Viscount Hastings 1931–1939', *Visual Culture in Britain*, vol. 14, no. 2, 2013, pp. 199–217; Jody Patterson, '"Marx on the Wall": Muralism and Anglo-American Exchange in the 1930s', *Tate Papers*, no. 27, Spring 2017. For Rivera's contemporary account of these events see 'The Stormy Petrel of American Art: Diego Rivera on his Art', *The Studio*, July 1933, pp. 23–26.

22 Hastings 2014, p. 168; Waugh 1978, p. 55.

23 Haskell 2020, p. 28.

24 See Marcia Matthews, 'George Biddle's Contribution to Federal Art', *Records of the Columbia Historical Society*, vol. 49, 1973–74, pp. 493ff.

25 The original John Reed Club Unemployed Artists Group had been renamed the Artists' Union (AU) in February 1934.

26 Hemingway 2002, pp. 59–64.

27 Junius Cravens, 'Artists Fight to Prevent Changes in Coit Tower Frescos', *San Francisco News*, 7 July 1934, p. 12.

28 Hemingway 2002, pp. 92–97.

29 Waugh 1978, p. 63.

30 'Earl's Heir Paints Picture for Workers College', *Daily Mirror*, 10 October 1935, p. 23.

31 *Marx House Bulletin*, November 1935, MML.

32 HB to ER, 3 March 1935, ESRO. HB exhibited three copper engravings at the exhibition: *The Tea Party*, *The Message* and *Lane in Devon* (cats 91–93).

33 See, for example, AIA Central Committee minute book, 15 December 1938, TGA 20143.

34 BR, 'British Artists Go Left', *International Literature*, no. 4, 1935, pp. 100–3.

35 Ibid.; the article concludes: 'Altogether it is clear that there is a left-ward movement growing among progressive artists of all sections. The need of the moment is for correct leadership and the creation of channels of activity and organisation which will enable these artists and students to unite in action against the capitalist class on progress on culture and the approach of fascism and war. It is this task which the AI has set itself and the results already achieved give justification for some optimism. Betty Rea, Secretary, London.'

36 The delayed Seventh World Congress was held in Moscow from 25 July to 20 August 1935, attended by over five hundred delegates from sixty-five Comintern-affiliated parties. This new line was in part facilitated by the May 1935 Franco-Soviet Treaty of Mutual Assistance.

37 *AI Bulletin*, June 1935, p. 1, TGA 8022/12.

38 For AL, see Arthur 2012, chs 1–3, from which this account is derived.

39 Arthur 2012, p. 37.

40 AL, 'Modern Art and Modern Society', in AIA 1935, pp. 53ff.

41 AIA 1935, p. 7.

42 *AI Bulletin*, June 1935, p. 3, TGA 8022/12.

43 Petropoulos 2015, pp. 64–87.

44 PLP and his wife, Mary Macnaghten (1903–1998), arrived in London on 22 March 1933, as evidenced by an entry in her sister Antonia Macnaghten's diary, family collection. After the Reichstag fire both had been arrested and interrogated by the Gestapo but released as foreign nationals (PLP being Hungarian, Macnaghten British). Leaving in haste forced PLP to abandon over 1,200 artworks which were subsequently lost during the war; for comprehensive coverage of PLP's life and work see Hartog et al. 2023 and peterlaszloperi.org.uk (accessed 30 August 2024).

45 *1935 Exhibition: Artists Against Fascism and War*, cat. nos 80, 81, private collection.

46 Petropoulos 2015, p. 52.

47 KC, 'The Future of Painting', *The Listener*, 2 October 1935, p. 547.

48 FU left Germany on 24 March 1933; Uhlman 1960, p. 134.

49 The three exhibitions at the Galerie Le Niveau in Boulevard Montparnasse ran from 12 October to 26 December 1935 under the titles *Villages*, *La Fantaisie dans l'Art* and *La Nuit*; FU's co-exhibitors included Derain, Dufy, Lhote, Renoir, Soutine, Utrillo and Vlaminck.

50 *Left Review*, vol. 1, no. 11, August 1935, pp. 446–63. The English delegation to the Congress consisted of E. M. Forster, Aldous Huxley and John Strachey, with Amabel Williams-Ellis and Ralph Fox the organizers of a group which included PB, HR and MS; their statement was also endorsed by Walter Greenwood, James Hanley, Winifred Holtby, Storm Jameson and Naomi Mitchison.

51 Aldous Huxley, catalogue foreword.

52 Muirhead Bone (1876–1953); Frank Dobson (1886–1963); Eric Kennington (1888–1960); Charles Cundall (1890–1971); Adrian Allinson (1890–1959); Lucien Pissarro (1863–1944); Ethel Walker (1861–1951).

53 *The Listener*, 2 October 1935, pp. 54–55; *Left Review*, vol. 2, no. 4, January 1936, pp. 161–64.

54 *Left Review*, vol. 2, no. 4, January 1936.

55 *AI Bulletin*, June 1935, p. 2, TGA 8022/12: 'French Exhibition: We regret that it was eventually impossible for us to send work for inclusion in the Anti-War, Anti-Fascist Exhibition in Paris. The exhibition was eventually shown in the French organisation's own headquarters, and there was not sufficient room for the inclusion of any foreign work.'

56 *AI Bulletin*, May 1935, 'Autumn Exhibition Preliminary Announcement', p. 3, private collection.

57 *Catholic Herald*, 22 November 1935, p. 10.

58 VW to CB, 19 February 1935, VW to QB, 27 February and 3 April 1935, in Nicolson 1979, pp. 381–82. VW opens the first of these letters: 'Mr Bluit of the Fascist Exhibition has been to see me about a letter you have written to the Committee' – evidently this was AB; see also Lilly 2003, pp. 29–54.

59 In Q. Bell 1995, p. 37, written four decades later, QB asserts that Angelica was apolitical to the point of finding politics 'a bore', a quality which recommended her to CB. QB goes on to say: 'Vanessa was even more ignorant of politics than her sister ... Yet Vanessa, compared to her daughter, was a veritable Rosa Luxemburg'; but this judgment is out of kilter with evidence that, in the 1938–39 period when she was a pupil at the Euston Road School, Angelica Bell had a significant involvement in the Artists' Refugee Group and solidarity activities with the Spanish, including the AIA's hoarding campaign in support of 'Foodships for Spain'. QB's memories, however, may attest to Angelica being unwilling to reveal her politics to CB.

60 For the evolution of JBe's politics at Cambridge see Stansky and Abrahams 1966, pp. 108–9.

61 See Lilly 2003, p. 30, note 2, for a description of the documentation held in the BL under Cambridge: Miscellaneous Institutions and Societies WP 7937 000578515; *International Literature*, vol. 1, no. 7, 1934, n.p.

62 VW diary, 20 February 1935, Woolf 1982, p. 280.

63 AB memoir held in Russian Intelligence (NKVD) Archives TONY File no 83895, vol. 1, p. 240, quoted in Carter 2001, pp. 101–2.

64 AB began writing regularly for the *Spectator* in 1933; Carter 2001, p. 88.

65 Hussey 2021, p. 161.

66 Hussey 2021, pp. 180ff., citing CB to VB, 10 June 1918.

67 The Tonypandy Riots of 1910–11 began when strikers confronted police during the long-running dispute to improve wages held down by the Cambrian cartel; after discussions with the War Office Churchill as Home Secretary reluctantly authorized deployment of the army to the area; over five hundred civilians and eighty police are thought to have been injured before the disturbances were suppressed.

68 In marrying Hannah Taylor Cory in 1874, William Heward Bell cemented his relations with the firm of Nixon, Taylor & Cory, a large coal-shipping concern and colliery owner based in Cardiff, where Hannah's father was a partner. William Bell's uncle John Nixon founded the company; the Bell forebears were small farmers in the Cheviots and after William Bell became a director of the company in 1901 the family accumulated capital from ownership of coal mines in Cynon Valley and Merthyr Vale.

69 C. Bell 1928, pp. 175–76.

70 Hussey 2021, p. 300.

71 AI membership reached 250 in the first half of 1936, *AIA Bulletin*, no. 18, July/August 1936, p. 1, private collection, and approximately five hundred by early 1937; it probably peaked at approximately nine hundred in 1939. For a further review of the Soho Square exhibition by FK, and the tensions involved in bringing different aesthetic tendencies into harness, see Pooke 2007, p. 117.

72 RGASPI F 541, Op. 1.D.50, conversation of the English artist Pearl Binder with M. S. Veleskayan, 2 December 1935.

73 *Left Review*, vol. 1, no. 8, May 1935, pp. 333–34, carried a review of the book by A. L. Morton; separately, the same issue published PB's lithograph *Chalking Squad*. The book was also favourably reviewed twice in the *Observer*, 10 March 1935, p. 6, and 31 March 1935, p. 8.

74 Mirsky 1935, p. 113: 'Bloomsbury liberalism can be defined as thin-skinned humanism for enlightened and sensitive members of the capitalist class who do not desire the outer world to be such as might be prone to cause them any displeasing impression.'

75 RGASPI F 541, Op. 1.D.50.

76 See McClean, 'England's Rivera', p. 206, for discussion of JH's *Welcome to Pearl Binder* painted at the private residence of D. N. Pritt and his wife Molly, who became the dedicatees of PB's *Misha and Masha* in 1936.

CHAPTER 4: CHARING CROSS ROAD

1 The American Artists' Congress exhibition took place at Herman Baron's ACA Gallery 10–23 November 1935. The gallery became the pre-eminent venue for one-person and group shows of social art in the second half of the 1930s; see Hemingway 2002, pp. 47–48 and 136–44. It was previously located at 1269 Madison Avenue, where it was the location for the exhibition *Twenty John Reed Club Artists on Proletarian and Revolutionary Themes* in November 1932.
2 *New Masses*, vol. 17, no. 1, 1 October 1935, p. 33. *New Masses* had a considerable readership in London, as evidenced by the fact that five speakers at the *Left Review* contributors' conference held at Conway Hall on 13 April 1935 referred to it as an exemplar for that publication; see *Left Review*, vol. 1, no. 9, June 1935, p. 367. The 'call' appeared in the same form in *Art Front*, November 1935, p. 6.
3 See Greening 2006, p. 67, for the role of Collet's Cardiff shop in Charles Street in this chain.
4 See Cooper and Haskell 2016, p. 174, quoting Romany Marie; for an overall analysis of *Art Front* and SD's role as editor and own writings therein see Monroe 1973, pp. 15–16.
5 SD's review, which opened 'The paintings of Salvador Dalí are completely successful', appeared in *Art Front*, January 1935, p. 7. It was followed the next month by reviews by Clarence Weinstock, who conceded that Dalí was 'a sophisticated illustrator', and Jerome Klein, for whom Dalí and the surrealists were 'neurotically incapable of giving their effort a point of leverage in the real world, having dodged the issue of revolutionary art'; both *Art Front*, February 1935, p. 8.
6 The 'call' also cited in its preamble the Old Court House in St Louis and the Abraham Lincoln High School, as well as the Museum of Modern Art and the Rockefeller Center, as among the 'important public and semi-public institutions [where] suppression, censorship or actual destruction of art works has occurred'.
7 'Morals in Murals', *Art Front*, July 1935, p. 3. Mural designs by Shahn and Block that had been developed with funds from the Temporary Emergency Relief Administration were rejected by the NYC Municipal Art Commission as 'psychologically unfit' and 'anti-social'; as SD noted in an editorial, murals funded by the Treasury Section were meeting 'with official approval in inverse order to their social and artistic worth'. Patterson 2020, p. 207, explains that the mural panels 'presented criminality as a socioeconomic issue and offered a politically charged perspective on the importance of reform within the corrections system ... their rejection became a cause célèbre in the New York cultural milieu, generating heated debate once again around issues of freedom of expression and censorship.'
8 The American Writers' Congress took place on 26–28 April 1935, out of which developed the League of American Writers. Its European counterpart was the Paris congress attended by PB, which took place in June 1935. The second International Writers' Congress took place in Valencia and Madrid during July 1937, by which time communist and socialist tensions were running high.
9 *Art Digest*, no. 10, 15 November 1935, p. 25.
10 See Haskell 2020, pp. 19–20 and 220. Orozco's 1931 murals filled four dining-room walls and one of an exterior lounge; two depicted political struggle in Russia, India and Mexico and two others an idealized post-revolutionary world of interracial harmony, productive labour and domestic tranquillity; because the latter featured a conference in which people of all races are presided over by a black person, it became a cause of controversy, leading to loss of some donor support for the school.
11 The public session speakers included SD, Lewis Mumford, Rockwell Kent, Aaron Douglas, Joe Jones, Margaret Bourke-White, Paul Manship, George Biddle, Heywood Brown, Francis J. Gorman and Peter Blume; subsequent days included, among many others, Meyer Schapiro, Lynd Ward, Weber, Ralph M. Pearson, Harry Gottlieb, Louis Lozowick, Margaret Duroc, Hugo Gellert, Boris Gorelick, Henry Billings, Orozco and Siqueiros.
12 The decision created a forty-six-member national executive committee; with twenty-six New York-based members, sixteen representing fifteen states, and four officers.
13 Baigell and Williams 1986, p. 18.
14 Baigell and Williams 1986, p. 62.
15 Baigell and Williams 1986, p. 215.
16 *AIA Bulletin*, no. 15, April 1936, private collection.
17 *Left Review*, vol. 2, no. 8, May 1936, pp. 381–84.
18 See Monroe 1974 for analysis of this resistance.
19 MB, 'An Equity for Artists?', *Left Review*, vol. 2, no. 7, April 1936, pp. 330ff.
20 *Left Review*, vol. 2, no. 9, June 1936, p. 473.
21 The meeting was held at Friends Meeting House, and the initial committee membership was listed in *AIA Bulletin*, no. 18, July/August 1936, as 'Messrs Misha Black, James Fitton, Rintow, Turner, Thomas Gray, Clay, Kinsman, Boswell, Lucas'.
22 Unpublished JF memoir, p. 144, privately held. PH had moved from 7 Camden Studios to 11 Pond Cottages by December 1932.
23 Sheeran 1986, p. 17.

24 *Left Review* had been formally established at a conference held at Conway Hall in February 1934, well ahead of its first issue in October 1934; as reported in *Left Review*, vol. 1, no. 9, June 1935, the meeting – variously described as a policy conference, a contributors' conference and a readers' conference – took place on 13 April 1935 at the same venue. The meeting concluded with Simon Blumenfeld, J. Crowther, JB, JF, Bob Ellis, Dr Rosenveld, Herbert Read, Barbara Nixon, John Summerfield, Alick West, PB, JH and Alec Brown joining the *Left Review* committee, which added West to the editorial board at its first meeting.
25 *Left Review*, vol. 2, no. 7, April 1936, p. 352; this also announced a new category of associate membership. Helen Wilson had now taken over as secretary, but by June the secretary is EW; by December JH had taken on role of organizing study circles, held at 9 Great Newport St WC2, on 'Working for Reproduction'.
26 *Left Review*, vol. 2, no. 9, June 1936, p. 418.
27 FEJ letter to PB, 2 February 1936, family collection.
28 *Left Review*, vol. 2, no. 10, July 1936, p. 536; a subsequent announcement in *Left Review*, vol. 2, no. 12, September 1936, added: 'Here is a new technique in the service of PEACE, not just another exhaustive and exhausting treatise ... Every page is a poster at first sight and a mine of information on closer acquaintance.'
29 It was nearly two years since Max Eastman's *Artists in Uniform* had broadcast doubts about freedom of expression in Soviet Russia, but Gide – who, before he hastened to Gorky's deathbed, had been expected in London to address the Writers International – was some months away from signalling his apostasy with publication of *Retour de l'USSR* in November 1936.
30 *Left Review*, vol. 2, no. 3, December 1935, p. 126. The series was jointly sponsored by AIA, *Left Review* and the Architects and Technicians' Organisation, with Wells Coates, Berthold Lubetkin, Alec Brown and MS the first speakers announced; BR was secretary to the series.
31 *Left Review*, vol. 2, no. 9, June 1936, p. 473.
32 KC, *New Statesman*, 22 December 1934; AB, *Spectator*, 2 November 1934. For a fuller discussion see Remy 1999, p. 34.
33 See Penrose 1981, part one: 'Finding A Way'.
34 Remy 1999, pp. 63 and 73–74; King 1960, pp. 160ff.
35 Danos and Gibelin 1986, pp. 63–72.
36 PN, *News Chronicle*, 7 June 1937, p. 10, reproduced in Causey 2000, pp. 139–40.
37 Ibid., p. 140.
38 Binyon 1983, p. 94.
39 AL, 'Surrealism and Revolutions', *Left Review*, vol. 2, no. 16, January 1937, p. 297.
40 Speech notes for PLP's contribution survive in the family collection curated by his grandson, the artist Peter Peri; AB became a significant supporter of PLP and the following year was instrumental in the staging of PLP's exhibition *The New Realism in Sculpture* at the Gordon Fraser Gallery in Cambridge in April 1937. FK, another speaker at the debate, wrote an introductory essay on the occasion of PLP's exhibition *From Constructivism to Realism*, which had been held at the Foyle Art Gallery in May 1936.
41 *AIA Bulletin*, no. 18, July/August 1936, p. 3, private collection.
42 The *Dutch Interiors* are a series of three paintings painted by Joan Miró in 1928, each inspired by Dutch golden age paintings. *Dutch Interior I* is a reinterpretation of Hendrik Martenszoon Sorgh's *Lute Player*; *Dutch Interior II* is a reinterpretation of Jan Steen's *Children Teaching a Cat to Dance*; and *Dutch Interior III* is a reinterpretation of *Young Woman at her Toilet*, also by Steen.
43 A report on the proceedings by Derek Kahn, *Left Review* assistant editor, appeared in *Left Review*, vol. 2, no. 10, July 1936, pp. 481–90, with PB sketches of John Strachey and H. G. Wells. Maxim Gorky died in Moscow the day before the congress opened, and the first show trial, with Zinovyev, Kamenev and Smirnov among the sixteen defendants accused of plotting with Trotsky to overthrow Stalin, concluded after six days on 24 August 1936, with all defendants found guilty and shot the following morning.
44 Ralph Fox, 'A Picture of Socialist Life', *Left Review*, vol. 2, no. 16, January 1937, p. 913.
45 PB was one of twenty-nine signatories to a tribute to Ralph Fox in *Left Review*, vol. 3, no. 1, February 1937, which led with news of his death and also previewed his posthumous *The Novel and The People*, Lawrence & Wishart, 1937. *Left Review*, vol. 3, no. 2, March 1937, pp. 67–68, carried a tribute to Cornford and his poem 'Full Moon at Tierz: Before the storming of Huesca'.
46 Elwyn-Jones 1983, pp. 49–51; these other expeditions to Europe enabled FEJ to write *The Battle for Peace*, published by the Left Book Club in August 1938, one of the most forensic and prescient pre-Munich analyses of the advance of fascism in Europe.
47 PB to FEJ, 22 December 1935: 'What my job is to tare [*sic*] down illusions ... to show things as they really are in England ... It will be much easier for me now I've found you Elwyn Bach, because I need love stability in my emotional life (and you too surely) and one's first task is to concentrate and direct one's energies in the right and continuous direction. Don't you think? No more Carol's, no more Jack's, no more Margaret Lane's ... and perhaps no more Naomi's either.' The first three names referred to Jack Driberg, PB's first husband, who was proving elusive when it came to finalizing a divorce, and two intimate female friends; 'Naomi' to an admirer of FEJ.

48 PB kept a book of work ideas, assignments and fees received. Prior to his death, PB and Ralph Fox were contemplating a book called *Workers*; PB also began preparatory work for a book described as *Left, Right* along with *Two Worlds*, a montage social-political book which was potentially intended for Bodley Head. In the event her next illustrated book, drawing on her Moscow sketchbooks, was Bertha Malnick's *Everyday Life in Soviet Russia*, Harrap, 1938, to which she contributed forty-four line drawings. While PB was in Moscow, FEJ had discussed working with ETH on a book about South Wales.
49 Uhlman 1960, pp. 186–88.
50 García 2010, p. 210. Page Croft was nothing if not consistent: he regarded General Dyer, the perpetrator of the Amritsar massacre in British India, as the 'gallant soldier whose action possibly saved the white inhabitants and loyal Indians from dreadful carnage'; Page Croft 1948, p. 149.
51 Uhlman 1960, p. 197. FU continued to exhibit at Galerie Le Niveau in Paris and travel back and forth after his move to England, a liaison that was subsequently germane to the formation of the FGLC in 1938–39.
52 Diana Page Croft to FU, 19 June 1936, quoted in Anna Müller-Härlin, 'An Unconventional Couple: Diana and Fred Uhlman and their support for Exiled Artists', in Bohm-Duchen 2019, p. 189.
53 Letter to EW, n.d. but 1935/36, quoted in Buchanan 2007, p. 65.
54 Buchanan 2007, p. 82; *Left Review*, vol. 2, no. 13, October 1936, p. 688.
55 Buchanan 2007, p. 82, and ch. 4 for full analysis. *Left Review*, vol. 2, no. 13, October 1936, p. 688, noted: 'She travelled widely, especially in the Tatra mountains, earning her living by making portraits of the inhabitants of the villages through which she passed. In the summer of this year she had planned a tour of this kind through the Sierra Guarra in Aragon.'
56 Nevinson exhibited *The Twentieth Century*; Peri the concrete frieze *Against Fascism and War* depicting a demonstration in Hyde Park and a bronze of a footballer; Rea *Mother and Child*; Pissarro *Les Chardons* and *Les Brusq*; Dismorr *Compositions nos 1 and 2*; Simon a print, *Cinema*; de Sausmarez a print, *Night*; Watson two oils titled *Suzanna* and *The Seine*; Weight an oil, *La Symphonie Tragique*; and Rowe an oil painting titled *Roadworkers*, now known only from a newspaper photograph; other AIA contributors were Michael Appleton, Stella Burford, V. Cunningham, Mervyn Franklin, Orovida and Helen Wilson.
57 FB talked enthusiastically about the potential for painting 'earth coloured towns only distinguishable from the hills by shadows', and 'not Tossa, the country inland' in her letters to EW of 31 July 1936 and her last letter of 7 August 1936; for FB letters see TGA 201023/2.
58 MML IBMA Box C 5/3, 10 September 1936.
59 NY memoir, TGA 20029/5/1; this account of NY in the 1930s draws directly on her unpublished autobiography.
60 Ibid., pp. 134ff., for death of FB and meeting BR.
61 Trevelyan 1957, p. 57.
62 For the 'Declaration on Spain' see Remy 1999, pp. 104–6.
63 The Duke of Alba to Franco, 16 June 1937, cited by García 2010, p. 219, note 43, in which Franco's representative in London conveyed Lord Hailsham's analysis that he, Sir Samuel Hoare, William Morrison, Sir Thomas Inskip, Leslie Hoare-Belisha and Neville Chamberlain were supporters, with Eden, Halifax, John Simon and Duff Cooper opposed to the Nationalists and the rest undecided.
64 *Left Review*, vol. 2, no. 16, January 1937, p. 895; and for reply by HR and Hugh Sykes Davies, *Left Review*, vol. 3, no. 1, February 1937, pp. 47–48.
65 DG, introduction to the exhibition catalogue, *Drawings by Felicia Browne*, TGA 7043/3/1. VB to JBe, 5 September 1936; see TGA 9311 for VB's letters to JBe in China.
66 TGA 7043/3/2.
67 AIA *Artists' News-Sheet*, no. 1, new series, November 1936, p. 2: 'Artists back to your sketchbooks!', PH collection, ESRO.
68 Buchanan 2007, p. 46, and ch. 3 for British medical aid to Spain.
69 VB to JBe, 10 October 1936, TGA 9311.83.
70 *Left Review*, vol. 2, no. 13, October 1936, pp. 675–77.
71 JB's account 'Cable Street: A Demonstrator's Impressions' and accompanying drawings were published in the Lawrence & Wishart house journal *The Eye*, no. 7, September–November 1936.
72 The first mention of the proposed congress occurs in *AI Bulletin*, no. 18, July–August 1936, in the context of a meeting to be held at Friends Meeting House on 11 August concerning the International Peace Campaign, where 'the AIA committee will propose that early in 1937 a *National Congress of Artists* shall be convened to discuss in a practical way what the profession can do for peace and cultural freedom, and that simultaneously an exhibition shall be held to show the unity of artists of all schools of thought on these questions. Further we shall propose that all groups of artists be invited to take part in the organising of the conference and exhibition.'
73 *AIA Bulletin*, no. 1, new series, November 1936, PH archive, ESRO.
74 Renamed Boswell Street sometime in 1938, presumably to avoid confusion as there were at least two other Devonshire Streets in inner London, along with numerous Devonshire Crescents, Mews etc. There are no residential listings in the Post Office Directories for number 42, not unusual for flats and rooms above shops; in 1934 the entry reads 'Cappelletti, Mrs Mary, fried fish shop' while in 1935 it reads

'A. Schiavetti, Fried Fish Shop', a listing that continues until 1940.
75 HR to PH, 23 October 1936, PH archives, ESRO. A. C. Sewter (1912–1983) had studied at the LSE and the Courtauld; in 1935 he was appointed arts assistant at the Leicester Museum and Art Gallery, where he remained until 1939, pursuing a progressive acquisition policy and emphasizing the purchase of contemporary British and European art. The painting first appeared in *Exhibition of Contemporary Art*, which ran at the Leicester Gallery from 1 May to 20 June 1936.
76 Helen Wilson had briefly occupied the role earlier in 1936, when PH made the first of two attempts to persuade HB to become secretary. Clara Zetkin (1857–1933) had visited London in 1896 and 1909; John S. Partington notes her final major political intervention occurred in 1932 when 'as oldest member of the German national assembly, she was President by Seniority of the Reichstag following the general election, holding the chair until a speaker of the house could be elected. Although a ceremonial position, the Nazi Party made vigorous attempts, including threats of assassination, to prevent a Communist holding the position, and when Zetkin took up the post, she spoke for an hour, condemning the rise of Nazism and looking forward to the day when she could open the national assembly of a German Soviet Socialist Republic'; John S. Partington, 'The International Socialist Women's Secretary in Wartime: Clara Zetkin and Britain, 1912–1915', in Marilyn J. Boxer and John S. Partington (eds), *Clara Zetkin: National and International Contexts*, Socialist History Society, 2012, pp. 22–34. Following the vote, she relinquished the speaker's chair to Hermann Göring and returned to Moscow at a time CR was there; he was also there when, on her death in June 1933, she was interred in the Kremlin wall, with Stalin as one of the opal bearers.

CHAPTER 5: GROSVENOR SQUARE

1 The catalogue, *Unity of Artists for Peace, Democracy and Cultural Development*, PH archive, ESRO, lists 724 paintings, drawings and sculptures by title, but correlation with works cited or illustrated in press reviews suggests that a sizeable number were omitted from the catalogue. The errata listed seventy-nine works that were displayed in halls and staircases overlooked at an earlier stage of compilation; the Peace Publicity section lists artists by name, not works, and there are other signs of the catalogue's hurried completion.
2 *Shelf Appeal*, April 1937; press cutting in TGA 901/37, which also holds the other reviews and press cuttings drawn on in this chapter.
3 For the Pitmen Painters in general see Feaver 1988. Robert Lyon, the tutor who supported the group's formation, had been a contemporary of PH and HB at the RCA, and HB had been involved in hosting the visit of nineteen members of the Ashington Group to London on 14–16 February 1936; HB to ER, 12 February 1936, in Ullmann 2008, p. 265.
4 AIA *Artists' News-Sheet*, new series, no. 3, p. 4, February 1937, private collection. MB urged that the commission should be extremely well informed on recent government-commissioned policy exercises on art, industry and education; the same source suggests that QB and NY were elected as chairman and secretary of the overall commission, but NY memoir, p. 143, TGA 20029/5/1, explicitly states that they held these offices in relation to the art education stream alone. CR had an overall role as chairman of the organizing committee.
5 Frank Rutter (1876–1937), prolific art critic, curator, gallerist and prime organizer of the Allied Artists' Association 1908–12, before becoming curator at Leeds City Art Gallery, where he was closely associated with Leeds University vice-chancellor Michael Sadler, another significant sponsor of the AIA 1937 Congress. Rutter died shortly before the event and was buried at Hampstead two days before the opening public meeting; a passionate advocate of art and artists and a born organizer, he was a veteran figure in sympathy with the AIA's agenda.
6 The only surviving cyclostyled copy known to this author of the resolutions put to the congress is found in PA's papers at ESRO, PEG 4.
7 AIA *Artists' News-Sheet*, new series, no. 4, April 1937, p. 4, private collection.
8 The exhibition was held at the New School for Social Research from 15 April to 6 May 1936. The material quoted here is from Harry F. Ward's catalogue contribution; for AAC exhibition activity see Hemingway 2002, pp. 125–30.
9 ACA Gallery, 11–18 October 1936; see Hemingway 2002, p. 125.
10 AAC 1936. The duplicate exhibitions were held simultaneously in December 1936; the selection was made by SD, Hugo Gellert, William Gropper, Wanda Gág, Yasuo Kuniyoshi, Margaret Lowengrund, Louis Lozowick, George Picken, Harry Sternberg, Lynd Ward and Max Weber. Each juror made an individual selection of one hundred prints, and the hundred receiving the highest number were included in both book and exhibition; the former included an introduction explaining the techniques involved, such as etching, wood engraving or lithography, as well as the intent of the initiative.
11 AAC 1936, p. 6.
12 AAC 1936, p. 7.
13 Langa 2004, p. 208; Monroe 1974, p. 8.
14 Monroe 1974, p. 8. While average employment on the WPA as a whole decreased by 11.9 per cent from January to June 1937, that on the four major art programmes increased by 1.1 per cent.

15 *Left Review*, vol. 3, no. 5, June 1937, p. 289.
16 The members were Hastings, Labour MPs Seymour Cocks and William Dobbie, and Isabel Brown, who was a member of the CPGB.
17 García 2010, pp. 158–64.
18 Van Hensbergen 2004, pp. 23–24.
19 AIA *Artists' News-Sheet*, January 1937, p. 1, private collection.
20 POUM, acronym for Partido Obrero de Unificación Marxista (Workers' Party of Marxist Unification).
21 Buchanan 2007, p. 89; García 2010, p. 160.
22 Penrose 1981, pp. 84–85.
23 The broadsheet was published by the British Surrealist Group with fifteen named signatories – of these, ten were exhibitors at Grosvenor Square (Eileen Agar, JT, RP, Norman Dawson, Merlyn Evans, Ernő Goldfinger, G. Graham, Charles Howard, HM and PN); other signatories included the poets David Gascoyne and Hugh Sykes Davies, Rupert Lee and Herbert Read.
24 Gwen Raverat in a positive review in *Time and Tide*, 24 April 1937, quoted with approval the formulation: 'As the present exhibition amply testifies, the Artists' International Association does not stand for uniformity of expression: for the dragooning of artists or the sinking of individuality. On the contrary the exhibition demonstrates the richness and variety of work that can be produced by the vanguard.'
25 *Universe*, 30 April 1937, cutting in TGA 01/37; the article's author is not credited, but its style and content (which rehearses the AIA's history since its foundation) suggests it may have been written by G. M. Godden, who in 1937 would also have been working on the second edition of her book *The Communist Attack on Great Britain*.
26 Cork 1987, pp. 196–201.
27 Cork 1987, p. 222; Lipke 1967, pp. 75–82.
28 Bomberg was a founder member of the LG in 1913; the two paintings were no. 124 *Rhonda* [*sic*] *Procession – Corpus Christi* and no. 131 *Rhonda* [*sic*] *Night*.
29 Rose 2002, pp. 198–99.
30 Lipke 1967, p. 81; Wilcox 1995, pp. 25–28.
31 The photograph first appeared in *Wolverhampton Express and Star* and *Glasgow Evening Citizen* on 8 April 1937 but was widely syndicated; see TGA 901/37 for further examples, and for syndicated JE letter.
32 These included, surprisingly, one in the *Catholic Herald*, 23 April 1937, where the notice 'Pacific Arts' generated controversy on the letters pagers and an editorial disclaimer about communist fronts; TGA 901/37.
33 This was highlighted in the *Northern Whig* preview, and followed up by an article on John Brand, the retired postman, in the *Evening Standard*, 16 April 1937: 'Began Painting at 9: at 81 he has won "Recognition"', TGA 901/37.
34 *Observer*, 25 April 1937, p. 16.
35 *Sunday Dispatch*, 11 April 1937, TGA 901/37.
36 *Daily Mail*, Irish edition, 15 April 1937, TGA 901/37.
37 For analysis see Griffiths 1980, part 3, pp. 308, 358 and 363.
38 *Sunday Dispatch*, 25 April 1937, anonymous interviewee but possibly CR; TGA 901/37.
39 Van Hensbergen 2004, p. 36; the officer was Michael Culmer-Seymour.
40 See Richardson 2021, p. 136, on revelation of this by historian Xabier Irujo in *Gernika, 1937: The Market Day Massacre*, University of Nevada Press, 2015. Logistical problems delayed Hermann Göring's plan by six days.
41 There has long been controversy over the numbers that died; Van Hensbergen 2004, p. 42, cites 1,645 dead and 889 injured; whatever the numbers, the intent was explicit.
42 Richardson 2021, p. 136; for Page Croft see García 2010, pp. 59–60, 128, 185, 190, 219, 231.
43 Richardson 2021, p. 142, is specific that this happened on 4 June 1937.
44 The etchings were *The Dream and Lie of Franco*; for the delegation see Van Hensbergen 2004, pp. 28–29.
45 The statement is attributed to Juan Negrín (1892–1956), physician and leader of the Spanish Socialist Workers' Party who replaced Largo Caballero as Prime Minister of the Republic on 17 May 1937, having served as finance minister in the Popular Front government since September 1936.
46 Russell 1968, pp. 129–30, quoted in Berthoud 1987, p. 162. RP's account of what is probably the same occasion possibly elides two visits, suggesting the visit was an evening one and took place shortly before the painting was transported to the Spanish Pavilion, yet it is consistent about Picasso's words and that it took place at a stage when Picasso was still considering adding colour to the otherwise black, white and grey-toned composition; Penrose 1981, p. 103.
47 Spalding 1983, p. 294. JBe left England for Spain on 7 June 1937, having waited for some time for Spanish Medical Aid to confirm a departure date.
48 QB's recollections are to be found in his preface to Watson 1994; further material in Kapp 2003, pp. 177–81. Artists listed on the programme and promotional material as supporters of *Spain and Culture* – and also supporters of the exhibition and congress – were VB, JE, DG, JH, EMK, HM, PN, Ben Nicholson and Edward Wadsworth.
49 See Martin 2014, pp. 51ff., for a good description of the event.
50 For a perceptive introduction to WT's life and work see Forge 1976. WT's extensive journals for these years, which give fascinating insight into his reactions to unfolding events, are held in University College London Special Collections.
51 Notice in *New Statesman & Nation*, 17 April 1937, TGA 901/37.
52 WT journals, 24 April 1937.
53 Forge 1976, p. 41.
54 *Manchester Guardian*, 2 July 1937, p. 22.

55 NY memoir, pp. 151–52, TGA 20029/5/1.
56 *Left Review*, vol. 3, no. 7, August 1937, p. 415; Radford 1987, p. 59.
57 P. Morton Shand, 'Second Thoughts on the Paris Exhibition', *The Listener*, 28 July 1937, p. 189.
58 Petropoulos 2015, pp. 287–89.
59 Van Hensbergen 2004, p. 72.
60 AB, 'From Bloomsbury to Marxism', *Studio International*, November 1973, p. 17; AB, 'Art in Paris', *Spectator*, 6 August 1937, p. 214.
61 Carter 2001, pp. 201ff. AB's public position at the time was encapsulated in the argument that 'a full realist must be able to devote himself to the painting of the most important facts or ideas of his time, the central realities of his period and paint them in a direct way', Day-Lewis 1937, pp. 103ff.; however, as Carter notes, a de luxe edition of *The Dream and Lie of Franco* purchased in 1937 was found among AB's possessions after he died. For the evolution of AB's view of Picasso and *Guernica* see *Spectator*, 9 April 1937, p. 664, and 8 October 1937, p. 584; *The Listener*, 28 July 1938, p. 182; Christopher Green, 'Anthony Blunt's Picasso', *Burlington Magazine*, January 2005, pp. 26–33; and Blunt 1969 in its entirety.
62 *Spectator*, 9 April 1937, p. 664.
63 *The Listener*, 28 July 1938, p. 182.
64 AB, 'The British Artists' Congress', *Spectator*, 30 April 1937, p. 806.
65 AB, 'The Realism Quarrel', *Left Review*, vol. 3, no. 3, April 1937, pp. 169–71.
66 The exhibition ran 1–24 June 1938. AB contributed a catalogue introduction to *The New Realism in Sculpture* at the Gordon Fraser Gallery, Cambridge, April 1937; see also *Spectator*, 5 June 1936, p. 1037.
67 Ewan Phillips (1914–1994); Radford 1987, p. 32. EP's extensive papers can be found at TGA 8217 and 9610.
68 Irmgard Burchard (1908–1964), Swiss painter. Patrons of the *20th Century German Art* exhibition included W. G. Constable, David Low, Sir Michael Sadler and HR, who chaired the organizing committee with AJ as president; other patrons included KC and John Rothenstein (respectively the directors of the National Gallery and the Tate Gallery), Sir Edward Marsh, Maillol, Picasso, Renoir, H. G. Wells, Virginia Woolf and Clive Bell and the Czech anti-fascist novelist and playwright Karel Čapek, who would die shortly after the betrayal of his country at Munich later in 1938.
69 TGA 920/10/3/4, Peter Thoene, with an introduction by Herbert Read, *Modern German Art*, Pelican Special, Penguin Books, 1938. Peter Thoene was a pseudonym for Oto Bihalji-Merin (1904–1993), the Serbian painter, writer, art historian; HR noted that modern German art was almost entirely unknown to the general public and almost entirely neglected by critics, collectors and dealers. The catalogue cited Cranach, Altdorfer and Grünewald as German predecessors and noted (p. 7): 'the artists represented here are the German equivalents of artists like Degas, Cezanne, Seurat, Matisse and Picasso in France, or of Walter Sickert, Augustus John, Jacob Epstein, Duncan Grant, Paul Nash and Ben Nicholson in our own country.'
70 TGA 920/10/3/4, p. 6; also, that the organizers were merely asserting that 'art, as an expression of the human spirit in all its mutations, is only great so far as it is free'.
71 Hitler's speech was made on 11 July 1938; AIA handbill, TGA 8214.
72 CR contributed an early critique in spring 1934 when he reviewed *Objective Abstractions* at the Zwemmer Gallery in *Viewpoint*, *Left Review*'s immediate predecessor; CR, 'The Position of Art Today', *Viewpoint*, April–June 1934, pp. 17–19. The artists involved included GB, WC, Ceri Richards, Ivon Hitchens, Geoffrey Tibble, Thomas Carr and Rodrigo Moynihan, who was the principal organizer.
73 Morris and Radford 1983, p. 43.
74 Laughton 1986, pp. 143–45, for a detailed analysis of how the venture emerged from a fusion of Claude Rogers's prospectus for starting a new art school, encouraged by Helen Anrep, and 'The Plan for Artists' circulated by GB and WC, with KC emerging as the *deus ex machina* backing two separate but simultaneous schemes where, to varying degrees, VP, WC and GB were subsidized as painters and Rogers financially backed to run an art school with their help.
75 WC, 'How I Paint', *The Listener*, 15 September 1937, p. 570: 'But such a direction was difficult for me to take wholeheartedly because my generation of painters had been taught to regard all movements except those away from realism as artistically reactionary.'
76 GB, 'Escape from Escapism', *Left Review*, vol. 3, no. 11, December 1937, pp. 663–66.
77 *The Listener*, 15 September 1937, p. 572.
78 *Left Review*, vol. 3, no. 11, December 1937, p. 666.
79 Forge 1976, pp. 43–44.
80 Hemingway 2002, p. 126.
81 Morris and Radford 1983, p. 43.
82 Remy 1999, p. 161: 'the surrealists' reaction was immediate and violent; their reply, in the following issue of the *News-Sheet* signed among others by Eileen Agar, James Cant, Sam Haile, Ceri Richards, Henry Moore, F. E. McWilliam, Penrose and Trevelyan threatened their withdrawal from the AIA if that was its official attitude. The AIA apologised saying they recognised the surrealists' "efficacy" and undeniable sympathy for the supporters of peace and democracy.'
83 AB, *Spectator*, 25 March 1938. PH, writing as 'Toros' in *Left Review*, vol. 3, no. 16, May 1938, p. 107, also reviewed the Wildenstein exhibition as 'too narrow for its title as cross-section of English painting' and as raising the question 'what is Social Realism?' without answering it; PH concluded 'social realism

means discoveries on a bigger and grander scale than these painters are achieving at present.'
84 Remy 1999, p. 161; King 1960, p. 170.
85 Humphrey Jennings (1907–1950), already a roving lensman for the *Daily Mirror*, was also part of the project as a photographer. A fourth painter was Michael Wickham, 'an impressionist, vivid Gauguin sort of stuff'; *The Listener*, 25 August 1938, pp. 398–400.
86 GB's *Bolton* appeared as cat. 36 at the AIA's Whitechapel exhibition the following year, and JT's works as cats 112 and 113, *The Potteries* and *The Potteries No. 2*.
87 George Orwell, 'Looking Back on the Spanish Civil War' (written autumn 1942), published in *New Road: New Perspectives in European Art and Letters, Volume 1*, Grey Walls Press, 1943.
88 Page Croft 1948, p. 293.
89 Trevelyan 1957, pp. 79–80.
90 Van Hensbergen 2004, p. 89.
91 NY memoir, pp. 153–55, TGA 20029/5/1; Morris and Radford 1983, p. 51.
92 Philip Evergood (1901–1973), socialist painter, etcher, lithographer who studied at the Slade 1921–23, before returning to USA; see Monroe 1974, p. 9, for specific occasion as AU President.
93 See Boswell 1947, pp. 25–38, for a survey of economic conditions and structures impacting artists in the late 1930s.
94 TGA 9610/3/14.
95 Mykhailo Lvovych Boichuk (1882–1937) was a Ukrainian modernist painter and leading member of the 'Executed Renaissance' generation; for Boichukism see Akinsha et al. 2023, pp. 42–47.
96 CC minutes, 7 December 1938, TGA 20143.
97 Now known only from a photograph, reproduced in Remy 1999, p. 119; the exhibition was *Surrealist Objects and Poems* of 1937. Dawson may have been referencing a cardboard cut-out of Chamberlain dressed in waders and fishing, which had featured in the British Pavilion at the 1937 Paris Exposition.

CHAPTER 6:
WHITECHAPEL HIGH STREET

1 TGA 20143. These meetings are recorded in detail in a minute book found among a collection of Morris Kestelman's uncatalogued papers; this covers sixty meetings that took place between autumn 1938 and June 1940 and provides hitherto unavailable but invaluable insight into the AIA between Munich and the Fall of France.
2 See Atkinson 2021, for comprehensive analysis of MB's career as exhibition designer, and esp. p. 44 for detail about New York assignment where MB, MG and Walter Landauer designed the Public Welfare Hall, the Maritime Hall and the china, leather and woollen trades sections of the British Pavilion. In the Maritime Hall MB represented 9,000 ships with tiny models on a gigantic world map to signify the global reach of British maritime trade; ER was recruited to work on this project, designing an extensive set of engraved copper symbols inlaid with enamel to represent peoples, places and commodities.
3 ES was a retiring member of previous CC; neither SH nor F. E. McWilliam were signatories to the 1937 Surrealist Manifesto, but both had exhibited at Grosvenor Square, SH with *Distressed Area*, cat. 259, and *Non-Payment of Taxes – Congo Christian Era*, cat. 233, and McWilliam with *Composition*, cat. 278.
4 'AIA: The first five years 1933–1948', brochure of December 1938, p. 4, col. 2, private collection.
5 This took place 16–28 January 1939.
6 With work largely selected from the Whitechapel exhibition, the itinerary included Southport, York, Bradford, Hanley, Kidderminster and Carlisle.

7 CC minutes, 8 November 1938, TGA 20143: 'A scheme to produce colour litho prints of the work of contemporary artists, at a price within reach of the majority, was mooted by Ewan Phillips as a recommendation from the Production Ctee. He showed that by printing sufficient quantities it would be possible to sell good colour litho reproductions at 2/6 each. After a long discussion upon the possibilities, it was agreed that the idea should be developed and a ctee was set up to deal with it as follows Ewan Phillips, Rowe, Coldstream, Stephen Bone and/or Mary Adshead. The first job will be to raise £50 to pay for 400 prints in 4 separate 100s to be used for getting orders for larger runs.'
8 OK to Ruth and Adolf Arndt, 20 October 1938, Kokoschka and Marnau 1992, pp. 157–58.
9 OK to HR, 17 May 1938, Kokoschka and Marnau 1992, p. 153.
10 CC minutes, 25 October and 8 November 1938, TGA 20143.
11 Bohm-Duchen 2019, p. 192; Brinson and Dove 2010, pp. 14–16.
12 This took place at Friends Meeting House, Euston Road; more than 250 attended the first public meeting, and over 500 a second on 12 May 1939 at the West Central Hall, at which J. B. Priestley gave an address, a Brecht one-act play was staged and Kokoschka read from his memoirs; Brinson and Dove 2010, p. 18.
13 Whitford 1986, pp. 132–34. The putsch led by Werner Kapp was an attempt to overthrow the Weimar Republic supported by monarchist and nationalist factions.
14 Van Hensbergen 2004, p. 90.
15 A march to the Cenotaph was held the next day, after which the International Brigaders dispersed to home cities and regions where further significant welcome ceremonies had been organized; some fifty Brigaders were repatriated a fortnight later. The International Brigade Memorial Trust at MML holds significant material concerning these events, including

film footage of the return to Newhaven and London.
16 EW to ER, ER to Diana Tuely, Ullmann 2008, pp. 414 and 417.
17 George Cadbury to EP, 9 January 1939, TGA 8217.
18 MML SC/ORG/LASC contains campaign literature and records of the extensive campaign mounted by the All London Aid Spain Council.
19 CC minutes, 28 February and 21 March 1939, TGA 20143.
20 Van Hensbergen 2004, p. 95.
21 *Daily Herald*, 18 February 1939, p. 5.
22 CC minutes, 3 January 1939, TGA 20143.
23 NY memoir, p. 150, TGA 20029/5/1.
24 The members of the initial AIA Advisory Council, which had a first meeting for some of its members on 23 February 1939 at Whitechapel, were James Bateman, VB, MB, Muirhead Bone, EG, DG, AJ, EMK, HM, PN, Lucien Pissarro and DL.
25 NY memoir, p. 150, TGA 20029/5/1. JT had taken part in experiments involving making art while taking mescaline at the Maudsley Hospital in 1936; Basil Beaumont and Herbrand Williams also took part, but only JT was a guide at Whitechapel, so I believe the figure recalled by NY was JT.
26 PLP contributed *Spain*, *Stormy Day* and *Group*, the latter in both steel and cement. HM *Reclining Woman* priced at £262.10; for HB's *Puppets for Spain*, exhibited alongside the sculpture, see Friend 2017, pp. 249–51.
27 'Tisa Schulenburg and the Pit University', *Classics and Class*, https://www.classicsandclass.info/product/194/, accessed 4 September 2024.
28 These activities represented the highpoint of GB's involvement; and his and WC's subsequent non-attendance at CC meetings meant that replacement members were co-opted on 18 April 1939, TGA 20143.
29 GB letter to his mother, 14 March 1939, Laughton 1986, pp. 198–99.

30 CC minutes, 14 February 1939, TGA 20143; EW reported that eight more banners on peacetime activities were in preparation and seven on refugee issues but effective arrangements for deployment were needed. See also Radford 1987, p. 11, and Morris and Radford 1983, p. 53.
31 *AIA News Sheet*, no. 39, March 1939, p. 2, private collection; CC minutes, 21 March 1939, TGA 20143.
32 TGA 20143, 22 November 1938, 7 and 15 December 1938, 24 January 1939 for early meetings and development.
33 Morris and Radford 1983, p. 55.
34 The June *AIA News-Sheet*, private collection, led with an article detailing how the AAC and the AU were resisting Republican pressure for cuts with sit-ins and demonstrations, concluding: 'The battle is by no means finished. The danger of the Federal Art Project being liquidated is more serious today than it has been or three years. The artists' organisations and trade unions are, however, determined that the Project, which was started as an emergency relief shall become part of the normally accepted life of the country.'
35 CC minutes, 18 April 1939, TGA 20143.
36 The issue was discussed at seven CC meetings between 4 April and 18 July 1939.
37 The memorandum, in TGA 8217, EP Papers, is an example of a worked-up proposal presented to the AIA by a member, in this case the English architect, architectural critic and novelist Robert Furneaux Jordan (1905–1978).
38 Mark Gertler gassed himself at 5 Grove Terrace, Highgate, on 23 June 1939, aged forty-seven. As well as his fears of imminent world war and anti-Semitism, his wife had recently left him, a recent exhibition had been poorly reviewed and he was reportedly still depressed after the death of his mother.
39 Hess's father and most of her siblings were strongly pro-Nazi, a fact that led some to interpret her

exclusion as stemming from family links to the Hitler regime; however, both the general tenor of British entry policy at this point, and the fact that she had been warned over her left-wing political activism suggest otherwise.
40 CC minutes, 11 July 1939, TGA 20143. At a prior meeting on 4 July it was agreed that the CC would be provided with copies of *Art Lies Bleeding* by Francis Watson, which attacked the AIA; it is possible that Watson's book encouraged Balneil's pressure on Whitechapel management.
41 *Tory MP* by Simon Haxey (a pseudonym) was published for Left Book Club in July 1939, and the *Time* review noted: 'Currently exciting comment in London is a provocative, 263-page book that analyses the tangled family, social, economic and political relationships of government supporters in the House of Commons'; *Time*, 7 August 1939.
42 Although advertised in the *AIA Bulletin* there is no evidence that this took place nor any mention of it in the CC proceedings; however, in the subsequent 1941 exhibition held in the Ministry of Shipping canteen, Keith Baynes exhibited a painting *Concarneau Harbour* featuring boats, which JG highlighted in his catalogue introduction for its 'emotional colour effect', TGA 7043/3/8.
43 NY memoir, pp. 159–61, TGA 20029/5/1; Rice et al. 1993, p. 31.
44 The CC met on 31 August and 5, 19, 23 and 30 September 1939. There is no extant record for the attendance at the first two of these meetings, but CR, EP, PH and MB were four of an unknown number of attendees.
45 *Emergency Bulletin No. 1* survives as a typewritten enclosure in TGA 20143.
46 'AIA Notice to Members of the Central Committee', typescript reporting the decisions taken on 5 September 1939 to absent committee members, an insert in TGA 20143. *Emergency Bulletin No. 2* was issued on 9 September 1939.

47 DL wrote, noting 'it is by no means proven that, since Litvinov retired, the Soviet Union had any intention of signing a pact with Britain'. EG deplored 'the AIA's constant preoccupation with politics' and wished it would confine itself 'to putting the artists' house in order'; EMK similarly saw the organization as becoming 'too political' and saw a Federal Union of Europe as the only end worth working for.
48 Harry Pollitt's pamphlet *How to Win the War* further summarizing his position was published on 12 September 1939, see Branson 1985, pp. 265–74, for analysis of the change of line.
49 *AIA Bulletin*, no. 58, December 1939, p. 2, TGA 7043/20/3, with letters from both the Ministry of Labour and the Home Office Civil Camouflage section saying their registers were full and no more applications would be accepted.
50 CC minutes, 19 September 1939, TGA 20143, mandated EP, BS, Olga Mitkevitch, EW, Walter Durac Barnett, Pamela Strain, Stephen Bone and NY, with twelve other non-CC names to be approached. PH, HB and Rivka Black made up a teachers and students subcommittee with six more names to be approached, including MG; this activity led to publication in late October of 'Your Work as an Artist in War-Time', TGA 7043/17/7, a printed text developed by Rowe which also served as both a recruiting leaflet and an application form.
51 The survey results led the *AIA Bulletin*, no. 58, December 1939, TGA 7043/20/3.
52 MB reported on the meeting with KC on 30 September 1939, TGA 20143.
53 KC to NY, 15 June 1937, MML SC/ORG/JCSR/2/2.
54 KC, 'The Artist in Wartime', *The Listener*, 26 October 1939, p. 810; KC to Humbert Wolfe, 3 October 1939, NG, Central Register 1939. The poet and author Humbert Wolfe (1885–1940) was also a senior civil servant in the Ministry of Labour.

55 The venue was the University Labour Club, Percy Street.
56 *AIA Bulletin*, no. 59, January 1940, p. 3, TGA 7043/20/4.
57 JH, HB, Henry Holzer, Freda Nichols and Pamela Strain were the candidates.
58 Information from carbon copy of memorandum prepared by PH on future of scheme, n.d. but February 1939, private collection.
59 At the launch of Everyman Prints, the committee consisted of BS, HB, Alicia Gray, JH, Kathleen Gardiner, Freda Nichols, Edmond Kapp and ES. PH had been heavily involved but was now teaching at the evacuated RCA in Ambleside.
60 CW's Everyman Print was strongly reminiscent of his painting *Tragic Symphony*, which had been exhibited at the Amsterdam exhibition, staged as to protest the Berlin Olympics, see p. 151 and ch. 4, n. 56
61 TGA 7043/20/6, p. 1.
62 'Two Letters on Finland', *AIA Bulletin*, no. 60, March 1940, p. 4, TGA 7043/20/5.
63 CC minutes, 6 February 1940, TGA 20143.
64 Brinson and Dove 2010, pp. 27–29. By this time local FGLC branches had also been set up in Birmingham, Glasgow, Leeds and Manchester, with the last having its own club room.
65 Brinson and Dove 2010, p. 28.
66 Wertheim's gallery was by now in financial difficulty and this was the last exhibition staged there.
67 Exhibitors included Walter Nessler, Fritz Kramer, Samson Schames, Georg and Bettina Ehrlich, Karel Vogel, Ernst Stern, S. Charoux, A. H. Huettenbach, Hilde Hamann, FU, Paul Hamann, OK and Joseph Murman; work by Max Ernst was also included as being by a refugee but not one in England.
68 'Activities Since 1938', supplement to *AIA Bulletin*, no. 72, July 1942, p. 2, TGA 7043/20/20.
69 OK to Ruth and Adolf Arndt, 20 October 1938, Kokoschka and Marnau 1992, pp. 157–58.

70 Whitford 1986, p. 173.
71 'Activities since 1938', p. 2. *AIA Bulletin*, no. 63, November 1940, p. 3, TGA 7043/20/8, describes the full range of activities; and no. 64, February 1941, p. 3, TGA 7043/20/9, reported that materials had been sent to twelve camps, along with the names of twenty artists known to have been released, including FU, FHKH, Paul Hamann, Berthold Wolpe, Ludwig Meidner and Fritz Kramer.
72 CC minutes, 21 March and 27 June 1939, TGA 20143.
73 CC minutes, 14 May, 10 and 17 June 1940, TGA 20143.
74 'Activities since 1938', pp. 1–2.
75 The Pilgrim Trust, approached by the Ministry of Labour after submission of the AIA–CIAD memorandum, supported the Recording Britain initiative with £6,000 in grants; the administration of the scheme was overseen by a committee consisting of Percy Jowett (RCA principal), KC (as director of the National Gallery) and Russell Flint (representing the Royal Academy); the work of ninety-seven artists led to a collection of 1,549 works being assembled. See *AIA Bulletin*, no. 65, May 1941, pp. 3–4, and no. 67, October 1941, pp. 1–2, for AIA interaction; TGA 70–50/115.
76 *AIA Bulletin*, no. 62, July 1940, p. 1, TGA 7043/20/7.
77 Addison 1977, p. 119; this pressure included David Margesson, Conservative Party chief whip, approaching the BBC directly and pressure being applied to Harold Nicolson, minister at the MOI.
78 *AIA Bulletin*, no. 63, November 1940, pp. 1–2, TGA 7043/20/8, reproduced excerpts from *The Times*, *Sunday Times*, *Telegraph*, *Observer*, *The Listener*, *Time and Tide*, *Architect and Building News* and *Daily Worker* reviews.
79 Brinson and Dove 2010, p. 61.
80 *AIA Bulletin*, no. 63, November 1940, p. 1, TGA 7043/20/8.
81 *AIA Bulletin*, no. 64, February 1941, p. 2, TGA 7043/20/9. The Advisory Council members

exhibiting were James Bateman, VB, DG, Lucien Pissarro, HM and PN; the other works added included paintings by Rouault, Freisz, Segonzac, Forain and EG (who had died two months before). After Liverpool, the exhibition moved to Derby; see *AIA Bulletin*, no. 65, May 1941, pp. 1–2, TGA 70–50/115, quoting local reviews.
82 PH Archive, ESRO.
83 CC minutes, 17 June 1940, TGA 20143.
84 Morris and Radford 1983, p. 65, for Leamington Spa.
85 CC minutes, 26 May and 3 June 1940, TGA 20143.
86 The convention's Credentials Committee announced that these delegates represented 1.2 million workers; for a critique see McLaine 1979, p. 57, and pp. 190ff. for Morrison's case for banning the *Daily Worker*.
87 JB and John Banting were members of the convention's Arts and Entertainment Professions group; see Croft 2020, p. 127.
88 *AIA Bulletin*, no. 65, May 1941, p. 4, TGA 70–50/115, which reproduces a spread of members' letters 'For and Against the People's Convention'.
89 Kapp 2003, pp. 226–27.
90 *AIA Bulletin*, no. 66, July 1941, p. 1.

CHAPTER 7: CAMDEN STREET AND SENATE HOUSE

1 Priscilla Thornycroft to PH, 11 July 1941, PH Archive, ESRO. PH had arrived in Ambleside on 16 November 1940; the exhibition was originally scheduled for 9 September 1941 but ran 16 September–9 October 1941.
2 Other members of the London organizing committee were MK, Thornycroft, George Downs, Russell Reeve, Mary Wykeham; *AIA Bulletin*, no. 65, May 1941, p. 1, TGA 70–50/115.
3 TGA 7043/3/10; *AIA Bulletin*, no. 67, October 1941, p. 2, TGA 7043/20/12, and 'Activities since 1938', supplement to *AIA Bulletin*, no. 72, July 1942, p. 4, TGA 7043/20/20.
4 FHKH interview, IWM Catalogue 9592/1986-12-12; CW and HR's use of Camden Studios may have been a temporary expedient or confined to studio use as both before and after 1941 they were resident at 17 Girdlers Road, Kensington.
5 WAAC minutes, 31 July 1941, quoted in Brian Frederick Foss, 'British Artists and the Second World War', PhD thesis, University College London, 1991, p. 344. In making this obtusely bizarre suggestion the WAAC members in question may have had in mind CW's 1932 painting *Allegro Strepitoso*, Tate T05836, which figured in the AIA exhibition at the Ministry of Shipping canteen.
6 CR fulfilled the chairman's role between August 1940 and January 1941.
7 CR applied and was rejected on 21 April 1941, during October 1943 and on 26 April 1944; Foss, 'British Artists', p. 454.
8 See Watson 1994, pp. 1–35.
9 TGA 7043/3/10.
10 TGA 7043/3/4/5; JB had eleven lithographs in this travelling show.
11 Croft 2020, p. 131.
12 *Poetry and the People*, June 1940, p. 24.
13 'In and Against the State' is the title of a 1979 pamphlet, published by Pluto Press, which discussed the experience of socialists working in the public sector, but the concept is germane to the AIA in the war years.
14 PH to RH, 10 November 1940, quoted in *The Artist as Evacuee: The RCA in the Lake District 1940–1945*, Wordsworth Trust, 1987, p. 39.
15 Cecil Day-Lewis, 'Where Are the War Poets?', in *The Complete Poems of C. Day-Lewis*, Sinclair-Stevenson, 1992, p. 335.
16 Downing 2022, p. 55; for a fuller discussion see Calder 1969, pp. 370ff.
17 For analysis see Brinson and Dove 2021, and in particular pp. 32–50 on refugee artists.
18 Discussions about employment of MB are at NA INF 1/132, 140, 152, 'Reorganisation of Displays and Exhibitions Division', cited in Atkinson 2021.
19 Addison 1977, p. 65; the slogan was devised by A. P. Waterfield, deputy secretary, MOI.
20 HB moved to Bath in July 1940, where she worked for the Admiralty Dept. of Cartography until September 1942; between 19 September 1942 and 20 October 1945 she worked in the MOI photograph division preparing exhibitions for home and neutral country consumption.
21 Laughton 1986, pp. 210 and 271.
22 Trevelyan 1957, p. 123.
23 Mary Petter took over as AIA secretary in November 1940. MP worked at AdPrint, where Walter Neurath, co-founder of Thames & Hudson, was director of books; MP's work included John Betjeman's *British Cities and Small Towns* in the 'Britain in Pictures' series. Neurath had been interned as an enemy alien in July 1940.
24 KR was already a member of the Exhibitions Committee when asked to join the CC; see CC minutes, 14 May and 17 June 1940, TGA 20143.
25 DC's photomontage skills were also deployed on CP posters urging miners to maximize production in support of a Second Front; Lindey 2018, pp. 65 and 86.
26 *AIA Bulletin*, no. 65, May 1941, p. 3, TGA 7043/20/10.
27 *AIA Bulletin*, no. 65, May 1941, p. 3, TGA 7043/20/10; 'Activities since 1938', p. 3.
28 TGA 7043/3/8.
29 *AIA Bulletin*, no. 65, May 1941, p. 3, TGA 7043/20/10.
30 CR exhibited three works: *H. Pinner, Sq Leader SP*, *Harry Page* and *George Thomas*, probably all recently created as a result of his service at the St Pancras depot of the Light Rescue Service.
31 Jan Stránský, introduction to Géza Szóbel, *Civilisation*, Penguin Books, 1942, p. 3.
32 Stránský in Szóbel, *Civilisation*, p. 2.

33 Brinson and Dove 2010, p. 63, citing NA KV2/1010.
34 Although OK was the instigator of two exhibitions of children's art as fundraisers for the Refugee Children's Evacuation Fund, he clearly kept his distance from the day-to-day running of both organizations, choosing to use his influence sparingly.
35 Radford 1987, pp. 140–47; Robert Radford, 'Kokoschka's Political Allegories', *Art Monthly*, no. 97, June 1986, pp. 3–6.
36 'Activities since 1938', p. 2, and *AIA Bulletin*, no. 68, December 1941, p. 3, TGA 70–50/115; *AIA and FGLC Exhibition of Sculpture and Drawings*, exh. cat., TGA 7043/3/9.
37 'Information from Civil Defence Artists, Eleventh Exhibition, 29 March–8 May 1942', catalogue insert, p. 2, private collection.
38 Kapp 2003, p. 220.
39 FHKH interview, IWM catalogue 9592/1986-12-12.
40 Brinson and Dove 2021, p. 43: citing 'Payments made to Architects and Designers', NA INF 1/133.2; in the first four months of 1943 FHKH received no less than £320 from the MOI alone.
41 The book was published in 1942; in the interim PB had drawn on her 1935–36 sketchbooks to provide forty line-drawn illustrations for Bertha Malnick's *Everyday Life in Russia*, published by Harrap two years later.
42 RH to PH, n.d., PH papers, ESRO.
43 Produced by Mary Wykeham, edited by John Banting and promoted by Nancy Cunard, *Salvo for Russia* was announced in the *AIA Bulletin*, no. 68, December 1941, p. 4, TGA 7043/20/12.
44 McLaine 1979, pp. 196–216, for detailed analysis and evidence of the MOI strategy in response.
45 Moore-Brabazon (1884–1964), Conservative MP for Wallasey 1931–42, had been appointed Minister of Aircraft Production in May 1941; in 1939, opposed to war with Nazi Germany, he attempted to co-ordinate activity with Oswald Mosley.

46 Catalogue, private collection. John Craxton contributed three works, *Mountain Waterfall*, *Tree and Ruins* and *Sawn-up Tree 1942*, cats 8–10, in what may have been his first significant exhibition. Peter Watson, his then patron, is thanked for his help in organizing the exhibition in the catalogue preamble; see also Collins 2021, p. 101.
47 *AIA Bulletin*, no. 63, November 1940, p. 2, TGA 7043/20/8; this was despite PH arguing 'that the experience of the AIA in organising large exhibitions representing all aesthetic schools showed that the difficulties of such an enterprise could be overcome'.
48 The CC members exhibiting included Badmin, LL, DC and KR; proceeds reported in the *AIA Bulletin*, no. 72, July 1942, TGA 7043/20/19, as more than £250 for Willow Road; no. 73, September 1942, TGA 7043/20/22, a net £2,600 at Hertford House.
49 CR had resigned as CC vice-chair on October 1941 'due to pressure of other work', and JH took over for the remainder of the 1941/42 year; *AIA Bulletin*, no. 67, October 1941, p. 4. EW had moved to Scotland.
50 *AIA Bulletin*, no. 72, July 1972, TGA 7043/20/19, gave full details of the new programme and was accompanied by a recruiting leaflet and the supplement 'Activities since 1938'.
51 Catalogue, TGA 7043/3/12.
52 *AIA Bulletin*, no. 70, March 1942, TGA 7043/20/17, reported extensively on KC's speech and summarized the press reviews.
53 Pooke 2007, pp. 171–73; FK was employed in the Ministry of Home Security unit run by J. D. Bernal, which produced the April 1942 HMSO publication *Quantitative Study of the Total Effects of Air Raids*.
54 Francis Klingender, *Russia: Britain's Ally, 1812–1942*, Harrap, 1942, p. 7.
55 Downing 2022, p. 286, quoting Field Marshal Lord Alanbrooke, *War Diaries 1939–1945*, Weidenfeld & Nicolson, 2001, p. 226.

56 Downing 2022, p. 291, quoting Macmillan 1984, pp. 313 and 347.
57 JB's sketchbooks discussed herein are held in TGA 8224.
58 TGA 7043/3/9.
59 Subsequently WAAC did purchase three works developed from JB's 1942–43 sketchbooks: *Crewe 2 a.m.*, *Sick Parade* and *A Corner of the NAAFI*, along with in February 1943, for 30 guineas, the two sketchbooks from which these larger drawings had been developed.
60 *AIA Bulletin*, no. 71, May 1942, pp. 1–2, TGA 7043/20/19; shortly after JB was transferred to the 33rd Hospital, which may indeed be the one he refers to in his letter to JG.
61 JB, quoted in *James Boswell: Drawings, Illustrations and Paintings*, Nottingham University Art Gallery, 1976, p. 25.
62 George Orwell in particular drew on DL's cartoons and used the term 'Blimps' as a shorthand for short-sighted conservative reactionaries and 'un-blimping' as a term for necessary reform of the officer cadre in the forces; see Davison 2009, pp. 257, 274, 365.
63 For the first critical elucidation of these connections see Richard Cork's essay in *James Boswell: Drawings, Illustrations and Paintings*.
64 *Our Time*, March 1942, p. 15.

CHAPTER 8: HOLLES STREET

1 *AIA Bulletin*, no. 71, May 1942, p. 2, TGA 7043/20/19; the piece concludes: 'British artists have a good record in the struggle against fascism and our association has played a leading part in organising artists in that struggle. By campaigning now for the democratisation of the services the AIA could help the development of the latent forces in the Army, Navy and Air Force and so by raising their efficiency and morale help bring the struggle to a rapid and victorious end. Yours fraternally James Boswell.'

2 *AIA Bulletin*, no. 72, July 1942, pp. 1–2, TGA 7043/20/1.
3 La Guardia commissioned Leo Friedlander to create four statues to celebrate Four Freedoms (religion, speech, press and assembly), which stood at the heart of the fair. Roosevelt subsequently commissioned Walter Russell to create a Four Freedoms monument at Madison Square Garden in New York.
4 MB to LL, 21 September 1943, TGA 7043/4/5.
5 For a comprehensive contemporary analysis of this programme, see G. S. Kallman, 'The Wartime Exhibition', *Architectural Review*, October 1943, pp. 95–106.
6 The *News Chronicle* delivered considerable publicity and at least £164 as a direct financial contribution.
7 *AIA Bulletin*, no. 74, November 1942, p. 2, TGA 7043/20/23, under the heading 'War Paintings Exhibition': 'The Exhibitions Committee has at last found suitable premises for this exhibition, though few members can possibly realise what difficulties, under the present circumstances, have had to be overcome. Thanks however to the co-operation of the Directors of John Lewis and the Marylebone County Council [*sic*] a grand site is now available.'
8 Davison 2009, p. 283; Kingsley Martin, *Critic's London Diary*, Secker & Warburg, 1960, p. 93.
9 Delivered on 10 November 1942 as part of address known as 'The End of the Beginning'; Charles Eade (ed.), *The War Speeches of Winston Churchill, Vol. 2*, Cassell, 1952, p. 344.
10 The Atlantic Charter was signed on 14 August 1941 following Roosevelt and Churchill's meeting in Newfoundland. Roosevelt's 'Four Freedoms' State of the Union Address had been made on 6 January 1941, articulating why the United States should abandon the isolationist policies that emerged from the First World War.
11 Imperial preference was a system of mutual tariff reduction enacted throughout the British Empire following the 1932 Ottawa Conference; it was a defensive response to the raising of tariff barriers globally following the financial crash of 1929, but did great damage to international trade.
12 Calder 1969, pp. 114–15.
13 Addison 1977, p. 222, citing memo by Nicolson, 17 July 1940, NA INF 1/862.
14 *AIA Bulletin*, no. 67, October 1941, p. 3, TGA 7043/20/12. The same *Bulletin* reported that of the thirteen members of CIAD elected as fellows to represent individual artists, ten were members of the AIA or its Advisory Council: Adrian Allinson, MB, Sir Muirhead Bone, Thomas Hennell, PH, HM, PN, Helen Mary Petter, Russell Reeve and KR. MG joined the AIA shortly after.
15 Addison 1977, p. 151, 17 October 1942; by August 1943 the *Architectural Review*, p. xiv, in a report on Abram Games's housing poster for the Army Bureau for Current Affairs, was noting that the Bureau 'has won the battle of the Beveridge Report' and that the ban had been overturned, reminding people of 'the bracing spirit in which army education is conducted by this body'.
16 Originally nineteen members including CR, JH and Helen Roeder, but these names no longer featured when the catalogue was finalized with a main committee including all the members of the Technical Committee and BS as chair, LL as treasurer and Kathleen Allen as secretary, plus RC, JF, EP, MK, Henry Carr, Margaret Lewis, Ruskin Spear and Priscilla Thornycroft.
17 The title 'For Freedom' was still in use when *AIA Bulletin*, no. 74, TGA 7043/20/23, was issued at the beginning of November 1942.
18 JB, *The Land of the Scorpion*, Lilliput, pp. 201–4, repr. in Feaver 2007, pp. 116–17.
19 See *James Boswell: Drawings, Illustrations and Paintings*, Nottingham University Art Gallery 1976, p. 25, and Feaver 2007, p. 76.

Eros is the drive of life, love, creativity, sexuality, self-satisfaction and species preservation; Thanatos, from the Greek word for 'death', is the drive of aggression, sadism, destruction, violence and death. The concepts play a key role in Freudian theory.
20 Trevelyan 1957, p. 185.
21 Laughton 1986, p. 262.
22 'War Artist Missing', *AIA Bulletin*, no. 73, September 1942, p. 4, TGA 7043/20/22; for the circumstances of ER's death see Friend 2017, pp. 300–2.
23 EW to LL, 3 February 1943, TGA 7043/2/3/7. EP had reviewed the Tate war-time acquisitions exhibition in *AIA Bulletin*, no. 71, May 1942, p. 3, TGA 7043/20/18, noting that works by AIA members EB, DG, Hennell, PH, AJ, OK, Le Bas, Methuen, HM, J. Nash, PN, Nicholson, VP, Piper and Rhoades had been acquired for the nation.
24 The series ran from 7 to 14 February 1943. TGA 7043/3/3 holds related correspondence and LL's extant handwritten summaries of the talks for AB's espionage activities at this time; see Carter 2001, pp. 275–77.
25 PH, foreword, in *Pictures to Live With: AIA Second Travelling Exhibition*, p. 2, TGA 7043/3.
26 NY memoir, pp. 159–61, TGA 20029/5/1; the school was Templefield, the price £10, and the picture was subsequently lost by the school, according to a note from NY on the verso of a surviving black-and-white photograph.
27 Of the 93 members, 39 are identifiable as men and 35 as women, while 19 are unclear from the catalogue; these figures do not include the Leamington Spa collective effort.
28 *Poster Design in War-time Britain Exhibition at Harrods Ltd Knightsbridge, arranged in collaboration with the Artists International Association*, FHKH archive, University of Brighton Design Archives; the exhibition toured subsequently to the Ashmolean Museum in Oxford and then to Newcastle.

29 These were Czechoslovakia, Norway, Yugoslavia, Greece, Poland and Belgium; also the USA (January 1942), the USSR (June 1942) and China (September 1942).
30 IWM 9592/1986-12-12, reel 1.
31 See Games and Webb 2013, p. 14.
32 Games and Webb 2013, p. 44.
33 MB to PN, n.d. but December 1942, TGA 70-50/9334; Bertram 1955, p. 251.
34 BS to PN, TGA 70-50/106; Bertram 1955, pp. 251 and 259.
35 IWM 9592/1986-12-12, reel 2.
36 JG in *The Studio*, June 1943, pp. 185–87.
37 'Perspex', in *Apollo*, April 1943, p. 84, identified it as an old picture of AJ's in the traditional 'essentially meaningless art for art's sake manner and therefore essentially meaningless' which 'the AIA should have had the courage to refuse'. JG (*The Studio*, June 1943, pp. 185–87) continued: 'Though the interweaving of the rhythms is brilliant, the tonal scheme has been left unfinished and one is tempted to ask oneself whether it can ever be finished or was the total scheme insufficiently weighed up before commencement.'
38 TGA 7043/3/14/9.
39 For Matvyn Wright's participation in the Auxiliary Fire Service exhibition held at the LCC Central School in autumn 1941, which subsequently toured to the USA, see *The Studio*, May 1941, pp. 146–49.
40 Brian Frederick Foss, 'British Artists and the Second World War', PhD thesis, University College London, 1991, p. 420.
41 JG in *The Studio*, June 1943, p. 185; 'Perspex' – writing in *Apollo*, April 1943, p. 84 – found it next in importance to JT's *Focal Point*, but added 'or at least it would be if only the artist had possessed that leisure, the artistic power and concentration upon craftsmanship that distinguishes the Flemish primitives, or perhaps a better comparison, the art of El Greco'.
42 RC in *Our Time*, May 1943, p. 28.
43 Now in the collection of People's History Museum, Manchester.
44 I am grateful to Joe Thornberry for this information, March 2024.
45 Tate, acc. no. NO5432.
46 Brinson and Dove 2010, p. 69; see also Harriet Atkinson, *Showing Resistance: Propaganda and Modernist Exhibitions in Britain, 1933-53*, Manchester University Press, 2024, ch. 6.
47 Radford 1987, p. 140.
48 *Apollo*, April 1943, pp. 84–85. For 'Perspex' there were generally 'too many pictures here that fall between the schools of propaganda and pleasure; too many for which one feels the wrong medium has been used'; the writer nevertheless urged 'Do not miss this for Liberty show', seeing it as 'a lively interesting and highly significant enterprise' and praising Carpenter's painting as 'extraordinarily suggestive of the foulness of the crime'.
49 From the final paragraph of Gabriel Peri's valedictory letter 'I Die so that France may live...' written during his last moments in the early hours of 13 December 1941 at Fort Mont Valérien, Suresnes, Paris.
50 *AIA Bulletin*, no. 71, May 1942, p. 2, TGA 7043/20/18, opened: 'I feel that artists in the Forces could play a very valuable part by recording the activity around them, but that they are hampered by the lack of help or recognition from the military authorities; such artists if given the chance, could produce work of more interest than the officially commissioned War Artists, because unlike the latter, who are always as it were "on the outside, looking in" they are living the life of the ordinary soldier, sailor or airman and experiencing all the vicissitudes of such a life.'
51 Peter Stanford, *C. Day-Lewis: A Life*, Continuum, 2007, p. 196.
52 IWM 1986-12-12, reel 2. JG in *The Studio*, June 1943, p. 186, added: 'Though some of the paintings make rather strange frame-fellows they are as it were pinned down to the single purpose with a poem brilliantly written round them by Mr Cecil Day-Lewis. His I feel is the major success of the exhibition, at least, considered as work done to a purpose.'
53 NY memoir, p. 200, TGA 20029/5/1.
54 RC in *Our Time*, May 1943, p. 30.
55 Eric Newton, 'Meals and Murals', *Architectural Review*, August 1943, p. 41.
56 *Spectator*, 26 March 1943, p. 291.
57 'Review of Reviews', *AIA Bulletin*, no. 77, May 1943, p. 2, TGA 7043/20/26.
58 *New Statesman & Nation*, 17 April 1943, p. 255.
59 *AIA Bulletin*, no. 76, March 1943, p. 3, TGA 7043/20/25.

AFTERWORD

1 For example *After Duty*, held at 84 Charlotte Street from 16 November to 18 December 1943; 'Watercolours by Sappers Carel Weight, Patrick Gieth, William Reed, Albert Patterson'.
2 Letter from JH to Robert Radford, quoted in Croft 1998, p. 43.
3 This trend is evident from as early as Rickaby 1978, p. 163: 'The War at once ended the AIA's position as a radical force which it had maintained over the previous six years.'

BIOGRAPHIES

This section summarizes basic biographical information for key individuals who participated in the Artists International, its AIA successor and initiatives the movement generated during its first decade. It is not exhaustive but highlights those whom both history and art history have tended to underestimate; thus Pablo Picasso, Diego Rivera, Kenneth Clark and Virginia Woolf are not listed below, despite their presence in the preceding narrative, nor are many others who played a more peripheral role. Some well-known artists whose engagement with the AIA has been overlooked are cited in truncated form.

Mary Adshead (1904–1995), painter, illustrator and muralist. Born in London, studied at the Slade 1921–24. Worked on mural design for the Shadwell Highways boys' club with Rex Whistler, with further mural, set and decorative commissions following. First solo exhibition as a painter at Goupil Gallery, London, 1930. Exhibited with AIA from *Artists Against Fascism and War* 1935 onwards. Worked as poster designer, created panels for the British Pavilion at the 1937 Paris Exposition. Active with ARC from 1938.

Eileen Agar (1899–1991), Surrealist painter. Born in Argentina, contemporary of Adshead at the Slade. Participated in major AIA exhibitions 1935, 1937, 1939; close during this period to PN and the group promoting the International Surrealist Exhibition 1936. Signed 'We Ask Your Attention' address to First British Artists' Congress.

Peggy Angus (1904–1993), painter, designer, teacher, community arts activist. Born in Chile, moved to London as a child. Founding member of the AI British Section after visiting USSR in 1932, and with PH instrumental in securing participation of RCA contemporaries including HB, ER, EB. Exhibited with AIA from inaugural Charlotte Street show 1934 to *For Liberty* 1943.

Edward Ardizzone (1900–1979), painter, illustrator and writer, especially of children's books. Born in French Indo-China to Italian father and English mother; attended Westminster School of Art while an office clerk, then attended JF's Central School lithography class. Present at founding AI meetings, contributed to hunger march cartoons but rarely thereafter. Official war artist from 1940.

Stanley Badmin (1906–1989), painter, etcher, notable for landscapes, townscapes, book illustration. Born in Sydenham, London; studied at Camberwell School of Art, 1922, then RCA 1924–27. Worked in USA, 1935; on return recruited to AIA by JH, exhibiting regularly. Close friend of PH; CC member 1938–42 and member of Production and Prints committees responsible for Everyman Prints. Worked on Recording Britain, 1941, and with MB on MOI exhibitions before RAF service from 1942.

John Banting (1902–1972), draughtsman, watercolourist, painter. Born in London, studied at Westminster School of Art, taking studio in Fitzroy Street near JH, JB, VB and DG. Member of Seven and Five Society and LG; developed Surrealist idiom. Participated in International Surrealist Exhibition 1936 and exhibited with AIA from 1939. Art editor of *Our Time* and its successor *Left Review* 1941–42. Involved with *Salvo for Russia* 1942, while working at MOI's Strand Films; elected to CC 1941.

Walter Durac Barnett (1876–1961), painter. Born in Leeds, attended Leeds School of Art; served in Artists' Rifles during Great War, then lived in London. Active in AIA recruitment, fundraising socials and support of AIA local groups; elected CC member 1938–41.

James Bateman (1893–1959), son of Lake District blacksmith, known for agricultural and pastoral paintings. Badly injured in Great War; taught at Goldsmiths in the 1930s as the threat of war returned. First participated in AIA exhibition 1935; AC member 1939, informed response to impending conscription. NEAC member, regularly exhibited at RA, made full RA 1942.

Edward Bawden (1903–1989), painter, illustrator, graphic artist. Joined AIA Peace Publicity Bureau in 1936, exhibited cartoons at Grosvenor Square 1937 and paintings at Whitechapel 1939; participated in 'Portraits for Spain' and travelling exhibitions.

Graham Bell (1910–1943), painter, journalist and writer. Born in South Africa, worked in London from 1931. Founder member of the Euston Road School and influenced leading members to participate in AIA. Elected to CC with WC in 1938, active organizing Whitechapel 1939 and writing catalogue preface for subsequent touring exhibition. Died serving in the RAF.

Quentin Bell (1910–1996), painter, potter, art historian. Born in Charleston, Sussex; after studying in Paris, returned to England in 1935, taking studio at 8 Fitzroy Street adjacent to JH. Close to AIA activist and secretary EW; active Spanish solidarity 1936. Convened AIA Education Commission preparing recommendations to First British Artists' Congress 1937; opposed pro-Soviet tendency in post-Munich period.

Vanessa Bell (1879–1961), painter. Exhibited with AIA from 1937, the year her elder son Julian died in Spain; joined AC on formation in 1939.

George Biddle (1885–1973), social realist painter, lithographer, muralist. Born in Philadelphia, studied in Munich and Paris, then worked in Europe, returning to USA in 1932. Worked on federal PWAP, which he helped to found as confidant of Franklin D. Roosevelt. Signed call for formation of AAC 1935.

Pearl Binder (1904–1990), artist, illustrator, writer, broadcaster. Born as Pearl Binderofski in Salford, first attending evening classes at Manchester School of Art after leaving school for factory work; gained graduate diploma. Moved to London in 1925; worked in Paris, creating distinctive book illustrations. Her first marriage to Jack Driberg encouraged a lifelong interest in anthropology. Lived in Whitechapel from 1930 becoming a highly original lithographer, producing East End and theatre scenes. Visited Soviet Union in 1933, 1934 and 1935–36, meeting CR there in 1933, linking up with Central School lithographers to form nascent AI. Active in organization of *The Social Scene* 1934, regularly exhibiting with AIA thereafter. After third visit to USSR created book of Soviet lives, having already met FEJ, her second husband. Made TV fashion broadcasts in 1937, which she co-presented with James Laver.

Helen Binyon (1904–1979), wood and metal engraver, puppeteer, watercolour painter, school and college art teacher. RCA friend of PA, who encouraged AIA participation; she in turn encouraged participation of ER and John Nash.

Active AIA organizer, exhibiting from 1935; CC member 1938–40. Worked at MOI from 1942.

Sir Misha Black (1910–1977), architect, organization builder, exhibition designer, teacher of industrial design; AI/AIA chair 1933–44. Born in Baku, Russian Empire (now Azerbaijan), moved to London aged two. Early success in display design, freelance prior to joining Bassett-Gray Design in 1934, thereafter IDP. Founder of DRU with MG and HR in 1943, leading member of MOI exhibitions division 1940–45; chair and financial guarantor of *For Liberty* 1943.

Anthony Blunt (1907–1983), art critic, art historian, teacher, spy. Contributed reviews to *AIA Bulletin* 1936, keen supporter of PLP as sculptor. Contributed to AIA 'Artist and War' lecture series in 1942 while working at MI5. Succeeded Kenneth Clark as Surveyor of the King's Pictures 1945.

Sir Muirhead Bone (1876–1953), painter, watercolourist, lithographer, engraver. Born in Scotland, studied at Glasgow School of Art, before moving to London in 1901. Britain's first official war artist in 1916; etchings achieved great popularity in the 1920s. Exhibited three works at AIA's *Artists Against Fascism and War* 1935, sponsor of 1937 Congress, joined AC on formation. Served numerous public bodies, Tate trustee, knighted 1937; support significant as AIA reached outward politically and upward generationally.

Stephen Bone (1904–1958), painter, watercolourist and wood engraver. Born in Chiswick, studied at the Slade 1922–24, where he met Mary Adshead; they married in 1929 and travelled extensively in Europe for work. Like his father, Muirhead Bone, exhibited with AIA from 1935, becoming secretary of ARC at inception in October 1938. Trenchant opponent within AIA of CP

position on Finland in 1940. Civilian camouflage officer 1939–43.

James Boswell (1906–1972), painter, graphic artist, political cartoonist, writer. Born in South Island, New Zealand; studied at RCA 1926, forging independent path as painter up to 1932 when turned to political activism joining CP. Modernist book cover designer and commercial art director for Asiatic Petroleum Company 1935. With AI from its 1933 inception, highly active CC member. Founding art editor of *Left Review* 1934, major contributor of visual content until its demise in 1938; subsequently *Our Time*. Made many lithographs, drawings and paintings of urban scenes in late 1930s and into war years. Served in the Medical Corps as radiographer in Scotland, Iran, Iraq and Egypt 1941–43; worked in army education 1944–45. Published *The Artist's Dilemma* in 1947.

Clive Branson (1907–1944), artist, poet, community activist. Born in Ahmednagar, British India, educated in England from the age of two; from 1926 attended the Slade, where he was close to WC and CR. Became a painter with the support of an inheritance, but abandoned painting for full-time political activism having been politicized by the events of 1929–32. From 1931 he had a lifelong partnership with Noreen Branson (née Browne), both taking a leading role in funding and establishing the AIA's ally the Marx Memorial Library and Workers' School 1933. As a CP member he was a clandestine recruitment co-ordinator for the International Brigades from 1936, volunteering himself once discovered; imprisoned by Nationalists 1938. On repatriation significant return to painting while living in Battersea. Conscripted January 1941; killed in Burma February 1944.

Felicia Browne (1904–1936), sculptor, graphic artist, feminist activist. Born in Surrey, studied at

St John's Wood Art School and then at the Slade 1921–28; contemporary of CB, WC, NY, CR. Moved to Berlin, living communally supporting fellow artists; travelled widely in Eastern Europe. Joined CP in early 1930, pursuing art and political activism in tandem; close friend of EW. Worked to unionize women in catering while waitressing. Travelled in France in spring 1936, then Barcelona; joined militia two weeks after military rebellion. Killed on the Aragon front late August; body abandoned, but satchel containing sketchbooks recovered and returned to EW as AIA secretary.

Jacob Burck (1907–1982), Polish-born painter, muralist, sculptor; from 1929 editorial cartoonist for US *Daily Worker*, which published a 248-page volume of his work as *Hunger and Revolt* in 1935. Regarded mural painting a key New Deal art form. Participated in JRC exhibitions; spoke on revolutionary art at opening of *The Social Viewpoint*. Signed call for formation of AAC 1935; resigned from CP in 1936 in protest at Soviet censorship.

Edward Burra (1905–1976), painter, draughtsman, printmaker. Participated in AIA exhibition 1934 at behest of PB, and again in 1937, but not thereafter. Principal reaction to Spanish Civil War was abhorrence of violence rather than adherence to Republic.

David Caplan (1910–1986), self-taught East End commercial artist, cartoonist as 'Davy' for the *Daily Worker*. Contributed *Liverpool Street* to AIA Everyman Prints. Worked with JB at Shell throughout WW2; CC member 1940–42. Made posters for CP, Soviet Embassy and MOI, with four examples included in 1943 exhibition *Poster Design in War-time Britain*.

Richard Carline (1896–1980), painter, draughtsman. Born in Oxford into a family of artists. Served in army during 1914 war, Royal Flying Corps in the Middle East, then as official war artist. Studied at the Slade 1921–24; exhibited annually with LG throughout inter-war years. Four visits to the USA cemented his admiration for socially engaged figurative art, especially muralism. Crucial link between AU/AAC in New York and AIA in London; consistent advocate of internationalism among artists. Active with ARC; worked in camouflage for Air Ministry during WW2.

Patrick Carpenter (1920–?), painter. Born in Chelsea, son of postman, active in student politics at Chelsea School of Art 1935–40. Joined AIA and CP 1937; conscripted as private, painting *Death of Gabriel Peri* for *For Liberty* while in barracks. Exhibited at Charlotte Street Centre 1944.

Sir William Coldstream (1908–1987), painter, documentary filmmaker. Born in Northumberland, studied at the Slade 1926–29. Found success as a painter, exhibiting with LAA and LG; believed abstraction was fracturing the relationship between the artist and society. Pivoted to documentary filmmaking 1935–37 with GPO Film Unit, returning to painting with the foundation of the Euston Road School in 1937. Elected to AIA CC with GB 1938, exhibiting at Whitechapel 1939. Enlisted with Royal Artillery 1940, transferring to Royal Engineers as camouflage officer; became official war artist 1943.

John Cole (1907–1988), potter, art teacher. Born in Woolwich, studied at Central School. Head of Beckenham School of Art during WW2; CC member 1942–43.

Jesse Collins (dates unknown), industrial designer and teacher, graphic artist. Colleague of MB at IDP 1935–99; active in SIA. Elected to AIA CC 1938, sitting on the Exhibitions Committee; designed poster for the 1939 Whitechapel exhibition. AIA treasurer 1940–41.

Ithell Colquhoun (1906–1988), Surrealist painter, poet, occultist. Born in Assam, India, studied at Cheltenham School of Art, then at the Slade 1927–30. Exhibited as AIA member 1939–42, member of London Surrealist Group 1939–40; contributed to *Salvo for Russia* 1942.

W. G. Constable (1887–1976), art historian, gallery director. Born in Derby, abandoned legal career for the Slade after being badly wounded in 1916. Guide at Wallace Collection, art critic for *New Statesman* and *Saturday Review*; worked at National Gallery 1923–31, latterly Assistant Director. Founding Director of the Courtauld Institute at London University 1931–37. Championed the touring exhibition *Art for the People*, sponsor and platform speaker at AIA British Artists' Congress in 1937. Moved to Massachusetts as curator of paintings at Boston Museum of Fine Art.

Charles Cundall (1890–1971), painter of genre scenes, potter. Studied at Manchester School of Art, then at RCA and the Slade before and after military service in WW1. Great facility with large panoramic canvases and crowd scenes; exhibited *Miners' Gala, Durham* at AIA's *Against Fascism and War* 1935. Painted *The Withdrawal from Dunkirk* in 1940 as official war artist; appointed full RA in 1944.

Stuart Davis (1894–1964), painter, muralist, campaigner. Born in Philadelphia, then lived in New Jersey and New York from 1905. Trained at Henri School, worked as *New Masses* illustrator. Progressed from naturalism and realism to relentless experimentation, making distinctive contribution to US modernism. Worked in Paris 1928–29; on return activist in UAG, AU, editor of *Art Front* and national secretary and national chairman of

AAC, having been a prime mover in its creation.

Cecil Day-Lewis (1904–1972), poet and laureate, novelist, publisher, academic. Born in County Laios, Ireland; member of Oxford Poets late 1920s; reacting to Depression. Member of CPGB 1935–38, editing *The Mind in Chains: Socialism and the Cultural Revolution* 1937; left CP disillusioned by Stalinist purges and show trials. Worked in MOI publications division 1941–44.

Jessica Dismorr (1885–1939), painter and illustrator known for abstract paintings. Born in Gravesend, Kent, attended the Slade 1902–3, with extended study in Paris. Member of the Vorticist Group 1914, Seven and Five Society and LG from 1926. Solo show at Mayor Gallery 1925; exhibited with AIA at Amsterdam 1936, Grosvenor Square 1937 and Whitechapel 1939. Took own life 29 August 1939.

Frank Dobson (1888–1963), sculptor and painter. Born in London, brought up in Hastings. Worked in Cornwall before serving in Artists' Rifles. Prominent in LG and for direct carving from 1920s; participated in AIA exhibitions from 1935 onwards, joined AC in February 1940.

George Downs (1901–1983), painter and holder of stocking stall in Caledonian Road. Born in east London. Admirer of Georges Braque, encouraged in his painting by JT. Exhibited with AIA from Whitechapel 1939, including Ministry of Shipping 1941, Charing Cross 1941, *For Liberty* 1943; elected CC member 1941–42.

Lord Frederick Elwyn-Jones (1909–1989), radical anti-fascist lawyer, Nuremberg prosecutor, long-serving Labour MP and Lord Chancellor. Born in Llanelli, Wales; met PB in 1935, married in 1937. Anti-fascist solidarity work in Europe led him to write *The Battle for Peace* for the Left Book Club, 1938, possibly the clearest country by country assessment of the political situation in Europe prior to the Munich crisis.

Philip Evergood (1901–1973), social realist painter, etcher, lithographer. Born in New York as Howard Blashki to English mother and Australian-Polish father; educated in England, leaving Cambridge University to study at the Slade 1921–23, where he met RC. Worked in Europe and USA from 1931 onwards, producing powerful political paintings. Signed call for formation of AAC 1935; highly active in AU and as link to AIA in London.

Hans Feibusch (1898–1998), painter, muralist, lithographer, often depicted religious subjects. Born in Munich; switched from medicine to art, training in Berlin and Paris before settling in Frankfurt, where as a Jew he was prevented from working. Moved to London in 1933, attending JF's Central School lithography class soon after arrival. LG member and early AIA adherent; provided one of fourteen core works in *For Liberty* 1943.

James Fitton (1899–1982), painter, lithographer, cartoonist, designer, art director. Born in Oldham, father machine worker blacklisted for trade union activity and appointed national organizer for Amalgamated Engineering Union 1920. JF left school at fourteen for insecure employment, took evening classes at Manchester School of Art for over six years, where his best friend was fellow student L. S. Lowry, eleven years his senior. Followed family to London, working as letterer, printers' studio assistant and freelance jobbing artist, making poster and commercial designs. Attended Central School evening classes from 1925 with A. S. Hartrick, a painter and leading lithographer from whom JF learned the latter skill; met his future wife Margaret Cook there. Exhibited paintings at LG, NEAC and RA throughout the 1930s; solo show at Tooths 1933, the year he succeeded to Hartrick's previous role teaching lithography at Central, combining this with a position at C. Vernon's advertising agency where he would work for many decades.

Margaret Fitton (née Cook, 1902–1988), painter and illustrator. Born in Willesden, studied at Central School. Illustrator for publisher Frederick Warne 1925–28. One of first eleven members of AI in 1933, participating in all major AIA exhibitions 1933–43. Exhibited with LG, NEAC, RA and Society of Women Artists, and at Storran Gallery, Senefelder Club and Art Institute of Chicago.

Abram Games (1914–1996), graphic designer. Born in Spitalfields, east London, studied at St Martin's School of Art before working in the studio system and establishing freelance practice as an innovative poster designer in the 1930s. Conscripted into the infantry in 1940, before being seconded to War Office Public Relations, where he developed instructional posters as a key forces communication tool.

Mark Gertler (1891–1939), painter. Born in Spitalfields, east London. Joined 'Portraits for Spain' scheme 1937; AIA delegate to IPC in January 1939. Took own life 23 June 1939.

Eric Gill (1882–1940), sculptor. Born in Steyning, Sussex. Exhibited in AIA exhibitions 1934, 1937, 1939; joined AC at inception 1939.

Jan Gordon (1882–1944), art critic, painter, travel writer (with wife Cora), principal art writer at the *Observer* 1934–42. Wrote catalogue introduction for *Exhibition of Modern Pictures* at Ministry of Shipping and Economic Warfare in 1941; thereafter active with AIA, elected to CC 1942–44.

Duncan Grant (1885–1978), painter. Born in Aviemore, Scotland. Sponsor of AIA's *Artists Against Fascism and War* 1935 and catalogue contributor to Felicia Browne memorial exhibition 1936; regular exhibitor with AIA and AC member from inception.

Milner Gray (1889–1997), industrial designer, consultancy industry leader. Born in Blackheath, London, studied at Goldsmiths. Founder member of SIA 1930, Bassett-Gray Group of Artists and Writers 1934, and IDP 1935; close colleague of MB. Head of MOI exhibitions division 1940–44.

Leonard Greaves (1918–1949), painter, teacher and writer. Attended London University then studied at Chelsea School of Art 1934–38, worked for two years as assistant lecturer at the National Gallery.

Sam Haile (1909–1948), ceramicist, Surrealist painter, militant pacifist and anti-imperialist. Born in London, studied at the RCA 1931–34; taught at Leicester, Kingston and Hammersmith Colleges of Art 1935–36. Exhibited with AIA 1937–39, elected to CC 1938–39; first organizer of travelling exhibitions. Moved to USA in 1939, conscripted 1943, transferred to British Army 1944.

Jack Hastings, 16th Earl of Huntingdon (1901–1990), painter, muralist, Labour peer and minister in post-war Labour government. Joined AIA after returning from USA, where he had assisted Rivera. Completed mural at Marx Memorial Library and Workers' School 1935; active organizing and financing British Artists' Congress 1937, financially supporting AIA initiatives thereafter.

F. H. K. Henrion (1914–1990), exhibition and poster designer, graphic artist. Born in Nuremberg, apprenticed in Paris at Atelier Paul Colin, before working in Palestine then settling in London in 1936. First worked with MB at IDP; interned as an enemy alien mid-1940. Recruited to MOI exhibitions division on release, as well as the US Office of War Information. Joined AIA 1941, elected to CC 1942–44; designed *For Liberty* exhibition 1943.

Barbara Hepworth (1903–1975), sculptor. Born in Wakefield. Exhibited four 1935–37 works at AIA exhibition 1937; supporter of First British Artists' Congress.

Gertrude Hermes (1901–1983). Exhibited wood engravings and sculpture with AIA 1935–39, and at LG and RA. Leading figure in SWE from mid-1920s alongside AIA supporters HB, CL, PN, ER.

Tisa Hess (1903–2001), woodcarver, teacher. Born in Mecklenburg, Germany, as Elisabeth von der Schulenburg, member of Prussian nobility; her four brothers supported the Nazis. Studied at Berlin Academy of Art, before marrying Fritz Hess, a Jewish businessman twenty years her senior, in 1928. Fled to Britain; met HM while living in Highgate and joined AIA. Worked in Durham coalfields 1936–37, teaching at Spennymoor Settlement. Elected CC member 1938; excluded from UK 1939.

James Holland (1905–1996), painter, illustrator, graphic artist. Born in Gillingham, Kent, son of a naval blacksmith; studied at Rochester College of Art, then RCA, where he formed lifelong friendship with JB, both living in Fitzroy Street in the early 1930s. Exhibited with LAA and LG on many occasions pre-war. Employed in commercial design, after entry to advertising through Jack Beddington at Shell. Distinctive graphic style, often using collaged statements; notable works depicting inner urban and dockside life. Prolific contributor with JB and JF to visual content of *Left Review*. Designed and led decoration of Peace Pavilion in Paris 1937. Exhibited at all major AIA events; highly active member of CC on continuing basis. Taught then worked at MOI exhibitions division from 1941.

Percy Horton (1897–1970), figurative painter, art teacher. Born in Brighton and was studying at Brighton Art College when detained as conscientious objector; vicious imprisonment 1916–17. Studied at RCA 1922–25 and as staff from 1929 onwards. CP member; taught at Crowndale Road Working Men's College Camden 1926–36. Part of AI founding group 1933, CC member, editor of *Bulletin*, frequently led AIA policy development. Curated mural exhibition at Tate Gallery 1939. Evacuee teacher with RCA at Ambleside during war years; post-war career at RCA then Ruskin Master of Drawing at Oxford.

Ron Horton (1902–1981), painter, printmaker, teacher, trade union activist; younger brother of PH. Studied at Brighton Art College 1919–23; moved to London, attending evening classes at St Martin's while working as a bookseller and sculptor's assistant, then RCA Painting School 1926–29. Member of CPGB from 1920 until death, continuously active on art education and AIA student participation.

Eitaro Ishigaki (1893–1958), painter. Born in Japan, lived in USA from age sixteen. Founding member of JRC; watched Rivera create *The Making of a Fresco* in San Francisco. His oil *Unemployed Demonstration (American Cossacks)* 1932, akin to Rowe's *Hunger Marchers* of the same year, was acquired by the Museum of Western Art, Moscow. Under the FAP painted murals *Human Rights in the United States* and *Emancipation of Negro Slaves* for Harlem Courthouse, removed in 1938 as portrayal of Washington and Lincoln deemed 'offensive'.

Augustus John (1878–1961), painter, etcher. Born in Tenby, Wales, studied at the Slade in the 1890s. Considered by many to be the pre-eminent British portraitist of the 1920s, by others in decline during the 1930s. His celebrity backing for AIA's *Artists Against Fascism and War* 1935 was nevertheless highly significant. Exhibited with AIA in 1937, the same year a stay in Jamaica led to renewed achievement. Participated in 'Portraits for Spain' 1938, exhibited at Whitechapel 1939 and joined AC at inception; exhibited in *For Liberty* 1943.

Morris Kestelman (1905–1998), painter, teacher, set and costume designer. Born in Whitechapel to Russian Jewish immigrants; studied at Central School 1922–25, taught by Bernard Meninsky, and then RCA. Began exhibiting with LG 1934; largely figurative, occasionally expressionist, later moved to abstraction. Period of intense involvement with AIA initiated with role as co-ordinator of War Pictures exhibition at Charing Cross 1941; elected CC member 1942–43.

Ronald Kidd (1889–1942), founder of NCCL and architect with AIA alliance. Prior career as radical bookseller, civil servant, journalist, advertising agent, actor and stage manager; witnessed disguised detective sergeant throwing missile at mounted police to provoke charge at hunger marchers. Addressed opening public meeting of First British Artists' Congress at Conway Hall 1937.

Francis Klingender (1907–1955), art historian, Marxist thinker. Born in Goslar, Germany, to British artist father; lived in England from 1926, studied sociology at London School of Economics, with doctoral thesis on clerical labour. Joined AIA 1933, contributing to *5 on Revolutionary Art* 1935, and *Left Review* and *Art Front*; supporter of First British Artists' Congress; made financial study of British film industry; researched impact of bombing for Ministry of Home Security 1941–42. Frequent lecturer for AIA; established AIA Charlotte Street Centre with partner Millicent Rose in 1944.

Dame Laura Knight (1877–1970), painter, watercolourist, engraver. Born Laura Johnson in Nottingham, attended Nottingham School of Art and RA Schools. Highly technically accomplished, she gained success with portraits, ballet and circus subjects. Her awareness of racism was heightened when visiting Baltimore, USA, in 1927; supported AIA's *Artists Against Fascism and War* in 1935, when already a Dame of the British Empire. The first woman to be elected a full RA in the modern era.

Alex Koolman (1907–1998), portrait and figure painter in oils and pastels. Early member of AIA, participated in *The Social Scene* 1934; member of SIA.

Roy Laurier (1912–?), commercial artist. Contributed to hunger march cartoons 1934, and *Left Review* 1935; remained active in AIA pre-war, including the 'Foodships for Spain' campaign. Resident in Chelsea in 1939, death date unknown.

James Laver (1899–1975), fashion expert, museum curator, poet. Born in Liverpool, educated in Oxford after war service. Employed at V&A from 1922 in department of engraving, illustration, design and painting, becoming keeper in 1938; literary output of light verse. Voluntary classes for Crowndale Road Working Men's College, Camden, where he reorganized art classes with PH. Early strong but anonymous supporter of AIA as civil servant; combined with PB in 1937 to deliver *Clothesline*, the first fashion TV broadcasts.

Edward Le Bas (1904–1966), painter and collector. Born in London, wealth derived from family steel business; studied architecture at Cambridge before painting in Paris and RCA from 1924, where he knew PN and BR. Collector of modern art; exhibited with LG 1932, solo exhibition at Lefevre 1936. Exhibited with AIA 1942 and at *For Liberty* 1943.

Feodora Leontinoff (1909–1956), academic, administrator. Born in New Zealand. Appointed secretary of National Institute of Economic Research 1940; AIA CC member 1938–39. Distinguished administrative and academic career as Mrs J. R. S. Stone before early death.

A. L. (Bert) Lloyd (1908–1982), folk singer, folk-song collector, briefly painter prior to journalism, scriptwriting, broadcasting. Born in Wandsworth, assisted emigrant to Australia aged sixteen, where self-educated while labouring. On return joined AI on formation, exhibiting in *The Social Scene* 1934; contributed to *Left Review* in the mid-1930s; co-wrote the influential BBC radio drama series *Shadow of the Swastika* 1940.

David Low (1891–1963), cartoonist. Published *Russian Sketchbook* after visit to USSR in 1932. Immense popularity meant his support for AIA as exhibitor, congress supporter and AC member was significant. Enjoyed great latitude to express own viewpoint in Beaverbrook's London *Evening Standard* on Austrian Civil War, Italian invasion of Ethiopia, the 1936 Summer Olympics and Spanish Civil War. In April 1934 invented character of Colonel Blimp satirizing reactionary supporters of National Government.

L. S. Lowry (1887–1976), artist. Born in Stretford, attended Manchester School of Art, where he formed close friendship with JF. Participated in AIA exhibitions from 1942. JF sponsored him as ARA 1955, full RA 1962.

Lowes Luard (1872–1944), painter. Born in Calcutta, abandoned mathematics at Oxford to study at the Slade as a contemporary of AJ. Lived and worked in Paris before and after 1914–18 war service, went to London 1934. Elected to AIA CC in 1939; crucial role as treasurer of war-time exhibitions.

Edward McKnight Kauffer (1890–1954), artist and graphic designer. Born in Montana, USA. Itinerant life as a scene painter from age thirteen; worked in Paris in 1913 and in London from 1914 when he became established in avant-garde painting circles. Post-war success as distinctive designer and illustrator. Early supporter of AIA, designing for documentary exhibition that accompanied *Artists Against Fascism and War* 1935; AC member 1939–40. Returned to USA mid-1940.

F. E. McWilliam (1909–1992), Surrealist sculptor. Born in County Down, Ireland, studied at Belfast College of Art and from 1928 at the Slade, where he turned from painting to sculpture. Exhibited with AIA 1937, 1939; created Chamberlain masks for Surrealist contingent on May Day 1938.

Lord Paul Aynsford Methuen (1886–1974), painter, zoologist. Born in Corsham. WAAC commissions during WW2; joined procurement and fine art branch set up to protect works of art during invasion and conquest of Germany. After 1942 destruction in the Blitz, rehoused Bath School of Art at Corsham Court as Bath Academy of Art.

László Moholy-Nagy (1895–1946), painter, photographer, sculptor, industrial designer, teacher. Born in Hungary, taught at Bauhaus 1923–28. Joined AIA soon after arrival in London in 1935; exhibited two works at Soho Square. Moved to USA in 1937, the year his work was included in Hitler's *Degenerate Art* exhibition.

Henry Moore (1898–1986), sculptor, artist. Born in Castleford, at RCA 1921–31 as student then teacher,

where he knew BR, PH. Exhibited with AIA from 1934; sponsor of *Artists Against Fascism and War* 1935, supporter 1937 Artists' Congress, AC member 1939 onwards.

Lewis Mumford (1895–1990), social critic, literary, architectural and cultural commentator. Born in Flushing, New York. Became known for his writings on the relationship between technology and society, publishing *Technics and Civilisation* 1934. Although left-aligned, his recruitment as an opening speaker signalled the breadth of ambition encompassed by the AAC and the alliance-building intentions of its organizers.

Donia Nachshen (1903–1987), illustrator, poster artist. Born in Ukraine, family fled pogrom in 1905. Studied at the Slade before considerable success as book designer in the 1920s and for *Radio Times*. Active in AIA from 1935, when served as treasurer.

Paul Nash (1889–1946), painter. Born in Kensington, studied at the Slade. Taught at the RCA 1924–25, with students including PA, HB, ER, EB. Participated in *Cambridge Anti-War Exhibition* 1933, exhibited with AIA 1934–42. Sponsored *Artists Against Fascism and War* 1935 and British Artists' Congress 1937; AC member 1939–46.

Walter Nessler (1912–2001), painter, graphic artist, painter and sculptor. Born in Leipzig, anti-fascist who left Germany in 1937; interned 1940, served in Pioneer Corps after release.

Eric Newton (1893–1965), writer, broadcaster and painter. Influential supporter of AIA while art critic for *Manchester Guardian* and *Sunday Times*; lectured in the AIA's 'Purposes of Art Today' series.

José Clemente Orozco (1883–1949), painter, muralist, lithographer,

political activist. Born in Ciudad Guzmán, Mexico. With Rivera and Siqueiros, a leading figure in the Mexican Mural Renaissance; active in FAP and, as ally of AU, addressed AAC in 1936.

Roland Penrose (1900–1984), painter, writer. Born in London. AIA ally over 1937 congress and exhibition; involved in formation of ARC 1938, and organization of *Guernica* tour 1939.

Peter László Peri (1899–1967), Constructivist artist, architect, sculptor, printmaker. Born in Budapest, moved to Berlin after failure of Hungarian revolution; exiled as communist after Nazi accession to power. Joined AI after arriving in London in 1933, exhibiting from *Artists Against Fascism and War* 1935; significant solo exhibitions as innovative social realist sculptor from 1936. War service in Civil Defence.

Ewan Phillips (1914–1994), art historian, curator, activist. Born in London, attended Goldsmiths College of Art and then the Courtauld; thesis on Expressionism laid the foundation for his role organising *20th Century German Art* exhibition 1938. Early member of AIA, previously beaten by police demonstrating against repression in Germany. Worked at Tate Gallery and then National Gallery assisting evacuation of art 1939. CC member 1937–40, active assisting refugee artists. War service in Intelligence Corps.

Lucien Pissarro (1863–1944), painter, illustrator. Born in Paris, worked mainly in London from the 1890s, where part of Camden Town Group. As eldest son of Camille Pissarro, a living link to the Impressionists, who had witnessed divisions among artists during the Dreyfus affair. Exhibited with AIA from 1935, his obituary concluding: 'For us in the AIA his loss is specially felt: a member of our Advisory Council, his generous support was never failing, and his sympathy for the younger generation was ever quick and warm.'

Betty Rea (1904–1965), sculptor, activist. Born in London; studied painting at Regent Street Polytechnic, then sculpture at RCA, where she became close friend of HM. As secretary, key player with MB, CR and JB in formulation of AIA 1935 strategy and implementation of many pre-1940 AIA initiatives. Made sculptural centrepiece of 'Four Freedoms' room at AIA exhibition *For Liberty* 1943.

Helen Roeder (1909–1999), painter, writer, administrator. Born in Richmond, Surrey, to German father and British mother; met life partner CW while both students at Goldsmiths. MB's secretarial assistant at IDP. AIA CC member 1939–40, responsible for ARC 1940, subsequently co-ordinating lobbying for release of artists detained as enemy aliens.

Cliff Rowe (1904–1989), artist. Born in Wimbledon, studied at Wimbledon School of Art 1918–20 and RCA 1920–22. Worked in advertising and commercial art while painting; exhibited with the Emotionists late 1920s. Graphic design for trade unions and CP. Worked in publishing in Moscow 1932–33; became prime mover in establishment of AI British Section on his return. Key figure in broad range of AIA activities during its first decade and beyond; chaired organizing committee of First British Artists' Congress 1937. Artistic output included many social realist paintings, cartoons, lithographs; served in Civil Defence during Blitz. Served on AIA CC 1933–43, frequently as vice-chairman, and as chair when MB threatened with internment 1940.

Kenneth Rowntree (1915–1997). Born in Scarborough, trained at the Ruskin and the Slade. Participated in Everyman Prints and worked for Recording Britain from 1940. Exhibited with AIA 1937, 1939, 1941 (Charing Cross, Ministry of Shipping), 1942, and commissioned for *For Liberty* 1943.

Maurice de Sausmarez (1915–1969), painter, teacher, writer on art. Born in Sydney, Australia; attended Christ's Hospital, then Willesden College of Art and RCA. AIA student activist, first exhibiting in *Artists Against Fascism and War* 1935, and regularly thereafter.

Ben Shahn (1898–1969), painter, graphic artist. Born in Kaunas, Lithuania, emigrated to USA aged eight; studied biology then art, travelled to study European modernists, turning to social realism on return to USA. Painted *The Passion of Sacco and Vanzetti* 1932 and assisted Rivera on Rockefeller Center mural; documented the Depression for Farm Security Administration. Signed call for formation of AAC 1935.

Meyer Schapiro (1904–1996), art historian. Born in Lithuania. Developed new art historical methodologies incorporating interdisciplinary approach. Signed call for formation of AAC 1935, delivering keynote address 1936.

Edith Simon (1917–2003), painter, printmaker and graphic artist, novelist, translator. Born in Berlin, emigrated to London aged fifteen; attended Central School evening lithography class 1933 while working multiple casual jobs. AIA member from founding meetings, typist for earliest AIA publications; exhibited with AIA including in 1937. First published as writer of children's fiction, novelist and translator pre-war.

Beryl Sinclair (née Bowker, 1901–1967). Contemporary of PH, ER and EB at RCA 1922–25; married journalist and editor Robert Sinclair in 1927. During WW2, a key AIA participant in CIAD and energetic and effective chair of AIA Exhibitions Committee.

David Alfaro Siqueiros (1896–1974), social realist painter, technically innovative muralist, lithographer, militant revolutionary. Born in Camargo, Mexico; joined rebel army at eighteen, travelled widely to study art in Europe. Early associate of Rivera; worked in USA on controversial New Deal projects. Fought in the Spanish Civil War; CP militant who participated in an attempt to assassinate Trotsky 1940.

Montagu Slater (1902–1956), journalist, playwright, novelist, poet. Born in Cumberland, educated at Oxford. Joined CP 1927, worked as journalist for *Liverpool Post*, then for *Morning Post* on moving to London. A founding editor of *Left Review* 1934, becoming close friend of JB. Wrote plays for Unity Theatre in 1930s and libretto for Britten's *Peter Grimes* 1942.

Géza Szóbel (1905–1963), painter, printmaker. Born in Komárno, Austro-Hungarian Empire (now Slovakia); studied in Prague and Paris. Influenced by Fauvism and Surrealism; briefly lived in Berlin where he absorbed Expressionism. Fought in the Battle of France as part of Free Czech forces; escaped to Britain in 1941 where he created art reflecting the horrors he witnessed in Nazi-occupied Europe; published by Penguin in 1942 as *Civilisation*.

Priscilla Thornycroft (1917–2020). Born in Golders Green, London, studied at the Slade mid-1930s, serving as student representative to AIA; CC member 1937–38. Produced striking posters for solidarity with Spain; highly active in support of Basque refugees and on AIA Production Committee.

William Townsend (1909–1973), painter, illustrator, diarist. Born in London, studied at the Slade 1926–29. Associated with the Euston Road

School, involved in peace movement and workers' education. Active with the AIA from 1935, exhibiting from 1937, including in *For Liberty* 1943 while serving with the Royal Artillery.

Julian Trevelyan (1910–1988), Surrealist painter, poet. Born in Dorking, studied at Cambridge, then art in Paris; travelled widely before settling in London in 1935. Engaged with both AIA and London Surrealists from 1936, signing Surrealist Manifesto to the First British Artists' Congress 1937 and exhibiting with AIA from 1937 onwards. Worked for Mass Observation's 'Worktown' project 1938; camouflage officer 1940–43.

Edith Tudor-Hart (1908–1973), Montessori teacher, photographer, communist activist and agent. Born as Edith Suschitzky in Vienna, studied photography at the Bauhaus, developing photojournalism practice. Excluded from Britain in 1930, returning as a married woman after Dollfuss coup; friend of PB from early 1930s. Participated in AIA exhibition *The Social Scene* 1934, and after. Active as recruiter for Soviet intelligence services, including AIA supporter Anthony Blunt.

John Tunnard (1900–1971), painter, designer, teacher. Born in London, studied at RCA 1919–23. Worked in retail and industry, taught at Central School from 1929; exhibited at RA, then with LG from early 1930s. Influenced by Constructivism, abstraction and Surrealism as he developed a strongly textured idiom. Active with AIA from 1935 onwards. As conscientious objector, served as Cornwall coastguard during WW2.

Fred Uhlman (1901–1985), socialist lawyer, painter and writer. Born in Stuttgart, Germany; forced to flee Nazi ascendancy in March 1933 for Paris, where he took up painting to subsist, developing naive style of great appeal. Solo and group exhibitions at Galerie Le Niveau from 1935. Met Diana Croft in Spain prior to outbreak of Civil War; the couple married in November 1936 after moving to London. Interlocutor between political émigré circles in London and Paris, and between FGLC and AIA; founder of FGLC 1939; interned for six months in June 1940. Exhibited in AIA's *For Liberty* 1943.

Dame Ethel Walker (1861–1951), painter, sculptor. Born in Edinburgh, studied at Putney School of Art, then at the Slade. Exhibited at the RA from 1900, and with NEAC and LG from 1936; represented Britain at Venice Biennale 1930–32. Participated in AIA exhibitions from 1935, joined AC 1939.

Elizabeth Watson (1906–1955), painter, activist. Born in London, studied at the Slade and the Académie Moderne in Paris in the 1930s, where she was taught by Léger and Marchand and became friends with QB. On return to London, succeeded BR as AIA secretary late 1935; organizer of Felicia Browne memorial exhibition 1936 and subsequent campaigns. Member of AIA team who painted the 1937 Paris Peace Pavilion; AIA CC member until 1941, vice-chair 1940. Served in the London Ambulance Service during the Blitz.

Max Weber (1881–1961), American modernist painter. Born in Białystok, Russian Empire, migrated to Brooklyn in 1891. Early exponent of Cubism, experimented with Fauvist, Cubist and Futurist styles before developing a personal style of 'figurative expressionism'; active in formation of AAC.

Carel Weight (1908–1997), painter, teacher. Born in Chelsea, London, studied at Hammersmith School of Art, then Goldsmiths College, before teaching at Beckenham School of Art 1932–39. First solo show 1934; exhibited with AIA from 1937, active assisting refugee artists. CC member 1939–41, exhibitions secretary for AIA early war-time shows. Paintings centred on suburban themes prior to conscription into Royal Armoured Corps 1941.

Hellmuth Weissenborn (1898–1982), painter, printmaker, illustrator. Born in Leipzig where, after army service 1917–18, he established career as artist and teacher; lost professorial post at Leipzig Academy in 1938 because of his wife's Jewish heritage. Arrived in London early 1939, participating in FGLC before being interned on the Isle of Man for six months. Exhibited with AIA from Charing Cross September 1941, beginning to teach at Beckenham School of Art that year after CW recommendation.

Tom Wintringham (1898–1949), activist, editor, military organizer. Born in Grimsby. Early supporter of AIA; reviewed 1934 AIA exhibition in *Left Review*, which he co-edited 1934–35. As CP member, organizer of International Brigades during Spanish Civil War; wounded in Spain, expelled from CP 1938. Organizer of Local Defence Volunteers (predecessor of Home Guard) 1940.

Nan Youngman (1905–1995), painter, educationalist, editor. Born in Maidstone, Kent, studied at the Slade 1924–27, then London Day College for teacher training. Developed new approach to children's art, which was exhibited at Lucy Wertheim's gallery in 1931, with a subsequent US tour. Participated in AIA exhibition 1935, highly active in AIA from 1936, CC member 1938–40. Founding activist of the allied Society for Education in Art and editor of the journal *Athene*; pioneering post-war county arts adviser in Cambridgeshire.

BIBLIOGRAPHY

AAC 1936
American Artists' Congress, *America Today: A Book of 100 Prints*, Equinox Cooperative Press, 1936

Addison 1977
Paul Addison, *The Road to 1945: British Politics and the Second World War*, Quartet Books, 1977

AIA 1935
Artists International Association, *5 on Revolutionary Art*, Wishart, 1935

Akinsha et al. 2023
Konstantin Akinsha, Katia Denysova and Olena Kashuba-Volvach (eds), *In the Eye of the Storm: Modernism in Ukraine, 1900–1930s*, Thames & Hudson, 2023

Andrew 2009
Christopher Andrew, *The Defence of the Realm: The Authorized History of MI5*, Allen Lane, 2009

Arthur 2012
Dave Arthur, *Bert: The Life and Times of A. L. Lloyd*, Pluto Press, 2012

Artmonsky and Webb 2011
Ruth Artmonsky and Brian Webb, *F. K. H. Henrion: Design*, ACC Art Books, 2011

Atkinson 2021
Harriet Atkinson, '"Lines of Becoming": Misha Black and Entanglements through Exhibition Design', *Journal of Design History*, vol. 34, no. 1, March 2021, pp. 38–53

Baigell and Williams 1986
Matthew Baigell and Julia Williams (eds), *Artists Against War and Fascism: Papers of the First American Artists' Congress*, Rutgers State University, 1986

Bell, C. 1914
Clive Bell, *Art*, Chatto & Windus, 1914

Bell, C. 1928
Clive Bell, *Civilisation*, Chatto & Windus, 1928

Bell, Q. 1995
Quentin Bell, *Elders and Betters*, John Murray, 1995

Berthoud 1987
Roger Berthoud, *The Life of Henry Moore*, Faber & Faber, 1987

Bertram 1955
Anthony Bertram, *Paul Nash: Portrait of an Artist*, Faber & Faber, 1955

Binder 1935
Pearl Binder, *Odd Jobs*, George Harrap, 1935

Binder 1936
Pearl Binder, *Misha and Masha*, Victor Gollancz, 1936

Binyon 1983
Helen Binyon, *Eric Ravilious: Memoir of an Artist*, Lutterworth Press, 1983

Blake 1984
Avril Blake, *Misha Black*, Design Council, 1984

Blunt 1969
Anthony Blunt, *Picasso's Guernica*, Oxford University Press, 1969

Bohm-Duchen 2019
Monica Bohm-Duchen (ed.), *Insiders/Outsiders: Refugees from Nazi Europe and their Contribution to British Visual Culture*, Lund Humphries, 2019

Borkenau 1937
Franz Borkenau, *The Spanish Cockpit: An Eye-witness Account of the Political and Social Conflicts of the Spanish Civil War*, Faber & Faber, 1937

Borkenau 1938
Franz Borkenau, *The Communist International*, Faber & Faber, 1938

Boswell 1947
James Boswell, *The Artist's Dilemma*, Bodley Head, 1947

Branson 1985
Noreen Branson, *History of the British Communist Party: Vol. 3, 1927–1941*, Lawrence & Wishart, 1985

Brinson and Dove 2010
Charmian Brinson and Richard Dove, *Politics by Other Means: The Free German League of Culture in London 1939–1946*, Vallentine Mitchell, 2010

Brinson and Dove 2014
Charmian Brinson and Richard Dove, *A Matter of Intelligence: MI5 and the Surveillance of Anti-Nazi Refugees, 1933–1950*, Manchester University Press, 2014

Brinson and Dove 2021
Charmian Brinson and Richard Dove, *Working for the War Effort: German-Speaking Refugees in British Propaganda during the Second World War*, Vallentine Mitchell, 2021

Buchanan 2007
Tom Buchanan, *The Impact of the Spanish Civil War on Britain*, Sussex Academic Press, 2007

Calder 1969
Angus Calder, *The People's War: Britain 1939–1945*, Jonathan Cape, 1969

Carter 2001
Miranda Carter, *Anthony Blunt: His Lives*, Macmillan, 2001

Causey 2000
Andrew Causey, *Paul Nash: Writings on Art*, Clarendon Press, 2000

Collins 2021
Ian Collins, *John Craxton: A Life of Gifts*, Yale University Press, 2021

Cooper and Haskell 2016
Harry Cooper and Barbara Haskell, *Stuart Davis: In Full Swing*, Prestel, 2016

Cork 1987
Richard Cork, *David Bomberg*, Yale University Press, 1987

Croft 1998
Andy Croft (ed.), *A Weapon in the Struggle: The Cultural History of the Communist Party in Britain*, Pluto Press, 1998

Croft 2020
Andy Croft, *The Years of Anger: The Life of Randall Swingler*, Routledge, 2020

Danos and Gibelin 1986
Jacques Danos and Marcel Gibelin, *June '36: Class Struggle and the Popular Front in France*, Bookmarks, 1986

Davison 2009
Peter Davison (ed.), *The Diaries of George Orwell*, Harvill Secker, 2009

Day-Lewis 1937
C. Day-Lewis (ed.), *The Mind in Chains: Socialism and the Cultural Revolution*, Frederick Muller, 1937

Denning 1996
Michael Denning, *The Cultural Front: The Laboring of American Culture in the Twentieth Century*, Verso, 1996

Downing 2022
Taylor Downing, *1942: Britain at the Brink*, Little, Brown, 2022

Eastman 1934
Max Eastman, *Artists in Uniform: A Study of Literature and Bureaucratism*, George Allen & Unwin, 1934

Egbert 1970
Donald Drew Egbert, *Social Radicalism and the Arts: Western Europe*, Alfred A. Knopf, 1970

Elwyn-Jones 1983
Frederick Elwyn-Jones, *In My Time: An Autobiography*, Weidenfeld & Nicolson, 1983

Ereira 1981
Alan Ereira, *The Invergordon Mutiny*, Routledge & Kegan Paul, 1981

Feaver 1988
William Feaver, *Pitmen Painters: The Ashington Group 1934–1984*, Ashington Group Trustees, 1988

Feaver 2007
William Feaver, *James Boswell: Unofficial War Artist*, Muswell Press, 2007

Forbes 2013
Duncan Forbes (ed.), *Edith Tudor-Hart: In the Shadow of Tyranny*, National Gallery of Scotland/Wien Museum, 2013

Forge 1976
Andrew Forge (ed.), *The Townsend Journals: An Artist's Record of his Times, 1928–51*, Tate Gallery, 1976

Friend 2017
Andy Friend, *Ravilious & Co: The Pattern of Friendship*, Thames & Hudson, 2017

Games and Webb 2013
Naomi Games and Brian Webb, *Abram Games: Design*, ACC Art Books, 2013

García 2010
Hugo García, *The Truth about Spain! Mobilizing British Public Opinion, 1936–1939*, Sussex Academic Press, 2010

Godden 1935
G. M. Godden, *The Communist Attack on Great Britain*, Burns, Oates & Washbourne, 1935 (revised edition 1938)

Goodwin et al. 2005
Inge Goodwin, Giles Sutherland and Antonia Reeve, *Moderation be Damned! Edith Simon*, Antonia Reeve, 2005

Görner 2020
Rüdiger Görner, *Kokoschka: The Untimely Modernist*, Haus Publishing, 2020

Greening 2006
Edwin Greening, *From Aberdare to Albacete: A Welsh International Brigader's Memoirs of his Life*, Warren & Pell, 2006

Griffiths 1980
Richard Griffiths, *Fellow Travellers of the Right: British Enthusiasts for Nazi Germany 1933–39*, Constable, 1980

Hannington 1936
Wal Hannington, *Unemployed Struggles, 1919–1936*, Lawrence & Wishart, 1936

Hartog et al. 2023
Arie Hartog, Dorothea Schöne and Veronika Wiegartz (eds), *Péri's People: Peter László Péri (1899–1967)*, Kunsthaus Dahlem, 2023

Haskell 2020
Barbara Haskell (ed.), *Vida Americana: Mexican Muralists Remake American Art, 1925–1945*, Yale University Press, 2020

Hastings 2014
Selina Hastings, *The Red Earl: The Extraordinary Life of the 16th Earl of Huntingdon*, Bloomsbury, 2014

Haxey 1939
Simon Haxey, *Tory MP*, Victor Gollancz, 1939

Hayburn 1972
Ralph Hayburn, 'The Police and the Hunger Marchers', *International Review of Social History*, vol. 17, no. 2, August 1972, pp. 625–44

Hemingway 2002
Andrew Hemingway, *Artists on

the Left: American Artists and the Communist Movement, 1926–1956, Yale University Press, 2002

Hussey 2021
Mark Hussey, *Clive Bell and the Making of Modernism: A Biography*, Bloomsbury, 2021

Jankowski 2020
Paul Jankowski, *All Against All: The Long Winter of 1933 and the Origins of the Second World War*, Profile Books, 2020

Kapp 2003
Yvonne Kapp, *Time Will Tell: Memoirs*, Verso, 2003

Kershaw 2015
Ian Kershaw, *To Hell and Back: Europe 1914–1949*, Allen Lane, 2015

Kidd 1940
Ronald Kidd, *British Liberty in Danger*, Lawrence & Wishart, 1940

King 1960
James King, *The Last Modernist: A Life of Herbert Read*, Weidenfeld & Nicolson, 1960

Kokoschka and Marnau 1992
Olda Kokoschka and Alfred Marnau (eds), *Oskar Kokoschka Letters, 1905–1976*, Thames & Hudson, 1992

Lambert 1938
R. S. Lambert (ed.), *Art in England*, Pelican Books, 1938

Langa 2004
Helen Langa, *Radical Art: Printmaking and the Left in 1930s New York*, University of California Press, 2004

Laughton 1986
Bruce Laughton, *The Euston Road School: A Study in Objective Painting*, Scolar Press, 1986

Lilly 2003
Amy M. Lilly, 'Three Guineas, Two Exhibits: Woolf's Politics of Display', *Woolf Studies Annual*, vol. 9, 2003, pp. 29–54

Lindey 2018
Christine Lindey, *Art for All: British Socially Committed Art*, Artery Publications, 2018

Lipke 1967
William Lipke, *David Bomberg: A Critical Study of his Life and Work*, Evelyn, Adams & Mackay, 1967

MacCarthy 1989
Fiona MacCarthy, *Eric Gill*, Faber & Faber, 1989

Macmillan 1984
Harold Macmillan, *War Diaries: The Mediterranean, 1943–45*, Macmillan, 1984

McLaine 1979
Ian McLaine, *Ministry of Morale: Home Front Morale and the Ministry of Information in World War II*, Allen & Unwin, 1979

McMeekin 2003
Sean McMeekin, *The Red Millionaire: A Political Biography of Willy Münzenberg, Moscow's Secret Propaganda Tsar in the West*, Yale University Press, 2003

Martin 2014
Simon Martin, *Conscience and Conflict: British Artists and the Spanish Civil War*, Pallant House Gallery, 2014

Mirsky 1935
Dmitri Mirsky, *The Intelligentsia of Great Britain*, Victor Gollancz, 1935

Monroe 1973
Gerald M. Monroe, 'Art Front', *Archives of American Art*, vol. 13, no. 3, 1973, pp. 13–19

Monroe 1974
Gerald M. Monroe, 'Artists as Militant Trade Union Workers during the Great Depression', *Archives of American Art*, vol. 14, no. 1, 1974, pp. 7–10

Monroe 1975
Gerald M. Monroe, 'The American Artists Congress and the Invasion of Finland', *Archives of American Art*, vol. 15, no. 1, 1975, pp. 14–20

Morris and Radford 1983
Lynda Morris and Robert Radford, *AIA: The Story of the Artists International Association 1933–1953*, Museum of Modern Art, Oxford, 1983

Nicolson 1979
Nigel Nicolson (ed.), *The Sickle Side of the Moon: The Letters of Virginia Woolf, Vol. 5: 1932–1935*, Chatto & Windus, 1979

Page Croft 1948
Brigadier-General The Lord Croft, *My Life of Strife*, Hutchinson, 1948

Patterson 2020
Jody Patterson, *Modernism for the Masses: Painters, Politics and Public Murals in 1930s New York*, Yale University Press, 2020

Penrose 1981
Roland Penrose, *Scrap Book, 1900–1981*, Thames & Hudson, 1981

Petropoulos 2015
Jonathan Petropoulos, *Artists Under Hitler: Collaboration and Survival in Nazi Germany*, Yale University Press, 2015

Pooke 2007
Grant Pooke, *Francis Klingender 1907–1955: A Marxist Art Historian Out of Time*, Gill Vista Marx Press, 2007

Radford 1987
Robert Radford, *Art for a Purpose: The Artists' International Association 1933–1953*, Winchester School of Art Press, 1987

Read 1938
Herbert Read, *Art Now: An Introduction to the Theory of Modern Painting and Sculpture*, Faber & Faber, 1938

Remy 1999
Michel Remy, *Surrealism in Britain*, Ashgate, 1999

Rice et al. 1993
Paul Rice, Marianne Haile, Victor Margrie and Eugene Dana, *Sam Haile: Potter and Painter*, Bellew Publishing, 1993

Richardson 2021
John Richardson, *A Life of Picasso: The Minotaur Years 1933–1943*, Alfred A. Knopf, 2021

Rickaby 1978
Tony Rickaby, 'Artists' International', *History Workshop Journal*, vol. 6, no. 1, Autumn 1978, pp. 154–68

Rose 2002
June Rose, *Demons and Angels: A Life of Jacob Epstein*, Carroll & Graf Publishers, 2002

Roth 1977
Herbert Roth, 'James Boswell: A New Zealand Artist in London', *Auckland City Art Gallery Quarterly*, no. 65, December 1977, pp. 2–13

Rothstein 1966
Andrew Rothstein, *A House on Clerkenwell Green*, Marx Memorial Library, 1966

Russell 1968
John Russell, *Henry Moore*, Allen Lane, 1968

Sheeran 1986
John Sheeran, 'James Fitton: An Appreciation', in *James Fitton RA*, Dulwich Picture Gallery, 1986

Skidelsky 1992
Robert Skidelsky, *John Maynard Keynes: The Economist as Saviour*, Macmillan, 1992

Spalding 1983
Frances Spalding, *Vanessa Bell*, Macmillan, 1983

Spalding 1993
Frances Spalding, *Duncan Grant*, Chatto & Windus, 1993

Spalding 2022
Frances Spalding, *The Real and the Romantic: English Art between the Wars*, Thames & Hudson, 2022

Stansky and Abrahams 1966
Peter Stansky and William Abrahams, *Journey to the Frontier: Julian Bell & John Cornford: Their Lives in the 1930s*, Constable, 1966

Trant 2004
Carolyn Trant, *Art for Life: The Story of Peggy Angus*, Incline Press, 2004

Trevelyan 1957
Julian Trevelyan, *Indigo Days*, MacGibbon and Kee, 1957

Uhlman 1960
Fred Uhlman, *The Making of an Englishman*, Victor Gollancz, 1960

Ullmann 2008
Anne Ullmann (ed.), *Eric Ravilious: Landscape, Letters and Design*, The Fleece Press, 2008

Van Hensbergen 2004
Gijs van Hensbergen, *Guernica: The Biography of a Twentieth-Century Icon*, Bloomsbury, 2004

Watson 1994
Elizabeth Watson, *Don't Wait for It, or, Impressions of War 1939–1941*, Imperial War Museum, 1994

Waugh 1978
Alec Waugh, *The Best Wine Last: An Autobiography Through the Years 1932–1969*, Allen, 1978

Wertheim 2022
Lucy Wertheim, *Adventure in Art*, Unicorn, 2022

Whitford 1986
Frank Whitford, *Oskar Kokoschka: A Life*, Weidenfeld & Nicolson, 1986

Wilcox 1995
Denys J. Wilcox, *The London Group 1913–1939: The Artists and their Works*, Scolar Press, 1995

Woolf 1982
Virginia Woolf, *The Diary of Virginia Woolf, Vol. 4: 1931–1935*, ed. Anne Olivier Bell, The Hogarth Press, 1982

ACKNOWLEDGMENTS

This book seeks to extend and rebalance the historical record of artistic activism during a decade spanning the popular front of the 1930s and the early years of the Second World War. It draws on several crucial resources, including the work and analyses of predecessors who ensured that the story of the AIA was not entirely lost and the voices of those involved were caught before they passed away; key contributors to this collective endeavour were Tony Rickaby for History Workshop in the late 1970s, Lynda Morris and Robert Radford in the 1980s and 1990s, and more recently Christine Lindey. References for their writings can be found in the Bibliography and citations for their research and that of many others in the Notes.

I owe a major debt of gratitude to descendants of the founding generation of AIA artists and activists for their time, hospitality and enthusiasm, and for making available previously unpublished material, biographical and autobiographical writings and works held in family collections. In particular I would like to thank Sandra and Joe Thornberry, Cliff Rowe's daughter and son-in-law; Joe has from the first been an encouraging and generous interlocutor as the research and writing have unfolded. Sal Shuel, James Boswell's daughter, has provided unflagging help, advice and invaluable support; my thanks also to her son, Simon Shuel. Judy Fitton, daughter of Margaret and James Fitton, and their granddaughter, Victoria Hilton, have been tireless in their assistance and encouragement, as have Jane and Jim Holland, the children of James Holland, the third of the 'three Jameses'. Pearl Binder's daughters, Lou Taylor and Jo Gladstone, have been ever supportive and willing to share insights and their own research, as have Will Rea and other members of Betty Rea and Nan Youngman's family network, and Antonia Reeve, Edith Simon's daughter. The painter Peter Peri has been a welcoming and willing guide to the life and work of his grandfather Peter László Peri, and in depositing her father Morris Kestelman's papers in the Tate Archive, the actor Sara Kestelman has enabled crucial evidence of the AIA's inner workings to come to light. On three occasions I was fortunate to meet the late Caroline Compton, Diana and Fred Uhlman's daughter, and I have warm memories of her interest and help. To all these and others, my profound thanks.

For help in accessing material held in archives and special collections, I would like to thank Neil Parkinson at the Royal College of Art; Adrian Glew and his colleagues at the Tate Archive; Meirian Jump and her colleagues at the Marx Memorial Library; Ralph Gibson at the Society for Co-operation in Russian and Soviet Studies; Eleanor King, Archivist, and Chris Whittick, former County Archivist, at the East Sussex Record Office; Sue Breakell and her colleagues at the Brighton University Design Archives; and staff at the London Library, the British Library, London University Special Collections, the People's History Museum, Manchester, and the National Art Library at London's Victoria and Albert Museum. My especial thanks to Katia Denysova for her crucial help in liaising with the Ministry of Culture and National Gallery of Ukraine, and to all those there working for cultural freedom at a time of extreme difficulty.

Working with Thames & Hudson's professional network is a privilege: my thanks to Roger Thorp for commissioning and championing the book; to Maria Ranauro for the energy of her commitment and the excellence of her picture editing; to Lisa Ifsits for yet again gracing a work of mine with superlative design, and to Steve O Connell for his arresting cover; to Felicity Maunder for the precision and sensitivity of her editing skills and to Howard Watson for their assiduous proofreading; to Kate Thomas for her careful stewardship of the images; and to Mohara Gill for integrating all our efforts while navigating the complexities of the production process. Many thanks to Robin Friend for his photography of works held in private collections; to Harriet Atkinson, Peter Brawne and Sophie Gibson for their insights into the history of design; to Julian Francis for sharing research; to Peter Eaves for his help at Tate Britain; and to Sara Cooper and Karen Taylor at the Towner Gallery for their ongoing professional collaboration and support.

I am extremely grateful to Frances Spalding for providing such a perceptive Foreword and for her very generous endorsement of the final product.

My greatest thanks go to Jenny Keating for her critical contribution, her encouragement, patience and enduring love, without which nothing would have been written.

PICTURE CREDITS

All images are from Private Collections unless otherwise stated.

pp. 1, 2, 6 Marx Memorial Library & Workers' School, London. Photo Karl Weiss. © Jack Hastings. Reproduced by permission of the Estate c/o Rogers, Coleridge & White Ltd., 20 Powis Mews, London W11 1JN
1.1 © Anna Sandra Thornberry, daughter of Clifford Hooper Rowe
1.2 Salford Museum & Art Gallery (1947-218). © Anna Sandra Thornberry, daughter of Clifford Hooper Rowe
1.3 Peggy Angus Archive, East Sussex Record Office
1.4, 1.5, 1.6 Collection of Borys Voznytskyi, Lviv National Art Gallery, Ukraine. © Anna Sandra Thornberry, daughter of Clifford Hooper Rowe
1.7 © Anna Sandra Thornberry, daughter of Clifford Hooper Rowe
1.8, 1.9 © The Estate of James Fitton
1.10–1.13 (all images) © The Estate of Pearl Binder
1.14 © The Estate of James Fitton
1.15, 1.16 © The Estate of James Boswell/Tate
1.17 © The Estate of James Holland
1.18–1.22 (all images) © The Estate of James Boswell/Tate
1.23, 1.24 © The Estate of Margaret Fitton
1.25 © The Estate of James Fitton
1.26 © The Estate of Edith Simon/Courtesy Antonia Reeve
1.27 © The Estate of Percy Horton
1.28 Sheffield Museums Trust/Bridgeman Images. © The Estate of Percy Horton
1.29, 2.1 © Anna Sandra Thornberry, daughter of Clifford Hooper Rowe
2.4 © 1934, The Ardizzone Trust
2.6, 2.7, 2.8 Photographs by Edith Tudor-Hart © The Estate of W. Suschitzky, courtesy Fotohof archiv
2.9 © The Estate of Peggy Angus. All Rights Reserved, DACS 2025

2.10 Manchester Art Gallery/Bridgeman Images
2.11 © The Estate of James Boswell/Tate
2.12 Museum of Fine Arts, Boston. Gift of William H Lane Foundation (1990.394). Photo 2024 Museum of Fine Arts, Boston. All rights reserved/Bridgeman Images. © The Estate of Stuart Davis/VAGA at ARS, NY and DACS, London 2025
2.13 Whitney Museum of American Art, New York. Gift of Edith and Milton Lowenthal in memory of Juliana Force (49.22). Digital image Whitney Museum of American Art/Licensed by Scala. © The Estate of Ben Shahn/VAGA at ARS, NY and DACS, London 2025
2.14 The Wolfsonian-Florida International University, Miami Beach, Florida, The Mitchell Wolfson, Jr. Collection (87.1462.5.2.2). Photo Lynton Gardiner. Hugo Gellert © The Estate of the Artist
2.15 Norton Museum of Art, West Palm Beach, Florida, Purchase R H Norton Trust (64.17). © Estate of Stuart Davis/VAGA at ARS, NY and DACS, London 2025
2.16, 2.17 © The Estate of James Fitton
2.18, 2.19 © The Estate of James Boswell/Tate
2.20, 2.21 © The Estate of James Holland
2.22 © The Estate of Pearl Binder
3.2 Fitzwilliam Museum, University of Cambridge/Bridgeman Images
3.3 © The Estate of James Boswell/Tate
3.4 © Anna Sandra Thornberry, daughter of Clifford Hooper Rowe
3.5 San Francisco Art Institute, formerly California School of Fine Arts. Photo Silicon Valley Stock/Alamy Stock Photo. © Banco de México Diego Rivera Frida Kahlo Museums Trust, Mexico, D.F./DACS 2025

3.6 Photo Lucienne Bloch (1909–1999), courtesy Lucienne Allen/Old Stage Studios. Diego Rivera © Banco de México Diego Rivera Frida Kahlo Museums Trust, Mexico, D.F./DACS 2025
3.7 Marx Memorial Library & Workers' School, London. Photo Karl Weiss. © Jack Hastings. Reproduced by permission of the Estate c/o Rogers, Coleridge & White Ltd., 20 Powis Mews, London W11 1JN
3.8 Royal Academy of Arts, London (03/451). Photo John Hammond. Dame Laura Knight © The Estate of the Artist/Bridgeman Images
3.9 Brighton & Hove Museums (FA000683). James Bateman © DACS 2025
3.10 Tate (N05133). © Tate
3.11 Tate (T00432). Photo Artgen/Alamy Stock Photo
3.12 Photo Christie's Images/Bridgeman Images
3.13 Tate (N06212). © Tate
3.14 British Museum, London (1990,1006.52). Reproduced with permission of The Trustees of the British Museum. © The Estate of Pearl Binder
3.15 © The Estate of James Boswell/Tate
3.17 © The Estate of Margaret Fitton
4.1 © The Estate of James Boswell/Tate
4.2 Harvard Art Museums/Fogg Museum, Gift of Bernarda Bryson Shahn, Photo President and Fellows of Harvard College (P1970.3921). © The Estate of Ben Shahn/VAGA at ARS, NY and DACS, London 2025
4.3 Hugo Gellert papers, 1916–1986. Archives of American Art, Smithsonian Institution, Washington DC
4.4 Museum of Modern Art, Wakayama, Japan
4.5 Photo Christie's Images/Bridgeman Images
4.6 Museo Nacional de Arte Moderno, Mexico City, Mexico.

Photo Album/Scala, Florence. David Alfaro Siqueiros © DACS 2025
4.7 The Estate of Stuart Davis Archives. © The Estate of Stuart Davis/VAGA at ARS, NY and DACS, London 2025
4.8 Harold Baumbach papers, 1934–1976. Archives of American Art, Smithsonian Institution, Washington DC
4.9, 4.10 © The Estate of James Holland
4.11 © The Estate of James Boswell/Tate
4.12, 4.13, 4.14 © The Estate of James Fitton
4.15 © The Estate of Margaret Fitton
4.16 British Council Collection (P3). Photo Artgen/Alamy Stock Photo
4.17 © The Estate of James Boswell/Tate
4.18 Scottish National Gallery of Modern Art, Edinburgh (GMA 3589). Photo National Galleries of Scotland/Bridgeman Images. © Successió Miró/ADAGP, Paris and DACS London 2025
4.19 Laing Art Gallery, Newcastle-upon-Tyne. Tyne & Wear Archives & Museums/Bridgeman Images
4.20 Birmingham Museum Trust, presented by the Contemporary Art Society, 1949 (1946P6). Photo Birmingham Museums Trust. © The Estate of the Artist/Bridgeman Images
4.25 Nan Youngman © A. Youngman/The Estate of the Artist
4.26 © The Estate of James Boswell/Tate
4.27 Leicester Museums & Galleries/Bridgeman Images © Anna Sandra Thornberry, daughter of Clifford Hooper Rowe
5.2 Photo Christie's Images/Bridgeman Images
5.3 Woodhorn Museum, Ashington, on loan from the Ashington Group Trustees (ASHMM 1989.17.53). Reproduced by courtesy of the Ashington Group Trustees
5.4 Woodhorn Museum, Ashington, on loan from the Ashington Group Trustees (ASHMM 1989.17.14). Reproduced by courtesy of the Ashington Group Trustees
5.5 Tate (N05038)
5.6 American Artists Congress Exhibition, Poster collection, Poster US 5422, Hoover Institution Library & Archives, Palo Alto, CA
5.7 National Gallery of Art, Washington DC. Reba and Dave Williams Collection, Art Purchase Fund (2008.115.31)
5.8 Amon Carter Museum of American Art, Fort Worth, Texas (1998.116). © Andrée Ruellan
5.9 National Gallery of Art Washington DC. Reba and Dave Williams Collection, Gift of Reba and Dave Williams (2008.115.3847). José M. Pavón © The Estate of the Artist
5.10 National Gallery of Art Washington DC. Reba and Dave Williams Collection, Gift of Reba and Dave Williams (2008.115.903). George Biddle © The Estate of the Artist
5.11 The State Art Collection, The Art Gallery of Western Australia. Purchased 1973 (1973/00P2)
5.12 Museo del Prado, Madrid (P000749)
5.13 Pallant House Gallery, Chichester. Hussey Bequest, Chichester District Council, 1985. Photo Bridgeman Images. © The Estate of David Bomberg. All Rights Reserved, DACS 2025
5.14 Tate (T03399). Barbara Hepworth © Bowness
5.15 Collection Buffalo AKG Art Museum, Room of Contemporary Art Fund, 1939 (RCA1939:12.1). © The Henry Moore Foundation. All Rights Reserved, DACS/www.henry-moore.org 2025
5.16 Scottish National Gallery, Edinburgh (GMA 4816). Photo Peter Nahum at The Leicester Galleries, London/Bridgeman Images
5.20 Reina Sofia, Madrid (RESERVA 2231/Folletos Caja 1793-10). © José Lino Vaamonde Valencia. MNCARS, Madrid. Donación J. Vaamonde Horcada (2001). Pablo Picasso © Succession Picasso/DACS, London 2025
5.21 DRU archives, now held by Scott Brownrigg
5.22, 5.23, 5.24 © The Peter László Peri Estate
5.25 Walker Art Center, Minneapolis, Minnesota. Gift of the T. B. Walker Foundation, Gilbert M. Walker Fund, 1942 (1942.1)
5.26 Manchester City Art Gallery (1944.49)/Bridgeman Images
5.27 Bolton Museum Collection. Purchased with the assistance of the Arts Council England/Victoria and Albert Museum Purchase Grant Fund, the Art Fund, and the Friends of Bolton Museum (BOLMG:2017.2). Julian Trevelyan © The Estate of the Artist/Bridgeman Images
5.28 Yale Center for British Art, Paul Mellon Fund (B1995.26)
5.29 Photo from an album in the Collection of Marjorie Weiner, courtesy Edmund Weiner and Antonia Reeve
5.30 The Murray Family Collection, UK and USA
5.31 © The Estate of Edith Simon/Courtesy Antonia Reeve
5.32 Collection of Harvey and Harvey-Ann Ross
6.2 Photo Felix Man/Picture Post/Hulton Archive/Getty Images
6.3 Private collection on long term loan to the Scottish National Gallery of Modern Art (GML 285). © Fondation Oskar Kokoschka/DACS 2025
6.4 Marx Memorial Library & Workers' School, London (Box A-4:S/28). © Succession Picasso/DACS, London 2025
6.5, 6.6 The Murray Family Collection, UK and USA
6.7 Photo James Austin/Bridgeman Images. Ben Nicholson © All rights reserved, DACS 2025
6.8 Photo Christie's Images/Bridgeman Images
6.9 The Murray Family Collection, UK and USA. Photo Michael Woods. All rights reserved 2024/Bridgeman Images
6.10 Tate (N05883). William Coldstream © The Estate of the Artist/Bridgeman Images
6.11 Tate (T00942)

6.12 Laing Art Gallery (TWCMS 2013.1785). Photo Tyne & Wear Archives & Museums/Bridgeman Images. Walter Durac Barnett © The Estate of the Artist

6.13 Laing Art Gallery (TWCMS 2013.1801). Photo Tyne & Wear Archives & Museums/Bridgeman Images. Elizabeth Spurr © The Estate of the Artist

6.14 Tate (T03834). © Fondation Oskar Kokoschka/DACS 2025

6.15 © Imperial War Museum (Art. IWM ART 15989 24). © The Estate of Hellmuth Weissenborn, courtesy Odile Weissenborn, New York

6.16 Laing Art Gallery (TWCMS 2013.1798). Photo Tyne & Wear Archives & Museums/Bridgeman Images. Geoffrey Rhoades © The Estate of the Artist

6.18 Laing Art Gallery (TWCMS 2013.1800). Photo Tyne & Wear Archives & Museums/Bridgeman Images. Lionel Maurice de Sausmarez © The Estate of the Artist

6.19 Laing Art Gallery (TWCMS 2013.1794). Photo Tyne & Wear Archives & Museums/Bridgeman Images. © The Estate of James Holland

7.1 © The Estate of Edith Simon/Courtesy Antonia Reeve

7.2 Royal Air Force Museum (FA00793). Carel Weight © The Estate of the Artist/Bridgeman Images

7.3 © The Peter László Peri Estate

7.4 National Railway Museum/Science & Society Picture Library - All rights reserved. With permission of The Board of Trustees of the Science Museum. © Anna Sandra Thornberry, daughter of Clifford Hooper Rowe

7.5 Photo Liss Fine Art/Bridgeman Images. © Anna Sandra Thornberry, daughter of Clifford Hooper Rowe

7.7, 7.8, 7.9 Geza Szobel © ADAGP, Paris and DACS, London 2025

7.10 Tate (T11789)

7.11 Julian Trevelyan © The Estate of the Artist/Bridgeman Images

7.12 © Crown Copyright. IWM (D 7027)

7.13 Museum of Modern Art, New York. Gift of Mrs. John Carter (287.1943). Digital image, The Museum of Modern Art, New York/Scala, Florence. Reproduced courtesy of the Henrion estate.

7.14 © The Peter László Peri Estate

7.15 © Crown Copyright. IWM (D 4372)

7.16 British Museum, London (2000,1125.17). Reproduced with permission of The Trustees of the British Museum. © The Estate of James Boswell/Tate

7.17–7.26 (all images) © The Estate of James Boswell/Tate

8.1 FHK Henrion Archive, University of Brighton Design Archives, by courtesy of the Henrion estate

8.2 FHK Henrion Archive (FHK-3-23-6), University of Brighton Design Archives, by courtesy of the Henrion estate

8.3–8.10 (all images) © The Estate of James Boswell/Tate

8.11 © Crown Copyright. IWM (Art.IWM PST 2802)

8.12 © Crown Copyright. IWM (Art IWM PST 2911)

8.13 FHK Henrion Archive (FHK-3-23-2), University of Brighton Design Archives, by courtesy of the Henrion estate

8.14 FHK Henrion Archive (FHK-3-23-1), University of Brighton Design Archives, by courtesy of the Henrion estate

8.15 FHK Henrion Archive (FHK-3-23-10), University of Brighton Design Archives, by courtesy of the Henrion estate

8.16 © Imperial War Museum (Art.IWM ART 16786). Morris Kestelman RA © Sara Kestelman

8.17 Marx Memorial Library & Workers' School, London. © Anna Sandra Thornberry, daughter of Clifford Hooper Rowe

8.18 Courtesy of the People's History Museum, Manchester. © Anna Sandra Thornberry, daughter of Clifford Hooper Rowe

8.19 FHK Henrion Archive (FHK-3-23-8), University of Brighton Design Archives, by courtesy of the Henrion estate

8.20 Kunsthaus, Zurich. Photo Bridgeman Images. © Fondation Oskar Kokoschka/DACS 2025

8.21 © The Estate of David Caplan

8.22 Tate (T15612)

8.23 Mackelvie Trust Collection, Auckland Art Gallery Toi o Tāmaki, purchased 1991 (M1991/31). © The Estate of John Tunnard. All rights reserved. DACS 2025

8.24 FHK Henrion Archive (FHK-3-23-9), University of Brighton Design Archives, by courtesy of the Henrion estate. Betty Rea © The Estate of the Artist

8.25 © J. Kamlani/The Estate of the Artist

INDEX

Figures in *italics* indicate illustrations; *n* indicates an endnote. Works including writings are listed by title under their creator's name, where known and singularly attributable.

Abstract art 44, 106, 109, 111, 126, 146, 165, 166, 220
Abyssinia 89, 110, 122, 156, 157, 170, 188, 231
Action Française 59
Adshead, Mary 115, 336
Advisory Council, AIA (AC) 9, n1.13, 209, 213, 219, n6.24, 225, 241, 245, 260, 268, 295
Agar, Eileen 115, n5.23, 5.82, 220, 266, 336
AIA American exhibition, proposed 209, 223, 224–5
AIA and FGLC Exhibition of Sculpture and Drawings 260
AIA Grosvenor Square exhibition 165–6, n5.1, 176, 179, n5.23, 181, 182, 185, 187, 188, 191, 195, 205, 220, 306
Albert Hall 89, 158, 190, 230, 266
Allies inside Germany 301
Allinson, Adrian 115, n8.14
All Union Society for Cultural Relations with Foreign Countries (VOKS) 15, 27, 1.45, 86, 103
Alpha Group 82, 138, 159; *It's Up to Us* 138, n4.28, *139*, 157; 'Three Jameses' desk diary 137
America Today 170, 176, n5.10–12
American Artists' Congress (AAC) 74, 125, n4.1, 126, 129–34, n4.11–12, 170, 176, 201–2, 206, 209, 225, n6.34, 238
American Writers' Congress 126, n4.8
Anglo-German Fellowship 303
Anglo-Soviet Alliance 264–5
Angus, Peggy n1.10, 27, n1.44, n1.55, n1.66, n1.76, 59, 63, 66, 91, 104, 248, 336; *Cement Works* 64; *Poison Gas* 115
Archer, David 125, 141
Ardizzone, Edward n1.55, n1.76, 241, 336; *Through the Hoop 56*
Army Bureau of Current Affairs (ABCA) 279, 283, n8.15, 292

Arp, Jean 141, 266
Art Front 126, n4.4–5, n4.7, *127*, *133*, 170, 177
Artists Against Fascism and War 9, 81, 104, 106, 113, 122, 141, 165, 191
Artists Aid China 289
Artists Aid Russia 266, *267*
Artists and Designers Collective, Leamington Spa 308–9
Artists' Committee of Action 125, 126
Artists Help Spain 158
Artists International Association (AIA) 7–8, 45, 89, 91, 113, 116, 118, n3.71, 133, 137, 145, 149, 151, 156, 158–9, 163, 165–6, 170, 179, 188, 191, 197, 199, 206–7, 212, 216, 220, 225–6, 229, 235, 238, 240, 242, 245, 247, 253–4, 255, 261, 268, 269–70, 272, 282, 304, 307, 309, 312; *AIA Bulletin* 201–2, 212, 215, 228, 235, 238, 241, 260, 263, 280, 288–9, 309, 311
Artists' International – British Section (AI) 8, 32, 44–5, 53–4, 58, 64, 78, 86–7, 89, 90, 96, n3.15, 104, 106, 109, 113, n3.71
Artists' News-Sheet 169–70, 178, 182, 219
Artists' Peace Campaign 192, 212
Artists' Refugee Committee (ARC) n3.59, 150, 198, 215, 235, 238, 248
Artists' Union (AU) n2.49, n3.25, 125, 126, 170, 206, 224, 225, n6.34
'Arts and the Dictators' 141, n4.30
Ashington Group 166, 182
Association des Écrivains et Artistes Révolutionaires (AEAR) 58, n2.13, 113
Association of Architects Surveyors and Technical Assistants (AASTA) 266
Athol, Duchess of 190
Atlantic Charter 281
Attlee, Clement 58, 215, 219, 242, 282
Aub, Max 188
Auden, W. H. n2.63, 150, 201
Austria 59, 63, 86, 87, 122, 138, 192
Ayrton, Michael 311

Badmin, Stanley 212, 223, 234, 255, n7.48, 336
Baldwin, Stanley 56, 192
Banting, John 220, n6.87, 250, 255, 264, n7.43, 266, 269, 336
Barcelona 150, 151, 215, 219, 220
Barnett, Walter Durac 209, 229, n6.50, 336; *Bread and Circuses 233*
Barry, Gerald 307
Bas, Edward Le 297, 341; *Bathers on the Serpentine* 297, *301*
Bassett-Gray 38, n1.67
Bateman, James 169, n6.24, n6.81, 336; *Thames Wharf 107*
Bauhaus 59, 194
Bawden, Charlotte 255
Bawden, Edward n1.10, 59, 158, 212, 242, 336
Beaverbrook, Max 106, 270
Beddington, Jack 36, 137
Bell, Angelica 35, 118, n3.59, 219
Bell, Clive 13, n1.11, 118, n3.59, 121, n3.67–8, 309; *Civilisation* 121
Bell, Graham 199, 201, 202, n5.86, 209, 211, 220, n6.28, 239, 255, 336; *Bury Them and Be Silent* 220; *The Café* 200
Bell, Julian 118, 122, 159, 190
Bell, Quentin n3.58, 115, 117, 118, n3.59, 150, 156, 166, n5.4, 186, 190, n5.48, 201, 212, 336
Bell, Vanessa 9, 35, n1.34, 63, 103, n3.59, 121, 158, 190, 201, n6.24, 234, n6.81, 260, 289, 337
Benton, Thomas Hart 71, n2.39
Bergamín, José 178, 188
Berlin Olympics 141, 151, 159
Bernal, J. D. 'Sage' 92, 104
Beveridge Report 282–3
Bevin, Ernest 123, 207, 242
Biddle, George 99, 102, 133, 337; *Sand! 175*
Bigge, John 45
Binder, Pearl 7–8, n1.19, 22, n1.29, n1.30, 23, n1.31–35, 24, 27, 31, n1.45–6, n1.66, n1.76, 62, 82, n2.65, 85, n2.72–3, 86, 87, n2.76, 91, 112, n3.50, n3.50, 122, n138, 141, 148, n4.7–8, 181, 234, 263, n7.41, 268, 311, 337; book and other illustrations: *Everyday Life in Soviet Russia* n4.48; *H. G. Wells* 148; *Misha*

353

and Masha 123, 148, 263; *The Real East End* 7, 23; *Russian Families* 263; prints: *The Bell Foundry 30*; *Chalking Squad* 94; *Down the Mine, South Wales* 116; *Evening in Aldgate* 29; *Jewish Bookshop, Wentworth Street 28*; *Love Lane, Shadwell* 85; *Odd Jobs* 23, 122; *Russian Railway Journey* 85; writings: 'English Artist in Moscow' 263

Binyon, Helen n1.10, n2.8, 104, n3.32, n5.3, 209, 211, n6.50, n6.57, n6.59, 255, n7.20, 268, 288, 337; *Puppets for Spain* n6.26, 223

Black, Rivka n6.50, 235

Blackshirts 53, n2.9, 159

Black, Sir Misha 7, 9, 11, n1.1, n1.2, n1.6, 12, n1.7, n1.8, n1.9, 15, n1.23, 32, 38, n1.67, n1.69, 42, 43, n1.76, 51, 64, 78, n2.51, 82, 92, 109, 113, 118, 136, 165, 186, 187, 192, 207, 209, 211, n6.2, 212, n6.24, 224, 225, 226, n6.44, 228, 230, 231, 232, 235, 238, 242, 248, 254, n7.18, 255, 262, 269, 270, n8.14, 284, 294–5, 311, 337; 'An Equity for Artists?' 136, 209; 'Personal Statement' 231

Blake, Betsy 198, 242

Der Blaue Reiter 199

Block, Lou 126

Block, Paul 176

Blum, Léon 142, 216

Blunt, Anthony 118, n3.58, 141, 145, 194, 195, n5.61, n5.66, 197, 202, 209, 241, 242, 289, 337

Boichukists 209, n5.95

Bomberg, David 181–2; *Ronda Bridge 180*

Bone, Edith 150, 155

Bone, Muirhead 115, 216, n6.24, 224, n8.14, 337

Bone, Stephen 115, 212, n6.7, 213, 223, 224, n6.50, 234, 337

Bonnard, Pierre 241

Boriswood 36, n1.61

Bosch, Hieronymus 299; *The Garden of Earthly Delights* 299

Boswell, James n1.1, 24, 32, n1.48, n1.49–53, 35, n1.55, n1.57, 36, n1.60, n1.61, n1.76, 46, 54, n2.8, 57, 64, 81, 82, n2.65–7, n3.15, 122, 124, 137, 159–161, n4.71, 186, 207, n5.93, 234, n6.87, 250, n7.10, 252, 253, 268, 270, 272–7, 279, n8.1, 284–5, 286, 311, 337; cartoons: *Church, Press and Army 136*; *Hatton Garden Luncheon* 83; *He hath made for us a pathway* 94, *94*; *His Majesty's Servants* 69, 85; *The Lonely Heart* 83, *83*; *Surrealist Exhibition London 1936 144*, 145; *You Gotta Have Blue Blood* 83, *83*, 85; drawings: *Bringing in a Casualty at Night* 273; 'Bull' Sketchbook *274–6*; *A Corner of the NAAFI* 288, n7.59; *Crewe 2 a.m.* 288, n7.59; *Depot Barber Shop* 250; 'Europa' Sketchbook *285–7*; *Fatigue Party* 250; *Leman Street Barricade* 160; *The Mind in Chains* 285, *285*; *The Night the Sergeant Copped It* 270; *Sick Parade* n7.59; *Steinmann Pin Going In* 273; *Taking Details from Casualty* 273; *Three Volunteers – You, You and You!* 250; prints: *The Fall of London* 38, *39*; *Empire Builders* 116, *117*, 137; *Marfa* 37; *The Street 124*; paintings: *The Entrance to Gordon Square 34*; *The Scala Stage Door 34*; writings: *The Artist's Dilemma* 207; 'Cable Street – A Demonstrator's Impressions' n4.71; 'Wanted a Goya' 252, 288

Bracken, Brendan 254, 307

Bracque, Georges 73, 142

Brancusi, Constantin 144

Branson, Clive n1.14, n1.70, 96, 259, 337; *Bombed: Women and Searchlights 258*, 259

Branson (née Browne), Noreen 96

Brenner, Anita 71

Bresson, Robert 144

Breton, André 142, 144, 145, 146, 188

Breughel, Pieter 299

Britain Today 211, 224, 239, 250

British Adult Education Institute 289

British Artists' Congress 117, 161, n4.72–3, 165, 166, 169, 170, 186, 187, 199, 207, 225, 312

British Restaurants 290, 307

British Union of Fascists (BUF) 43, 53, 56, 86, 161, 187

Browne, Felicia 150, n4.55, 153, 155, n4.57–60, 156, 157, 159, 161, 163, 170, 215, 337; *Drawings by Felicia Browne* 158; drawings of Republican militia and supporters *154*

Brown, Isabel 178, n5.16

Brownrigg, George; *Dawn 168*

Brücke, Die 199

Buchanan, Tom 151

Buñuel, Luis 142

Burchard, Irmgard 198, n5.68

Burck, Jacob 93, 338

Burford, Stella 211

Burra, Edward 45, 64, 144, 338

Cable Street, Battle of 159–161

Cadmus, Paul, *Shore Leave 172*

Cambrian cartel 121, n3.67

Cambridge anti-war exhibitions 50, 116, 118, *119*, 122

Camden Studios 247, 268

Camden Town Group 35, 113, 115

Čapek, Josef 213

Caplan, David 'Davy' 255, n7.25, n7.48, 294, 338; *Gabriel Peri* 303

Carline, Richard 115, 206, 209, 224, 260, n8.16, 338

Carpenter, Patrick n3.12, 211, 303–4, n8.50, 305, 338; *The Death of Gabriel Peri* 303, *304*, n8.48

Casati, Cristina 96, 98, 99, 102, 158

Catholic Herald 80, 116, n5.32

Central Committee, AIA (CC) 150, 198, 207, 209, 211, n6.1, n6.3, 213, 215, 220, 225, 228, 229, 231, 232, 238, 242, 245, 247, 248, 250, 255, 260, 268, 280, 291, 311

Central Institute of Art and Design (CIAD) 230, 239, 255, 266, 268, 269, 282, n8.14

Central School of Art and Design 12, 23, 27, 46, 137

Chamberlain, Neville n4.63, 192, 205, 213, 219, 226, 227, 229

Charing Cross Booking Hall 247, 249, 250, 253, 256, 261–3, 265, 269, 270, 272

Charlotte Street 7, 43, 51, 64, 80, 89, 105, 156, 311; AIA Centre 270, 288

Chirico, Giorgio de 141, 144

Chosak, Bessie 73–4, 126

Churchill, Winston 85, 237, 245, 254, 265, 266, 271, 281–3, 292, 307

Citrine, Walter 207

Civil Defence Artists 261

Clark, Helena 269

Clark, Kenneth 111, 115, 141, 201, 219, 229, 230, n6.54, 234, 236, n6.75, 241, 254, 256, 261, 270, 288, 289

Clough-Williams, Amabel 82, n3.50

Clynes, John 24, n1.39

Coit Tower 102, 126

Coldstream, William n1.54, 90, 96, 150, 199, 201, n5.75, 202, 209, 211, n6.7, 220, n6.28, 223, 255, 285, 338;

Inez Spender 223; *Thomasson Park, Bolton* 203
Cole, John 260, 338
Collins, Doris 301
Collins, Jesse 212, 219, 224, 240, 255, 338; *AIA Annual Exhibition Whitechapel Art Gallery* 210
Colquhoun, Ithell 220, 256, 264, 289, 338
Communism 8, 79, 80, 106, 112, 229
Communist Party of Great Britain (CPGB) 14, 36, 91, 92, 102, 150, 161, 163, 207, 228, 229, 242, 294
Constable, W. G. 165, 186, 338
Contemporary Poetry and Prose 141, 157
Conway Hall 141, 145, 170, 177, 187, 209, 235
Cornford, John 49, 148
Co-operative Publishing Society of Foreign Workers 15, 21
Council for Civil Liberties 58, 106, 311
Council for Encouragement of Music and the Arts (CEMA) 250, 289
Courbet, Gustave 197
Courtauld Institute 165, 186, 241
Coxon, Raymond 182
Craxton, John 266, n7.46
Croft, Henry Page 149, n4.50, 188, 205, 281
Croix-de-Feu 59
Crowndale Road Working Men's College 46, 166, 247, 289
Cundall, Charles 115, 169, 338; *Durham Miners' Gala* 115
Czechoslovakia 192, 231, 235, 291

Daily Herald 219
Daily Mail n2.9, n2.74, 185
Daily Worker 8, 18, 137, 138, 148, 155, 185, 245, 249, 250, 255, 299
Daladier, Édouard 192, 216
Dalí, Salvador 126, 141, 144
Daumier, Honoré 24, 170, 197, 262
Davis, Stuart 71, 73–78, n2.46, 74, n2.47, n2.51, 102, 125, n4.5, n4.7, 134, 170, n5.10, 176, 224, 338; *Adit, No. 2 or French Factory* 71, *72*
Dawson, Norman n5.23, 207, 209, n5.97; *British Diplomacy* 209
Day-Lewis, Cecil n2.63, 253, 304–5, 339; 'The cry for help ...' 305, n8.52, 307
Degenerate Art 112, 193, 198
Derain, André 241

Design Today 92, n3.11
Desnoyer, François 115
Dickens, Ronald 284
Dismoor, Jessica 151, n4.56, 220, 339; *Superimposed Forms* 221
Dix, Otto 112
Dobson, Frank n1.54, 115, 220, 223, 270, 339
Dollfuss, Engelbert 62, 123
Dooley, Pat 14–15
Downs, George n7.2, 256, 266, 339; *Cycle Race* 256
Driberg, Jack n1.34, 87
Duchamp, Marcel 144
Duddington, J. N. 226
Dunlop, Ronald Ossory 12, n1.10
Durer, Albrecht 170

Eden, Anthony n4.63, 219
Ellis, Fred 86, 87
Éluard, Paul 144, 188
Elwyn-Jones, Lord Frederick 87, 122–3, 138, 148, n4.46–7, 263, 311, 339; *The Battle for Peace* n4.46
Emotionist Group 13, n1.13, 32
Empire Marketing Board 135
Epstein, Jacob 158, 159, 181, 185, 197
Equipment of a Division 281
Ernst, Max 141, 142, 144, 156, 188
Eurich, Richard 224
Euston Road School n3.59, 199, 201, n5.74, 220, 252, 299
Evergood, Philip 206, n5.92, 224, 339; *American Tragedy* 208
Everyman Prints 176, 212, n6.7, 224, 232–5, *233*, 236, *239*, *243*, 244
Exhibition of 20th Century German Art 198–99, 209, 213, n.5.68–9
Exhibitions Committee, AIA 211, 225, 238, 239, 279–80, 284, 289–90, n8.16, 295
Expressionism 110, 126, 303

Federal Art Project (FAP) 102, 134, 135, 176, n5.14, 206, 224, 225, n6.34, 229, 239
Feibusch, Hans 27, n1.76, 54, 182, 295–6, 339; *Resurrection* 295
Finland 234–5
Fitton, James 23, n1.36, 24, n1.37–40, 27, 32, n1.76, n2.8, n2.65, 83, 124, 126, 137–8, 148, 182, 185–86, 224, 248, 254, 268, n8.16, 289, 311, 339; cartoons: *A New Use for Perambulators* 79, 83; *For Charity* 79, 83; paintings: *The Canal Bridge* 42; poster and cover designs: *Russian Oil Products* 24, *25*; *It's Up to Us* 138, *139*; prints: *May Day* 24, *26*; *Trapeze II* 33
Fitton (née Cook), Margaret n1.66, n1.76, 137, 186, 195, 268, 289, 311, 339; *Duck Pond, Dulwich* 140; *Ironing and Airing* 41; *Man in a Wicker Chair* 40; *Rhubarb Pie* 120
Fitzroy Street 35–6
Flesch, Hans 215
'Foodships for Spain' n3.59, 216
Force, Juliana 73
For Intellectual Liberty 224
For Liberty 262, 279, n8.7, 284, 286, 288–90, n8.27, 291, 295–309
Forster, E. M. 15, n1.61, 112, 113, n3.50, 123
Fox, Ralph n2.64, n3.50, 148, n4.44–5; *France Faces the Future* 148
France 59, 138, 142, 165, 264
Franco, General Francisco 146, 149, 158, 181
Free German League of Culture (FGLC) 150, n4.51, 215, n6.12, 235, n6.64, n6.67, 238, 241, 259, 301
Freedman, Barnett 24, 158
Friell, James 'Gabriel' n2.67
Freud, Lucian 199
Freundlich, Otto 166; *Komposition* 167
Fry, Maxwell 270, 292
Fry, Roger 31, n1.54, 56

Gabo, Miriam 209
Games, Abram 291–2, 339; *Your Britain – Fight for it Now* 293
Gardiner, Clive 309
Garside, Jean 66
Gascoyne, David 142; *A Short Survey of Surrealism* 142
Gauguin, Paul 73
Gellert, Hugo 74: *Us Fellas Gotta Stick Together or The Last Defence of Capitalism* 76
General Post Office 135, 137, 291
Germany 15, 86, 148, 181, 227
Gernika 187, n5.40–1, 192
Gertler, Mark 182, 216, 224, 225, n6.38, 339
Giacometti, Alberto 144, 156, 188
Gide, André 112, 148, 4.29; *Retour de l'USSR* 148, n.4.29
Gill, Eric 64, 67, 80, n2.58, 91, 93, 158, n6.24, 228, n6.81, 242, 339;

INDEX 355

Prospero and Ariel 80; *Stations of the Cross* 80
Gillet, Paul 255
Gilray, James, *The Plum-pudding in Danger* 260
Ginesi, Edna n1.14, 182
Goebbels, Joseph 110, 182
Goldfinger, Ernő n5.23, 266
Goldring, Douglas 67, n2.27
Gollancz, Victor 123, 166, 242; *The Betrayal of the Left* 245
Gooden, G. M. 79–81, n5.25; *The Communist Attack on Great Britain* 80
Gordon, Jan 185, n6.42, 256, 269, 272, 296, n8.52, 339
Gorelick, Boris 176
Gottlieb, Harry 224, 225
Goupil Gallery 13, 15
Gowing, Lawrence n3.12, 220; *Non Combatants* 223
Goya, Francisco 38, 170, 178, 220, 253, 258; 262, 289; *Disasters of War* 38, 258, 277, 279; *The Third of May 1808* 178 *179*
Grant, Duncan 35, n1.54, 36, 91, 103, 113, 118, 150, 158, 182, 185, 190, 201, n6.24, n6.81, 260, 289, 340; *After Goya* 223; *Drawings by Felicia Browne* n4.65
Gray, Milner n1.67, 229, n6.50, 230, 248, 254, n8.14, 340
Greaves, Leonard 239–40, 340
Greco, El, *The Holy Trinity* 194
Grierson, John 93
Gris, Juan 110
Gropius, Walter 110
Gropper, William 74
Grosz, George 70, 73, n2.68, 112, 277

Haile, Sam n1.55, n5.82, 211, n6.3, 219, 220, 231, 232; *Non-Payment of Taxes, Congo, Christian Era 184*; *Surgical Ward* 227
Hamann, Paul 235, 237, n6.71
Hannington, Wal n1.25, 53
Hartrick, A. S. 23–24, 46
Hastings, Viscount Jack 96, 97, 98, n3.19, 102, 103, 123, 158, 166, 178, 186, 213, 216; *The Worker of the Future Clearing Away the Chaos of Capitalism 1, 2, 6, 100–1, 102–3*
Havinden, Ashley 311
Hayter, Stanley William 156
Heartfield, John 215
Hélion, Jean 110, 142, 166

Hendy, Philip 289
Henrion, F. H. K. n6.71, 248, 254, 262, n7.40, 269, 284, 291, 295, 304, 305; *Artists Aid Russia Exhibition 267*
Hepworth, Barbara n1.14, 45, 115, 166, 182, 220, 266; *Ball, Plane and Hole 183*
Hermes, Gertrude 220, 340
Hess, Tisa 220, 225, 226, n6.39, 340
Hillier, Tristram 45
Hitler, Adolf 31, 54, 56, 70, 110, 111, 112, 126, 151, 156, 157, 187, 212, 227, 231, 245, 247, 254, 263, 264, 303
Hodgkins, Frances n1.75, 266
Hogarth, William 170, 272
Hogarth Group 92, n3.12, 225, 311
Holbein, Hans 277; *The Dance of Death* 277
Holland, James 32, n1.50–1, 35, n1.55, n1.58–9, 36, n1.60, n1.76, n2.8, 82, n2.65, 83, 84, n3.12,118, 124, n4.25, 145, 150, 192, 209, 212, 224, 232, n6.57, n6.59, 254, 255, 269, n8.16, 311, 340; cartoons: *Happy Days 135 135*; *Incitement to Disaffection 85*; *The tumult and the shouting dies 94*; *With a Ladder and Some Glasses 84, 84*; drawings: *Comment on Guernica 192*; *Docks 36*; *Midday Meeting 192*; *Our Heritage, the Sea 135*; *The Sailor's Return 84, 84*; prints: *Newsreel 244*
Holzer, Henry 232, n6.57
Horton, Percy n1.55, n1.76, 46, n3.12, 109, 113, 134, 137, 145, 158, 163, 165, 166, n5.3, n5.83, 207, 212, 225, n6.44, 228, 229, n6.50, 230, 232, n6.59, 234, 241, 247, n7.1, 252, 253, 263, n7.47, 272, n8.14, 289, 340; *The Invalid 108*; *The Postman 47*; *Unemployed Man 48*, 163
Horton, Ron n1.76, n3.12, 225, 247, 253, 263, 340
Hunger Marchers 18, 49, 53, 54, 56
Hunger, Fascism and War 102
Hurricane Lamp Gallery 13, n1.12
Huxley, Aldous n1.12, 15, 112, 113, n3.50, 123, 141

Incitement to Disaffection Bill 58, 79, 84
Independent Labour Party (ILP) 91, 178
Industrial Design Partnership (IDP) 38, n1.67, 211, 248

International Brigade 148, 149, 158, 181, 215, n2.16, 259, 292
International Bureau of Revolutionary Artists (IBRA) 68, 80, 86, 87, 104, 122
International Labour Defence 11, n1.4
International Literature n1.65, 45, 104
International Surrealist Exhibition 142–7, 148, 157, 190
Invergordon Mutiny 11, 14, n1.17
Isle of Man 237, 262
Ishigaki, Eitaro 129, 340; *Soldiers of the People's Front – Zero Hour 128*
Île de Ré 206, 226

Jarrow March 56, 161
Jellet, Mainie 220
Jennings, Humphrey 202, n5.86
John, Augustus n2.12, 91, 106, 113, 117, 158, 197, 201, 213, 216, n6.24, 224, 263, 264, 266, 296–7, 340; *King Feisal 117*; *The Return of the Fisherman 296, 297*, n8.37
John Lewis Oxford Street 280–1, 294
John Reed Clubs (JRC) 68, 70, 71, 102, n3.25, n4.1, 126

Kandinsky, Wassily 24, 166
Kapp, Edmond 234
Kapp, Yvonne 245
Kauffer, Edward McKnight n1.55, 122, 142, 185, n6.24, 228, n6.47, 242, 342; *5 on Revolutionary Art 88*; *Cambridge Exhibition Against War and Fascism 119*
Kennington, Eric 115
Kernn-Larsen, Lisa 266
Kestelman, Morris n6.1, 247, n7.2, n8.16, 299, 305, 341; *Lama Sabachthani? 298*, n8.41, *301*
Keynes, John Maynard 15, 35, n1.54, 103, 121, 165
Kharkov 21, n1.26
Kidd, Ronald n2.3, 58, n2.29, 186, 341
Klee, Paul n1.75, 112, 144, 266
Klingender, Francis n1.76, 46, 49, 54, 93, 109, 209, 262, 270–1, n7.53–4, 311, 341; *Marxism and Modern Art* 270; 'Our Tradition' 262; *Russia: Britain's Ally* 270
Knight, Dame Laura 91, 106, 113, 115, 224, 341; *Dawn 105*
Knight, Harold 115
Kokoschka, Oskar 63, 213, 215, 236, 237, 242, 259–60, n7.34, 299, 305;

356 INDEX

The Crab 236, 237; *Private Property* 236; *The Red Egg* 260; *Self-Portrait of a Degenerate Artist* 213, *214*; *What We Are Fighting For* 299, *301, 302*, 303
Kollwitz, Käthe 70
Koolman, Alex 219, 248, 341
Krokodil 31, 87
Kukriniksy 92, 263

Labour Party 57, 148, 282
Lacasa, Luis 188, 193–4
La Guardia, Mayor Fiorello 176, 206, 280, n8.3
Laning, Edward, *Unlawful Assembly, Union Square* 70
Laurier, Roy 54, n2.8, n3.12, 219, 341; *It is a Fascist Scheme!* 57
Laver, James 106, 166, 289, 341
Lavery, John 181
Leach, Bernard 260
League Against Imperialism 49
League of Nations 15, 89
Left Book Club 166, 226
Left Review 81, 84, 85, 109, 122, n4.2, 134–5, 137–8, 4.24, 145, 158, 159, 177, 201, 250, 255, 276
Léger, Fernand 24, 115, 166, 258, 266
Leighton, Clare n1.66, 64, 169
Leningrad 27, 87, 263, 266, 284, 290
Lenin, Vladimir Ilyich 51, 99, 103
Leontinoff, Feodora 211, 341
Lhote, André 115, 142
The Life and Death of Colonel Blimp 277
Light Rescue Service 249
The Link 187
The Listener 63, 263
Lithographers Union 232
Lloyd, Albert Lancaster n1.76, n2.64, 109, 113, 145, 158, 341; *5 on Revolutionary Art* 109; 'The Red Steer' 109
Lockyer, Mildred 255
Loewenthal, Helen 269
London Artists' Association (LAA) 35, n1.54, n1.56
London County Council (LCC) 18, 216
London Economic Conference 31, n1.47
London Group (LG) 24, n1.38, 25, n1.55–6, 115, 137, 155, 166, 181–2, 207, 213, 268
London Mercury 67, 106

London Passenger Transport Board 135, 137, 159, 207, 253, 290
Lorca, Federico García 157, 194
Low, David 106, 122, 151, 165, 187, 219, n6.24, 225, 228, n6.47, 277, 341
Lowry, L. S. 24, 289, 341
Luard, Lowes 239, 242, 255, n7.48, n8.16, 289, 341
Lubetkin, Berthold 292
Lucas, James n1.76, 46, 66, 67, n3.12, 136, 212
Lyon, Robert n5.2

MacDonald, Ramsay n1.17, 24, n2.2, 56, 58
McWilliam, F. E. n5.82, 211, n6.3, 220, 342
Madrid 179, 188
Magritte, René 144
Maisky, Ivan 266, 271, 301
Manchester School of Art 7, 23
Manchuria 14, 18, 170, 231
Man, Ray 142, 144
Marc, Franz 199; *Blue Horses 198*, 199
Marchand, Jean 115, 241
Marchant, Cicely 13
Marchmont Street 51, 93
Martin, Kingsley 281
Marx Memorial Library and Workers' School n2.29, 79, 96, n3.18, 102, 103
The Masses 73, n2.46
Mass Observation 202
Masson, André 149, 266
Matisse, Henri 73, 241
Mayor Gallery 45, n1.75, 83
Means Test 18, 53, 54
Meblin, Anna 21, 31, n1.76, 49, n1.79, 51, n2.28, 91, n3.7, 161
Medley, Robert 64, 67, 195
Meninsky, Bernard 182
Mesens, E. L. T. 142
Methuen, Lord Paul Aynsford 270, 342
Miles, May Tilney n1.3, 15, n1.19, 17
The Mind in Chains 285, 305
Ministry of Agriculture 291
Ministry of Food 255, 262, 308
Ministry of Home Security 237, 255, 270, 291
Ministry of Information (MOI) 230, 231, 253, 254, 255, 262, 264, 266, 268, 277, 280–2
Ministry of Labour 230, 239
Ministry of Shipping and Economic Warfare 256

Ministry of War Transport 255
Miró, Joan n1.75, 141, 146, 156, 194, 202, 266; paintings: *Le Carnaval d'Arlequin* 146; *Dutch Interior 1* 146, n4.42; *Maternity* 147; *The Reaper* 146; *Catalan Peasant* 194; prints: *Aidez Espagne* 146
Mirsky, D. S., *The Intelligentsia of Great Britain* 123, n3.74
Mitkevitch, Olga 211, n6.50, 232
Moholy-Nagy, László 104, 110, 158, 185, 342; *AI2 111*; *K VII 111*; *K VIII 111*
Moore, Henry n1.54, 45, 64, 91, 106, 110, 113, 118, 141, 142, 144, 146, 157, 166, 179, 182, 188, 190, n5.82, 216, n6.24, 220, n6.24, 241, n6.81, 266, n8.14, 342; *Reclining Figure 183*
Morris, Lynda 8, 347, 349
Morrison, Herbert 216, 219, 242, 245
Mortimer, Raymond 309
Morton, A. L. 109
Moscow 8, 11, 16, 21, 22, 27, 31, 38, 91, 92, 122, 141, 190, 226, 263, 265, 270, 289, 311
Mosley, Oswald 56, n7.45
Motesiczky, Marie-Louise 311
Moynihan, Rodrigo 191, 220; *Pursuers Have No Mercy* 223
Munich 192, 205, 209, 212, 226, 231
Murder in Camp Hohenstein 55
Musgrave, Noel 109
Mumford, Lewis 133, 342
Museum of Modern Art (MoMA), New York 74, 99
Museum of Western Art and Fine Arts, Moscow 7, 86
Mussolini, Benito 54, 56, 121, 157

Nachshen, Donia 92, 342
Nash, John 115, 201, 223, 224
Nash, Paul n1.54, 42, 44, 45, 64, 91, 106, 113, 115, 141, 142, 144, 145, 146, 157, 158, 166, 179, 182, 185, 207, 209, n6.24, 220, n6.81, 266, n8.14, 289, 294–5, 342; *The Archer Overthrown 177*; *Coronilla* 90; *Landscape of the Megaliths 143*
National Congress of Action 53, 54, 57
National Conservatism 179, 225, 253, 292, 312
National Gallery 21, 230, 247, 270, 272, 288, 289
The National Government 14, 51, 54, 58, 78, 135, 149, 181, 231

National Joint Committee for Spanish Relief 190, 216
National Socialism 15, 111, 199, 312
National Unemployed Workers' Movement (NUWM) 53, 54, 56, 57
Nazi-Soviet Pact 226–7
Nessler, Walter 262, 342; *Age of Chaos* 262; *Destruction* 262; *Devastated Area* 262
Nevinson, C. R. W. 151; *The Twentieth Century 152*, n4.56
Newbould, Frank 292; *Your Britain – Fight for it Now 293*
New Burlington Galleries 142, 156, 198, 199, 205, 215
New English Art Club (NEAC) 24, 115, 166, 268
New Masses 70–71, n.2.46, 125, n.4.2
New Programme, AIA 269, 279
New School for Social Research 129, 170, n5.8
News Chronicle 156, 185, 280, n8.6, 307
New Statesman 141, 191
Newton, Eric 261, 270, 290–1, 309, 342
New York World Fair 211, n6.2, 238, 280
Nichols, Freda 232, n6.57, n6.59
Nicholson, Ben 45, 115, 266; *Composition, 1933* 221
Nicholson, Winifred 224
Nicolson, Harold n6.77, 282
Norman, Montagu 302–3
Novembergruppe 199

Observer 185, 256
The Olympics under Dictatorship 151
On Duty in the Desert 288
Orozco, José Clemente 70, 132, 342; *A Call for Revolution and Universal Brotherhood* 132; *The Unemployed 130*
Orwell, George 205, n5.87, 245, n7.62, 281; *Homage to Catalonia* 207
Our Time 250, 277
Ozenfant, Amédée 166, 266

Palkovská, Olda 213, 215, 236
Paris 58, n3.55, 149, 150
Paris International Exposition 1937 146, 188, 192–3; Peace Pavilion 192, *193*
Parton Street 92, n3.15, 94, 125, 141

Pasmore, Victor n1.14, n1.54, 199, 201, 220; *It Cannot Be Long Now* 223
Pavón, José M., *14th Street 174*
Peace Ballot 89, 155, 191, 192
Peace Publicity Bureau 136, n4.21, 165, 185
Pearson, Ralph 176
Penrose, Roland 141, 142, 143, 157, 166, 178, 179, n5.23, 182, 188, 190, 202, n5.82, 213, 215, 224, 264, 266, 342
Peoples' Convention 242, 245, n6.86, n6.88, 249, 250, 263
Peoples' Olympiad 151
Peri, Gabriel 255, 294, 303–4
Peri, Peter László n1.76, 54, 66, 110, n3.44, n4.40, 151, n4.56, 195–7, 202, 220, n6.26, 248, 249, 260, 268, 311, 342; exhibitions: *London Life in Concrete* 197, 248; *The New Realism in Sculpture* 197; paintings: *Nazi Photographing Hanged Couple* 268; sculpture: *Against War and Fascism* 115; *Chess* 197; *Fishing* 196; *The Rescue Men* 249; *Road Worker* 260; *Sawing* 196; *Spain* 223; *Tube Scene* 260
Petter, Helen Mary 241, 242, 255, n7.23, 269, n8.14
Pevsner, Nikolaus, *Pioneers of the Modern Movement* 163
Phillips, Ewan n1.76, 197, 209, 212, n6.7, 213, 216, n6.44, 228, 229, n6.50, 242, 255, 269, n8.16, n8.23, 342
Picasso, Pablo 68, 73, 110, 142, 144, 146, 156, 157, 178, 183, 188, 190, n5.46, 191, 193, 194, 202, 215, 216, 266; *The Dream and Lie of Franco* 195, n.5.44, n.5.61; *Guernica* 146, *189*, 190, 194, 195, 205, 215, 216, 277; *Harlequin* 182; *Weeping Woman* 191
Pick, Frank 254
Piper, John 115, 166, 191, 264, 266, 309; *Abstract I* 114
Pissarro, Lucien 115, 151, n4.56, 158, n6.24, n6.81, 342; *Chemin de l'Hubac, Toulon 113*
Pitmen Painters 166, n5.2
Poland 227, 291
Pollitt, Harry 11, n1.5, 163, 229, n6.48
Popular Front 106, n3.36, 125, 142, 188

Porter, Freddie 32, 35, n1.54
'Portraits for Spain' 198, 212, 215–16
Poster Design in War-time Britain 284, 290–4, n8.28
Prado 157, 178, 194
Preece, Patricia 223
Pressburger, Emeric 277
Priestley, J. B. n1.61, n2.53, n6.12, 219, 240
Pritt, D. N. n2.12, 123, n3.76
Public Works of Art Project (PWAP) 78, n2.49, n2.52, 135
'The Purpose of Art Today' 270

Quirt, Walter, *The Future Belongs to the Workers* 70–1

Radford, Robert 9, 302, 347, 349
Raverat, Gwen n5.24, 234
Ravilious, Eric n1.10, 59, 63, n2.24, 91, 104, 158, 212, 216, 248, 288, n8.22; *Cement Works* 66
Ray, Peter 284, 295
Rea (née Bevan), Betty n1.55, n1.66, n1.76, 91–2, n3.12, 94–5, 104, n3.35, 113, 122, 125, 151, 156, 165, 207, 209, 211, 213, 216, 220, 226, 228, 232, 255, 268, 306–7, 343; *5 on Revolutionary Art* 88, 89, 110, 122, 141; 'Children and Art in Soviet Russia' 92; *New World?* 297, 306, *307*
Read, Herbert 44, n1.73, 67, 68, 104, 106, 110, 112, n3.50, 118, 141, 142, 143, 145, 155, 157, 163, 169, n5.23, 182, 185, 195, n5.69, 202, 207, 209, 213, 260
Realism 165, 201, 197
Recording Britain 239, n6.75, 261
Red Army 8, 17, 31, 264
Red Cross United Artists' Exhibitions 261, 268
Reeve, Russell n7.2, 255, n8.14
Refregier, Anton, *American Artists Congress Exhibition* 171
Refugee Artists and their British Friends 259
Regent Street Polytechnic 91
Rembrandt, Harmenszoon van Rijn 170
Renau, José 188
Reynolds Illustrated News 185
Rhoades Geoffrey, *Blackout 239*
Rhoades, Joan 170
Rhonda Valley, Wales 115, 118
Richards, Ceri n5.82 219, 220
Richardson, Marion 155

358 INDEX

Rickword, Edgell 82, n2.64
Rimmington, Edith 220; *Family Tree* 222
Rivera, Diego 74, 96, 97, 98, n3.21, 103, 195; *Detroit Industry* 98, 195; *The Making of a Fresco Showing the Building of a City* 97, 98; *Man at the Crossroads* 99, *99*, 103
Robeson, Paul 190, 192
Rockefeller, John D. 74, 125
Roeder, Helen 248, n7.4, 255, n8.16, 343
Rogers, Claude n1.54, 191, 199, 220, 285
Roosevelt, Franklin Delano 68, 70, 74, 99, 134, 262, 280, n8.3, 281–2, n8.10, 284, 291
Rose, Millicent 270
Rothenstein, John 236, 289
Rothenstein, Michael 2 66
Rothenstein, William 13, 15, 32, 46
Roughton, Roger 157
Rousseau, Henri 266
Rowe, Cliff (Clifford Hooper) 8, 11, n1.6, 12, 13, n1.10, 14, n1.16, 15, 16, n1.21, 17, n1.22, n1.23, 21, n1.28, 22, n1.30, 24, 31, 32, n1.55, 38, n1.76, 46, 49, n1.79, n2.8, 67, 91, n3.12, 93, 118, 151, n4.56, 161–3, 165, 169, n5.4, 185, 207, 209, 212, n6.7, 219, 220, 223, n6.44, 228, 232, 234, 238, 239, 242, 248–9, n7.6–7, 250, 255, 256, 268, 269, n7.49, 270, n8.16, 301, 305, 311, 343; drawings: *Lenin and the Peasants* 21, *22*, 161; paintings: *Factory Gate Meeting 300; Freedom of Speech 300, 301; The Fried Fish Shop* 161–3, *162*, n4.74, 249; *Still Life* 13; *The Struggle between the Unemployed and the Police Forces* 8, 15–21, *16–17, 19, 20*; *Woman Cleaning, St Pancras Yards 251*; poster and cover designs: *9th Congress of Trade Unions* 17; *Cambridge Exhibition Against War and Fascism 50; The Development of Socialist Methods and Forms of Labour* 17; *Jubilee* 94, *95*; *The Spirit of Invergordon* 10, 11–12; *Why We Are Marching! 52*; prints: *Harry Page* n7.30; *H. Pinner, Sq Leader SP* n7.30; *George Thomas* n7.30; *The Call Out 250, 251; Moonlight Incident* 250; *Next Morning* 250; *The Raid* 250; *Stretcher Party* 250, 270; writings: 'The Position of Art Today' n5.72
Rowntree, Kenneth 239, 240, 242, 255, n7.24, n7.48, n8.14, 299; *Freedom of Worship 297*, 299
Royal Academy of Arts (RA), London 24, 142, 181, 213, 261
Royal Armoured Corps 259
Royal College of Art (RCA) 12, n1.10, 32, 35, 46, 58, 91, 241, 247, 253
Ruellan, Andrée, *City Market 173*
Rust, William 255
Rutter, Frank 169, n.5.5

Sadler, Michael 165, n5.5
Salvo for Russia 264, n7.43
Sausmarez, (Lionel) Maurice de 115, 151, n4.56, 343; *A Garden – God Wot! 243*
Schapiro, Meyer 71, 343
Schwitters, Kurt 112, 266
Scroggie, William 211
Security Services (MI5) 11, n1.16, 24, 237, 250, 254, 305
Sert, Josep Lluís 146, 188, 192
Seven and Five Society 115
Sewter, A. C. 163, n4.75
Shahn, Ben 74, 126, 129, 343; *The Passion of Sacco and Vanzetti 75*
Shell Oil (Shell-Mex / Asiatic Petroleum) 116, 135, 137, 207, 290
Shostakovich, Dimitri 266, 284
Sickert, Walter 35, 241
Simon, Edith 27, n1.42, n1.66, 43, 45, n1.76, 54, 151, n4.56, 219, n6.3, n6.59, 248, 343; *Incendiary Bombs 246; Isle de Ré Bed 206; Self-portrait 43*
Sinclair, Beryl n1.55, 226, n6.50, 234, n6.59, 239, 240, 255, 260, 266, n8.16, 290, 294, 297, 343; *Air, Light, Land and Water* 297
Siqueiros, David Alfaro 70, 132, 177, 343; *Art Front 133; Peasant Mother (Madre Campesina) 131*
Slade School of Art 96, 150, 191
Slater, Montagu 82, n3.50, 115, 116, 160, 277, 343
Smith, Matthew 261
Socialist Realism 21, 31, 141, 158
The Social Scene 64–68, n2.26, 71, n2.55, 80, 89, 105, 259
The Social Viewpoint in Art 68, 71, 74, n2.68
Society for Cultural Relations between Peoples of the British Commonwealth and the Union of Soviet Socialist Republics (SCR) 15, 292
Society for Education in Art 311
Society of Industrial Artists (SIA) n1.67, 136, 206–7, 229, 230, 311
Soho Square 89, 104, 111, 113, 115, 116, 117, 134, 151, 170, 191
Soviet Union (USSR) 7, 11, 15, 21, 78, 79, 86, 92, 112, 209, 227, 231, 235, 245, 247, 264, 271
Spanish Civil War 123, 136, 138, 150, 156, 157, 177, 205, 259, 270
Spanish Medical Aid 158, 159, 177, 182, 190, 215
Spanish Republic 157, 194, 205, 220
Spear, Ruskin 115, n8.16
Spectator 118, 194, 195, 202, 309
Spencer, Gilbert 253
Spencer, Stanley 103, 241
Springer, Roselle 126
Spurr, Elizabeth 242; *Washing Day 233*
Stalingrad 264, 284, 301
Stalin, Josef 21, 123, 163, 228, 263, 265
The Studio 66, 78
Sunday Dispatch 185, 187
Surrealism (Surrealists) 44, 109, 126, 141, 142, 145, 146, 157, 165, 179, n5.23, 181, 182, 195, 201, 202, n5.82, n5.97, 220, 252, 236, 306
Sutherland, Graham 241, 264, 295
Szóbel, Géza 258–9, 343; *Back to the Dark Ages 257; Civilisation 259; Execution of Hostages 257; Jewish Procession 257; Poste de Mitrailleuses 258; Refugiés 258; La Route Nationale 13 Juin 258*

Tanguy, Yves 144
Tennant, Trevor 242, 255
Ternovets, Professor n1.29, 31
Terry, Phyllis 241, 255
Thornycroft, Priscilla n3.12, 212, 232, 247, n7.1, n7.2, 255, n8.16, 343
Tibble, Geoffrey 191
Time and Tide 185, 291
The Times n1.13, n1.14, 240
Topolski, Feliks 289
Townsend, William n1.14, n1.55, 191, n5.50, 205, 212, 343
Trafalgar Square 21, 53, 59, 271
Travelling Exhibition No. 1 211, n6.6, 223; *No. 2* 241

Travelling exhibitions 269, 289–90
Trenchard, Lord Hugh 53, n2.2–3, 85, 97
Trevelyan, Julian n1.55, 144, 150, 156, n5.23, 202, n5.82, 205, 212, 219, 220, 255, 256, 263, 264, 266, 285, 344; *Bolton 203*; *Camouflage 264*
Trotsky, Leon 103, 161
Tudor-Hart, Alex 59, 62, 63, 122
Tudor-Hart (née Suschitzky), Edith 59–63, n2.16–21, 67, 115, 122, 148, 343; *An Arrest, Vienna 61*; *Die Bühne 62*; *Prater Ferris Wheel, Vienna 63*; *Karl-Marx-Hof, Vienna* n2.15, *60*; *Der Kuckuck 62*; *Sedition 62*, 63, 163
Tunnard, John 115, 182, 266, 306, 344; *Focal Point 306, 306*

Uhlman (née Croft), Diana 149–50, 187, 213, 236, 270
Uhlman, Fred 112, n3.48–9, 149–50, n4.51, 215, 235, 237, n6.71, 270, 281, 289, 344
Unemployed Artists Group (UAG) 71, 74, 78
Unemployment Bill 51, 54
Unit One 42, 44, n1.73, n1.75, 104, 115
Universe 181, n5.25

Vaillant-Couturier, Paul n2.13, 112
Van Gogh, Vincent 73, 80, 197
Vernon's Advertising 136, 137
Vienna 24, n1.40, 58, 59, 123
Voluntary Printing Unit 224, 232
Volunteer for Liberty 177

Wadsworth, Edward 45, n2.8, 166
Walker, Dame Ethel n1.13, n1.55, 169, 344; *Vanessa 169*
Walkington, Norman 66
War Artists Advisory Committee (WAAC) 230, 239, 242, 250, 272, 288
Watson, Elizabeth 115, n4.25, 150, 151, n4.56, 156, 158, 159, 163, 186, 190, n5.48, 192, 209, 211, n6.30, 229, n6.50, 238, 250, 255, 269, 344; *Bombed in the City 256*
Waugh, Alec 102–3
Waugh, Evelyn 254
Weber, Max 132–3, 344; 'The Artist, His Audience and Outlook' 132

Weight, Carel n1.55, n3.12, 151, n4.56, 232, 234, 239, 240, 248–9, n7.4, n7.5, 255, 260, 299, 305, 344; *Allegro Strepitoso* n7.5, 256; *Blockade* 234, n6.60; *It Happened to Us! 248*, 249, n7.5; *The Land of Ears 297*, 299; *La Symphonie Tragique 153*, n4.56; *Transcription of Goya's Unhappy Mother* 223
Weissenborn, Hellmuth 237, 344; *View from Internment Camp, Douglas, Isle of Man* 237, 240
Wells, H. G. 15, n1.61, 58, 148, 219
Wertheim, Lucy n1.14, 155, 235, n6.66
West, Alec 93
Whistler, Rex 103
Whitechapel 122, 211, 216, 219, 220, 223, n6.40, 236
White, Ethelbert 106, 158, 182
Whitney, Gertrude 73
Wight, Clifford 97, n3.20, 102; Coit Tower murals 102
Wilson, Harry, *Ashington Colliery, Northumberland 168*
Wilson, Helen 109, n4.25, n4.56, n4.76
Wimbledon School of Art 12
Wintringham, Tom 67, 78, 81, n2.64, 84, 155, 344
Wincott, Len 12
Wolfe, Edward n1.54, 182
Wolfe, Humbert 230, n6.54
Woolf, Leonard n1.19, 121
Woolf, Virginia 15, n1.19, 63, 117, 118, n3.58, 121, 123
Workers Educational Association 191
Workers Film and Photo League 46, 64, n2.29
World Disarmament Conference 31, n1.47
Wright, Matvyn 297–9, n8.39; *Fear Motive 297*, 299
Writers International 21, n2.13, n2.64, 112, 123, 137, 148, n4.43
Wykeham, Mary n7.2, 255, n7.43, 266

Youngman, Nan n1.14, n1.55, 91, n3.12, 96, 115, 150, 155, n4.59–60, 166, n5.4, 186, 192, 195, 209, 211, 215, 219, 226, 229, n6.50, 232, 255, 268, 270, 290, 307, 344; *The First Siren 290*, n8.26; *Gleaning at Godmanchester 308*; *Self-portrait 157*

Zadkine, Ossip 115, 142
Zetkin, Clara 163, n4.76
Zwemmer, Anton 141, 252